The Institutions of the European Union

THE NEW EUROPEAN UNION SERIES

Series Editors: John Peterson and Helen Wallace

The European Union is both the most successful experiment in modern international cooperation and a daunting analytical challenge to students of politics, economics, history, law, and the social sciences.

The EU of the twenty-first century continues to respond to expanding membership and new policy challenges—particularly in transnational arenas such as climate change, energy security, and crisis management—as well as political and institutional controversies. The result is a truly new European Union that requires continuous reassessment.

THE NEW EUROPEAN UNION SERIES brings together the expertise of leading scholars writing on major aspects of EU politics for an international readership.

The series offers lively, accessible, reader-friendly, research-based textbooks on:

POLICY-MAKING IN THE
EUROPEAN UNION

INTERNATIONAL RELATIONS AND
THE EUROPEAN UNION

THE MEMBER STATES OF THE
EUROPEAN UNION

THE ORIGINS AND EVOLUTION
OF THE EUROPEAN UNION

THE INSTITUTIONS OF THE
EUROPEAN UNION

THE EUROPEAN UNION:
HOW DOES IT WORK?

The Institutions of
the European Union

THIRD EDITION

Edited by

John Peterson

Michael Shackleton

OXFORD
UNIVERSITY PRESS

OXFORD

UNIVERSITY PRESS

Great Clarendon Street, Oxford OX2 6DP,
United Kingdom

Oxford University Press is a department of the University of Oxford.
It furthers the University's objective of excellence in research, scholarship,
and education by publishing worldwide. Oxford is a registered trade mark of Oxford University Press
in the UK and in certain other countries

Impression: 1

British Library Cataloguing in Publication Data

Data available `

Library of Congress Cataloging in Publication Data

Data available

ISBN 978-0-19-957498-8

Printed in Great Britain
on acid-free paper by
Ashford Colour Press Limited, Gosport, Hampshire

■ OUTLINE CONTENTS

PART III   Integrating Interests

▌ DETAILED CONTENTS

▋ PREFACE

The first edition of this book was only the second to appear in the Oxford University Press 'New European Union' series, after Helen and William Wallace's milestone in the EU literature, *Policy-Making in the European Union*. The shelf on which these two books once sat alone now groans under the weight of no fewer than five other volumes, including a new sixth version of *Policy-Making* (2010). Whereas we once faced 'only' the (already daunting) task of living up to the high standards set by Wallace and Wallace (recently joined by Mark A. Pollack and Alasdair R. Young), we now find ourselves having to be good enough to avoid letting down a stable of other authors and editors who, together, have made the New European Union series an essential set of works for any student of European integration. Quite a lot of the blame for putting us under so much pressure lies with Professor Helen Wallace, the series co-editor, whose energy, enthusiasm, razor-sharp mind, and all-around good citizenship never cease to amaze us.

We owe a large debt to our colleagues at Oxford University Press for helping to keep the project on track. Catherine Page has been an absolute joy with whom to work. She has worked hard to ensure that this book, along with others in the series, finds the audience that it deserves. Our great regret that she is leaving OUP, making this the last book on which she will work with us, is balanced considerably by our satisfaction in seeing her embark on the UK civil service's European fast-stream programme. And the past efforts of Catherine's predecessors—Ruth Anderson, Sue Dempsey, and Angela Griffin—have not been forgotten. Joanna Hardern's professionalism in seeing this volume of the book through the production process was exemplary.

Our authors have almost invariably worked to a high standard, while patiently coping with our active editorship and constant urgings to respect the next deadline. We have learned much from them and are enormously grateful to each for the part that they played in making this project a success. Some of the work of some contributors to past editions—Brian Crowe, Kathleen McNamara, Neill Nugent, and Michael E. Smith—may live on in this edition, so we must thank them for their past efforts. We also are in considerable debt to Amy Marshall for her highly valued and highly skilled help in preparing the final text.

Our final expression of thanks is to our families: Elizabeth, Miles, and Calum in Edinburgh, and Jan near Oxford, with Katie and Lucy now further afield. They have now put up with literally years of the two of us neglecting them while we conferred, debated, and cajoled each other and our authors about this project. We dedicate the final product to them.

John Peterson

Michael Shackleton

New to this edition

- The book in its third edition has been fully updated to cover the institutional changes prompted by the Lisbon Treaty and to address the key issues raised by the eurozone crisis.
- A number of new contributors have been added to ensure that the book continues to bring together the foremost scholars in the field.

▍ LIST OF BOXES

▌ LIST OF FIGURES

▌LIST OF TABLES

LIST OF ABBREVIATIONS

ABM	activity-based management
ACER	Agency for the Cooperation of Energy Regulators
ACP	African, Caribbean and Pacific countries
AFSJ	Area of Freedom, Security, and Justice
ALDE	Alliance of Liberals and Democrats for Europe
AMP	annual management programme
APS	annual policy strategy
ARLEM	Euro–Mediterranean Assembly of Local and Regional Authorities
BBC	British Broadcasting Corporation
BCC	Budgetary Control Committee (of the European Parliament)
Benelux	Belgium, the Netherlands, and Luxembourg
BIS	Bank for International Settlements
BRIC	Brazil, Russia, India, and China
BSE	bovine spongiform encephalopathy
BVerfGE	German Federal Constitutional Court *(Bundesverfassungsgericht)*
CAP	common agricultural policy
CATS	*Comité Article Trente-six* (Article 36 Committee)
CCMI	Consultative Commission on Industrial Change
CCP	common commercial policy
CDR	career development review
CDU/CSU	German Christian Democratic Union/Christian Social Union
Cedefop	European Centre for the Development of Vocational Training
CEECs	Central and Eastern European countries
CEPOL	European Police College
CEPS	Centre for European Policy Studies
CESR	Committee of European Securities Regulators
CFCA	Community Fisheries Control Agency

CFI   Court of First Instance

CFP   common fisheries policy

CFSP   common foreign and security policy

CHMP   Committee for Medicinal Products for Human Use

CJEU   Court of Justice of the European Union

COA   Court of Auditors

COCOBU   European Parliament's Committee on Budgetary Control

Cocor   *Commission de Coordination du Conseil des Ministres*

COMP   Committee for Orphan Medicinal Products

CoR   Committee of the Regions

Coreper   Committee of Permanent Representatives

COSI   Standing Committee on Internal Security

CPI   consumer prices index

CPMP   Committee for Proprietary Medicinal Products

CPVO   Community Plant Variety Office

CSCE   Conference for Security and Cooperation in Europe

CSDP   common security and defence policy

CSP   Confederation of Socialist Parties of the European Community

CST   Civil Service Tribunal

CVMP   Committee for Veterinary Medicines

DAS   statement of assurance (also known as SOA)

DG   Directorate-General

DG RELEX   Directorate-General for External Relations

DTI   Department of Trade and Industry (UK)

EA   European Alliance

EAGGF   European Agricultural Guidance and Guarantee Fund

EASA   European Aviation Safety Agency

EAW   European arrest warrant

EBA   European Banking Authority

EBRD   European Bank for Reconstruction and Development

EC	European Community
ECA	European Court of Auditors
ECB	European Central Bank
ECDC	European Centre for Disease Prevention and Control
ECHA	European Chemicals Agency
ECHO	European Community Humanitarian Office
ECHR	European Convention on Human Rights
ECJ	European Court of Justice
Ecofin	Council of Economic and Finance Ministers
ECON	Economic and Monetary Affairs Committee (of the European Parliament)
ECOWAS	Economic Community of West-African states
ECR	European Conservatives and Reformists; European Court Reports
ECSC	European Coal and Steel Community
ECtHR	European Court of Human Rights
ecu	European currency unit
EDA	European Defence Agency
EDC	European Defence Community
EDF	European Development Fund
EEA	European Environment Agency
EEAS	European External Action Service
EEC	European Economic Community
EESC	European Economic and Social Committee
EFA	European Free Alliance
EFC	Economic and Financial Committee
EFD	Europe of Freedom and Democracy
EFGP	European Federation of Green Parties
EFSA	European Food Safety Authority
EFTA	European Free Trade Association
EGP	European Green Party
EIB	European Investment Bank

EIF	European Investment Fund
EIGE	European Institute for Gender Equality
EIOPA	European Insurance and Occupational Pensions Authority
ELDR	European Liberal, Democrat, and Reform Party
EMA	European Medicines Agency
EMI	European Monetary Institute
EMS	European monetary system
EMSA	European Maritime Safety Agency
EMU	economic and monetary union
ENISA	European Network and Information Security Agency
EP	European Parliament
EPC	European Political Community; European political cooperation
EPP	European People's Party; European Public Prosecutor
EPP–ED	European People's Party and European Democrats
EPSO	European Personnel Selection Office
ERA	European Railway Agency
ERDF	European Regional Development Fund
ERPA	European Research Papers Archive
ESC	*See* EESC
ESCB	European System of Central Banks
ESDP	European Security and Defence Policy
ESMA	European Securities and Markets Authority
ESRB	European Systemic Risk Board
ESS	European Security Strategy
ETA	*Euskadi ta Askatasuna*
EU	European Union
EUL–NGL	Confederal Group of the European United Left/Nordic Green Left
EU-OSHA	European Agency for Safety and Health at Work
Euratom	European Atomic Energy Community
Eurofound	European Foundation for the Improvement of Living and Working Conditions
Eurojust	EU Judicial Cooperation Unit

Europol	European Police Office
Eurostat	European Statistical Office
FAC	Foreign Affairs Council
G/EFA	Greens/European Free Alliance
G7	Group of Seven
G8	Group of Eight
G20	Group of Twenty
GAC	General Affairs Council
GAERC	General Affairs and External Relations Council
GATT	General Agreement on Tariffs and Trade
GDP	gross domestic product
GNP	gross national product
GNSS	global navigation satellite systems
GSA	European GNSS Agency
HICP	harmonised index of consumer prices
HMPC	Committee on Herbal Medicinal Products
HR/CFSP	High Representative for common foreign and security policy
IGC	intergovernmental conference
IIA	inter-institutional agreements
IMF	International Monetary Fund
IR	international relations
IRA	Irish Republican Army
ISS	Institute for Security Studies
JHA	justice and home affairs
JPC	judicial and police cooperation
LI	liberal intergovernmentalism
LSE	London School of Economics and Political Science
MEP	Member of the European Parliament
MFA	European Minister for Foreign Affairs
MP	Member of Parliament
MPC	Bank of England's Monetary Policy Committee

NATO	North Atlantic Treaty Organization
NGO	non-governmental organization
NI	new institutionalism
NPM	new public management
NRA	national regulatory authority
NSS	US National Security Strategy
ODS	Czech Civic Democratic Party
OHIM	Office for Harmonization in the Internal Market (Trade Marks and Designs)
OLAF	*Office de la Lutte Anti-Fraude* (European Anti-Fraud Office)
OMC	open method of coordination; (US Federal Reserve) Open Markets Committee
OSCE	Organization for Security and Cooperation in Europe
PCA	partnership and cooperation agreements
PES	Party of European Socialists
PNR	passenger name record
PoCo	Political Committee
PPE	European People's Party
PSC	Political and Security Committee (also known as COPS)
PSOE	Spanish Socialist Workers' Party
QMV	qualified-majority voting
REACH	registration, authorization, and restriction of chemicals
RegLeg	Conference of Presidents of Regions with Legislative Power
RRF	rapid reaction force
S&D	Progressive Alliance of Socialists and Democrats
SAI	supreme audit institution
SCA	Special Committee on Agriculture
SCIFA	Standing Committee on Immigration, Frontiers and Asylum
SDP	Social Democratic Party
SEA	Single European Act
SGCI	*Secrétariat Général du Comité Interministériel pour les Questions de Coopération Économique Européenne* (France)
SGP	stability and growth pact

SIS	Schengen information system
SMEs	small and medium-sized enterprises
SNP	Scottish National Party
SOA	*see* DAS
SWIFT	Society for Worldwide Interbank Financial Communication
TARGET	Trans-European Automated Real-time Gross Settlement Express Transfer System
TCN	third-country national
TEU	Treaty on European Union (Maastricht Treaty)
TFEU	Treaty on the functioning of the European Union
UCLAF	*Unité de Coordination de la Lutte Anti-Fraude* (Anti-Fraud Unit)
UK	United Kingdom
UKIP	United Kingdom Independence Party
UN	United Nations
US	United States
WB	World Bank
WEU	Western European Union
WMD	weapons of mass destruction
WTO	World Trade Organization

▌ LIST OF CONTRIBUTORS

ANDREW BYRNE	Universities of Köln and Edinburgh
PHILIPPE DE SCHOUTHEETE	University of Louvain
RENAUD DEHOUSSE	Institut d'Etudes Politiques (Paris)
ANDREW GEDDES	University of Sheffield
FIONA HAYES-RENSHAW	College of Europe (Bruges)
NIKLAS HELWIG	Universities of Köln and Edinburgh
DERMOT HODSON	Birkbeck College (University of London)
LIESBET HOOGHE	University of North Carolina (Chapel Hill)
CHARLIE JEFFERY	University of Edinburgh
GEORGE KARAKATSANIS	European Court of Auditors
HUSSEIN KASSIM	University of East Anglia
R. DANIEL KELEMEN	Rutgers University
BRIGID LAFFAN	University College Dublin
JEFFREY LEWIS	Cleveland State University
PAUL MAGNETTE	Minister for Climate and Energy, Belgium
GIANDOMENICO MAJONE	University of Pittsburgh
NIAMH NIC SHUIBHNE	University of Edinburgh
JOHN PETERSON	University of Edinburgh
TAPIO RAUNIO	University of Tampere
CAROLYN ROWE	Aston University
MICHAEL SHACKLETON	Maastricht University, formerly European Parliament

CHAPTER 1

The EU Institutions: an Overview

John Peterson and Michael Shackleton

▌ Summary

The European Union (EU) straddles accepted categories of political organization. It is neither a state nor an 'ordinary' international organization. What sets the EU apart, perhaps above all, is its unique institutions: they resemble no other bodies found at the national or international level. Now, perhaps more than ever, Europe's institutions *are* Europe's politics. The point was illustrated by the political crisis that began when the EU's Constitutional Treaty, designed to reform the Union's institutions to cope with enlargement, was soundly rejected in referenda held in France and the Netherlands in 2005. The crisis continued when the Lisbon Treaty, which contained many of the same institutional reforms, took years (and yet another referendum defeat in Ireland) before it was finally ratified in late 2009. This chapter introduces contending definitions of 'institution'. It also presents competing approaches to studying them. It argues that understanding politics always begins with understanding institutions, not least in the EU.

Introduction

The EU remains one of the most elusive of all subjects of study in the social sciences. It is neither a state nor an 'ordinary' international organization (see Wallace *et al.* 2010), but rather a unique experiment embedding the national in the European and the European in the national (Laffan *et al.* 2000). What distinguishes the EU above all is its institutions: they have no close analogues at either the national or international levels.

The EU exists to provide collective goods—such as an internal market, a single currency, and international power—which the Union's member states cannot deliver (or not as well) on their own. The EU's institutional system is both the central mechanism for achieving those goals and the locus of disagreement about the future development of the Union. The point was illustrated by the political crisis that began when the EU's Constitutional Treaty was soundly rejected in referenda held in France and the Netherlands in 2005. The crisis continued when the Lisbon Treaty, which contained many of the same institutional reforms, required years (and another referendum defeat in Ireland) before it could be ratified in 2009. The primary goal of both treaties was to reform the EU's institutions to allow them to work efficiently despite the Union's radical enlargement from fifteen to twenty-seven (plus) member states after 2004. Perhaps even more than when Ludlow (1992) first made the argument decades ago, Europe's institutions were shown to be Europe's politics: battles over the political direction of the EU morphed into clashes about how its institutional system can and should work.

To illustrate, the Constitutional Treaty—a traditional Treaty between EU member states, but meant to be more permanent than its predecessors—was portrayed by its supporters as simply a pragmatic attempt to rationalize the EU system to cope with enlargement. Yet it became a lightning rod for Eurosceptics opposed to closer European integration. Much the same could be said about the Lisbon Treaty, even if it was eventually ratified more than four years after it was agreed.

Most academic work on European integration highlights the highly variable capacity of the EU to govern effectively in different phases of its development. The standard story holds that Europe integrated surprisingly rapidly in the 1950s and early 1960s. Then, in the 1970s and early 1980s, the Community became immobilized by economic crisis and a set of rules that made decision-making almost impossible. During this period of so-called Eurosclerosis, it seemed the Community could accomplish nothing very important. Then, dramatically, European integration was given fresh impetus by the so-called single market project, which sought to transform (then) twelve national economies into a single, seamless European one. Before the project's 1992 target date for completion, even more dramatic changes were unleashed by the collapse of the Warsaw Pact and Soviet Union in 1989–91. West European governments responded by agreeing the Maastricht Treaty, which contained bold commitments to economic and monetary union, a 'common' European foreign and security policy, and a political union. Suddenly, it seemed the EU could accomplish *anything* (Laffan *et al.* 2000: 4). Twenty years later, turmoil surrounding the sovereign debt of weaker members of the eurozone (spanning the EU's monetary union), the Union's continued weakness in foreign policy, and Europe's loss of economic competitiveness to emerging states such as China and India all raised questions about whether the EU had again become immobilized, perhaps as never before.

These perceptions of total breakdown and dramatic advance are both products of failed imagination: lack of it during the Eurosclerosis period; overactivity in the 1990s; and a failure to imagine that the EU might, as it always has in the past, eventually recover from repeated crises in the early twenty-first century. The EU has always been somewhere between inert and ideal. In its relatively recent past, it successfully introduced the euro, thus reinforcing the identity of the Union in the minds of millions of Europeans (if not always positively[1]). It also negotiated the entry of twelve new member states in 2004–07, with more in the waiting room (particularly Croatia) after that, thus exporting its liberal democratic habits to Europe's east and south.

But the EU also made few strides towards the goal that it set itself in Lisbon in 2000 to make the Union the most dynamic economy in the world. It was entirely unable to agree a common European response to the 2003 war in Iraq. Its former Commissioner for Trade, Peter Mandelson, once opined that 'nothing divides us more than Russia' (Bouchard and Peterson 2011: 20), widely viewed as the most important geopolitical challenge facing the EU. The 2010–11 crisis in the eurozone threatened, according to some, the Union's very existence. What spans the EU's successes and failures, its potential and shortcomings, its state-centrism and Europeanness is its institutions.

There is no single, accepted definition of 'institution', but rather a variety of contending ones. The EU's treaties have followed the European tradition of defining institutions as organizations that enjoy special legal status. The Lisbon Treaty designates seven: the European Parliament (EP); the Council (of Ministers); the European Commission; the Court of Justice (ECJ); the European Court of Auditors (ECA); the European Council; and the European Central Bank (ECB). (Lisbon granted the ECB and the European Council formal status as 'institutions' for the first time.) If we were to use this definition, this book would be much shorter and narrower in focus than it is.

Yet institutions are often defined in a far broader sense in the study of politics, as 'extending beyond the formal organs of government to include standard operating procedures, so-called soft law, norms and conventions of behavior' (Bulmer 1994: 355). According to this perspective, 'institutions do not think, have preferences or act, but are sets of commonly accepted formal and informal norms that constrain political actors' (Marks 1996: 22). In this sense, virtually anything that is accepted as 'normal' could be considered institutionalized. Coverage of all that fits under this definition in the EU would result in a book far longer than this one.

We take a middle way. First, we conceive of institutions as arenas in which power and influence are exercised, regardless of the precise legal status of the organizations that preside over them. Second, we invite our readers to think of institutions not only in terms of specific people and premises, but also as rules and practices.

We begin by explaining why the study of institutions has been brought 'back in' to the study of politics in recent years. We then develop the argument that the EU's institutions provide an essential and revealing window into Europe's politics (see Box 1.1). Our next task is to consider how and why the Union's institutions have changed and yet endured over time. Finally, we set out some of the book's major themes, and conclude with advice on how this book might be read.

BOX 1.1   Perceptions of the EU institutions

Each man begins the world afresh. Only institutions grow wiser. They store up collective experience ... From this experience and wisdom, men subject to the same laws will gradually find ... not that their natures change ... but that their behaviour does.

Jean Monnet (1950, quoted in Duchene 1994: 401)

What a model our institutions, which allow every country irrespective of its size to have its say and make a contribution, offer the nations of Eastern Europe.

Jacques Delors (1989, quoted in Nelsen and Stubb 1998: 60–1, 197)

Supranational institutions—above all, the European Commission, the European Court, and the European Parliament—have independent influence in policy-making that cannot be derived from their role as agents of state executives.

Gary Marks, Liesbet Hooghe, and Kermit Blank (1996: 346)

All along [the] road, the European institutions—the Council, the European Parliament, the Commission, and the Court of Justice—have provided sterling service, to which we must pay tribute. At the same time ... the process of European union is showing signs of flagging.

Valery Giscard d'Estaing (2002: 5)

Like other reformers, political leaders in the EU try to make institutions more rational and efficient, more humane, representative, responsive, transparent and accountable ... The motivations of EU reformers are complex and shifting. They want many, different and not necessarily consistent things.

Johan Olsen (2003: 50)

From my own experience, the EU's institutions are far more autonomous than institutionalist theory (much of it focused on the American institutions) would lead one to believe. Much, much more.

José Manuel Barroso (2007, quoted in Peterson 2008b: 69)

Why study institutions?

The social sciences came of age in the early twentieth century by focusing intensely, often exclusively, on institutions. In political science, the overwhelming emphasis was on formal structures of government and systems of law-making. Political analysis began—and often ended—by describing institutions in great detail. Methodology was generally not a matter for debate nor was the behaviour of political leaders, officials, or citizens. As Rhodes (1995: 42) suggests, 'the focus on institutions was a matter of common sense, an obvious starting point … and therefore there was no need to justify it'.[2]

Everything changed in the 1950s and early 1960s. First, the so-called behavioural revolution was unleashed (see Sanders 2010). Behaviouralists condemned the traditional emphasis on institutions as too narrow, unscientific, and atheoretical. Traditional institutionalist analysis not only failed to explain policy or power; it also suffered from 'hyperfactualism'—reverence for 'facts' amounted to theoretical malnutrition (Easton 1971).

For behaviouralists, institutions were relatively uninteresting compared to the *behaviour* of political actors. Institutions had no political interests or personalities of their own. In a sense, behaviouralists assumed that an institution was just a car waiting for a driver. What was far more interesting than studying the car was studying the behaviour of the agents—political leaders, parties, voters—competing to seize power, control institutions, or drive the car. Behaviouralists sought to make political science a true science, often through the use of statistics and quantitative analysis. Institutions—leaving aside some notable exceptions (see Allison and Zelikow 1999)—more or less disappeared from the radar screens of most political scientists.

The second big change was a shift in the study of international relations. Traditionally, scholarship had focused mostly on competition (especially military) between sovereign states in what was assumed to be a Hobbesian and anarchic international system (see Morgenthau 1948). However, the postwar creation of the United Nations (UN) and the Bretton Woods institutions (the General Agreement on Tariffs and Trade, or GATT, the World Bank, and the International Monetary Fund, or IMF) led to a blossoming of scholarship on international cooperation. In time, Europe became the primary focus of this scholarship as the continent embarked on ambitious experiments in (especially economic) integration. 'Neofunctionalists' theorized that modest steps towards cooperation would lead to more ambitious moves in a process that was, in many ways, self-sustaining (see Haas 1958; Lindberg 1963).

However, the dawning of the so-called 'second cold war' (Halliday 1983), a period of heightened international tension in the early 1980s, made most international organizations—including the apparently Eurosclerotic Community—seem too weak to foster much meaningful cooperation. The focus shifted towards explaining renewed conflict, especially between the United States and Soviet Union (see Waltz 1979). Europe was politically and—along with institutionalism—academically marginalized.

Then, beginning in the mid-1980s, institutions began to be rediscovered. A groundswell of academic momentum developed behind the idea that institutions were important but neglected, and that it was time to bring them 'back in' to the study of politics (see Skocpol 1985; March and Olsen 1989). In some respects, the so-called 'new' institutionalism was a rebellion against behaviouralism. Neoinstitutionalists insisted that political behaviour was determined in fundamental ways by the nature of political institutions, how they are constructed, and how power is distributed between them.

The basic neoinstitutionalist argument is that institutions *matter*. They define group loyalties in any political system and help to determine how political debates are structured. They are not just cars waiting for drivers. In particular, institutions—even ones that are formally apolitical—can develop their own interests, agendas, and priorities. They act with considerable autonomy despite being formally controlled by political actors, such as governments. Actual policy outcomes can reflect the *agency*—the determined pursuit of favoured choices—of institutions more than of the preferences of governments. One reason why is that the policy priorities of governments are often disputed or vaguely defined, thus allowing scope for formally apolitical institutions to set the agenda.

The new institutionalism is more a *perspective* on politics than a fully developed theory. Still, neoinstitutionalism has emerged as a leading, even (arguably) dominant, perspective on European integration and politics (Cowles and Curtis 2004; Pollack 2009). If nothing else, it is accepted as a viable alternative to state-centric or intergovernmental approaches derived from the study of international relations (see Moravcsik 1998; Moravcsik and Schimmelfennig 2009). The latter assume, reasonably, that the EU has a strong intergovernmental backbone. Policy debates are mostly debates between national actors pursuing national interests.

Yet battles over EU policy are mostly fought out far from national capitals and governments. Nearly all actors in EU politics have multiple identities and mixed loyalties, to their member state, political party, or the interests of the policy sector in which they work. Institutional affiliations thus give actors a sort of anchor or orientation that may override others. Neoinstitutionalist treatments argue that EU politics have to be understood in terms of institutional competition (and cooperation) between, above all, the Council, the Commission, the EP, and the ECJ, and not just in terms of *intergovernmental* competition (and cooperation) between the Union's member states.

There are at least three main variants of institutionalism (see Hall and Taylor 1996; Peters 1996; Pollack 2009). Historical institutionalists focus on how EU governance has evolved over time (Armstrong and Bulmer 1998; Lindner and Rittberger 2003; Sanders 2006). This work highlights the importance of emergent institutional norms, such as the Council's ingrained habit of seeking unanimity on any measure regardless of whether qualified-majority voting (QMV) applies (see Golub 1999; Hayes-Renshaw and Wallace 2006). Such norms can constrain political decision-making and produce 'path dependence'—a concept central to all variants of institutionalism—which happens when 'initial policy choices … restrict subsequent [policy] evolution' (Armstrong and Bulmer 1998: 55). Path dependence is particularly powerful when consensus is required to change an existing policy or institution. Historical institutionalists, as neofunctionalists before them, insist that European integration must be studied as an historical process, in which actors often apply a high 'discount rate' to the future. Thus, today's decisions sometimes are taken with little regard for tomorrow's consequences. In these circumstances, member governments can become locked in to policy paths on which they have set the Union, with its institutions becoming guardians of long-established policies and 'not simply passive tools of the Member States' (Pierson 1996: 132; see also Pierson 2004).

A second, sociological variant of institutionalism shares with the historical version a preoccupation with the Union's 'uneven institutional history' (Fligstein and McNichol 1998: 88; see also Fligstein 2008). Yet sociological institutionalists assign even greater weight to norms, conventions, and ideas. For example, Parsons (2003: 1) explains why the EU 'stands out as the major exception in the thinly institutionalized world of international politics' by examining how certain ideas about how solutions could be connected to problems became institutionalized in postwar Europe. The political effects have been powerful, since the 'institutionalization of certain ideas gradually reconstructs the interests of powerful actors' (ibid.: 6).

Sociological institutionalists share important assumptions with constructivists. The latter insist that preferences in EU policy debates are 'constructed' through the social interaction of actors in Brussels and Strasbourg as much as (or more than) they are determined prior to such interactions (see Christiansen et al. 2001; Risse 2009). More generally, sociological institutionalism holds that institutions matter because they determine what is considered appropriate behaviour by actors, which itself has powerful implications for political and policy outcomes.

A third variant of institutionalism builds on rational choice theory (see Farrell and Heritier 2005; Pollack 2006). Rational choice institutionalists argue that institutions matter most when they become subject to what economists call 'increasing returns'—that is, they generate sufficient benefits that member governments, which themselves rationally calculate their own interests, face disincentives to abandon or reformulate them. Thus, the ECJ has been able to pursue legal integration even beyond the collective preferences of member governments because of the high costs to member states of seeking to overrule it or of failing to comply with its judgments (Garrett 1995). Rational choice institutionalism sometimes draws on principal–agent theory, which seeks to explain how and why governments, or 'principals', solve collective action problems by delegating functions to international institutions, which then act as their 'agents', although usually with a variety of mechanisms put in place to control or monitor their behaviour (see Majone 2000; Pollack 2003, 2009).[3]

The point here is not that neoinstitutionalism, in one or more of its variants, is the only—or even best—way in which to study the EU's institutions. In fact, the contributors to this volume deploy a range of different theoretical approaches. The point is rather that institutions are worth studying because, as is now widely acknowledged across all the social sciences, institutions matter.

Why study the EU institutions?

If institutions matter, they may matter even more in the European Union than in other political systems. Why? We can think of at least eight reasons.

First, the EU is probably the most powerful non-state actor in the contemporary international world (see Josselin and Wallace 2001; Cowles 2003). Its institutions generate a wide array of policies that impact upon EU states and their citizens (as well as many beyond Europe) directly and in ways that are unmatched by any other international organization. Every day, EU citizens in seventeen states (at the time of writing) use the currency that was adopted as a result of a series of decisions taken by EU leaders meeting in the European Council. Air passengers in Europe whose flights end up being cancelled are now often entitled to compensation, mostly due to the stubborn insistence of the EP that they should be. One of the largest proposed corporate mergers in history, between the *American* firms General Electric and Honeywell, was scuppered by a decision of the European Commission. In short, the EU is enormously powerful, and not only because it combines the power of twenty-seven (as of 2012) European states, including several major powers. Much of the EU's power is vested in its institutions.

Second, the EU's institutional structure has uniquely blended continuity and change. The institutions established in the 1950s (see Table 1.1) have retained many of their essential characteristics, revealing how deeply ingrained established institutional norms and cultures have become. In most policy areas, the Commission retains to this day a virtual monopoly on the right to present legislative proposals, a power it has held since the origins of the European Economic Community (EEC). For its part, the EP has evolved from a mostly toothless, consultative body to an effective co-legislator with the Council. Meanwhile, a remarkable burgeoning of new bodies started with the European Council and European Court of Auditors in the 1970s, and continued with a seemingly endless array of decentralized agencies that sprang up beginning in the late 1990s (see Table 1.1).

Third, the EU's institutions matter because they are the vehicles used by the Union's member governments to enforce the terms of the bargains that they make with each other. But they are more than just passive instruments, or cars waiting for drivers. The powers that they have accrued over time—arising from the *acquis communautaire*, or the full set of rights and obligations deriving from EU treaties,

TABLE 1.1   An institutional timeline

	Start of activities	Title of institution	Location
1950			
	1952	Council of Ministers	Brussels/Luxembourg
		ECSC High Authority	Luxembourg
		European Court of Justice	Luxembourg
		ECSC Parliamentary Assembly	Strasbourg/Luxembourg
	1958	European Commission	Brussels/Luxembourg
		Economic and Social Committee	Brussels
		European Investment Bank	Luxembourg
		Committee of Permanent Representatives (COREPER)	Brussels/Luxembourg
1960			
	1962	European Parliamentary Assembly changes its name to European Parliament	Strasbourg/ Luxembourg/Brussels
	1965	Merger Treaties create a single Commission	Brussels/Luxembourg
1970			
	1974	European Council (formally established by Paris Summit)	
	1975	European Centre for the Development of Vocational Training	Berlin (since 1995 Thessaloniki)
		European Foundation for the Improvement of Living and Working Conditions	Dublin
	1977	European Court of Auditors	Luxembourg
1980			
	1989	Court of First Instance	Luxembourg
1990	1990	European Environment Agency	Copenhagen
	1994	Committee of Regions	Brussels
		Office for Harmonization in the Internal Market	Alicante
		Translation Centre for the Bodies of the European Union	Luxembourg
	1995	European Ombudsman	Strasbourg
		European Training Foundation	Turin
		Community Plant Variety Office	Angers

Cont. ➤

Cont.			
		European Agency for Safety and Health at Work	Bilbao
		European Medicines Agency (EMA)	London
		European Monitoring Centre for Drugs and Drug Addiction	Lisbon
	1998	European Monitoring Centre on Racism and Xenophobia	Vienna
		European Central Bank	Frankfurt
	1999	European Anti-Fraud Office (OLAF)	Brussels
		Europol	The Hague
2000	2000	European Police College (CEPOL)	Bramshill
		European Agency for Reconstruction	Thessaloniki
	2001	European Data Protection Supervisor	Brussels
	2002	Eurojust	The Hague
		European Maritime Safety Agency	Lisbon (since 2004)
		European Aviation Safety Agency	Cologne (since 2004)
		European Food Safety Authority	Parma (since 2004)
		European Institute for Security Studies	Paris
		European Union Satellite Centre	Torrejon de Ardoz
	2003	European Personnel Selection Office (EPSO)	Brussels
	2004	European Network and Information Security Agency	Heraklion
	2004	European Defence Agency (EDA)	Brussels
	2005	Community Fisheries Control Agency (CFCA)	Vigo
	2005	European Agency for the Management of Operational Cooperation at the External Borders (FRONTEX)	Warsaw
	2005	European Centre for Disease Prevention and Control (ECDC)	Sweden
	2006	European Railway Agency (ERA)	Valenciennes
	2007	European Chemicals Agency (ECHA)	Helsinki
	2007	European Institute for Gender Equality (EIGE)	Vilnius
	2007	European Union Agency for Fundamental Rights (FRA)	Vienna
	2007	The European GNSS Supervisory Authority (GSA) (renamed GNSS Agency in 2010)	Brussels

Cont. ➤

Cont.			
	2008	European Institute of Innovation and Technology (EIT)	Budapest
2010	2011	European Banking Authority (EBA)	London
	2011	European Securities and Markets Authority (ESMA)	Paris
	2011	European Insurance and Occupational Pensions Authority (EIOPA)	Frankfurt

Note: Institutions in bold are designated in the treaties as 'EU institutions'.

laws, and regulations—give the Union's institutions substantial autonomy. For example, the ECJ has had an intensely powerful impact on the shape and direction of European integration both through its own judgments and its integration of national courts into a single system of judicial review (Weiler 1999; Alter 2001). More generally, the EU's institutions are an important reason why European states continue to respond to their interdependence by cooperating (while competing, sometimes fiercely, over the details).

Fourth, the Union's institutions not only manage, but also provide direction. More than the international secretariats of any other international organization, the EU's institutions possess rational-legal authority to make rules. They also create social knowledge in less formal ways: defining shared European tasks; creating new categories of actor (such as refugees or EU citizens); forming new interests for actors or reshaping old ones; and transferring new models of political and administrative organization across Europe (see Barnett and Finnemore 1999). Of course, political direction comes mostly from member governments and is channelled via the European Council and Council of Ministers. But there is scope for agency by the Commission and Parliament, each of which has its own political agenda and priorities that cannot be reduced to the sum total of those of the EU's member governments.

Moreover, the Commission, Parliament, and other EU institutions also act to integrate interests, including those of actors who either oppose or act independently of their home government. Certainly, it is easy to overestimate the EU as a Brussels-based system of politics in which national interests or institutions are marginalized or blended together. As Wallace *et al.* (2010: 9) argue:

much of EU policy is prepared and carried out by national policy-makers and agents who do not spend much, if any, time in Brussels. Instead, what they do is consider how EU regimes might help or hinder their regular activities, and apply the results of EU agreements on the ground in their normal daily work. If we could calculate the proportions, we might well find that in practice something like 80 per cent of that normal daily life was framed by domestic preoccupations and constraints.

At the same time, the EU has given rise to a multilevel polity in which the boundary between politics in national capitals and Brussels is blurred. The Union's institutions have aided and abetted this blurring by providing opportunities for interests, including ones that lack influence at the national level, to join their counterparts across Europe in pursuing common objectives. Many truly pan-European interests have been nurtured, sometimes manufactured, by the Union's institutions. Some lobbies have been energized by their perceived need to respond to agency on the part of the EU's institutions. Witness, for example, the resolute lobbying effort of the European chemicals industry in response to the Commission's proposed REACH (registration, evaluation authorization, and restriction of chemicals) Regulation, which threatened the industry with significant new costs.

Fifth, the EU's institutions are worth studying because they are powerful, yet often unloved or misunderstood by European citizens. Arguably, popular disillusion with the EU's institutions is no more severe—some evidence suggests less—than is disillusion with national institutions and politics.[4] Still, the EU's institutions are clearly not as accepted or well known as national institutions are by European citizens. Average voter turnout in EP elections has fallen with each successive poll. After the French and Dutch voted against the Constitutional Treaty by surprisingly large margins in the 2005 referenda, one seasoned observer detected a 'collapse of self confidence and general morale in the EU institutions' (Palmer 2005; see also Tsakatika 2005). However, its President, José Manuel Barroso, fought back by urging member governments to break their habit of blaming all of Europe's ills on the EU: 'If you attack Brussels six days of the week, can you really expect citizens to support it on Sunday?'[5]

Sixth, the EU's institutions not only link Brussels to national EU capitals, but also link Europe to the wider world of international politics and, particularly, an extensive network of international organizations. As the world's largest trading power, the EU is a crucial player in the World Trade Organization (WTO), and the twentieth member of the G20 (all other members are states). The creation of a European Security and Defence Policy (ESDP) has required extensive interaction with the North Atlantic Treaty Organization (NATO). As the Iraq war illustrated, the EU continues to disappoint those who wish to see it become, in Tony Blair's memorable phrase, 'a superpower, not a super-state'. Yet the Lisbon Treaty has equipped the Union with a potentially powerful, new foreign policy machinery. The post held by Javier Solana, of 'High Representative' for the Common Foreign and Security Policy (CFSP), from 1999 to 2009, was transformed into something like an EU Minister for Foreign Affairs—and was even given that title in the Constitutional Treaty before Lisbon reverted to the more familiar designation of High Representative. The first holder of the post, Catherine Ashton, became both Vice-President for External Affairs of the Commission and chair of the Council of Foreign Ministers. Her post thus combined the intergovernmental with the supranational as no EU post had ever done. Ashton also became head of the new European External Action Service (EEAS), something like a nascent EU foreign ministry, which experienced considerable—even severe—early teething problems, but ones that were predictable given that it drew officials from multiple EU institutions as well as national ministries (see Chapter 13). Nevertheless, the EEAS gave the Union the chance to transform its marginalized delegations in foreign national capitals—almost exclusively staffed by the Commission—into 'real' embassies with expertise, resources, and clout to match or even surpass those of its member states. EU governments clearly were cautious about unleashing the full potential of the EEAS or the High Representative: Ashton was a surprise choice with no previous foreign policy experience. But agreement to create these new institutions by twenty-seven member governments illustrated a remarkable depth of will in Europe to try, at least, to make the EU a more effective global actor.

More generally, the Union's institutions are increasingly powerful actors in the so-called 'international community', a world once almost exclusively dominated by sovereign states. One effect is to allow Europe (sometimes, at least) to wield its formidable, collective power. Perhaps ironically, in an era during which the EU appears to be losing ground in foreign affairs to emerging powers such as China, India, Russia, and Brazil, there are tentative signs that European national capitals were responding to incentives to maximize their power by wielding it collectively more often through the EU.

Seventh, and somewhat paradoxically, EU politics are largely a product of competition between its institutions, but the Union's institutions are inescapably interdependent. The EU's decision rules are designed to foster collective responsibility for the Union's policies. Little of importance may be agreed without the joint consent of the Commission, EP, and Council—with appeal to the ECJ always likely when such consensus is not achieved. The Lisbon Treaty spells out far more explicitly than ever before aims that *all* of the EU's institutions share collectively: to advance the EU's objectives, promote its values, serve the interests of the Union, its citizens and member states, and ensure the consistency, effectiveness, and continuity of its policies. It explicitly states that all EU institutions should work in 'full mutual cooperation'.

Thus our understanding of the Union runs up against hard limits when we study them as separate and autonomous entities. In practice, they form a series of networks, differing in structure and membership in different policy sectors, with each bound together by both formal and informal rules (see Keohane and Hoffmann 1991). Even an institution that is formally designated as independent, such as the European Central Bank (ECB), cannot be understood without reference to the decisions taken by the European Council and the Council of Economic and Finance Ministers (Ecofin) at its inception. In line with institutionalist assumptions, these decisions have heavily structured the kind of decisions the ECB could take as it battled—together with eurozone finance ministers—to cope with the fallout from the global financial crisis post-2008 or the subsequent calamities in the eurozone in 2010–11.

Institutional interdependence is clearly uneven across policy sectors. For example, the EP has little power—other than budgetary—to determine the substantive output of the CFSP. The Commission acts with considerable independence in competition policy. There exists no single mode of EU policy-making (see Wallace 2010). The traditional Community method—which gives distinct and exclusive powers to the Commission, EP, and Council—has often been found inappropriate for new policy tasks, such as freeing labour markets or creating the common security and defence policy (CSDP). These and other objectives have been pursued via the so-called 'open method of coordination' (OMC), which usually involves peer review of national policies as a way in which to disseminate best practices, with policy change occurring voluntarily (as opposed to being imposed by new EU rules) when it occurs at all.

The record of the OMC has been, at best, mixed. More generally, it is easy to conclude that the EU is suffering from 'a crisis of governance' (Eberlein and Kerwer 2004: 135), given its radical enlargement, attempts to tackle problems that are not readily solvable by traditional methods, and the turmoil surrounding the euro. Whether or not new policy modes such as the OMC are just stages on the way towards the embrace of the tried and true Communitarian model (see Wessels 2001), the trend is towards finding new, non-traditional ways in which to encourage collective action on the part of multiple EU institutions. Good examples include the High Representative who, in addition to having two institutional homes in the Council and Commission, is also chair of the Board of Directors (which itself consists of EU defence ministers) of the European Defence Agency (EDA) and chair of the 'P5+1'—a sort of contact group of great powers (including the EU) focused on nuclear diplomacy with Iran. Another example is the European data protection supervisor, who both oversees how the institutions apply the EU's own privacy rules and coordinates a network of data protection officers appointed by each EU institution.

Last, but not least, the Union's institutions are worth studying because they are a testing ground: they will go far towards determining history's verdict on the EU's success in managing enlargement. Since the first edition of this book was published, twelve new states have joined the EU, bringing with them eleven new official languages and increasing the number of language combinations from 110 to 506. No other international organization has ever had to face a challenge on this scale. To illustrate the point, trade officials stressed the gravity of China's accession to the WTO in 2001. Yet even admitting a state with a market of 1.3 billion consumers whose language was not an official WTO working language did not come close to posing the challenges posed by the EU's 2004–07 expansions: mathematically, the WTO would have to have admitted around 105 new states alongside China to stand comparison to what the EU did over the course of just three years. The possible institutional effects of EU enlargement are a central theme of this volume.

'Frustration without disintegration': the persistence of the EU system

We have argued that the EU's institutions are both important and essential to understanding the European Union. It also must be acknowledged that the EU is home to considerable institutional weakness and dysfunction. By no means is the Union alone amongst international organizations in having institutions that sometimes appear obsessed with their own internal rules or neglectful of their missions (Barnett and Finnemore 1999). Yet European citizens who express stronger support for a united Europe in the abstract than for the EU in practice[6] exhibit a sort of collective common sense. It is perfectly plausible to be pro-European, but to believe that the EU's institutional system does not work very well. To illustrate, the EU flag was widely displayed at many 'non' rallies during the 2005 French referendum campaign on the Constitutional Treaty (Palmer 2005).

Part of the problem may be historical. Many of the EU's institutions were created for a Community of six states, not a Union of twenty-seven (plus). Even in the original EEC, very different ideas about what kind of polity the EU should be created scope for weak compromises and institutions that were dysfunctional almost from the moment of their creation (see Lindner and Rittberger 2003). In these circumstances, it could be argued that the EU's institutions have adapted remarkably well to successive enlargements. Yet the 2004–07 enlargements clearly marked a step-level change. The Constitutional Treaty was intended to be a quasi-permanent solution to the problem of modernizing the EU's institutional system so that it could cope with enlargement. Its rejection by French and Dutch voters—as well as the extended battle to ratify the Lisbon Treaty—revealed that Europe remains far from a consensus about what kind of polity the EU should become. In France, in particular, the Union's radical enlargement has generated considerable angst about a '"disembodied" Europe' and 'nurtured feelings that the French state was losing its homogeneity and coherence, while protective frontiers were also progressively disappearing' (Lacroix 2010: 114). More generally, the EU has, arguably, relied for far too long on an institutional system that is long past its sell-by date.

Another part of the problem is political. Without a government (or opposition), the Union often seems unable to steer the European project. For one thing, the project has always depended for its sustenance on appearing to be apolitical, consensual, or uncontroversial. For another, the capacity of the EU's institutions—with the arguable exception of the European Council (see Chapter 3)—to give political impulses to the Union are strictly limited. For all of the capacity of the EU's institutions for agency, political leadership of Europe must inevitably come mostly from national capitals.

A third and related problem is managerial. The 1980s saw the Commission under the presidency of Jacques Delors show genuine political leadership. However, Delors and his College of Commissioners took little interest in efficient management. Amidst charges of mismanagement and nepotism, the collective resignation of the Commission under Delors' successor, Jacques Santer, in March 1999 was a low point in the institutional history of the EU. It illustrated that the EU's lack of hierarchy and reliance on informal networks had serious costs. For students of public management, it was axiomatic that 'pluralistic policy networks are undermanaged because the constituent organisations do not invest in the capacities needed to manage their mutual interdependence' (Metcalfe 2000: 13). For students of the EU, it was hard to resist Metcalfe's conclusion that 'the substandard performance of the system is everyone's problem and no-one's responsibility' (*ibid.*).

Yet there was little question that the Commission was far better managed (if not necessarily better led) by the end of Romano Prodi's presidency in 2004. Prodi's Vice-President and Commissioner for Administrative Reform, Neil Kinnock, piloted an ambitious programme of reforms (see Spence 2000; Kassim 2004b; Kassim *et al.* 2012). Meanwhile, the Council was taking its own steps to better manage its agenda and make itself more transparent. The Court was revamping itself to cut down on its backlog of cases.

One view of these developments is that they reflect the steady maturation of the EU's institutions into modern, high-performance bodies as the Union itself slowly, but steadily, comes of age politically. This view focuses more on long-term process than short-term crises. It assumes that no Constitutional Treaty was ever going to be greeted with universal enthusiasm. It also reminds us that, after all, the version rejected by the French and Dutch in 2005 had been agreed within a broadly inclusive constitutional convention that produced the most transparent and readable European treaty in modern history (see Norman 2005). Implicitly, this view assumes that political consensus on institutional reform was solid enough to make it possible for nearly all of the Constitutional Treaty's provisions to appear unchanged, and then to be approved, in the Lisbon Treaty. For example, the rotating Council presidency system (a source of discontinuity in the work of the Council) was reformed. The Commission kept its virtual monopoly right of legislative initiative. For the first time, the European Council has a sitting President, chosen by the other members, with a mandate for two-and-a-half years.

These two portraits that we have painted—of institutional weakness and fresh dynamism—are less incompatible than they appear. First, consider how one of the primary functions of the EU's institutions, integrating political interests, has often *not* been abetted and sometimes has been actively resisted by member governments. Naturally, perhaps, EU governments wish to retain their own, favoured, primary relationships with voters and interest groups. The result is that the EP and Commission lack powerful, independent sources of authority and support. They also lack resources. The EP has nothing approaching the resources of say, the US Congress (with its large Congressional Research Service, General Accounting Office, and so on). The Commission has one official per 10,000 EU citizens, while national civil services average 300 per 10,000 (Leonard 2005: 15). There are clear limits to the willingness of the Union's member governments to delegate control of the European project.

Second, the EU almost never makes a hard decision today that can be put off until tomorrow. Barroso was explicit in stating that making a success of the so-called Lisbon process of economic reform would be one of the priorities of his (first) Commission. Yet its fate clearly was overwhelmingly determined by difficult decisions that had to be taken at the national level, many of which continue to be avoided (see EU 2004).

Third, and finally, it is impossible to banish path dependency from EU governance. Even after attempts to constitutionalize the EU seemed to go so badly wrong in the mid-2000s (Skach 2005), 'frustration without disintegration' remained an apt description for how the EU's institutional system remained suboptimal, but never stopped working (Scharpf 1999). The desires amongst European governments to make the Union work better but to avoid a genuine process of state-building were both time-honoured impulses by this point, however contradictory they sometimes seemed to be.

The EU's institutions have always, from their earliest origins, operated in a highly contested environment. There is no universal agreement about what the European Union is or ought to be, and never has been. Is it a particularly elaborate international organization that enables states to achieve certain goals more efficiently than they could otherwise do? Or does it now transcend the state, in some areas emerging as more than the sum of its parts? Since academics as well as practitioners (see Box 1.1) give different answers to these questions, they inevitably disagree as to what the Union's institutions—individually and collectively—exist to do.

One thing should be clear from our analysis thus far: the EU's institutions cannot simply be seen as a purely functional set of bodies designed to achieve certain common purposes. If they were, they could be judged purely on the basis of efficiency. Yet the EU's institutional system no longer rests 'on a single principle of legitimacy, but several' (Lord and Magnette 2004: 199). European integration has become a highly political exercise and the EU's institutions have evolved into highly political animals. Arguments about how to make the EU more efficient often ignore widespread doubts about the legitimacy of the Union as a whole (see Habermas 2009).

Thus we encourage our readers to look beyond debates about what each institution should do. Can the EU withstand new demands to be more open and transparent even as it digests radical enlargement? Is the EU a model for the world or a one-off? Are its best days behind it? Answering each of these questions begins, inevitably, by understanding its institutions.

Conclusion

Most leading texts on the EU offer a straight review of what the Treaty designates as institutions, with one chapter each on the Council, Commission, EP, and so on. Less weighty institutions, such as the Court of Auditors and Committee of the Regions, are covered in a composite, 'lest we forget' chapter. This book does not present a simple, standard, one-institution-per-chapter dash across the EU's institutional landscape. Instead, after a historical overview (in Chapter 2) of the attempts at EU institutional reform, we offer three grouped sections of chapters that examine how different institutions:

- provide political direction (Part I);
- manage the Union (Part II); and
- integrate interests (Part III).

Each of these chapters begins with an analysis of the origins and development of the institution specified, followed by an overview of its structure and functions. Each author then reflects on their institution's powers, before considering how it fits into the EU's wider institutional system. Each considers which theories of European integration and EU governance help us best to understand the institution. None ignores the crucial questions of how his or her institution is likely to be changed by enlargement or the Lisbon Treaty.

Some EU institutions—particularly the Commission, Council, and EP—perform more than one function, and thus analysis of them is spread across more than one chapter. The reader who wants to understand the institutions 'one by one' (or the teacher who wants to teach them that way) should not hesitate to read, say, Chapter 5 on the College of Commissioners together with Chapter 8 on the Commission's services. But we encourage the reading of chapters together in the sections into which they are grouped. The effect, we hope, is to help our readers to come to grips with the intensity of both inter-institutional cooperation *and* competition in the performance of the Union's three core functions, and thus to come to grips with the politics of European integration.

NOTES

1. One third of Dutch no voters in the June 2005 referendum cited the euro as a reason for rejecting the Constitutional Treaty. See *Financial Times*, 2 June 2005, p. 6.

2. The story of the social sciences that we present here is one that fits the English-speaking world better than the European continent, where intellectual trajectories have been rather different (see Jørgensen 2000).

3. Arguably (and certainly in strict legal terms), it is incorrect to describe the EU's institutions as 'agents' because they have been attributed wide discretion—not only executive power—and their powers cannot be clawed back by governments, short of closing down the EU altogether. We are grateful to Kieran Bradley for making this point to us.

4. To illustrate the point, the annual Eurobarometer poll of European public opinion in spring 2008 indicated that levels of trust in the EU's institutions were measurably higher than for national governments or parliaments (with an even wider gap, in favour of the EU, between levels of 'mistrust'). See standard *Eurobarometer 69: 4—The European Union and its Citizens*, available online at **http://ec.europa.eu/public_opinion/archives/eb/eb69/eb69_part2_en.pdf**

5. Quoted in *Financial Times*, 9 June 2005.

6. Consistent majorities of European citizens express precisely this view in biannual Eurobarometer surveys (available online at **http://europa.eu**) of public opinion.

FURTHER READING

For alternative perspectives on the EU's institutions, see (particularly on the effect of enlargement) Best *et al.* (2008; in French) Doutriaux *et al.* (2010), and Wallace (2010). The best and most comprehensive coverage of the institutions given in any basic EU text is Nugent (2010). Good overviews of the neoinstitutionalist literature—in which March and Olsen (1989) remains seminal—are Hall and Taylor (1996) and Peters (1996). Essential applications of neoinstitutionalism to the EU are Pierson (1996), Armstrong and Bulmer (1998), and Pollack (2003).

Armstrong, K. and Bulmer, S. (1998) *The Governance of the Single European Market* (Manchester: Manchester University Press).

Best, E., Christiansen, T., and Settembri, P. (2008) (eds) *The Institutions of the Enlarged European Union: Continuity and Change* (Cheltenham and Northampton, MA: Edward Elgar).

Doutriaux, Y., Lequesne, C., and Ziller, J. (2010) *Les Institutions de l'Union Européenne après le traité de Lisbon* (Paris: Lavoisier).

Hall, P. A. and Taylor, R. C. R. (1996) 'Political science and the three new institutionalisms', *Political Studies*, 44/5: 936–57.

March, J. and Olsen, J. (1989) *Rediscovering Institutions* (New York: Free Press).

Nugent, N. (2010) *The Government and Politics of the European Union* (7th edn, Basingstoke and New York: Palgrave).

Peters, B. G. (1996) *Institutional Theory in Political Science* (London and New York: Continuum).

Pierson, P. (1996) 'The path to European integration: a historical institutionalist analysis', *Comparative Political Studies*, 29/2: 123–63.

Pollack, M. (2003) *The Engines of European Integration: Delegation, Agency, and Agenda Setting in the EU* (Oxford and New York: Oxford University Press).

Wallace, H. (2010) 'An institutional anatomy and five policy modes', in H. Wallace, M. A. Pollack, and A. R. Young (eds) *Policy-making in the European Union* (6th edn, Oxford and New York: Oxford University Press).

WEB LINKS

http://ec.europa.eu/
The European Commission's website is the best place to start any search for basic information on the EU's institutions, because it contains links to all of the websites of the Union's other institutions.

http://eiop.or.at/erpa
The European Research Papers Archive (ERPA) is a valuable research tool, offering access to papers posted on the websites of several leading EU research institutes (including the European University Institute in Florence, Italy, and the Harvard Law School) and reliably containing work in the neoinstitutionalist vein.

CHAPTER 2

Institutional Change in the European Union

Renaud Dehousse and Paul Magnette

▋ Summary

EU institutions have frequently been reformed since the origins of what is now the European Union, and particularly so in the last twenty years. This chapter explains why and how this quasi-constant change has taken place. It begins by identifying four phases in this history: the founding, consolidation, adaptation, and rationalization of the institutional system. It then assesses the respective weight of state interests, ideas, and institutions in this process. In retrospect, institutional change in the EU appears to have followed a functionalist logic, leading to complex compromises that, in turn, prompt regular calls for 'simplification' and democratization.

Introduction

It is widely recognized that the dynamics of European integration owe much to the originality of its institutional structure, in which the delegation of powers to supranational institutions has been more intensive than in 'classical' international organizations. However, European institutions themselves have changed significantly since the creation of the European Coal and Steel Community (ECSC) in 1951. The European Union (EU) of 2012, with twenty-seven member countries, had a population of roughly 500 million people. Several treaty changes had recently taken place, and new institutions created. The EU deals with a much wider range of issues than its forerunners of some fifty years ago did. New problems—such as the need to democratize the European political system—have emerged.

The aim of this chapter is to understand how the institutional setting has evolved. To this end, we will begin by reviewing the main changes that have taken place, covering not only the grand 'constitutional moments'—that is, the intergovernmental conferences (IGCs) that have marked the history of European integration—but also the changes that have taken place in the meantime. We will then focus more closely on the European Convention, which took place at the beginning of this century, to determine the extent to which this new episode of treaty reform really differed from earlier ones and what impact it had on the Lisbon Treaty that followed. Finally, we will discuss the main factors that have affected the dynamics of institutional change.

The four phases of institutional development

The institutional system of the European Union has been in constant evolution since its creation in the 1950s. The IGCs that were concluded by the signing of the Treaties of Paris (1951) and Rome (1957) were merely the first of a long series of inter-state negotiations. Indeed, institutional change can be seen as a quasi-permanent feature of the integration process, with many institutional adaptations taking place without treaty reform in the periods between IGCs.

The EU's institutional history can be divided into four phases. These 'stages' are not precisely delimited. But each does have its own peculiarities and consequently its own dynamics of change.

The foundations

Contrary to many other polities, the EU's institutional system was not brought about by a dramatic revolution inspired by a clear doctrine. The long decade between the end of the Second World War and the signature of the Treaty of Rome in 1957 was, in hindsight, a period of trial and error, which gave rise to an unprecedented system via the accumulation of partial compromises. Contrary to what the official historiography would lead us to believe, what is now called the 'Community model' was not born overnight; there was no sudden conversion of European elites to Jean Monnet's plans. Between 1948 and 1957, European leaders were actually torn between competing visions of Europe's future, each reflecting a particular institutional model.

For example, the 'constitutional approach' was a widely shared objective in the founding years. At the Congress of Europe held in The Hague in May 1948 (a private initiative gathering dozens of European movements that had mushroomed in the two preceding years), many voices supported the idea that a European constitutional assembly should be convened to define the basic rules governing relations among European countries. The institutional conceptions of these federalist movements were largely inspired by the American model: the idea that Europe should have its own 'Philadelphia'[1] was their leitmotif. In the following months, however, a clear opposition emerged between governments supporting a federal vision and those conceiving Europe's future in more classical intergovernmental terms. This divide, which echoed the debates of the interwar period, showed that Europe was not ready to adopt anything like the 1787 US Constitution. Ultimately, in May 1949, ten European governments managed to sign the Treaty establishing the Council of Europe. Even before it was signed, however, it was clear for most of its members that the consensus on which it was based was so narrow that it would end in deadlock.

The Schuman Declaration of May 1950, which launched the idea of a more modest European Coal and Steel Community, signalled a change of strategy: the states most interested in deeper European cooperation shifted to a functionalist approach. Although very classical in some respects—confining cooperation to a limited field is a standard practice in international organizations—this approach was founded on an original institutional philosophy. The cornerstone of ECSC institutional architecture was the delegation of powers to an international High Authority, the independence of which was guaranteed, and to a court with much wider powers than other international jurisdictions. In addition, the governments gathered in the Council of Ministers could renounce the classic international practice of unanimity in favour of qualified-majority voting (QMV). By virtue of these 'supranational' elements (a word used both in the Schuman Declaration and in the ECSC Treaty), the 'Community model' entailed greater transfer of powers than other international organizations. It nevertheless fell short of a federal model, given among other things the absence of a direct link to the people (although there was a provision in the Treaty for member states to create such a link—see Chapter 6).

A hybrid institutional system always gives rise to competing interpretations and the Community model was no exception. Many supporters of the functionalist approach hoped that integration would be a dynamic process: that cooperation would extend to other fields due to issue linkages and spill-over effects, so that, ultimately, the functionalist approach could lead to the adoption of a real constitution. In the months following the signing of the Paris Treaty, the dynamics of

European integration did, in fact, seem to accelerate. In an international context marked by the intensification of the cold war, the six member states of the ECSC ('the Six') agreed to try to extend their cooperation to the military field, and negotiated a new treaty establishing a European Defence Community (EDC). In the framework of these negotiations, the governments of the Six also agreed to set up a constitutional assembly (prudently called an 'ad hoc assembly') to define a broader institutional framework inspired by federal principles. Set up in order to gather the various forms of cooperation under a single constitutional umbrella, this assembly came to be known as the European Political Community (EPC). In March 1953, the assembly chaired by Paul-Henri Spaak adopted a draft constitution inspired by federalist principles (Griffith 2001). However, this constitutional phase was short-lived. Only a year later, the EDC Treaty was rejected by the French National Assembly following a heated public campaign, and the EPC sank with it. The rejection of the EDC Treaty led to a revival of the functionalist approach. The 'relaunch' of European integration at the Messina Conference and the subsequent creation of the European Economic Community (EEC) in March 1957 were, in part, a reaction to this failure.

The negotiations that gave rise to the Treaties of Paris and Rome were but the first in a long series of diplomatic bargains between the member states. They took the classic form of IGCs, rather than constitutional assemblies. Formally, the governments never departed from the canons of international practice. The outcome, arrived at through discrete and complex negotiations, was not a constitution, but a treaty agreed upon by 'the High contracting parties'. As such, it could enter into force only after being ratified by all member states. In these conferences, in which each country was represented by a delegation of government officials, mixing diplomats and experts drawn from economic ministries, everything had to be decided by consensus. National experts gathered in working groups to examine the details of the arrangements, while the heads of delegation—usually senior diplomats—met regularly to assess the progress of the negotiations and settle the most sensitive issues in close consultation with foreign ministers. In addition, the heads of state and governments met bilaterally or multilaterally to provide the political impetus and address the most contentious issues. Mindful of the political crisis generated by the ratification of the EDC Treaty, the national delegations worked in closer contact with national parliamentarians, party leaders, and interest groups during the Brussels IGC of 1956–57. But the conference nevertheless remained classically intergovernmental. Its deliberations took place behind closed doors and were almost entirely invisible to ordinary citizens, while the Community institutions merely acted as outside advisers.

In retrospect, this founding decade seems characterized by a constant oscillation between a 'constitutional way' and a functionalist approach. In the end, the repeated failures of the former consolidated the latter (Magnette 2005a). The governments of the member states accepted some limitations on their sovereignty in order to improve the efficiency of their cooperation. But they nevertheless retained control of the process of institutional change.

The consolidation of the Community model

The first decade after the foundation was a period of sharp differences among the Six, which paradoxically strengthened the European Community (EC)'s institutional system. Several governments still hoped to expand the scope of their cooperation and to strengthen the Community institutions, whereas France, under President Charles de Gaulle, was fundamentally concerned with preventing encroachments on its sovereignty. In these circumstances, the Community model was subjected to both centripetal and centrifugal forces.

In the early 1960s, two well-known episodes of the European saga, the rejection of the Fouchet Plans and the 'empty chair' crisis, showed that any attempt to alter the balance between intergovernmentalism and supranationality in the Community model would be opposed by at least one member state. In 1961–62, de Gaulle thought that he could reassert French hegemony by creating a political community based on pure intergovernmental cooperation. The Fouchet Plans, named after de Gaulle's special envoy to European capitals, contemplated both the extension of the scope of European cooperation to military issues and the creation of an administrative secretariat, which was largely seen as a potential rival for the supranational European Commission. These plans were thwarted, however, by the opposition of the Benelux countries (Belgium, the Netherlands, and Luxembourg). Although they had initially feared the supranational High Authority, which they saw as a Trojan horse of French influence, the three small states now realized that a strictly intergovernmental Community would weaken them. In the absence of a supranational agenda-setter and independent monitoring of treaty implementation, it would be harder to resist French dominance.

Advocates of supranationalism were no more successful, however. In 1964, the ambitious Commission President Walter Hallstein sought to strengthen the Commission and the European assembly's powers, believing that he could force France to accept more supranationality in exchange for a consolidation of the common agricultural policy (CAP). But Hallstein had underestimated de Gaulle's capacity for resistance. France deserted Council meetings for six months, before imposing on its partners the so-called 'Luxembourg compromise': a declaration (released only in the form of a press release) that stated that any member state could block any proposal that threatened its 'vital' national interest. The agreement made the use of QMV practically impossible, thereby significantly reducing the Commission's room for manoeuvre (see Chapter 5).

Similarly, the European Court's foundational case law, which gave the Community legal order a quasi-constitutional authority, was paralleled by the reinforcement of intergovernmental influence over decision-making. In a series of landmark cases, and in spite of opposition from several governments, the Court ruled that European law could be invoked directly by private plaintiffs (*direct effect*) even where this was not explicitly contemplated by the treaties, and that it should enjoy *supremacy* in case of conflict with national law (see Chapter 7). This jurisprudence enhanced the pressure on national governments, which now realized that decisions taken in common could limit their freedom of action. In this new legal context, the Commission's prerogatives took on a new dimension: its powers to set the agenda upstream and to monitor the implementation of EU decisions by the national administrations downstream seemed less innocuous (Stein 1981). Moreover, during the same period, a number of ECJ rulings enabled integration to proceed irrespective of deadlocks in the Council (Dehousse 1998). However, these developments in the legal sphere were compensated for by the evolution of policy-making structures. The creation of the Committee of Permanent Representatives (Coreper) and the gradual extension of its tasks enabled governments to control the Commission's power of initiative. Their influence in the executive phase was made possible by another ad hoc development: the establishment of an ever denser network of committees composed of national civil servants to 'assist' the Commission—a phenomenon known in Eurospeak as 'comitology' (Pedler and Schaefer 1996; Joerges and Vos 1998). Like the Luxembourg compromise, these developments confirmed the Community's partly intergovernmental character, in the face of an ever stronger legal supranationalism (Weiler 1981).

The 1960s was thus a paradoxical period in terms of institutional development. Divergences between member states did not allow formal amendment of the treaty, except for the 1965 decision to merge the institutions of the three European communities (the ECSC, the EEC, and the European Atomic Energy Community, or Euratom) without altering their powers. Nonetheless, crucial developments did take place during this same period: the 'constitutionalization' of the Community legal order compensated for the member governments' stronger grip over the policy process. Ultimately, these tensions ended up strengthening the original matrix; the Community model demonstrated its stability by resisting any attempt to strengthen either intergovernmentalism or supranationality.

The 'relaunch': institutional change through task extension

The two decades that followed saw considerable expansion of the European Community. Three consecutive enlargements doubled the number of member states, rendering decision-making more difficult. At the same time, they also created demands for new policies, which ended up pushing in favour of substantial changes.

The 1970s were perceived as a period of relative stagnation due to a severe economic crisis and the institutional strains created by the first enlargement. However, the resignation of General de Gaulle created a political climate more favourable to change. The Treaty revision agreed in Luxembourg in 1970 endowed the EC with its own financial resources, thereby ensuring the financing of the CAP. It also saw an increase—the first in a long series—in the powers of the European Parliament (EP), which was given a significant role in the adoption of the EC budget. At the Paris Summit of 1972, heads of state and government decided to 'relaunch' the integration process by developing policies more in tune with citizens' expectations, such as environmental and consumer protection, and regional development. This decision served to justify the development of a series of policies that went beyond economic integration.

While reflections on the institutional development of the Community were not entirely absent, they failed to trigger any real momentum. At Monnet's instigation, the meetings of heads of state and government were institutionalized with the creation—amid some controversy—of the European Council. A 1976 decision made the direct election of members of the European Parliament (MEPs) possible, realizing an idea first mooted three decades earlier at the Hague Congress. The first directly elected Parliament rapidly pressed for bolder reforms. In 1984, it presented a 'Draft Treaty on European Union' that was clearly inspired by federalist ideas. While several of the ideas contained in that project were picked up in ensuing reforms, it was not even discussed by most of the national parliaments to which it had been sent for consideration.

The Parliament's pressure in favour of institutional reform was, however, exploited by another actor. As soon as Jacques Delors was nominated President of the Commission from 1985, he began searching for a new strategic concept capable of imparting a fresh dynamic to the integration process. Many of the options contemplated at the time—monetary union, joint defence, or institutional reforms—seemed out of reach, as each faced opposition in some national capitals. Delors (2004) and his aides therefore settled for a seemingly more modest plan: the completion of the internal market by the end of 1992. As much of the preparatory work had already been done by the previous Commission, a road map detailing a long series of directives aiming to remove obstacles to free movement was presented to the European Council within a few months. The strength of this approach was that it did not appear to require any major transfer of legal competence or budgetary resources to the European level. Moreover, the emphasis placed on the concept of mutual recognition of national standards, developed by the European Court of Justice (ECJ) in its famous *Cassis de Dijon* ruling (1979), gave the programme a deregulatory flavour. This idea appealed to the UK's Conservative government headed by Margaret Thatcher, which strongly opposed further transfers of power to the Community (Dehousse 1988).

Having secured the member states' support for its 1992 programme, the Commission was then in a good position to obtain the treaty changes that were needed to facilitate its implementation. A large majority of governments supported the Commission's agenda in a vote (the first ever) during the 1985 Milan European Council, where it was decided to convene an IGC. Despite the initial furore among those countries that opposed such a move (the UK, Denmark, and Greece), fears were soon allayed by the pragmatic nature of the proposals tabled by the Commission, which for the most part focused on making it possible to implement the 1992 programme (De Ruyt 1987). The 1985 IGC was both short and largely structured by the Commission's proposals, two features that did not reappear in the IGCs that were to follow (Moravcsik 1998). The Single European Act (SEA), which it elaborated, contained mostly incremental changes: new tasks for the Community (environmental, research, and regional development policies); a closer association of the EP with law-making through the establishment of the so-called cooperation procedure (see Chapter 6); and, above all, the shift to QMV for much of the 1992 legislation. The harvest seemed meagre to the pro-integration camp (Pescatore 1987), but it was sufficient to inject the EC with a new dynamic. Thanks in part to the open texture of several new legal bases, a number of new policy areas were able to develop, which themselves conveyed to European people the feeling that the Community could influence their daily lives.

This episode suggests that when the Commission, acting as a 'policy entrepreneur', is able to 'soften up' the relevant policy community by getting it used to new ideas, it may then make the most of opportunities to push forward its preferred reform proposals (Kingdon 1984). This dynamic was confirmed in the lead-up to economic and monetary union (EMU). When it appeared that the single market was making substantial progress, the Commission began to argue that it needed to be supplemented by greater coordination of macroeconomic policies. Otherwise, the liberalization of capital movements would lead to major disruption (Padoa-Schioppa *et al.* 1987). Delors realized that this prospect had little chance of materializing without the support of central bankers. Thus, he convinced the European Council to create a working party, made up of the governors of the central banks, to discuss the establishment of EMU. This committee, chaired by Delors himself, largely supported the Commission's view and began a gradual move towards a single currency (Committee for the Study of Economic and Monetary Union 1989). The Committee's plans were endorsed by the European Council in June 1989, despite British reservations (compare Box 3.8 in Chapter 3).

The IGC that led to the Maastricht Treaty (1991) largely followed the Delors Committee's blueprint on EMU, emphasizing the establishment of a European Central Bank (ECB), the autonomy of which was protected by the Treaty, and a process of economic policy convergence that was regarded as indispensable prior to the creation of a single currency. But it did not stop there. In the meantime, the collapse of communism in Eastern Europe and the rapid move towards German unification completely modified the context in which the integration process was taking place. Eager to anchor Germany firmly in Europe, French President Mitterrand and German Chancellor Kohl suggested convening a second IGC to deal with the creation of a 'political union' (that is, a pact on non-economic policies and institutional questions), but achievements in this framework were less spectacular. Incremental changes were made to the Community's institutional structure: more majority voting, the opening of new areas to Community intervention, and the advancement of the legislative prerogatives of the EP, notably through the creation of a codecision procedure (see Chapter 6). In addition, the EP was granted the right to approve the appointment of the Commission, a power that went largely unnoticed at the time, but subsequently proved to be of great importance. In contrast, the member states did not consent to any delegation of power in relation to issues of 'high politics', such as foreign policy or immigration policy. The newly created European Union was therefore given a complex structure, the EC being supplemented by two inter-governmental 'pillars' in which the role of supranational institutions was strictly limited. In the view of the masters of the treaty, 'political decisions' were therefore to remain primarily in the hands of national governments.

This mixed result confirmed the experience of the previous decades: transfers of sovereignty are more readily accepted when they are approached in a functional manner, the emphasis being on substantive issues. When institutional issues are handled separately, however, negotiations are likely to end up with a lowest-common-denominator result, as the following IGCs were to confirm.

Adjusting the institutional system

After the monumental changes decided in Maastricht and the intense debates that followed, a period of relative institutional stability might have been expected. In fact, the opposite happened: two IGCs took place in the second half of the 1990s, leading to the Treaties of Amsterdam (1997) and Nice (2000). Even before the latter was ratified, pressure for further reforms led to the convening of a European Convention, which drafted a 'Treaty establishing a Constitution for Europe', signed in Rome in October 2004. How can one account for this acceleration in the pace of change?

Contrary to the previous phase, this period was not characterized by major new projects. The difficult ratification of the Maastricht Treaty had revealed widespread dissatisfaction within the European public and generated a 'spirit of subsidiarity', with many European leaders arguing that the EU should resist the temptation to regulate all matters from Brussels and leave more discretion to national authorities. Instead, institutional change was motivated by two concerns: a desire to respond to criticism of the EU's 'democratic deficit' by bringing the EU institutional architecture closer to European democratic standards, and the need to prepare for the enlargement to Central and Eastern European countries (CEECs).

Meeting these two challenges proved tricky, given the considerable heterogeneity of member states' preferences. The divergences between these preferences largely explain the sustained pace of treaty changes (Moravcsik and Nicolaïdis 1999). The Maastricht Treaty had, in fact, foreseen the 1996 IGC: forced to accept the 'pillar' structure by a minority of their peers, several pro-integration governments obtained the guarantee that the institutional setting would be revisited four years later. This scenario was repeated in Amsterdam in 1997 and in Nice in 2000: unable to reach a comprehensive agreement, but unwilling to abandon their claims, a group of governments ensured that the process of institutional revision continued.

Democratic concerns were not the main difficulty. As will be seen, European governments tend to share a vision of democracy in which the parliamentary element plays a key role, which makes compromises easier. Indeed, from the SEA to the Lisbon Treaty, the most stable trend in institutional change has been the increase in the powers of the EP.

The reforms aiming to help the EU to adjust to its new membership have proved much more controversial. This problem was unprecedented; whereas earlier enlargements had meant incorporating a maximum of three countries at a time without altering the initial balance between large and small states, the 2004 enlargement involved ten countries, of which nine were small states. Mechanical adjustments were therefore not sufficient; they would have led to an excessive increase in size of both Commission and the EP, and given too much influence to the small states in the Council. Strategic disagreements made compromise difficult. Since unanimity was required for treaty changes, the pro-integration camp, which found strong support in the Commission and the Parliament, argued that consolidating the institutional structure was a necessary precondition of enlargement. In contrast, the CEECs, having recently recovered their sovereignty, were anxious not to have it diluted in the EU. Other countries, such as the UK, Denmark, and Sweden, hoped that enlargement would counterbalance the integration that had taken place over the course of the previous decade.

The problem was addressed unsuccessfully during the Amsterdam negotiations. The Nice IGC in 2000 confirmed the sensitivity of the issues. The large countries tried to reassert their influence to avoid being constrained by coalitions of smaller states, while the latter resisted attempts to reduce their weight in the EU institutions. The classic federal dilemma between equality of states and equality of population became more tense than ever. As the EU regime is based on a complex balance of state representation in the three poles of the institutional triangle, changes made at the level of one institution rendered adaptations indispensable in the others, as well as in the balance of power among the institutions. The large states were willing to abandon their right to appoint a second Commissioner (see Chapter 5), but only to the extent that this loss was compensated by having their positions strengthened in the two other institutions. This crucial issue could not be solved in Nice. After protracted bickering, a complex compromise was reached, including a redistribution of seats in the EP, the eventual downsizing of the Commission, and a re-weighting of votes in the Council. This agreement was the focus of intense criticism, however, so that these issues re-emerged as one of the central contentions of the treaty reform negotiated in the years that followed.

What did the Convention method change?

On 9 May 2000, Joschka Fischer, then German Minister for Foreign Affairs, made a speech in Berlin, calling for the adoption of a European constitution—and thereby sparking intense debate on the institutional future of the EU. In the ensuing months, the leaders of most member states made their own views public.

Those who advocated transforming the procedure of treaty change made a twofold argument. In terms of substance, the EU's institutional system had to undergo thorough reform before the next enlargement (Dehaene *et al.* 1999). In terms of process, the Nice Summit had demonstrated the limits of the IGC process: more inclusive and more transparent methods were required. The precedent of the first Convention—set up in 1999 to draft a Charter of Fundamental Rights—offered an alternative model consistent with a 'constitutional' perspective on the issues at stake, given that it comprised European and national parliamentarians, and operated in public. The assumption underlying this argument was that a new process would produce a new outcome. One year after the bitter compromise reached in Nice, the governments of the member states seemed to subscribe to this idea when, at the Laeken European Council (2001), they agreed to create a new body to prepare a blueprint for the next IGC and to reflect, among other things, on the constitutionalization of the EU. The European Convention comprised a broader range of actors, a number of whom were independent from national governments (the two Commissioners, most of the MEPs, and MPs drawn from the domestic opposition, making up about a third of the members). Half a century after its foundation, the EU appeared ready to resume the constitutional work abandoned after the abortive attempts of the 1950s.

Two years later, the Convention had adopted its draft 'Treaty establishing a Constitution for Europe'. EU governments signed the 'Constitutional Treaty' in Rome on 24 October 2004. To what extent did the transformation of the process shape the eventual outcome?

Of course, supporters of the convention model had a vested interest in this process. The EP and the Commission which, until then, were deprived of a formal role in treaty reforms,[2] expected their representatives to be associated as full and equal partners with governments. Likewise, the representatives of the smaller member states had discovered in previous IGCs that their ability to shape the final outcome of the negotiations was limited (Moravcsik and Nicolaïdis 1999). Resorting to their veto power, while possible in theory, was extremely costly. They hoped that the framework of the Convention (composed of over a hundred members and in which government representatives would have to negotiate with MEPs, Commissioners, and national parliamentarians) would mean that the influence of large countries would be lessened and the range of opportunities to forge alternative coalitions broadened. Obviously, expectations of this kind were strongest among those governments who wanted to go beyond the status quo—namely, the Benelux countries, Finland, Greece, and Portugal.

On the other side of the fence, governments from bigger member states (with the exception of Germany) were less inclined to change the rules of the game. They were nevertheless all aware of the limits of the IGC method. The setting up of the Convention was therefore accompanied by safeguards enabling governments, acting collectively and individually, to remain in control of future developments. First, the Convention would only be a preparatory body, all decisions remaining with the IGC. Second, national representatives would make up three-quarters of the membership. Finally, the Convention's President would be appointed by, and report to, the European Council.

The Convention was thus the middle ground between the intergovernmental tradition and the constitutional approach that had been supported by the federalist movements since the 1950s. However, the Convention was free to organize its own work and it had to deliberate in public—a factor that, according to students of constitution-making, renders the crude expression of naked interests more difficult (Elster 1998). On the other hand, the conventioneers knew that their text would be only a draft, and that it could be altered by the IGC that would follow.

From his inaugural speech up until the conclusion of the Convention eighteen months later, the chairman, former French President Valéry Giscard d'Estaing, dwelled on the originality of this experience. He insisted on the need *not* to reproduce the patterns of former IGCs, in which member states sought to maximize their gains 'without regard for the overall picture'. Instead, he tried to convey what he called a 'Convention spirit':

If your contributions genuinely seek to prepare a consensus, and if you take account of the proposals and comments made by the other members of the Convention, then the content of the final consensus can be worked out step by step here within the Convention.

(Giscard d'Estaing 2002: 14)

To some extent, this strategy was successful, at least in the first part of the Convention's work. The majority of the conventioneers shared Giscard's ambitions, and looked for a comprehensive compromise. They took the time to deliberate on each and every issue in plenary sessions, and to examine the most technical issues in more detail within smaller working groups. They were helped by a rather flexible Presidium, which coordinated their work, and by an efficient Secretariat, which provided them with detailed notes on the state of the EU. The flexibility of this organization, the absence of obvious pressures from governments, and the collective willingness of most members to reach an ambitious outcome, as well as the 'constitutional ethos' surrounding their work, all combined to make compromises possible on several issues that former IGCs had been unable to settle. These included the abolition of the pillars, the consolidation of the treaties, the EU's legal personality, the simplification of decision-making procedures, and the incorporation of the Charter on Fundamental Rights into the draft Constitution. All of these points were agreed without contention in the early stages of the Convention's work (Magnette 2005b). True, none of these elements were totally new and original, and the legal clarity of the text was often disputable (Jacqué 2004), but the Convention nevertheless succeeded where the three previous IGCs had failed.

But, by the autumn of 2002, when discussions on institutional issues were initiated, the pendulum moved back to traditional forms of diplomatic bargaining. Most government representatives started openly to defend their briefs, to build coalitions among themselves, and to use thinly veiled threats of vetoing in the IGC. All Convention members were well aware of this threat. Neither political parties nor institutional representatives were able to develop coherent positions, except in a few specific instances. Instead, two classic cleavages dominated the debate (Magnette and Nicolaïdis 2004): the traditional opposition between 'federalist' and 'intergovernmentalist', as well as that between large and small countries. With the exception of Germany, the former sought to strengthen the role of the European Council, and thereby the role of governments in the decision-making process; meanwhile most small states defended supranational institutions and the rotating presidency of the Council. A Franco–German compromise, made public in January 2003, sought to reconcile the two views by combining the French demand for a 'permanent' European Council President with the German desire to see the Commission President elected by the Parliament. The final compromise, reached through typical intergovernmental negotiation (with MEPs kept on the sidelines), reflected the Franco–German proposal. When the proposed reform was supported by a very large majority, a government that was isolated on points that could not easily be presented as non-negotiable 'red lines' (as was the UK on the incorporation of the Charter of Fundamental Rights) was generally forced to make unilateral concessions.

The Presidium played an important role in shaping the final outcome. On the one hand, like presidencies in IGCs (Tallberg 2004), it acted as an organizer and a mediator with the support of the Convention's Secretariat, seeking to forge a compromise on a step-by-step basis. It chose to do so, however, not by leaving options open until a last-minute package deal could be made, but rather by submitting a single negotiating text that became the reference or the status quo, with the burden of proof being put on the dissenters. On the other hand, since the Presidium was a collective organ rather than a single presiding member state, it could present its viewpoints as 'the best possible compromise'. Potential vetoes were forestalled and actual ones ignored—such as the Spanish and Polish opposition to the idea of a double majority (50 per cent of states, 60 per cent of population) that would replace the system of weighted votes agreed on in Nice. These tactics succeeded in bringing about a 'consensus' that might have eluded a traditional IGC. But they also left a decidedly bitter taste for many delegates, which in the end may have deprived the Presidium proposal of the kind of legitimacy that a more negotiated text would have had. Unsurprisingly, the governments of Poland and Spain, the objections of which had been ignored, subsequently played a major role in the failure of the Brussels Summit in December 2003. Indeed, the IGC was not a mere rubber-stamping exercise: it had to settle these contentious issues and governments used this opportunity to re-examine several aspects of the draft treaty, rejecting some of the Convention's innovations and adding new ones.

Even though the reference to a Constitution suggested a radical break with the past, continuity was the main theme of the new document. Not only did it require ratification by all member countries before it could come into force, but intergovernmental negotiations and unanimous ratification were also deemed necessary for future modifications. Many of the innovations contained in the text had actually been discussed in previous IGCs, and the elements that consolidated the supranational institutions (more QMV and more codecision) were similar to those of earlier interstate bargains. Above all, several of the changes introduced, from the full-time President of the European Council to the status of the double-hatted Foreign Minister, who would also be a member of the Commission and accountable to the European Council, showed a clear reluctance to allow the development of a strong executive at the European level. The contention that 'all institutions have been strengthened' simply showed an inability to choose between a supranational and an intergovernmental approach.

The Lisbon Treaty: back to basics?

Despite (or perhaps because of) its fundamental ambiguity, the Constitutional Treaty became a source of concern in some circles, particularly among those who felt left behind by an integration process that did not seem to respond to their day-to-day problems. These feelings of alienation appear to have played a major role in the rejection of the treaty in France and the Netherlands, where referenda were organized (Dehousse 2005; Sauger *et al.* 2007). This time was not the first time that a proposed reform was rejected in a referendum: the Danes, at the time of the Maastricht Treaty, and the Irish, on the occasion of the Nice Treaty, had done so in the past. Yet the shock was particularly brutal in this case. Not only did the failure of the draft Constitutional Treaty leave the Union with the institutions carved in Nice, which many argued would not work efficiently with twenty-seven member countries, but the campaign had also brought to the fore a deep mistrust vis-à-vis European institutions that appeared too remote to be controlled. To make things worse, given the intensity of the debate in countries in which referenda were held, it could hardly be argued that the negative outcome was to be attributed to a lack of interest. There was therefore little point in organizing a new referendum to verify the people's feelings. At the same time, no threat of exclusion was deemed to be possible against France or the Netherlands, as founding members of the EU.

These elements are recalled here for they largely conditioned the way out of the crisis. On the one hand, the Commission reverted to a functionalist rhetoric, advocating an emphasis on a 'Europe of results' (Barroso 2007). On the other, in his successful bid for the French presidency, Nicolas Sarkozy announced that he would, if elected, seek his partners' support for a 'modifying treaty' that, while abandoning the state-like symbolism of the Constitutional Treaty, would preserve most of its substance. Having rallied a large majority of voters, he could legitimately claim to have been given a mandate to implement this solution, which the other member states were broadly happy to accept.

The Lisbon Treaty therefore appears as a return to the logic of incremental change that has dominated the history of European integration since the 1950s. Technically, it consists of amendments to its forerunners. In substance, it extends earlier reforms: more majority voting in the Council; more powers to the EP; the completion of the transfer of justice and home affairs (JHA) to the 'first pillar'; an improved synergy (so one hopes) between the 'Community method' and the policy regime applied to foreign policy. All are important reforms, for sure, but none appears to have been designed to achieve a major transformation of the EU policy system. The Lisbon Treaty essentially leaves the balance of power unchanged. Although the Parliament's powers have been consolidated, the EU has stopped short of a real parliamentary system since the Commission still owes prime allegiance to the European Council.[3] Typical features of the Community method—such as the Commission's right of initiative and QMV—have been extended. But, at the same time, the newly created President of the European Council has rapidly emerged as a potentially powerful rival of the Commission. Once more, ambiguity appears to be one of the essential attributes of the eventual compromise.

The dynamics of institutional change

The history of institutional change in the European Union shows that its motivations and dynamics vary widely over time. The process responds to various logics. It is nevertheless possible to identify three permanent factors of change and the conditions under which they may influence the negotiation. The classical trilogy of interests, institutions, and ideas (Hall 1997) serves as a helpful guide.

The weight of interests

That institutional change has largely been shaped by state interests should not come as a surprise. After all, when the EU was created, it took the form of an inter-state agreement that, like most treaties, could be modified only with the assent of all parties. Economic interests played a key role in this process, as the states saw the construction of Europe as a means to reassert their influence in an increasingly interdependent world (Milward 1992). Domestic concerns clearly impinged upon governments' attitudes whenever reforms were contemplated. France's farming interests, Germany's industries, and the need to foster free trade for export-oriented Benelux countries featured prominently in the European agenda of their respective governments. The most important stages of the integration process have therefore been associated with the key interests of the member states. Institutional changes have generally responded to an instrumental logic rather than to some kind of grand design. Governments, having defined a series of objectives, bargained to reach 'substantive agreements concerning cooperation, and finally selected appropriate international institutions in which to embed them' (Moravcsik 1998: 5).

The contours of institutional evolution have also been shaped by states' desire to retain some control over the process. Intergovernmental bodies were thus given a central role: the position of the Council of Ministers in decision-making was consolidated by structures such as Coreper, the web of intergovernmental committees, and the European Council. More recent developments, such as the Maastricht pillar system or the creation of the High Representative for foreign policy, were clearly inspired by reluctance to relinquish power in sensitive areas. Representative concerns are apparent in the design of every European institution, including the supranational ones: nationals of all member countries sit in the Commission and on the Court's bench. Balance among states has certainly been a key point in most institutional negotiations and, from the outset, QMV within the Council of Ministers was based on a system of weighted votes balancing the equality of states and demographic size. The three biggest states made sure that they would need only one ally to block a decision, while preventing the three small ones from forming a blocking minority. Fifty years later, these strategic concerns are as salient as ever, as shown by the drafting of the Constitutional Treaty. The debates on the composition of the Commission (should it include one national of each member state or should it be reduced in size?), on the presidency of the Union (should the system of rotation among member states be maintained, or should it be replaced by a permanent chair?), and on the reform of QMV (should the system of weighted votes be maintained or should it be replaced by a more proportional double majority?) were all clearly dominated by the governments' ambitions to maximize their weight in the EU's decision-making bodies.

While the emphasis on states' interests has occupied a central place in the analysis of European integration, it should not blind us to the importance of other factors. On several occasions, states have decided that their interests were better served by mechanisms that could facilitate their negotiations (the Commission's monopoly of initiative), reduce transaction costs (majority voting in the Council), or ensure that joint decisions would be implemented fairly by their partners (the enforcement powers of the Commission and the Court). Furthermore, supranational actors have often used their (formal or informal) powers to foster their own interests as an institution, as discussed below.

The role of institutions

Understood in their broadest sense, as the rules that structure political relationships (Steinmo 2004), institutions have also considerably influenced the dynamics of change. This point is quite clear in the case of formal rules: the requirement of unanimity for any amendment to the treaties means that governments must take the final crucial steps in the negotiations. They can also use the threat of non-ratification by their legislature to obtain concessions from their partners. Likewise, the change in the rules of the game reflected in the setting up of the convention allowed for the development of a new dynamic, which largely explains why the convention could reach an agreement on issues where previous IGCs had failed. There are also informal rules affecting the way in which actors behave. Smaller countries know that the veto power they enjoy can be used only sparingly, and preferably not without allies when a major reform is at stake. This explains why Belgium in Nice, or even Poland at the 2004 IGC, ended up accepting agreements that they had forcefully opposed.[4]

While these principles are valid in many international regimes, the weight of institutions is of particular relevance at EU level, because of the political clout enjoyed by its supranational organs. They are endowed with a substantial degree of autonomy, and thus are naturally inclined to promote interests of their own. As was seen earlier, through its rulings on direct effect and supremacy, the ECJ has conferred a federal structure on the European legal order. In so doing, however, it has considerably increased its own role in the integration process (Dehousse 1998). The Parliament's stubborn insistence on the need to address the 'democratic deficit' was, of course, underpinned by its eagerness to improve its own institutional position.[5] Likewise, we have seen that even if it is deprived of any formal role in IGCs, the Commission can at times shape the contours of the final agreement, by acting as a policy entrepreneur or as a mediator between national preferences. The SEA is the best illustration of this kind of dynamic. One year before the conclusion of that treaty, three member states had opposed any extension of majority voting in the so-called Dooge Committee. It was the Commission that developed the idea that enabled a breakthrough, and it did so by drawing inspiration from principles laid dowm in the path-breaking *Cassis de Dijon* case law of the ECJ (1979). Thus, even if one accepts the centrality of interstate negotiations in the cumbersome process of institutional change, one must recognize that state preferences are not static and can be influenced by the action of supranational institutions (Dehousse and Majone 1994).

When do ideas matter?

In addition to state interests and institutional constraints, ideas can, at times, contribute to shaping the EU's institutional system. All of the actors of the EU political system have their own views of what the system should look like. In some cases, those views are derived from the actors' broader perceptions of the nature of the EU. Since its origins, two competing interpretations of the 'meaning' of European integration have proved very significant: the federalist doctrine remains influential in some circles, particularly in the founding member states; others see the EU as a functional organization, designed to maximize economic state interests in an increasingly interdependent world economy—a view that underlies British leaders' perceptions of the EU, and which is also widespread in Nordic and Central European countries. These two 'models' are, in key respects, the poles of the debate. They structure, positively or negatively, the ongoing discussion on the EU's *raison d'être*, very much like the 'federalist' and 'anti-federalist' doctrines that dominated constitutional debates in the US for decades. As such, they bear their own institutional patterns. In some cases, governments may support an institutional reform that defies their own short-term interests—such as when the Benelux countries defend the extension of the EP's prerogatives, although they are less over-represented in this institution than in the Council—because it is part of their broader vision of the EU.

A country's perceptions of institutional structures will very often also reflect its own national political culture. When German leaders support the parliamentarization of the EU's regime, they tend, explicitly or not, to project the constitutional balance of the Federal Republic (Kohler-Koch 2000). French politicians, on the other hand, tend to perceive the European Council as a collective 'head of state', and to consider the Commission–European Council duopoly as a European equivalent of the Fifth Republic's dualist executive (Quermonne *et al.* 1999). The Nordic insistence on the transparency-enhancing mechanisms of the EU system (the ombudsman, parliamentary scrutiny, and the publicity of the Council's deliberations) is another example of the importation of national traditions into the EU (Gronbech-Jensen 1998).

Although some of these ideas have found their way into the EU treaties, they remain secondary factors of change. In most cases, the governments' positions depend on how they perceive their own interests. When the long-term implications of an institutional decision are unclear, however, ideas may be influential. This phenomenon may notably explain the gradual consolidation of the EP's powers— one of the most original aspects of EU institutional evolution, strengthened even though it may undermine the influence of member states. Some governments were prompted to support this consolidation by an ideological bias in favour of parliamentary democracy (Dehousse 1995); others made what they considered symbolic concessions with no foreseeable impact on their interests (Pollack 1997; Moravcsik 1998; Rittberger 2001). Needless to say, governments' expectations can, at times, prove wrong: one of the 'minor' concessions made to parliamentary orthodoxy in the Maastricht Treaty—the conferral on the EP of the right to approve the appointment of the Commission—allowed the assembly to gain significant leverage over the European executive (Magnette 2001).

It should not come as a surprise that, generally, 'federalist ideology is still required to account for the general institutional structure of the EC' and particularly 'its quasi-constitutional form' (Moravcsik 1998: 153). As one legal theorist puts it, 'A good deal of legal development (and this includes constitutional development) is autonomous ... The decision actually taken is chosen out of habit, or out of respect for the constitutional practices and traditions' (Raz 2002: 156). When they think of the EU's overall institutional order, governments tend to reason, like the lawyers of the EU institutions, in the conceptual terms with which they are familiar. This reasoning has facilitated agreement on reforms aiming to 'simplify' the institutional and legal order of the EU by making it more compatible with classic constitutional canons. Like most other polities, the EU oscillates between institutional complexity prompted by pragmatic concerns to accommodate divergent interests, and institutional rationalization driven by the leaders' will to clarify the rules of the game (Olsen 2002). This oscillation may help us to understand why, at the turn of the century, EU leaders collectively flirted with the 'constitutional' idea, only to abandon it as soon as it appeared that it met with sustained opposition in some countries.

Conclusion

The institutional history of the European Union can be read in several ways. On the one hand, the system has substantially evolved: successive enlargements and expansion of the tasks delegated to the Union have created regular pressures for adaptation. On the other, it has demonstrated remarkable stability: the EU has not become a centralized superstate, nor have member states done away with the atypical powers enjoyed by the European Commission (such as its right to initiate legislation). On several occasions, attempts to consolidate the powers of the supranational institutions have been balanced by governments' determination to see their role in the system preserved.

Institutional change has been mostly incremental. For all of the surrounding rhetoric, even the Constitutional Treaty signed in 2004 could not really be seen as marking a rupture in the history of European construction, as it largely built on innovations introduced at earlier stages. IGCs have been the key moments in this evolution, but they cannot be understood independently from the rest of the process. Their successes have owed much to the institutional adjustments that have taken place between conferences (Héritier 2007). Their failures have paved the way for continuing tensions.

This gradualism is largely the result of a process in which governments retain the central role because they must agree to all formal changes. For the same reason, functionalism has been the main force in this evolution. Governments had to agree on joint objectives prior to any major transfer of powers to the European level. Agreed objectives, however, are but one part of the story. The complexity of the system has generated pressures for simplification and legitimation as part of a process in which ideational factors play an important role. The European Commission has, at times, succeeded in influencing the preferences and negotiation strategies of the member states. The coexistence of these contrasting forces largely accounts for the schizophrenic nature of an institutional evolution simultaneously characterized by a consolidation of intergovermentalism and the conferral of ever-larger powers onto the European Parliament. The rigidity of the 'constitutional charter' is another explanation for the fundamental ambiguity of most reforms: unanimity being required for any change, they must appeal both to supranationalists and supporters of states' rights. In all likelihood, the same structural factors will impinge upon future changes and prevent a radical simplification of European institutional architecture as long as each member country retains a right of veto on proposed changes. Calls for more flexibility have been made, advocating, for example, more transparency in the treaty revision process or stressing the necessity to do away with unanimity. But so far they have fallen on deaf ears.

At any rate, a decade of institutional discussions has made clear that there is no real consensus on what the ultimate organization of the Union should look like. For all of its ambiguity, the Lisbon Treaty was widely seen as a kind of plateau from which it would not be easy to move. Enlargement has made the Union more diverse, and the many changes brought about by globalization appear to have created in public opinion a strong ambivalence vis-à-vis the integration process. In such conditions, the prospects for large-scale reform remain limited. However, external factors may well decide otherwise. The recent turmoil on the financial markets is quite telling in this respect. There is little doubt that EU member states were satisfied with the somewhat unbalanced system set up in Maastricht at the time that economic and monetary union was created, with a centralized monetary policy on the one hand, and loosely coordinated macroeconomic governance on the other. Yet by questioning the credibility of this system, the markets have forced reluctant governments to accept the principle of a reform that is likely to lead to a greater degree of centralization. Either the European leaders will be able to devise a reform that will meet their concerns, or they might ultimately threaten the existence of the euro, with devastating consequences for the single market. Of all possible options, the status quo is the most unlikely, despite the intrinsic rigidity of the current quasi-constitutional arrangement.

NOTES

1. The US Constitution was drafted by delegates of the thirteen states gathered in Philadelphia in 1787.

2. Although two members of the EP had been nominated as members of the Westendorp group that prepared the negotiation of the 1996–97 IGC, the MEPs themselves acknowledged that this minimal form of participation did not give them the opportunity to influence the outcome significantly, since this group only identified 'questions' and 'options', and all decisions were left to the IGC. In 1994, before the enlargement that took place the following year, some MEPs had also suggested that the EP should threaten to refuse its 'assent' to the treaty changes to force the governments to adopt the reforms that they advocated, but these MEPs could not form a majority within the Parliament. Their threats were thus far from credible.

3. See the new Art. 17, para. 7, of the Treaty on European Union (TEU).

4. In Nice, as part of the new Treaty, Belgium was asked to accept to have fewer votes under QMV than the Netherlands, with which it had always had numerical parity in the past (despite Belgium's population being only about two-thirds that of the Netherlands). Poland had to accept a new QMV system in the Constitutional Treaty that was far less favourable to it numerically than the system in the Treaty of Nice.

5. This does not mean that the EP proved able to impose its views upon the governments. In only two cases was the EP really able to do this successfully. The first concerns the Commission's appointment, after the 1992 Maastricht Treaty gave the EP the power to approve the candidate for Commission President nominated by member governments. As a result, the MEPs were able to use the threat of refusing this approval to press their case for being consulted on the College's appointment as a whole. The second case

concerns their influence in the codecision procedure, also created by the Maastricht Treaty. The MEPs managed to prevent the Council making systematic use of the possibility to put its position to a vote in the Parliament after failed conciliation negotiations, by firmly rejecting the one Council text (relating to voice telephony in the summer of 1994) on which it was invited to vote. In Amsterdam in 1997, governments brought these practices, established by the Parliament, into alignment with the Treaty (Hix 2002a). But these are exceptions that cannot be generalized. In many other cases, the claims supported by the majority in the EP (for example, approval of appointments to the ECJ and consolidating budgetary power by giving the EP rights over revenue) were not followed up by governments (Costa 2001).

 FURTHER READING

There is no systematic overview of institutional change in the EU available in the current literature. In-depth historical accounts can be found in Moravcsik (1998), which remains the classic presentation of the liberal intergovernmentalist interpretation. For more recent periods, see Moravcsik and Nicolaïdis (1999), and Magnette and Nicolaïdis (2004). Analyses of individual institutions can be found in Kassim *et al.* (2012) for the European Commission, Costa (2001), (in French) and Corbett *et al.* (2011) for the EP, Hayes-Renshaw and Wallace (2006) for the Council, and Dehousse (1998) for the Court. On the role of ideas in the founding period, Parsons (2003) offers a stimulating view, as does Rittberger (2001), who offers an institutionalist reading.

Corbett, R., Jacobs, F., and Shackleton, M. (2011) *The European Parliament* (8th edn, London: John Harper).

Costa, O. (2001) *Le Parlement Européen, Assemblée Délibérante* (Brussels: Editions de l'Université de Bruxelles).

Dehousse, R. (1998) *The European Court of Justice: The Politics of Judicial Integration* (Basingstoke and New York: Palgrave).

Hayes-Renshaw, F. and Wallace, H. (2006) *The Council of Ministers* (2nd edn, Basingstoke and New York: Palgrave).

Kassim, H., Peterson, J., Bauer, M., Dehousse, R., Hooghe, L., Connolly, S., and Thompson, A. (2012) *The European Commission of the 21st Century* (Oxford and New York: Oxford University Press).

Magnette, P. and Nicolaïdis, K. (2004) 'The European Convention: bargaining under the shadow of rhetoric', *West European Politics*, 27/3: 381–404.

Moravcsik, A. (1998) *The Choice for Europe: Social Purpose and State Power from Messina to Maastricht* (Ithaca, NY: Cornell University Press).

Moravcsik, A. and Nicolaïdis, K. (1999) 'Explaining the Treaty of Amsterdam: interests, influence, institutions', *Journal of Common Market Studies*, 37/1: 59–85.

Parsons, C. (2003) *A Certain Idea of Europe* (Ithaca, NY: Cornell University Press).

Rittberger, R. (2001) 'Which institutions for post-war Europe? Explaining the institutional design of Europe's first Community', *Journal of European Public Policy*, 8/5: 673–708.

PART I

Providing Direction

CHAPTER 3

The European Council

Philippe de Schoutheete

▌ Summary

Since its creation in 1974, the European Council has played a fundamental role in the development of European integration. It gives political guidance and impetus to the Union, takes the most important decisions, gives high visibility to external policy positions and declarations, and plays a major role in amending the treaties. Its composition gives it an intergovernmental character, yet successive decisions at that level have increased the supranational character of the Union. The European Council has been, for more than thirty years, a formidable locus of power, and the Lisbon Treaty gives it the formal status of an institution of the Union under the leadership of a permanent President.

Introduction

With the entry into force of the Lisbon Treaty, the European Council became an institution of the European Union. It brings together heads of state or government (a formula designed to cover the situation of the French and Finnish presidents, both of whom are heads of state and chief executives) together with its own President and the President of the Commission. The High Representative of the Union for Foreign Affairs and Security Policy is also present. Ministers or a member of the Commission can be invited to attend when the agenda so requires. Apart from a very small number of European civil servants, nobody else is allowed in the meeting. This is the essence of the European Council: a limited number of political figures, including the chief executives of all member states, meeting in a closed room with no assistants.

The Treaty specifies that the European Council 'shall provide the Union with the necessary impetus for its development and shall define the general political directions and priorities thereof'. In fact, over the years, it has been involved in detailed decision-making on a great number of issues. The Treaty and the Rules of Procedure indicate that the European Council shall meet at least four times a year. In fact, regular use of informal meetings and occasional meetings in the margins of summits with third countries lead to more frequent contacts, particularly in times of crisis. Under the French presidency in 2008, heads of government met practically every month.

European Council meetings are held in Brussels in the Justus Lipsius building, which also houses the Council, and where the President of the European Council has his offices. A separate building for the European Council, in the immediate proximity, is planned for completion in 2012. In exceptional circumstances, meetings may be organized outside Brussels.

Two points about the European Council should always be kept in mind:

- As an institution of the Union, the European Council has, in some circumstances, the power and the obligation to adopt acts having legal effect, which was not the case before the Treaty of Lisbon. The European Court of Justice (ECJ) has, as it always has, the power to rule on the legality of such acts. The European Council now therefore needs to pay due attention to legal form and this explains why its first act, when the Lisbon Treaty entered into force, was formally to adopt rules of procedure, which previously did not exist.

- When adopting treaty changes, as they did in Maastricht, Amsterdam, Nice, and Lisbon, the participants meet not as a European Council, but as an intergovernmental conference (IGC) at the level of heads of state or government.[1] This legal distinction is not generally understood by public opinion and frequently ignored even by participants.

Origins

Heads of government have always played an important role in the development of European integration. The legendary Belgian Foreign Minister, Paul-Henri Spaak (1969: II.95) described a meeting in Paris in February 1957, on the eve of the signature of the Treaty of Rome, in which heads of government had to settle the last politically sensitive issues: 'It went on day and night. I had to run from one to the other, pleading, looking for compromises. Finally at dawn on 20 February a solution was found.' This sounds no different from some present-day European Councils. But regular meetings of what was to become the 'European Council' were only decided at a summit in Paris in December 1974 (see Box 3.1), and the first such meeting was held in Dublin in March 1975.

At the time, two reasons were put forward as justifications for the decision. Community institutions were felt not to be working as well as they should, especially since the Luxembourg compromise of 1965 was in practice blocking majority voting. The first enlargement of the Community (the UK, Ireland, and Denmark) was likely to make decision-making more ponderous. The creation of a regular (as opposed to an occasional) source of strategic direction and political impulse made sense in this context.

Foreign ministers were (already) finding it difficult to coordinate the activities of a growing number of Council formations. Moreover, the first efforts at foreign policy coordination, or European political cooperation (EPC), posed a problem. Some

---

BOX 3.1   The origins of the European Council

Conclusions of the Paris Summit meeting, December 1974

- Recognizing the need for an overall approach to the internal problems involved in achieving European unity and the external problems facing Europe, the Heads of Government consider it essential to ensure progress and overall consistency in the activities of the Communities and in the work on political co-operation.

- The Heads of Government have therefore decided to meet, accompanied by the Ministers of Foreign Affairs, three times a year, whenever necessary, in the Council of the Communities and in the context of political cooperation. The administrative Secretariat will be provided for in an appropriate manner with due regard for existing practices and procedures.

- In order to ensure consistency in Community activities and continuity of work, the Ministers of Foreign Affairs, meeting in the Council of the Community, will act as initiators and coordinators. They may hold political co-operation meetings at the same time.

Source: Bulletin of the European Communities (1974), no. 2

member states—France in particular—were insisting that Community institutions should have no authority whatsoever in this new activity. Clearly, some form of over-all coordination would be needed if the 'European Union', as it was beginning to be called, were to develop in a coherent manner in various directions. Introducing the heads of government as the ultimate source of authority, with foreign ministers at their side, was felt to be the only way—or, at least, the least controversial way—in which to ensure coordination and consistency.

As is frequently the case for important decisions, personalities also played a role in the creation of the European Council. Valéry Giscard d'Estaing (1988), newly elected President of the French Republic, wanted to continue playing a significant role in European affairs and convinced the new West German Chancellor, Helmut Schmidt. Jean Monnet, whose influence in all Community countries was considerable, came to the conclusion that regular meetings of heads of government were needed and his views were instrumental in securing the agreement of the smaller member states.

In any institutional framework, the regularity of meetings makes a fundamental difference. Before 1974, summit meetings were important occasions on which sig-nificant decisions were taken, but with little or no lasting impact on the working of Community institutions. Since then, and increasingly as time has gone by, European Council meetings have come to mark the rhythm of EU activities. Commission papers are put forward, Council reports approved, and parliamentary resolutions voted in view of this or that European Council. It has played a leading role in the European integration process. By the end of the twentieth century, it was being called the arbiter of systemic change, the principal agenda-setter, and the core of the EU's executive (Ludlow 1992), or the primary source of history-making decisions (Peterson and Bomberg 1999). At that time, however, the European Council was not an institution of the Union: it exercised great power without any legal treaty basis for that power. That is a paradox to which the Lisbon Treaty has put an end.

Composition

The composition of the European Council has been significantly altered by the new Treaty. Foreign ministers, who had been *de jure* participants in the European Council from the very beginning, have lost that capacity. The justification generally given for that decision is, simply, size: in an enlarged Union, the presence of two members per delegation leads to a meeting of sixty-plus people around the table, which becomes difficult to manage and loses that intimate character to which participants have always attached great importance. It should be noted, however, that foreign minis-ters get a sort of proxy presence in the European Council through the presence of the High Representative, who is chair of the Foreign Affairs Council. Moreover, foreign ministers, as well as finance ministers, can be called to take part in the discussion of agenda points relevant to their competence.

Although the restricted composition of the European Council is confirmed, even enhanced, by the Treaty, practice allows a small amount of flexibility. In the absence of a head of government, a minister (even, in rare cases, a permanent representative) may take her seat. The French Prime Minister sometimes replaces, and sometimes assists, the President of the Republic. Over the years, a limited number of officials from the presidency, the Council Secretariat, or the Commission have gained a seat in the room, or even, in the case of the Secretary General of the Council, at the table (see Figure 3.1). Two delegates per delegation are issued red badges, which allow them to enter and submit a note or whisper a message, but they may not stay. Other members of national delegations, who should number no more than twenty, do not have access to the conference room: they are confined to a 'blue' zone.

The debate in the European Council is relayed to the outside world by a system of note-takers, who are officials from the Council Secretariat sitting in the conference room. At regular intervals, they are replaced and then give an oral briefing to the Antici groups[2] (that is, the group of personal assistants of the permanent representatives), sitting in an adjacent room, to which other members of national delegations do not have regular access. Each Antici then transmits his or her notes to his or her own delegation, in the 'blue' zone. This indirect dissemination of information guarantees that national delegations know something of the proceedings inside, but with

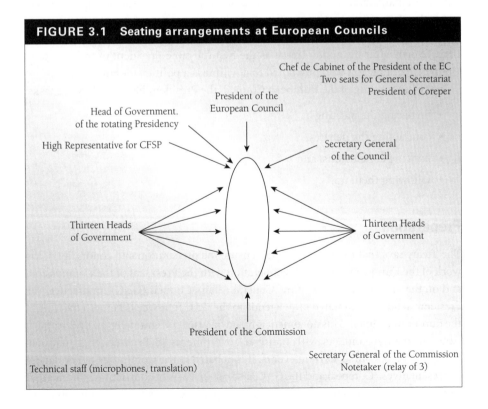

FIGURE 3.1   Seating arrangements at European Councils

Chef de Cabinet of the President of the EC
Two seats for General Secretariat
President of Coreper

President of the European Council

Head of Government. of the rotating Presidency

High Representative for CFSP

Secretary General of the Council

Thirteen Heads of Government

Thirteen Heads of Government

President of the Commission

Secretary General of the Commission
Notetaker (relay of 3)

Technical staff (microphones, translation)

considerable delay and in a way that makes direct attribution of specific words to any participant nearly impossible. Peter Ludlow (2000: 15) has compared the physical arrangements at a European Council 'to a vast temple in some oriental rite', in which high priests officiate in seclusion while lesser participants remain in other parts of the building. Such an extraordinary system would not have survived if heads of government were not happy with the result: namely, that they operate at some distance, both in space and time, from the views and comments of their assistants.

The President

The European Council is chaired by a President elected for a two-and-a-half-year period, renewable once. That is another major change introduced by the Lisbon Treaty: previously, it had been chaired by the head of government of the country holding the rotating presidency. Here, again, the justification given is linked to size. Combining the duties and responsibilities of a national head of government with the duties and responsibilities linked to the preparation and chairmanship of the European Council has always been somewhat problematic. The difficulty has increased with the enlargement of the Union because views and interests are more varied, personal relationship between participants less intimate, and contacts more time-consuming. The main advantage of a 'dedicated' president is that he or she has more time. Shortly after his appointment as the first full-time President of the European Council, Herman Van Rompuy noted that '[t]ime is a politician's prime material'.

In the functioning of the European Council, the President has the following tasks:

- preparing the meetings;
- conducting the debates;
- drawing conclusions; and
- following them up.

Preparation

The Treaty says that the President shall ensure the preparation and continuity of the work of the European Council in cooperation with the President of the Commission, and on the basis of the work of the General Affairs Council (GAC). In practice, the President sends an annotated draft agenda to the GAC four weeks before a meeting of the European Council. This document is based on prior commitments of the European Council, regular contacts with national governments in Brussels or in national capitals, and, of course, current events. It is debated in the Committee of Permanent Representatives (Coreper) and the GAC, also on the basis of contributions from other Council formations. The President then prepares draft guidelines, decisions, or conclusions of the European Council that are examined in a last GAC meeting held five days before the European Council. The aim of this procedure is to concentrate the debate on those politically sensitive points on which heads of government must decide themselves. The resulting agenda is not absolutely binding, because there is no way of preventing a head of government from raising a subject that he or she wants to raise. But, in general terms, the authority of the President is respected.

Debates and decision-making

Proceedings of the European Council, initially largely informal, were codified by a set of rules adopted at the Seville European Council in June 2002. They are now formalized by the Rules of Procedure adopted on 1 December 2009 (see Box 3.2). Those changes have undoubtedly been beneficial and have increased the efficiency of the European Council as a decision-making body.

Although there are exceptions (the Nice Summit lasted four days), most European Councils extend over a two-day period. They will frequently begin with a dinner held separately for heads of government and foreign ministers. On this occasion, foreign ministers will normally discuss a few specific points of international relations. Prime ministers may have a freewheeling discussion on European affairs, recalling the fireside chats of the early European Councils, or they may have a preliminary exchange on politically sensitive issues such as nominations. The next day, after a 'family' photograph, the meeting begins with an address by the President of the European Parliament (EP). This custom, introduced in the late 1980s, has always had high symbolic value for the EP. It can, at times, lead to a short and sharp debate: for example, in October 2010, a somewhat fraught exchange occurred between UK Prime Minister David Cameron and EP President Jerzy Buzek on the 2011 EU budget. For the rest of the day, the full European Council meets to debate the different points on the agenda and to approve the draft conclusions.

It is up to the President 'to ensure that business is conducted smoothly'. If the discussion gets bogged down, the President may well interrupt the meeting and hold bilateral conversations (known as 'confessionals') with each delegation. The President can also encourage two or more delegations to get together to solve a specific problem. Any procedural suggestion that seems likely to get results is usually accepted, at least on an experimental basis.

As a rule, decisions are taken in the European Council by consensus. However rules of procedure are adopted by a simple majority, as is the decision to call an IGC. Major appointments, such as the President of the Commission or the High Representative, require a qualified majority. Unanimity applies to common defence. If absent, a member of the European Council can delegate his or her voting power to another member, but none may exercise more than two votes. The Presidents of the Commission and the European Council do not take part in votes. On urgent matters, and if all members agree, decisions may be taken by written procedure at the initiative of the President.

BOX 3.2   **Rules of procedure for voting**

In those cases where, in accordance with the Treaties, the European Council adopts a decision and holds a vote, that vote shall take place on the initiative of its President.

The President shall, furthermore, be required to open a voting procedure on the initiative of a member of the European Council, provided that a majority of the members of the European Council so decides.

The presence of two thirds of the members of the European Council is required to enable the European Council to vote. When the vote is taken, the President shall check that there is a quorum. The President of the European Council and the President of the Commission shall not be included in the calculation of the quorum.

Where a vote is taken, any member of the European Council may also act on behalf of not more than one other member. Where the European Council decides by vote, its President and the President of the Commission shall not take part in the vote.

Source: Article 6 of the Rules of Procedure, adopted on 1 December 2009

Consensus is obtained when a proposal is put on the table and no objection is formulated. Unanimity implies that a proposal be put to a vote and that no negative vote be registered. In theory, the difference lies therefore in the formality of the procedure. In practice, formal votes are extremely rare, so the difference is meaningless. Nevertheless, the Treaty maintains the distinction: guidelines in the field of common foreign and security policy (CFSP) are adopted by unanimity; guidelines in the area of freedom, security, and justice (AFSJ) are adopted by consensus.[3] One wonders why?

Treaty texts normally specify a procedure other than consensus when decisions by the European Council are to have legal effects (see Box 3.3). This is presumably due to the fact that, in legal terms, consensus is an uncertain concept. But here, again, the rule is not absolute. On cooperation in criminal matters, a special procedure (known as an 'emergency brake') allows the European Council to suspend the normal legislative procedure.[4] That is a decision having legal effects, so it is taken by consensus.

Follow-up

In the course of accession negotiations, it has been customary to invite heads of government from candidate countries for lunch and/or a brief session on the second day of a summit. In former years, it was quite frequent to see special guests (for example, the UN Secretary General or the head of a friendly government) invited to a meeting in the margins of a European Council. This practice, which is time-consuming, is now frowned upon under the Rules of Procedure. It is allowed only in exceptional circumstances and with the unanimous agreement of the members of the European Council.

BOX 3.3	European Council decisions that are not taken by consensus

- Article 7, para. 2 TEU: persistent breach of Union values*
- Article 14, para. 2 TEU: composition European Parliament*
- Article 15, para. 5 TEU: election and ending the term of office of the President of the European Council**
- Article 17, para. 5 TEU: modifying the number of Commissioners*
- Article 17, para. 7 TEU: proposal for President and appointment of the Commission**
- Article 18, para. 1 TEU: appointment and ending the term of office of the High Representative**
- Articles 22, para. 1, and 26, para. 1 TEU: identification of strategic interests, objectives and general guidelines for CFSP*
- Article 31, para. 3 TEU: *passerelle* clause for CFSP*
- Article 42, para. 2 TEU: establishment of a common defence*
- Article 48, para. 3 TEU: decision to examine amendments to the treaty and decision not to convene a Convention***
- Article 48, para. 6 TEU: simplified treaty revision for internal EU competences (TFEU Pt III)*
- Article 48, para. 7 TEU: simplified treaty revision (general *passerelle* clause)*
- Article 50, para. 3 TEU: withdrawal of a member state (extension of the period)*
- Article 86, para. 4 TFEU: powers of the Public Prosecutor*
- Article 253, para. 3 TFEU: rules of procedure of the European Council***
- Article 236 TFEU: configurations and presidency of the Council**
- Article 244 TFEU: rotation of Commissioners*
- Article 283, para. 2 TFEU: appointment of the board of the European Central Bank**
- Article 312, para. 2 TFEU: *passerelle* clause for multiannual financial framework*
- Article 355, para. 6 TFEU: amending the status of overseas territories*

*Unanimity; **Qualified majority; ***Simple majority
TEU: Treaty on European Union (Maastricht Treaty); TFEU: Treaty on the Functioning of the European Union (Treaty of Rome)

Conclusions reached by the European Council are encapsulated in a final document. Traditionally, these texts were known as 'presidency conclusions', but the time spent on them shows that everyone is aware of their importance for the daily working of the Union. In practice, if a conclusion of the European Council can convincingly be quoted in support of any argument, at any level of the Union, it is most likely to be decisive. In one exceptional case (Athens in 1983), disagreement was such that no conclusions could be drafted. The Rules of Procedure now imply that

---

BOX 3.4   **Minutes of the European Council**

Minutes of each meeting shall be drawn up; a draft of those minutes shall be prepared by the General Secretariat of the Council within 15 days. The draft shall be submitted to the European Council for approval, and then signed by the Secretary-General of the Council.

The minutes shall contain:

- a reference to the documents submitted to the European Council;
- a reference to the conclusions approved;
- the decisions taken;
- the statements made by the European Council and those whose entry has been requested by a member of the European Council.

Source: Article 8 of the Rules of Procedure, adopted on 1 December 2009

---

the drafting, and later approval, of minutes of each meeting contain references to the conclusions and the official text of statements and declarations (see Box 3.4).

The last, but certainly not least important, act of a European Council is to give press conferences. Frequently, each national delegation gives its own press conference to a number of journalists who commute from one delegation to another. By comparing notes on sometimes contradictory statements, experienced hands will frequently get a clear picture of the actual debate. This practice led Roy Jenkins (1989: 75), President of the Commission from 1977 to 1981, to call European Councils 'a restricted meeting with full subsequent publicity'.

In the days following a European Council, the President, accompanied by the President of the Commission, reports to the European Parliament on the meeting. Although this exercise tends to repeat information already available in the press, it has contributed to a better understanding between the institutions. It alleviates the sense of frustration that the European Parliament initially entertained vis-à-vis the European Council concerning activities over which it exerted no control and little influence.

The Lisbon Treaty gives the President of the European Council a new and most important task: to see that European Council decisions and conclusions are effectively implemented. As a result, the President is now frequently entrusted with follow-up tasks that would probably, in previous years, have been given to the Commission. Chairing the Task Force on Economic Governance, which drafted a report for the European Council in October 2010, is one example. It is now clear that the President has become a major player in the working of the European Council. Herman van Rompuy has been quite successful in defining the nature of his job, which was initially unclear, and his relations with other major players.

Special meetings

- *Extraordinary meetings*   It has always been the case that the European Council could meet in exceptional circumstances at short notice. Such was the case after the 9/11 terrorist attacks on the United States (21 September 2001), at a crucial moment in the Iraq crisis (17 February 2003), when war erupted in Georgia (1 September 2008), or in Libya (11 March 2011).

- *Informal meetings*   The first informal meeting was called by the Spanish presidency at Formentor (Mallorca) in September 1995 to discuss the issues of the ongoing IGC. The purpose of informal meetings is to allow for the sort of confidential exchange of views and brainstorming that a growing workload has gradually eliminated from regular meetings. Informal meetings are usually shorter than formal meetings. As a rule, there are no presidency conclusions, although, in some cases, official declarations have been issued. One of the first acts of the newly appointed Van Rompuy was to call an informal meeting in Brussels on 11 February 2010, which led to a statement on the Greek financial crisis.

- *Thematic meetings*   Meetings can be called on a specific subject such as justice and home affairs (JHA) (Tampere, October 1999), or economic and social affairs (Lisbon, March 2000). Spring meetings of the European Council are supposed to be devoted mainly to the implementation of the Lisbon Agenda on the economic, social, and environmental situation of the Union. In fact, heads of government cannot avoid dealing with issues of immediate relevance. In practice, thematic meetings differ only slightly from the ordinary ones.

Legal nature and characteristics

Before the Lisbon Treaty, the legal nature of the European Council was the object of much academic debate (see Taulègne 1993: 92–100). Part of the problem came from the fact that, for the first twelve years of its existence (1974–86), the European Council met, and exercised significant power, without any legal basis in the treaties. In a highly structured legal system, such as the Community, this phenomenon was indeed strange. The Lisbon Treaty has clarified the legal nature of the European Council: it is now an institution of the Union, just like the Parliament, the Commission, or the Court.

However, the European Council needs to be considered not only as an institution, in legal terms, but also as an essential locus of power. This idea helps to explain some of its key characteristics: its authority, its informality, its flexibility, the special relationship between participants (including the impact of seniority), and the ambivalence of its intergovernmental character.

- *Authority*   The European Council brings together political personalities who, in their national capacity, are ultimate decision-takers. Collectively, they consider themselves, in the European context, as having a similar task. Essentially, they come together to take decisions and they expect these decisions to be respected. That is a fact that other participants have to take into account.

- *Informality*   The European Council has always attached the highest importance to the informality of its meetings. It works on the basis of restricted sessions in which heads of government sit alone, face to face, frequently addressing each other by their first names. In the 1970s, Chancellor of West Germany Willy Brandt wanted summit meetings to be like a fireside chat (*Kamingespräch*). Roy Jenkins (1989: 74) considered the European Council to be 'a surprisingly satisfactory body, mainly because it is intimate'. With time, and as a result of enlargement, meetings have tended to become more structured and more formal. Specific papers are, in practice, actively debated. But the principle of privacy and direct contact—quite frequently confrontational—remains.

- *Flexibility*   In the past, European Councils did not have formal rules of procedure and did not hesitate to depart from rules that they themselves had formulated. They now have formal rules, but, in some regards, these rules are relatively flexible. It is to be expected that heads of government will, at times, want to make use of that flexibility.

- *Seniority*   Because participants are relatively few in number and personal relations are important, the balance of power in the European Council is influenced by seniority. Newcomers will not be able to pull their full weight at first meetings. Heads of government from smaller member states can expect to exert more influence after several years of being present, particularly after they have led a successful presidency. The case of Jean Claude Juncker, Prime Minister of Luxembourg since 1995, is an example of the representative of a small member state exercising considerable influence, certainly due to his personal qualities, but also because of his seniority.

- *Intergovernmental character*   In the abstract, all heads of government are equal, just as their states have equal status in international law. But because the European Council is a locus of power, the fact that some participants have in fact more power (because they represent a more powerful country) is immediately apparent and implicitly understood by all. Put simply, 'the intergovernmental nature of the European Council is more marked than that of the sectoral Councils' (Hayes-Renshaw 1999: 25). However, the President of the Commission, who is not an intergovernmental figure, is *de jure* a member of the European Council and has, at times, exercised considerable influence on its decisions. Highly important decisions concerning Union affairs and favouring supranational integration, such as the creation of the euro, have been taken at that level and could not have been taken at any other. To describe the European Council as strictly intergovernmental is therefore to deny a good deal of ambivalence.

Perhaps because of this ambivalence, theories of European integration have some difficulty in accommodating the role of the European Council. Its composition and the power that it wields would seem, at first sight, to confirm liberal intergovernmentalist theory, best developed by Andrew Moravcsik. Liberal intergovernmentalist theory explains European integration as a succession of bargains between the bigger member states, based on national interests, domestic politics, and the constraints of the world environment. According to this view:

the creation of the European Council was explicitly designed to narrow rather than to broaden the scope for autonomous action by supranational actors ... Its major consequence was to transfer policy initiative away from the more rule-governed Commission and Parliament ... Bargaining outcomes reflect the relative power of states rather than supranational entrepreneurship.

(Moravcsik 1998: 488, 310, 485)

One may indeed consider, along with Moravcsik, successive intergovernmental conferences as 'bargains' concluded by member states at the highest level. However, the fact is that the Union has obviously more supranational elements today than it did in 1974. If supranational actors 'have only a rare and secondary impact' on negotiations (Moravcsik 1998: 485), how is this transfer of power to be explained?

Historical institutionalism, on the other hand, considers that institutions themselves 'structure political situations and leave their own imprint on political outcomes' (Thelen and Steinmo 1992: 9). According to this view, actors are assumed not to be entirely aware of, or concerned about, the long-term institutional consequences of the decisions that they take. To explain the integrative impact of the European Council over a quarter of a century in this way presupposes, however, a lasting degree of political naivety not normally associated with heads of government. The European Council is master of its own agenda and can quite easily change one of its own decisions if unforeseen consequences become apparent. When the Treaty of Lisbon was ratified, there was consensus in the European Council that no new treaty change would be considered in the next few years. Less than a year later, it changed its mind and, in view of developments in the financial crisis, decided to pursue a modification of the Treaty. As we can see, theoretical models have difficulty reconciling the different and sometimes contradictory aspects of the European Council.

Functions

The Treaty says that the European Council 'shall provide the Union with the necessary impetus for its development and shall define the general political directions and priorities thereof. It shall exercise no legislative function' (Art. 26 TEU). In CFSP, it should 'identify the Union's strategic interest, determine the objectives of and define general guidelines' (Art. 68 TFEU). In the AFSJ, it shall 'define the strategic guidelines for legislative and operational planning' and shall 'discuss a conclusion on the broad guidelines of the economic policies of the Member States and the Union' (Art. 121 TFEU). Several clauses specify various other competences for the European Council in treaty revision, breaches of human rights, appointments, Council formations, and so on. These texts undoubtedly give a clearer view of the tasks of the European Council than was the case in previous treaties. But it can be argued that they still do not adequately reflect the role of ultimate negotiator and, at times, detailed decision-maker that is so frequently that of the European Council.

The fact is that functions of the European Council go well beyond the official texts. They can be described under the following headings:[5]

- strategic guidelines;
- decision-making;
- foreign policy;
- the open method of coordination; and
- amending the treaties.

Strategic guidelines

As we have seen, the most traditional function of the European Council is to provide political guidance and impetus across the whole spectrum of Union activities. Indeed, this was the main reason given for its creation. It is mentioned both by the Tindemans report[6] (1976) and by the Stuttgart Declaration (1983). In the early texts, the accent was put on ensuring consistency between Community affairs and other forms of European activity. At a time (before the Treaty of Maastricht) when these branches were completely separated, the European Council was indeed the only place where some form of consistency could be ensured.

This task implies the right to launch new fields of activities. In Rome, in December 1975, the European Council decided to initiate cooperation in the fight against terrorism and organized crime. In Hanover, in June 1988, it appointed a group to look into economic and monetary union (EMU). At Lisbon, in March 2000, it opened up a new field of action in social affairs and economic policy. Gradually, it has acquired a sort of monopoly in this respect: 'Nothing decisive can be proposed or undertaken without its authority' (Taulègne 1993: 481).

Basically, the European Council fixes the agenda of the European Union and is the place where strategic orientations are given. This is true for all fields of activity. It is the European Council that approves common strategies in the framework of CFSP, as it has done vis-à-vis Russia and Ukraine. As far as the Community is concerned, orientations leading to the completion of the internal market and to EMU were defined at that level. One specific example of political guidance is the enlargement process. Momentous decisions were taken at Copenhagen in December 1993 on Central and Eastern European countries, and in Brussels in December 2004 on Turkey. They could not have been taken at any other level. Another recent example is to be found at the onset of the Greek financial crisis in February 2010. Heads of government issued a statement that, in effect, gave political guidance on the issue to the Ecofin Council, the Commission, Greece, and other eurozone members (see Box 3.5).

Decision-making

It was certainly not the initial intention of the member states that the European Council should serve as ultimate decision-taker, nor as a court of appeal for settling problems too complex or too politically sensitive to be resolved at the Council level. Quite the contrary: both the Tindemans report on European Union (1976) and the

---

BOX 3.5	Political guidance of the European Council on the Greek crisis

Informal meeting, 11 February 2010

All euro area members must conduct sound national policies in line with the agreed rules. They have a shared responsibility for the economic and financial stability in the area. In this context, we fully support the efforts of the Greek government and their commitment to do whatever is necessary, including adopting additional measures to ensure that the ambitious targets set in the stability programme for 2010 and the following years are met. We call on the Greek government to implement all these measures in a rigorous and determined manner to effectively reduce the budgetary deficit by 4% in 2010. We invite the Ecofin Council to adopt at its meeting of the 16th of February the recommendations to Greece based on the Commission's proposal and the additional measures Greece has announced. The Commission will closely monitor the implementation of the recommendations in liaison with the ECB and will propose needed additional measures, drawing on the expertise of the IMF. A first assessment will be done in March. Euro area Member states will take determined and coordinated action, if needed, to safeguard financial stability in the euro area as a whole. The Greek government has not requested any financial support.

Source: Statement by the Heads of State or Government of the European Union. 11 February 2010

BOX 3.6	Detailed decision-making on the financial perspective, 2007–2013

Conclusions of the European Council meeting on 21 December 2005

The European Council reached agreement on the Financial Perspective 2007–2013 as set out in doc. 15915/05. That document covers 35 pages governing allowable expenditure over the six year period, with detailed numbers and tables. It had been, as always, hotly debated in the previous months. The responsibility of the European Council is further underlined in the following excerpt from the conclusions 'The European Council has treated the Financial Perspective 2007–2013 as an overall negotiation package including expenditure, revenue and the review clause. The European Council shall ensure the global nature of this agreement'. In other words, the European Council is not only the ultimate decision taker, it also guarantees participants that the application of that decision will not be selective.

Dooge report[7] on institutional reform (1985) stated that this should *not* be the case. Official texts, like the Stuttgart Declaration (1983), steer clear of giving to the European Council a decision-making capacity. But, in fact, over the years, that is exactly what it has acquired and exercised.

Examples abound. Successive European Councils wrestled in the early 1980s with the intractable British budgetary problem until a solution was finally found at Fontainebleau in June 1984. 'Virtually every decision that affected the development of the internal market since the early 1980s was taken by the European Council' (Sbragia 1991: 63). The 'packages' around the financial perspectives of the Union (Delors I, Delors II, Agenda 2000, Financial Perspective 2007–2013), which involve an element of distributive bargaining between member states, have always been settled at the top level (see Box 3.6). The same is true of decisions concerning the seat of European institutions: Edinburgh in December 1992; Brussels in October 1993 and December 2003. The reason generally given for this evolution is the incapacity of the GAC (composed of foreign ministers) to coordinate the activities of other councils. This failure compels the European Council to step in as arbiter. However, it is also the case that heads of government, although accepting in principle that their role should be one of mere guidance, have not in practice refused to deal in substance with the growing number of problems arising on their agendas. After all, decision-making is a sign of power, and power is not something that successful politicians tend to eschew.

The open method of coordination

The open method of coordination was established by the European Council at Lisbon in March 2000 (and is generally known as the 'Lisbon process'). It was aimed at a range of socio-economic challenges, for which the policy powers remain located at the level of national or subnational government in the member states, and for which the scope for agreement depends on soft prescriptions rather than hard law. The approach provided for a central role of the European Council—especially its spring meeting, which was to become a forum for comparing different national experiences and experiments in economic reform, making use of guidelines, timetables, indicators, benchmarks, periodic monitoring, and peer review to exercise a strong guiding and coordinating role. The European Council thereby deliberately undertook a new responsibility and a new role. This approach, located somewhere between the classical intergovernmental cooperation and the Community method, has been called 'intensive transgovernmentalism' in which 'the primary actors are leading national policy-makers, operating in highly interactive mode and developing new forms of commitment and mutual engagement' (Wallace 2002: 341).

The aims of the original Lisbon process—creating the most competitive economy in the world—were overambitious. Stated objectives for 2010 were not reached. This is partly due to negative developments in the world economy, but also partly due to methodological failure. The European Council has not, in fact, been able to deliver. In an evaluation document in 2010, the Commission noted tactfully that 'ambitions endorsed at the highest political level have not always resulted in faster decision-making or in avoiding dilution'.[8] The successor programme, adopted in 2010 under the name 'Europe 2020', tasks the European Council with overall assessment of progress and debates on main strategic priorities, which is more in line with the traditional functions of that institution.

Foreign policy

Formulation of foreign policy has always been one of the primary tasks of the European Council. Its very first meeting at Dublin in March 1975 approved a declaration on Cyprus and one on the Conference for Security and Cooperation in Europe (CSCE.). Over the years, European Councils have approved a great number of statements on foreign policy, covering events in all parts of the world and developments in all fields of diplomacy. Some of these statements were made at a time of existing or impending crisis, such as those made in Berlin in March 1999 on the eve of NATO air strikes in Yugoslavia, in September 2008 when armed conflict was breaking out in Georgia, and in March 2011 just before intervention in Libya (see Box 3.7).

The present Treaty confirms that tradition by saying that the European Council should identify the Union's strategic interest, and determine the objectives of and define general guidelines for the CFSP, including for matters with defence implications. It adopts the necessary decisions by unanimity. The Treaty adds that, if international developments so require, 'the President of the European Council shall convene an extraordinary meeting of the European Council in order to define the strategic lines of the Union's policy in the face of such developments'.

It can be argued that, in the past, European Council conclusions contained an excessive number of foreign policy declarations (between fifteen and twenty in some cases) and that this proliferation diminished the impact of such statements.

BOX 3.7   Foreign policy

Declaration adopted on Libya, 11 March 2011

The situation in Libya remains a cause for grave concern. We express our strong solidarity with the Libyan people and the victims. We firmly condemn the violent repression the Libyan regime applies against its citizens and the gross and systematic violation of human rights. We welcome UN Security Council Resolution 1970 and the referral of the situation in Libya to the International Criminal Court. The use of force, especially with military means, against civilians is unacceptable and must stop immediately. The safety of the people must be ensured by all necessary means. The European Council expresses its deep concern about attacks against civilians, including from the air. In order to protect the civilian population, Member States will examine all necessary options, provided that there is a demonstrable need, a clear legal basis and support from the region. Those responsible will be held accountable and face grave consequences. We will work with the United Nations, the Arab League, the African Union and our international partners to respond to the crisis. We call for the rapid holding of a summit between the Arab League, the African Union and the European Union.

Colonel Qhadaffi must relinquish power immediately. His regime has lost all legitimacy and is no longer an interlocutor for the EU. The European Union has adopted restrictive measures against the country's leadership and against entities holding sizeable assets controlled by the regime, and stands ready to adopt further sanctions.

Source: Declaration adopted by the Extraordinary European Council, 11 March 2011

There is no doubt, however, that member states have, at times, used the European Council effectively as a means of expressing forcefully common positions on international affairs. It is clear, for example, that the message demanding that the siege of Sarajevo be lifted, sent by the Cannes European Council in June 1995, was to be taken seriously precisely because it was sent, in no uncertain terms, at the level of authority that might, if necessary, decide the use of force.

When acting in this external capacity, the European Council operates in fact like a 'collective head of state'. This was used in the Convention as an argument in favour of a more permanent presidency of that body, in order to avoid the disadvantages of the six-month rotation. It translated into an Article of the Treaty[9] that says that the President of the European Council shall, at his or her level and in that capacity, ensure the external representation of the Union on issues concerning its CFSP, without prejudice to the powers of the High Representative of the Union for Foreign Affairs and Security. This is not the clearest of treaty texts, nor the easiest to implement, as was shown when the UN General Assembly refused in September 2010 to give the floor to Herman Van Rompuy in a debate at head-of-government level. Areas of potential conflict clearly exist: with the High Representative, with the President of the Commission, and probably also with the rotating presidency. But in the first months of implementation, these treaty provisions were not overly conflictual. In March 2010, a practical arrangement on external representation at presidential level was formalized between Presidents Van Rompuy and Barroso.

Amending the treaties

As we have seen, heads of government have always played some role in treaty negotiations. This tradition began with the negotiation of the Treaty of Rome. But, over time, that role has become predominant: the European Council has become 'the key forum for determining treaty reforms' (Wallace and Wallace 2000: 20).

In the negotiation of the Single European Act (SEA; 1985–86), the input of heads of government was limited. The main top-level decision was that the Act would indeed be 'single', that it would incorporate in one document Articles relating to political cooperation *and* Community activities, which had been negotiated separately. This decision was important in terms of political symbolism and it was appropriate that it should be taken by heads of government. But the texts themselves had been negotiated and largely finalized at the level of officials or foreign ministers.

In the Maastricht negotiations (1990–91), several important points of substance were decided only at the highest level and at the last minute. The contribution of heads of government was therefore more significant than had previously been the case. Nevertheless, a large amount of work had been done both by finance ministers, on the articles on monetary union, and by foreign ministers, notably on the second pillar relating to CFSP.

In the Amsterdam negotiations (1996–97), and again in the negotiations leading to the Treaty of Nice, foreign ministers had little impact. Practically all of the problems not resolved at the level of personal representatives went to the European Council. Its direct contribution was not limited to basic issues: at Amsterdam, it included points such as the status of public credit institutions in Germany or crisis meetings of the Political Committee.

The Lisbon Treaty negotiations followed a different path. Most of the substantial amendments introduced by that document can be traced back to the Constitutional Treaty as it emerged from the Convention in 2004. It is, nevertheless, true that important modifications were made to the draft treaty on issues such as majority voting and reinforced cooperation or defence, and that these modifications were largely decided at head-of-government level. It is at that level also that the decision was taken to redraft a text in order to overcome the situation created by negative referenda in France and the Netherlands. The Lisbon Treaty introduces the possibility of modifying certain treaty Articles through a simplified revision procedure—that is, without going through the process of an IGC.[10] It also accepts that the decision-making procedure foreseen in treaty Articles could be changed from unanimity to qualified majority, and from special to ordinary legislative procedure.[11] Similar clauses, known as *passerelle* clauses in EU jargon, exist for foreign and security policy and for the multi-annual financial framework.[12] They have existed in various forms since the Treaty of Maastricht, but have never been used, and it is open to doubt whether they will prove more attractive in future. They reflect the conviction, widespread in the Convention and confirmed by the difficulties encountered in the last ratification process, that, in future, formal treaty modifications will become increasingly difficult to achieve. It is worth noting that, in all circumstances, the trigger mechanism for a treaty revision of any sort is a unanimous decision by the European Council. That institution thus remains central to all forms of treaty modification.

Strengths and weaknesses

For over a quarter of a century, the European Council has been the guiding force of the European integration process. Time and time again, the most difficult problems have been debated, and solutions have been found, at that level. The European Union would not be what it is today if heads of government had not been systematically involved in major decisions.

But top-level decision-making has its limits and its dangers. Dangers relate to the irretrievable character of mistakes. Limits are about the nature and the quantity of decisions to be taken.

Negotiation at the highest level is risky: miscalculations or tactical errors occur and cannot, in most cases, be corrected. It is clear, for example, that, in Rome in December 1990, Mrs Thatcher's insistence on having a separate paragraph for the UK in the presidency conclusions enabled the other member states to define monetary union as they wished, which was not her intention (see Box 3.8).[13]

When considering the limits of the decision-making capacity of the European Council, two points are significant, as follows.

- *The number of meetings*   It is reasonable to assume that, in view of their other obligations, it will always be difficult for heads of government to meet more frequently than five or six times a year on a regular basis.[14] Even if occasional meetings can, at times, be arranged in the margin of other international activities, it is far from clear that such a limited number of meetings, however intense, are sufficient to deal effectively with the governance of an increasingly complex multinational entity. European Councils are frequently short of time and dominated by unforeseen current events.

- *Consensus*   Some modifications have been introduced, but decision-making in the European Council remains, in general, based on consensus—that is, on a relatively inefficient procedure. European Councils frequently fail to reach decisions, creating 'leftovers' and postponing decisions to a future date.

BOX 3.8	A tactical error: Rome, October 1990

The main point on the agenda was the state of preparation of the IGC and, in particular, monetary union. A major point in the debate was whether the future currency (then called the 'ecu', or European currency unit) should be:

- a common currency—that is, a currency circulating in parallel with, but not supplanting, national currencies (pounds, francs, Marks, and so on);
- a single currency—that is, a currency taking the place of national currencies.

On this fundamental point, no agreement was reached on the first day of the European Council. The draft presidency conclusions, circulated early on the second day, were based on the principle of a *common* currency. When questioned before the meeting started, the presidency answered that it had reluctantly come to the conclusion that the British Prime Minister would not in any circumstances accept conclusions based on a *single* currency. Given the previous day's discussions, it was difficult to question that judgement. At the beginning of the meeting, Mrs Thatcher declared that the presidency draft conclusions on monetary union were unacceptable, the UK would not be party to conclusions based on that draft, and that they required a separate paragraph in which the British point of view would be described.

   This changed the deal completely. Frantic activity was noted in the corridors, with several delegations putting pressure on the presidency. Italian Prime Minister Giulio Andreotti, who was in the chair, stated in the course of discussion that the presidency had changed its mind and would propose conclusions based on the principle of a *single* currency. When Mrs Thatcher protested, he answered (with a Sicilian smile) that since the UK would not be party to that part of the conclusions and would have a paragraph of its own, it could hardly expect to influence the formulation preferred by other member states.

   The European Council conclusions were as follows: 'The Community will have a single currency which will be an expression of its identity and unity.' A separate paragraph notes British dissent. If, as seems to be the case, the strategic objective of the UK government at the time was to prevent the birth of a single currency, Mrs Thatcher made a serious tactical error. At this level, tactical errors are irretrievable.

   Today, the euro is a single currency.

In practical terms, the limits of the European Council are particularly apparent when it is amending the treaties. The important point, not always well understood even by participants, is that the work of the European Council as treaty negotiator is different in nature from its other functions. When it gives political guidance or impetus, when it makes foreign policy statements, or debates economic policy or financial frameworks, decisions are political. They may now have legal effect, but they are not legal in nature. When it acts as negotiator, however, the European Council is directly modifying the Treaty, the basic law of the Union. It is, in fact, legislating. That is a completely different task.

   The structure and the modus operandi of the European Council are well adapted to collective bargaining, the crafting of compromises, the definition of general guidelines,

and to the drafting of political statements. It is not well adapted to a legislative function. Hectic night sessions with no assistants in the room, multilingual debate on
texts that appear and disappear from the negotiating table without having been studied in depth, and across-the-board compromises on unrelated issues at the break of
dawn cannot lead to clear legal texts. The complexity and confusion of the treaties
(with numerous protocols and declarations annexed to the final act of each IGC)
must be partly attributed to the way in which they are negotiated. It regularly takes
legal and linguistic experts, under the guidance of Coreper, several weeks to establish in legal terms what has been decided. The fact is that no civilized nation legis-
lates in such an uncoordinated and risky way. As Tony Blair famously remarked at
the end of the Nice European Council, 'We cannot go on like this'.

This and other weaknesses have been apparent for a number of years. Still there
was, for a very long time, very little criticism of the functioning of the European
Council. At Helsinki in December 1999, heads of government approved welcome
and substantial changes in the working methods of the Council, but barely mentioned the European Council. Two years later, the Laeken Declaration included a
variety of institutional points that it directed to be considered by the forthcoming
Convention, but it was silent on the European Council. It was not before 2002
that critical voices began to be heard, in the Convention, both in academic circles[15] and in the institution itself. In March of that year, the Barcelona European
Council heard strong words from the Secretary-General of the Council. Javier
Solana considered that, for some years, the European Council had been side-
tracked from its original purpose and had spent too much time on low-level drafting work, and that its meetings had been reduced to 'report-approval sessions or
inappropriate exercises in self-congratulation'. This led to the Rules of Procedure
adopted at Seville in June 2002 and, later, to the very substantial modifications,
proposed in the Constitutional Treaty and finally introduced by the Treaty of Lisbon, which are described in this chapter. The European Council is undoubtedly
strengthened by becoming a formal institution, with a reduced number of participants, a permanent President, and some clarification of its competences and decisions. Some observers even consider that it has been excessively strengthened to
the detriment of the Commission and institutional balance. But those modifications tend, in fact, to bring law in line with reality and to remedy perceived weaknesses in the previous modus operandi.

Conclusion

In many ways, 'the whole European Union system revolves round the European
Council' (Ludlow 2000: 15). It is 'the only institution which has overall political
leadership on all EU affairs' (Piris 2010: 208). The dates of its meetings, announced
well in advance, mark the rhythm of the Union's various activities in the same way

as religious feast days marked the rhythm of daily life in medieval Christendom. Foreign governments, the press, and business organizations study presidency conclusions to gauge the health, the dynamics, future orientations, and potential actions of the Union.

In successive meetings over the years, it has largely fashioned the Union as we know it today. And the fact is that, even if the European Council is basically intergovernmental in nature, the system to the establishment of which it has so largely contributed is not mainly intergovernmental. Forty years later, the Union is much larger, much more integrated, and more supranational than it was in the 1970s. With hindsight, it is clear, therefore, that Monnet was justified in advocating its creation. Those who feared, at the time, that it would lead to an intergovernmental system dominated by a *directoire* of major partners were proven wrong: 'The European Council worked its way into the Community decision-making process without deeply undermining the institutional balance' (Werts 1992: 295).

What are the underlying reasons that have led to this result? For most of the time since 1974, France and Germany have been governed by leaders strongly committed to mutual cooperation and to furthering European integration. They found enough support for this ambition in the Benelux and other member states to push the Union forward, even in the face of winds of scepticism blowing from the UK or Scandinavia. Monetary union is a typical example. Moreover, for a long time, from 1985–95, the Commission was chaired by Jacques Delors, a man who had developed a real talent for harnessing the power of the European Council to further the dynamics of integration (see Chapter 5). In the absence of any of these conditions, the results would have been very different.

It is also worth noting that the sequence of events that rocked the global financial system after 2008 has confirmed and reinforced the role of the European Council in the EU's decision-making process. In the second half of 2008, under the activist leadership of France's President Sarkozy, the European Council met practically every month and delivered results that were generally considered, at the time, to be an adequate response to the very difficult situation created by the bankruptcy of Lehman Brothers (de Schoutheete 2009). The sovereign debt crisis in the eurozone in 2010 shows a similar trend, and also the peaceful emergence of regular meetings limited to the heads of government of the eurozone countries and chaired by Van Rompuy, a development that would, in other times, have caused an outcry not only from member states outside the eurozone, but also from the Community/Union orthodox. It must be significant that when talking about better economic governance in the eurozone, public discourse immediately refers to heads of government, not to finance ministers.

Efforts were made in the Lisbon Treaty to adapt the European Council to new challenges in an enlarged Union. Time will tell whether those adaptations are sufficient. There is no doubt that an increase in the number of participants weighs on the working of the European Council, as it does on other institutions of the Union. The informality, direct contact, and personal trust that characterized early meetings are difficult to maintain in a larger body. Unofficial preparatory caucuses or other forms of *directoire* become more tempting, and cause dismay.

Three conclusions seem appropriate.

- Management of the European Union could not be assured without a top-level institution of this type: the European Council has played a fundamental role in European integration and will continue to do so.

- It is therefore appropriate that the European Council should become a treaty institution: it brings law in line with political necessity and practice.

- But top-level meetings have their limits and are not a panacea: agendas can become overburdened and participants overconfident. European Councils will certainly play a significant role in resolving future problems of European governance—but they will be only a part of the solution to that most difficult problem.

NOTES

1. See Articles 15 and 48, para. 4 TEU.

2. This group, which plays an important role in the coordination of Coreper II activities, is named after Massimo Antici, an Italian diplomat who was, in 1975, its first chairman.

3. Articles 26, para. 1 TEU, and 68 TFEU.

4. Articles 82 and 83 TFEU.

5. These distinctions are somewhat arbitrary and they frequently tend to overlap. Some authors identify no fewer than nine different functions (Bulmer and Wessels 1987: 76–80). Elsewhere, they are counted as three (Dinan 2000: 190), six (Nugent 1999: 201), or even twelve (Werts 1992: 120–2). This variety is, of course, a consequence of the absence of clear legal texts, but the ground covered is basically the same.

6. Leo Tindemans was prime minister of Belgium in December 1974 when he was asked by the Paris Summit to draft a report on European Union, which he presented in early 1976.

7. James Dooge, a former Irish foreign minister, was asked by the Fontainebleau European Council in June 1984 to chair a group to draft a report on institutional reform. The report, presented in 1985, prepared the negotiation of the SEA.

8. COMM SEC (2010) 114 final.

9. Article 15, para. 6 TEU.

10. Article 48, para. 6 TEU.

11. Article 46, para. 7 TEU.

12. Articles 31, para. 3 TEU, and 312, para. 2 TFEU (respectively).

13. Information is provided mainly by a series of interviews conducted in 1997 by the British Broadcasting Corporation (BBC) for the preparation of a documentary on monetary union called *The Money Makers*.

14. In 2010, there were five formal meetings of the European Council and one informal; in 2009, there were four formal meetings and two informal.

15. See, for example, Grant (2002) and de Schoutheete and Wallace (2002).

FURTHER READING

For well over ten years, Peter Ludlow has set himself the task of making an extensive commentary on each formal meeting of the European Council, on which he has become a major expert. In 2010 and 2011, his briefing notes, published by EuroComment (**http://www.eurocomment.be**) under the generic title *A View from Brussels*, underlined the impact that the new President was having on the functioning of the institution. Older publications are now dated because of changes introduced by the Lisbon Treaty, described in Piris (2010). The situation before and during the Convention, at which those changes originated, can be found in de Schoutheete and Wallace (2002) and Norman (2003).

de Schoutheete, P. (2011) *El Consejo Europeo*. In *Tratado de Derecho y de Politicas de la Union Europea* (vol. III, Madrid: Aranzadi).

de Schoutheete, P. and Wallace, H. (2002) *The European Council* (Paris: Notre Europe), available online at **http://www.notre-europe.com**

Ludlow, P. (2002) *The Laeken Council* (Brussels: EuroComment).

Ludlow, P. (2010) *A View from Brussels: Briefing Notes on the European Council* (Brussels: EuroComment).

Ludlow, P. (2011) *A View from Brussels: Briefing Notes on the European Council* (Brussels: EuroComment).

Norman, P. (2003) *The Accidental Constitution: The Story of the European Convention* (Brussels: EuroComment).

Piris, J.-C. (2010) *The Lisbon Treaty: A Legal and Political Analysis* (Cambridge: Cambridge University Press).

WEB LINKS

http://www.european-council.europa.eu

The European Council website gives detailed information on its activities, including press releases, basic documents, and presidency conclusions since 1993. The home page of the President includes major speeches and a number of videos.

CHAPTER 4

The Council of Ministers

Fiona Hayes-Renshaw

▌ Summary

In the Council of Ministers (the Council), national interests are articulated, defended, and aggregated by representatives of the member governments, the ministers of which exercise legislative and budgetary functions in tandem with the European Parliament (EP). The Lisbon Treaty has introduced new rules affecting the rotating presidency of the Council, exercised by each member state in turn for a period of six months. The Council is supported by an international Secretariat, based at the institution's headquarters in Brussels. Qualified-majority voting (QMV) has become the normal decision-making rule. However, most decisions continue to be taken by consensus, a fact that can now be verified empirically as a result of the Council's policy of legislative transparency. The 2004 enlargement of the European Union provided the impetus for changes to the Council's organization and working methods. The implementation of the Lisbon Treaty has also had an effect on the Council's role, working methods, and relationships with the other EU institutions.

Introduction

The buildings programme in Brussels provides a neat metaphor for the Council of Ministers' position in the institutional set-up of the European Union. Housed from 1971 to 1995 in the rather nondescript Charlemagne building beside the much more impressive Berlaymont (Commission) headquarters, the Council then moved into the purpose-built Justus Lipsius building across the Rue de la Loi from the Berlaymont. Significant adaptations to its headquarters were required to deal with increased numbers as a result of the 2004 enlargement. Thus, in 2007, the Council Secretariat's twenty-three translation units were moved into the newly built Lex building further along the Rue de la Loi. In addition, the Résidence Palace building, which lies between the Justus Lipsius and Lex buildings, is being refurbished for use by the European Council, a very physical reminder of its separateness from the Council following the entry into force of the Lisbon Treaty.

This chapter examines the inhabitants of, and visitors to, the Council's headquarters in Brussels. First, the present-day Council is traced back to its origins in the 1951 Treaty of Paris. Second, the structure of the institution is explored, in order to identify those individuals who together constitute its horizontal and hierarchical layers. As this volume contains separate chapters on the European Council (Chapter 3) and the Committee of Permanent Representatives, or Coreper (Chapter 14), this chapter will concentrate on the remaining layers of the Council hierarchy: the ministerial Council; the preparatory bodies (the working parties and senior committees apart from Coreper); the presidency; and the Council Secretariat. The third section describes the formal and informal powers of the Council and its members, the ways in which its work is coordinated, and the means available to its members to exert influence and affect its output. The Council's relationships with the European Council, the Commission, and the European Parliament (EP) are examined in the subsequent section, as is the vexed question of the Council's accountability. In the final section, the Council's role in the context of the EU as a whole is analysed, as are the ways in which it has dealt with change over the past decade. The effects on the Council of the implementation of the Lisbon Treaty since December 2009 are a constant theme of the chapter.

The origins of the Council

The Council of the European Union can trace its origins back directly to the (Special) Council of Ministers provided for in the 1951 Treaty of Paris, which established the European Coal and Steel Community (ECSC). The creation of a body representing the governments of the member states was a direct and rather obvious attempt to temper the powers of the ECSC's innovative supranational High Authority (the fore-runner of the present-day European Commission). When the founding treaties of the two new European Communities were negotiated and adopted six years later, a slightly altered version of the ECSC blueprint was agreed, and the Council of the European Communities was born.

Despite the shared name, the powers of the old and new Councils could not have been more different. The ECSC's Special Council was required merely to exchange information with and consult the High Authority. In contrast, the 1957 Treaties of Rome provided that the Council should 'ensure coordination of the general economic policies of the member states and have power to take decisions'.

This enhanced role derived from the increased assertiveness of member governments vis-à-vis the more supranational elements of the European Communities. This confidence has become still more marked in recent years. It is reflected not only in the additional formal and informal powers acquired by the Council, but also in the changes that have been made to its structure and working methods (documented in successive treaties and in the Council's internal Rules of Procedure).

The Council hierarchy

In the past, it was customary to represent the Council hierarchy as a layered triangle. At its top was the European Council, followed by the ministers, then by Coreper and several other senior preparatory bodies, and, at the base, a large number of working parties. Each of these levels was headed by the rotating Council presidency and the whole structure was underpinned by a general Secretariat. The Lisbon Treaty established the European Council as a separate institution with its own semi-permanent President and created a cross-institutional High Representative who now chairs the Foreign Affairs Council. Nevertheless, both continue to be connected via political and administrative ties to the main Council hierarchy.

The ministers

Although we speak of 'the' Council of Ministers, in practice it meets in ten different configurations, each one dealing with a distinct policy area (see Box 4.1). Every Council is composed of the relevant minister(s) from each of the member states and, with the exception of the Foreign Affairs Council, is chaired by a representative of the member state currently holding the presidency (see below). The Commission is invited to attend, and is represented by one or more Commissioners. Officials from the member states, the Commission services, and the Council Secretariat accompany the ministers, the Commissioners, and the presidency, to advise and assist them in their deliberations.

BOX 4.1	Council configurations and frequency of meetings, 2004 and 2010

The post-Lisbon Council officially meets in ten configurations, the previously conjoined General Affairs and External Relations Council having been split into its component parts. In practice, the agenda items of the sectoral Councils are usually grouped according to policy sector, in order to enable ministers with distinct portfolios to attend separate parts of the session.

Configurations	No. of meetings in 2004	No. of meetings in 2010
General affairs and external relations (GAERC) (including European security and defence policy and development cooperation)	26	–
Foreign affairs	–	15
General affairs	–	11
Economic and financial affairs (Ecofin) (including the budget)	11	11
Agriculture and fisheries (AgFish)	10	11
Justice and home affairs (JHA) (including civil protection)	9	6
Transport, telecommunications, and energy (TTE)	5	6
Employment, social policy, health, and consumer affairs (EPSCO)	4	4
Competitiveness (Comp) **(Internal market, industry, and research)** (including tourism)	4	6
Environment (Env)	4	4
Education, youth, and culture (EYC) (including audiovisual affairs)	3	3
TOTAL	**76**	**77**

Source: Council website

The Council is a busy body. In March 2010, it held its 3,000th regular meeting since the entry into force of the Merger Treaty on 1 July 1967. It now meets formally between seventy-five and eighty times a year, normally at the Council's headquarters in Brussels. However, in April, June, and October every year, the Council's meetings are held in Luxembourg, the grossly inefficient result of a 1965 political agreement on the seat of the institutions. Each presidency is also entitled to schedule a number of informal ministerial meetings, which normally take place in the presidency member state and serve as an opportunity to showcase the country. Indeed, the twenty-five informal ministerial meetings organized by the Spanish presidency in the first half of 2010 read like the national tourist board's list of must-visit destinations! The Polish presidency in the second half of 2011 opted to hold informal Council meetings in a different Polish city each month, thereby limiting the number of cities involved and making the Council more visible in each one.

Special mention should be made of the informal Eurogroup, the official existence of which was recognized in Protocol 14 of the Lisbon Treaty. It has been chaired since 2005 by Jean-Claude Juncker of Luxembourg. The Eurogroup brings together the finance ministers of the eurozone member states (which numbered seventeen in 2011), the Commissioner for Economic and Monetary Affairs, and the President of the European Central Bank (ECB). The elected chairman of the Eurogroup Working Group also attends the monthly meetings, which normally take place the evening before the full Economic and Financial Affairs Council (Ecofin), and deal with issues relating to the economic and monetary union (EMU). The Council Secretariat assists the Eurogroup President and provides logistical support to the meetings.

The preparatory bodies

Council meetings are prepared by committees and working parties, composed of officials from each of the member states and a representative of the Commission. Coreper, the most senior of these committees, is formally responsible for preparing the work of the entire Council and fulfils an important horizontal coordination function (see Chapter 14). Other senior bodies coordinate work in particular policy areas, such as the Economic and Financial Committee (EFC) and the Special Committee on Agriculture (SCA).

Officials from the national ministries represent their governments in the 160 or so specialized working parties and ninety or so subgroups that constitute the base of the Council hierarchy. Some of these officials are based in Brussels in their national permanent representations (see Chapter 14), while others travel to Brussels from their national capitals for meetings. All are experts in their policy fields, operating on the basis of instructions from their home ministries. The Commission is represented by officials from the relevant Directorate-General (DG) in the 4,000 or so working party meetings that take place every year.

Most of the preparatory bodies are chaired by an official from the rotating Council presidency (see below). A small number have a fixed (elected) chair. Some are presided over by a representative of the High Representative and still others by an official from the Council Secretariat.

The presidency

The presidency of the Council rotates every six months among the member states according to a pre-established order, which also determines the place their representatives occupy at the table in meetings throughout the Council hierarchy (see Figure 4.1). The current order of rotation came into effect on 1 January 2007 and

FIGURE 4.1   Seating arrangements in the Council of Ministers, 2012

Places at the Council table are assigned following the pre-established order of rotation of the Council Presidency among the member states. The representatives of the Commission sit at one end of the table, facing the chairperson (or the representative of the Presidency-in-office) at the other end. The national delegation of the Presidency member state sits on the President's immediate right, followed by the representative of the member state next in line for the Presidency, and so on. All delegations move one place to the left at the beginning of a new presidential term, on 1 January and 1 July every year (see below). Acceding member states have to be slotted into the rotation order and a place made available for them at the various tables within the Council hierarchy

JANUARY–JUNE 2012		JULY–DECEMBER 2012	
Presidency		Presidency	
(Denmark)		(Cyprus)	
Denmark	Poland	Cyprus	Denmark
Cyprus	Hungary	Ireland	Poland
Ireland	Belgium	Lithuania	Hungary
Lithuania	Spain	Greece	Belgium
Greece	Sweden	Italy	Spain
Italy	Czech Republic	Latvia	Sweden
Latvia	France	Luxembourg	Czech Republic
Luxembourg	Slovenia	Netherlands	France
Netherlands	Portugal	Slovakia	Slovenia
Slovakia	Germany	Malta	Portugal
Malta	Finland	UK	Germany
UK	Romania	Estonia	Finland
Estonia	Austria	Bulgaria	Romania
Bulgaria		Austria	
Commission		Commission	

covers the period up to July 2020, unless another decision is taken in the meantime (see Box 4.2).

Taking on the Council presidency directly affects large numbers of civil servants from the member state in question. A chairperson and a national spokesperson must

| BOX 4.2 | Order of presidency rotation, 2007–20 |

The Lisbon Treaty institutionalized what had existed in embryonic form in the years immediately preceding its entry into force: a system of team presidencies, whereby groups of three member states exercise the Council presidency over a period of eighteen months. Each member state takes its turn in the chair for a period of six months and offers material support to its team colleagues during their time in office. The grouping of the member states is intended to reflect a general balance of geographical situation, economic weight, and 'old' and 'new' members. The Spanish–Belgian–Hungarian trio was the first to operate according to the Lisbon rules, starting in January 2010. They drew up a common presidency programme spanning the entire eighteen-month period and, in a further indication of their collective approach, shared a common presidency logo. The pre-agreed order of rotation (fixed in 2004 and reproduced below) may be amended only by the Council, acting by a qualified majority.

Germany	January–June	2007
Portugal	July–December	2007
Slovenia	January–June	2008
France	July–December	2008
Czech Republic	January–June	2009
Sweden	July–December	2009
Spain	January–June	2010
Belgium	July–December	2010
Hungary	January–June	2011
Poland	July–December	2011
Denmark	January–June	2012
Cyprus	July–December	2012
Ireland	January–June	2013
Lithuania	July–December	2013
Greece	January–June	2014
Italy	July–December	2014
Latvia	January–June	2015
Luxembourg	July–December	2015
Netherlands	January–June	2016
Slovakia	July–December	2016
Malta	January–June	2017
United Kingdom	July–December	2017
Estonia	January–June	2018
Bulgaria	July–December	2018
Austria	January–June	2019
Romania	July–December	2019
Finland	January–June	2020

be provided for virtually every meeting at each level of the Council, a particular challenge for smaller member states with limited personnel. A coordinating unit is normally created in the presidency capital that, with the Council Secretariat, is responsible for ensuring coherence and consistency across the entire range of issues being discussed in the Council hierarchy. The national permanent representation in Brussels becomes the operations centre for all Brussels-based activity during that member state's presidency.

The Council Secretariat

The General Secretariat of the Council (to give it its official title) is a relatively small and ostensibly politically neutral body. It has undergone a period of profound change over recent decades, not least moving into its own purpose-built buildings on the Rue de la Loi in Brussels. Because of its unprecedented magnitude, the 2004 enlargement provided the necessary impetus for implementing reforms to the Secretariat's structure and working methods, the avowed aim being to create a slimline Secretariat capable of taking on the extra tasks resulting from increased numbers and extensions to the Council's (and consequently its own) scope of activities.

The Council Secretariat is headed by a Secretary-General, who is appointed by agreement of the Council. Javier Solana, the (Spanish) incumbent from 1999 to 2009, combined this role with that of the High Representative for the common foreign and security policy (CFSP), while a Deputy Secretary-General (Frenchman Pierre de Boissieu) was responsible for the day-to-day running of the Secretariat. With the creation of the new post of EU High Representative for Foreign Affairs and Security Policy by the Lisbon Treaty, the Secretary-General of the Council is once again responsible 'only' for running the Council Secretariat. Uwe Corsepius, a German national, replaced Pierre de Boissieu as Secretary-General in July 2011.

The main body of the Secretariat is divided into eight DGs, the largest being responsible for personnel and administration. Six DGs are organized on a functional basis, according to the Councils that they serve, and the eighth is responsible for press, communication, and transparency. A horizontal legal service serves all levels of the Council hierarchy and a number of specialized units are directly answerable to the Secretary-General. Some 600 officials (of whom about 200 were military personnel) were transferred from the Council Secretariat to the new European External Action Service (EEAS), which started work in January 2011 under the leadership of the new (British) High Representative (and Vice-President of the Commission) Catherine Ashton.

The Secretariat is staffed by about 3,500 independent, international civil servants, recruited by open competition from among the nationals of the member states. A small number of national officials and experts are seconded to the Secretariat from the member states. The Secretariat has more than doubled in size since the early 1980s (when it numbered about 1,600 officials)—a direct result of extensions in the scope of the Council's activities and successive enlargements.

What does the Council do?

The Council has four main functions, as follows.

- *Legislative*   It passes laws, mostly legislating jointly with the EP under the ordinary legislative procedure, or codecision.

- *Budgetary*   Together with the EP, it constitutes the authority that agrees the EU's budget.

- *Policy-making*   It provides the mandate for the High Representative to carry out the EU's CFSP.

- *Coordination*   It coordinates the broad economic policies of the member states.

The Council fulfils these functions mainly by reference to formal rules laid down in the treaties and in its internal Rules of Procedure. These formal rules have been supplemented over the years by informal conventions and rules of the game that govern the work of the Council, the presidency, and the Secretariat, as well as their relations with the Commission and the EP.

Formal and informal powers

The ministers and preparatory bodies

The Council is the EU's principal legislative and policy-making institution. It is formally charged with decision-making across virtually all areas of Union activity. Specific decision-making procedures and voting rules apply to the different areas of Council activity, entailing a greater or lesser role for the EP, and unanimity or some form of majority voting in the Council itself.

In fulfilling its decision-making functions, the Council as a body represents and attempts to aggregate the interests of all of the member governments. The reconciliation of conflicting interests within the Council is achieved through a continuous process of negotiation, in the course of which the Commission proposal on the table is discussed in detail, national positions are articulated and defended, coalitions are formed, and compromises are advanced. In addition to these internal deliberations, the Council must also negotiate with the other institutions involved in the legislative process, in particular the EP (see Chapter 6).

The ministers' deliberations are prepared first by one or more working parties of national officials, and finally by Coreper or another senior committee. At their meetings, the ministers adopt without discussion those items on the agenda that have been the object of agreement at Coreper or working-party level (the so-called 'A points'), and engage in detailed discussions on those still requiring agreement (the so-called 'B points'). Following discussion in the Council, an agenda item may either be adopted or else referred back down to a senior committee or a working party for further discussion, before reappearing on the Council's agenda for discussion and/or adoption.

Legally speaking, there is only one Council. In effect, this means that any grouping of ministers may take a final decision on any issue coming within the scope of the Council as a whole. Thus, the Agriculture and Fisheries Council of 21–22 December 2010 agreed the fishing quotas for 2011, but also approved a number of other items that had previously been prepared by the relevant sectoral Councils. They included a regulation on EU officials' remuneration and pensions, a decision regarding a transitional mechanism for preferential trade arrangements within the World Trade Organization (WTO), and the authorization of an air services agreement with the republic of Cape Verde.

Most of the detailed negotiation and much of the actual agreement tends to occur at various levels below that of the ministerial Council itself. Insiders have estimated that, in some Council configurations, the ministers only actively discuss between 10 and 15 per cent of all of the items on their agendas, with the rest being discussed by Coreper and the working groups. Häge (2007) has produced figures to show that the decision-making input of ministers may in fact be much higher than this, but acknowledges the inherent difficulty in identifying the level within the Council hierarchy at which agreement is actually reached. There is no controversy, however, about who legally takes the final decision. Implicit indicative voting may occur in senior preparatory bodies or even in some working parties, but it is the ministers themselves who take—and they alone who are legally authorized to take—the final decision in the name of the Council.

Ministers vote in the Council on the basis of simple majority, qualified majority, or unanimity, depending on the rules governing the issue in question as laid down in the treaties. Under simple majority voting, which is normally used for procedural issues, each member state has a single vote, and fourteen votes in favour are required to adopt a measure in the EU of twenty-seven. (The Commission representative and the Council President do not vote.) In the reduced number of policy areas in which unanimity is now required (such as taxation, foreign policy, defence, and social security), an unhappy member state can either exercise a veto by voting against, or can choose to abstain from voting without preventing agreement by the others (an abstention, in effect, counts as a 'yes').

Qualified-majority voting (QMV) is now the usual voting rule in the Council, accounting for some 80 per cent of all legislative acts adopted annually. Under the current (Nice Treaty) system of QMV, each member state is allocated a set number of votes in approximate relation to its size, and specific thresholds have to be attained in order to adopt or block a measure (see Table 4.1). The votes are described as 'weighted' because when for example Germany votes, its voice counts as twenty-nine votes, whereas Malta's only counts as three. In addition to using its votes to support or vote against a measure, a member state also has the right to abstain from voting, thereby making the construction of a qualified majority or a blocking minority more difficult to achieve. The threshold for the achievement of a qualified majority has always been set at about 70 per cent of the total number of votes, implicitly also requiring a majority of the member states.

TABLE 4.1	Qualified-majority voting in the Council, EU27	
Member state	**Weighted votes (Nice Treaty rules)**	**Percentage of EU population in 2011 (Lisbon Treaty rules)**
Germany	29	16.32
France	29	12.91
United Kingdom	29	12.37
Italy	29	12.04
Spain	27	9.18
Poland	27	7.62
Romania	14	4.28
Netherlands	13	3.31
Greece	12	2.26
Belgium	12	2.16
Portugal	12	2.12
Czech Republic	12	2.10
Hungary	12	2.00
Sweden	10	1.87
Austria	10	1.67
Bulgaria	10	1.51
Denmark	7	1.10
Slovakia	7	1.08
Finland	7	1.07
Ireland	7	0.89
Lithuania	7	0.67
Latvia	4	0.45
Slovenia	4	0.41
Estonia	4	0.27
Cyprus	4	0.16
Luxembourg	4	0.10
Malta	3	0.08
Total	**345**	**100.00**
Qualified majority	255 (62% of total EU population)	55% of the member states (15 of 27) 65% of total EU population
Blocking minority	91	At least four member states

The need to attribute votes to acceding member states and to set new thresholds in the wake of enlargements has in the past given rise to some of the most bitter bargaining ever witnessed among the member states. The 2001 Treaty of Nice sought to rectify this state of affairs by adding a possible third requirement, namely that the member states constituting the qualified majority should represent at least 62 per cent of the total population of the EU. Official population figures for each of the member states are now agreed on an annual basis in order to facilitate the calculation of this latter figure (see Table 4.1 for the figures relating to 2011). This population requirement was deemed likely to increase the leverage of the larger member states in general and Germany in particular.

In an effort to simplify matters, the Lisbon Treaty did away with weighted votes per se and provided for a so-called 'double majority' system. Under this new regime, a qualified majority will have to be made up of at least 55 per cent of the member states (fifteen countries in an EU of twenty-seven), representing at least 65 per cent of the total population of the EU. In order to ensure that a small number of the most populous member states (such as France, Italy, and the UK, which together represent some 37 per cent of the total EU population) cannot collectively block a decision, the Lisbon Treaty further provides that a blocking minority must consist of at least four member states. The Lisbon voting system is due to enter into force on 1 November 2014. However, for a transitional period of almost three years after that, any member state may request that an act be adopted in accordance with the qualified majority rules laid down in the Treaty of Nice. The Lisbon Treaty rules will thus only come into full effect from 1 April 2017 onwards. ·

Much time and effort has been expended over the years by national officials and academics on the details of the Council's voting rules, and the implications for individual member states' voting strength and possible winning coalitions. Yet voting in the Council has not always occurred in the past, even under QMV, and did not often take the form of a show of hands or, more recently, the pressing of electronic buttons. Instead, the President tended to allow all delegations to have his or her say on the point under discussion, then summed up and, if necessary, proposed a form of words that reflected the views of the majority of member states, often in the form of a compromise. He or she then frequently concluded the debate by asking whether any delegation was opposed to the decision reached. If no one objected, the measure was deemed to have been adopted in line with the President's conclusions.

From the late 1990s onwards, the Council was obliged under new transparency rules to publish the results of any votes actually taken and to identify those Council members that had contested them. As a result, an important body of firm data became available against which to test what had previously been only hypothesis and anecdotal evidence. Analysts got to work, giving rise to an entirely new and rich vein of research. The empirical data made it possible to demonstrate conclusively, for example, that only about a fifth of decisions technically subject to QMV were explicitly contested at ministerial level, and that even when decisions were contested, the number of 'no-sayers' normally fell far short of a blocking minority (see Hayes-Renshaw and

TABLE 4.2   Unanimity under qualified-majority voting, 2004–10

Year	Number of legislative acts adopted under QMV	Contested			Uncontested (adopted unanimously with no abstentions or votes against)	Percentage of adopted legislative acts subject to QMV agreed unanimously
		Adopted with abstentions only	Adopted with votes against and abstentions	Total contested		
2004	158	10	24	34	124	78.5
2005	101	7	13	20	81	80.2
2006	167	12	19	31	137	82.0
2007	122	14	23	37	85	69.7
2008	199	16	13	29	170	85.4
2009	212	18	24	42	170	80.2
2010	51	6	7	13	38	74.5

Source: Figures supplied by the Council Secretariat

Wallace 2006). Unanimous agreement continues to be the general rule today, despite the greater number of member states involved as a result of enlargement and the increased amount of issues subject to QMV (see Table 4.2).

⎨ The Lisbon Treaty obliges the Council to deliberate and vote in public on draft legislative acts (Art. 16, para. 8 TEU), and under Art. 7 of the Council's Rules of Procedure the outcomes of all votes in the Council are represented on the Council's website 'by visual means'. In practice, a visual display of the votes cast by the ministers (green for a 'yes', red for a 'no', and yellow for an abstention) facilitates a quick reckoning of the level of consensus or contestation on individual dossiers. The Council Secretariat is working on a database containing all of the voting records in a user-friendly form that, it is hoped, will help all interested in the voting statistics to interpret them.

The presidency

Exercising the rotating presidency of the Council has always been an important task, but the list of its overall duties has tended to increase in recent years, in line with the Council's expanded scope of activities (see Box 4.3). In addition, more member states mean that negotiations have become more time-consuming and, at times, more conflictual. Exercising the presidency today can therefore be a rather daunting prospect, particularly for small or new member states.

Arguably, the main task of the rotating presidency is to be, or at least to be seen to be, neutral. Specifically, this aim is achieved by the presidency member state fielding

---

BOX 4.3   Duties of the presidency

The main formal task of the presidency is the management of the Council's business over the duration of its six-month period in office. This involves a number of different duties, including:

- working with the two other members of the presidency trio (and, where necessary, the preceding or successor presidency trio) to elaborate and then carry out its part of their common presidential programme;
- convening formal and informal meetings at ministerial and official levels;
- providing chairpersons for the vast majority of all meetings held throughout the Council hierarchy;
- ensuring the businesslike conduct of discussions at all meetings;
- liaising with the President of the European Council and the High Representative for Foreign Affairs and Security Policy in order to ensure the coherence of the Council's work;
- acting, together with the President of the European Council and the High Representative for Foreign Affairs and Security Policy, as spokesperson for the Council within and outside the Union;
- constituting the main point of Council contact for the Commission, EP, and other bodies involved in decision-making, including speaking on behalf of the Council in trialogues and conciliation meetings;
- ensuring that all of the Council's legislative and other obligations are met; and
- aiding the reaching of agreement in negotiations within the Council (with the help of Coreper, the Council Secretariat, and the Commission).

In fulfilling all of these tasks, the presidency is assisted by the Council Secretariat and works closely with the Commission services.

---

two delegations for each meeting it chairs: one to chair and manage the meeting; the other to articulate and defend the national position. This job can place a heavy burden on national resources, particularly when a small member state is in the chair. The introduction of 'compromises from the chair' (often with substantive input from the Council Secretariat) when negotiations get bogged down is further evidence of the neutrality of the presidency, as is the fact that the President does not vote.

The presidency can and does play a critical role in shaping the Council's agenda (see Tallberg 2008; Warntjen 2008), but its ability to impose its own interests on the rest of the EU is limited by the fact that Council activities are now programmed on a multi-annual basis, requiring close cooperation within and between presidency trios. A presidency member state needs to tread carefully in attempting to highlight certain issues, since its colleagues will not look kindly on a presidency that appears to use (or abuse) the office too flagrantly for its own ends.

It has become a point of pride for outgoing office-holders to be viewed by their colleagues as having conducted a 'good' presidency. Such judgements are obviously subjective, but a number of objective criteria can be employed as measuring devices. For example, it is possible to gauge whether Council business was dealt with efficiently and impartially, whether the main objectives outlined in the presidency programme were achieved, and whether unpredictable events were dealt with calmly, efficiently, and effectively. All presidencies produce a 'scoreboard' at the end of their period in office, seeking to show that they have indeed fulfilled these criteria in carrying through EU business.

The Council Secretariat

The changing role of the Council Secretariat is evident in the description of its basic formal functions contained in both the earliest and the most recent versions of the Council's Rules of Procedure. Originally charged with 'assisting' the Council, it is now required to be 'closely and continually involved in organizing, coordinating and ensuring the coherence of the Council's work and implementation of its 18-month programme. Under the responsibility and guidance of the Presidency, it shall assist the latter in seeking solutions'.[1]

Some 85 per cent of the Secretariat's staff is engaged in the technical and logistical organization of the Council's work. This task involves convening meetings, preparing meeting rooms, and producing and distributing documents (including their translation, photocopying, and archiving). The remainder of the Secretariat's staff is engaged in the substantive preparation of the Council's work: drawing up agendas; preparing briefing notes for the presidency; advising the presidency on questions of substance, procedure, and legality; helping to draft amendments; and producing reports, minutes, or press releases on meetings held within the Council hierarchy. In fulfilling all of these functions, the Secretariat is at the service of the presidency, but is independent both of it and of the member governments.

Coordinating the work of the Council

In the European Communities of the 1950s, a General Affairs Council (GAC) composed of the national ministers for foreign affairs was given overall responsibility for coordinating the work of the Council as a whole. This task was relatively easy when the number of policy areas (and member states) involved was small. However, the gradual expansion in the scope of the European Communities and then the EU resulted in the creation of a large number of specialized Council configurations and an increasing fragmentation of Council activity.

Some of these specialist Councils took on the leading role in important policy discussions, thereby undermining the central coordinating function of the GAC and its position as the most 'senior' of the Council formations. The most notable example was Ecofin. Its powerful national ministers (usually for finance) played a central role in discussions (and crucial decisions) on such important issues as EMU and taxation.

The GAC was also responsible for foreign affairs, and this part of its agenda expanded rapidly, particularly in the 1990s following the formalization of the CFSP and the greater representational role vis-à-vis third countries attributed to the GAC by the 1992 Treaty on European Union (TEU). The foreign ministers were less inclined to spend time on coordinating the work of a growing number of technical Councils, preferring instead to focus on the foreign policy questions on which they were better qualified to speak. Consequently, the European Council frequently found itself debating issues that, in an ideal and more efficient world, would have been settled by the foreign ministers in the GAC. It was also the European Council that increasingly set the EU's agenda, with the GAC frequently being reduced to the position of a senior organ of execution for the decisions of the heads of state or government.

Over the years, the need to ensure proper coordination of the work of the various Council configurations became more obvious and pressing. This problem was merely one aspect of a more general discussion on Council reform that took place at various levels between the European Councils held in Helsinki in December 1999 and Seville in June 2002. The Seville conclusions attempted to facilitate coordination by, inter alia:

- creating a General Affairs and External Relations Council (GAERC), which would hold separate meetings, possibly on different dates, with separate agendas, in order to distinguish its coordinating from its foreign policy responsibilities;

- explicitly making the general affairs formation of the GAERC responsible for preparing and ensuring the follow-up of meetings of the European Council (including the coordinating activities necessary to that end); and

- reducing the number of Council configurations from sixteen to nine.

The effect of the Seville reforms on the preparation of European Council meetings was generally viewed as positive, but criticism of the more general coordination by the GAC of the work of the other Council configurations continued to be expressed.

The Lisbon Treaty responded by splitting the GAERC into two distinct bodies: a General Affairs Council (GAC) and a separate Foreign Affairs Council (FAC), the former chaired by the rotating presidency and the latter by the High Representative. Article 2.2 of the Council's Rules of Procedure provide that the GAC shall:

- ensure consistency in the work of the different Council configurations;

- prepare and ensure the follow-up to meetings of the European Council, in liaison with the President of the European Council and the Commission;

- be responsible for overall coordination of policies, institutional and administrative questions, horizontal dossiers that affect several of the European Union's policies, such as the multiannual financial framework and enlargement, and any dossier entrusted to it by the European Council, having regard to operating rules for the EMU.

On paper at least, the new GAC would appear to be central to the work of the Council, in effect acting as the political equivalent of Coreper. A year after the entry into force of the Lisbon Treaty, however, there was little evidence of the GAC flexing its newly acquired muscle. This feebleness may have been partly due to the fact that its agenda was rather slim: there was not much going on in the area of enlargement and, with the arrival of a President of the European Council, it was not the only body involved in the preparation of European Council meetings. Things may change with the commencement of discussions on the multi-annual financial framework, when conflict with the economic and finance ministers over ownership of the dossier is likely to arise.

The GAC's coordinating function was also still the subject of criticism, largely due to its composition. While it is chaired by the foreign minister of the member state currently holding the rotating Council presidency, the representatives of the other member states in the GAC can range from the national permanent representative, to a state secretary for European affairs, to the foreign minister. Because of the less-elevated positions of many of the GAC's members, it is felt that they are less close to their respective prime ministers than the national foreign ministers, and therefore lack the necessary clout required to fulfill an effective coordinating role. The 2009 Dehaene Report[2] had proposed that the prime minister or head of state of the rotating presidency member state should chair the GAC in order to give it greater clout, but this suggestion has not been followed.

Exerting influence in the Council

The Council's central position in the Union in general and, in the process of EU decision-making in particular, endows it with a large degree of influence over other institutions and authorities. But the Council is not a monolithic body. It is composed of the representatives of twenty-seven very different governments, the member states of which differ according to size, economic weight, length of EU membership, administrative culture, negotiating style, and attitude to European integration (inter alia). Despite these differences, they continue to reach agreement. So who wields influence within the Council and what form does this influence take?

In the small number of areas in which unanimity is the rule, influence is shared equally among the Council members. Since any national representative can block agreement, the interests of all have to be taken into account. Under QMV, numbers matter, and those member governments with the largest number of votes (or biggest populations) could be expected to wield the greatest amount of influence. However, safeguards have been built into the system to ensure that the smaller member states, working together, have as much chance as the larger ones to exert influence over the final outcome. Indeed, the big member states are frequently out-voted in the Council, as Table 4.3 demonstrates.

However, raw statistics on roll-call voting, such as those contained in Table 4.3, need to be interpreted with some caution, as Hagemann (2008) has demonstrated: taken alone, they are unreliable indicators of member states' attitudes. While they

TABLE 4.3 Losing the vote in the Council under QMV, 2004–10 (abstentions and votes against by member state)

	Austria	Belgium	Bulgaria	Cyprus	Czech Rep.	Denmark	Estonia	Finland	France	Germany	Greece	Hungary	Ireland	Italy	Latvia	Lithuania	Luxembourg	Malta	Netherlands	Poland	Portugal	Romania	Slovakia	Slovenia	Spain	Sweden	UK	Total
Abstentions																												
2004	4	5	–	0	0	0	1	0	1	5	3	0	0	3	1	1	2	0	0	2	0	–	0	0	4	2	3	37
2005	1	0	–	1	1	0	0	0	0	2	3	0	0	1	0	1	1	0	0	1	3	–	1	0	1	2	2	20
2006	0	3	–	1	1	0	1	0	1	3	1	1	0	1	0	0	0	0	2	1	0	–	0	1	0	1	1	23
2007	1	0	1	1	0	2	0	2	2	1	1	2	1	1	3	1	1	0	0	1	0	2	0	0	2	1	3	31
2008	3	4	0	2	2	0	2	1	3	3	2	1	3	1	2	3	2	3	2	1	1	0	0	0	2	1	5	41
2009	1	1	0	0	4	2	1	3	0	3	0	1	2	0	0	0	0	2	2	1	3	2	1	1	2	0	5	39
2010	0	1	0	0	3	1	0	0	0	1	1	4	0	0	0	0	0	1	0	3	1	0	1	3	1	2	4	27
Total	**10**	**14**	**2**	**4**	**11**	**5**	**5**	**7**	**8**	**18**	**9**	**9**	**7**	**7**	**6**	**6**	**6**	**6**	**4**	**11**	**6**	**4**	**3**	**6**	**12**	**9**	**23**	**218**
Votes against																												
2004	4	5	–	0	0	5	0	0	1	2	0	0	2	2	0	2	4	0	2	0	2	–	0	0	3	3	1	39
2005	0	0	–	0	1	4	0	1	1	0	2	0	0	4	0	2	0	3	0	2	1	–	0	0	0	4	1	26
2006	2	1	–	1	2	4	0	0	0	1	2	2	1	0	1	3	0	3	4	4	1	–	3	0	0	5	2	42
2007	2	2	0	2	2	4	2	2	1	0	4	2	2	3	1	1	2	0	0	3	2	0	3	0	2	2	5	49
2008	2	1	0	1	0	4	0	0	0	5	1	1	0	1	1	0	1	1	1	1	0	0	0	1	0	1	0	20
2009	5	0	0	0	0	5	4	0	0	5	0	0	2	2	3	0	0	0	1	1	0	1	4	0	1	1	3	40
2010	1	0	1	0	0	1	0	0	0	0	0	0	0	0	0	0	0	0	1	0	0	0	0	0	0	1	0	10
Total	**16**	**9**	**2**	**4**	**5**	**27**	**6**	**4**	**4**	**16**	**9**	**3**	**7**	**12**	**6**	**8**	**7**	**7**	**9**	**12**	**7**	**1**	**10**	**1**	**5**	**17**	**12**	**226**

Source: Figures supplied by the Council Secretariat

indicate *how* a particular member state voted at the end of the decision-making process, they do not explain *why* it acted in the way it did. By conducting interviews with participants and examining the statements of the member states attached to the record of the vote, it is possible to discern whether, for example, a member state disagreed with the decision, but decided for whatever reason not to prevent its adoption.

Influence can also be exerted by large and small member states alike in more informal (and less easily quantifiable) ways, such as by putting forward compromise proposals acceptable to a majority of the member governments, forming coalitions with like-minded states, and making their point of view known to the Commission, the presidency, and the Council Secretariat. The formation of coalitions within the Council is an intrinsic part of the decision-making process under QMV, in which qualified majorities and blocking minorities matter, if only for the purposes of calculating which member states need to be won over in order to achieve a consensus. For many years, it was customary to claim that coalitions in the Council were constantly shifting and tended to be issue-driven rather than power-driven. With the publication of systematic records of voting now spanning more than a decade, however, some emerging patterns of coalition formation have been identified (see Naurin and Wallace 2008). Again, such findings need to be approached with caution: while roll-call votes represent a precise public choice on the part of national representatives in the Council, they constitute only one aspect of a member state's preferences and bargaining behaviour at EU level.

Dealing with the other institutions

The notion of an inherent institutional balance is a popular one in the EU, particularly when new powers are at stake, such as when a new treaty or inter-institutional agreement is being negotiated or implemented. Supporters of one or other EU body watch even more carefully than usual in order to ensure that new arrangements do not have a detrimental effect on the position of 'their' institution. When assessing inter-institutional relations in the EU, however, it is important to distinguish between outward protestations or manifestations of discord, and a close and cooperative working relationship that has developed over the years between the various institutions, particularly since the introduction of the codecision procedure.

The Council and European Council

The Lisbon Treaty's institutionalization of the European Council and the appointment of its first semi-permanent President have had the effect of setting the European Council apart from the Council of Ministers. Nevertheless the two bodies remain closely linked, both physically and administratively. Herman Van Rompuy and his private office are housed in the Council's headquarters, the Justus Lipsius building in Brussels, although (at the time of writing) the intention is that they will move into a separate building dedicated to the European Council, the Résidence Palace, when its renovation is complete.

The European Council's work continues to be prepared by the GAC and Coreper, supported by the Council Secretariat, and (a point driven home repeatedly in the European Council's internal rules of procedure) in cooperation with the rotating presidency of the Council of Ministers. The draft conclusions of each European Council meeting are discussed in advance in a restricted session of Coreper, which is attended by one or more officials from the European Council President's private office. By means of these conclusions, the European Council frequently 'tasks' (the new in-house buzzword) the Council to do certain things by a certain date, and it falls to the GAC and Coreper to ensure that these obligations are fulfilled. A good deal of Council–European Council cooperation is therefore inherent to, and already written into, the relationship. It is to be expected that this cooperation will develop even more behind the scenes in the years to come.

In the year after the appointment of its first President, the European Council met more frequently than usual. More regular meetings had implications for those parts of the Council hierarchy that prepare and are responsible for the follow-up to its meetings. It remains to be seen whether this increase will continue, or was a temporary aberration in response to the particular political and economic circumstances in 2010–11.

The Council and Parliament

The Council–EP relationship is based on the natural rivalry that exists between all executives and legislatures, even though neither institution closely resembles national models of such bodies. A large part of the inter-institutional tension in the EU setting is a result of the EP's historically unremitting and largely successful campaign to wrest increasing amounts of legislative and budgetary power from the reluctant grasp of the Council. Successive inter-institutional agreements (IIAs) on budgetary discipline and the introduction of multi-annual financial frameworks have done much to reduce the number and ferocity of the disputes between the two arms of the budgetary authority. Budgetary disputes still flare up from time to time, but the hostilities have tended to be muted by agreed rules of engagement. It remains to be seen whether times of economic hardship will result in a resumption of hostilities and what effect this will have on Council–EP relations.

In contrast, the EP has had to fight harder and longer for legislative powers, which it has won in increments via court cases, IIAs, and treaty reform. The introduction and simplification of the codecision procedure in the 1990s, and its continued extension to more and more areas of EU activity (most recently to a large number of JHA issues under the Lisbon Treaty), have gradually transformed the Council–EP relationship from one of permanent confrontation to one of both formal and informal cooperation. The EP is now a real co-legislative authority with the Council. But there is less agreement between the two over the EP's repeated depiction of the post-Lisbon Council as the second chamber in a bicameral system.

The cooperation between the two institutions is subject to complicated procedures that can (and frequently do) give rise to tensions between them. Sometimes, these tensions flare up into full-scale inter-institutional battles or failures in decision-making—the negotiations over the creation of the EEAS in 2010, and the rejection by the EP of the SWIFT (Society for Worldwide Interbank Financial Telecommunication) agreement and of the Novel Foods Directive in 2010–11 are recent examples. Generally speaking, though, the prevailing spirit between the Council and the EP is probably best described as one of wary interdependence.

The wariness on the part of the Council arises from its experience of the EP's (no doubt understandable) determination and evident ability to gain the maximum amount of influence from newly acquired formal powers. The entry into force of the Lisbon Treaty was no exception, with the Council and EP engaged in a number of disputes over issues such as comitology and access to documents, causing blockage on certain dossiers. The extent of the EP's new powers under the Lisbon Treaty appears to have come as something of a surprise to the Council, putting it repeatedly on the defensive (CEPS/Egmont/EPC 2010: 44). However, given the underlying relationship between the two institutions, the most likely outcome of at least some of these disputes is their eventual resolution by means of IIAs, although others may prove more difficult to resolve.

The bedrock of the Council–EP relationship is the now well-established codecision procedure, transformed by the Lisbon Treaty into the ordinary legislative procedure. If it is to operate smoothly and efficiently, this rather complex procedure requires constant contact between the main protagonists. Whenever feasible, the Council is now content to reach agreement as swiftly as possible, thereby reducing the number of issues that end up in formal (and time-consuming) conciliation. Great efforts are therefore made to ensure that the work of both institutions proceeds in parallel. Much informal negotiation goes on behind the scenes in advance of trialogue meetings, bringing together representatives of the Council, Commission, and EP at presidential and official levels (see Chapter 6).

Despite a small number of sometimes spectacular failures, there is now a growing and rather positive balance sheet of agreements reached between the Council and the EP under the codecision procedure, proof of the greater cooperative spirit that now underpins their entire relationship. Codecision statistics released by the institutions are impressive, with a significant increase in the number of dossiers agreed at first reading and an important drop in the number of dossiers that end up in conciliation. As with all statistics, however, these figures merit more in-depth investigation, since early agreements can be reached for many different reasons.

What is beyond doubt is that there is very real evidence of increasing cooperation and growing mutual trust between the Council and the EP, at least in those areas in which codecision is well established. This trend should not be interpreted as evidence of the Council and the EP being hand in glove on all issues, however; rather, it is a case of the Parliament choosing its battles more judiciously than in the past. There is still some resistance within the Council to EP-inspired suggestions for greater collaboration, often entailing increased availability of the presidency (as the representative of the Council) at EP plenary sessions and committee meetings. This aversion to establishing any precedent that might have the effect of extending the institutional obligations laid down in the Treaties—and thereby increasing the EP's current and future role and powers—informs the Council's general approach in its dealings with the EP.

The Council and Commission

Council–Commission relations have always been typified by a complex mixture of cooperation and competition. Public skirmishes between the Council and Commission have frequently been presented as battles for dominance between a more supranationalist and a more intergovernmentalist concept of the integration process. Yet this political rhetoric coexists with very real cooperation, the result of a long and close working relationship across all areas of EU activity.

The entry into force of the Lisbon Treaty has required new forms of Council–Commission cooperation, the long-term effects of which remain to be discerned. The new High Representative for Foreign Affairs and Security Policy, Catherine Ashton, straddles both institutions, being both a member (indeed a Vice-President) of the Commission and the President of the Foreign Affairs Council. She oversees the EEAS, composed of permanent officials from both the Commission and the Council Secretariat, as well as seconded officials from the national foreign ministries. The creation of this new position and innovative body gave rise to long and complex negotiations between the two institutions about administrative issues that might appear trivial (even petty) to outsiders, but which had (and continue to have) very real resonance for serving officials. Relations between the High Representative and the EEAS, on the one hand, and the Council (specifically the rotating presidency and the Council Secretariat), on the other, got off to a (probably predictably) rocky start. It is to be hoped that a suitable modus vivendi will emerge between these bodies in the years to come as the relationship settles down and acquires its own distinctive rhythm.

The day-to-day reality of Council–Commission relations at the level of officials is much more mundane and reassuring, bearing in mind that the relationship differs between policy arenas. As regards issues subject to the so-called 'Community method', the two institutions are required to cooperate because they are so clearly interdependent. Thanks to its right of initiative, the Commission is responsible for producing the proposals on which most Council debates are based, but it is reliant on the Council (increasingly in tandem with the Parliament) to adopt the measures it has proposed. Accordingly, it attends meetings at all levels of the Council hierarchy, acting both as protagonist and mediator in an attempt to have its proposals adopted. As one of the potential architects of compromise between conflicting positions in the Council, the Commission delegation can be regarded by beleaguered member governments in the Council as their greatest ally on particular issues under discussion.

Indeed, the support of the Commission can be helpful for both the Parliament and the Council in their dealings with each other, and the Commission is well placed to play a brokerage role between them. However, on the actual substance of negotiations on dossiers, the feeling in the Council is that the Commission tends more often to be on the side of the EP than that of the member governments. The Council therefore viewed with some disquiet a framework agreement concluded in October 2010 between the Commission and the EP on relations between them during the 2009–14 legislative period.[3] The Council was of the opinion that the Commission, under pressure from the EP, had agreed to act beyond its Treaty obligations in certain areas, thereby according powers to the EP not conferred on it by the treaties. The Council claimed that this would have the effect of limiting the autonomy of the Commission and its President, consequently modifying the institutional balance established by the treaties. Its misgivings were further reinforced by the Commission President's constant references to 'the two Community institutions par excellence', an indication of the special relationship that he perceived between the Commission and the EP.

The Council and accountability

The democratic accountability of the Council has always been an issue of concern to both proponents of and detractors from European integration. Whereas the members of the EP are directly elected, the members of the Council take their seats *ex officio* in their capacity as national ministers, elected on issues often unrelated to those that they discuss and upon which they decide in the Council. While the Commission can be voted out of office by the EP, the Council as a body has permanent tenure, although the individuals who make it up may (and frequently do) change following elections or cabinet reshuffles in their national capitals.

The EP's lack of direct control over the Council has been a source of some frustration for MEPs down the years, who have responded by trying to ensure the presence of representatives of the Council in various EP fora. The rotating Council presidency is the EP's main interlocutor at plenary sessions, in committee meetings, and in the codecision process, including conciliation. The EP would prefer such appearances to be much more regular and the discussions to be more in-depth—but the Council continues to resist attempts to draw it into greater degrees of collaboration.

Recent improvements regarding legislative transparency have increased the accountability of the Council, in the sense that video-streaming (via the Council's portal[4]) and the publication of the outcomes of votes have made it possible to check how national ministerial representatives defend their positions and exercise their votes in the Council. However, there is no public access to meetings below ministerial level, at which most of the pre-agreement discussion and negotiation continues to take place. The nagging feeling persists that the transparency provisions, far from shining a spotlight on decision-making in the Council, have instead had the effect of moving the real negotiations out of the range of the cameras and microphones.

BOX 4.4	Public access to Council documents

The following figures relate to the documents listed in the Council register, but not directly available to the public (some 25 per cent of the total).

	1999	2001	2003	2005	2007	2009
Number of requests for documents	889	1,234	2,830	2,100	1,964	2,666
Percentage of requested documents supplied	83.7	88.2	87.3	81.2	78.9	77.5

Source: Council annual reports on access to documents

Arguably, this outcome was predictable in an institution that has consistently made the case for privacy when key negotiations between member governments are taking place.

One area in which a good deal of progress has undoubtedly been made, however, is on public access to the Council's internal documents. An electronic register of Council documents has been operational since January 1999 and, by the end of 2009, contained over 1 million documents (all language versions taken together). Some 75 per cent of these documents are public, in the sense of being directly available by downloading or on request, while special rules apply for sensitive documents. Council documents, depending on their nature, are either made available as soon as they are circulated within the Council (some 70 per cent of all Council documents produced in 2009) or else after the final adoption of the act.

Members of the public interested in documents not directly available via the register can apply to the Council Secretariat in writing to request a copy of them. In most of these cases, full or partial access is granted (see Box 4.4). Where a document reflecting the positions of national delegations is still subject to discussions within the Council or its preparatory bodies, partial access to the document (the blacking out of the names of delegations) has been granted since 2001, although the European Court of Justice (ECJ) has now outlawed this practice (and the Council is appealing the decision).[5]

The Council in context

The Council and the EU system

In this chapter, the Council has been presented as a club of member governments, and as the locus of persistent competition among them for influence. The Council is regarded as the central body by those who stress the importance of national interest as the factor explaining outcomes in the EU. Indeed, the Council as it exists and operates today may be viewed as one of the living symbols of the continuing power of the member states in the EU, and of the desire of the national governments to remain at the centre of the process of European integration. Since it is also representatives of the member governments who constitute the intergovernmental conferences (IGCs) that initiate constitutional reform in the EU, we can expect the Council to endure and to continue to play a central role in the larger EU.

Despite being the EU's intergovernmental institution par excellence, however, this chapter has also attempted to show that, in reality, the Council is a unique blend of the intergovernmental and the supranational. It represents member state interests that are aggregated under conditions frequently owing more to supranationality than to intergovernmentalism, and it is not necessarily the interests of the larger member states that determine the final outcomes. In addition, the Council as an institution works closely with the Commission and the EP, the views of both of which inform its work and impinge in important ways on its output.

Theorizing the Council

Spanning as it does the supranational and intergovernmental camps, the Council embodies the enduring tension between the two approaches as explanatory tools for understanding the construction of the EU. Realist and liberal intergovernmentalist observers can find plenty of instances in which 'state interests' inform negotiating preferences, while constructivists and rational choice scholars argue that the predominant modes of decision-making are based on deliberation and bargaining (Warntjen 2010). The behaviour of the ministerial and official representatives who comprise the Council may be better explained by sociology and anthropology than by regional integration or negotiation theories, but the outcome of their conduct continues to be a testimony to 'collective purpose, collective commitment and collective ideas' (Hayes-Renshaw and Wallace 1997: 2).

Throughout the Council hierarchy, the reconciliation of conflicting national interests is pursued by means of a continual process of negotiation. Given that the ministers' deliberations in Council are prepared by Coreper, a similar general ethos informs their approach (see Chapter 14). However, the consensual reflex in the Council is tempered by the fact that the ministers are more high-profile actors than the permanent representatives; they are required to justify their actions to their national constituents and, given the transparency rules that now govern their formal meetings, they can be directly monitored to ensure that they are indeed 'defending the national interest'. Thus, while consensus is the most usual mode of ministerial agreement whatever the formal rule, abstentions, 'no' votes, and statements in the Council minutes are all utilized to signal national dissatisfaction with the legislative act being adopted when earlier negotiation has not succeeded in having the national viewpoint taken into account, for whatever reason.

Two opposing suggestions for the Council linger in the debate over EU institutional reform. One advocates that it should become an explicitly representative and legislative rather than an executive institution; the other asserts that the Council should be made even more explicitly dominant, as the core of executive power within the EU. The Lisbon Treaty has neither resolved this argument nor clarified the situation. It is likely that the Council will have to continue to serve both camps, with all of the constitutional and operational ambiguities that this implies.

Coping with change

Enlargement is no novelty for the EU, or indeed for the Council, which, by 2011, had had to adapt to new members on six separate occasions. An increase in numbers has always necessitated adjustment in the Council and elsewhere, both in terms of socialization (of old and new members alike), and in terms of adaptation of working methods, systems, and structures. The prospect of the 2004 enlargement had given rise to some disquiet and much discussion regarding the capacity of the Council physically to deal with such an unprecedented number of new arrivals. Consequently, the Seville reforms agreed in 2002 were supplemented by a code of conduct on working methods in an enlarged Council, agreed in March 2003 and now incorporated into the Council's Rules of Procedure.[6]

Contrary to the predictions of many, the Council did not grind to a halt as a result of large-scale enlargement. Yes, negotiations are more complex because of the greater number of positions that have to be taken on board before agreement can be reached, but more efficient working methods have been introduced and adhered to by newer and older member states alike. A consensual reflex continues to underpin negotiations within the Council, with member states finding ways other than abstentions and 'no' votes in which to register their dissatisfaction with adopted decisions that they cannot (or choose not to) block.

Arguably, the entry into force of the Lisbon Treaty is having less impact than enlargement did on the way in which the Council actually operates on a day-to-day basis. The changes to the presidency demand greater efforts of coordination among the relevant actors in order to ensure consistency in the Council's actions across all of its areas of activity, while the extension of the codecision procedure to new areas of policy-making draws the Council into closer and more regular contact with the EP in order to adopt legislation in those areas. But these are changes in degree rather than a fundamental alteration to the way in which the Council conducts its business in the post-Lisbon EU.

Conclusion

The Council has always occupied a central position in the institutional structure of the EU, because of both its composition and the functions attributed to it. Successive treaty changes have altered some aspects of its role and relationships with the other institutions, while repeated enlargements of the EU have compelled the Council to assess the way in which it transacts its business and to introduce reforms to its operating procedures. The implementation of the Lisbon Treaty is but the latest stage in this ongoing process of adaptation.

The Lisbon-inspired changes to the Council's internal presidency arrangements have not done away with the six-month rotating presidency. But they will require sustained coordination between the various bodies in order to ensure a coherent and consistent approach in decision-making. The earliest date for the implementation of the double-majority system of voting in the Council is November 2014, and it may not come into effect fully until April 2017. In the meantime, consensus continues to be the most usual means of reaching agreement in the Council, a fact that can be verified by means of the voting figures now routinely produced by the Council under its transparency provisions.

The institutionalization of the European Council, the addition of the role of Vice-President of the Commission to that of the High Representative, and the extension of the EP's legislative powers under the Lisbon Treaty will have implications for the Council's relationship with each of these institutions. A state of flux in the so-called institutional balance is to be expected until such time as a mutually acceptable modus operandi is agreed, whether formally or informally. In the meantime, outward protestations or manifestations of inter-institutional discord are likely to coexist with the close and cooperative working relationship that has developed behind the scenes between the EU's institutions over the years, particularly since the introduction of codecision.

NOTES

1. Article 23.3 of the Council's Rules of Procedure, adopted on 1 December 2009 and available in OJ L 325/35-61 of 11 December 2009.
2. The Dehaene Report on the impact of the Treaty of Lisbon on the development of the institutional balance of the European Union was commissioned by the Committee on Constitutional Affairs of the European Parliament and adopted in plenary session in March 2009.
3. See OJ L 304/47-62, 20 November 2010.
4. **http://video.consilium.europa.eu/**
5. The specific provisions regarding public access to Council documents are laid down in Annex II to the Council's Rules of Procedure.
6. See Annex V, entitled 'Council working methods'.

FURTHER READING

The best recent book on the Council is an edited volume by Naurin and Wallace (2008), which focuses on conflict dimensions, modes of interaction, and power and leadership in the Council. Earlier, more general, textbooks on all aspects of the Council's organization and role include Hayes-Renshaw and Wallace (2006) and Westlake and Galloway (2005). Milton and Keller-Noëllet (2005) provide the detailed background to the Council-related provisions in the Lisbon Treaty. Interesting empirical data on Council voting practices is presented in pieces by Häge (2007) and Hagemann (2008). Finally, articles in the two joint studies produced by CEPS/Egmont/EPC contain the views of insiders on the expected (2007) and actual (2010) consequences of the entry into force of the Lisbon Treaty on the Council and its relations with the other institutions.

CEPS/Egmont/EPC (2007) *The Treaty of Lisbon: Implementing the Institutional Innovations*, available online at **http://www.ceps.eu/files/book/1554.pdf**

CEPS/Egmont/EPC (2010) *The Treaty of Lisbon: A Second Look at the Institutional Innovations*, available online at **http://www.ceps.eu/ceps/download/3736**

Häge, F. M. (2007) 'Committee decision-making in the Council of the European Union', *European Union Politics*, 8/3: 299–328.

Hagemann, S. (2008) 'Voting, statements and coalition-building in the Council from 1999 to 2006', in D. Naurin and H. Wallace (eds) *Unveiling the Council of the European Union: Games Governments Play in Brussels* (Basingstoke: Palgrave Macmillan).

Hayes-Renshaw, F. and Wallace, H. (2006) *The Council of Ministers* (2nd edn, Basingstoke and New York: Palgrave Macmillan).

Milton, G. and Keller-Noëllet, J. (2005) *The European Constitution: Its Origins, Negotiation and Meaning* (London: John Harper).

Naurin, D. and Wallace, H. (2008) (eds) *Unveiling the Council of the European Union: Games Governments Play in Brussels* (Basingstoke: Palgrave Macmillan).

Westlake, M. and Galloway, D. (2005) *The Council of the European Union* (3rd edn, London: John Harper Publishing).

WEB LINKS

http://www.consilium.europa.eu
The Council's website contains a wealth of information on its structure, output, and day-to-day activities, including direct access to most of its documents. It also contains a link to the website of the current Council presidency.

http://www.councildata.cergu.gu.se
Another useful website for those interested in quantitative research on the Council, which contains links to published research based on systematic empirical data, with the laudable aim of making these data sets more easily accessible to researchers.

CHAPTER 5

The College of Commissioners

John Peterson

▌ Summary

No institution closely resembles the European Commission. It is a distinct hybrid: the European Union's largest administration and main policy manager, as well as a source of political and policy direction. This chapter focuses on the Commission's most 'political' level: its College of Commissioners. Yet, Commissioners are unelected, independent (in theory) of member governments, and often portrayed as unaccountable technocrats. The Commission seemed in a permanent state of decline after 1999, headed by Presidents who were perceived as weak, ineffective, or both. The appointment of José Manuel Barroso as President in 2004, and his reappointment in 2009, at least spurred debates about whether the Commission could be revived. However, the rejection of the Constitutional Treaty in the 2005 referenda and bruising political rows over the crisis in the eurozone in 2010–11 revealed how much the Commission's fate is determined by factors over which it has little or no control.

Introduction

The European Commission may be the strangest administration ever created. Despite brave attempts to compare it to other bureaucracies (see Page 1997), the Commission is in many respects a *sui generis* institution. Legally, the Commission is a single entity. In practice, it is a unique hybrid. It is given direction by a political arm, or College, of Commissioners. But the College is unelected. Its members act independently of the states that appoint them (at least in theory) and even swear an oath of independence when appointed. The College exists alongside a permanent, formally apolitical administration, or what are known as the Commission's services or Directorates-General (DGs). This book squarely confronts the Commission's duality by focusing here on the College and devoting a separate chapter (Chapter 8) to the services.

Even if they are unelected, Commissioners 'are appointed via a highly politicised process ... are almost invariably national politicians of senior status, and are expected to provide the Commission's political direction' (Nugent 2001: 3). At times, the College—the President, the Commissioners, and their advisers—has provided political direction to European integration, particularly during the earliest days of the European Economic Community (EEC) and again in the 1980s. More recently, it has become almost accepted wisdom that 'the decline of the Commission ... has continued ... and there seems little possibility that the situation will be reversed' (Kassim and Menon 2004: 102; see also de Schoutheete and Wallace 2002; Tsakatika 2005; Dinan 2011: 117–18). The Commission has always been powerful as a designer and manager of EU policy. But its role has never been uncontested (Lequesne 1996; Spence 2006; Kassim *et al.* 2012). The central theme of this chapter is that the Commission and most of what it does is highly politicized, despite its ambitions to be an 'honest broker' and independent guardian of the EU's treaties.

The origins and history of the College

The forerunner of today's European Commission was the High Authority of the European Coal and Steel Community (ECSC). Its first President was the legendary Jean Monnet (1978; see also Duchêne 1994). Provisions in the 1951 Treaty of Paris that gave the High Authority significant independent powers to regulate markets for coal and steel bore Monnet's own fingerprints. The ECSC thus established that common European policies would be managed, and European integration given political impulse, by a non-partisan, central authority.

The High Authority was larger than Monnet wanted it to be: nine members—two from France and West Germany and one from all other member states (plus a co-opted ninth member). Thus a precedent was set for national representation in what was meant to be a supranational administration. Over time, the High Authority became much less nimble and more bureaucratic than Monnet wanted it to be (Nugent 2001: 21–2). Partly in protest, Monnet resigned before the end of his term.

The design of common institutions for the new EEC was one of the most difficult issues in negotiations on the Treaty of Rome. A Dutch proposal sought to give the EEC a supranational administration that would be even more independent of member governments than the ECSC's High Authority. However, it ran into opposition, particularly from France, and the Dutch suggestion ended up being 'almost the reverse of what was finally decided' (Milward 1992: 217–18). Compared to the High Authority, the new European Commission (the label 'High Authority' was discarded as too grandiose) was subject to considerably tighter political control by a Council of (national) Ministers.

The Treaty assigned three basic functions to the Commission: overseeing the implementation of policies, representing the Community in external trade negotiations, and (most importantly) proposing new policies. The Commission's monopoly on the right to initiate policies, along with its prerogative to 'formulate recommendations or deliver opinions on matters dealt with in this Treaty', gave it licence to act as a sort of engine of integration, or a source of ideas on new directions that the Community might take. Alongside the European Court of Justice (ECJ), the Commission was also designated as a guardian of the Treaty, and tasked with ensuring that its rules and injunctions were respected.

The early Commissions were small (nine members) and united by a 'dominating sense of team spirit' (Narjes 1998: 114; see also Dumoulin 2007). Between 1958 and 1967, only fourteen different men[1] served as Commissioners, supported by two cabinet advisers (with four advising the President). Walter Hallstein, foreign policy adviser to the first West German Chancellor, Konrad Adenauer, became the Commission's first President. Hallstein was both a political heavyweight and a forceful leader, repeatedly referring to himself as the equivalent of a 'European Prime Minister'. The Commission achieved considerable policy success during this period, laying the foundations for the common agricultural policy (mere agreement on the CAP was considered a success), representing the Community in the successful Kennedy Round of world trade talks, and convincing member government to accelerate the timetable for establishing the EEC's customs union.

A watershed in the history of the Commission was reached in 1965. A year away from a scheduled extension of qualified-majority voting (QMV) as a decision rule in the Council, the Hallstein Commission proposed a new system of financing the CAP through 'own resources', or revenue directly channelled to the Community rather than cobbled together from national contributions. The plan proposed to give new budgetary powers both to the Commission and the European Parliament (EP). It became a pretext on which French President Charles de Gaulle could pull France out of nearly all EEC negotiations for more than six months. De Gaulle's hostility to Hallstein's federalist rhetoric and actions, which included receiving foreign ambassadors to the EEC with a red carpet, was highly personal, but also reflected deep-seated French anxiety about a resurgent (West) Germany (see de Gaulle 1970: 195–6).

The so-called 'empty chair' crisis ended and France returned to EEC negotiations after the Luxembourg compromise was agreed in 1966 (with Luxembourg holding the Council presidency). The agreement, made public only in the form of a press re-lease, stated that 'where very important interests are at stake the discussion must be continued until unanimous agreement is reached'. Any member government could invoke the compromise in any negotiation if it felt that its 'very important interests' were at risk. The upshot was to give political blessing to unanimous decision-making in the Council, and generally to hobble the Commission.[2]

De Gaulle insisted that Hallstein be replaced as President of the Commission, which itself became a single, integrated administration for all three previously dis-tinct 'Communities'—the EEC, the ECSC, and the European Atomic Energy Community (Euratom)—in 1967. Headed by low-key Belgian Jean Rey, the new Commission initially contained fourteen members (reduced to nine in 1970). The next decade was a lean time for the Commission, both because of weak presidential leadership (see Table 5.1) and the EEC's more general lack of dynamism. In retro-spect, the Community may have actually achieved more in the 1970s than it appeared at the time (see Nugent 2001: 35–8). Still, Western Europe suffered through a series of economic crises, and the Community itself was widely seen as dilapidated.

TABLE 5.1 The Presidents of the Commission	
President (nationality*)	**Period of tenure**
Walter Hallstein (D)	1958–67
Jean Rey (B)	1967–70
Franco Maria Malfatti (I)	1970–72
Sicco Mansholt (N)	1972–73
François Xavier-Ortoli (F)	1973–77
Roy Jenkins (UK)	1977–81
Gasthon Thorn (L)	1981–85
Jacques Delors (F)	1985–95
Jacques Santer (L)	1995–99
Romano Prodi (I)	1999–2004
José Manuel Barroso (P)	2004–

*Note that the Presidency has been held by a non-national of one of the original EEC6 only twice.

By the late 1970s, a critical mass of member governments was persuaded that the Commission should be led by a political figure, or one who was a potential Prime Minister in his or her own country. Thus Roy Jenkins, a senior member of the UK's governing Labour Party, was appointed as President in 1977. Jenkins was the first President to be nominated in advance of the College as a whole, thus giving him scope to influence the composition of his team.

Jenkins' record was ambiguous. On the one hand, member governments frequently disregarded his advice and there is little dispute that he 'was not a great success at running or reforming the Brussels machine' (Campbell 1983: 195). On the other, Jenkins raised the external policy profile of the Commission by insisting (against French resistance) that the Commission President should attend Group of Seven (G7) economic summits. Jenkins also worked tirelessly with German Chancellor Helmut Schmidt and French President Valéry Giscard d'Estaing to build a consensus in support of the European monetary system (EMS). The EMS helped to keep European currency values stable in the 1980s after enormous exchange rate turbulence in the 1970s. It was an important forerunner both to the freeing of the Community's internal market and, later, monetary union.

Before the 1979 election of Margaret Thatcher as UK Prime Minister, Jenkins seemed a candidate to be the first Commission President since Hallstein to be reappointed to a second four-year term.[3] However, reappointing Jenkins became politically untenable when Thatcher doggedly pursued the so-called 'British budgetary question' (arising from the size of its net EU budgetary contribution), which preoccupied the Community for no fewer than five years. It cast a dark cloud over the Commission presidency of former Luxembourg Prime Minister Gaston Thorn, whose tenure marked a retreat in the direction of the lacklustre, post-Hallstein Commissions.

Thorn was replaced in 1985 by former French Finance Minister Jacques Delors. Thatcher accepted the nomination of Delors, a French Socialist, on the strength of his role in France's economic policy U-turn of the early 1980s, when it abandoned protectionism and increased public expenditure in favour of market liberalism. Delors carefully reflected on how the Community could be relaunched via a headline-grabbing, political project. Working closely with Lord (Arthur) Cockfield (1994), the former British Trade Minister and Commissioner for the internal market, Delors opted for an integrated programme to dismantle most barriers to internal EU trade by the end of 1992. Seizing on converging preferences amongst the EU's largest member states for economic liberalization (Moravcsik 1991), as well as the strong support of the European business community, the 1992 project gave European integration renewed momentum. A substantive overhaul of the Community's founding treaties was agreed in the 1986 Single European Act (SEA), which gave the Commission significant new powers—notably by extending the use of QMV in the Council.

Delors then convinced European leaders, despite the scepticism of many, to allow him to chair a high-level committee of (mostly) central bankers and to relaunch long-dormant plans for economic and monetary union (EMU). Progress towards

EMU was uninterrupted by the geopolitical earthquakes that shook the European continent in late 1989. German unification was handled with skill and speed by the Delors Commission (Spence 1991; Ross 1995), which also stepped forward to coordinate Western economic aid to the former Warsaw Pact states. By spring 1990, with a round of treaty revisions to create EMU on course, French President François Mitterrand and German Chancellor Helmut Kohl threw their combined political weight behind the idea of separate, parallel set of negotiations to create a political union. By this point, Delors was accepted by Kohl, Mitterrand, and even Thatcher as a political equal in the European Council.

The second half of Delors' ten-year term was a far less happy time for the Commission. Member governments agreed mostly intergovernmental mechanisms for making new internal security and foreign policies via the (Maastricht) Treaty on European Union, denying the Commission its traditional Community prerogatives in these areas. Delors also shouldered some of the blame for the 1992 Danish rejection of the new treaty, after suggesting that the power of small states would inevitably be weaker in a future EU (Nugent 2001:46–7). By the time Delors left Brussels in 1995, a critical mass of member governments wanted a less-visionary successor.

After a tortured selection process,[4] Jacques Santer, Prime Minister of Luxembourg, was chosen to replace Delors. Santer promised that his Commission would 'do less, but do it better'. Yet, it inherited a full agenda, including the launch of the euro, Eastern enlargement, another round of treaty reforms, and negotiations on the Union's multi-annual budget and structural funds for regional development. The Santer Commission generally handled these issues well. Its stewardship of the launch of EMU in particular seemed 'enough to earn any Commission President a proud legacy' (Peterson 1999: 61).

In fact, Santer's legacy was hardly a proud one. For all of the dynamism of the Delors era, the Commission had become far more focused on policy initiation than on effective management. Presiding over an administration that had become inefficient and sometimes chaotic, the Santer era culminated in the dramatic mass resignation of the College in March 1999 after the publication of a report of a Committee of Independent Experts (1999a), convened by the EP, on charges of fraud, mismanagement, and nepotism (see Box 5.1).

Santer's resignation in spring 1999 came at a particularly difficult moment. The Berlin Summit, at which a series of major decisions needed to be made on the EU's seven-year budget, structural funds, and agricultural reform, was about a week away. A political crisis over Kosovo was deepening. The German Council presidency thus undertook a whirlwind tour of national EU capitals to seek a swift decision on replacing Santer. In Berlin, after 10 minutes of discussion, the European Council agreed that the new Commission President should be former Italian Prime Minister Romano Prodi.

Prodi was by no means free to choose his own College. Nevertheless, armed with new powers granted to the Commission President by the Amsterdam Treaty (see below), Prodi had more influence over its composition than had most of his predecessors. He

| BOX 5.1 | The fall of the Santer Commission |

Jacques Santer's troubles began in earnest in late 1998 after the publication of a damning Court of Auditors' report, which suggested that large amounts of EU funding had gone missing. Around the same time, press reports appeared alleging that Research Commissioner (and former French Prime Minister) Edith Cresson had given plum advisers' jobs in the services to unqualified personal cronies. Characteristically, Cresson dismissed them as part of an Anglo-German 'conspiracy'. A motion of censure tabled under the EP's treaty powers to sack the entire Commission was defeated (by 293 votes to 232) after Santer accepted that a Committee of Independent Experts would investigate charges of fraud and mismanagement within the Commission. At this point, according to Leon Brittan (2000: 10), a veteran of the Delors and Santer Commissions, the Commission began 'to sleepwalk towards its own destruction'. Santer told the EP that the College would implement the recommendations of the Experts' report, regardless of what they were, in a clear sign of the Commission's political weakness.

The Experts had exactly five weeks in which to investigate the Commission, yet produced a report that was painstaking in detail. Its most serious charges—leaving aside those against Cresson—concerned improprieties that had occurred during the Delors years. Bitter animosity between Delors and the Experts' chair, former head of the Court of Auditors André Middlehoek, was palpable in the report, which drew conclusions that seemed to go well beyond the evidence it contained. The report built to a crescendo with the devastating charge that it was 'becoming difficult to find anyone who has even the slightest sense of responsibility' for the work of the Commission (Committee of Independent Experts 1999a: 144). The EP's largest political group, the Socialists, announced that it would vote to sack all twenty Commissioners, thus making the outcome of any vote all but inevitable.

A series of efforts were mounted by individual Commissioners to isolate Cresson, including a bid by Santer to convince the French President and Prime Minister, Jacques Chirac and Lionel Jospin, respectively, to ask her to step down. None succeeded. Thus Santer insisted that the entire Commission, as a collegial body, had to resign. The President was defiant in a subsequent press conference, claiming that the Experts' report was 'wholly unjustified in tone'.[5] Whether or not Santer's combativeness was ill-judged, his fate was sealed by a stroke of bad luck: an English interpreter mistakenly communicated Santer's claim (in French) that he was *blanchi*, or exonerated, from personal charges against him in the Experts' report, to the non-French press as a claim that he was 'whiter than white'. It became widely seen as a political necessity that Santer had to go, and quickly.

Ironically, the Commission under Santer had undertaken a series of reforms that made it—on balance—better managed than it had been under Delors (see Cram 1999; Peterson 1999; Metcalfe 2000; Nugent 2000: 49–50). But the efforts were far from enough to cure the Commission of pathologies that had festered under Delors. The Experts' report exposed the Commission as everyone's favourite scapegoat in Brussels. More generally, the fall of the Santer Commission showed, in the words of one of its members, that 'in economic and monetary terms Europe is a giant in the world. But politically we are very young.'[6]

ended up with a less charismatic College than that of Santer, but one in which expertise was matched to portfolio to an extent unseen in the Commission's history.

One EU ambassador spoke for many in Brussels in claiming that Prodi's economic team was 'collectively the best the Commission has ever had'.[7] One of two Vice-Presidents, Neil Kinnock, was charged with implementing an ambitious series of internal reforms of the Commission (Kassim 2004b). Prodi himself helped to shift the debate on Eastern enlargement to the point at which EU governments—at the 1999 Helsinki Summit—decided to open accession talks with no fewer than twelve applicant states on a more-or-less equal basis.

Yet Prodi's weakness as a political communicator was probably his Commission's most glaring liability (Peterson 2004). Kinnock's administrative reform programme encountered bitter resistance in the services, among whom morale seemed to sink ever lower. The Commission was marginalized first in the negotiations that yielded the Treaty of Nice, and then in the Convention on the Future of Europe that drafted a new Constitutional Treaty (see Box 5.2). The most charitable comments that could be made about Prodi himself were that he mostly avoided interfering in the work of a highly competent College.

The leading candidate to replace Prodi in 2004, Belgium's Prime Minister Guy Verhostadt, received powerful Franco-German backing, but was opposed intractably by the UK, thus reawakening divisions over the previous year's invasion of Iraq. Eventually, Portuguese Prime Minister José Manuel Barroso emerged as a consensus candidate to lead a new, expanded College, with each member state in an EU of twenty-five appointing one member. Barroso's allocation of powerful economic portfolios to liberals and previous support for the Iraq war were both controversial. Barroso, as Santer

---

BOX 5.2	**The Commission and the Convention on the Future of Europe**

Most accounts of negotiations on the 2000 Treaty of Nice concur that the Commission had little impact on the outcome (see Gray and Stubb 2001; Peterson 2002: 81). At the Nice Summit itself, Prodi was bullied mercilessly by the summit's chair, Jacques Chirac, revealing how low the Commission President's standing in the European Council had sunk. Two participant-observers concluded that Nice marked the end of a decade during which the Commission never managed to agree a unified position on its own composition in four different rounds of debate (Gray and Stubb 2001: 19).

A rather different version of events starts with the observation that the Commission—leaving aside Delors' influence on the SEA and blueprint for EMU—never contributed much before to what were, after all, revisions of treaties between member states (not EU institutions). The Treaty of Nice was not unkind to the Commission, giving future Presidents more authority to reshuffle portfolios, ask for resignations, and 'ensure that [the College] acts consistently, efficiently and on the basis of collective responsibility'. One seasoned observer insisted that Nice showed that European leaders 'agree[d] that a more efficient Commission, including in particular a more powerful President, is highly desirable' (Ludlow 2001: 18).

Cont. ➤

Cont.

Still, deep dissatisfaction with the Treaty of Nice was revealed in the Laeken Declaration, agreed only a year later and which put the EU on the road to its grandiosely titled 'Convention on the Future of Europe'. Decision-making within the Convention quickly became dominated by its thirteen-member Praesidium, an inner-circle steering group, two members of which (Michel Barnier and Antonio Vitorino) were Commissioners under Prodi. Most of its other members were committed pro-Europeans who could be counted as 'natural allies' of the Commission and backers of the EU institution that most purely 'represented the European interest' (Norman 2003: 161).

At the end of the Convention—as well as the subsequent intergovernmental conference (IGC)—it was (again) possible to come to very different conclusions about how well the Commission had fared. Both Vitorino and Barnier contributed significantly to the Convention. In particular, Barnier surprised many with his successful chairing of a working group on defence, perhaps because he assumed the classic role of honest broker, with the Commission having 'no realistic aspirations to get involved in defence policy' (Norman 2003: 116). The Commission's basic legislative and watchdog roles were preserved in the Constitutional Treaty, which even extended its powers (particularly justice and home affairs, or JHA, policies). A late political compromise in the IGC meant that the College would comprise one Commissioner per member state until at least 2014. But a leaner, more cohesive Commission (equalling two-thirds of the number of states or, say, eighteen in an EU of twenty-seven) was in prospect eventually on the basis of equal rotation between member states. Finally, a proposal backed by the Commission was accepted to make the Union's new Minister of Foreign Affairs a Vice-President in the College (as well as chair of the Foreign Affairs Council), with responsibility for all of the Commission's external activities, thus putting down a marker for an institutional arrangement that 'stuck' despite the Constitutional Treaty's eventual fate.

A less generous interpretation was that the Convention revealed the Prodi Commission at its worst. Divisions sprouted within the College about what the Commission's strategy should be. Little or no attempt was made to ensure that Commission staff put to work on the Convention—numbering considerably more than the Convention's own Secretariat—worked together (Norman 2003: 267). Most damagingly, the Commission produced two very different contributions to the Convention at a crucial stage in late 2002: one an official communication; the other a maximalist, full draft treaty prepared in secret by Prodi's own hand-picked operatives and code-named 'Penelope'. In presenting the Commission's official paper, Prodi downplayed Penelope as a 'feasibility study, a technical working tool' for which his College had 'no political responsibility' (Norman 2003: 167).

Still, Prodi instructed (the visibly infuriated) Barnier and Vitorino to push for language on several Treaty articles that conformed with Penelope. In the end, when consensus emerged within the Convention in June 2003 on the resolution of outstanding issues, the Commission was almost entirely marginalized. Norman's (2003: 267) verdict was that it 'marked an unhappy end to an unhappy Convention for the Commission President'.

before him, also found himself on the sharp end of muscle-flexing by the EP, which threatened to vote to reject his Commission after the initial Italian nominee, Rocco Buttiglione, outraged MEPs by airing his conservative views on gays and women (see Box 5.3 later in this chapter). By most accounts, Barroso handled the affair badly, before finally securing the EP's approval of a redesigned College. Hopes that Barroso could restore the Commission's position sank, and fell further when the Constitutional Treaty was rejected by French and Dutch voters in May 2005 referenda. Meanwhile, political rows blazed over the EU's budget and economic policy direction. The early Barroso years showed that the Commission's position serves as a barometer of European integration, but also that its ability to influence the process is determined by broad political and economic forces over which it has little or no control.

Barroso's first term in office illustrated the point: the Commission became focused on its buoyant policy agenda, but launched no new, major initiative besides deciding to recommend Bulgaria and Romania as the EU's newest member states (they joined in 2007). Barroso himself dominated the College as perhaps no other President previously had, transforming the Commission's Secretariat-General—its service responsible for management of the Commission—into almost an extension of his private office. A large-scale attitudinal survey of Commission officials in 2008 found a considerable majority agreeing that the 'Sec-Gen', as it is known in Commission parlance, had become both more 'political and influential' in the life of the Commission, even if officials were more split on whether it was too process-focused or biased[8] (see Figure 5.1). Despite resentment within the Commission of his personal dominance and alleged lack of ambition, he worked successfully to ensure the ratification of the Lisbon Treaty, in the process showing considerably better political communication

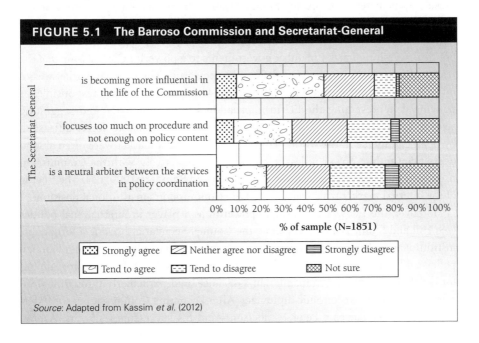

FIGURE 5.1   **The Barroso Commission and Secretariat-General**

Source: Adapted from Kassim *et al.* (2012)

skills than had Prodi. He was re-nominated for a second term by member states in 2010, thus becoming the first Commission President since Delors to serve two terms.

The structure of the College

Basic norms established over fifty years govern appointments to the College and the relationship between its three basic elements: the President, the College itself, and Commissioners' cabinets.

The President

A biographer of Roy Jenkins starkly concluded that:

The presidency of the ... Commission is an impossible job. Indeed it can hardly be called a job at all—the President has a number of conflicting responsibilities, but no power. By no stretch of the imagination does it resemble the Prime Ministership of Europe.

(Campbell 1983: 181)

This claim initially seemed to be challenged by the appointment of Prodi, a former Prime Minister of a large member state. Yet, less than a year after his appointment, Prodi was forced to deny rumours that he was considering leaving the Commission to fight a forthcoming Italian domestic election. The only other Italian to have been Commission President, the barely remembered Franco Maria Malfatti, had done precisely that and left Brussels early in the 1970s. Had the Commission gone back to the future?

In a sense, the legacy of Delors continued to haunt Brussels, both in terms of the political aversion of many member governments to a powerful Commission *and* the reality of a Commission that was irreversibly powerful. The internal market was, if by no means complete, at least a political fact. The Commission was responsible for policing it, representing the EU in international trade diplomacy, and suggesting steps towards its full realization. The enormously powerful market forces unleashed by open commerce in the world's largest single capitalist market were often able to overwhelm public power unless it was wielded collectively, with the Commission usually in the lead (see Pollack 1997; Peterson and Bomberg 1999: 67). The freeing of the internal market truly transformed the Commission's institutional position.

Moreover, the EU was increasingly powerful as a player in international politics (see Hill and Smith 2011). Over time, the Council Secretariat became a formidable institutional rival and clearly superior to the Commission on most questions of foreign policy. Still, the Commission packed a punch as purveyors of the EU's programmes for development aid and humanitarian assistance, and particularly through its lead role in international economic diplomacy. After becoming Commissioner for External Trade under Barroso, Peter Mandelson—and his successors Catherine Ashton and (in Barroso's second College) Karel De Gucht—could plausibly be considered more powerful than perhaps twenty or so prime ministers of the EU's smaller states.

Finally, the Commission remained an honest broker between many diverse and competing interests in a system that relied fundamentally on consensus. Arguably, the Commission stood to be empowered in an expanded EU of twenty-seven or more member states, around three-quarters of which were small states (with about 17 million or fewer citizens), since the Commission had always been the traditional defenders of the 'smalls'. Pointedly, Barroso vowed to defend the newest EU countries—all small states besides Poland—from protectionist pressures from long-time member' states, some of which Barroso claimed had 'not yet changed their chip to an enlarged Europe'.[9]

The days when Barroso's job could 'hardly be called a job at all' may be gone, but no Commission President ever makes his or her own luck. How much any President can accomplish is determined by a variety of factors over which he or she has little or no control. Even Delors was successful only because of three propitious contextual variables: a (brief) receptivity to European solutions, international changes (especially German unification), and a favourable business cycle from 1985 to 1990 (Ross 1995: 234–7). These factors helped Delors to exert 'pull' within the European Council, in which the Commission President is the only member who does not head a state or government. Crucially, Delors (and perhaps Jenkins, at least on EMS) was viewed as a political equal in the European Council. There is no evidence that either Santer or Prodi—former prime ministers themselves—ever were. The case of Barroso is more arguable.

In any case, the Commission has become more *presidential* over time. Successive treaty revisions have given the Commission President—considered 'first amongst equals' only during Delors' time—a progressively stronger grip over the College. Prodi tried to focus on broad political themes, giving himself no specific policy portfolio (unlike Santer, who retained overall responsibility for EMU and external policy), while also seeking to expand his own influence by inserting many of his 'own' people into key positions of authority within the Commission's services. The collective identity of the College seemed a secondary consideration, with Prodi declaring: 'I want each Commissioner to be a star, a big star, in his or her own policy area.'[10]

Yet few argued that it was also more effective or cohesive. Prodi's political misjudgements were frequent and his communication skills poor. His inability to form coalitions with (especially large-state) European leaders led to charges that he had failed to reverse 'the weakness of a Commission that ha[d] not fully recovered from the trauma of the Santer resignation' (de Schoutheete and Wallace 2002: 17).

For his part, Barroso insisted that his would be a dynamic, reform-minded Commission subject to a strong presidential lead. Promising that his College would be more policy-focused and team-oriented, Barroso argued that any effort to restore the position of the Commission had to respect the premise that 'the basic legitimacy of our union is the member states'.[11] Yet even after recovering from the Buttiglione affair (see Box 5.3), Barroso came under attack from the political left, particularly in the EP where he was accused of pursuing a 'neo-conservative agenda' and privileging a 'liberal Atlantic' clique within the Commission.[12] Barroso's defence of small and

BOX 5.3	The Rocco Buttiglione affair

Views on José Manuel Barroso's prospects fluctuated wildly in the first days after his nomination. Barroso was few people's first choice for the job. Immediately after he was chosen, he was subjected to hard lobbying by France and Germany, which wanted him to designate their nominees as 'super-Commissioners', provoking fears of another weak Commission President.

Barroso's early surprise announcement of the distribution of jobs in his College, and his wry comment that he needed twenty-four 'super-Commissioners', temporarily silenced his critics. After first offering the powerful JHA portfolio to the French nominee, Jacques Barrot (who was firm in wanting an economic job), Barroso designated the Italian nominee, Rocco Buttiglione, JHA Commissioner. An arch-Catholic and close confidante of the Pope, Buttiglione aired ultra-conservative views on homosexuality (calling it a 'sin') and women (who 'belonged in the home') at his EP confirmation hearing, leading the Parliament's Civil Liberties Committee to vote to recommend his rejection. Barroso tried to appease MEPs by delegating Buttiglione's responsibilities for civil liberties to a committee of other Commissioners. Yet opinion within the EP did not measurably shift. Barroso then made things worse, stating that he was 'absolutely convinced' that his Commission would be approved since only 'extremist' MEPs could possibly vote against it.[13] Ultimately, he had no choice but to withdraw his team from consideration by the EP in order to avoid a humiliating rejection.

Barroso's political instincts seemed to return in subsequent weeks. He was helped by Buttiglione's decision to stand down, as well as Latvia's withdrawal of its original nominee, Ingrida Udre, who was dogged by allegations of corruption. Fresh nominations by both states—particularly Italy's choice of its Foreign Minister Franco Frattini to replace Buttiglione—allowed Barroso to propose a new-look College, which was overwhelmingly approved by the EP. Afterwards, Barroso could claim that 'we have come out of this experience with strengthened institutions',[14] including a stronger Commission and, of course, an emboldened EP.

For their part, religious organizations were outraged, with one insisting that the affair showed 'how little trust there is at the heart of the EU'.[15] Supporters of the Parliament accused Barroso of going too far to try to appease European leaders, particularly Italy's Prime Minister Silvio Berlusconi. A more mundane, but inevitable, conclusion was that as long as each state in an EU of twenty-seven or more nominates one Commissioner, any nominee for President will find himself or herself trying to build a team from a large group that includes many (a majority in Barroso's case) whom he or she has never met before. In Barroso's own words, 'it is like a blind date'.[16]

new EU states provoked French President Jacques Chirac to respond to rising Euro-scepticism in France (in advance of the failed 2005 referendum on the Constitutional Treaty) by attacking the Commission. Yet Barroso's reappointment to a second term was testimony to his skills as a consensus-builder and political communicator. He also ranked well above his predecessors—although (predictably) behind Delors—when Commission officials were asked to rate his performance in an extensive survey of officials (see Figure 5.2).

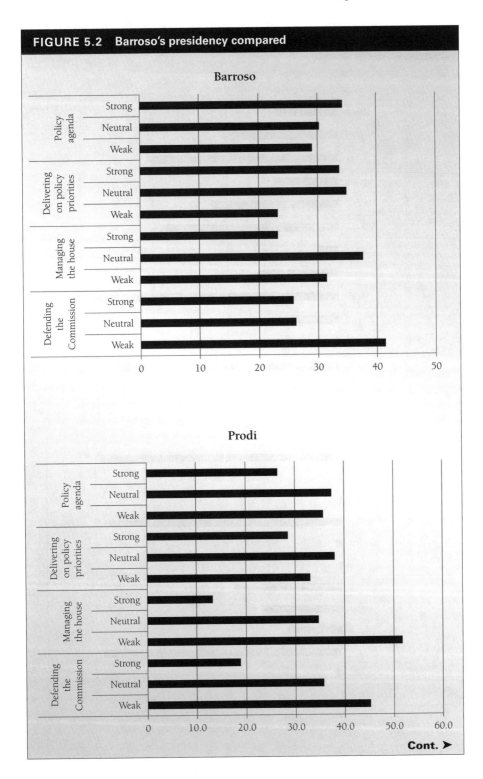

FIGURE 5.2   Barroso's presidency compared

Cont. ➤

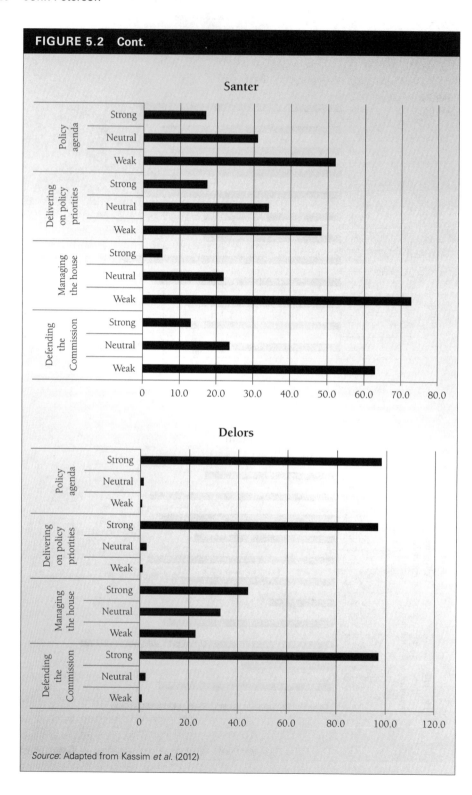

FIGURE 5.2   Cont.

Santer

Delors

Source: Adapted from Kassim et al. (2012)

The College

The appointment of the College is often a fraught and highly politicized exercise (see Peterson and Bomberg 1999: 40–1). The compositions of the Jenkins and Prodi Commissions were shaped in important ways by the nominees for President himself. Nevertheless, provisions in the Amsterdam Treaty[17] that lent weight to Prodi's own preferences in 1999 still 'did not prevent governments from having the upper hand over "their" nomination(s)' (Nugent 2001: 83). Barroso did not appear to influence many choices about who was nominated to his first Commission until he was forced to ask for fresh nominees following the Buttiliogne affair (see Box 5.3). Nor did he seem to influence many choices about who would serve in his second Commission, although he insisted—in the face of criticism for (inter alia) assigning the internal market portfolio to Frenchman Michel Barnier—that 'I do not give portfolios to countries. I attribute portfolios to individuals'.[18]

The institutional design of the EU is intended to create collective, inter-institutional responsibility for what the Union does. It has given rise to a gradual strengthening of the EP's right to vet the choice of member governments' nominees to the College. The Santer, Prodi, and Barroso I and II Commissions (after the reconfiguration of the former) all were ultimately confirmed by large margins (of around 300 votes). Yet the provisions of the Lisbon Treaty reinforce the formal powers of the EP: it now officially elects the presidential nominee and member states are legally obliged to take account of the results of the most recent EP election in choosing a nominee for President. Even these changes, however, pose no threat—in advance of any move to a smaller Commission—to the basic principle that 'each national government is free to select a national Commissioner' (Devuyst 2005: 53).

Collective responsibility is not only built into the EU's institutional system generally; it is also a cardinal principle *within* the College. All members must publicly support all decisions and actions of the Commission. They even take an 'oath' of independence from the government that nominates them. These principles are often difficult to uphold. In contrast to governments, the College is never united by shared party-political, national, or ideological affinities. In fact, no one has ever really explained what is meant to hold it together besides a commitment to 'Europe' (see Coombes 1970).

Formally, the College decides by simple majority votes. In a College of twenty-seven, as many as thirteen Commissioners could vote against a motion, but then have to support it publicly. Our knowledge about how often the College votes is primitive and frequent voting cannot necessarily be equated with more division in the College. However, when the College votes, it is usually an admission that the majority view must be forced on at least a few Commissioners. By most accounts,[19] voting was more frequent in the Santer Commission than in Delors', perhaps because the latter was more clearly dominated by its President. In the Prodi Commission, insiders noted 'a culture of avoiding votes' in a College the members of which were 'very focused on their own responsibilities and relatively unconcerned with some larger "big vision"' (Peterson 2008b: 69). Barroso took pride in noting that his first College never had to resort to a single vote.

The single most important factor in determining the cohesiveness of the College remains the strength of presidential leadership. The Prodi Commission was the first in which, according to the Amsterdam Treaty, the College worked 'under the political direction of the President'. Nevertheless, one of its members denied ever having a single substantive discussion with Prodi on any issue related to his own (economic) portfolio, adding: 'Prodi got out of the way, but we needed a sort of control tower. We only avoided a lot of plane crashes at the last minute, and some we did not avoid' (quoted in Peterson 2006: 505).

Barroso appeared to think that his College needed more of a collective identity and more teamwork on actual policy. He thus announced the formation of five 'clusters' of Commissioners in key areas: the Lisbon Agenda; external relations (both chaired by Barroso himself); communications; equal opportunities; and competitiveness. Yet, in an early indication of how such devices do not guarantee a cohesive College, Barroso's Commissioner for the internal market, Charlie McCreevy, publicly attacked the Commissioner for Enterprise, Günter Verheugen, dismissing the latter's doubts about the proposed Services Directive as a case of 'some Commissioners … who like to speak out of both sides of their mouth … from one day to the next'.[20]

Collective responsibility has become more difficult to enforce as the College has become, over time, a more politically weighty group of individuals. The Santer Commission reinforced the trend towards 'increasing politicisation of the College' (MacMullen 2000: 41), with its inclusion of six former prime ministers, foreign ministers, or finance ministers. Prodi's College contained more policy specialists, with a majority coming to the Commission after being national ministers for agriculture, finance, European affairs, and so on. The Barroso I Commission pushed back in the direction of high-powered generalists, with its three former prime ministers, five former foreign ministers, and three former finance ministers. Notably, nearly all who had held such high-level posts hailed from small states, and the verdict on Barroso's first College was that it lacked 'big stars', as Pascal Lamy, Chris Patten, and Antonio Vitorino had been considered to be in their policy areas under Prodi. His second College (see Table 5.2) was, if anything, even more populated by low-key technocrats, thus making it likely that it would be even more dominated than his first by the President himself.

The cabinets

One of the Commission's most vexed problems has always been the proper role of cabinets. In principle, cabinets are meant to act as a bridge between the College and the services, and thus between the political and apolitical. Most national civil services contain some analogue in the form of party-political, temporary appointees to civil services. Yet members of cabinets in the Commission have tended to be particularly vilified as agents of their member state, as opposed to the Commission as an

TABLE 5.2	The Barroso II Commission		
Commissioner (Nationality)	**Portfolio(s)**	**Relevant previous post(s)**	**Party affiliation in home country (EP party group*)**
José Manuel Barrosso (Portugal)	President	Prime Minister	Social Democratic Party (EPP)
Catherine Ashton (UK)	Vice President & High Representative for Foreign and Security Policy	EU Trade Commissioner	Labour Party (PES)
Joaquín Almunia (Spain)	Vice President, Competition Policy	Employment and Social Security Minister; EU Economic and Monetary Affairs Commissioner	Socialist Workers' Party (PES)
Siim Kallas (Estonia)	Vice President, Transport	Estonian Prime Minister, EU Commissioner for Administration	Estonian Reform Party (ALDE)
Neelie Kroes (Netherlands)	Vice President, Digital Agenda	Transport, Public Works and Communications Minister, EU Competition Commissioner	People's Party for Freedom and Democracy (ALDE)
Viviane Reding (Luxumbourg)	Vice President, Justice, Fundamental Rights and Citizenship	MEP, EU Commissioner for Information, Society and Media	Christian Social People's Party (EPP)
Maroš Šefčovič (Slovakia)	Vice President, Inter-institutional Relations and Administration	Slovakian Ambassador to the EU	Party of the Democratic Left (PES)
Antonio Tajani (Italy)	Vice President, Industry and Entrepreneurship	MEP, President of EPP	Forza Italia (EPP)
Lásló Andor (Latvia)	Employment, Social Affairs and Inclusion	University Economics Professor, Advisor to Prime Minister	Socialist Party (PES)
Michel Barnier (France)	Internal Market and Services	Foreign and Environment Minister, EU Regional Policy Commissioner, MEP	Union for a Popular Movement (EPP)
Dacian Cioloş (Romania)	Agriculture	Agriculture Minister	Democratic Liberal (EPP)
John Dalli (Malta)	Health and Consumer Policy	Minister for Economy, Finance Minister	Nationalist Party (EPP)

Cont. ➤

Cont.

Maria Damanaki (Greece)	Maritime Affairs and Fisheries	MP, President of Greek political party	Socialist Party (PES)
Karel De Gucht (Belgium)	Trade	Deputy Prime Minister, EU Commissioner for Development	Flemish Liberal and Democratic Party (ALDE)
Štefan Füle (Czech Republic)	Enlargement and European Neighbourhood Policy	European Affairs Minister	Czech Social Democratic Party (PES)
Maáire Geoghegan-Quinn (Ireland)	Research and Innovation	Minister for Justice, European Court of Auditors	Fianna Fáil (ALDE)
Kristilina Georgieva (Romania)	International Cooperation, Humanitarian Aid and Crisis Response	World Bank	Citizens for European Development of Bulgaria (EPP)
Johannes Hahn (Austria)	Regional Policy	Minister for Justice, Science and Research	People's Party (EPP)
Connie Hedegaard (Denmark)	Climate Action	Environment Minister	Conservative People's Party (EPP)
Janusz Lewandowski (Poland)	Budget and Financial Programming	MEP	Civic Platform (EPP)
Celia Malmström	Home Affairs	European Affairs Minister, MEP	Liberal People's Party (ALDE)
Günther Oettinger (Germany)	Energy	Minister-President, Baden-Württemberg	Christian Democratic Union (EPP)
Andris Piebalgs (Latvia)	Development	Finance Minister, EU Energy Commissioner	Latvian Way (EPP)
Janez Potočnik (Slovenia)	Environment	European Affairs Minister, EU Research Commissioner	None
Olli Rehn (Finland)	Economic and Monetary Affairs	MEP; EU Enlargement Commissioner	Centre Party (ALDE)
Algirdis Šemeta (Lithuania)	Taxation and Customs Union, Audit and Anti-Fraud	Finance Minister	Homeland Union-Christian Democrats (EPP)
Androulla Vassiliou (Cyprus)	Education, Culture, Multilingualism and Youth	Vice-President, European Liberal Democrats	United Democrats (ALDE)

*Here, we show the affiliation of national parties to party groups within the EP to give a sense of the political balance—especially between Commissioners with ties to centre-right (EPP), socialist (PES), or liberal (ALDE) parties—within the College. See also Chapter 15.

institution. In the past, cabinets were usually (not always) packed with officials—often quite young—who shared their Commissioner's nationality, leaving aside a few non-nationals. Many were hand-picked by governments in national capitals. Tensions between the cabinets and services were rife, especially during the Delors years. One abiding complaint about cabinets was that they intervened aggressively in personnel decisions, acting as lobbyists for national capitals in securing senior posts in the services.

Prodi himself was widely accused of violating the spirit of new meritocratic rules on appointments by placing his own hand-picked operatives in powerful posts. Still, Prodi instituted major changes at the level of cabinets, which were reduced in size to six officials from as many as nine previously (Prodi's own cabinet numbered nine). Each Commissioner was required to appoint a head (*chef*) or deputy head (*adjoint*) who hailed from a member state other than his or her own. Leading by example, Prodi chose as his own *chef* an Irishman, David O'Sullivan (later to become Secretary-General).

Under Prodi, a significant number of new faces appeared in the cabinets, with only about a third having previous cabinet experience.[21] The Commission trumpeted the fact that all cabinets had officials of at least three different nationalities, and that almost 40 per cent were women (a big increase on past totals). Cabinets, along with their Commissioners, were moved out of a central office in Brussels by Prodi and into the same buildings as the services for which their Commissioner was responsible, thus making Commissioners more like national ministers.

Barroso brought Commissioners and cabinets back together when the Commission's Berlaymont headquarters were reopened in 2004 after being refurbished and cleared of asbestos. The move was widely expected after complaints that separating Commissioners' office made it harder for them to strike deals and build coalitions. However, Barroso stuck with Prodi's rules on cabinet appointments, and the influx of (twelve) Commissioners from post-accession states made for an unusually large influx of fresh faces at this level. How much the traditional role of cabinets changed in the process was open to question, with one EU ambassador observing that 'the cabinets still channel impulses from national capitals, and they probably always will'. However, survey data presented in Kassim *et al.* (2012) suggest quite definitively that there is far less mutual animosity between the *cabinets* and services now than there was in the past.

The Commission's powers

The main source of the Commission's power has always been its monopoly right to propose legislation. The Commission also has significant independent powers within the CAP and on external trade and (especially) competition policy. In the latter case, the College often acts as judge and prosecuting attorney—and sometimes jury—on cases of state aids to industry, mergers, and anti-competitive practices by firms. The Commission has considerable powers to set the agenda for policies that 'flank' the internal market, such as cohesion or research policies.

Two important sources of Commission influence—as opposed to power—are its prerogative to deliver opinions on any EU matter and its obligation to publish an annual report on the activities of the Union. Both give the Commission scope to influence policy debates or steer the EU in specified directions. Generally, however, the Commission must earn its respect by the quality of its analysis, and particularly its judgement of what will play in national capitals and with relevant policy stakeholders (including industry and non-governmental lobbies). For example, the Barroso Commission was challenged in its first months in office by a revolt by some member states over the Services Directive that it inherited from its predecessor, forcing a highly unusual redrafting of its proposal.

Over time, the Commission has become increasingly accountable to the EP. Besides its powers to confirm the College (and its President) and to sack the Commission, the EP retains the informal right to scrutinize the activities of the Commission, with individual Commissioners expected to appear regularly before its policy-specialized committees. The emergence of the codecision procedure (see Chapter 6) as the 'ordinary' legislative procedure post-Lisbon has had the effect of upgrading the institutional position of the EP at the expense of the Commission. When the EP and Council cannot agree, the Commission risks being marginalized unless it is sensitive to the positions of both of the other institutions and acknowledges their dominance of the procedure. More generally, the EP has 'gained a greater ability not only to hold the Commission more accountable, but also to get the Commission to do things it would not otherwise do' (Stacey 2003: 951).

Historically, the ECJ has usually ruled in the Commission's favour when it has been asked to settle competence disputes. Several underpinnings of the 1992 project became doctrine as the result of individual ECJ decisions, which the Commission then used in the design of new policies (see Armstrong and Bulmer 1998). However, a landmark case in early 1994 saw the Court rule against the Commission in a dispute with the Council over competence on new external trade issues such as services and intellectual property. The Commission also suffered a series of painful court defeats on its competition policy judgements under Prodi, leading to a sweeping overhaul of the EU's regime for state aids to industry under Barroso.

The Commission's most important power may be its right of initiative, but increasingly the Commission's most important role is that of a *manager* of policies set by other institutions. The twenty-first century has found the Commission sharing responsibility for more EU policies, often acting as a broker and facilitator within organizational networks linking the member states and other EU institutions. To cite a prominent example, the launch of the Lisbon Agenda of economic reform in 2000 granted few significant new competences to the Commission. However, it allowed just enough room for the Commission to catalyse new initiatives to convince Barroso (five years later) that a revamped Lisbon strategy focused on 'jobs and growth' should be his Commission's top priority. It was also indicative that the Barroso Commission welcomed the proposals of a UK-convened 'Better Regulation Task Force' (2004) to create an informal body composed of officials from the Commission, EP, and Council that could fast-track moves to simplify legislation or adjust it informally to suit changing circumstances. More than ever, the Commission's work was concerned with advocacy and persuasion within horizontal policy networks, rather than hierarchical compulsion or coercion.

The College in context

The mass resignation of the Santer Commission was clearly a defining event in the life of the institution. Afterwards, one former Commissioner lamented the Prodi Commission's 'astonishing weakness'. A senior official in the services claimed: '[N]o one is defending the Commission in any major national capital. The Commission as a whole is losing heart.' After its first year, Peter Mandelson (2005) claimed that the Barroso College was finding its feet, but had found its position eroded by a 'pincer movement': a loss of leadership to the Council and loss of the internal Commission agenda to the services, which had become more autonomous in the void created by the demise of the Santer Commission.

If the Commission was really so weak, intergovernmentalist accounts of EU politics—which tend to make three arguments about the Commission—could be marshalled to explain why. First, it makes little difference who is Commission President. Second, the Commission is only powerful when and where national preferences converge. Third, the Commission is empowered only to the extent that member government want to ensure the 'credibility of their commitments' to each other (Moravcsik 1998: 492; see also Moravcsik and Schimmelfennig 2009). There is little dispute, amongst scholars as well as practitioners, that the Commission has traditionally had little influence over most 'history-making' decisions about the broad sweep of European integration.

In contrast, institutionalist theory—now long-established as 'the leading theoretical approach in EU studies' (Cowles and Curtis 2004: 305)—paints a portrait of a Commission that is often powerful in day-to-day policy debates (see Pierson 1996). According to this view, policy decisions in complex systems such as the EU are difficult to reverse, and policy often becomes locked into existing paths and 'path-dependent'. Thus, even as the Stability and Growth Pact (the economic rulebook governing EMU) was rewritten in 2005 amidst frustration over the Commission's reprimands of governments running profligate budget deficits, the Commission lost none of its existing mandate or authority over EMU.

Some variants of institutionalism combine insights from rational choice and principal–agent theories (see Pollack 2003, 2009). They hold that the principal authorities in EU politics—the member governments themselves—make rational choices to delegate tasks to the EU's institutions, which then become their agents in specific policy areas. This body of theory sheds light on the tendency for the EU to make policy by means other than the traditional 'Community method' of legislating (see Devuyst 1999), according to which only the Commission can propose. One of the least flattering features of the Prodi Commission was its frequent insistence that the Community method was the only legitimate path to making EU policy, even in areas such as common foreign and security policy (CFSP), in which its use was politically unthinkable. There was little dispute that some new policy modes, particularly the so-called 'open method of coordination' (OMC), relying on benchmarking, league tabling, and designating the Commission as a scrutinizer of national policies rather than a proposer of EU policies, produced few tangible, early results (see Borràs and Jacobsson 2004; Dehousse 2004). Yet EU principals (national governments) were clearly moving towards new kinds of delegation, with the Commission cast as a different kind of agent. The Europe 2020 programme under the second Barroso presidency, designed to 'complete' the single market and promote sustainable development, relied—as the Lisbon process had—far more on soft law and the OMC than on actual legislation, with the Commission (again) cast in the role of a sort of coxswain.

Increased affinity for new policy modes is also reflected in the creation of a variety of new regulatory agencies, some of which have assumed some of the traditional roles of the Commission (see Chapter 10). EU governments increasingly seem to want new kinds of agents—not just the Commission—to whom they can delegate cooperative policy tasks. Usually, however, the Commission retains the job of identifying and seeking to solve coordination problems within policy networks of (inter alia) private actors, consumer and environmental groups, and national and European agencies.

Advocates of multilevel governance as an approach to understanding the EU have long contended that the Commission enjoys a privileged place at the 'hub of numerous highly specialized policy networks of technical experts', even retaining 'virtually a free hand in creating new networks' (Marks *et al.* 1996: 355, 359). Metcalfe (2000: 838) argues that 'the Commission will have to be reinvented as a network organization adept at designing the frameworks of governance and developing the management capacities needed to make them work effectively'. There is little doubt that, in so far as the Commission provides direction to the EU of the future, it will largely do so as a coordinator of networks that seek to make national policies converge (see Héritier 1999; Kohler-Koch and Eising 1999; Peterson 2009), as opposed to replacing them with EU policies.

The College after enlargement

Barroso's Colleges reflected a new political reality in an EU of twenty-seven or more: even if all Commissioners are formally equal, the idea that none is more powerful than another is now a practical fiction. If Commissioners from large member states tend to be more successful or powerful, it may be less because of blatant political activism by their national capitals than because they operate in wider networks of contacts (Joana and Smith 2002). Commissioners from small states can 'punch above the weight' of their home country if their performance earns them the respect of their peers and EU member governments. Still, no one pretends that Commissioners from, say, Germany and Malta start out as equals.

To their credit, member governments in the 2004–07 accession states mostly appointed top members of their political classes to the College. Of the first thirteen appointed by new EU states, six were former prime ministers, foreign ministers, or finance ministers, and several others had been European affairs ministers or national ambassadors to the EU. Thus most had in-depth knowledge of how Brussels worked from their involvement in negotiating their own state's accession.

Barroso's Commissions found the President's reformist agenda mostly backed by Commissioners whose states had undergone radical, and often painful, reforms to enter the EU. Moreover, Barroso's pledge to defend 'new' EU countries seemed part of a strategy to challenge the status quo on key EU issues. For example, Barroso's first Budget Commissioner, Dalia Grybauskaite, raised eyebrows with her assessment that inherited proposals on the structural funds, which targeted more than half of regional funding for the pre-2004 EU15, were 'difficult to defend'.[22]

The institutional effects of the 2004–07 enlargements on the Commission, as well as the rest of the EU, will only be revealed years after the event (see Peterson 2008a). Yet there were reasons to think that enlargement might be digested more easily by the Commission than other EU institutions, the numbers of which were swelled by a relatively larger influx of new and inexperienced members (see Best *et al.* 2008). At the level of the College, and possibly even more so within the services, enlargement at least held out the prospect of revitalizing and renewing the Commission with a new breed of reform-minded Europeans.

Conclusion

Any analysis of the Commission must consider the normative question of what kind of organization the College should be: a policy entrepreneur; an honest broker; a manager of decisions taken by others; or an engine of integration?

Increasingly, the Commission seems to have outgrown the last of these roles. It might be argued that there is no other institution that has the independence to identify new directions that European integration needs to take. Moreover, there is historical evidence suggesting that the Commission's declining fortunes can be reversed: after all, it appeared entirely moribund after Hallstein and before Delors.

The Commission spent much of the Prodi era focused on its own institutional position. With its basic role mostly preserved, it can be argued that the Commission now needs to focus on *policy*, as opposed to grand designs. Yet it has become increasingly difficult, especially in an EU of twenty-seven or more, to design single, EU-level policy solutions. As a top former Commission official suggested in 2005, 'most of Europe's worst problem are now micro-level problems. They need to be solved at that level'.

In this context, the EU's added value is mostly as a laboratory for policy learning and transfer. Logically, the new EU will have to adopt new policy modes—and particularly more, and more intensive, exchange and cooperation within networks of national, or even subnational, agencies (see Wallace 2010). The Union's institutions—including the Commission—will need to embrace more collective types of leadership and advocacy of new policy ideas. The Lisbon Treaty (in Art. 9) now gives a clear political signal that the EU's institutions must 'practice mutual sincere cooperation' if the Union is to thrive.

In an enlarged EU, the Commission may be even better placed than it was in the past to act as a truly honest broker. It may rarely exercise control over new cooperative networks or reclaim its old function as an engine of integration, but it will logically remain at the centre of many EU policy networks. In any event, it will often find itself in a unique position to steer debates in ways that serve collective European interests, as difficult as they may be to identify clearly in the new EU.

NOTES

1. The College remained a men-only club for a shockingly long time. The first women Commissioners were Christiane Scrivener (France) and Vasso Papandreou (Greece), who were appointed to the Delors Commission in 1989.

2. The Luxembourg compromise was accompanied by a range of new restrictions on the Commission, including a bar on making proposals public before the Council could consider them and the requirement that the Commission could receive the credentials of non-EEC ambassadors to the Community only alongside the Council.

3. It is not clear that Jenkins ever wished to serve another term. His 1979 Dimbleby lecture (halfway through his term as Commission President) foreshadowed his ambition to form a new British political grouping—eventually, the Social Democratic Party (SDP)—of which he became co-leader three years later. By 1980, even Belgium—which originally favoured his reappointment—decided that the 'gap between [Thatcherite] Britain and the rest of the Community was so great that the time had not arrived when any Englishman could be President of the Commission indefinitely' (Jenkins 1989: 601). The Commission's term in office was later extended to five years by the Maastricht Treaty so as to align its tenure with that of the EP.

4. Santer was literally no one's first choice, but was chosen after the nominations of Ruud Lubbers (Prime Minister of the Netherlands), Leon Brittan (Commissioner under Delors), and Jean-Luc Dehaene (Prime Minister of Belgium) were all rejected, with the UK under John Major prominently vetoing Dehaene.

5. Santer was not alone in making this claim. Respected Belgian Commissioner for competition policy Karel van Miert attacked the Experts' report as 'unjust and incorrect' (Santer and van Miert, both quoted in *Financial Times*, 17 March 1999). For his part, Brittan (2000: 11) insisted that the Experts had added 'unnecessary and crude journalistic icing ... to what was a perfectly well-baked and freestanding cake'.

6. Unattributed quote in *Financial Times*, 17 March 1999.

7. This quote (and all others not referenced as otherwise in this chapter) is taken from interviews conducted as part of the research for this chapter in November–December 2000, March 2001, November 2003, June 2004, and January–April 2005. The interviewees included two Commissioners, two former Commissioners, one national ambassador, a former Secretary-General, cabinet officials (eight from the Prodi Commission, including three *chefs* and two deputy *chefs*), and a diverse range of senior officials in the services.

8. Data collected as part of The European Commission in Question project, funded by the UK Economic and Social Research Council (grant no. RES-062-23-1188) and conducted by the author along with Hussein Kassim, Michael Bauer, Renaud Dehousse, Liesbet Hooghe, Sara Connolly, and Andrew Thompson. The online survey was administered by the polling organization YouGov in September and October 2008. A sample of 4,621 policy administrators was drawn from a population of over 14,000. The sample was stratified to ensure proportionality by gender, age, and nationality; officials from the ten new member states were oversampled. The response rate was 41 per cent (1,901 responses). Iterative proportional fitting was used to create a weighted sample that reflects the population distributions by gender, age, nationality, and DG location. For further information, see online at **http://www.uea.ac.uk/psi/research/EUCIQ** or see Kassim *et al.* (2012).

9. Quoted in *Financial Times*, 15 March 2005, p. 8.

10. Quoted in *Financial Times*, 19 July 1999, p. 9.

11. Quoted (respectively) in *Financial Times*, 2 March 2005, p. 6, and 7 February 2005, p. 17.

12. President of the EP Socialist group Poul Nyrup Rasmussen and veteran French Socialist MEP Jean-Louis Bourlanges, quoted (respectively) in *Financial Times*, 2 March 2005, p. 6, and EurActiv.com, 3 September 2003, available online at **http://www.euractiv.com**

13. Quoted in *Financial Times*, 22 October 2004, p. 1.

14. Quoted in BBC News (2004) 'MEPs approve revamped Commission', available online at **http://news.bbc.co.uk/1/hi/world/europe/4021499.stm**

15. See commentary by the European Evangelical Alliance, available online at **http://www.europeanea.org/TheButtiglioneAffair.htm**; see also Weigel (2004).

16. Quoted in *Financial Times*, 19 December 2004, p. 8.

17. The Amsterdam Treaty promised that members of the College would be chosen 'in common accord' with the nominee for President—not only 'in consultation' with them, as in the past.

18. Quoted in *European Voice*, 3 December 2009, p. 6.

19. One former Commissioner interviewed for this chapter insisted that there were 'far more votes under Delors and tight votes'. Another indicated that 'voting wasn't very frequent' in the Delors Commission. Previous interviewees with experience of successive Commissions estimated that there were more votes taken under Santer than Delors (see Peterson 1999: 62).

20. Quoted in *Financial Times*, 4 March 2005, p. 6.

21. As is generally the case in the Commission, personnel records on cabinet members are incomplete, thus making precise comparisons impossible. However, using data presented in Hill and Knowlton (2000), a total of thirty-four (out of all 123 cabinet officials) had previous experience working in cabinets, or 28 per cent of the total, compared to seventy-four with no previous cabinet experience, or 60 per cent of the total. The data showed no previous information on the former positions held by fifteen cabinet officials.

22. Quoted in *Financial Times*, 24 February 2005, p. 10.

FURTHER READING

The most comprehensive work on the Commission, based on an unprecedentedly large data set on the attitudes of Commission officials, is Kassim *et al.* (2012). Spence (2006) and Dimitrakopoulos (2004) are also useful. Nugent (2001) is still very good on the history of the Commission, as is Dumoulin (2007), while Delors (2004) offers an insider's view. Coombes (1970) and Ross (1995) rank as classics that are worth revisiting. A typically downbeat assessment of the declining position of the Commission is Tsakatika (2005), which may be contrasted with Barroso's own view (Peterson 2008b); Peterson (2008a) offers a view on the likely impact of enlargement on the Commission.

Coombes, D. (1970) *Power and Bureaucracy in the European Community* (London: Croon Helm).

Delors, J. (2004) *Mémoires* (Paris: Plon).

Dimitrakopoulos, D. G. (2004) (ed.) *The Changing European Commission* (Manchester: Manchester University Press).

Dumoulin, M. (2007) (ed.) *The European Commission, 1958–72: History and Memories* (Brussels: European Commission).

Kassim, H., Peterson, J., Bauer, M., Connolly, S., Dehousse, R., Hooghe, L., and Thompson, A. (2012) *The European Commission of the 21st Century* (Oxford and New York: Oxford University Press).

Nugent, N. (2001) (ed.) *The European Commission* (Basingstoke and New York: Palgrave).

Peterson, J. (2008a) 'Enlargement, reform and the European Commission: weathering a perfect storm?', *Journal of European Public Policy*, 15/5: 761–80.

Peterson, J. (2008b) 'José Manuel Barroso: political scientist, ECPR member', *European Political Science*, 7/1: 64–77.

Ross, G. (1995) *Jacques Delors and European Integration* (New York and London: Polity Press).

Spence, D. (2006) (ed.) *The European Commission* (London: John Harper).

Tsakatika, M. (2005) 'The European Commission between continuity and change', *Journal of Common Market Studies*, 43/1: 193–220.

WEB LINKS

http://ec.europa.eu/

The Commission's own website is a treasure trove that handles some 2 million 'hits' per month.

http://www.epc.eu
http://www.european-voice.com

The sites of the European Policy Centre and *European Voice* offer insiders' insights from Brussels.

http://www.cec.org.uk
http://www.eurunion.org

It is often useful to see how the Commission's delegations in EU member states and non-EU member states present the Commission's line in capitals beyond Brussels.

CHAPTER 6

The European Parliament

Michael Shackleton

▌ Summary

The European Parliament (EP) is the European Union's only directly elected institution. For much of its history it was relatively weak. But since the first direct elections in 1979, its powers and status have grown with remarkable speed, culminating in the changes agreed under the Lisbon Treaty. It is now arguably one of the most powerful parliaments in the world, enjoying a relationship of equals with governments in the Council, as well as the ability to exercise significant control over the Commission. And yet many argue that, despite the changed status of its one directly elected body, the EU still suffers from a 'democratic deficit'. This chapter will examine these issues by looking at how the EP has evolved, how it is structured, what influence it exercises, and what kind of body it is becoming within an enlarged Union of twenty-seven or more states.

Introduction

The rejection of the SWIFT Agreement (on data access and protection) by the European Parliament (EP; see Box 6.1) was the first major use of the new powers that the EP had obtained under the Lisbon Treaty. It illustrated in a graphic way how the Parliament could act to shape the overall direction of the European Union, even in the face of the opposition of all twenty-seven EU governments and the European Commission. It was, however, an outcome that should not be seen as simply the product of a single treaty; rather, it was the result of developments stretching back over the whole history of the EP, which differentiate it from all of the other institutions discussed in this book. The Parliament is the only one of the EU bodies that were created in the 1950s, the role of which has been radically revised over the last half-century, with tasks and responsibilities that very few imagined likely before the 1990s.

This chapter therefore confronts three main issues:

- how and why the Parliament has been able to acquire such a range of additional powers;

- what difference the inclusion of a directly elected institution has made to the evolution of the EU; and

- what kind of institution the EP is becoming and how far can it resolve the so-called 'democratic deficit'.

BOX 6.1   **The SWIFT Agreement**

On 11 February, the EP rejected the SWIFT[1] Agreement between the United States and the European Union. This agreement was designed to give the US access to data about the international money transactions of EU citizens as part of its efforts to combat terrorism. A large majority in the Parliament (378 to 196) considered that the provisions of the Agreement did not provide an adequate balance between security needs and civil liberties. In particular, members felt that the Agreement was unfair in that it did not apply to US citizens, was not firmly restricted in time, and did not provide for the right of appeal against misuse of data.

A striking feature of the debate was the greater seriousness with which the US government appeared to treat the EP as compared with EU governments. US Secretary of State Hilary Clinton rang the President of the EP in advance of the vote to express her concerns. Some weeks after the vote, US Vice-President Jo Biden came to speak to the full Parliament to allay its worries and to prepare for the revision of the Agreement. In July 2010, the Parliament gave its approval to a new version that provides for judicial redress, as well as for a limited period of data retention.

The empowerment of the EP has occurred because it has proved easier to agree a gradual extension of the institution's role than to say no to the claims of a representative institution with democratic credentials based on direct elections. What difference has the Parliament made? The EP has changed the direction of many EU policies; it has also opened up a debate about whether the Union meets the standards of representative democracy. As for the 'democratic deficit', successive decisions taken to develop the Parliament have, above all, strengthened its role as a legislator. This strengthened role reinforces its position in relation to the other institutions in Brussels—notably the Council of Ministers and the Commission—but cannot, by itself, resolve the broader issue of the legitimacy of the EU. The debate about the democratic nature of the Union is about the kind of political structure that European governments and citizens want the Union to become and whether they want the same things: an issue that lies at the centre of EU politics.

Historical evolution

The story of the Parliament has been told as a transition from 'fig-leaf to co-legislature' (Corbett *et al.* 2005: 1). This change is reflected symbolically in the Parliament's physical surroundings. It has moved from renting premises in Strasbourg that it shared with the parliamentary assembly of the Council of Europe, to become the effective owner of two substantial building complexes in Brussels and Strasbourg, both of them with parliamentary chambers (known as 'hemicycles' because of their shape) equipped to seat 750 members. At the same time, as Table 6.1 indicates, the formal powers of the EP have developed dramatically between 1951, when the Six signed the European Coal and Steel Community (ECSC) Treaty, and 2009, when the Lisbon Treaty, signed by twenty-seven states, came into force.

When the ECSC was established, a parliamentary body was far from the centre of discussion (Smith 1999: 27–44). The crucial institution was the High Authority, given supranational powers in the management of coal and steel. The creation of a parliamentary institution, called the Common Assembly, was something of an after-thought, perceived as the least imperfect way in which to address the issue of accountability. The Assembly's only significant power was that of supervising the Authority. However, the potential for the institution to evolve towards something more influential was reflected in the provisions governing its election. Member states could choose whether to have direct elections to the Assembly or to allow their national parliaments to select members. The possibility of a direct link to the electorate distinguished the institution from the outset from other international parliamentary bodies, such as the Council of Europe's parliamentary assembly.

The Treaty of Rome brought significant change. Specific provision was made for direct elections: it was no longer a matter for each member state to decide. No timetable was laid down, but the commitment to abolish the system of nominated

TABLE 6.1   Main treaty changes affecting the European Parliament

	Election of MEPs	Legislative and budgetary role	Appointment and scrutiny of executive
ECSC Treaty (1950)	Choice between direct elections or national parliaments to select members		Right to dismiss High Authority
Rome Treaty (1957)	Specific provision for direct elections (implemented in 1979)	Right to be consulted and to give its opinion to the Council	
Budgetary Treaties (1970 and 1975)		Right to reject budget, modify level of expenditure, and approve/disapprove accounts ('discharge')	
Single European Act (1985)		'Cooperation procedure' providing right to a second reading of legislation 'Assent procedure' to approve enlargement and some international agreements	
Maastricht Treaty (1992)		'Codecision procedure' with conciliation to apply to fifteen legal bases Right to invite Commission to present a legislative proposal	Right to approve Commission as a whole Committees of inquiry, appointment of Ombudsman and ECB President to report to EP committee
Amsterdam Treaty (1997)		Simplification and extension of codecision to thirty-two legal bases	Right to approve Commission President
Nice Treaty (2000)		Extension of codecision to thirty-seven legal bases	
Lisbon Treaty (2007)		Extension of codecision to ninety legal bases and now called 'ordinary legislative procedure' Budget procedure amended to give joint control with Council over whole budget Consent procedure (formerly 'assent') for international trade agreements Joint control with Council over delegated legislation	Commission President elected by EP on basis of proposal of European Council that 'takes into account the elections to the European Parliament'

members was made legally binding. The Assembly was also given advisory, as well as supervisory, powers and thus was given its first glimpse of legislative power. These two changes did not have an immediate effect. It took over twenty years for direct elections to be organized and the Parliament's formal legislative powers were not altered for nearly thirty years. Nevertheless, a trajectory for further development in the Parliament's powers was laid down.

Subsequent changes in the Parliament's role were closely linked with other modifications to the EU's structure. Treaty revisions introduced in 1970 and 1975 gave the EP budgetary powers, including the right to reject the budget (a right it was to exercise in 1979 and 1984), to amend it within certain fixed limits, and to approve (or not approve) the annual accounts. The essential source of these changes was the decision to alter the basis for financing the European Community. It was agreed that the EU would move away from a system of national contributions linked to each country's gross national product (GNP) to a system of 'own resources', whereby the revenue available for financing European policies legally belonged to the Community. Under these circumstances, there was a strong body of opinion amongst the governments of the Six—notably the Dutch—that national parliaments could no longer exercise effective control over Community finance and that the task should be passed onto the EP. Already at this stage, the idea of the EP enjoying the kind of rights at EU level traditionally exercised at national level by parliamentarians was proving difficult to resist, with sceptics faced with the task of suggesting a convincing alternative.

However, the Parliament was still composed of national parliamentarians, working there on a part-time basis. The attempt to give life to the provisions of the Treaty of Rome on direct elections posed a difficult dilemma. It was well described in the Vedel report on the enlargement of Parliament's powers:

[I]f one cannot imagine a Parliament with real powers which does not draw its mandate from direct universal suffrage, it is even more difficult to imagine the election through direct universal suffrage of a Parliament without extended powers. In this way, two equally desirable objectives are making each other's implementation impossible.

(Vedel 1972: 59)

This dilemma persisted until the election of Valéry Giscard d'Estaing as President of France and Helmut Schmidt as West German Chancellor within five days of each other in May 1974. The subsequent Paris Summit agreed to hold direct European elections after 1978, thereby giving effect to the option that Vedel had considered the more difficult to imagine. Direct elections paved the way for an extension of the Parliament's legislative powers. A critical moment was the 1980 *Isoglucose* judgment of the European Court of Justice (ECJ). This judgment annulled a piece of Community legislation adopted by Council on the grounds that the EP had not yet given its opinion. The Court made it clear that Council could not adopt Community legislation before receiving Parliament's opinion. Moreover, the Court made a link between the democratic character of the Community and the Parliament's right to be consulted, which the Court described as:

the means, which allow the Parliament to play an actual part in the legislative process of the Community. Such a power represents an essential factor in the institutional balance intended by the Treaty. Although limited, it reflects at Community level *the fundamental democratic principle* that the peoples should take part in the exercise of power through the intermediary of a representative assembly. [Emphasis added]

The right to be more than simply consulted came with the Single European Act (SEA), which provided the treaty base for the establishment of a single European market by 1992. To accelerate the process, member states created a new 'cooperation' procedure, with more majority voting, under which Parliament was entitled to two readings of proposed legislation, rather than one. Moreover, provided that the Commission was persuaded to back Parliament's amendments, the Council could overrule the EP only by unanimity.

The precise form of Parliament's involvement in the legislative procedure was not preordained. The Vedel Report had argued against the idea that the Parliament should be given the right to amend legislation and instead suggested giving it the right to say 'yes' or 'no' to legislation presented to it by the Council. In fact, such a power of 'assent' was granted to the Parliament in the SEA for non-legislative issues. Although restricted to the accession of new member states and the conclusion of a limited number of agreements with non-EU countries, the Parliament was called to give its assent to international agreements thirty times within the first two years of the SEA being ratified. It was subsequently asked to vote on new accessions in 1995, 2003, 2005, and 2007.

The Maastricht Treaty ushered in a new and transformational procedure, generally described until recently as 'codecision' (although the Lisbon Treaty has dubbed it the 'ordinary legislative procedure'). It made the EP and Council legal equals in the legislative process, and provided for joint decision-taking and direct negotiations between Parliament and Council, as well as the possibility for the EP to reject draft legislation if such negotiations were to fail. Supporters of stronger EP powers argued, successfully, that, with more majority voting in Council, the position of national parliaments was weakened. A greater role for the EP would improve the democratic legitimacy of EU legislation, by ensuring that it had the support of European citizens and not only their governments.

Maastricht also gave the EP:

- the right to approve (or not to approve) the Commission before it took office;
- extended formal powers of control by providing for the establishment of committees of inquiry;
- empowerment to appoint a European Ombudsman; and
- formal provision to invite the Commission to present a legislative proposal, thereby giving the EP a limited form of legislative initiative.

Member states thereby proved receptive to the argument that the broader agenda set for the EU at Maastricht should be matched by a reinforced role for the Parliament.

The process of parliamentarization was still only partial, but the ongoing process of treaty revision provided the EP with the opportunity to continue pressing for an expansion of its role, and it did so with considerable success. Under the Amsterdam Treaty, codecision was extended from fifteen to thirty-two treaty legal bases and simplified to make it possible to reach agreements more quickly. This development can be partly explained by the Parliament proving more 'responsible' than some in EU national capitals had imagined or predicted it would be, readily accepting the obligations imposed by the Treaty. At the same time, the direct negotiations provided for under codecision proved remarkably successful in facilitating agreement. As a result, more reticent member states, such as the UK and Denmark, became less nervous about extending Parliament's prerogatives and accepting the arguments of those, such as Germany, which argued that its powers needed to be expanded to increase the democratic legitimacy of the Union.

The Amsterdam Treaty also legitimized existing practice by giving the EP the formal right to approve the European Council's nominee as Commission President. Thus, by 1999, the Parliament possessed a set of rights to influence the nomination of the Commission. These rights complemented the power of dismissal that originated in the ECSC Treaty, nearly fifty years earlier.

The negotiations over the Nice Treaty were dominated by the dispute over the relative weight of member states in the Council and Commission in an enlarged Union, with a related, but less central, argument about the number of seats that each member state should have in the Parliament. However, agreement emerged to extend codecision, if only marginally, to thirty-seven treaty legal bases, with the possibility of limited further extension thereafter by unanimous Council decision. This extension, agreed in November 2004, applied to parts of the justice and home affairs (JHA) pillar that had been explicitly excluded from the scope of codecision under Maastricht (see Chapter 12).

The position of the Parliament was subject to major debate and revision in the course of the European Convention and in the 2004 Constitutional Treaty. Although the Treaty was rejected, following negative votes in referenda in France and the Netherlands in 2005, the process that led four years later to the entry into force of the Lisbon Treaty saw no one seriously contest the principle that the changes proposed for the EP be retained. The most significant of these was the effective acceptance of the link between qualified-majority voting (QMV) in the Council and the application of codecision. The procedure was extended to ninety legal bases, including the common agricultural and fisheries policies (CAP and CFP, respectively), the common commercial policy (CCP), and JHA. The centrality of this way of making EU laws was recognized by renaming it the 'ordinary legislative procedure'.

The Treaty gave the Parliament two other important powers: the right to share power with the Council on all EU spending in the annual budget negotiations; and the right to approve virtually all international agreements, including all trade agreements. In addition, the Lisbon Treaty laid down that the Commission President be elected by the Parliament on the basis of a European Council proposal, 'taking into account the elections to the European Parliament and after having held the appropriate consultations' (Art. 17, para. 7). The EP was not given the right to elect the Commission President on its own, but the suitability of a candidate would henceforth be judged in the light of the political composition of the Parliament after direct elections. Such a link was effectively established already in 2004 when the largest group in the Parliament (the European People's Party) argued successfully that the new President should come from a party represented in its ranks, thereby establishing a precedent that was repeated in 2009, when President José Manuel Barroso was proposed for a second time by the European Council and approved by the Parliament.

Aggregating interests

It is one thing to be granted significant powers; it is another to use them effectively. More than any other EU institution, the Parliament faces difficulties in aggregating interests in an extraordinarily heterogeneous environment. Before the first direct EP elections, there were 198 members of the European Parliament (MEPs), from nine states; by 2009, the number of members had more than tripled to 736 from twenty-seven states. The total is due to rise still further to 751 by 2014, when the next European elections will take place. No elected parliamentary chamber in Europe has as many members, with such major differences in the number of citizens that each member is expected to represent (see Table 6.2).

How can such a large, heterogeneous institution take effective decisions? The EP does not contain a government, and cannot rely on those parliamentarians who belong to the party or parties of a government to ensure that a particular political programme is enacted. And yet it is remarkably successful in overcoming the clash between efficiency and diversity. In the ten years from 1999 to 2009, for example, it managed to reach agreement with the Council on more than 800 pieces of codecision legislation and failed to agree on fewer than ten occasions.

Leadership structures

The Parliament does have leadership structures, but they are not critical to the exercise of influence by the institution. The President, elected every two-and-a-half years, has the task of chairing the plenary (with the help of fourteen Vice-Presidents), representing the institution vis-à-vis other institutions and the outside world, and overseeing the Parliament's internal functioning. He or she also chairs two leadership bodies: the Conference of Presidents and the Bureau. The Conference,

TABLE 6.2   Number of MEPs per member state and ratio to population

Member state	Population (million)	Seats in 2009 elections	Number of inhabitants per MEP at 2009 elections	Seats in line with Lisbon Treaty	Number of inhabitants per MEP under Lisbon allocation
Germany	82.0	99	830,000	96 (–3) 99 to 2014	854,000 830,000 to 2014
France	64.4	72	885,000	74 (+2)	862,000
United Kingdom	61.6	72	850,000	73 (+1)	838,000
Italy	60.0	72	828,000	73 (+1)	817,000
Spain	45.8	50	906,000	54 (+4)	839,000
Poland	38.1	50	762,000	51 (+1)	747,000
Romania	21.5	33	653,000	33	653,000
Netherlands	16.5	25	656,000	26 (+1)	631,000
Greece	11.3	22	510,000	22	510,000
Belgium	10.7	22	485,000	22	485,000
Portugal	10.6	22	483,000	22	483,000
Czech Republic	10.5	22	472,000	22	472,000
Hungary	10.0	22	457,000	22	457,000
Sweden	9.3	18	510,000	20 (+2)	459,000
Austria	8.4	17	490,000	19 (+2)	439,000
Bulgaria	7.6	17	449,000	18 (+1)	424,000
Denmark	5.5	13	421,000	13	421,000
Slovakia	5.4	13	415,000	13	415,000
Finland	5.3	13	408,000	13	408,000
Ireland	4.4	12	367,000	12	367,000
Lithuania	3.3	12	281,000	12	281,000
Latvia	2.3	8	284,000	9 (+1)	252,000
Slovenia	2.0	7	289,000	8 (+1)	253,000
Estonia	1.3	6	223,000	6	223,000
Cyprus	0.8	6	132,000	6	132,000
Luxembourg	0.5	6	81,000	6	81,000
Malta	0.4	5	82,000	6 (+1)	68,000
TOTAL EU27	499.5	736	–	751 (754 until 2014)	–

Source: adapted from Corbett (2012)

composed of the chairs of all of the political groups, agrees, inter alia, the draft agenda of plenary sessions, settles conflicts of competence between committees, and determines whether or not to send delegations outside the EU. The Bureau, composed of the Parliament's fourteen Vice-Presidents, deals with internal financial, organizational, and administrative matters.

An important task of the President, Conference, and Bureau is to manage the centrifugal forces at work in the institution. But they all have only limited means at their disposal and can find themselves disavowed by the Parliament as a whole. In March 2011, for example, the plenary voted in a secret ballot—by just short of an overall majority—to reduce from twelve to eleven the number of weeks that it spends in Strasbourg every year. It did so by deciding to hold two 'plenary' or full sessions during the same week in October, instead of during separate weeks, in 2012 and 2013. This decision ran contrary to the wishes of the leaders of the two main groups (the European People's Party and the Socialists and Democrats), who were faced with a secret vote that backbenchers supported to enable them to express their feelings on this delicate issue.

Political groups

The key agents in the aggregation of interests are the EP's political groups (see also Chapter 15). Since 1952, members have sat not in national groups, but in groups created to reflect shared political affiliation. This structure serves to counteract the logic of the Council whereby political differences are constructed on national lines. It is also a structure that has proved remarkably stable, with members from new member states normally being assimilated into existing groups rather than forming completely new ones. In 2011, there were seven political groups, only one more than in 1979 before direct elections.

Within the group structure, there is a mixture of competition and cooperation. On the one hand, there is evidence of high levels of group cohesion, with members eager to find agreement with their colleagues in the same group. Hix *et al.* (2007) have drawn attention to a substantial increase in Left–Right competition in the EP. They have shown that party allegiance is much more important than nationality in determining how members vote and that members vote the party line more often than do, for example, US legislators. Contrary to the expectations of many, the addition of members from twelve new member states has not served to undermine significantly the coherence of the groups. In practice, being a member of a group encourages all to follow the group line in most circumstances (see also Ringe 2010).

The obligations imposed by the treaties also create strong incentives for groups to find agreement across party lines. Consider the measures that require an absolute majority of MEPs (half of all members plus one) to vote in favour:

- to reject or adopt amendments to the Council's draft budget or to its position at second reading under the ordinary legislative procedure (codecision);
- to give consent to international agreements;

- to approve the accession of new member states; and

- to adopt a motion of censure on the Commission.

No group has anything approaching such a majority: the largest group, the European People's Party, would be a hundred votes short even if all of its members were to be present and were to vote in the same way. Thus a strong bargaining culture between the groups has evolved. For some, this development is to be regretted. As two former MEPs (one who is, at time of writing, now UK Deputy Prime Minister) commented, 'political argument is usually displaced by detailed horse-trading to secure the widest possible cross-party support for a given position or set of amendments' (Clegg and van Hulten 2003: 14). Alternatively, this practice can be seen as an effective way of aggregating interests, and perhaps the only way of ensuring that the Parliament has significant influence in the policy process.

The committee system

Most of the detailed work of the EP is conducted within twenty policy-specialized committees, the political composition of which closely reflects that of Parliament as a whole. These committees enjoy a high level of autonomy under the Parliament's rules. All legislative proposals are referred directly, without debate, from the plenary to one of the committees, which then organizes the examination of a proposal before it returns to the plenary for a vote. Only one committee can normally be responsible for a proposal (a procedure for associating other committees can be applied in special cases) and only its amendments can be considered in plenary. Other committees can table amendments in the responsible committee, but do not get a second chance in plenary. The responsible committee appoints a *rapporteur* who follows a legislative proposal from its inception to the conclusion of the procedure. On the basis of the work and report of the rapporteur, the committee comes to adopt a position that will normally prevail in the plenary, unless the members of the committee are unable to overcome their own differences and the vote on a proposal is very close.

The committees provide an effective mechanism for finding agreement across political groups. But they also embody two other important features that differentiate the Parliament from the Council. First, all committee meetings are—and, since 1999, must be—held in public. The Parliament has traditionally offered a contrast between its own way of operating and the often less-transparent mechanisms of the Council. The result can be very full meeting rooms, with all those who wish to influence the shape of proposals—lobbyists, national governments, or officials from the Council Secretariat—free to observe the evolution of debate. Second, the detailed work in the committees provides an opportunity for those interests that fail to win the argument in the Council or the Commission to have a second chance. The fact that the Parliament does not necessarily mirror the majorities in the Council, with opposition parties often making up the largest number of MEPs from a member state, means that such efforts to influence policy can sometimes succeed. In both respects, the Parliament offers a distinctive model for reaching political agreement at EU level.

Exercising influence

To look at what the Parliament is doing on a day-to-day basis is to be confronted with a bewildering array of reports, debates, and questions. To identify the importance of the Parliament's role, it is useful to distinguish between different kinds of decision (see Peterson and Bomberg 1999): history-making; policy-making; and policy-implementing. Using this distinction, we can establish that the Parliament is more likely to have an effect on outcomes at the level of policy-making than on history-making and policy-implementing decisions.

History-making decisions

Most of the major decisions in the EU are taken at the level of the European Council (see Chapter 3). In this framework, the EP is an outsider: it is not present in European Council meetings except for the relatively brief appearance of its President at the start of the proceedings. It does not have the formal right to say 'yes' or 'no' to the outcome of an intergovernmental conference (IGC), which is ultimately determined by the European Council. Despite repeated calls to be given such a right of consent, ratification of the results of an IGC remains a purely national affair, determined by parliamentary vote and/or referendum.

Two powers given to the Parliament after the European Council has taken its decision can be described as 'history-making' ones. As we have seen, the EP has the right, since Amsterdam, to approve the candidate proposed by the European Council as President of the Commission. It also has to give its consent to the accession of new member states. The possibility of the Parliament not approving a Commission President cannot be ignored. In 1994, Jacques Santer was approved by a majority of only twenty-two, despite very heavy lobbying by national governments. After the decision at Nice that the President of the Commission be chosen in the European Council by qualified majority, the opportunity for the Parliament to influence the choice has grown. The largest group in the Parliament is always likely to press for a candidate from its ranks to be chosen.

However, this may not be enough to ensure that the whole Commission will win the approval of the Parliament. In October 2004, for example, President Barroso came to the Parliament to say that he needed more time before asking it to vote on his new Commission. He knew that, following the previous hearings of the individual Commissioners, he was unlikely to gain the support of the Parliament for the 'investiture' of his College, as required by the treaties (see Chapter 5). Within a matter of days, he had reshuffled its composition, with the nominees from two countries replaced, paving the way for the Parliament to give its approval by a large majority the following month.

Regarding the accession of new member states, the right of consent will continue to be of importance as long as new states seek to join the EU. It is a right that is perhaps most empowering during accession negotiations, when the Parliament can influence individual issues and try to shape the overall debate. In December 2004, Parliament's vote in favour of opening negotiations with Turkey 'without undue delay' (407 votes in favour, 262 against, and twenty-nine abstentions) gave a sense of the balance of political opinion across Europe. The EP's vote paved the way for the formal decisions of the European Council later the same week. However, the slowing of the pace of the negotiations with Turkey since then has reflected deep-seated divisions amongst the member states, which the Parliament has very limited opportunities to affect. Hence the Parliament can have some influence on a limited number of history-making decisions, but its role is undoubtedly more restricted than it is on policy-making decisions.

Policy-making decisions

The Maastricht agreement on the codecision procedure established the principle of the Parliament as a joint legislator with the Council in a limited number of areas. The Lisbon Treaty that came into force some sixteen years later provided the opportunity for the renamed 'ordinary legislative procedure' to apply to all areas of policy, with the exception of proposals involving taxation or the revenue sources of the Union. The overall shape of the procedure and the possibilities that it offers are presented in Figure 6.1.

Two central features of the codecision procedure should be underlined:

- First, the EP and the Council have *equal status*, with neither institution able to oblige the other to accept its position throughout the three readings available to come to an agreement.

- Second, the two parties are obliged to *negotiate* to find a solution in the knowledge that if no agreement is reached at the end of the three readings, the procedure comes to an end. Such a prospect necessarily concentrates the minds of the negotiators.

These general principles have gone hand in hand with significant changes in the behaviour of the two institutions over the nearly twenty years of the procedure's existence. In particular, there has been a marked move towards reaching agreements as early as possible without having recourse to conciliation or even a second reading. Between 2004 and 2009, nearly 70 per cent of all codecision procedures were concluded at first reading, with 25 per cent requiring a second reading and fewer than 6 per cent going to conciliation. These tallies contrast with the situation in the previous legislature, when as many as 22 per cent of procedures went to conciliation, half were resolved at second reading, and less than 30 per cent were agreed at first reading (European Parliament 2009a).

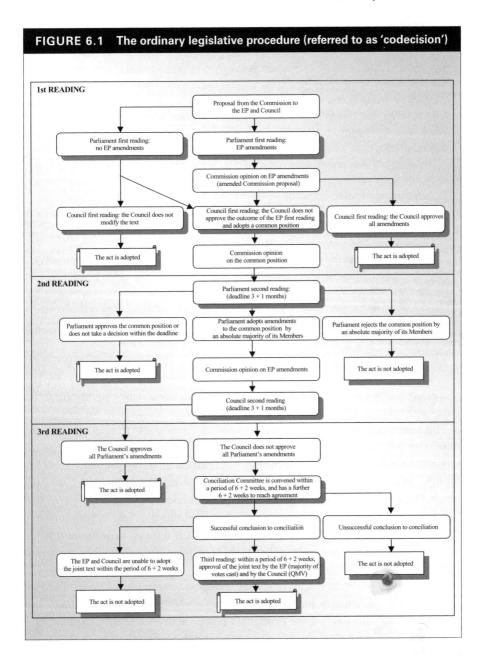

FIGURE 6.1   The ordinary legislative procedure (referred to as 'codecision')

The trend towards early agreement has continued since the 2009 elections. It seems to have become an established part of the legislative landscape, despite the concerns of some that such agreements make the decision-making process more complex and potentially threaten the legitimacy of the decisions taken (see Farrell and Heritier 2007; Rasmussen 2007). However, the change in the rhythm of the

---

BOX 6.2   The Alternative Investment Fund Managers Directive

The Parliament received a Commission proposal to establish EU-wide rules for alternative investment funds (otherwise known as 'hedge funds') in April 2009. A draft report was tabled by the Economic Committee in June 2010, but it was not until six months later, in November, that the EP voted at first reading. After very intensive discussions, it approved a text negotiated with the Council and thereby avoided the need to go to a second reading or beyond.

The length of the negotiations reflected significant differences between Parliament and Council, as well as between governments in the Council. The EP introduced provisions not in the original proposal designed to deter private equity investors from attempting to take control of a company solely in order to make a quick profit. It also pushed for strict liability of depositaries, key players in the running of the funds, to ensure that damages can always be claimed by the investors.

The Parliament also got agreement on a marketing passport to be granted to non-EU players, enabling fund managers to market to investors across the Union without seeking permission from each member state. In so doing, it made common cause with a number of governments, including the British, but to satisfy others, including the French, it gained the support in Council for the position that non-EU players should come from a jurisdiction that meets certain minimum regulatory standards.

---

procedure has not prevented the EP from continuing to exercise a significant influence on the shape of legislation, as Box 6.2 indicates.

This reinforced level of cooperation between Parliament and Council has had two important consequences in terms of the EP's level of influence. First, it has enhanced its status in relation to the other institutions. In particular, its own enhanced role has brought to an end the Commission's position as the privileged interlocutor of the Council, giving greater prominence to its role as an honest broker between the two legislative bodies. Formally, the Commission still retains the right to withdraw any proposal until the Council has acted; in practice, it is difficult now to see it being prepared to challenge the two branches of the legislative authority if they are able to agree on the shape of legislation.

Second, the Parliament has become the centre of attention for the Council and, in particular, for the country holding the presidency. No six-month presidency can hope to operate effectively if the permanent representatives and their deputies (see Chapter 14) do not devote major effort to the search for solutions with the Parliament. A central part of that effort is to organize so-called 'trialogue' meetings with the Parliament, in which the two sides, aided by the Commission, meet in restricted session to identify points of difference and to look for solutions. Making such an effort is not always comfortable for presidencies, especially for those of large states that may have high and specific ambitions for their terms in office. But the logic of the ordinary legislative procedure renders it inevitable and leads to a result that both parties are also obliged to defend in the ECJ in the event of a challenge.

Indeed, the changed status of the Parliament can mean that the Council is obliged to work with it beyond what the Treaty formally requires. To illustrate the point, when the member states were discussing the overall structure of the European External Action Service (EEAS) during 2010, they found themselves driven to involve the EP, even though the latter formally had only a right to submit an opinion. This result was a reflection of the Parliament's power of codecision over the budget, staff and the financial regulation of the EEAS; it was impossible to separate these detailed elements from the broader framework. As a result, as one participant in the negotiations has noted, 'the whole package became de facto subject to codecision' (Christoffersen 2011: 33).

Policy-implementing decisions

The implementation of Community policies involves thousands of individual decisions in any one year. No parliamentary body can hope to follow all of these decisions in detail. However, the EP has consistently pressed for scrutiny rights equivalent to those of the Council over the implementing bodies, known as 'comitology committees', which are chaired by the Commission and bring together representatives of all of the member states. The EP has consistently argued that it should be informed about the work of these committees and should have the opportunity to block draft decisions with which it disagrees.

The comitology debate may seem arcane, but it raises essential questions about the openness and accountability of the EU system. The decisions involved are not simply technical: in the early 1990s, for example, the level of controls needed to stop the spread of bovine spongiform encephalopathy (BSE, or 'mad cow disease') was decided in a comitology committee: the Veterinary Committee. All such decisions are taken very far from the public gaze, remaining in the hands of the Commission and national experts. Advocating a more powerful role for the EP was therefore designed to improve the transparency of the system.

This argument became more intense after codecision was introduced. With the Council able to block draft comitology decisions and take an implementing decision itself, the legislative parity of the two branches in policy-making clearly did not extend to policy implementation. The Council claimed that its role in policy implementation related to its executive functions and that it therefore was in a different institutional position from that of the EP.

Over a long period, member states did gradually agree to strengthen the Parliament's rights. These moves culminated in the Lisbon Treaty, which placed the EP on an equal footing with the Council for a new category of policy-implementing decisions, known as 'delegated acts' (Corbett *et al.* 2011: 330). However, the decision did not cover all comitology activity and the dispute between the institutions continues. These differences of view show that the Parliament still exercises less-effective influence over policy-implementing decisions than it does over policy-making.

The Parliament and the 'democratic deficit'

The crisis provoked by the 'no' votes on the Constitutional Treaty in referenda held in France and the Netherlands in 2005 was particularly keenly felt in the Parliament. The EP had championed the Convention as an original and better way of preparing an IGC. It had achieved equal status with the Council for virtually all EU legislation, and it had voted by a very large majority in favour of the results of the IGC. For the first time in its history, its acquisition of broader powers was blocked.

Critical outsiders suggested that there was a wider lesson to be learnt. *The Economist* (2005) suggested that the referenda results 'cruelly exposed the fantasy that the EP is the answer to the disconnect between political elites and ordinary citizens'. It contrasted unfavourably the turnout in France and Holland for the referenda (70 per cent and 63 per cent, respectively) with the much lower figures in the 2004 European elections (see Table 6.3).

Despite the subsequent 'rescue' of the contents of the Constitutional Treaty via the Lisbon Treaty, the shape of the argument about the role of the Parliament has not significantly changed. Indeed, the fact that overall turnout fell again (if only by a small percentage) in the 2009 elections served to confirm for many that the Parliament could not hope to become the democratic link between European citizens and the EU institutional structure. Critics of the EU insisted on this point regardless of however much the EP's own role in that structure was strengthened.

At the root of the argument lie very different perspectives on the nature of the EU and the possibilities for closing the 'democratic deficit'. At least three such perspectives can be identified, each offering a different remedy for the democratic failings of the EU. Yet all share the idea that the structure of the institutions is not a technical question, but one with political values at its core. In this sense, the French and Dutch referenda results brought into the open a debate that had remained half-hidden.

A first perspective is often referred to as the 'no demos' thesis. It suggests that democracy is a chimera outside the national context because the peoples of Europe are not bound together in the same way as national communities—which form a *demos*, or common people or populace—which share common histories and cultures (Siedentop 2000). If there is no European demos, there can be no democracy at the European level. From this point of view, the EP can only be an expensive irrelevance.

The most militant advocates of this point of view do not look for a solution within the structures of the Union; they would rather return to the kind of non-binding international cooperation found in the Council of Europe. Milder versions of the thesis accept the existence of the EU institutions, but look to reinforce significantly the role of national parliaments. There were strong voices, for example, before and during the Convention in favour of this approach. Joschka Fischer, then German Foreign Minister, and Tony Blair both argued in 2000 that the EP should have two chambers: one made up of directly elected members; the other, of members of national parliaments.

TABLE 6.3　Turnout in European Parliament elections

	1979	1981	1984	1987	1989	1994	1995	1996	1999	2004	2007	2009
EU	62.0	–	59.0	–	58.4	56.7	–	–	49.5	45.5		43.0
Luxembourg	88.9	–	88.8	–	87.4	88.6	–	–	87.3	91.3		90.8
Belgium	91.4	–	90.7	–	90.7	90.7	–	–	91.0	90.8		90.4
Malta	–	–	–	–	–	–	–	–	–	82.4		78.8
Italy	85.6	–	82.5	–	81.1	73.6	–	–	69.8	71.7		65.0
Denmark	47.8	–	52.4	–	46.2	52.9	–	–	50.5	47.9		59.5
Cyprus	–	–	–	–	–	–	–	–	–	72.5		59.4
Ireland	63.6	–	47.6	–	68.3	44.0	–	–	50.2	58.6		58.6
Latvia	–	–	–	–	–	–	–	–	–	41.3		53.7
Greece	–	81.5	80.6	–	80.0	73.2	–	–	70.2	63.2		52.6
Austria	–	–	–	–	–	–	–	67.7	49.4	42.4		46.0
Sweden	–	–	–	–	–	–	41.6	–	38.8	37.8		45.5
Spain	–	–	–	68.5	54.7	59.1	–	–	63.0	45.1		44.9
Estonia	–	–	–	–	–	–	–	–	–	26.8		43.9
Germany	65.7	–	56.8	–	62.3	60.0	–	–	45.2	43.0		43.3
France	60.7	–	56.7	–	48.8	52.7	–	–	46.8	42.8		40.6
Bulgaria											29.2	39.0
Finland	–	–	–	–	–	–	–	57.6	30.1	39.4		38.6
Portugal	–	–	–	72.4	51.1	35.5	–	–	39.9	38.6		36.8
Netherlands	58.1	–	51.0	–	47.5	35.7	–	–	30.0	39.3		36.7
Hungary	–	–	–	–	–	–	–	–	–	38.5		36.3
UK	32.3	–	32.6	–	36.4	36.4	–	–	24.0	38.5		34.7
Slovenia	–	–	–	–	–	–	–	–	–	28.3		28.4
Czech Republic	–	–	–	–	–	–	–	–	–	28.3		28.2
Romania											29.5	27.7
Poland	–	–	–	–	–	–	–	–	–	20.9		24.5
Lithuania	–	–	–	–	–	–	–	–	–	48.4		21.0
Slovakia	–	–	–	–	–	–	–	–	–	17.0		19.6

Source: Adapted from Corbett (2011)

The Lisbon Treaty did not see the creation of a second parliamentary chamber at European level. There has been a consistent majority against creating such a new institution, not least because it would be likely to face the same kind of organizational and political weaknesses that confronted the EP before it was directly elected.[2] However, the Treaty did reinforce the position of national parliaments and gave them, for the first time, a treaty-based role in the legislative procedure. They are now explicitly invited to state whether a draft legislative act complies with the principle of subsidiarity, whereby action at European level should be restricted to areas in which an EU objective can be better achieved at the Union level. If sufficient parliamentary chambers consider the principle to be breached, then the EU institutions are obliged to confirm whether they think the proposal should go forward.[3] So far, there has been no instance of a majority of national parliaments objecting to an EU proposal in this way. But the fact that the possibility exists reflects the continuing desire of many in national political life to have a chance to exert influence at European level and to assert their primacy in terms of legitimating EU actions in a world in which there is no recognizable European demos.

A second perspective suggests that the EU system needs to be less consensual and more politicized to become democratic. On this view, the EU will be democratic only if European elections are fought by cohesive Euro-parties that present rival agendas for EU policy action. The winning parties would form the executive and the parties would act cohesively to ensure that their office-holders implement their electoral programme (Hix 2002a, 2002b, 2008).

Such a vision of the future corresponds to the classic parliamentary model found in all EU member states. It can be seen as a natural development from the existing structure of the EP's powers. Indeed, efforts are already in progress to alter the process whereby a candidate for Commission President emerges in a way that reinforces a party logic. The main European political parties have agreed that they will each nominate a candidate for the post in advance of the 2014 European elections (see Chapter 15). The intention is that the candidates will present the manifesto of their political family, along with their own priorities for the Commission if they are appointed, and thereby provide voters with a clearer reason for voting for one party rather than another. The procedure would not eliminate the need for the European Council and the EP to find a candidate for the Commission President after the elections. As Hix (2008) has shown, the outcome need not be an automatic one. Nonetheless, it would create a different dynamic and directly link the electoral process with what the EU institutions subsequently do.

However, there are important obstacles to the success of this device. National political parties are likely to be reluctant to support fully such nominations, which weaken their own control of the electoral process. Moreover, there is a clear potential for conflict between candidates nominated by European political parties and individuals who might be favoured inside the European Council. In the event of a dispute between the two bodies, it is not clear that the Parliament would be victorious. In 1994, when many in the Parliament were unhappy with the nomination of

Jacques Santer as Commission President, pressure exercised by national governments succeeded in ensuring that the choice of the European Council prevailed.

Moreover, there is the broader issue of the relationship between Parliament and Commission. As Magnette (2001: 308) has pointed out:

the Commission is not subordinate to a parliamentary majority that can *sanction* it, but rather scrutinised by MEPs who can only try to *influence* it. The pyramidal and hierarchic structure of the parliamentary state is replaced, here, by horizontal relations of mutual control. [Emphasis original]

Parliament itself has always wanted to uphold the role of the Commission as a separate institution. It has, for example, consistently supported the Commission's right of legislative initiative and not sought to acquire such a right for itself.

Last, but not least, the Commission is not an executive in the same sense as a national government is. Executive roles in the EU are split, a tendency accentuated in the Lisbon Treaty, which has created the post of President of the European Council to be filled every two-and-a-half years. Whatever that person's mandate and relationship with the Commission President, it is difficult to imagine the creation of traditional mechanisms of parliamentary control and accountability applying to him or her. Parliament can only ever hope to have very partial control over the executive at European level. Hence the politicization of the EU structure can be expected to make only restricted progress.

A third narrative sees the democratic credentials of the Union depending neither on the reinforcement of the role of national parliaments, nor on the creation of partisan politics at European level; rather we should acknowledge how far the EU as a whole has already progressed in establishing a democratic system. As Corbett (2012: 157) has commented, 'the EU is unique in how far it goes to try to apply democratic principles at a level wider than the national state'. It is a system that provides for very broad involvement of parliamentary assemblies in the adoption of legislation, which assures a high level of parliamentary scrutiny of the action of the executive, and which goes to considerable lengths to guarantee the rights of minorities. The democratic added value of the system derives from the high premium that it places on the search for compromise among competing interests. The Parliament contributes to the proper functioning of the system, but it should not be seen as the sole source of its democratic credentials.

From this point of view, the fact that the EP does not have a right of legislative initiative comparable, for example, to what is found in national parliaments simply underlines the different character of the EU rather than showing that the Union lacks a 'proper' democratic Parliament. The European system is one that continues to search for new ways of giving expression to the wishes of EU citizens, which can involve the EP only peripherally. Thus the Lisbon Treaty created the European Citizens' Initiative, enabling 1 million EU citizens from a significant number of member states (subsequently defined as at least a quarter) to call upon the Commission to come forward with a legislative proposal. This provision reflects a readiness to envisage a limited dose of direct democratic participation alongside the more traditional representative tradition in a way that is familiar in several member states.

One argument in support of the dispersion of power implicit in such arrangements is that it reinforces the search for balance between a remarkably wide variety of interests, with all able to identify with one or other part of a divided system of government. The introduction of a logic of partisanship, based on the decisions of a political majority within a parliamentary government, would severely test such a balance. Those who argue that there is no European demos are right to point to a limited sense of belonging in the EU: without such a sense of belonging, it is very hard to envisage a political system at European level deriving its legitimacy from majority decisions adopted on the basis of the programme of one political family. EU institutions reflect a general resistance to the centralization of power, a resistance reflected in the kind of role that the Parliament plays. Even in the legislative arena, where its powers have been so significantly strengthened, the EP cannot decide the contents of legislation alone: power and influence are shared.

How does this vision of a diffuse polity fit with the evidence of turnouts at European elections, the clearest opportunity for European citizens to take part in the development of the Union? It is one of the ironies of recent years that the steady growth in the powers of the EP has been matched by a steady decrease in the level of participation in European elections. In the 2009 direct elections, as Table 6.3 shows, the average level of turnout fell for the sixth time running, with increases in ten countries outweighed by drops in turnout in sixteen others, with six countries (all from Central and Eastern Europe) registering less than 30 per cent participation.

Declining turnouts are a feature of many democratic systems, but, in any case, should the tendency be any surprise, given the second-order nature of the elections? Even with all of the new powers in the Lisbon Treaty, the legislature at EU level continues to operate within a much narrower sphere than does the US Congress. Most of the political issues that affect European citizens directly, such as health care, education, or taxation, are still discussed and decided at national level. MEPs are unlikely ever to have the kind of powers enjoyed by members of Congress in influencing, for example, the location of government investment in their constituencies. More generally, the collective character of decisions in the EU makes it difficult for voters to identify whom to reward or punish for particular policy outcomes when they participate in European elections. Election turnout, from this point of view, need not be considered particularly poor.

At the same time, the third perspective that stresses how far the EU has gone in creating a democratic system beyond the nation-state level cannot guarantee that it receives public support. The severe tensions generated by the financial crisis have provoked considerable dissatisfaction with the EU in many member states. It is not only how a system works and who is involved that counts, but also what the system generates in terms of policies. Because there is no longer what has been described as a 'permissive consensus', the limited sense of belonging to the EU felt by most of its citizens poses a difficulty for the acceptance of controversial decisions that have, or are perceived to have, a direct and negative effect on people's lives. The EP alone cannot provide a solution to this difficulty.

Conclusion

This chapter has pointed to four general insights into the workings of the Parliament. First, it has shown the power of the democratic idea as driving change in the Parliament's powers. Governments have found it extremely difficult to resist an increase in the role of the EP, because they have not easily been able to formulate an alternative for addressing the 'democratic deficit'. This consensus has now found its expression in a new section of the Lisbon Treaty on democratic principles, which underlines that 'the functioning of the Union shall be founded on representative democracy' (Art. 10). The commitment to such ideas has to be integrated into an explanation of institutional change.

Second, we have seen that the shape of the EU's institutions is 'path-dependent', or heavily influenced by earlier decisions. Direct elections can be traced back to the provisions of the ECSC Treaty in the early 1950s. Similarly, the establishment of codecision in the Maastricht Treaty established a trajectory for the Parliament effectively to become one branch of a bicameral legislature under Lisbon.

Third, the chapter has contested the notion that major decisions in the EU are taken exclusively by governments. The Parliament has been able to use its legislative powers to alter the shape of outcomes sought by the Council and has started to exercise influence over the choice of the Commission President, as well as the shape of the Commission. Such developments are difficult to reconcile with a purely liberal intergovernmentalist perspective.

Finally, we have stressed the importance of consensus mechanisms within the Parliament, as well as those that link it to the other institutions. The result is the spreading of responsibility to ensure that support for policy change is broad amongst a very diverse set of competing interests. Democracy in the EU seems unlikely to develop on the basis of the same kind of majoritarian processes as exist at national level.

 NOTES

1. SWIFT stands for the Society for Worldwide Interbank Financial Communication; it is based in La Hulpe, outside Brussels in Belgium.

2. Julian Priestley, former Secretary-General of the Parliament, takes on those who favour a reinforced role for national parliaments and the creation of a Congress of national parliaments in an article entitled 'Right question, wrong answer', *European Voice*, 28 July 2011, p. 12.

3. See Lisbon Treaty, Protocol No. 1, on the role of national parliaments in the European Union, and Protocol No. 2, on the application of the principles of subsidiarity and proportionality.

→ FURTHER READING

There is a growing range of books and articles on the European Parliament. Corbett *et al.* (2011) is now in its eighth edition and provides a detailed account of the internal workings of the institution. Judge and Earnshaw (2008) place the role of the Parliament in a wider perspective, considering its formal and informal influence, as well as its effectiveness as a representative body. Rittberger (2005) offers an in-depth analysis of the reasons why governments have been willing to delegate powers to the institution. Ringe (2010) considers how policy choices are made inside the Parliament and why the political groups are able to overcome their internal heterogeneity. Corbett (1998) offers a more historical account of how the institution consciously set out to develop its powers during the 1980s and 1990s, a view that can be compared with the Vedel Report (1972), which looked forward to an unknown future for the institution.

Christoffersen, P. S. (2011) 'The creation of the European External Action Service: challenges and opportunities', in *The European Union after the Lisbon Treaty* (Maastricht: Monnet Lecture Series Three).

Corbett, R. (1998) *The European Parliament's Role in Closer Integration* (Basingstoke: Palgrave).

Corbett, R., Jacobs, F., and Shackleton, M. (2011) *The European Parliament* (8th edn, London: John Harper).

European Parliament (2009) 'Activity report of the delegations to the Conciliation Committee for the period 1 May 2004 to 13 July 2009', Presented by Vice-Presidents R. Kratsa-Tsagaropoulou, A. Vidal Quadras, and M. Rothe, available online at **http://www.europarl.europa.eu/code/information/activity_reports/ activity_report_2004_2009_en.pdf**

Farrell, H. and Héritier, A (2007) 'Codecision and institutional change', *West European Politics*, 30/2: 285–300

Judge, D. and Earnshaw, D. (2008) *The European Parliament* (2nd edn, London: Palgrave Macmillan).

Rasmussen, A. (2007) 'Early conclusion to the co-decision legislative procedure', *European University Institute Working Papers MWP 2007/31*.

Ringe, N. (2010) *Who Decides, and How? Preferences, Uncertainty, and Policy Choice in the European Parliament* (Oxford: Oxford University Press).

Rittberger, B. (2005) *Building Europe's Parliament: Democratic Representation beyond the Nation-state* (Oxford: Oxford University Press).

Vedel, G. (1972) *Report of the Working Party Examining the Problem of the Enlargement of the Powers of the European Parliament* (Brussels: Bulletin of the European Communities, Supplement 4/72) (the 'Vedel Report').

⊕ WEB LINKS

http://www.europarl.europa.eu
The EP website provides up-to-date material on the workings of the institution. It is divided into five sections, looking at the news from the Parliament, what the EP is and how

it is structured, who the MEPs are, what the EP produces (reports, amendments, minutes, records of debates. etc.), and an online video link to parliamentary debates.

http://www.europarltv.europa.eu

Since 2008, the Parliament has also run a web TV channel that offers (in twenty-two languages, using subtitles) background interviews and analysis on what is happening in the Parliament, provides easily accessible material for younger audiences, and enables the viewer to discover more about how the Parliament works. The channel is fully integrated into the Parliament's main website.

http://votewatch.eu

The Parliament website hosts access to Votewatch, a project run from the London School of Economics and Political Science (LSE) that provides a means of checking how MEPs have voted, as well as verifying how cohesive the groups have been on particular issues and over time.

CHAPTER 7

The Court of Justice of the European Union

Niamh Nic Shuibhne

▌ Summary

This chapter sketches a biographical profile of the Court of Justice of the European Union. It outlines how the Court is composed, 'who' the Court is, and how judges are appointed. It then focuses on what the Court does and how the Court functions in a practical sense. How is its workload organized? How long does it take before the Court issues a judgment? The chapter offers some reflections on the nature and influence of the Court, and locates it in a wider institutional picture, especially its relationship with national courts and the Strasbourg-based European Court of Human Rights (ECtHR). It also reflects on changes brought about by successive EU enlargements and the Lisbon Treaty. The Court was not radically reformed by Lisbon; arguably, the practical difficulties that the Court faces through the sheer increase in its size as a result of EU enlargement created the real challenges that it now faces.

Introduction

The Court of Justice of the European Union (CJEU) is the EU's judicial institution. Although confusingly depicted in the singular, the CJEU actually comprises three distinct courts: the Court of Justice; the General Court; and the Civil Service Tribunal. All three courts have their institutional seat in Luxembourg, in a burgeoning complex of court buildings.

History and development

The Court of Justice (often referred to as the 'European Court of Justice', or the ECJ) is the most well known of the three courts and it is the European Union's original judicial institution. It was established in 1952 to resolve disputes for the European Coal and Steel Community (ECSC). Its role was then consolidated and expanded with the adoption of the Treaty of Rome, when it became the sole judicial institution of the European Economic Community (EEC) too. Mainly because of long-held concerns about workload, a second court, the Court of First Instance (CFI), was established in 1989. The Lisbon Treaty renamed this second court the General Court.

Through the Nice reforms, the Treaty was amended in 2003 to provide also for the establishment of 'specialized courts'. The intention here was to offer a structure for the creation of new courts that would focus only on certain types of case. The Civil Service Tribunal, created in 2005, exemplifies this point: it hears and determines just one type of dispute—that is, cases between the EU and the staff of its institutions, bodies, and agencies. In other words, it is a forum for employment disputes.

Structure and functions

The composition of the Court

Both the ECJ and the General Court are composed of twenty-seven judges each. The number of judges has always increased in direct proportion to each EU enlargement. Both courts have always included one judge from each EU member state, but this principle has been articulated as an express requirement only since the Nice Treaty. It is interesting to note a slight difference between the rule for the ECJ ('one judge from each Member State') and for the General Court ('*at least* one judge per Member State', emphasis added), leaving open an (as yet) untapped potential for General Court expansion quite separately from any further EU enlargement.

The Civil Service Tribunal has seven members. The Tribunal's founding instrument provides that the appointment of judges must ensure a balanced composition on as broad a geographical basis as possible from among nationals of the member states and, interestingly, with respect to the national legal systems represented. On the latter point, it is important to remember that the member states operate with different forms of legal system internally. Ireland, for example, has a common law system with a written constitution. Germany also has a written constitution, but its legal system reflects the civil law tradition. The UK does not have a written constitution and has different legal systems operating within its borders (common law in England and Wales, for example, but a mixed legal system in Scotland).

The ECJ also has eight Advocates General.[1] When a case that arrives at the ECJ is thought to raise an especially complex or new legal question, an Advocate General is instructed to prepare an advisory opinion to help the ECJ to reach its decision. These opinions set out in detail both the factual background to the case and the possible legal options available to the Court. But the Advocate General's views are not binding. The Court is always free to depart from either the reasoning used or the actual decision proposed. Typically, however, it does not. But an important proviso is relevant here: while we often speak of the Court 'following' its Advocate General, judgments rarely, in fact, make express reference to opinions. No one can really say, then, whether the opinion is being followed or the conclusions of the Court are arrived at independently.

At present, five member states (France, Germany, Italy, Spain, and the UK) have a permanent Advocate General at the ECJ. The remaining three spaces rotate as non-renewable six-year positions across the remaining twenty-two member states. Despite the contrast with the Treaty-guaranteed equality of member state representation that is now built into judicial appointments, the unevenness of the Advocate General appointment process has never caused serious political discord.

The General Court does not have distinct Advocates Generals. Its Rules of Procedure provide that General Court judges can themselves perform this function. They do so on an ad hoc basis, whenever an advisory opinion is felt to be necessary.

Judicial appointments

At the time of writing, the ECJ was composed of twenty-two male and five female judges, with six male and two female Advocates General. The age range of its members spans 47 to 73, and members' biographies reflect a diverse range of professional backgrounds in legal practice, public service, other (national and international) institutional roles, and academia.[2]

How are judges and Advocates General actually chosen and appointed? Most importantly of all, they are required by the Treaty to be 'persons whose independence is beyond doubt'. Independence is an essential characteristic of the judicial function in general. In the EU context, each member state is represented by having 'its' judge at both the ECJ and General Court, but, critically, each judge must then be an independent member of the EU judiciary.

Judicial independence at the CJEU is enhanced by the fact that all three courts operate as *collegiate* institutions. The publication of just one judgment in each case exemplifies this collective responsibility, by ensuring that the views or arguments put forward by any of the individual judges when the case was being discussed are never revealed. This feature is a point of contrast with most national judicial systems, in which dissenting opinions, directly attributed to the relevant individual judge, are normally published alongside the majority judgment. Interestingly, dissenting opinions are also part of the system at the European Court of Human Rights (ECtHR).

Apart from the three rotational Advocate General positions, all other judicial appointments are made for a period of six years and are renewable. Partial replacements of ECJ and General Court membership take place every three years. This practice is designed to ensure a degree of institutional continuity notwithstanding any new appointments.

According to the Treaty, all judges and Advocates General must be appointed 'by common accord of the Member States'. Since Lisbon, however, a panel must first comment on the suitability of proposed judicial candidates. The panel must consist of seven persons chosen from among former members of the Court of Justice and the General Court, members of national supreme courts and lawyers of recognized competence, one of whom shall be proposed by the European Parliament (EP). This new step in the approval of judicial appointments certainly fits with broader Lisbon ambitions of greater accountability, representation, and transparency.

Finally, there is a subtly nuanced difference in the Treaty-specified basis of qualification for judicial appointment to each court. The requirement of independence is common to all CJEU judicial appointments. To be eligible for appointment to the ECJ, candidates must 'possess the qualifications required for appointment to the *highest* judicial offices in their respective countries or be jurisconsults of recognised competence' (emphasis added).[3] This requirement would typically be understood to mean eligibility for supreme court positions. For the General Court, it is possession of 'the ability required for appointment to *high* judicial office' (emphasis added); for specialized courts, it is 'the ability required for appointment to judicial office'.

This sliding scale of required expertise reflects a sort of hierarchy. More specifically, it suggests that the ECJ sits at the institutional apex of the EU judicial architecture, with authority then flowing downwards to the General Court, and, finally, downwards again to any specialized courts that have been (or might in future be) established. This notion of a hierarchy of courts fits comfortably with how we understand national legal systems too.

What the Court does

Lawyers talk about what courts can and cannot do in the language of 'jurisdiction'. A court's jurisdiction normally has two important meanings: substantive and procedural. First, *substantive jurisdiction* means the subject matter on which a court is permitted to hear disputes. We saw earlier that the Civil Service Tribunal, for example, may hear and resolve only staff disputes between the EU and its employees. That is its substantive jurisdiction.

The ECJ and General Court both have a much broader jurisdiction. They can hear cases on any aspect of EU law unless the treaties expressly exclude something from their jurisdiction. One of the most basic rules here is that disputes must typically have EU relevance, often as a result of the given situation having a cross-border dimension. In other words, the CJEU normally has no jurisdiction to hear disputes in which the facts are wholly internal to one member state. The Treaty provides for only very limited exceptions to this general rule (for example, claims about gender discrimination in employment situations).

The Lisbon Treaty has brought about some fundamental changes to substantive Court jurisdiction. The Lisbon reforms were, in general, praised for the unification of the different facets of the EU in macro or structural terms (notably, through the merging of the EC and EU) and for managing the implications of this unification in policy terms. Under the former three-pillar EU structure, the jurisdiction of the ECJ and General Court was very limited with respect to police and judicial cooperation in criminal matters, and also disputes involving visas, asylum, and immigration. Now, after a transitional period of five years has passed, these limitations will dissolve and the Court will have full jurisdiction on legal questions that arise from action in these EU policy fields. This development is subject to an exception, in that the Court cannot review:

the validity or proportionality of operations carried out by the police or other law-enforcement services of a Member State or the exercise of the responsibilities incumbent upon Member States with regard to the maintenance of law and order and the safeguarding of internal security.

(Article 276 TFEU)

Judicial second-guessing of national action by the CJEU is therefore precluded, suggesting recognition of a protected sphere of national security sovereignty for the member states.

Restrictions on jurisdiction also remain in place in relation to the common foreign and security policy (CFSP). The default position here is that the Court does *not* have jurisdiction, but the Lisbon Treaty did introduce significant exceptions. The Court now has jurisdiction to monitor the delimitation of Union and member state competences in this field. Again, this provision fits with the broader Lisbon Treaty objective of setting out more clearly how the exercise of exclusive and shared competences should be worked out. The Court may also hear actions brought against Council decisions providing for restrictive measures against natural or legal persons in connection with, for example, combating terrorism. Overall, this new role for the Court reflects its significant contribution towards ensuring both institutional and member state compliance with principles of constitutional importance, such as the boundaries of EU competence and the protection of fundamental rights.

Second, the jurisdiction of the Court of Justice has an important *procedural* meaning. The legal vocabulary for procedural jurisdiction speaks of 'forms of action before the Court'. This boils down to two critical questions: what types of legal action can each of the courts hear and who can initiate them?

As a general rule, and addressing the second question first, the ECJ is typically the court to which only the EU institutions and the member states have access for *direct actions* (that is, legal actions actually initiated in the ECJ itself). By contrast, the General Court is the forum in which direct actions initiated by a natural (that is, human) person or legal person (that is, a company or an organization) are heard. Other disputes arrive in Luxembourg following their initiation elsewhere. The most important of these *indirect actions* before the ECJ is the preliminary rulings procedure (see below).

The ECJ also has jurisdiction to hear appeals (only on points of law, not fact) against judgments of the General Court. The General Court, in turn, may hear appeals from the Civil Service Tribunal. This *appellate jurisdiction* is a further marker of court hierarchy.

Finally, the Court also has jurisdiction to hear a number of special procedures, such as disciplinary actions (for example, dismissal of the European Ombudsman) or actions for damages against EU institutions.

To unpack the first question in more detail—*what* the forms of action are—the following sections look first at two direct actions (enforcement proceedings before the ECJ and actions for judicial review). The key features of the preliminary rulings procedure—an indirect action—are then outlined.

Enforcement proceedings

Legal discourse on EU integration often centres on the idea of *effectiveness*. In other words, if the EU were a purely political organization, without any input from law or any sense of legal obligation, could European integration have been achieved as effectively and intensively as it has been to date? Is it more effective to persuade member states to act in a certain way, or to force them? After all, it is a hallmark of modern Western democracies that their courts are obeyed (see Weiler 1999).

In fact, enforcement proceedings (also called 'infringement proceedings') combine both political persuasion and legal obligation. The action is initiated against a member state when there is an alleged failure to fulfil binding obligations to which the State has committed under EU law. In theory, member states can launch proceedings against each other, but the Commission initiates almost all of these actions[4] (see Box 7.1).

Actions for judicial review

Direct actions for judicial review require the input of the Court in determining the legal propriety of binding EU acts (a regulation or directive, for example).[5] Member states and the other EU institutions can initiate their actions for judicial review before the ECJ. Actions brought by natural or legal persons must begin in the General Court.

BOX 7.1	**Enforcing state commitments**

The enforcement proceedings mechanism provides an interesting example of how the Commission and the Court work together and share responsibility for ensuring that the member states fulfil the obligations they assume under EU law. The political phase managed by the Commission is essential. Ultimately, however, the bite of law lies in wait.

The Commission can commence infringement proceedings against a member state either on its own initiative or in response to a complaint that it has received. It is important always to remember that failure to fulfil an obligation can arise only where the relevant commitment is a legally binding one. The mechanism enables, and indeed encourages, the resolution of enforcement issues through channels of political negotiation between the Commission and the state involved. The judicial phase is, in other words, the stage of last resort. Moreover, even when disputes have *not* been resolved satisfactorily at the political stage, the Commission still retains complete discretion about whether to proceed to the ECJ or not. The political stage involves a series of letters and other communications (detailed in the Treaty) between the Commission and the relevant member state. Firm time limits within which a state must respond to the case set out against it by the Commission are also enforced.

If the situation is not resolved to the satisfaction of the Commission after the necessary political steps have been exhausted, the Commission may then decide to go ahead and launch legal proceedings against the member state before the Court of Justice. If the Court goes on to find against the member state, which it does in over a hundred enforcement actions annually (typically, more than half of all such cases initiated), and if, even then, the state fails to remedy the breach of its EU obligations, the Commission can embark on a second round of enforcement proceedings. The difference here is that the Court can then impose steep financial sanctions on the state.

The Commission has published guidance on the calculation of these financial penalties, which can involve per diem penalty payments or lump sums, and which run into millions of euro in total. The Commission recommends the amount of financial sanction that it wishes to apply in each case, but the decision rests with the Court. In one of the highest fines ever imposed by the Court, in an environmental law compliance case, France was presented with a 'bill' running into hundreds of millions of euro.[6] Since the coming into force of the Lisbon Treaty, there are two changes in this procedure. First, the Court can vary, but no longer exceed, the amount proposed by the Commission. Second, if the infringement of EU law at issue involves a state's failure to notify the Commission that it has transposed an EU directive (which it is legally obliged to do), then sanctions may be imposed at the end of 'round one'.

The purpose of judicial review is to ensure that the EU legislative institutions comply with Treaty rules (on law-making procedures and voting requirements, for example) and general principles of EU law (such as the requirements of proportionality and non-discrimination on the grounds of nationality) when carrying out their law-making activities—in legal vocabulary, to check that they have not acted ultra vires (that is, beyond the extent of their authority) in fulfilling those functions. The ultimate objective of the action is to have either the entire EU act or the offending part of that act annulled.

Four conditions must be met in order to bring a successful action for judicial review. First, the act in question must be a 'reviewable act'. The Court has interpreted this provision to mean that the act must be intended to produce legal effects. A directive or regulation will always fall into this category, but even a letter, for example, might be looked at by the Court and tested for any binding legal intention.

Second, anyone bringing an action for judicial review must have *locus standi* (that is, the legal standing to do so). Different actors have different levels or degrees of legal standing before—and therefore, different levels of access to—the Court. Member states, the Council, the Commission, and the EP are *privileged applicants*—that is, they can challenge any legal act before the ECJ; they do not have to show that the act has any particular impact on them. The Court of Auditors, the European Central Bank (ECB), and the Committee of the Regions (CoR) are semi-privileged applicants. This means that they can challenge acts only on the basis of protecting their prerogatives—that is, the act in question must have potential impact on their own powers or functions.

The legal standing of natural and legal persons is the most difficult—and contentious—aspect of legal standing. No court is an absolutely open forum; all litigants have to establish their legal standing to bring a court action, in national courts too. The critical question is whether the conditions for access to the courts, and thus access to justice, are properly balanced between the need to ensure an appropriate workload for courts (on the basis of the 'floodgates' argument—that is, that if courts were completely open, then they would be flooded with mostly nonsensical claims) and appropriate respect for the fundamentally important value of appropriate judicial protection.

Natural or legal persons normally have standing to challenge acts that have been directly addressed to them (for a company, for example, a decision of the Commission imposing a fine on it for breach of EU competition rules). If natural or legal persons want to challenge acts of more general application (such as an EU regulation or directive), the odds are stacked against them. In such a scenario, the person in question must fulfil the criteria of 'direct and individual concern'; these words signify two distinct tests.

The test of direct concern demands a clear relationship of cause and effect between the act itself and its impact on the applicant, with no intervening discretion on the part of member states. This test rules out any individual challenges to EU directives through the direct action for judicial review, since directives must *always* be transposed into national law through the adoption of national (thus intervening) measures. EU regulations, on the other hand, are self-executing. As soon as the institutions adopt them, they have legal effect in the member states. This direct applicability suggests that individuals have standing to challenge their legality before the General Court. Normally, the second test—of 'individual concern'—rules this out. The ECJ has determined that any applicant seeking to challenge an EU regulation will have to show himself, herself, or itself to be a member of a closed class—that is, a finite group of persons affected by the measure to which not even a future or hypothetical expansion of membership is possible.[7] Ironically, then, the greater the number of persons affected or *potentially* affected by an EU measure, the smaller the chance that any of them can actually challenge that act directly before the General Court.

There has been stringent criticism of this situation within the academic literature and also in the opinions of some of the Court's own Advocates General.[8] Nevertheless, the Court has held fast to its narrow understanding of direct, and especially individual, concern. The Court has always stressed that the system of judicial remedies available under EU law must be looked at in the round. Thus, although individuals might have more limited access to the Court of Justice through direct actions, the possibility of raising questions about the validity of EU law through national courts has always existed in parallel (that is, through the preliminary rulings procedure). But this solution is an imperfect one, since it demands that someone must get themselves involved in a national dispute in the first place and must then persuade the national court about the possibility of illegality, so that the court will be content to refer the question to Luxembourg.

Second, the Court has pointed out repeatedly that the tests of direct and individual concern are both in the Treaty. If the member states wanted to amend the Treaty in order to change the rules on legal standing, it was entirely within their powers to do so. This claim is difficult to argue with, and now, through the Lisbon Treaty, the rules have finally been softened to enable natural or legal persons to 'institute proceedings against … a regulatory act which is of direct concern to them and does not entail implementing measures'. It was hoped that this change would cover EU regulations, thus going some way towards restoring the balance in favour of judicial protection and lending more credence to the Court's claim about the 'completeness' of the EU forms of action when they are taken together as a comprehensive system of remedies.

The third of the four conditions for direct actions of judicial review is that the applicant must adhere to a strict time limit: the action must be initiated within two months (normally, of the publication of the measure or of its notification to the applicant).

Finally, there must be actual grounds for review. In other words, the applicant must have good arguments as to the illegality of the act being challenged. This test might involve, for example, an argument that the institution in question did not have legal authority to adopt the act being challenged, or that the act is not compatible with the substantive provisions of the Treaty on which it has been based.[9]

Finally, if the challenge is well founded, the Court will declare that the act (or the relevant part of the act) is void. The action for judicial review represents, overall, the provision of legal checks on the exercise of political power. EU law sets down the substantive and procedural parameters within which the institutions can develop and implement their policy choices; the action for judicial review enables the Court to establish that these parameters are respected.

The preliminary rulings procedure

Accounting for more than half of the ECJ's entire caseload,[10] the Court's judgments under the preliminary rulings procedure have pronounced some of its most significant statements on the nature and purpose of EU law. The profoundly important principles of the primacy of EU law (meaning that, in the case of a conflict, EU law must prevail over national law) and of its direct effect (meaning that EU law can be invoked directly by litigants in national courts) both emerged in cases decided under this form of indirect action.

The purpose underlying the preliminary rulings procedure is to ensure uniform application and interpretation of EU law by the national courts and tribunals in all of the EU member states.[11] The procedure establishes a line of communication between national judicial institutions and the ECJ that can be invoked in two instances:

- *interpretation* of the treaties or of acts of the institutions, bodies, offices, or agencies of the Union; and
- the *validity* of those acts.

In the former scenario, a national court or tribunal is typically asking the ECJ for clarification on the meaning or scope of EU law to the extent that EU law is relevant to the dispute before it. In situations concerning validity, the national court is essentially raising the same questions as those considered under a direct action for annulment—but, crucially, without the same constraints regarding legal standing or time limits. If the legality of an EU directive adopted thirty years ago is relevant to a case before a national court involving two private individuals, then that court can send those questions to Luxembourg.

Whether the issue before the national court relates to interpretation or validity, that body formulates a question or questions for transmission to the ECJ. The ECJ publishes an online guide to assist national courts in making their references. The ECJ will not answer questions in a limited range of circumstances: those in which there is no genuine dispute at national level (that is, the case is contrived purely to ascertain the ECJ's interpretation of EU law); those in which the questions sent are too vague; or those in which the referring court has not supplied the ECJ with sufficient information.

The ruling given by the ECJ under this procedure is 'preliminary' in the sense that the practical application of the ruling—that is, the final resolution of the national dispute—rests with the referring national court. Indeed, proceedings before that body have to be suspended pending the ECJ judgment. But the judgment is legally binding on the national court: the latter is the only court that can resolve the dispute, but it must apply the legal answers given by Luxembourg. The ECJ has also established that an interpretation of EU law given in the context of one particular preliminary ruling has binding legal effects throughout all member states. The ECJ has thus constructed a system akin to precedent within EU case law.

The average duration of the ECJ phase, from receipt of question(s) to publication of judgment, is now approximately seventeen months. The reduction of delay in Court proceedings has been a clear institutional priority for the CJEU over recent years, as evidenced by the Court's Annual Reports.[12] The ECJ Rules of Procedure also make provision for an accelerated preliminary rulings procedure and an urgent preliminary rulings procedure. The latter mechanism was first used in 2008 and it has enabled the Court, where the requisite conditions for urgency are genuinely established (three times in 2008; twice in 2009), to respond to questions from national courts in just over two months.

As for the interpretation of EU law, most national courts have discretion about whether or not to refer questions to the ECJ. National judges need trigger the preliminary rulings procedure only if they deem the input of the ECJ to be *necessary* to enable them to resolve the national dispute before them. They are perfectly entitled to interpret EU law themselves. For final courts of appeal, however, the referral of questions is mandatory, unless the correct application of EU law is so obvious as to leave no scope for reasonable doubt. This safeguard is in place to ensure that 'bad' interpretations of EU law do not get trapped in national law because of the mistaken interpretation offered by, for example, national supreme courts (which all other national courts would then be obliged to follow, save a subsequent reference to Luxembourg). But national courts can never themselves declare EU acts to be invalid and thus if any question about the validity of an EU legal measure is raised, it must be referred to the ECJ.

In terms of uptake, the preliminary rulings procedure has been an astounding success. National courts and tribunals at all levels in all member states (some more than others, of course) continue to engage with the mechanism and the number of pending preliminary rulings is, at the time of writing, higher than ever. The access to the ECJ given to lower courts and tribunals within national judicial hierarchies has been a particularly significant feature of the procedure. This level of openness has gone some way towards the embedding of EU law in national legal structures. It has also seen substantive results in lower-level cases involving individuals (through the access to Luxembourg afforded, for example, to employment and also migration tribunals). The ECJ continues to build its substantive contribution to EU law primarily through its judgments in such cases.

How does the Court work?

Judicial chambers

Since the ECJ and General Court both have twenty-seven judges, we can immediately dispel any image of 'the Court' in trying to understand the organization of its work in practical terms. Both courts function instead through a system of eight *chambers*. Most cases are heard by either a three-judge chamber or a five-judge chamber. Each chamber elects its own chamber president (every three years for a five-judge chamber; every year for a three-judge chamber). The judges are members of more than one chamber at any given time, thus enabling them to sit on both three-judge and five-judge chamber cases. A single judge can also hear cases under limited circumstances in the General Court.

The 'Grand Chamber' is the formation used when a member state or an institution that is a party to the proceedings so requests, or for more legally significant cases. The minimum composition of the Grand Chamber is thirteen judges, comprising the President of the ECJ/General Court and the presidents of the eight chambers, with the remaining places being filled on a rotational case-by-case basis.[13] The judges themselves elect the Presidents of the ECJ and the General Court, each for a renewable three-year term. Vassilios Skouris, the Greek judge, was elected President of the ECJ in 2003 and then re-elected twice; Marc Jaeger, the Luxembourg judge at the General Court, became its President in 2007. At the ECJ, the task of being 'First' Advocate General, a position denoted primarily for administrative and workload distribution purposes, also rotates. The 'full court' of twenty-seven judges still exists in theory and it must sit for certain hearings (for example, in disciplinary hearings provided for by the treaties). But the full court was not assigned any cases, in either the ECJ or General Court, in the six years after 2005. In effect, the Grand Chamber has absorbed the role previously played by the full court (of, then, fifteen members) before the 2004 EU enlargement.

The organization of the ECJ and General Court into chambers is clearly essential. It ensures that their respective workloads can be managed both effectively and efficiently. In the majority of cases, three or five judges can resolve the dispute appropriately. The Court has also been under constant pressure to reduce the duration of its proceedings, especially in the preliminary rulings procedure, so that pending national disputes can be resumed and resolved more speedily, which should in turn encourage more national courts to engage with the process.

With so many chambers delivering so many judgments at any one time, however, and with few opportunities for all members of the ECJ or of the General Court to engage in meaningful collective debate or discussion, there is an acute concern about the need to ensure consistency and coherence in judicial decision-making. The 2009 annual report from the ECJ showed that, from 2005 to 2009, five-judge chambers resolved more than half of all cases (57 per cent) and chambers of three judges determined a third of cases. The Grand Chamber delivered only 8 per cent of the ECJ's judgments. Again, the Court applies a system of precedent, which means that its decisions should 'add up' coherently overall. At the ECJ at least, the burden of piecing the developing case-law narrative together as systematically as possible falls increasingly on the eight Advocates General. There is merit in both the speedy delivery of justice and the securing of legal certainty, but both values need to be balanced against each other: speedy 'bad' case law is not worth the price paid.

BOX 7.2	From case to judgment at the ECJ

Once a case is lodged at the CJEU, the preliminary documents (national court questions, for example) are sent for translation into the EU's twenty-three official languages. This first step reflects the logistical complexities of applying EU case law uniformly in twenty-seven member states. Each case is assigned a 'language of the case' into which all case documents are translated. As a general rule, the applicant selects the language of the case, unless the defendant is a member state or a natural or legal person.

For preliminary rulings, the parties, as well as any of the member states or the institutions, have two months within which to submit written observations. Several submissions will be received in contentious cases. For direct actions, the application is served on the defendant, who has one month in which to lodge a defence. The applicant may then lodge a reply and the defendant a rejoinder, both, again, within one month.

In all cases, a Judge-Rapporteur is appointed by the President. The Judge-Rapporteur prepares an initial report summarizing all aspects of the case. The parties are asked to state whether (and, if so, why) they wish an oral hearing to be held. The ECJ decides collectively to what type of chamber the case should be assigned and whether a hearing should be held. If an oral hearing is held, the parties present strictly time-limited arguments in public.

Some weeks later, for ECJ cases, the Advocate General delivers his or her opinion in open court. But if it was considered that the case raised no new question of law, the Court will have proceeded to judgment without an opinion. Originally, an opinion was delivered in all cases before the ECJ. In 2009, just over half of the cases were resolved without an opinion.

The judges deliberate on the basis of a draft judgment prepared by the Judge-Rapporteur. Judicial deliberations take place in private, however, through the Court's common working language (French). Decisions are taken by majority.[14] The voting mechanism is outlined in the Rules of Procedure, but no record of dissent is made public.

The judgments themselves are quite formulaic. They begin with an outline of national (where relevant) and EU law, followed by a summary of the dispute, the legal arguments, and any observations submitted, and then the findings of the Court—that is, its legal reasoning and the decision actually taken on the various questions of EU law raised. The legal kernel of the judgment is repeated briefly in bold at the end of the text.

Judgments are published on the Court's website on the day on which they are delivered. Judgments are usually published in twenty-two languages (they do not have to be published in Irish unless it is the language of the case), but not always on the day of delivery, reflecting the enormity of the translation effort. The judgment in the language of the case has authoritative legal effect if there is any question about diverging meanings across different languages. Most judgments are also later published in the *European Court Reports* (ECR).

Judgments of the ECJ are sometimes criticized because of the absence of detailed reasoning. Especially when compared to the more fluid (and often very lengthy) Advocate General opinions, they can appear very clipped. Neither does the Court make as much effort as it might to relate the case to relevant previous case law, so that the bigger jurisprudential picture is not always as clear as it could be. From a different perspective, however, when the application of a legal solution that works both for the specific case at issue, but also as a precedent across twenty-seven states, in mostly translated versions, is taken into account, then perhaps the simpler the text, the better. This demonstrates why it is essential to try to ensure a good balance of representation of the different legal systems and legal approaches of the member states in the composition of the chambers—something that is difficult to achieve within the enlarged Court.

From the outside, we can only imagine what deliberations are actually like: polite and ordered exchanges of concise views, or passionate exchanges of detailed arguments? No doubt the walls of the Court have seen both, depending on the case at hand. Is the flow of judicial discussion inhibited by the need to use one common language, with which judicial competence and comfort levels must surely vary, at least initially? We will never know. Judges pledge to preserve the independence of the Court through an oath of secrecy. Moreover, the force of this oath outlasts the tenure of their appointment.

The influence of the Court

How can we assess the Court of Justice in institutional terms? Can the Court's contribution to European integration be quantified? How can we measure the influence of its case law? These questions are critical. Interestingly, however, they tend to be tackled by lawyers through very different theoretical and practical lenses from the integration criteria usually applied in political science.

As a starting point, lawyers tend to *assume* both the relevance and value of law and judicial institutions. In particular, law is conceptualized as having a neutral quality. It is a product of rational reasoning and it is thereby insulated from political vagaries. This neutrality is seen then to confer a considerable perception of authority on legal decisions that, in turn, feeds into a neutral perception of courts in institutional terms. But it is not that simple and there are a series of interrelated questions to which lawyers seek answers. When evaluating the Court of Justice in institutional terms, key debates bear much resemblance to discourse on court behaviour in general. Is the ECJ an activist court, or not? (Should *any* court be an activist court or not?) Does the Court of Justice make law? (*Should* courts make law?) And if courts do make law, is this function an expression of, or, instead, an undue trampling on, political functions? Or is it something else? Here, we are mainly in the territory of well-developed debates about the balance between legislative and judicial functions, and the respective roles of elected and unelected officials.[15]

There is an added edge to discourse on the Court of Justice, however, as we try to decipher whether it has its own integration agenda. Even if that could be shown to be true, the question arises whether the progression of that agenda is acceptable or even possible in the interests of institutional legitimacy and overall institutional balance. In a polity besieged by charges of a democracy deficit, unelected ECJ judges annulling legislative decisions of, collectively, the Commission, Council, and EP can be all the more difficult to swallow.

At a very basic level, Art.19(1) TEU establishes the core function of the Court of Justice: 'It shall ensure that in the interpretation and application of the Treaties the law is observed.' This deceptively clear sentence has generated controversies of its own: notably, what is 'the law'? The Court has always applied an expansive interpretation of 'the law' to include some amorphous legal sources (such as often unwritten 'general principles of EU law'). We know that it has also attached deep significance to the objective of building an 'ever closer union', a phrase noted only in the preambles to both of the EU treaties. It is an empirical fact that many of the Court's judgments have resulted in the outcome that best fits with a preference for deeper levels of European integration. It is also true, however, that those decisions have often required very sparse or ambiguous Treaty provisions to be 'interpreted'. In having resort to the *stated* political ambition of moving towards an 'ever closer Union', can the Court really be criticized for furthering that objective through its case law too? Is this furthering really a displacement of political preferences? And all the more in the enlarged Court, in which 'the Court' is itself an elusive phenomenon, can the Court be said even to have a particular or agreed institutional vision anyway?

It would be astonishing if the judges and Advocates General at the CJEU were not aware of broader political issues and considerations underpinning the cases before them. We can be sure that they are. But it does not automatically follow that the Court somehow abuses its position within the overall EU institutional balance.

The ECJ and other courts

In the preliminary rulings procedure, we saw how the Court of Justice must engage with the submissions of member states and the other EU institutions. We also can see how dependent it is on national courts and tribunals. Only national courts can keep asking questions, the answers to which in turn shape the shifting boundaries of EU law.

Furthermore, the Court of Justice is not the *only* transnational court in town, given the presence of the ECtHR in Strasbourg. The ECtHR sits in an unusual position vis-à-vis the Court of Justice through both courts' engagement with the setting of rights protection standards within a partially overlapping Europe. The European Convention on Human Rights (ECHR) binds all twenty-seven of the EU member states, but it also applies to an additional twenty European states. This connection could become even more complex in the future, because the EU was compelled, by the Lisbon Treaty, to seek accession to the ECHR. These negotiations were ongoing at the time of writing. For the first time, this membership will formally introduce a degree of external judicial supervision of the work of the Court of Justice.

The relationship with national courts

Academics have discussed the relationships between all of these interlocking courts for many decades now (see, for example, Alter 2001). For example, does the preliminary rulings procedure reflect dialogue or hierarchy? This question, which is often phrased in the language of judicial pluralism ('dialogue') and judicial federalism ('hierarchy'), asks whether the national courts are equal partners in the procedure or whether, given the ultimately binding authority of the ECJ's response, they are merely bit players in the Court's construction of the narrative of EU law. The most accurate answer probably reflects a bit of both. The Court of Justice retains the final word in a legal sense, but it is dependent on the national courts to send questions in the first place.

Over the years, courts and tribunals at the lower levels, in particular, have engaged very healthily with the preliminary rulings procedure. But the measure of success here is simply that of the volume of questions sent. It would entail empirical research on a massive scale (both geographically and linguistically) to discover what happens when the judgments from Luxembourg are then *applied* back in the referring court forum. In other words, how 'obedient' are national courts, really? The Commission instigated enforcement proceedings against one member state (Italy) for persistent failures on the part of its national courts to engage with EU law. But it is difficult to get an accurate sense of how well (or otherwise) EU law is applied in general. Moreover, any sense of this application will be even more opaque for the vast majority of cases in which EU law might be relevant— that is, in cases in which national courts determine that a reference to the ECJ is not 'necessary' at all and instead interpret (or dismiss) the EU legal issue by themselves.

The reception of EU case law within national constitutional courts or other courts at the apex of national judicial hierarchies (such as the Supreme Court in the UK) is a more documented phenomenon. Taking the primacy of EU law as a case study, we can clearly see the continuing coexistence of *parallel* claims about the authority that underpins this fundamental legal principle. Lower courts, in general, are used to being lower: they can resolve the legal dispute before them, but they are still links in an appellate court chain. The highest courts within national systems have more to lose within the supranational EU legal order. They give up their more typical role of having the final say on legal questions, especially questions closely connected to national constitutional principles.

The Court of Justice attributes the principle of primacy to the nature of the EU itself. From this, the Court derived a 'new legal order' that the member states sought to create. It also placed itself and the tenets of EU law at the apex of supranational EU legal authority, so that only it could determine the outcome of any such cases of conflict. It is critical to remember, however, that the 'new legal order' is the Court's own description of things.[16] National constitutional courts tend to take a different stance. They *allow* rather than subjugate themselves to primacy. They permit the operation of primacy in practice so as to give effect to the temporary tolerant will of their national parliaments. This point is extremely clear in the *Solange* doctrine of the German Federal Constitutional Court (*Bundesverfassungsgerichts*, or BVerfGE) in particular,[17] a position that has been altered subtly over the years, but which nonetheless continues to inform how that Court characterizes its relationship with the Court of Justice. This perspective has been articulated most recently in the German Federal Constitutional Court's decision (in 2009) on ratification of the Lisbon Treaty. That judgment reaffirmed the sovereignty of the member states. It acknowledged the temporary transfer of limited sovereignty to the EU so that agreed political objectives can be achieved through the actions of the Union's institutions, where appropriate. It also understood the purpose of primacy in securing the effectiveness of progress towards realizing those objectives. But it located these decisions at the level of the states themselves—not the EU in general, and not the ECJ more specifically.

An attempt to codify the principle of primacy expressly in the treaties was undertaken through the Constitutional Treaty. This ambition did not reappear as part of the Lisbon Treaty. However, Declaration No. 17 attached to the Lisbon Treaty states:

The Conference recalls that, in accordance with well settled case law of the Court of Justice of the European Union, the Treaties and the law adopted by the Union on the basis of the Treaties have primacy over the law of member states, under the conditions laid down by the said case law.

The Declaration also incorporates a 2007 Opinion from the Council Legal Service, which notes that:

According to the Court, this principle is inherent to the specific nature of the European Community. At the time of the first judgment of this established case law [*Costa*] there was no mention of primacy in the treaty. It is still the case today. The fact that the principle of primacy will not be included in the future treaty shall not in any way change the existence of the principle and the existing case law of the Court of Justice.

Perhaps this softer, more mutual accommodation—in which national judicial institutions operationalize and legitimize the primacy of EU law as a consequence of national political choices, while the Court of Justice continues to evolve the distinctiveness of the also-sovereign (partially, at least) EU legal order—is a good example of judicial pluralism in practice. The downside is that it works only while it works. The shadow of national court revolt continues, however faintly, to shade the Court of Justice's perception of the primacy of EU law.

The Court of Justice and the ECtHR

It is often remarked that the Court of Justice invented the idea of fundamental rights as general principles of EU law as a compromise in order to respond to challenges from national constitutional courts in the 1970s. At that time, it was trying to bed down the nascent principle of primacy. Whatever the motivation(s), however, this profoundly important judicial work led ultimately to the drafting and adoption of the EU Charter of Fundamental Rights. The Charter has now acquired the same legal standing as the treaties through Lisbon.

The Court of Justice had, early on, drawn from the ECHR, and the jurisprudence of the ECtHR interpreting the Convention, as sources of inspiration for EU fundamental rights protection. It thus recognized the authoritativeness and expertise of the Strasbourg Court, while ensuring that it could nonetheless develop its own distinct case law. This approach also threads through the Charter, which makes it clear that the standards of protection as set by the ECHR and Strasbourg Court are the threshold below which EU law cannot go, while emphasizing that EU protection can, however, go further. But we saw that the Lisbon Treaty also requires the EU to accede to the ECHR, raising fascinating questions about the next phase of the relationship between the two courts.

Quite apart from complex questions about how Strasbourg supervision of Luxembourg jurisprudence would work in practice (Would there be an 'EU judge' in Strasbourg, for example? Would cases be referred from Luxembourg in something like a new preliminary rulings system?), the prospect of EU accession to the ECHR potentially dilutes, rather than enhances, the pluralist relationship that has evolved thus far. There are not, in fact, many examples in Court of Justice case law in which it departed from ECtHR jurisprudence. And the engagement works both ways: although not, of course, as a legally binding source, the ECtHR actually referred to the Union's Charter of Fundamental Rights before the ECJ did so itself.

In one strand of its case law, the ECtHR has indicated that it is prepared to review EU measures for compatibility with ECHR standards of fundamental rights protection. This pledge is designed to ensure that the member states—that is, Council of Europe members acting 'behind' the EU measure—have not unduly relinquished their responsibilities under the ECHR. But that is not the same as a more direct supervisory role. And it is not the same as having one, more definitive institutional voice on the meaning and standards of fundamental rights protection in the EU legal space. How will the Court of Justice cope with these changes? Will it respond well to the more formalized engagement that will most likely have to ensue? It will be interesting to watch this next chapter in the story of the Court of Justice unfold, observing its responses to legal instruction and not just charting its profile as the legal instructor.

Conclusion

The contribution of the Court of Justice's case law to the furtherance of EU integration may well be controversial, but, at least at the level of fact, it is probably uncontested. Through the development of the primacy of EU law, in particular, the Court copper-fastened the idea that EU law was going to be effective law. Member state promises were not going to rest two-dimensionally on Treaty paper. The Court has consistently emphasized the seriousness of the commitments entered into by the member states themselves. It has striven also to ensure the uniform application of EU law across all of the member states in so far as is practically possible. In doing so, however, it has inevitably established, consciously or otherwise, its own critical role in fulfilling these functions.

   The Court of Justice is also, in practical terms, very different from its ancestor 1952 institution. For starters, it is now three courts. It is a considerably enlarged institution, which must balance the application of effective and efficient working methods against fundamental requirements such as the legal certainty of its case law. It is not yet apparent that the enlarged Court has really grappled with these contemporary challenges in a systematic way.

   Finally, it is worth remarking that few lawyers have engaged seriously with theories of European integration or governance in their analyses of the Court of Justice. Equally, few political scientists have engaged seriously with the Court's own extensive outputs (its judgments) in shaping their perspectives of the Court as an institution. Notable exceptions are included in the guide to further reading at the end of this chapter. But there is clearly much scope for meaningful and rich interdisciplinary research on all of these questions.

 NOTES

1. Although Declaration No. 38 attached to the Lisbon Treaty provides that an increase to eleven Advocates General has been agreed by the member states. Declaration No. 38 also provides that Poland will become the sixth member state to have a permanent

Advocate General at the ECJ should the number of such posts be increased overall from eight to eleven.

2. The biographies of all members of the Court of Justice can be found online at **http://curia.europa.eu/jcms/jcms/Jo2_7026/**; for the General Court, see **http://curia.europa.eu/jcms/jcms/Jo2_7035/**; for the Civil Service Tribunal, see **http://curia.europa.eu/jcms/jcms/T5_5240/**

3. There is no official definition of the term 'jurisconsult', but it is normally considered simply to mean someone who has legal expertise. This might refer to a practising lawyer, for example, or to a legal academic.

4. The details of this procedure are set out in Art. 258 TFEU.

5. The action is detailed in Art. 263 TFEU.

6. In Case C-304/02 *Commission v. France* [2005] ECR I-6263, France was required by the Court to pay a penalty payment of €57,761,250 for each six-month period by the end of which it had not fully complied with the Court's previous judgment (delivered on 11 June 1991) and a lump-sum penalty of €20 million.

7. The Court expressed this principle as follows in its classic decision in Case 25/62 *Plaumann v. Commission* [1963] ECR 95, 107:

   if that decision affects them by reason of certain attributes which are peculiar to them or by reason of circumstances in which they are differentiated from all other persons and by virtue of these factors distinguishes them individually just as in the case of the person addressed.

8. For an overview of the problems caused by the Court's stance, see also the Opinion of Advocate General Jacobs in Case C-50/00 *P Unión de Pequeños Agricultores* [2002] ECR I-6677. Focusing specifically on the changes brought about by the Lisbon Treaty, but also sketching the debates prior to these reforms, see Balthasar (2010).

9. A famous example of a legislative act being annulled occurred in the *Tobacco Advertising Case* (Case C-376/98 *Germany v. Parliament and Council* [2000] ECR I-8419), in which the Court found that a directive prohibiting several forms of tobacco advertising, including advertising methods confined to one member state, such as cinema adverts, exceeded the competence to harmonize internal market standards provided for in the Treaty. A revised directive, focusing more expressly on cross-border advertising, was upheld by the Court in a second challenge (Case C-380/03 *Germany v. Parliament and Council* [2006] ECR I-11573).

10. In 2010, there were 385 references for a preliminary ruling, from a total of 631 new cases.

11. The procedure is outlined in Art. 267 TFEU.

12. See also the preface to the ECJ's proposal in May 2011 for amendments to its Rules of Procedure, available online at **http://curia.europa.eu/jcms/upload/docs/application/pdf/2011-05/en_rp_cjue.pdf**

13. In March 2011, the Court published proposals for reform of the chamber system, available online at **http://curia.europa.eu/jcms/upload/docs/application/pdf/2011-04/projet_en.pdf**

14. In the original EEC of six member states, there were seven ECJ judges for precisely this reason.

15. For further discussion of these themes and a useful bibliography, see Wasserfallen (2010).

16. This depiction comes from its landmark decisions in Case 26/62 *Van Gend en Loos v. Nederlandse Administratie der Belastingen* [1963] ECR 1 and Case 6/64 *Costa v. ENEL* [1964] ECR 585.

17. In a series of cases, the BVerfGE suggested that it would not review EU law for compatibility with the German Constitution 'so long as' threshold levels of protection of fundamental rights and other basic constitutional principles were embedded in EU law and the EU institutional structure (see Order of 29 May 1974 (*Solange I*) 37 BVerfGE 271; Order of 22 October 1986 (*Solange II*) 73 BVerfGE 339; Order of 12 October 1993 (*Maastricht*) 89 BVerfGE 155).

 FURTHER READING

Craig and de Búrca (2011) is one of the most comprehensive texts on EU law. There are specific chapters on the Court of Justice and also on, for example, the primacy of EU law. See also Alter (2001) for a political-science perspective on the evolution of primacy. Arnull (2006) is invaluable in two senses: first, he covers the organization of, and procedures before, the Court in analytical, as well as factual, depth; he then uses substantive case studies to demonstrate the influence of the institution through its material outputs. The premise of Maduro and Azoulai (2010) is a fascinating one: the collection selects cases that are considered to be 'classics' within ECJ output and then offers parallel comments on each from a range of different perspectives (present and former members of the Court, for example, but also academics who are not specialists in EU law). Weiler (1999) has written extensively on the Court's relationship with the broader development and integration of the Union. Burrows and Greaves (2007) is one of the few in-depth studies of the role of the Advocate General. Finally, looking outwards from Luxembourg, Slaughter (2004) locates the Court of Justice within a wider global 'community of courts'.

Alter, K. J. (2001) *Establishing the Supremacy of European Law* (Oxford and New York: Oxford University Press).

Arnull, A. (2006) *The European Union and its Court of Justice* (2nd edn, Oxford: Oxford University Press).

Burrows, N. and Greaves, R. (2007) *The Advocate General and EC Law* (Oxford: Oxford University Press).

Craig, P. and de Búrca, G. (2011) *EU Law: Text, Cases and Material* (5th edn, Oxford: Oxford University Press).

Maduro, M. and Azoulai, L. (2010) (eds) *The Past and Future of EU Law* (Oxford: Hart).

Slaughter, A.-M. (2004) *A New World Order* (Princeton, NJ: Princeton University Press).

Weiler, J. H. H. (1999) *The Constitution of Europe* (Cambridge: Cambridge University Press).

WEB LINKS

http://curia.europa.eu/

The Court's website provides access to all cases brought before the Court of Justice since 1953 and the General Court since 1989. The annual reports of the Court of Justice are also available on this website. It is a hugely valuable source of statistics and also institutional commentary on both the functioning and case law of the three CJEU courts. The annual reports detail the types of case that have arrived before the Court, how long it takes to get to judgment, which countries have enforcement proceedings pending against them, and so on. There are also valuable tables and charts covering statistical trends over the Court's history.

PART II

Managing the Union

CHAPTER 8

The Commission's Services

Liesbet Hooghe and Hussein Kassim

▌ Summary

The European Commission has always been considered one of the 'engines of Europe.' However, an increasingly sceptical public, the managerial challenge of Eastern enlargement, and allegations of mismanagement have forced the Commission to rethink its role. In 2000, the Commission embarked on an administrative overhaul to professionalize its services. According to some observers, this reform was to lead to the 'normalization' of the Commission into a traditional bureaucracy—but has it? How has the reform programme affected the organization, functions, and people of the Commission services? We conclude that the reforms have probably not weakened the Commission's capacity nor will to play a policy role, although we note distinct changes in appetite: the Commission bureaucracy has become more wary of bold political initiatives.

Introduction

Commentaries on the European Commission tend to focus more on the College, the political arm of the Commission (see Chapter 5), than on the services, the Commission's permanent bureaucracy. This disparity is not surprising. Commentaries on national political systems also tend to pay more attention to political executives than to bureaucracies. But in the case of the Commission, it is unwise to focus overly on the College, for the Commission services are not a normal bureaucracy. They exercise a central role—sometimes in a leading and sometimes in a supporting capacity—in virtually everything the Commission does. Few initiatives are launched, proposals made, or decisions taken by the Commission without being extensively examined and approved by the services.

The Commission was initially designed by the founding fathers to be one of the 'engines of Europe', and it has generally lived up to this role. But, over the past decade, European integration has changed dramatically. Three exogenous shocks—the emergence of an increasingly politicized climate, the resignation in 1999 of the Santer College, and the 2004 'Big Bang' enlargement—have forced the Commission to rethink its role. This rethinking provided the context for a reform programme, launched in 2000 by Commissioner Neil Kinnock, which reshaped the organization and the culture of the Commission services.

This chapter examines how the reform programme has affected the Commission's role as the engine of Europe. Has the institution been weakened, as some anticipated? How have the reforms affected the organization and functions of the services, and how have they influenced the people who work within them? We bring to bear evidence from a large-scale survey among Commission officials (N = 1,901) conducted in 2008 that taps into their political beliefs and attitudes on reform.[1]

Origins and evolution

The Commission's services have their origins in the High Authority of the European Coal and Steel Community (ECSC). Jean Monnet, the High Authority's first President, wanted it to be small and informal. Shortly after becoming President, Monnet (1978: 405) remarked to a fellow member of the High Authority: 'If one day there are more than two hundred of us, we shall have failed.'

Monnet's hopes were quickly dashed. Following its foundation in 1952, the High Authority rapidly acquired more staff, a more formal organization, and more bureaucratic procedures than Monnet had envisioned. When, in 1957–68, the Commissions of the European Economic Community (EEC) and the European Atomic Energy Community (Euratom) were established, their administrations were built on the High Authority model. With the mergers of the High Authority and the two Commissions in 1967, the single Commission that we know came into existence. Over the intervening years, the Commission's services have expanded their tasks as the European Union has come to touch on many aspects of European citizens' lives. Yet core features of the services have remained durable, as follows.

- The services have always been relatively impartial (that is, neutral in their policy stances, save perhaps for a certain pro-integration bias) and independent (that is, autonomous from national and sectoral interference). This impartiality has facilitated close working relationships with a host of governmental and non-governmental organizations. More than any national or international administration, the work of the Commission is intimately interwoven with that of national, regional, and local administrations.

- The administrative structure, organized around the Brussels equivalent of ministries, Directorates-General (DGs), has remained essentially unchanged. The number of DGs—and services (such as the Legal Service, Anti-Fraud Office, and so on) increased from fifteen in 1958 to forty-five by the late 1990s. By mid-2011, there were twenty-five DGs, nineteen services, and four types of agency.[2]

- The Commission has always been small in size compared to national administrations. There are good reasons for this. National governments have been reluctant to keep the EU's administrative budget in step with the expansion in tasks. Also, the Commission rarely implements EU policies and does not undertake much routine administration—two common bureaucratic activities that require large numbers of civil servants. In 1959, there were just over 1,000 full-time staff in the EEC Commission for a population of 172 million; in 1970, there were close to 5,300 in the merged Commission. By 1990, the number had increased to 16,000 for 343 million; by mid-2011, there were 22,500 full-time officials for half a billion EU citizens in twenty-seven member states. In addition, the Commission employs some 8,400 temporary agents, contract agents, and seconded officials.[3]

- Recruitment has been primarily meritocratic. Officials are recruited through competitive procedures, although this method has not always been applied strictly at the most senior levels. National governments have often insisted on a broadly proportional representation of their nationals in the top layers of the bureaucracy, and some key posts, such as the Directors-General for agriculture, development, or trade, have until recently tended to be reserved for particular nationalities. Commissioners, too, sometimes bend the rules of competitive recruitment to reward cabinet members with a permanent appointment.

- The services have consistently been involved in political, as well as administrative, activities, with the relative importance of the political being greater than in national administrations. Preparing EU legislation, managing funds, or conducting trade negotiations—tasks undertaken mainly by the services—have significant political ramifications. Monnet intended the Commission to set the agenda for Europe, and the services have generally lived up to his expectations.

What kind of bureaucracy does this make the Commission—or 'the House', in the language of Commission officials? The most core features can be traced back to three diverse bureaucratic models.

The Monnet model

Jean Monnet had a strong hand in shaping the early years of the Commission services. His vision was to recreate at European level a planning commission, based on the French *Commissariat du Plan* he had headed after the Second World War. The *Commissariat* was composed of a small high-level team of civil servants and experts outside the normal bureaucratic hierarchy, whose main job was to produce five-year national economic plans. In the same vein, Monnet wanted the High Authority to be made up of a small, organizationally flexible and adaptable, multinational nucleus of individuals. It was to be their role to develop ideas, and to stimulate and persuade others, but to leave implementation to national administrations. As François Duchêne (1994: 240) put it in his biography of Monnet, there was 'a comic incompatibility of humour between Monnet and routine administration'. Monnet did not want a permanent core of civil servants.

This Monnet spirit is still palpable. By and large, Commission officials focus on designing policies and rely on national or regional administrations to implement most EU legislation. They are an exceptionally diverse and multinational collection of people. And though officials have career tenure, the Commission is more inclined than national administrations to attract experts from outside.

National bureaucratic models

Monnet was never able to mould the High Authority wholly according to his vision. From the start, the nature and range of its responsibilities and the watchful eye—if not suspicion—of member states meant that it came to have much in common with national bureaucracies. That is to say, from an early stage the services were strongly shaped by Weberian principles and modes of operation. Hierarchy, formality, and impartiality became key organizational principles.

Particular national bureaucratic traditions have also fed into the shaping of the services. The strongest national signature remains French, which, while weaker now than in the early years of European integration, is still apparent in the Commission's organizational structure and terminology. For example, the terms for senior positions are borrowed from the French model: *directeur-général*; *directeur-général-adjoint*; *directeur*; *conseiller*; and *chef de cabinet*.

International organization models

The Commission also has features of an international bureaucracy. Indeed, the League of Nations and the United Nations secretariats were models for the High Authority. The influence of international organization bureaucratic models is evident in the special work conditions of Commission officials, such as their relatively high pay and special status in the host country. Generous terms of employment are designed to help officials to resist outside pressures. In return, Commission officials (as well as Commissioners) pledge neither to seek nor receive instructions from their home state. Like international civil servants, Commission officials also benefit from tax privileges and limited immunity against prosecution, although some of these privileges have been curtailed by the most recent personnel reform.

The international legacy is also evident in persistent conundrums that the Commission faces, including:

- how to wed meritocracy with national representation;
- how to guarantee officials' impartiality while recognizing their national allegiances; and
- how to provide political entrepreneurship in the absence of electoral accountability.

The Commission has always been an amalgam of diverse traditions, but these are now partially under revision. The unstated purpose is to make the Commission services look more like any other professional administration. However, as we describe below, after a decade of reform, the threads of continuity appear as strong as those of change.

Powers, structure, and functioning

What is the role of the services in the Commission as a whole? What are their powers and functions, and how are the services organized? As we will see, the basic structural features have remained relatively untouched by the Kinnock reforms launched in 2000. The thrust of the reform pertains to how the services organize their work—both in-house and in relation to member states, third parties, and the public—as well as to how they recruit and promote personnel, to which we turn in the next section.

The College and the services

If political and administrative tasks could be disentangled, the College would be responsible for politics and the services for administration. In the wake of the Santer College's resignation in 1999 (see Chapter 5), Commission President Romano Prodi sought to make the distinction between political and administrative tasks clearer by 'reducing the grey areas which currently tend to blur demarcation lines of autonomy and responsibility between those performing more political tasks and those more involved with administration' (Prodi 1999).

In practice, the role of the services is not easily separated from that of Commissioners and their cabinets. There are a number of reasons why. To begin with, what is 'a political decision', and what is 'routine' or 'administration'? So, for example, deciding whether a new product is subject to an existing EU law on product standards may appear to be an administrative matter. However, the decision may be contested by important economic or social interests.

Second, Commissioners usually rely on the services for information, advice, and the preparation of documentation. The services are the main repository of accumulated wisdom in the Commission. While Commissioners and cabinets come and go, the services hold the fort.

Third, Commission officials are often the hub of policy networks involving key EU actors, and therefore inevitably influence political choices.

Finally, and arguably most importantly, Commissioners have to contend with a strong tradition of policy entrepreneurship among Commission officials, since the administration as a whole enjoys a monopoly on the right of initiative: no EU legislative decision may be made unless the Commission decides to propose it. Monnet's intent to create a team of creative thinkers echoes powerfully. This ethos is reinforced by the fact that officials often have career reasons to defend their right to make policy.

Powers and functions

The role of the European Commission is described in the Treaty establishing the European Community. The Commission has a constitutional obligation to set the legislative agenda in the European Union (Art. 211). Again, its most important power is that it has exclusive formal competence to initiate and draft EU legislation. The Council of Ministers and the European Parliament (EP) may request the Commission to draft an initiative, but the Commission can, and sometimes does, refuse to do so. The Treaty also instructs the Commission to serve the European interest, and it requires the Commission to be independent from any national government.[4]

Most powers and functions of the Commission apply to the services as well as to the College, and they combine to put the services in a position that is unparalleled among international and national civil services. It is true that ultimate political responsibility for Commission actions lies with the College, but, in practice, the services have considerable leeway to act on behalf of the Commission. Commissioners and their cabinets usually simply do not have the time, information, or political will to monitor their civil servants or to control their actions fully. Over 85 per cent of 'Commission' decisions are adopted without being put on the College of Commissioners' agenda for discussion.

The Commission's powers and functions can be grouped under six headings:

- policy initiator;
- legislative facilitator;
- executive roles;
- legal guardian;
- mediator and broker; and
- external representative and negotiator.

Policy initiator

The single most important power of the Commission is its virtually exclusive Treaty right to draft legislative proposals. This prerogative guarantees the Commission pole position in initiating policies. The Commission maintains this position whether it deals with broadly based policy initiatives or proposals to develop/revise narrow 'technical' policies.

Many different actors in addition to the Commission may attempt to initiate EU policy. The European Council and the Council of Ministers regularly request policy papers from the Commission. The EP can prod the Commission to start initiatives. Member states, especially when they occupy the Council presidency, table policy documents and proposals at Council meetings. Interest groups make policy submissions to relevant DGs. However, to be turned into legislation, such proposals must be picked up by the Commission. No other body can draft legislation or direct how the Commission should respond to requests to bring forward legislative drafts.

There are a couple of dents in the Commission's monopoly of initiative. Most importantly, the Commission does not initiate legislation in common foreign and security policy (CFSP) and in some areas of police cooperation. In all other fields, the Council and Parliament can request legislation, although the Commission has the power to refuse, as it did in 2008 over transnational collective conventions. Since the Lisbon Treaty, EU citizens are also able to request the Commission to legislate in an area via a petition carrying 1 million signatures, but any such request is not binding.

Legislative facilitator

The Commission also acts as a key legislative facilitator. It is the only institution present throughout the legislative process—at meetings in the Council of Ministers, in the Parliament, and at inter-institutional meetings. This continuing presence gives it knowledge not only of what the legislators in the Council and the EP ideally want, but also what they are prepared to accept.

The bulk of EU legislation now uses the ordinary legislative procedure (previously called the codecision procedure). The Commission initiates a proposal and, after consultation of national parliaments and, where required by the Treaty, the Committee of the Regions (CoR) or the Economic and Social Committee (EESC), it engages in a layered negotiation game with the EP and the Council of Ministers that can stretch over three rounds. In the first two stages (first reading and second reading), the Commission's legislative role is pivotal: it can withdraw its proposal, amend it, or raise the voting hurdle in the Council of Ministers by accepting amendments passed by the Parliament. Once the Council and the EP convene in a conciliation meeting, which is the third and last stage, the Commission loses the right to withdraw its proposal and it can also no longer raise the bar to unanimity in the Council if it disagrees with the Parliament's amendments. At that point, it is charged with taking 'all the necessary initiatives with a view to reconciling the positions of the European Parliament and the Council' (Art. 294, para. 11 TEU). These are the legal rules, but political practice has diverged. In the recent political climate of resurgent intergovernmentalism, it has become increasingly difficult for the Commission to withdraw its proposal if not requested to do so by Parliament or Council.

The bottom line is pretty clear: with the exception of the few policy areas mentioned above, every initiative begins with the Commission. No national bureaucracy and virtually no other international governmental body has this kind of authority. Comparative examples that spring to mind are the Commission in the Economic Community of West-African States (ECOWAS) and, within much narrower parameters, the General Secretary of the International Monetary Fund (IMF).

Executive roles

In a few policy areas, the Commission has direct implementation responsibilities. The most important of these is competition, in which it has to decide, for example, whether state aids and certain types of takeover or merger are permissible under EU law. In most policy areas, however, the Commission relies on national or regional governments, or external agencies, to do the work. About 80 per cent of the EU budget is implemented by third parties. The Commission's role in respect of this 80 per cent is largely limited to putting an implementation framework in place—that is, rules that tell national or regional governments or agencies how to implement EU legislation.

Such implementation frameworks—for example, rules prescribing how to test technical product standards, or how to set prices for agricultural products—must normally be channelled through a so-called comitology committee, of which there were 266 in 2009.[5] The comitology network is densest in enterprise and industry, environment, transport and energy, justice and security, and health and consumers. Here, member state representatives, scientific experts, and interest-group representatives watch closely how the Commission monitors the implementation of EU policies by third parties. Comitology is the living embodiment of how different institutions and different levels of government have become intertwined. Unilateral action by one institution has become virtually impossible.

Legal guardian

The Commission—along with the European Court of Justice (ECJ)—is also charged with ensuring that EU law is applied uniformly throughout the member states. The Commission is heavily dependent on 'whistle-blowing' to be made aware of possible breaches of EU law. Its limited resources mean that only a relatively small number of likely breaches can be pursued all the way to Court. The usual approach is to resolve the matter informally. But, from time to time, the Commission organizes dawn raids on suspected firms, which, if found guilty, may end up paying hefty fines. The Commission may impose fines of up to 1 per cent of a company's total turnover for the preceding business year for failure to provide accurate information or refusal to submit to an inspection. Since the 1993 Maastricht Treaty, the Commission can also take member states to court. The first fine imposed on a member state was in July 2000, when the ECJ ordered the Greek government to pay €20,000 for each day of continued non-compliance with a 1992 Court judgment concerning the disposal of toxic and dangerous waste at a plant on the island of Crete.

Mediator and broker

EU decision-making involves a multiplicity of actors eager to influence policy. Within this multilevel system, there is a strong need for mediation and brokerage, for which the Commission is particularly well placed. The Commission tends to have the best overall understanding of the positions of decision-making actors—a knowledge that stems from its contacts across the EU and its extensive involvement in EU policy processes. It is also more likely to be perceived as impartial, in contrast with, for example, the Council presidency, parliamentary groups, or interest-group representatives.

External representative and negotiator

The Commission negotiates trade matters on behalf of the EU. It takes the lead during enlargement negotiations and shares responsibilities with member states in foreign policy, development policy, and the external dimensions of such policies as transport, environment, and competition.

The Commission's influence depends on the character of the policy. It is greatest in policy areas such as those that:

- fall under what used to be called the first (EC) pillar (notably trade and the single market);
- have been subject to extensive transfer of competence, such as enlargement;
- do not normally raise too much political sensitivity, such as development;
- require impartial leadership, such as competition; and
- require technical expertise, such as agriculture or environment.

Structure

The Commission services are organized into DGs and general and internal services. DGs are normally concerned with policy sectors, such as trade, environment, competition, or climate action. Other services usually handle horizontal tasks, such as the Secretariat General, the Legal Service, and the Publications Office, or they have a specific mandate, such as fighting fraud or compiling statistics. A recent development is the creation of agencies set up for a fixed period to manage Community programmes, such as the European Research Council or the Executive Agency for Health and Consumers.

The Commission's most senior official is the Secretary General. There have been only five Secretaries General in the history of the Commission: Émile Noël (1958–87; French); David Williamson (1987–97; British); Carlo Trojan (1997–2000; Dutch); David O'Sullivan (2000–05; Irish); and, since 2005, Catherine Day (also Irish and the first woman to hold this post). The Secretary General is the captain on the ship. She and her services ensure that all parts of the Commission coordinate activities, act in accordance with formal procedures, and liaise properly with other institutions—notably the Council of Ministers and the EP—and outside bodies. Under Émile Noël and, to a lesser extent, David Williamson, the Secretary General was also a formidable policy-shaper. Several important new policy ideas—including cohesion policy, justice and home affairs (JHA) policy, asylum policy, and foreign policy—were nursed in the Secretariat General. The two subsequent Secretary Generals interpreted their role in more strictly managerial terms. Catherine Day has steered between these poles and has, perhaps more than her predecessors, understood her role to be to extend the arm of the Commission President into the services.

Each DG or service is headed by a Director General, who may be assisted by one or more deputies. Directors General give instructions to Directors, who head a Directorate. An average-sized DG has between three and five directorates, each of which is composed of between three and seven units—the lowest organizational level in the Commission. A typical unit contains between twelve and fourteen officials, of whom, aside from the unit head, between four and six work on policy development, two or three are assisting clerks, and between three and five are mainly involved in secretarial and other administrative work. These people are often supplemented by one or two contractual positions.

The Commission under pressure

In the first decade of the twenty-first century, the Commission's services came under intense pressure to reform. This pressure was largely a consequence of three external shocks to the system.

The first shock was the demise of the 'permissive consensus' on European integration. The Danish 'no' and the very narrow French 'yes' in referenda on the 1992 Maastricht Treaty heralded a new era—one in which European integration had become more politically contentious (Hooghe and Marks 2009). Governments found it increasingly difficult to control debate on key issues of European integration. Should national sovereignty be diluted? Should further market integration be implemented? Should the EU be expanded? More people, from political parties to ordinary citizens, wished to have their say. The Convention on the Future of Europe was intended to bring the Union closer to citizens and involve them in a debate about the form that integration might take. But the 'no' votes in the 2005 referenda on the Constitutional Treaty in France and the Netherlands signalled that the exercise had not succeeded. Politicization has weakened the Commission's claim to be the primary agenda-setter for Europe (Kassim and Menon 2004). In a polity that struggles to be democratic, decisions by unelected Commission officials have questionable legitimacy. There has therefore been increased pressure on the Commission to justify what it is doing and to be more deferential to elected politicians. Under the (first, at least) Barroso presidency, it did precisely that.

Second, the EU moved towards the most challenging enlargement in its history to include a swathe of former communist states. With the 2004 and 2007 enlargements, the EU faced a policy environment in which problems became more diverse across the Union, resources scarcer, decisions more contentious, and implementation more haphazard. No institution has been left unaffected by enlargement, but the impact on the Commission services has been particularly great. The Commission has invested extensive personnel resources in the accession process and it will continue to do so for some time to come. It has also been overhauling its own organization to make space for new nationals. Such an exercise is never popular among existing staff, since it diminishes promotion opportunities. Moreover, there is considerable disillusionment among recruits from the new member states. Personnel reforms by the Commission that adversely affected both pay and promotion came into force on the same day as the accession of ten new members. A survey conducted in 2008 reveals that two-thirds (66.4 per cent) of staff either disagreed or strongly disagreed with the proposition that the personal implications of 'enlargement [were] handled with equity and fairness' (Kassim *et al.* 2012).

Finally, the EU struggled through a major institutional crisis in 1999, provoked by alleged malpractice in the Commission services. In March 1999, the Santer College resigned in the face of allegations of nepotism, fraud, and mismanagement of funds. The immediate cause was the publication of a report by a Committee of Independent Experts (1999a), which had been established at the EP's insistence to investigate accusations of maladministration in the Commission. Most media attention was directed to those parts of the Committee's report that detailed acts of favouritism by some Commissioners, but the real message of the report was that there were serious performance problems in the Commission services. A second Experts' Report, published in September 1999, exposed in great detail shortcomings in financial management (Committee of Independent Experts 1999b). This report provided the immediate context for a comprehensive reorganization of the services.

The reform programme

Aims

Against a backdrop of politicization, enlargement, and the 1999 resignation crisis, the Commission moved to overhaul its administration. The incoming Prodi College (1999) was compelled by the European Council to make internal Commission re-form a top priority. Prodi himself announced a number of measures soon after his nomination as Commission President. But one of his first acts was to persuade Neil Kinnock, a Commissioner in the Santer Commission and a former leader of the Brit-ish Labour Party (which he had reformed), to oversee the reform task as Vice Presi-dent. Under the banner of modernization, Kinnock moved quickly to begin preparing a blueprint. The outcome was the reform White Paper, which set out a comprehen-sive programme and was adopted by the College in May 2000.

In the introduction to the White Paper, the Commission stated that:

We want the Commission to have a public administration that excels so that it can con-tinue to fulfill its tasks under the Treaties with maximum effectiveness. The citizens of the Union deserve no less, the staff of the Commission want to provide no less. To fulfill that objective, we must keep the best of the past and combine it with new systems designed to face the challenges of the future. The world around us is changing fast. The Commission itself, therefore, needs to be independent, accountable, efficient and trans-parent, and guided by the highest standards of responsibility.

(Commission 2000, Part I: 3)

The central aims were to make the Commission more professional, more efficient, and more focused on core tasks.

Content

Box 8.1 outlines the main goals and measures of the reform programme. The Com-mission's basic organizational structure has remained unchanged. However, new systems have been introduced, operational principles amended, and the internal organization of individual DGs altered, with departments compelled to create new divisions or units responsible for managerial functions.

One set of measures is aimed at making the Commission more 'service-oriented' and more accountable to its principals—the EP, member states, interest groups, and Europe's citizens. The Commission has ensured faster payment of invoices, increased electronic access to documents, and adopted guidelines for consultation with civil society. Perhaps the single most important change is the introduction of a system of centralized strategic policy planning, which aims to ensure greater coordination, more predictability, and better matching of resources to objectives. The system tries to achieve a sensitive balancing act. On the one hand, the Commission's (2000: 5) responsibility to conceptualize policy is reinforced so as to 'fulfil its institutional role as the motor of European integration'; on the other, the Commission is induced to do less by prioritizing core tasks.

BOX 8.1	The Commission's internal reform programme

PRINCIPLES AND GOALS	MOST IMPORTANT MEASURES
SERVICE-ORIENTED COMMISSION CULTURE Five core principles: • Independence from national and sectoral interests • Clear division of responsibility • Accountability • Efficiency • Transparency	• New codes of conduct for Commissioners and for relations between Commissioners and departments • Faster payment of invoices: no more than sixty days later • Framework agreement on relations with European Parliament • Whistleblower's charter • Improved public access to documents • Guidelines for consultation of civil society groups; public listing of interest groups in committees or working groups • E-Commission: electronic accessibility of documents and contacts
PRIORITY SETTING, ALLOCATION, AND EFFICIENT USE OF RESOURCES • Strategic planning • Externalization of non-core tasks	• Introduction of new public management-influenced principles • Activity-based management (ABM): new system that organizes what Commission does in substantive rather than budgetary categories • Annual policy strategy (APS) combined with annual management programme (AMP): Commission sets policy priorities and allocates resources in APS, which provides basis for departments' AMPs and is updated every three months • Detailed, regularly updated job descriptions for each official • New rules for externalization of non-core tasks: devolution to executive EU agencies, decentralization to national administrations, and contractual outsourcing to private parties
A MERITOCRATIC PERSONNEL POLICY • Merit above nationality • Managerial training • Mobility and flexibility	• Staff reform: two-track career structure, reorganization of non-permanent staff, changes in pay and pension provisions • Training: fourfold increase of budget, management skills criterion for promotion • New statute for seconded national officials • Senior management: open competition, merit and experience, no national quotas, compulsory mobility • Transitional rules for enlargement candidates
EFFECTIVE FINANCIAL MANAGEMENT • Decentralization • Faster and simpler procedures	• Separation of financial control and internal auditing; creation of two centralized services—one to help DGs to manage their finances, the other to conduct internal auditing • Financial accountability decentralized to DGs, if feasible down to official who decides a particular action • Enhanced cooperation with national administrations • Strengthening of OLAF, the anti-fraud office

Source: **Kassim (2004b)**

At first sight, this new system seems at odds with the Monnet tradition of policy activism and political entrepreneurship. But the implications of the new rules are ambivalent. To the extent that the services' energies are refocused on 'core functions such as policy conception, political initiation and enforcing Community law' and 'away from managing programmes and projects and directly controlling the latter' (Commission 2000: 5), the services may end up doing *less* hands-on routine administration and *more* policy initiation—and that would be close to Monnet's heart.

There have also been major changes in personnel policy. Meritocracy is now given clear preference over the claims of nationality in recruitment and promotion. Structures and procedures have been put in place intended to make it more difficult for national governments to interfere with Commission personnel policy. Research on promotion in the wake of the reform suggests that the reform has succeeded in giving the Commission a new independence from the member states in the appointment of senior officials (Egeberg 2003). The Kinnock reforms also encourage mobility throughout the services, especially at the most senior levels, where Directors General can no longer spend more than five years in the same post, and management training is mandatory.

Finally, there has been a comprehensive overhaul of the Commission's financial management and control procedures. Under the old system, an official wanting to implement a particular proposal was compelled to secure a 'visa' to approve the associated expenditure from a central finance department. In other words, policy-making took place independently of financial planning or budgetary awareness, and there was no incentive for policy officers to incorporate financial planning or value for money in their decision-making. The reform has decentralized financial responsibility to units and even to individual officials, separated financial control and auditing, simplified accounting procedures, and reorganized and intensified cooperation with national administrations, which are often the culprits in the mismanagement of EU funds.

The thrust of the reform reflects principles of the new public management (NPM) philosophy, which applies principles and practices from the private sector, such as competition, cost-effectiveness, outsourcing, and customer satisfaction, to public service (Hood 1991). Thus the Commission has followed the wave of NPM-inspired reforms that has swept across most democratic states since the 1980s. Because its direct delivery functions are limited, the Commission has not adopted the model wholesale. Nevertheless, the effect has been to shift the Commission in the direction of the Anglo-Saxon bureaucracies and away from the Franco-German influences that have historically shaped its practices (Balint *et al.* 2008; Kassim *et al.* 2012: ch. 8).

Externalizing Commission work

A particularly contentious aspect of the reform programme concerns the externalization of financial, administrative, and support tasks to agencies outside the Commission. Externalization is not a new phenomenon; many subsidy programmes in agricultural or regional policy have been managed by contractors, who organize (but do not decide on) project selection and administer funds. The main purposes of externalization are to allow Commission staff to concentrate on policy-making, and to save money. However, the Commission is walking a fine line between economizing, on the one hand, and ensuring accountability, on the other. This was the flashpoint in the 1999 crisis, when the Commission was accused of having encouraged mismanagement in outsourced offices because it did not have proper supervision in place.

The reform package distinguishes between three kinds of externalization: devolution to EU agencies; decentralization to national administrations; and outsourcing through contracts with private parties. For each category, rules of engagement and oversight have been standardized and tightened. The basic principle is that the Commission remains responsible for making policy, but external agents take on implementation. By streamlining the rules, Kinnock paved the way for a substantial increase of externalization, even over and beyond substantive policy programmes and into administration. For example, in January 2003, the DG for Personnel spun off part of its tasks to three offices: one for the payment of all Commission staff, and the other two for managing Commission buildings and infrastructure in Brussels and Luxembourg. The Commission justified the decision by pointing out that externalizing these tasks should shave 18 per cent off operational costs.

Streamlining personnel policy

Contrary to the myth that Brussels is a sprawling bureaucracy, the Commission services are small in size, totalling just under 31,000 officials in 2011. The Commission's core of full-time officials consists of about 12,600 policy-making officials who make policy, negotiate with other EU institutions and outside bodies, and represent the EU abroad. Prior to the reforms, these officials were known as 'A-category' officials in what was a four-category personnel career structure. Now, they are described as 'administrators' in a two-grade system. There are also about 700 temporary agents at administrator level. Members of Commission cabinets fall into this category, as do individuals attracted to meet temporary staff shortages or to provide short-term expertise (for example, to evaluate Commission-funded research programmes).

Administrators are assisted by administrative assistants, clerks, and translators, of whom there are about 11,300 in total. Before the personnel reforms, these people populated 'B' and 'C' grades; they are now called 'assistants', and constitute the second group of the new two-track system. There are also some 3,500 researchers, half of whom are employed in the Ispra/Varese facilities of the Commission in northern Italy on fixed-term contracts. Just over 70 per cent of Commission staff reside in Brussels; the other 30 per cent work in Luxembourg (such as for the Statistical Office), in Italy, or in one of the manifold EU agencies across the Union. The 2,000 officials previously located in the 120 Commission delegations in third countries have been absorbed into the new European External Action Service (EEAS).

One goal of the reform programme is to scale down non-*fonctionnaire* numbers by reducing temporary staff, and by off-loading non-core tasks to national administrations or to contract staff. Conversely, two important categories outside the core are set to grow: seconded national officials; and contract agents. Seconded national officials are usually sent from national or regional civil services to work in the Commission for up to four years (until the Kinnock reform, up to three years). Exceptionally, they may be detached from the private sector or from non-profit organizations. New rules make it easier for DGs to attract national officials, although the number is not to rise above 30 per cent of a DG's permanent policy-making staff. Secondment allows the Commission to attract specialist expertise from national administrations or from the private sector. It also gives national, regional, or local civil servants the opportunity to gain experience with EU programmes, which is particularly important for new member states. There were just over 1,000 seconded national officials in the Commission in 2011.

The second category to expand consists of contract agents. Most of these agents work in the outsourced agencies: some are temporarily employed as in-house 'consultants', 'experts', or 'advisers' (previously called 'auxiliary staff'), whilst others are locals working in the various Commission representations and delegations in and outside the EU. Before the reforms began to take effect, the Commission employed about 1,250 contract agents. There are now close to 5,900.

Seconded national officials and contract agents are cheaper for the Commission than permanent staff. Seconded national officials are almost 'freebees': they receive their salary from their national employer, and only a top-up for daily living expenses from the Commission. Contract staff are usually paid 10–15 per cent less than comparable Commission staff. It is also easier for managers in the departments to employ a seconded national official or contract agent than to rely on the Commission's time-consuming procedures for recruiting full-time administrators.

The Commission also hosts about 1,200 trainees per year—known as *stagiaires*. These are usually graduate students, who spend up to five months in the Commission gaining work experience. Competition for these jobs is cut-throat, especially for popular DGs such as external relations or press and communication. To be appointed, it can help to know someone in the services who can make a recommendation from the long list of candidates. *Stagiaires* perform supportive tasks, which can range from copying, to researching background information, to assisting discussions in Commission committees.

Recruitment and training

The reform programme leaves existing recruitment policy basically intact, but upgrades training. Nearly all new officials in policy-making positions are recruited by written and oral examination: the *concours*. Competition is intense and there are usually, for each vacancy, well over a hundred qualified candidates—that is, people with a good academic qualification and high proficiency in at least one language in addition to their mother tongue. Candidates who pass the *concours* are placed on a reserve list from which they may be cherry-picked by an interested DG. Nationality is in principle not a criterion, but overrepresented nationalities, such as Belgians and Italians, find it more difficult to jump from the reserve list to a permanent job.

A minority of middle- and higher-level officials are recruited directly. The rules for recruitment from outside have been tightened and, as a result, there are fewer external appointments: between 2000 and 2002 the figure was about 20 per cent among the most senior level (Directors-General) and about 8 per cent among Directors, down from about 50 per cent in the mid-1990s. All vacancies need to be posted publicly and require a competitive process. There are good reasons for maintaining flexibility at senior levels. For one thing, recent member states would otherwise have to wait a very long time before they would have nationals in the senior ranks. Lateral appointments also make it possible to attract scientific or managerial talent to take on specialist jobs.

The biggest change in personnel policy is the virtual elimination of nationality as a criterion for the Commission's top management. National quotas—'geographical balance' is the official expression—used to be very strict at the most senior level and included informal country flags for some key positions. For example, Germans were usually in strategic positions in the Competition DG, French officials were prominent in the Agriculture DG, Italians in economic and monetary affairs posts, and British in external affairs positions (Page 1997: 54). However, the rules now explicitly state that merit and experience should prevail over nationality: 'The nationality of the outgoing post holder is not a factor in the appointment of the new occupant' (Commission 2002). The only nod to nationality is that 'each nationality should have at least one post as Director General, Deputy Director General or equivalent', although this aspiration is not always fulfilled.

The training budget has increased substantially. Much attention is given to enhancing managerial skills, with candidates for senior posts now needing to demonstrate solid management experience. The development of financial reporting and accounting skills has also been prioritized.

Assessing the reform

Although the design and enactment of the reform was an historic accomplishment, wide-ranging and implemented within a remarkably short timeframe, the extent to which it has succeeded in securing its objectives is not amenable to any clear-cut judgement. Certainly with respect to two of its chapters—financial management and control, and the staff rules—the reform has led to a replacement of practices and procedures that were antiquated and problematic (see Stevens 2001: ch. 5). In personnel policy, the reform has strengthened the Commission's independence from national governments. Yet while the underlying principles—greater accountability and better management accounting in financial management; merit and performance in staff policy—may be sound, their implementation has not necessarily been sure-footed. The new system of appraisal, especially its career development review (CDR), was regarded as fundamentally flawed and the changes introduced by the Barroso Commission—tagged by critics 'the reform of the reform'—have seemingly created new difficulties.

An important criterion in judging a reform is whether it has carried officials along with it. The evidence in the case of the Commission is, at best, mixed. Aside from the emphasis on training, which has been warmly welcomed by staff, officials appear not to be impressed (see Kassim *et al.* 2012: ch. 7). They generally register negative opinions on most elements of the reform programme. There are, however, some exceptions. Senior managers—Directors General, deputy Directors General, and Directors—are supportive of the reform, which introduced new tools that make it easier for them to perform their steering role. Officials from member states in which NPM-style reforms have been introduced—the UK and Ireland, as well as the Scandinavian countries and the countries of Central and Eastern Europe—tend also to take a more positive approach. More surprising, perhaps, is that longer-serving officials, as well as the most recently recruited, are more supportive of the reform.

At the same time, it is important to recall that administrative reform is a precarious enterprise, that it can rarely be deemed entirely successful, and that positive evaluations are, in fact, rare (see Wright 1997; Pollitt and Bouckaert 2004). Certainly, support among bureaucrats is likely to be variegated. Moreover, reform of a multinational administration, especially one the supranational responsibilities of which distinguish it from most international secretariats, presents very particular challenges. To summarize, while it would be an exaggeration to claim that the Commission has been transformed into a modern administration, it has taken important steps in that direction.

Commission officials' attitudes to EU governance

The Treaty creates clear expectations for Commission officials. It prescribes that they must put the Union's interest first, set the agenda for the EU, and promote the Union's interest independently from national pressures. The Commission's internal staff regulations reinforce these prescriptions by instructing that:

an official shall carry out his duties and conduct himself *solely with the interests of the Communities in mind*; he shall neither seek nor take instructions from any government, authority, organization or person outside his institution. ... *He shall carry out the duties assigned to him objectively, impartially and in keeping with his duty of loyalty to the Communities.* [Emphasis added]

(Commission Staff Regulations 2005, Art. 11)

These norms have roots in the pioneering days. The Commission's autonomy, all-European focus, and its exclusive power of initiative were crucial to Monnet's conception of the Commission as the engine of Europe, and he persuaded member states to enshrine them in the Treaty. In the early 1960s, Émile Noël, the Commission's first Secretary-General, institutionalized them in Commission staff rules and practices.

The norms were not challenged head-on by those seeking to reform the Commission. Thus the 2000 White Paper on reforming the Commission (2000: 7) states that:

the original and essential source of the success of European integration is that the EU's executive body, the Commission, is supranational and independent from national, sectoral or other influences. This is at the heart of its ability to advance the interests of the European Union.

But some observers anticipated that one by-product of the reform, intended or not, would be a cooling of the political agenda-setting ambitions of Commission officials. In other words, the Commission bureaucracy would become more like a normal civil service executing orders given elsewhere.

Sixty years after the Commission's inception, to what extent do Commission officials still subscribe to Monnet's core philosophy? Has the most challenging decade in the Commission's existence weakened core norms? What has been the effect of the administrative reform, if any, on Commission attitudes? Have officials from the new member states adopted those traditional norms? We bring to bear evidence from three surveys of Commission officials in 1996, 2002, and 2008. The first two surveys were conducted among the senior ranks of the Commission bureaucracy: Director-Generals, Deputy Director-Generals, Directors, and principal advisers (Hooghe 2002, 2005.) The 2008 survey polled a representative sample of the Commission bureaucracy (Hooghe 2012; Kassim *et al.* 2012).

Agenda-setting, nationality, and primacy

To determine whether Monnet's core ideas have survived, we first have to be clear about what we mean by 'Monnet's ideas'. A narrow understanding emphasizes features of the Commission's immediate environment: the extent to which the Commission (rather than member states or the EP) initiates policy, and the role of nationality in the Commission's daily operation. A broader conception also considers the location of the Commission in the future EU institutional architecture—as the *primus inter pares* in a federal Union, the servant in an intergovernmental polity, or an indispensable, but not all-powerful, player in a multilevel system of governance. Surveys of Commission officials' attitudes enable us to monitor changing views on these elements over time.

Let us follow first senior officials, for whom we have data for 1996, 2002, and 2008. There is a noticeable upward trend in support for Commission agenda-setting power from 1996 to 2008 (see Table 8.1). Large majorities of senior Commission officials (between 60 and 85 per cent) find it desirable that the Commission retains its monopoly of initiative rather than shares it with the EP. Interestingly, while previous surveys detected a tendency among senior officials to give precedence to management

TABLE 8.1 Commission officials and support for Monnet norms (percentages)

Monnet norms	1996 (senior officials)	2002 (senior officials)	2008 (senior officials)	2008 (rank-and-file)	2008 (new member states)	2008 (old member states)
Agenda-setting						
Commission should *not* give up sole right of initiative to European Parliament	62.1	83.7	72.8	56.0	50.9	60.9
Administration or management should *not* be the Commission's priority	42.9	36.6	86.5	78.1	78.4	80.2
Nationality in Commission						
Qualifications should prevail over national quotas/posts should *not* be distributed according to national quotas or geographical balance*	74.7	62.4	44.0	48.3	31.1	53.2
The Commission's role in the EU institutional architecture						
Member states should *not* be the central pillars of the EU	65.0	83.7	81.9	78.6	75.2	80.4
College of Commissioners should be the government of the European Union	48.6	60.2	41.9	38.8	33.8	42.2

Note: Percentage supporting a statement: N = 105 in 1996; N = 93 in 2002; N = 186 (senior officials), N = 1540 (rank-and-file), N = 418 (new member states), and N = 1292 (old member states) in 2008. For details on the 1996 and 2002 surveys, see **http://www.unc.edu/~hooghe**. For details on the 2008 survey, see Hooghe (2012) and Kassim *et al.* (2012).

*Statement wording varies over time (see text).

over initiative, the 2008 survey observes a counter-movement away from management towards initiative. Contrary to what many pundits claim, politicization, enlargement, and the Commission crisis have (thus far) not weakened the view that the Commission should be able to initiate policy; on the contrary, this preference has intensified.

One major objective of the administrative reform programme was to focus attention on administrative management. This move ran counter to Monnet, who saw a basic contradiction between the need to provide political leadership and the duty to administer, and, when forced, relegated the Commission's administrative and managerial tasks to second place—a choice not always appreciated by his colleagues. By the mid-1990s, the Commission's senior officials were not so sure about the wisdom of Monnet's choice. The glorious years of Commission leadership under Jacques Delors (1985–95) left a sour aftertaste when, a few years later, accusations of mismanagement and nepotism were slung at the College and the Commission bureaucracy. Many senior officials had seen it coming and supported a correction (Hooghe 2001). As Table 8.1 shows, already in 1996—before the Santer crisis—a majority of senior Commission officials wanted to make management and administration a priority. By 2002, at the cusp of the administrative reform, support for this view had grown, with only 37 per cent of officials agreeing with the statement that administrative management should *not* be a priority. The administrative reform was implemented in the subsequent years. However, by the end of 2008, the overwhelming majority of senior officials (86 per cent) wanted the Commission to focus *more* on initiative again. Perhaps the administrative managerial pendulum had swung far enough or perhaps the challenges of enlargement had made the Commission leadership change its mind.

Most Commission officials explain the need for strong Commission agenda-setting power in pragmatic terms. They argue that Commission leadership tends to produce better results than member state guidance. Time and again during interviews, officials contrast the relatively smooth handling of enlargement or climate change, in which the Commission has taken the lead, with well-documented examples of inefficient or botched member state guidance, such as the failure to manage the break-up of Yugoslavia, the aborted attempt to negotiate external trade in services, deadlocks in immigration and asylum policy, and, more recently, the financial crisis. Furthermore, many top officials warn that enlargement will grind EU decision-making to a halt unless the Commission gains more power and can preserve its right of initiative.

Monnet also emphasized the need for officials to be independent of national interests. The strongest tool for this is a personnel policy that allocates posts on the basis of merit instead of nationality. Administrative reform has reinforced this shift by asserting that merit, not national quotas, should determine promotion and recruitment, especially at the highest ranks. In Table 8.1, support amongst senior officials for this principle is considerable, but it softened from 75 per cent in 1996 to 62 per cent in 2002. In 2008, the support base had shrunk to a plurality of senior officials (44 per cent, with another 17 per cent neither agreeing nor disagreeing). Direct comparison is complicated because the question wording changed between 2002 and 2008. In 2008, the question was whether posts should be 'distributed according to geographical balance'; in 2002, it was whether posts should be 'distributed across nationalities proportionate to their respective populations'. So the sharp dip in support may be caused in part by a change in the question—but it is difficult to believe that this alone explains the sea change.

Interviews reveal that many top officials take a more nuanced view than either Monnet or the administrative reform on nationality in the Commission. Officials resent *parachutage*, the practice of appointing individuals outside the normal recruitment procedures, but see merit in geographical balance. As *parachutage* has become a thing of the past, the once-deep suspicion against national colonization has mellowed.

As late as the mid-1990s, 35–40 per cent of top positions were filled by outsiders parachuted from national administrations, diplomatic services, or from Commissioners' cabinets into the Commission's top bureaucracy. These individuals bypassed competitive examinations or conventional internal promotion procedures, and blocked careers for officials who had worked their way up through the ranks. Moreover, there were no guarantees that these parachuted officials had the necessary skills for the task or that they would be independent from the national capital that landed them the job. One outcome of the 2002 personnel reform is the virtual elimination of *parachutage* and, in the rare occasions that it is still used, it is subject to competitive examination.

Geographical variation among Commission officials, on the other hand, ensures a range of views in policy-making and bestows greater legitimacy on EU policy. A policy blind to the realities of a diverse multilevel polity could do more harm than good. Senior officials' instincts about how to balance national sensitivities and impartiality have been honed by the hard school of the last decades. A Commission that speaks in a foreign tongue is vulnerable to Eurosceptic rhetoric, while a Commission perceived to be the handmaiden of particular national interests loses credibility. That is one reason why officials make a sharp distinction between talking with compatriots and making policy for compatriots. While the former finds broad approval, the latter meets widespread reticence. When asked in 2002, only 12 per cent believed that Commission autonomy would be better served if officials were to avoid contact with compatriots, but 80 per cent agreed that national policy dossiers are better *not* handled by officials of the same nationality.

In 2008, we asked a slightly more probing question: namely, whether it is problematic for Commission officials to manage dossiers of special interest to their own member states. We found that an absolute majority (53 per cent) finds it unproblematic. Allocating national dossiers to nationals remains contested, but sometimes it is wise to strike a balance between the ideal and the practical. As a top official observed, there are not many non-Estonian officials who speak Estonian, and so to the extent that good policy relies on local knowledge, one needs to use the human capital that one has. Moreover, one major outcome of the new personnel policy is that even when geographical balance influences hiring and promotion, it happens after candidates have gone through the fire of meritocratic examination.

The last two statements in Table 8.1 gauge Commission official preferences on the constitutional future of Europe. The first echoes de Gaulle's call for intergovernmentalism, and the second taps Monnet's (or Hallstein's—see Chapter 5) notion of supranationalism/federalism. If Monnet's political ideas were to determine Commission preferences about Europe's architectural design, one would expect to see solid majorities opposing member states being central pillars and solid majorities supporting the idea of the Commission as a sort of 'government for Europe'. The expectation that member states should *not* run the EU is confirmed (from 65 per cent in 1996, to 84 per cent in 2002 and 82 per cent in 2008), but support for the Commission as the embryonic European government is less widespread than expected (49, 60, and 42 per cent, respectively). On basic issues of EU governance, senior Commission officials are distinctly divided.

It may be surprising that a plurality of the Commission's bureaucratic leadership is lukewarm on a federal Europe with a government-like Commission. One reason appears to be our tendency—in academia as well as in public debate—to oversimplify the array of Europe's jurisdictional options. Often, the choice is presented as one of federalism/supranationalism and intergovernmentalism/state-centrism, which prevents us from picking up plurality.

Supranationalists are those who agree that the College of Commissioners should be the government of Europe and disagree that member states should remain the central pillars. Intergovernmentalists disagree with the former and agree with the latter. But many officials believe that *neither* the College of Commissioners *nor* the member states should be the kernel of European government, or they believe that *both* should lead Europe. This third group does not want to be lumped together with one of the other two. We call them 'institutional pragmatists' on account of the fact that they prefer to side-step institutional battles. They favour a jurisdictional design in which Commission and member states are interlocking and complementary institutions: the Commission on account of its monopoly of initiative; the member states on account of their legitimacy to legislate and implement EU policy.

Table 8.2 shows how each of these visions finds a constituency among senior Commission officials and how it has done so since the mid-1990s. One group supports a proto-federal or supranational EU, which conceives of the Commission as the primary authority. Another favours a more intergovernmental or state-centric Union that reserves that role for the member states. A third wants a multilevel polity that conceives the

TABLE 8.2	Supranationalists, institutional pragmatists, and intergovernmentalists among senior Commission officials		
	1996	**2002**	**2008**
Supranationalists	35.2%	53.1%	39.3%
Institutional pragmatists	37.0%	26.1%	33.5%
Intergovernmentalists	22.2%	8.8%	12.6%

Note: N = 105 in 1996; N = 93 in 2002; N = 186 in 2008

Commission and member states as complementary institutions. Plurality, not hegemony or polarity, describes most aptly the political views of senior Commission officials.

Rank and file vs top, and East vs West

The 2008 poll surveyed the whole Commission, thus providing us with an opportunity to explore the breadth and depth of Monnet norms across the Commission. To what extent do the rank and file share the views of the senior bureaucracy? We were also interested in whether officials from the most recent member states have the same or different preferences than their Western colleagues. As of June 2011, 24.2 per cent of Commission policy-makers (AD grades) came from the twelve most recent member states (EU12), a group sizeable enough to shift the preferences of the Commission services.

The last four columns in Table 8.1 compare rank and file with senior officials and new with 'old' member state officials, respectively. In all but one instance, rank and file are less in favour of Monnet positions than are senior officials. The one exception is that relatively junior officials are somewhat more circumspect about applying geographical balance to hiring and promotion. On no dimension is the difference particularly striking.

The differences are greater between officials from new member states and those from the EU15. In every instance, EU12 officials are less supportive of Monnet norms than officials from the EU15, and the distinctions are particularly great on geographical balance and on whether the College of Commissioners should be the government of Europe. Supranationalism is considerably less popular among officials from the new member states (30.2 per cent against 38.6 per cent for the EU15), intergovernmentalism slightly more (14.7 per cent against 12.8 per cent), and institutional pragmatism about the same (30.8 per cent against 30.1 per cent). Almost one in four new member officials (24.2 per cent) declare neutrality or have no position on whether power should reside with the Commission or with the member states.

All in all, Monnet's vision seems to have resilience in the Commission. But it is less entrenched among rank and file than among senior officials, and it musters considerably less support among officials from the newer member states. Are the differences we detect early tidings of impending change? Or will they wash out as junior and middle management move up the ranks, and as EU12 officials carve out work experiences and careers at the heart of the EU? Perhaps only time will tell.

Conclusion

After an eventful decade—shaped by politicization, enlargement, and administrative reform—the Commission services have emerged more unchanged than changed. The reforms have put the organization on a more professional footing, most particularly by upgrading on-the-job training, focusing more on managerial skills, scrapping national quotas and country flags, and decentralizing accountability. However, contrary to what pundits had thought, there are few signs that these changes have weakened the Commission's traditional role of being the engine of Europe. A central purpose of the reforms has been to free the 12,600 Commission administrators from routine administration and implementation, so that they can focus on initiating policy—in the spirit of Jean Monnet's original ideas.

The many changes in staff policy and work practices seem to reaffirm, not weaken, the special role of the Commission in the EU architecture. And thus organizational change paves the way for institutional continuity. Surveys of the Commission's senior officials before and after the reform corroborate this conclusion. Support for agenda-setting—understood here as a preference for a privileged role for the Commission in setting Europe's agenda—has grown among Commission officials.

Does this trend suggest that more policy may flow from the services? This result is unlikely since a major goal of the reform programme has been to constrain the Commission's penchant for policy entrepreneurship. Measures such as the introduction of the Commission's annual policy strategy and its associated annual management programme are designed to entrench this restraint, by compelling Commission officials to pursue initiatives within the guidelines set by the College. Combined with the 'completion' of the internal market, and a market-liberal turn in the College and among top Commission officials, these measures may well keep the Commission services' entrepreneurship within bounds. But perhaps most decisive are a political environment of resurgent nationalism and a receptive College of Commissioners. Strong signals are sent to the Commission services to tread lightly.

NOTES

1. Data collected as part of The European Commission in Question project, funded by the UK Economic and Social Research Council (grant no. RES-062-23-1188) and conducted by the authors, along with Michael Bauer, Sara Connolly, Renaud Dehousse, John Peterson, and Andrew Thompson. The online survey was administered by the polling organization YouGov in September and October 2008. A sample of 4,621 policy administrators was drawn from a population of over 14,000. The sample was stratified to ensure proportionality by gender, age, and nationality; officials from the twelve new member states were oversampled. The response rate was 41 per cent (1,901 responses). Iterative proportional fitting was used to create a weighted sample that reflects the population distributions by gender, age, nationality, and DG location. For further information, see online at **http://www.uea.ac.uk/psi/research/EUCIQ** or see Kassim *et al.* (2012).

2. **http://ec.europa.eu/about/ds_en.htm**

3. **http://ec.europa.eu/civil_service/about/figures/index_en.htm**

4. Both the injunction to serve the 'European interest' and the Commission's independence are set out in Art. 213, para. 2.

5. Annual report from the Commission on the working of committees during 2009 (COM (2010) 354 final).

FURTHER READING

The academic literature on the Commission has grown considerably in recent years. The list of further reading provided here concentrates on sources that include extensive discussions and analyses of the services. The full findings from the 2008 survey of Commission officials is reported in Kassim *et al.* (2012).

Balint, T., Bauer, M., and Knill, C. (2008) 'Bureaucratic change in the European administrative space: the case of the European Commission', *West European Politics*, 31/4: 677–700.

Committee of Independent Experts (1999a) *First Report on Allegations Regarding Fraud, Mismanagement and Nepotism in the European Commission*, 15 March (Brussels: European Parliament).

Committee of Independent Experts (1999b) *Second Report on Reform of the Commission: Analysis of Current Practice and Proposals for Tackling Mismanagement, Irregularities and Fraud*, 10 September (2 vols, Brussels: European Parliament).

Egeberg, M. (2003) *Organising Institutional Autonomy in a Political Context: Enduring Tensions in the European Commission's Development* (Oslo: ARENA Working Paper series 04/02).

Hooghe, L. (2001) *The European Commission and The Integration of Europe: Images of Governance* (Cambridge: Cambridge University Press).

Hooghe, L. (2005) 'Many roads lead to international norms, but few via international socialization. a case study of the European Commission', *International Organization*, 59/4: 861–98.

Hooghe, L. (2012) 'Images of Europe: how Commission officials conceive their institution's role', *Journal of Common Market Studies*, 50/1: 87–111.

Kassim, H. and Menon, A. (2004) 'EU member states and the Prodi Commissions', in D.G. Dimitrakopoulos (ed.) *The Changing Commission* (Manchester: Manchester University Press).

Kassim, H., Peterson, J., Bauer, M., Connolly, S., Dehousse, R., Hooghe, L., and Thompson, A. (2012) *The European Commission of the 21st Century* (Oxford: Oxford University Press).

WEB LINKS

http://europa.eu/about-eu/institutions-bodies/european-commission/index_en.htm
The Commission's website.

http://ec.europa.eu/reform/index_en.htm
Provides access to Commission (2004) *Reforming the Commission: Reform of Europe's Public Services.*

http://ec.europa.eu/civil_service/docs/toc100_en.pdf
Provides access to Commission (2005) *Staff Regulations of Officials of the European Communities: Conditions of Employment of Other Servants of the European Communities.*

CHAPTER 9

Managing the Euro: the European Central Bank

Dermot Hodson

▌ Summary

With the launch of the single currency in January 1999, the European Central Bank (ECB) assumed complete control over euro area monetary policy.[1] The Bank is a unique case among European Union (EU) institutions, boasting as it does a higher degree of independence than either the European Commission or the European Court of Justice (ECJ), yet assigning national central banks a key role in its decision-making structures. The ECB's idiosyncratic institutional design reflects the historical role played by national monetary authorities in EU macroeconomic policy, the desire of member states to lock in the benefits of price stability, and the power of ideas in relation to central banking. The ECB's distinctive decision-making structure also raises concerns that it will act too conservatively in its conduct of monetary policy and about the Bank's uneasy relationship with other EU institutions.

Introduction

The European Central Bank (ECB) opened the doors of its Frankfurt-based head-quarters in May 1998. Seven months later, the launch of the single currency saw the Bank assume full control over the formulation and implementation of monetary pol-icy in the euro area. It was not until the Lisbon Treaty entered into force in December 2009, however, that the Bank was formally recognized as an institution of the Euro-pean Union (EU), under Art. 13 TEU. The euro's first decade bore witness to a lively debate over the ECB's exact status in EU law, with some scholars claiming that eco-nomic and monetary union (EMU) involved the creation of a new institutional order in its own right (Zilioli and Selmayr 2000). Even the ECB sought to establish a *sui generis* institutional status in its dealings with the European Court of Justice (ECJ) (Goebel 2006) and the Convention on the Future of Europe (Hodson 2011).

The ECB's strategy of institutional isolationism can be viewed as an attempt by an embryonic EU actor to test the scope and limits of its statutory independence. The Bank enjoys considerable autonomy under the Treaty, which prohibits monetary authorities from seeking or taking instructions from member states or from institu-tions, bodies, offices, or agencies of the EU (Art. 130 TFEU). The limits of ECB au-tonomy were soon discovered, however, with the ECJ ruling in 2004 that central bank independence 'does not have the consequence of placing the ECB beyond the reach of the rules of the Treaty'.[2] The ECB's new designation under the Lisbon Treaty implies, furthermore, that the Bank is bound to practise 'sincere mutual cooperation' with other EU institutions and to uphold the objectives, interests, and values of the people and member states of the Union (Art. 13 TEU).

Although the ECB's status as an EU institution is now beyond doubt, the Bank is likely to be no less protective of its independence in consequence. Calls for the ECB to be made more accountable to politicians are commonplace. The two leading candidates in the 2007 French presidential elections, for example, publicly urged euro area monetary authorities to pay greater attention to growth, employment, and exchange-rate developments. The victor in this contest, Nicolas Sarkozy, toned down his criticism of the ECB at the request of Angela Merkel, but the German Chancellor herself is not immune to the occasional public criticism of euro area monetary policy. The global financial crisis, which began in mid-2007 with the col-lapse of the US sub-prime mortgage market, piled further pressure on the ECB. In the months and years that followed, Frankfurt found itself in the front line of efforts to secure economic recovery, to stabilize the financial system, and, ultimately, to save the single currency.

This chapter examines the ECB's emergence and evolution as an institution of the EU. It begins with an overview of the Bank's mandate, tasks, and key decision-making bodies, before employing historical, rational choice, and sociological insti-tutionalism to shed light on different aspects of the ECB's unique design. This overview is followed by a discussion about how institutional variables have influenced the ECB's performance as a central bank and its place in the EU's legal order. The first of these sections asks whether warnings of a status quo bias in ECB decision-making were borne out in the global financial crisis. The second discusses the democratic checks and balances on euro area monetary policy and explores the ECB's interaction with the European Parliament (EP) and the Eurogroup.

The ECB's mandate and tasks

Not to be confused with the 'other' European banks (see Box 9.1), the ECB's primary objective is to maintain price stability in the euro area and, without prejudice to this goal, to support economic policy (Art. 127 TFEU). The Treaty does not specify what is meant by 'price stability', leaving the ECB to define and refine this objective as it sees fit. The ECB's definition of price stability—a year-on-year increase in the harmonized index of consumer prices (HICP) for the euro area of below 2 per cent—has been criticized by some commentators for lacking precision (Buiter 1999). The Bank

---

BOX 9.1   The 'other' European banks

Established by the Treaty of Rome in 1958, the European Investment Bank's (EIB) overarching objective is to 'contribute ... to the balanced and steady development of the internal market in the interest of the Union' (Art. 309 TFEU). To this end, the Bank gives loans and guarantees for a wide range of projects, financed not through the EU budget, but by borrowing on capital markets. The fact that the twenty-seven EU member states are shareholders in the EIB ensures that such borrowing takes place at favourable interest rates.

The projects funded by the EIB vary according to the EU's shifting policy priorities. The global financial crisis, for example, saw a significant increase in lending to small and medium-sized enterprises (SMEs). Under the Bank's corporate operational plan for 2011–13, particular emphasis was placed on projects that contribute to the implementation of the Europe 2020 Strategy, EU climate change policy, and external policy (EIB 2011). The third of these three priorities echoes the outcome of the 2010 Camdessus Report, which called for greater coherence between EIB lending and EU foreign policy.

The EIB is, alongside the EU and some sixty-one countries, a shareholder in one of the 'other' European banks: the European Bank for Reconstruction and Development (EBRD). Founded in 1991, the EBRD was assigned a key role in promoting the transition from central planning to market economics in Central and Eastern Europe following the end of the cold war. Today, the EBRD functions as a development bank for 'countries committed to and applying the principles of multiparty democracy, pluralism and market economics'.[3] Although this mandate refers specifically to Central and Eastern European countries, the EBRD's shareholders responded to the Arab Spring by taking steps in May 2011 to extend the Bank's lending to the Middle East and North Africa.

offered a partial concession on this point in 2005, when it announced that it would pursue inflation rates below, but close to, 2 per cent over the medium term.

The Treaty is even more opaque about how the ECB is supposed to support economic policy, stating only that such efforts should contribute to the objectives of the Union, as laid down in Art. 3 TEU. That the Article in question includes such lofty aims as peace, social justice, and human rights, as well as more grounded objectives such as balanced growth and full employment, makes it virtually impossible to judge the ECB's compliance with its secondary objective. For critics, the ECB's mandate is biased towards the pursuit of low inflation at the expense of higher growth and employment (Randzio-Plath 2000), although Frankfurt's supporters insist that no such trade-off exists, in the long term at least (Issing 2008).

Compared with other central banks, the ECB is more independent than most, but less transparent than some (see Box 9.2). As regards independence, the ECB's statutes are embedded in a hard-to-revise treaty as compared with the more malleable legislative acts underpinning the US Federal Reserve, the Bank of Japan, and the Bank of England. That the ECB can choose its own definition of 'price stability' gives it an added layer of independence that monetary authorities such as the Bank of England, which is assigned an inflation target by the Chancellor of the Exchequer, lack. As regards transparency, the ECB has a more clear-cut price stability mandate than the Federal Reserve, which is required to 'maintain long-run growth of the monetary and credit aggregates commensurate with the economy's long-run potential to increase production, so as to promote effectively the goals of maximum employment, stable prices, and moderate long-term interest rates'. The ECB's definition of price stability is vaguer than that of the Bank of England, however: while Frankfurt targets year-on-year price increases below 2 per cent, its counterpart in the City of London targets increases of precisely 2 per cent.

The ECB's primary task is to define and implement euro area monetary policy (Art. 127 TFEU). This brief typically involves the setting of short-term interest rates, although the global financial crisis saw the ECB resort to unconventional monetary policies (see below). The ECB, furthermore, holds and manages the official foreign reserves of the member states, which includes the foreign currency and gold reserves of national central banks. The Bank also promotes the smooth operation of European payments and settlements systems through initiatives such as the Trans-European Automated Real-Time Gross Settlement Express Transfer System (TARGET; see Quaglia 2009).

The ECB is required, under Art. 127 TFEU, to contribute to 'the smooth conduct of policies pursued by the competent authorities relating to the prudential supervision of credit institutions and the stability of the financial system'. In principle, this remit gives the ECB no more than a supporting role alongside national authorities in identifying risks to the euro area's financial system, but these limits have not prevented some in the upper echelons of the Bank from making the case for the creation of a supranational financial authority (see Padoa-Schioppa 1999). Reforms enacted in the light of the global financial crisis stopped short of this ideal, but still

BOX 9.2	The ECB in comparative context			
Bank	**ECB**	**US Federal Reserve**	**Bank of Japan**	**Bank of England**
Legal statutes	Maastricht Treaty (1993)	Federal Reserve Act of 1993	Bank of Japan Act 1997	Bank of England Act 1997
Mandate	'The primary objective of the ESCB shall be to maintain price stability. Without prejudice to the objective of price stability, the ESCB shall support the general economic policies in the Community.'	To 'maintain long-run growth of the monetary and credit aggregates commensurate with the economy's long-run potential to increase production, so as to promote effectively the goals of maximum employment, stable prices, and moderate long-term interest rates'.	Monetary policy should be 'aimed at achieving price stability, thereby contributing to the sound development of the national economy'.	'In relation to monetary policy, the objectives of the Bank of England shall be (a) to maintain price stability, and (b) subject to that, to support the economic policy of Her Majesty's Government, including its objectives for growth and employment.'
Numerical target/definition	'Price stability is defined as a year-on-year increase in the Harmonised Index of Consumer Prices (HICP) for the Euro area of below 2%.'	No numerical target	A year-on-year change in the consumer prices index (CPI) in an approximate range of 0–2%.	The inflation target of 2% is expressed in terms of an annual rate of inflation based on the consumer prices index (CPI).
Numerical target/definition set by	ECB	N/A	Bank of Japan	Chancellor of the Exchequer

significantly extended the ECB's competence in this domain. As of December 2010, the ECB President has been in charge of a new European Systemic Risk Board (ESRB), which is responsible for monitoring the EU's financial system and has the authority to issue early warnings if systemic risks are foreseen (see Box 9.3).

The task of conducting euro area exchange-rate policy, finally, is shared by the ECB and the Economic and Financial Affairs Council (Ecofin). The authority to enter the single currency into an exchange-rate regime with a third country—imagine, for example, a situation in which the euro were pegged to the dollar—lies with Ecofin, but this decision must be based on a recommendation from the ECB or the Commission (Art. 219 TFEU). Ecofin is also empowered to formulate general orientations on the exchange-rate policy of the euro area in relation to third countries, although it falls to the ECB to carry out specific foreign-exchange operations (Arts 219 and 127 TFEU).

BOX 9.3   **The European Systemic Risk Board**

The ESRB, which was launched in December 2010, is responsible for:

the macro-prudential oversight of the financial system within the Union in order to contribute to the prevention or mitigation of systemic risks to financial stability in the Union that arise from developments within the financial system and taking into account macro-economic developments, so as to avoid periods of widespread financial distress.

(Regulation (EU) No. 1092/2010, OJ L 331/1, 24 November 2010)

If this opaque mandate has the potential to create confusion over the precise role of the ESRB, then so too does its governance structure. Of particular concern is the unwieldy size of the ESRB Governing Council, which has no fewer than thirty-seven voting members: the ECB President, who was appointed chair for the period 2010–15; the ECB Vice President; the national central bank governors of the twenty-seven EU member states; the heads of the European Banking Authority (EBA), the European Insurance and Occupational Pensions Authority (EIOPA), and the European Securities and Markets Authority (ESMA); the chair and the two vice-chairs of the ESRB Advisory Scientific Committee; and the chair of the ESRB Advisory Technical Committee.

The ESRB's statutes emphasize the impartiality of its activities. Members of the Board are both required to act in the interests of the EU as a whole and prohibited from seeking or taking instructions from member states, EU institutions, or any other public or private body in the exercise of their responsibilities. The ESRB is, furthermore, subject to comparatively few checks and balances, being required only to keep the European Parliament abreast of its activities and to examine specific issues at the invitation of the Parliament, the Council, or the Commission. Buiter (2009), for one, is sceptical about such arrangements, arguing that supervisors should not be afforded the same degree of independence as central banks because supervision is inherently more politicized than monetary policy.

In practice, Ecofin has been reluctant to issue formal recommendations on the exchange rate for fear that they might be seen as impinging on the independence of the ECB. Instead, euro area finance ministers have developed an informal approach to exchange-rate policy based on the adoption of 'terms of reference' by euro area finance ministers. Although these pronouncements carry no legal weight, they provide political cover for the ECB to conduct exchange-rate policy. A case in point is the ECB's joint intervention in exchange-rate markets alongside the US Federal Reserve and the Bank of Japan in September 2000. Frankfurt's first move of this kind, this intervention followed a non-binding communiqué from euro area finance ministers stating that '[a] strong euro is in the interest of the Euro area' (Eurogroup 2000).

The decision-making bodies of the ECB

Responsibility for euro area monetary policy formally lies with the Eurosystem, which includes the ECB and the national central banks of euro area members (Art. 282 TFEU). The Eurosystem, in turn, is a member of the European System of Central Banks (ESCB), which also consists of monetary authorities from member states that do not share the single currency. The ESCB is made up of three key decision-making bodies: the Executive Board; the Governing Council; and the General Council (see Table 9.1).

The ECB Executive Board runs the Bank on a day-to-day basis. Among its most important tasks is the preparation of ECB Governing Council meetings, thus giving the Executive Board significant agenda-setting powers in relation to Eurosystem business. The Executive Board also plays a lead role in policy implementation, putting monetary policy decisions into practice through measures taken by Frankfurt in close cooperation with national central banks.

The six members of the ECB Executive Board are appointed for an eight-year, non-renewable term of office by the European Council. This decision is based on a qualified-majority vote (QMV) on a recommendation from the Council of Ministers following consultation with the EP and the ECB Governing Council (Art. 11, Protocol 4 TFEU). The only formal criteria for selecting ECB Executive Board members is that they should be chosen from persons of recognized standing and professional experience in monetary or banking matters (*ibid.*). In practice, appointments to the Executive Board have been subject to informal deals, especially between the euro area's largest member states (see Box 9.4).

By far the most important Executive Board member is the ECB President, who is responsible for chairing meetings of the Governing Council and representing the ECB externally (Art. 11, Protocol 4 TFEU). The ECB President's signature also adorns euro banknotes, making him or her the public face of the single currency. The first President of the ECB was Wim Duisenberg, a former head of De Nederlandsche Bank. Duisenberg took office in May 1998 and was succeeded in November

TABLE 9.1   The governing bodies of the European System of Central Banks

General Council	Governing Council	Executive Board	European Central Bank Board Member/National Central Bank Governor
	x	x	ECB President
	x	x	ECB Vice President
	x	x	Four other board members
x	x		National Bank of Belgium
x	x		Banque de France
x	x		Banca d'Italia
x	x		Banco de Portugal
x	x		Banco de España
x			Bulgarian National Bank
x			Bank of Latvia
x			Sveriges Riksbank
x	x		Oesterreichische Nationalbank
x	x		Bank of Finland
x	x		Central Bank of Ireland
x	x		De Nederlandsche Bank
x	x		Central Bank of Cyprus
x	x		Deutsche Bundesbank
x	x		Banque Centrale du Luxembourg
x	x		National Bank of Slovakia
x			Czech National Bank
x			Bank of Lithuania
x			Bank of England
x			Danmarks Nationalbank
x			National Bank of Poland
x	x		Bank of Estonia
x	x		Bank of Greece
x	x		Central Bank of Malta
x	x		The Bank of Slovenia
x			Magyar Nemzeti Bank
x			National Bank of Romania

BOX 9.4	**Appointments to the ECB Executive Board**

In May 1998, an eleventh-hour bilateral agreement between French President Jacques Chirac and German Chancellor Helmut Kohl in the margins of the European Council saw Germany's preferred candidate, Wim Duisenberg, become the first ECB President. Known as 'the longest lunch in EU history', this agreement saw Wim Duisenberg step aside in the middle of his eight-year term, allowing France's nominee, Jean-Claude Trichet, to become ECB President in November 2003.

Subsequent appointments to the ECB Executive Board sought, not without controversy, to reserve a seat for candidates from large member states, with Eugenio Domingo Solans (Spain), Tommaso Padoa-Schioppa (Italy), and Otmar Issing (Germany) each replaced by a compatriot. The two remaining seats on the Executive Board have traditionally been rotated between candidates from smaller euro area countries. The vice-presidency of the ECB was initially held by a Frenchman, Christian Noyer, but this role has been occupied by a central banker from a smaller state since 2002.

It was initially assumed that a German candidate would succeed Jean-Claude Trichet as ECB President in 2012, with Axel Weber treated as the heir apparent until his unexpected resignation as President of the Bundesbank in April 2011. Germany proved unable or unwilling to field an alternative, leaving Mario Draghi, President of the Banca d'Italia, to emerge as a compromise candidate. Draghi won the backing of EU finance ministers in May 2011 and the approval of the EP's Economic and Monetary and Affairs Committee a month later, paving the way for his investiture as the third President of the ECB in November 2011.

2003 by Jean-Claude Trichet, former governor of the Banque de France. Trichet served his full eight-year term, before being succeeded in November 2011 by Mario Draghi, former President of the Banca d'Italia.

The ECB Governing Council includes the six members of the ECB Executive Board and the national central bank governors of euro area members. The Governing Council's most important function is to formulate the monetary policy of the euro area. It also determines the ECB's role in international financial institutions and fulfils its advisory function, which allows the ECB to submit opinions on EU and national legislation that may be relevant to its sphere of competence.

As of 2011, all members of the Governing Council retain the right to cast a single vote on monetary policy matters, with decisions approved, in principle, by a simple majority. Under this arrangement, the ECB Executive Board has seen its relative voting power diminish as the number of euro area members (and, by implication, national central bank governors on the ECB Governing Council) has increased from eleven in 1999 to seventeen in 2011. To offset this tendency, a set of reforms were adopted in May 2004 that will eventually cap the total number of votes exercised by national central bank governors. Under this set-up, which will take effect once the euro area has eighteen members, voting rights will rotate between national central bank governors, with the speed of rotation varying according to the relative size of a member state's economy and financial sector. This system will ensure that national central bank governors from large economies have a vote more often than their counterparts from small economies. Executive Board members, in contrast, will retain their voting rights in the Governing Council on a permanent basis.

The General Council of the ECB consists of the Bank's President and Vice President and the national central bank governors of the twenty-seven EU member states. Initially designed as a transitional body, the General Council was given responsibility for certain practical aspects of the ECB's work, such as the collection of statistical information, until such time as all EU member states have adopted the single currency (Art. 46, Protocol 4 TFEU). This seldom-seen body came to prominence during the global financial crisis by virtue of its advisory role in relation to financial supervision. It was on the basis of this role that EU finance ministers decided, in June 2009, that the President of the ESRB should be chosen from the ECB General Council. This means, that the Governor of the Bank of England or the head of another central bank from outside the euro area could, in principle, serve as chair of this important new body.[4]

Explaining the ECB's institutional design

Each of the three main variants of new institutionalism (see Chapter 1) can explain different aspects of the ECB's distinctive design. Historical institutionalism, with its belief that past institutional choices influence present policies, can, for example, help us to understand the prominent role played by national central banks in the governance of the Eurosystem. Rational choice institutionalism, with its emphasis on intergovernmental bargaining and commitment devices, helps to explain the very high degree of independence granted to the ECB. Finally, sociological institutionalism offers important insights into the influence of economic ideas on the governance of the ECB.

Beginning with historical institutionalism, the role of national central banks in EMU shows signs of path-dependence that can be traced back to the signature of the Treaty of Rome in 1957. No reference was made at the outset of the European Economic Community (EEC) to the goal of monetary union, but the Treaty's modest provisions on macroeconomic policy coordination did envisage collaboration between national central bankers on matters related to the balance of payments. National central bank governors wasted little time in putting such provisions into effect, initiating informal discussions in January 1958 (Maes 2006). These discussions paved the way for the creation of the Committee of Governors of the Central Banks of EEC member states in May 1964.

Few central banks were independent of national governments during this period—the Bundesbank was a notable exception—but these circumstances did not prevent the Committee of Governors from keeping its distance from

Brussels. Significant in this respect was the decision of national central bank governors to meet in the margins of the Bank for International Settlements (BIS) in Basle, far from the gaze of EEC institutions. The Commission was given observer status on the Committee of Governors, but its official was excluded from discussions in Basle of highly sensitive policy matters (Andrews 2003).

In December 1969, EEC leaders finally agreed on the goal of EMU, inviting Luxembourg Prime Minister Pierre Werner to work out a detailed policy plan. Such was the influence of the Committee of Governors by this point that its chair, Hubert Ansiaux, was invited by Werner to produce an opinion on the technical aspects of preparations for monetary union. It was in the light of this opinion that the Werner Committee proposed, in effect, to upgrade the Committee of Governors to the status of an EEC institution with responsibility for the conduct of monetary policy in EMU.

The international economic turmoil that followed the first oil shock in October 1973 put paid to the Werner Plan, but the Committee of Governors continued to wield significant influence in EEC macroeconomic policy. This influence was evident, for example, in the Committee's key role in the management of the European monetary system (EMS), a fixed exchange-rate regime launched by member states in March 1979. The relaunch of EMU at the Hanover European Council in June 1988 saw national central banks given a more significant role still, with the governors invited to draw up a blueprint for a single currency under the leadership of Commission President Jacques Delors.

The reluctance of national central banks to cede control over monetary policy was evident in the final report of the Delors Committee, which called for the creation of a European System of Central Banks that would include a central monetary authority and national central banks (Committee for the Study of Economic and Monetary Union 1989). EC leaders endorsed this vision of EMU, even inviting the Committee of Governors to draw up the statutes of the ESCB in the intergovernmental conference (IGC) on EMU launched in December 1990.

The Maastricht Treaty, signed in February 1992, codified a three-stage plan for EMU in which national central banks played a central role. Stage 1, which began in July 1990, saw the Committee of Governors given a more hands-on role in the coordination of monetary policies. Stage 2, which began in January 1994, saw the Committee of Governors integrated into the Council of the European Monetary Institute (EMI), which took charge of practical preparations for EMU. These preparations culminated in June 1998 with the launch of the ECB, which saw the Council of the EMI transformed into the ECB Governing Council. Stage 3 of EMU, which was launched in January 1999, saw the Governing Council take charge of euro area monetary policy, thus giving national central bank governors a major say in EU macroeconomic policy a little over four decades after informal cooperation between these institutions was initiated.

Historical institutionalism can explain the involvement of national central banks in the decision-making structures of the Eurosystem. But it is arguably less clear about the reasons why EMU involved such a dramatic increase in central bank independence in the EU. Rational choice institutionalism fares better here, with Moravcsik (1998) pointing to the importance of preference formation, intergovernmental bargaining, and institutional choice in the design of EMU's governance architecture.

Moravcsik's essential point about preference formation regarding EMU is that Germany had only a little to gain from a single currency, while France stood to gain a lot. In the case of the former, it seemed unlikely that EMU could outperform domestic macroeconomic policy. The Bundesbank, in particular, had a formidable track record at achieving price stability, even if some in the business community saw a single currency as a response to the progressive appreciation of the Deutschmark against some European currencies. In the case of the latter, the Banque de France was already shadowing the monetary policy of the Bundesbank as part of its efforts to keep inflation under control. EMU was therefore seen by political leaders and interest groups alike as a way in which to reassert a degree of shared sovereignty over French macroeconomic policies.

The intensity of France's preferences for EMU was such, Moravcsik (1998) contends, that its negotiators were willing to make significant concessions to Germany during intergovernmental bargaining over the Maastricht Treaty. A deal breaker in this regard was Germany's demand that EMU attach a very high degree of importance to the pursuit of price stability. This commitment was essential in allaying domestic concerns—especially in the upper echelons of the Bundesbank—that a single currency would be soft on inflation. To this end, it was agreed not only that the Maastricht Treaty would assign an unequivocal price-stability mandate to the ECB, but also that EU member states would be required to keep inflation under control and meet convergence criteria before being admitted to the euro area.

On the issue of institutional choice, Moravcsik (1998) rejects the argument, neo-functionalist in its reasoning, that the delegation of monetary policy to the ECB was a matter of necessity for the successful management of the single currency. He suggests, rather, that the framers of the Maastricht Treaty chose to delegate policy-making powers in this area to an independent institution rather than a political forum such as Ecofin because the former provided a more credible commitment to the anti-inflationary intergovernmental bargain on which EMU rests. The ECB, in other words, was given a high degree of autonomy over monetary policy because member states willed it so.

Scholars looking at these issues through the lens of sociological institutionalism challenge this line of reasoning. The economic case for an independent ECB, McNamara (2002) suggests, is a 'rational fiction' that is based on a narrow reading of the causes of inflation and the distributional consequences of interest-rate decisions. The emergence of independent central banks in the euro area and elsewhere, she suggests, can be viewed as a symbol of economic credibility aimed at financial markets, as well as the product of an epistemic community with a shared understanding of monetary policy.

Verdun (1999) also sees an epistemic community at work in the design of the ECB's price-stability mandate. The Delors Committee, she argues, consisted not only of policy-makers with an authoritative claim to knowledge about central banking issues, but also a shared set of causal beliefs about the importance of stable prices for sustainable economic growth. It was by virtue of these beliefs, Verdun argues, that the Delors Report insisted on the pursuit of price stability above all other goals as a *sine qua non* for EMU.

The ECB and the global financial crisis

For economists, a striking feature of the ECB's institutional design is the sheer number of decision-makers involved in euro area monetary policy. Even after the Governing Council begins to rotate voting rights, twenty-one people will have a direct say over the setting of short-term interest rates and other aspects of monetary policy. This number is well above the norm for central banking, with twelve members of the US Federal Reserve Open Markets Committee (OMC), for example, having the right to vote at any one time. Decision-making is even more streamlined in the Bank of England's Monetary Policy Committee (MPC), which has just nine voting members.

Blinder (2007) sees advantages and disadvantages to a committee-based approach to central banking. On the plus side, empowering groups rather than individuals guards against the risks of extreme preferences for either low inflation or low unemployment, and pools knowledge about the complex working of the economy in general and monetary policy in particular. On the minus side, Blinder acknowledges that committees can be cumbersome and that there is a risk of 'group think' as the individuals involved come to share the same understanding of the economy. ECB watchers have tended, by and large, to err on the side of pessimism, with Gros (2003), for one, warning of a status quo bias in monetary policy in the presence of multiple veto players.

There has been no greater test to date of the ECB's responsiveness to changing economic circumstances than the global financial crisis that began in August 2007 following the collapse of the US sub-prime mortgage market. The Bank showed itself to be surprisingly supple during the opening phase of the crisis, providing €94.8 billion in emergency liquidity support to forty-nine European banks a matter of hours after BNP Paribas sounded the alarm over worldwide liquidity shortages. That the ECB Governing Council made this decision by conference call at the height of the summer holidays is all the more impressive, and points towards a degree of contingency planning that was not discernible in the actions of all central banks at this time.

The Bank's response to the later stages of the global financial crisis was more characteristically cautious. The ECB Governing Council waited until June 2008 to alter its monetary stance—the US Federal Reserve, by comparison, started slashing interest rates in August 2007—and even then the Bank's Governing Council took the astonishing decision to raise the interest rate amid mounting concerns over inflationary pressures. Within a matter of months, it became clear that the euro area was in recession and that the threat of deflation loomed, leaving the ECB with little choice but to begin a series of belated interest-rate cuts that brought the cost of lending to unprecedented lows.

The ECB was also slow to embrace the use of unconventional monetary policies in comparison with other central banks. In June 2009, Frankfurt unveiled a plan to purchase €60 billion euro-denominated covered bonds (long-term debt securities backed by mortgages or public sector loans). This plan involved a fairly modest sum when compared with the US Federal Reserve's $800 billion 'credit easing' programme and the Bank of England's £200 billion asset purchase facility, even after the ECB increased its bond purchases by €40 billion in late 2011. The ECB's covered-bond scheme was also more modest in its ambitions, as it could be used to purchase only one class of private-sector asset. The Fed's 'credit easing' programme, in contrast, was used to purchase, inter alia, debt securities backed by car loans, credit cards, student loan debt, and mortgage-backed securities held by federal agencies.

The effect of the financial crisis on member states was delayed, but devastating. Having seen all euro area post-budget deficits below 3 per cent of GDP as late as mid-2008, all countries found themselves in breach of this limit just two years later. The reasons for this reversal of fiscal fortune were manifold, but included the unforeseen costs of bank rescue packages and fiscal stimulus packages, the effects of a sudden shortfall in stamp duties once housing bubbles burst, and, in some cases, downright dishonesty over the true state of public finances prior to the crisis. Greece fared worst initially, finding itself on the brink of sovereign default in early 2010 after the budget deficit for the preceding year was revised from 3.9 to 15.4 per cent.

The ECB was in the vanguard of the international response to this crisis, joining forces with the European Commission and the International Monetary Fund (IMF) to negotiate the technical details of a €110 billion financial rescue package with Greece in May 2010. Frankfurt's decision to enter the political fray reflected the seriousness of this situation and perhaps also an attempt to ensure that euro area monetary policy would not be compromised by conditions attached to the rescue package. That the Bank was not entirely successful in doing so was suggested by the ECB's announcement in May 2010 that it would henceforth accept Greek bonds as collateral in credit operations, irrespective of the country's sovereign credit rating—a move that the Bank had hitherto resisted. These measures provided temporary respite to Greece. But they came too late to prevent the sovereign debt crisis from spreading to other euro area members. EU member states' response was to commit up to €500 billion to a joint EU–IMF initiative to provide financial assistance to any euro area member that might need it. Ireland became the first country to tap these funds in November 2010, with Portugal following suit in May 2011. The ECB's contribution to this self-styled 'overwhelming display of financial force' came in the form of the securities markets programme, which allowed the Bank to intervene in markets for public and private debt securities. By the end of 2011, the ECB had spent more than €200 billion through this programme but neither this sum nor other EU and IMF commitments were enough to allay financial market fears that the euro area might collapse under the weight of soverign debt.

The securities markets programme laid bare the perils of monetary policy-making by committee, with dissenting voices emerging from the ECB Governing Council about the effectiveness and appropriateness of bond purchases. Axel Weber, President of the Bundesbank, was the most vocal opponent, voting against the securities markets programme, and warning of potential risks to price stability and the dangers of blurring the divide between monetary and fiscal policies. This disagreement may have been a factor in Weber's dramatic resignation as Bundesbank President in February 2011, a move that ruled the German out of the running to succeed Jean-Claude Trichet as ECB President (see Box 9.4).

The euro area's sovereign debt crisis also inflamed tensions between euro area monetary and fiscal authorities. One source of conflict surrounded the ECB's decision in April 2011 to raise interest rates amid persistent inflationary pressures in the euro area and rapid economic recovery in Germany. More serious still was the ECB's stubborn stance against calls by German Finance Minister Wolfgang Schäuble, among others, for bondholders to bear some of the burden through a partial restructuring of Greek debt. Fearful that such a decision could further inflame the euro area's fiscal difficulties, the ECB insisted that Greece persevere with plans to bring government borrowing under control through drastic expenditure cuts and emergency revenue-raising measures. Whatever route is ultimately taken, the prospects of a rapid resolution to Greece's fiscal predicament, in particular, and the euro area's sovereign debt crisis, in general, are slim, leaving the single currency in a precarious state.

The ECB and other EU institutions

As EU institutions and central banks go, the ECB is subject to comparatively few checks and balances. While members of the European Commission and ECJ judges serve renewable terms of five and six years, respectively, members of the ECB Executive Board are appointed for eight years, after which they cannot be rehired. If this rule gives the ECB an added layer of political protection, so too does the fact that the EP is powerless to remove members of the Bank's Executive Board. Only the ECJ can call for the removal of Executive Board members who are guilty of serious misconduct or otherwise in breach of the requirements for the performance of their duties, and only then with the prior approval of the ECB Governing Council (Art. 11, Protocol 4 TFEU).

The ECB's remarkable degree of statutory independence has understandably raised concerns about the legitimacy of EMU. For Verdun and Christiansen (2000), the problem is not so much that the ECB lacks democratic accountability, because this characterization is true to a greater or lesser extent of all independent central banks, but the fact that the Bank lacks the 'societal embeddedness' of other monetary authorities. By this, Verdun and Christiansen mean that the ECB is unable to look to the kinds of beliefs and values that allowed the Bundesbank, for example, to seek legitimacy by appealing to collective memories of hyperinflation, and through the interaction of its conservative monetary policies with Germany's coordinated wage bargaining and generous welfare-state policies.

The failure of EMU's architects to embed the ECB in a 'wider European polity', Verdun and Christiansen (2000) warn, leaves the euro's legitimacy dangerously dependent on its perceived economic benefits and hence on short-term economic fluctuations. Subsequent empirical works chimes with this analysis, with Deroose *et al.* (2007) finding a correlation between popular support for the euro on the one hand, and expectations about future economic developments on the other. The perception that the euro cash changeover in 2002 caused prices to rise sharply, although it was not borne out by the economic data, also appears to have weighed heavily on support for the single currency in some countries.

For its part, the ECB has sought to enhance its legitimacy by reaching out to the EP. The Treaty envisages only a limited role for the EU legislature in the oversight of the Bank. For example, the ECB President is required to present an annual report on its activities to the Parliament and, along with other Executive Board members, appear before competent committees if requested to do so (Art. 285 TFEU). But these provisions have not stopped the two sides from developing a close working relationship. Of central importance in this regard is the so-called 'monetary dialogue', which sees the ECB President appear before the EP's Economic and Monetary Affairs (ECON) Committee at least four times per year to present the Bank's views on the economic situation.

Few commentators expected the monetary dialogue to amount to much, but it has proved to be a mutually beneficial forum. For the ECB, the monetary dialogue offers further evidence of the Bank's commitment to transparency and a public platform from which to expound on policy issues in a non-technical way. It was noteworthy in this regard that ECB President Jean-Claude Trichet used an extraordinary hearing of the ECON Committee in August 2007 to explain monetary policy responses to the unfolding financial crisis. For the EP, the monetary dialogue offers a chance to (be seen to) hold the ECB to account, as well as a foothold in an area of EU policy-making in which the legislature has limited competence. Although it is difficult to measure the precise impact of the monetary dialogue, Amtenbrink and Van Duin (2009) argue that it has achieved a level of oversight for euro area monetary policy beyond that envisaged in the Treaty, even if doubts remain about whether the ECB is being held sufficiently to account.

The surprising success of the monetary dialogue can be explained by a number of factors. First, the ECB President has demonstrated a commitment to this forum by presenting carefully prepared statements, and answering most questions in a full and frank way. The Bank also offered an early concession to the ECON Committee by agreeing in 2000 to make public the macroeconomic forecasts prepared by ECB staff. Second, ECON has upgraded its expertise on monetary policy by inviting high-profile economists to contribute to the preparation of the monetary dialogue.

Third, the ECON Committee has itself operated in a highly transparent manner, publishing a transcript of the monetary dialogue, as well as the briefings of its outside experts, on its external website.

The ECB has been altogether more guarded in its dealings with other EU institutions. A case in point is the Bank's uneasy relationship with the Eurogroup, an informal meeting of euro area finance ministers that gathers in advance of Ecofin. A key rationale for the launch of the Eurogroup in December 1997 was to facilitate a behind-closed-doors dialogue between euro area finance ministers and the ECB President, with the Commissioner for Economic and Monetary Affairs also in attendance. Initially, such discussions were said to have been fairly one-sided, with the ECB President keen to lecture finance ministers on the importance of fiscal discipline, but finance ministers reluctant to criticize the ECB openly out of respect for its independence (Puetter 2006).

The appointment of Luxembourg Prime Minister Jean-Claude Juncker as the first permanent President of the Eurogroup in January 2005—prior to which, euro area finance ministers took it in turns to chair—marked the beginning of a more combative approach to the ECB. Tensions came to a head in November 2005 when Juncker let it be known in public that euro area finance ministers saw the ECB's anticipated increase in interest rates as 'not particularly necessary' (Atkins *et al.* 2005). Such comments did not deter the ECB from increasing interest rates in December 2005, but neither did they discourage Juncker from publicly seeking an enhanced dialogue on euro area issues with the ECB President. This request received short shrift from Frankfurt, with Jean-Claude Trichet insisting that the proposed measures were incompatible with the independence of the ECB.

Economists are divided on the issue of whether public criticisms of ECB monetary policy by euro area politicians will be damaging to the ECB's credibility over the long term. Lamfalussy (2006), for one, sees such criticisms as signalling a growing disregard among euro area politicians for the ECB's independence. Kenen (2006) is more sanguine, arguing that the Treaty is designed to protect the ECB from coercion rather than criticism. Whatever its effects on the credibility of the ECB, the mere fact that such criticism was aired reveals the Eurogroup's failure to keep discussions of the euro area monetary and fiscal policy mix behind closed doors. It suggests that euro area policy-makers are failing to pay sufficient attention to the interaction between monetary and fiscal policies, and the need for a cooperative solution for achieving price stability and higher sustainable growth.

For political scientists, the ECB's reluctance to strengthen the Eurogroup provides one indication of the Bank's ambivalent attitude towards the pursuit of European integration (Hodson 2011). Although Frankfurt has, as noted above, consistently championed the case for greater EU and ECB involvement in the area of financial supervision, it has often criticized calls for the euro area to move towards a system of economic government. A concern for its price stability mandate would appear to be at play here, with ECB Executive Board member Jürgen Stark arguing in January 2008 that the real motivation behind such calls is 'to establish political influence on monetary policy in the euro area and thereby to undermine the independence of the ECB' (Stark 2008).[5]

Whatever the reasons for its unease, the ECB's ambivalence about the European project challenges rational-choice institutionalist assumptions that EU institutions have more intense preferences for European integration than member states, whether for self-interested or ideological reasons (see Pollack 2003). One of two implications could be drawn from this finding: on the one hand, it could be argued that the ECB behaves differently from other EU institutions by virtue of its specific responsibilities in relation to monetary policy; on the other, it could be argued that the ECB illustrates the potential of delegation to function-specific agencies (Wallace 2010: 94) with well-defined preferences as a way of avoiding at least some of the problems of accountability associated with the traditional engines of European integration (see Chapter 10).

Conclusion

Under the Lisbon Treaty, the ECB has finally been recognized as an EU institution—but it remains a most unusual one. The autonomy afforded to the ECB in the pursuit of this goal also goes well beyond the independence enjoyed by the Commission and the ECJ, leading Pollack (2003: 392) to describe the Bank as 'without doubt the most spectacular example of delegation in the European Union since the EEC Treaty of 1957'.

For an EU institution, the ECB also has a surprisingly decentralized governance structure, with national central bank governors outnumbering Executive Board members by a ratio of almost three to one when it comes to decisions on monetary policy. The ECB's decisiveness in the opening phase of the global financial crisis challenged claims that the size of the Governing Council would produce inertia, but the Bank's subsequent reluctance to cut interest rates and embrace unconventional monetary policies lent support to such views. In spite of this hesitancy, the ECB found itself immersed in efforts to maintain the credibility of the single currency in the midst of a sovereign debt crisis, with the decision to purchase government bonds seemingly a step too far for some members of the Governing Council.

The ECB faces few checks and balances compared to other EU institutions, with some scholars warning of a legitimacy deficit at the heart of monetary union. For its part, the ECB has gone further than the Treaty requires in developing a close working relationship with the European Parliament. Whether the EP ECON Committee's monetary dialogue can be said to hold the ECB to account is a matter of debate, but it has proved to be a mutually beneficial exercise for both sides. The Bank has been much more cautious in its dealings with other EU bodies, with periodic calls for the Eurogroup to become an economic government forever falling foul of Frankfurt. What this caution means for EMU's legitimacy is uncertain, but it challenges conventional assumptions about EU institutions' commitment, for reasons of self-interest or ideology, to the pursuit of ever-closer union.

NOTES

1. Thanks to John Peterson and Michael Shackleton for helpful comments on an earlier draft of this chapter. The usual disclaimer applies. The term 'euro area' is used throughout this chapter, because it is the preferred term in Brussels and appears in the treaties; the alternative term widely used in the press is 'eurozone'.

2. Case C-11/00 *Commission of the European Communities v. European Central Bank* [2003] ECR I-7147, [126].

3. Article 1, Agreement establishing the European Bank for Reconstruction and Development.

4. The ESRB's statute states only that the Vice-President of the ESRB should be chosen from the General Council, but there is an agreement to revisit the appointment procedure for the Presidency before the end of 2013 (Regulation (EU) No. 1092/2010, OJ L 331/1, 24 November 2010).

5. These warnings notwithstanding, there are signs that the sovereign debt crisis may have shifted thinking in some parts of the ECB, with Jean-Claude Trichet floating the idea of an EU finance ministry, with budgetary, regulatory, and surveillance powers, towards the end of his tenure as President.

FURTHER READING

See Hodson (2010) for a short introduction to EMU and its relevance for debates about EU policy-making. For a more detailed introduction to the economics of EMU, see De Grauwe (2007). De Haan *et al.* (2005) offer a detailed economic analysis of the ECB's early years, with Buiter (1999) and Issing (1999) engaging in a lively debate about democratic accountability at the ECB and the Bank of England. Howarth and Loedel (2005) and Quaglia (2008) explore the ECB from a political science perspective. Hodson (2011) includes a detailed discussion of the ECB's ambivalent relationship with the EU's institutional order. Dyson and Featherstone (1999), Moravcsik (1998), and McNamara (1998) offer alternative perspectives on the ECB's creation.

Buiter, W. (1999) 'Alice in Euroland', *Journal of Common Market Studies*, 37/2: 181–209.

De Grauwe, P. (2007) *The Economics of Monetary Union* (7th edn, Oxford: Oxford University Press).

De Haan, J., Eijffinger, S., and Waller, S. (2005) *The European Central Bank: Credibility, Transparency, and Centralization* (Cambridge, MA: MIT Press).

Dyson, K. and Featherstone, K. (1999) *The Road to Maastricht: Negotiating Economic and Monetary Union* (Oxford: Oxford University Press).

Hodson, D. (2010) 'Economic and monetary union', in H. Wallace, M. Pollack, and A. Young (eds) *Policy-making in the European Union* (6th edn, Oxford: Oxford University Press).

Hodson, D. (2011) *Governing the Eurozone in Good Times and Bad* (Oxford: Oxford University Press).

Howarth, D. and Loedel, P. (2005) *The European Central Bank: The New European Leviathan?* (Basingstoke: Palgrave Macmillan).

Issing, O. (1999) 'The Eurosystem: transparent and accountable or "Willem in Euroland"', *Journal of Common Market Studies*, 37/3: 503–19.

McNamara, K. (1998) *The Currency of Ideas: Monetary Politics in Europe* (Ithaca, NY: Cornell University Press).

Moravcsik, A. (1998) *The Choice for Europe: Social Purpose and State Power from Messina to Maastricht* (Ithaca, NY: Cornell University Press).

Quaglia, L. (2008) *Central Banking Governance in the European Union: A Comparative Analysis* (London: Routledge).

 ## WEB LINKS

http://ec.europa.eu/dgs/economy_finance
http://www.ecb.eu
http://www.europarl.europa.eu/activities/committees/homeCom.do?body=ECON
Key official websites include those of the European Commission's Directorate General for Economic and Financial Affairs, the ECB itself, and the European Parliament's ECON Committee.

http://www.economist.com
http://www.ft.com
The *Financial Times* is the journal of record on EU affairs, with *The Economist* counting as another important publication.

http://www.eurointelligence.com
http://www.voxeu.org
Eurointelligence and VOX EU offer intelligent commentary on EMU-related issues by leading scholars in the field, with the former also offering a subscription-based daily news briefing on euro area issues.

CHAPTER 10

Managing Europeanization: the European Agencies

R. Daniel Kelemen and Giandomenico Majone

▌Summary

Over the past two decades, the European Union has established over thirty agencies in a wide variety of policy areas, with headquarters spread out across the member states. EU agencies are now well established as an integral part of the EU's model of governance. This chapter analyses why EU agencies have been created and what impact they are having on European governance. EU leaders have delegated regulatory powers to agencies both in response to functional pressures and because of political motivations relating to inter-institutional politics in the EU. The chapter spotlights the development and operation of three particular European agencies: the European Environment Agency (EEA); the European Medicines Agency (EMA); and the European Food Safety Authority (EFSA).

Introduction

This chapter examines the rise of European Union (EU) agencies. EU agencies—
sometimes also labeled 'authorities', or 'centres'—are 'EU level public authorities
with a legal personality and a certain degree of organizational and financial autonomy that are created by acts of secondary legislation in order to perform clearly
specified tasks' (Kelemen 2005: 175). Over the past two decades, the EU has established over thirty agencies in a wide variety of policy areas, with headquarters spread
out across the member states. With the establishment of these agencies, the EU has
quietly managed to expand its regulatory capacity without directly increasing the
size or capacity of the EU's primary executive organ—the European Commission.
Today, EU agencies employ over 4,000 staff members and their budgets total over
€1.25 billion. EU agencies are now well established as an integral part of the EU's
model of governance. This chapter analyses why EU agencies have been created and
what impact they are having on European governance.

Development

The first EU agencies (the European Centre for the Development of Vocational
Training, or Cedefop, and the European Foundation for the Improvement of Living
and Working Conditions, or Eurofound) were created in the 1970s, but these were
operational, rather than regulatory, bodies. The 1990s produced a second wave of
agencies, this time dealing with regulatory issues, including the European Environment Agency (EEA) and the European Medicines Agency (EMA; discussed below).
A third wave of agency creation started at the beginning of the twenty-first century
with the creation of the European Food Safety Authority (EFSA), the European Maritime Safety Agency (EMSA), the European Aviation Safety Agency (EASA), and the
European Railway Agency (ERA). It has continued with the recent creation of EU
authorities in the fields of securities, banking, and pension regulation. Most European regulatory-type agencies of the second and third generation advise the Commission on the technical or scientific aspects of regulatory problems, but have not
been given the formal authority to take final and binding regulatory decisions. In
addition to the regulatory agencies on which we focus in this chapter, the EU has
also established a handful of executive agencies that perform managerial tasks on
behalf of the Commission. It has also set up a number of agencies focusing on foreign and security policy, and justice and policing, such as the European Union Institute for Security Studies (EUISS), the European Defence Agency (EDA), the EU
Judicial Cooperation Unit (Eurojust), and the European Police College (CEPOL).
While this chapter focuses exclusively on EU agencies with some regulatory dimension (see Table 10.1), the creation of these regulatory agencies should be understood

TABLE 10.1 European regulatory agencies

	Start of activities	Mission	Location	Official website
European Environment Agency (EEA)	1990	To collect and disseminate information on the state and trends of the environment at European level; to cooperate with relevant scientific bodies and international organizations	Copenhagen	**http://www.eea.europa.eu/**
Office for Harmonization in the Internal Market (Trade Marks and Designs) (OHIM)	1993	To contribute to harmonization in the domain of intellectual property, and, in particular, the domain of trade marks	Alicante	**http://oami.europa.eu/**
European Medicines Agency (EMA)	1993	To protect and promote public and animal health through the evaluation and supervision of medical products for human and veterinary use	London	**http://www.ema.europa.eu/**
Community Plant Variety Office (CPVO)	1994	To implement the regime of Community plant variety rights, a specific form of industrial property rights relative to new plant varieties	Angers	**http://www.cpvo.europa.eu/**
European Agency for Safety and Health at Work (EU-OSHA)	1994	To provide the Community bodies, the member states, and stakeholders with all relevant technical, scientific, and economic information; to create a network linking up national information networks and facilitate the provision of information in the field of health and safety at work	Bilbao	**http://osha.europa.eu/**
European Union Agency for Fundament Rights (FRA)	1997/2007	To provide EU and member state institutions with assistance and expertise on fundamental rights when implementing Community law, and to support them in formulating and taking measures	Vienna	**http://fra.europa.eu/**

Cont. ▶

Cont.

European Food Safety Authority (EFSA)	2002	To provide independent scientific advice on all matters with a direct or indirect impact on food safety; to carry out assessments of risks to the food chain; to give scientific advice on genetically modified (GM) non-food products and feed	Parma	http://www.efsa.europa.eu/
European Aviation Safety Agency (EASA)	2002	To assist the Community in establishing and maintaining a high level of civil aviation safety and environmental protection in Europe; to promote cost-efficiency in the regulatory and certification processes; to promote worldwide Community views regarding civil aviation safety standards	Cologne	http://easa.europa.eu/
European Maritime Safety Agency (EMSA)	2002	To provide technical and scientific advice to the Commission in the field of maritime safety and prevention of pollution by ships; to contribute to the process of evaluating the effectiveness of Community legislation	Lisbon	http://emsa.europa.eu/
European Network and Information Security Agency (ENISA)	2004	To assist the Community in ensuring particularly high levels of network and information security; to assist the Commission, the member states, and the business community in meeting the requirements of network and information security, including those of present and future Community legislation	Heraklion	http://www.enisa.europa.eu/
European Railway Agency (ERA)	2004	To provide the member states and the Commission with technical assistance in the fields of railway safety and interoperability, in particular by carrying out continuous monitoring of safety performance, and producing a public report every two years	Lille/Valenciennes	http://www.era.europa.eu/

European Centre for Disease Prevention and Control (ECDC)	2004	To work with national health protection bodies to strengthen and develop continent-wide disease surveillance and early warning systems; to develop authoritative scientific opinions on risks posed by new and emerging infectious diseases	Stockholm	**http://www.ecdc.europa.eu**
European GNSS Agency (GSA)	2004	To manage the public interests and to be the regulatory authority for the European GNSS (Global Navigation Satellite Systems) programmes	Brussels	**http://www.gsa.europa.eu/**
Community Fisheries Control Agency (CFCA)	2004	To strengthen the uniformity and effectiveness of enforcement by pooling EU and national means of fisheries control, and monitoring resources and coordinating enforcement activities	Vigo	**http://cfca.europa.eu/**
European Institute for Gender Equality (EIGE)	2006	To support the work of EU institutions in promoting gender equality by collecting and analysing data, facilitating dialogue between stakeholders, and raising public awareness	Vilnius	**http://www.eige.europa.eu/**
European Chemicals Agency (ECHA)	2007	To coordinate registration, evaluation, authorization, and restriction processes under the REACH regulation; to ensure consistency in chemicals management across the EU, and to provide technical and scientific advice and information on chemicals	Helsinki	**http://echa.europa.eu/**
European Securities and Markets Authority (ESMA)	2010	To safeguard the stability of the EU's financial system by ensuring the integrity, transparency, efficiency, and orderly functioning of securities markets, as well as enhancing investor protection	Paris	**http://www.esma.europa.eu/**

Cont. ▶

Cont.

European Banking Authority (EBA)	2010	To safeguard the stability of the financial system, the transparency of markets and financial products, and the protection of depositors and investors; to work with national regulators to prevent regulatory arbitrage, strengthening supervisory coordination and promoting supervisory convergence; to provide advice to the EU institutions on banking and financial regulation	London	http://www.eba.europa.eu/
European Insurance and Occupational Pensions Authority (EIOPA)	2010	To support the stability of the financial system, transparency of markets and financial products, as well as the protection of insurance policyholders, pension scheme members, and beneficiaries	Frankfurt	https://eiopa.europa.eu/
Agency for the Cooperation of Energy Regulators (ACER)	2011 (planned)	To provide advice to EU institutions on energy-related issues; to take binding individual decisions on terms and conditions for access and operational security for cross-border infrastructure if NRAs national authorities cannot agree	Ljubljana	http://www.acer.europa.eu/

Source: Official home page of the Agencies: **http://europa.eu/agencies/index_en.htm**

as part of a broader trend in the EU toward delegating authority to autonomous bodies outside the structure of the European Commission.

Why EU agencies?

When they agree to regulate a field at the EU level, EU law-makers in the Council of Ministers and European Parliament (EP) have a number of options in setting up bodies that can be tasked with making and implementing regulation (Coen and Thatcher 2008; Kelemen and Tarrant 2011). First, they can simply delegate to the European Commission, as member state governments did for most of the EU's history when they decided to delegate regulatory tasks to the EU level. Second, law-makers can delegate tasks to specially established networks of national regulatory authorities (NRAs), as did securities regulators when they delegated certain regulatory tasks to the Committee of European Securities Regulators (CESR) in 2001. Finally, they can delegate to EU agencies outside the structure of the European Commission, as in the case of the European Environment Agency, the European Medicines Agency, or the more recently created European Securities and Markets Authority (ESMA). What then explains law-makers' design choices and the increasing popularity of EU agencies?

Delegation and policy credibility

First, compelling functional reasons exist for delegating regulatory powers to agencies: namely, to enhance the credibility of long-term policy commitments. *Political uncertainty* and *time inconsistency* are the main causes of the credibility problem. Political uncertainty is a direct consequence of the democratic process. One of the defining characteristics of democracy is that it is a form of government *pro tempore* (Linz 1998). The requirement of elections at regular intervals implies that the policies of the current majority can be subverted by a new majority with different and perhaps opposing interests; hence the uncertainty about future policies.

The other threat to policy credibility—time inconsistency—occurs when a government's optimal long-run policy differs from its preferred short-run policy, so that the government in the short run has an incentive to renege on its long-term commitments. In the absence of some binding commitment, the government will use its discretion to pursue what appears now to be a better policy. If the policy-makers have the possibility of revising the original policy to achieve such short-term gains, economic actors will recognize this incentive and change their behaviour accordingly.

One way of enhancing the credibility of long-term policy commitments is to delegate the implementation of those objectives to politically independent institutions.

The delegation of regulatory powers to some agency distinct from the government itself can serve as a means whereby governments can commit themselves to regulatory strategies that would not be credible in the absence of such delegation (Gatsios and Seabright 1989). In the EU context, member states may agree that it is in their long-term interests to cooperate on harmonizing regulation in a particular area in order to integrate the market, but they will face short-term incentives to defect from their agreements. To make their policy commitments credible, member states may have an incentive to delegate to a politically independent, supranational regulatory authority. Indeed, in a general sense, this is the very *raison d'être* for the European Commission.

These considerations explain why there may be a functional need for independent regulatory bodies at the European level, but they do not by themselves explain the creation of EU agencies. They do not tell us how agencies will be structured, what powers will be delegated to them, or why new, autonomous agencies—rather than the European Commission itself—will be tasked with regulation. While functional considerations play a key motivating role, the process of agency design is ultimately driven by political considerations. The design of EU agencies is the result of political compromises involving EU law-makers in the Council of Ministers, the European Parliament, and the European Commission.

The politics of agency design

With the drive to complete the single market project by 1992, the EU's regulatory agenda expanded rapidly—increasing significantly the scale of regulatory functions (information-gathering, analysis, issuance of rules to implement directives, monitoring of enforcement, and so on) that needed to be performed (or at least coordinated) at the European level. These regulatory burdens might have been dealt with simply by expanding the European Commission—adding to its staff and budget. This choice is what the Commission itself and its allies in the EP would have preferred, but among the member states there was widespread opposition to any substantial expansion of the European Commission. Quite simply, many governments would not permit the establishment of a substantially larger, centralized EU bureaucracy in Brussels.

In this political context, Commission President Jacques Delors proposed what would become the first in a wave of new EU agencies: the EEA (discussed below). For the Commission and EP, the idea of establishing autonomous European agencies was an attractive second-best means through which to expand the EU's regulatory capacity—given that expansion of the Commission itself was unacceptable to member governments. Delegating routine information-gathering and regulatory tasks to agencies was attractive to the Commission, because it allowed the Commission to focus its limited resources better on its core tasks, such as policy development and enforcement. Moreover, many of the responsibilities granted to EU agencies would not be in any sense taken away from the European Commission; instead, agencies would perform tasks that might otherwise have been performed by so-called 'comitology committees', which advised the Commission. But member states extracted a price for acquiescing in the establishment of these new agencies: as we will see, the member states demanded considerable intergovernmental oversight of the agencies—through the creation of management boards that were to be dominated by appointees of member state governments. In other words, with the creation of EU agencies, the European Commission got the expansion of EU regulatory capacities that it wanted, while the member states maintained substantial intergovernmental control over these new entitities.

Over the course of the past decade, the politics of agency design have shifted as a result of the growing power of the EP. Along with the growth of its legislative power, the Parliament has strengthened its oversight of the Union's executive organs—including the EU agencies. The EP has scrutinized agency budgets and has demanded that agencies follow formal and transparent regulatory procedures. In essence, the Parliament is acting to ensure that the European agencies will operate in a far more transparent manner than the obscure comitology committees that have so long operated in the shadows of EU governance.

Finally, in a broader sense, the rise of EU agencies has coincided with and facilitated a shift in the role of the European Commission. The Commission used to be viewed as the EU's independent, regulatory bureaucracy. But just as more and more routine regulatory tasks were being delegated to EU agencies, the Commission itself was experiencing a progressive politicization. As the Commission comes to depend on the political support of the EP, it begins to look less like a politically independent, supranational regulatory bureaucracy and more like a nascent parliamentary government.

Legal obstacles to delegation

European agencies do not have the powers granted to American regulatory bodies, and even lack the more limited competence enjoyed by the regulatory authorities of many member states. Thus the regulation setting up the European Environment Agency (EEA) does not include regulatory functions in the agency's mandate.[1] The task of the EEA is mainly to provide information that may be useful in framing and implementing environmental policy. Even those agencies with more substantial regulatory powers, such as the European Medicines Agency, the European Aviation Safety Agency, or the more recently established European Securities and Markets Authority, do not, formally speaking, have discretionary decision-making powers. For example, the European Medicines Agency (EMA), does not take decisions concerning the safety and efficacy of new medicinal drugs, but submits opinions concerning the approval of such products to the European Commission, which takes the final legal decision.[2] Similarly, the European Food Safety Authority (EFSA) is allowed only to assess risk, not to manage it.[3] Only the Commission can make final determinations concerning the safety of the food that Europeans—and others who enjoy EU exports—eat.

Ostensibly, the primary reason why European agencies are not granted broader powers is that the European Court of Justice (ECJ) has prohibited it. In a 1958 ruling,[4] the
ECJ established the 'Meroni doctrine', holding that Community law prohibits the delegation of discretionary powers to bodies—including European agencies—that are not
established in the EU treaties. Thus member states can establish new bodies with discretionary powers—such as the European Central Bank (ECB) or Europol—in EU
treaties, but they cannot do so through normal secondary legislation. The Commission
(2001) has interpreted the doctrine as follows: 'Agencies cannot be granted decision-
making power in areas in which they would have to arbitrate between conflicting public interests, exercise political discretion or carry out complex economic assignments.'

But political considerations back up this legal obstacle. Some of the political actors
involved in the design of European agencies prefer not to see them take on discretionary regulatory powers. In other words, there is considerable political support for the
Court's Meroni doctrine. While some member states would be happy to transfer more
rule-making power from the Commission to agencies, the design of EU agencies and
decisions over which powers they will exercise require the agreement of the Commission and EP as well. The Commission, for its part, prefers to maintain ultimate decision-
making authority; it is enthusiastic to see routine regulatory tasks delegated to EU
agencies in large part because it knows that, under the Meroni doctrine, it retains the
last word. Over time, however, we can observe a gradual decrease in the constraints
imposed by the Meroni doctrine and a gradual increase in the authority delegated to
EU agencies. A number of the EU agencies established in recent years—from the European Aviation Safety Agency, to the European Chemicals Agency (ECHA) and the
European Securities and Markets Authority—have been granted regulatory powers
that would seem to push them into the realm of discretionary decision-making.

The growing role of agencies

The European Environment Agency and the other agencies established in the mid-
1990s were ad hoc experiments in institutional innovation, but over the past decade
EU agencies have become an integral aspect of the EU's regulatory landscape. Today,
proposals to expand EU regulation substantially are regularly accompanied by plans
for the establishment of an EU agency. As plans for new agencies proliferated, the
Commission called for the establishment of a common framework on which to
model them. The 2001 White Paper on European Governance contained a section
on 'Better application of EU rules through regulatory agencies', and called for the
establishment of a common framework for the creation, operation, and supervision
of agencies. The following year, the Commission proposed such a framework for the
agencies and, in 2005, a draft inter-institutional agreement on EU agencies was
published. However, adoption of the agreement was blocked in the Council. In
2008, the Commission finally withdrew the stalled agreement and presented a new

Communication on European agencies that promised to relaunch the debate about their place in governance. Representatives of the Commission, EP, and Council subsequently met to discuss issues concerning the structure, supervision, and operations of the agencies; however, at the time of writing, they had not agreed on any uniform framework for European agencies.

While the Council, Commission, and Parliament have been unable to agree on a standard template for agencies, they nonetheless have continued to create new ones. In recent years, agencies have been created in sectors such as energy—the European Agency for the Cooperation of Energy Regulators (ACER)—and financial market regulation—the European Securities and Markets Authority, the European Banking Authority (EBA), and the European Insurance and Occupational Pensions Authority (EIOPA)—in which member states had long resisted the establishment of new agencies (see Table 10.1). In these fields, in which regulatory decisions entail substantial distributional consequences, member states had previously sought to rely on networks of national regulatory authorities to provide necessary coordination without establishing EU bodies that might constrain national regulatory discretion. However, disastrous regulatory failures and a growing acceptance that the network model alone was inadequate led member states to agree to link these networks to powerful EU agencies (Kelemen and Tarrant 2011).

The politics of institutional choice: the birth of the European Environment Agency

In January 1989, Commission President Jacque Delors proposed the establishment of a European Environment Agency, to strengthen the Community's information-gathering, monitoring, and implementation capacity. Member states, European institutions, and environmentalist groups all voiced support for the proposal, but were deeply divided over specific structural choices—especially those concerning the regulatory powers and effective independence of the new agency. Many in the EP favoured a body with regulatory 'teeth'. In varying degrees, all member states opposed the idea that the agency could monitor the implementation of European environmental legislation by national regulators, preferring to restrict its task to the collection of environmental information and to networking with national, European, and international research institutions. The position of the Commission was ambivalent. On the one hand, officials in the Directorate General for the Environment (DG Env) were concerned about the criticism of industry and of some member states that the Commission's environmental proposals were not grounded in 'good science'. They were even more concerned by the poor implementation of environmental directives. Hence the idea that the EEA could become a sort of inspectorate of national environmental inspectorates had a number of influential supporters

within the Commission. On the other hand, this institution was reluctant to sur-
render regulatory powers to an agency operating at arm's length. In a 1989 proposal,
the Commission outlined four functions for the new body:

- to coordinate the enactment of European Community (EC) and national
  environmental policies;
- to evaluate the results of environmental measures;
- to provide modelling and forecasting techniques; and,
- to harmonize the processing of environmental data.

Because of the expected opposition by the member states, no inspection tasks were
contemplated.

This proposal was quite distant from the EP's 'ideal point'. The fact that Beate
Weber, the *rapporteur* of the Parliament's Environmental Committee, travelled to
Washington DC to gain first-hand knowledge of the US Environmental Protection
Agency (EPA) suggests the model of regulatory agency that European parliamentarians had in mind. The EP Environmental Committee maintained that the EEA
should be given power to police environmental abuses, to supervise national enforcement of EC environmental regulations, and to carry out environmental impact
assessments on certain Community-funded projects. Also, the composition of the
management board became a point of contention. According to the EP, environmental groups should be represented on the board, alongside representatives from the
member states, the Commission, and the EP itself, and the board should be allowed
to take decisions by majority vote.

Comparing the preferences of the main political actors—member states, Commission, EP—with the provisions of the regulation setting up the agency, we see that the
member states clearly won the contest over the structure and powers of the agency.
The decisive influence of the national governments is revealed by the composition
of the management board, which was to be dominated by member state appointees.
As mentioned, the main task assigned to the agency is to provide the EU and the
member states with environmental information and, in particular, 'to provide the
Commission with the information that it needs to be able to carry out successfully
its tasks of identifying, preparing, and evaluating measures and legislation in the
field of environment'.[5] The wording is sufficiently vague, however, to make it unclear whether the agency would be allowed to directly influence policy formulation,
for example by evaluating alternative proposals for regulatory measures. Political
compromise produced an institutional design characterized by uncertain competences, unresolved conflicts, and failure to deal with the serious implementation
problems of EU environmental policy. The compromise over the creation of the EEA
established a model that then provided a rough template for subsequent agency proposals. Each agency was created in distinctive political circumstances, and the details of the powers granted to agencies and the oversight structures put in place
varied as a result. However, a number of key elements of the design of the EEA have

been replicated in other agencies. For example, agency management boards have continued to be dominated by representatives of member state governments and the agencies have served as hubs of regulatory networks that include (rather than replace) national regulatory authorities.

From committees to agency: the development of the European Medicines Agency

Our next example provides valuable insights into how obscure comitology committees have been transformed into a structure in which they become the operational arm of European agencies and link up with national authorities to form transnational regulatory networks. The first attempt by the EC to regulate the testing and marketing of pharmaceutical products was a directive introduced in 1965 with the dual objective of protecting human health and of eliminating obstacles to intra-Community trade. This directive established only the principle that no medical drug should be placed on the market without prior authorization, and defined the essential criteria of safety and efficacy for drug approval.

The second phase of regulatory developments began in 1975, with another directive setting up the 'multi-state drug application procedure' and establishing the Committee for Proprietary Medicinal Products (CPMP). This Committee composed of national experts has played, and continues to play, a key role in the EU approach to the regulation of pharmaceuticals. Under the multi-state procedure, a firm that had received a marketing authorization from the regulatory agency of a member state could ask for the recognition of that approval by at least five other member states. The agencies of these countries had to approve or raise objections within 120 days. In the case of objections, the CPMP had to be notified, and would express its non-binding opinion within sixty days. The procedure did not work well: the national agencies did not appear to be bound either by the decisions of other regulatory bodies or by the opinion of the CPMP. Subsequent simplifications failed to streamline the approval process, as national regulators continued to raise objections against each other almost routinely. Hence firms generally chose to continue to seek authorization from each national agency separately.

A different approval process was introduced in 1987 for biotechnology and other high-tech products. This new 'concertation procedure' required that the application for the authorization be filed both with the national authorities and with the CPMP. The country in which the authorization had been filed acted as *rapporteur*, but unlike the old multi-state procedure, no decision on the application was to be made by any member state before the CPMP had expressed its opinion. The final decision remained with the member states, however. The evaluation of the application, led by the *rapporteur* country, was carried out at the same time in all of the member states—hence the name 'concertation procedure'. The new process was an advance with respect to the old practice, but was nevertheless problematic for firms because, as with the previous procedure, there was a tendency for delays in the notification of decisions following the CPMP opinion. Waiting for all countries to notify their decisions following the Committee's opinion could result in serious delays in a firm's ability to start marketing a new drug.

In 1995, the problematic multi-state and concertation procedures were replaced by three new approaches and a new agency (see Box 10.1). The multi-state procedure was replaced by a decentralized procedure, which continues and reinforces the principle of mutual recognition introduced in 1975. Meanwhile, the concertation procedure was replaced by the centralized procedure set out in the same regulation that also established the EMA (see Box 10.2).[6]

Under the centralized procedure, applications are made directly to the agency, leading to the granting of a European marketing authorization. Use of this procedure is compulsory for products derived from biotechnology and optional for other innovative medicinal products. The EMA is also called on to arbitrate disputes arising under the decentralized (mutual recognition) procedure. Opinions adopted by the EMA in either the centralized procedure or following arbitration lead to binding decisions formally adopted by the Commission.

The technical work of the agency is carried out by the Committee for Medicinal Products for Human Use (CHMP, the successor of the old CPMP), by the Committee for Veterinary Medicines (CVMP), and by two smaller and newer bodies: the Committee for Orphan Medicinal Products (COMP), established in 2001 and charged with reviewing designation applications from persons or companies who intend to develop medicines for rare diseases ('orphan drugs'); and the Committee on Herbal Medicinal Products (HMPC), established in 2004 to provide scientific opinions on traditional herbal medicines. A network of some 3,500 European experts underpins the scientific work of the EMA, and of its committees and working groups.

The CHMP (and similar rules apply to the CVMP) is composed of two members nominated by each member state for a three-year renewable term. These members, in fact, represent the national regulatory authorities. Although Commission representatives are entitled to attend the meetings of the Committee, the Commission is no longer represented, no doubt to emphasize the independence of the CHMP.

In keeping with the political compromise common to the establishment of all EU agencies, the new EMA was put under the control of a management board dominated by member state appointees. When the EMA was restructured in 2004, member states acquiesced to the Parliament's demand that EP and stakeholder representatives be added to the Agency's management board, although member state representatives still held a majority. Also, the Council agreed to the Parliament's demand that the nominee for the position of agency executive director appear before the Parliament prior to her or his formal approval by the Council.

In fact, the Committee has become more important, as well as more independent, since the establishment of the EMA. In the new situation, Committee members have

BOX 10.1	An overview of the European authorization system

Human and animal health

The European system for the authorization of medicines for human and veterinary use has been in place since 1995. It is designed to promote both public health and the free circulation of pharmaceuticals. Access to the European market is facilitated for new and better medicines—benefiting users and European pharmaceutical research.

EMA: a network agency

The European system is based on cooperation between the nationally competent authorities of the member states and the European Medicines Agency. The EMA acts as the hub of the system, coordinating the scientific resources made available by member state national authorities, including a network of thousands of European experts.

The EMA is designed to coordinate the scientific resources of the member states, acting as an interface between the national competent authorities rather than as a highly centralized organization.

The European procedures

The European system offers two routes for authorization of medical products, as follows.

Centralized procedure	Decentralized procedure
Applications are made directly to the EMA, leading to the granting of a European marketing authorization. Use of this procedure is compulsory for products derived from biotechnology.	Applicable to the majority of conventional medicinal products. Applications are made to the member states selected by the applicant and the procedure operates by mutual recognition of national marketing authorizations. Where mutual recognition is not possible, the EMA is called upon to arbitrate.

Opinions adopted by the EMA scientific committees in either the centralized procedure or following arbitrations lead to binding decisions adopted by the European Commission. Purely national authorizations remain available for medicinal products to be marketed in one member state.

greater incentives to establish the Agency's, and their own, international reputation than to defend national positions. Using Alvin Gouldner's (1957–58) terminology, we may say that the agency creates a favourable environment for the transformation of national regulators from 'locals' (that is, professionals who have primarily a national orientation) to 'cosmopolitans', who are likely to adopt an international reference-group orientation. It does so by providing a stable institutional focus at the European level and a forum in which different risk philosophies are compared and mutually

---

BOX 10.2   **The EMA mission statement**

The mission of the European Medicines Agency is to foster scientific excellence in the evaluation and supervision of medicines, for the benefit of public and animal health. Working with the Member States and the European Commission as partners in a European medicines network, the European Medicines Agency:

- provides independent, science-based recommendations on the quality, safety and efficacy of medicines, and on more general issues relevant to public and animal health that involve medicines;

- applies efficient and transparent evaluation procedures to help bring new medicines to the market by means of a single, EU-wide marketing authorisation granted by the European Commission;

- implements measures for continuously supervising the quality, safety and efficacy of authorised medicines to ensure that their benefits outweigh their risks;

- provides scientific advice and incentives to stimulate the development and improve the availability of innovative new medicines;

- recommends safe limits for residues of veterinary medicines used in food-producing animals, for the establishment of maximum residue limits by the European Commission;

- involves representatives of patients, healthcare professionals and other stakeholders in its work, to facilitate dialogue on issues of common interest;

- publishes impartial and comprehensible information about medicines and their use;

- develops best practice for medicines evaluation and supervision in Europe, and contributes alongside the Member States and the European Commission to the harmonisation of regulatory standards at the international level.

---

adjusted, and by establishing strong links to national and extra-European regulatory bodies. Overall, the EMA has been highly successful at least in so far as pharmaceutical manufacturers report satisfaction with the Agency's centralized procedure and many companies seek centralized authorizations (Kelemen and Tarrant 2011).

The pursuit of regulatory credibility: the European Food Safety Authority

The food sector is an area in which EC regulation dates back to the earliest days of the Community. Traditionally, policy on food safety was developed by the Commission, assisted by a large number of comitology and expert committees. Several

BOX 10.3	The EFSA mission statement

- To provide independent scientific advice on all matters with a direct or indirect impact on food safety.
- To carry out assessments of risks to the food chain, and scientific assessments of any matter relating to the safety of the food supply.
- To give scientific advice on genetically modified non-food products and feed, and on nutrition, in relation to Community legislation.
- To provide scientific opinions which will serve as the scientific basis for the drafting and adoption of Community measures.
- To cooperate with the Commission and the member states in order to promote effective coherence between risk assessment, risk management, and risk communication.

regulatory failures—of which the bovine spongiform encephalopathy (BSE, or 'mad cow disease') epidemic attracted the greatest public attention—revealed the inadequacy of the traditional approach. The BSE outbreak exposed serious shortcomings in the overall coordination of European policies on agriculture, the internal market, and human health. In 1996, the EP set up a temporary Committee of Inquiry into BSE. The Committee concluded that both the Council and the Commission had neglected their duties, and that the UK government had exerted pressures on the Commission's veterinary services in order to avoid Community inspections and to prevent the extent of the epidemic being made public. The Commission was criticized for having given priority to the management of the beef market rather than to the risks to human health posed by BSE, and for having downplayed the problem despite concerns raised by a number of experts. The Committee of Inquiry also noted that there had been severe problems with the workings of the Commission's Scientific Advisory Committee.

Responding to these and other criticisms, in 1997 the Commission issued a Green Paper on the general principles of food law in the EU. It was followed in 2000 by a White Paper on food safety, proposing the creation of what became the European Food Safety Authority in the context of a reform of the entire food safety system, 'from farm to table'. The EFSA was to take on responsibilities relating to the risk assessment and risk communication parts of the regulatory system envisaged by the Commission. However, risk management, comprising legislation and control, was not to be transferred to the agency. The EFSA was to be: guided by the best science; independent of industrial and political interests; open to public scrutiny; scientifically authoritative; and closely linked to national scientific bodies. The reform proposals contained in the White Paper on food safety formed the basis of a regulation that laid down the general principles and requirements of food law, established the EFSA, and sets out its mission (see Box 10.3).

The organizational design of the EFSA is broadly similar to that of the EMA: a management board, an executive director, a scientific committee, and a number of scientific expert panels and their working groups. There are, however, some important differences that are best understood in light of the credibility crisis of EU food safety regulation following the BSE crisis and the rising power of the EP. The BSE crisis had exposed the potential dangers of interference by national officials in objective risk assessments. Under pressure from the Parliament, the member states agreed to put the EFSA under control of a management board that did not guarantee each member government a representative. The EFSA Board comprises fourteen members appointed by the Council—in consultation with the Parliament, from a list drawn up by the Commission—plus an additional representative of the Commission. Four members must have a background in organizations representing consumer and other interests in the food chain, and no member is an official government representative. Instead, the principle of one representative per country has been retained in the composition of the advisory forum, which assists the executive director and advises on scientific matters, priorities, and work programmes.

The tension between the desire to enhance regulatory credibility by appealing to independent scientific expertise, and the refusal to delegate regulatory powers to the EFSA, has been temporarily resolved by the doubtful expedient of an organizational separation of risk assessment (the function assigned to the Authority) and risk management, which remains the responsibility of the Commission. However, the separation of risk assessment and risk management is problematic, because while the two functions are conceptually distinct—one dealing with scientific issues; the other with economic, legal, and political issues—they are closely intertwined in practice. The setting of rational regulatory priorities, for example, entails economic, political, and scientific judgements that cannot be easily separated. Again, the determinations of the risk analysts can effectively pre-empt the decisions of the risk managers. Thus it is often impossible to determine with certainty whether a 'dose–response function'—measuring the probability of an organism's response to different levels of toxicity—follows a linear or a non-linear model, yet the scientists' choice of one or the other model is crucially important to the determination of an acceptable level of risk (Majone 2003). Because risk assessment and risk management are so difficult to separate in practice, the refusal to set up a regulatory agency fully responsible for food safety entails a serious accountability deficit, without solving the credibility problem.

Independence and accountability

In any democracy, there is a tension between the desire for regulatory bodies to be simultaneously independent and accountable. As we saw at the beginning of this chapter, the desire for policy credibility provides an important functional motivation for agency independence. However, in a democratic polity, when regulatory powers are entrusted to a non-elected body, there is understandably a desire to balance this independence with a healthy dose of accountability. The basic problem is always how 'to control and validate the exercise of essentially legislative powers by administrative agencies that do not enjoy the formal legitimacy of one-person, one-vote election' (Stewart 1975: 1688). Law-makers can try to ensure some measure of accountability by giving the agency very specific instructions in the laws that they ask it to implement, putting in place a variety of oversight and judicial review mechanisms, and imposing rigid administrative procedures that force the agency to act in an open and transparent manner (McCubbins *et al.* 1987).

From the outset, EU agencies have been subject to a variety of control mechanisms designed to ensure that they cannot deviate too far from the will of their political masters. This oversight has long been evident in the composition of agency management boards, whereby member states ensured that their representatives could keep a watchful eye over agency operations. As the power of the EP has grown over the past decade, it too has asserted itself as a political master of the EU agencies. This assertion has been evident both in the EP's scrutiny of agencies' budgets and in the Parliament's demands that the agencies adopt more formal, transparent, and judicially enforceable administrative procedures. The impact of these demands is evident in the regulations founding a number of the recently created EU agencies. For example, the European Aviation Safety Agency and the European Chemicals Agency, both of which have been given authority to make decisions concerning the safety of products, are required to follow detailed, transparent procedures, to give reasons for their decisions, and to provide applicants access to a board of appeal to contest decisions. Substantial accountability mechanisms have been put in place, and certainly the EU agencies operate in a far more transparent and accountable manner than the comitology committees that preceded them.

The network model

It is clearly impossible to transpose to the EU the American model of federal agencies operating independently from the regulatory authorities of the states. Regardless of what one thinks of the alleged legal obstacles to the adoption of such a model, it is certain that the member states would reject it. However, again and again, member states have proven themselves willing to construct systems in which the national regulators become components of EU-wide networks, coordinated by European agencies.

The model in which an EU agency serves as the coordinating hub of a network of national regulatory authorities (NRAs) should not be confused with a model of governance that relies exclusively on a network of national regulatory authorities in the absence of a European agency. Some scholars (see Eberlein and Grande 2005) and many practitioners have argued that EU-wide networks of national regulators provide an effective alternative to establishing more formal, centralized EU agencies. In some sectors, such as energy and financial market regulation, many national governments long resisted calls for the establishment of EU agencies by insisting that networks of NRAs could achieve the needed cooperation and harmonization. However, the actual experience with such networks—in fields from pharmaceuticals, to telecoms, to energy, to financial market regulation—has been unimpressive. EU networks regularly fail to deliver regulatory harmonization, because pursuit of national self-interests regularly trumps the impact of 'professionalization' and other normative pressures that network governance theorists claim should facilitate effective cooperation. Indeed, it is for this very reason that some of these loose, ineffectual networks have eventually been subsumed into more centralized structures under the leadership of a European agency (as in the fields of medicines, energy, and financial services regulation).

The success of the network model has been crucial to the proliferation of EU agencies. By relying on networks of national regulatory authorities, EU agencies render themselves less threatening to those who oppose centralization of power. Nevertheless, by creating and coordinating networks of national regulatory authorities, the EU agencies can encourage the spread of common regulatory norms and practices across the member states. Ultimately, the agencies manage to harness the capacities of existing national regulatory authorities to serve European ends.

Conclusions

As shown by many chapters in this volume, the rate of institutional innovation in the EU, after fifty years of integration, is still remarkable. The present chapter has revealed a certain amount of change. What is particularly striking in the case of regulatory agencies, however, is the gap between the quantitative and the qualitative dimension of change. While the number of European agencies created since the early 1990s matches the scale of parallel developments in many member states, the majority of these new European bodies lack the powers normally granted to their national counterparts. The reason for this discrepancy must be sought in the politics of inter-institutional relations in the EU, and ultimately in the logic of the Community method.

Each European institution is the bearer of a particular interest that it strives to protect and promote, and the nature of the prevailing interest determines the structure of decision-making. Thus when the framers of the Rome Treaty deemed that national interests should have precedence in an area of particular interest to national sovereignty, such as fiscal harmonization, they required a unanimous vote in the Council. Where, on the other hand, it appeared that national interests had to be reconciled with the supranational interest, it was decided that the Council should legislate by qualified majority. Again, where it was thought that the supranational interest should prevail, the Commission was given an autonomous power of decision.

In most areas of regulation, design of new regulatory agencies today requires the agreement of the Council, the EP, and the Commission, each of which can simply refuse to propose reforms that would undermine its own authority. The precise terms of the compromise between these institutions varies in the case of each agency, and they have failed thus far to agree on a standard template. Nevertheless, the basic outlines of a model of EU agencies has emerged and now become a vital feature of the Union's regulatory landscape. EU agencies rely heavily on national regulatory authorities, but the agencies provide central leadership and harness these authorities into pan-European networks.

NOTES

1. Council Regulation 1210/90 of 7 May 1990 on the establishment of the European Environment Agency and the European Environment Information and Observation Network.

2. Council Regulation 2309/93 of 22 July 1993 laying down Community procedures for the authorization and supervision of medicinal products for human and veterinary use and establishing a European Agency for the Evaluation of Medicinal Products.

3. Regulation 178/2002 of the European Parliament and the Council of 28 January 2002 laying down the general principles and requirements of food law, establishing the European Food Safety Authority and laying down procedures in matters of food safety.

4. Case 9/56 *Meroni v. High Authority* [1957–58] ECR 133.

5. Article 2 of Regulation 1210/90.

6. See Regulation 2309/93.

FURTHER READING

Recent examples of the burgeoning literature on regulatory agencies in Europe are the volumes edited by Zwart and Verhey (2003), and by Gerardin *et al.* (2005). Freedman (1978) considers only US institutions, but still provides the most extensive discussion of the legitimacy problems of regulatory agencies. Recent developments in risk regulation, with special emphasis on food safety, are discussed in Majone (2003). The Community method and its implications for institutional reform are analysed by Majone (2005). Shapiro (1997) and Kelemen (2002) provide early accounts of the politics of EU agency design. Kelemen and Tarrant (2011) and Rittberger and Wonka (2010) provide more recent analyses, while Groenleer (2009) provides a detailed, book-length analysis of the development of EU agencies.

Freedman, O. (1978) *Crisis and Legitimacy* (Cambridge: Cambridge University Press).

Gerardin, D., Munoz, R., and Petit, N. (2005) (eds) *Regulation through Agencies: A New Paradigm of European Governance* (Cheltenham: Edward Elgar).

Groenleer, M. (2009) *The Autonomy of European Union Agencies: A Comparative Study of Institutional Development* (Delft, The Netherlands: Eburon).

Kelemen, R. D. (2002) 'The politics of "Eurocratic" structure and the new European agencies', *West European Politics* 25/4: 93–118.

Kelemen, R. D. and Tarrant, A. (2011) 'The political foundations of the Eurocracy', *West European Politics*, forthcoming.

Majone, G. (2003) (ed.) *Risk Regulation in the European Union: Between Enlargement and Internationalization* (Florence: European University Institute).

Majone, G. (2005) *Dilemmas of European Integration: The Ambiguities and Pitfalls of Integration by Stealth* (Oxford: Oxford University Press).

Rittberger, B. and Wonka, A. (2010) 'Credibility, complexity and uncertainty: explaining the institutional independence of 29 EU agencies', *West European Politics*, 33/3: 730–52.

Shapiro, M. (1997) 'The problems of independent agencies in the US and the EU', *Journal of European Public Policy*, 4/2: 279–91.

Zwart, T. and Verhey, L. (2003) (eds) *Agencies in European and Comparative Law* (Antwerp: Intersentia).

 WEB LINKS

http://europa.eu

http://europa.eu/agencies

The official EU website is the place to start any search for basic information on its institutions and bodies, and this page links directly to the various different European agencies. (See also Table 10.1 for more specific links.)

CHAPTER 11

Financial Control: the Court of Auditors and OLAF

George Karakatsanis* and Brigid Laffan

▍ Summary

This chapter analyses two of the European Union's organizational entities designed to protect the financial interests of the Union: the European Court of Auditors (ECA), a full EU institution since the 1993 Treaty on European Union (TEU); and OLAF, the EU's Anti-Fraud Office, which is a department (service) of the European Commission. The chapter examines their origins, how their internal structures have evolved, their powers, and their place in the institutional landscape of the Union. Their growing importance arises from the expansion of the EU budget, evidence of mismanagement and fraud against the financial resources of the Union, the emergence of an accountability culture in the EU, and enlargement.

Notwithstanding institution-building and a tightening of the regulatory environment, there remains a lack of clarity in roles under shared management practices between the Commission and the member states—especially since the costs of controls solely burden the latter, while effective implementation of reforms is still in question.

Introduction

The focus in this chapter is on the bodies of the European Union (EU) that were created to protect the interests of Europe's taxpayers in relation to the Union's public finances: the European Court of Auditors (ECA) and OLAF (*Office Européen de Lutte Antifraude*, known in English as the European Anti-Fraud Office). The two bodies are very different. The ECA, established as one of the institutions of the European Communities since the Treaty of Maastricht, is a public audit institution that, as the EU's external auditor, is charged with carrying out the audit of EU finances. OLAF is not an EU institution; rather it is a specialist body with a remit to combat fraud.[1] The Court of Auditors, based in Luxembourg, is already more than thirty years old, dating back to 1977. In contrast, OLAF is a much newer body, created only in 1999. The European Parliament (EP), exercising its role of fostering political accountability, played an important part in the establishment of both institutions.

Member states were persuaded that an independent audit body was warranted given the emergence of an EU budget with supranational characteristics. The creation of the Court represented polity-building at the EU level. The fight against fraud assumed greater salience as the size and reach of the EU budget expanded. Peterson (1997) highlights the challenge facing the EU that arises from the coexistence of pooled sovereignty and divided accountability. The two bodies are part of an important contribution to improving the accountability for EU spending, while taking account of pooled sovereignty.

Financial management—and, in fact, management more generally—tends to be marginalized in scholarly discussions of the EU (Bauer 2002). We should not forget, however, that it was a pronounced failure of management that led to the first resignation of an entire Commission in the history of the Union. The political crisis that culminated in March 1999 with the departure of the Santer Commission had its origins in deep-rooted and perennial problems of financial management in the EU (MacMullen 1999; see also Chapter 5). Moreover, a continuing stream of sensational newspaper headlines highlighting the smuggling of animals, cigarettes, or liquor acted to undermine public confidence in the effectiveness of EU institutions and its policy regimes. Whistle-blowers working in European institutions have featured prominently in public disclosures about financial management in the Union. One of the most prominent of these, Marta Andreasen, who worked for some time as an accountant of the Commission, was subsequently elected in 2009 as a member of the European Parliament (MEP) and is a member of the Parliament's Committee on Budgetary Control (also popularly known by its French acronym, COCOBU).

Following the 1999 crisis, the next Commission under Romano Prodi was given a strong mandate by the European Council to make financial management more robust in the Commission. The Prodi Commission embarked on a series of structural and managerial reforms, known as the 'Kinnock reforms', because Vice President Neil Kinnock was given the lead role in the Commission reform programme (for more details, see Chapter 8). Although committed to reform, the Prodi Commission was not immune to problems of financial management. The Eurostat investigations, discussed below, put considerable pressure on Prodi.

Effective management of the EU budget poses a considerable challenge to the EU and the member states. While overall responsibility for management rests at EU level (that is, with the Commission), over 80 per cent of expenditure management is shared with the member states. The budget, amounting to some €122.9 billion in payment appropriations in 2010, is largely managed by the member states, with only some 12 per cent managed directly by the Commission and an additional 6 per cent spent on the administrative costs of running the institutions. Management and control of the budget is therefore not only—or even primarily—a task for the EU's institutions, but can occur only if member states have the capacity and willingness to protect the financial interests of the Union.

OLAF's annual reports highlight various cases of fraud and corruption, such as misuse of parliamentary expenses by an ex-MEP and fraudulent import activities (OLAF 2009: 9–12). OLAF also continues to have to assert its right to conduct investigations involving the EU institutions. In March 2011, following allegations that a number of MEPs had accepted money for amending legislation, OLAF attempted to launch an investigation. The EP questioned OLAF's legal right to investigate the MEPs, but appeared to back down when faced with a legal justification from OLAF.

Combating fraud, corruption, and waste—much of it transnational—is a formidable task. The Court of Auditors and OLAF operate in a challenging environment, given the complexity and reach of the EU budget. The future of OLAF has become bound up with discussion of the establishment of a European public prosecutor, an office designed also to protect the financial interests of the Union.

The origins of the institutions

Both the Court and OLAF evolved from pre-existing bodies with responsibility for financial control and fighting fraud. The Court of Auditors replaced two audit bodies: the European Communities Audit Office and the Auditor of the European Coal and Steel Community (ECSC). OLAF evolved from the Commission's internal anti-fraud unit known as UCLAF (*Unité de Coordination pour la Lutte Antifraude*), established in 1988 by the Delors Commission. Both were created as a response to the perceived weakness of their precursors, as well as to broader changes in the EU as a whole.

The provision for a Court of Auditors in the 1975 Budget Treaty was directly related to the transition from national contributions to a system based on 'own resources', an independent revenue base. In addition, the granting of the power of the purse to the EP was seen to require a related shift in the locus of financial auditing. The political argument in favour of a Court of Auditors was made in 1973 by

President of the EP's Budgetary Committee, Heinrich Aigner, who argued that a more supranational EU budget necessitated an independent EU audit body. His case was reinforced by a series of well-publicized frauds against the EU budget, and the limited and patchy nature of the financial investigation undertaken by the Audit Board and the ECSC Auditor (Wallace 1980: 101–2; Strasser 1992).

The establishment of OLAF in 1999 can be traced back to 1988 when the Delors Commission felt compelled to create UCLAF in response, notably, to repeated requests from the Parliament to the Commission to enhance its fight against fraud. For many years, it was a largely symbolic response to the problem of fraud, rather than a serious anti-fraud unit. With an initial staff of ten, in addition to temporary agents from the member states, UCLAF could do little more than coordinate the anti-fraud units in the big-spending Directorates-General (DGs)—that is, those for agriculture, customs union, and structural funds. The need to go beyond a symbolic response was heightened by repeated reports of fraud against the EU budget in the media, in reports from the UK's House of Lords, in the Court of Auditors' reports, and in UCLAF's own annual reports (Laffan 1997a).

In 1993, Commissioner Peter Schmidhuber was given direct responsibility for combating fraud and a new director, Per Brix Knudsen, was appointed to UCLAF. The EP insisted in that same year that all anti-fraud divisions in the Commission should be integrated into UCLAF rather than dispersed throughout the organization. After 1994, consolidation took place alongside an increase in the number of staff in UCLAF (sixty permanent staff and sixty-two contract staff by 1997), with the effect that all those with responsibility for combating fraud in the Commission were finally within one chain of command.

The decision in 1998 to create OLAF was taken as the relationship between the Commission and Parliament worsened on the whole question of the Commission's management capacity. The prospect of a new body failed to ward off attacks on the Commission in the EP and from the Committee of Independent Experts that it established in January 1999 (see Box 5.1). After the Santer Commission resigned in March 1999, the Prodi Commission immediately identified the European Anti-Fraud Office (which became OLAF) as a central plank in its response to the criticisms of the Commission's ability to combat fraud (Pujas 2003: 778–97). The Committee of Independent Experts had been critical of UCLAF, finding that 'its intervention sometimes slows the procedures down, without improving the end result' (Committee of Independent Experts 1999a). This was followed by a 2005 special report of the Court of Auditors (ECA Special Report No. 1/2005) highlighting the potential for improved efficiency in the operations of UCLAF's successor body (OLAF). In March 2011 and after OLAF had carried out approximately 4,500 investigations since its establishment, the Commission adopted a proposal to reform the organization with the aim of improving its efficiency, effectiveness, and accountability, while safeguarding its investigative independence.

As the external auditor of the EU budget, the Court of Auditors audits the accounts of all revenue and expenditure of the Union, and all bodies, offices, or agencies set up by the Union. This function is typical function of any external audit body, but what are atypical are the powers conferred on the Court by the treaties to provide assurance not only as to the reliability of the accounts, but also as to the legality and regularity of the underlying transactions. By doing the latter, the Court conducts detailed on-the-spot checks in the places where expenditure has actually taken place. It is through this provision that many irregularities are revealed and reported in the Court of Auditor's annual reports. In case the Court happens to run across a fraudulent case through its examination of underlying transactions, it reports it to OLAF for investigation and subsequent action. OLAF's role is more functional, with the emphasis on protecting the financial interests of the Union via its role in combating fraud, corruption, or any other illegal activity.

The structure of the institutions

The European Court of Auditors

The Court of Auditors consists of twenty-seven members, one per member state, the members' cabinets (four staff per member, a head of private office, and an *attaché*, plus two assistants), and about 557 auditors, who form the operating core of the organization. In 2010, 63 per cent of the 889 total staff were assigned to audit departments called audit chambers. There are five chambers: three are related to internal EU policies, one to external actions, and the fifth is a chamber that deals with horizontal issues such as coordination and audit methodology. The Council appoints the members of the Court to a six-year renewable term after consultation with the EP. The members elect a President from amongst their number for a three-year renewable term.

The Parliament's Budgetary Control Committee holds formal investiture proceedings on appointments to the Court, which have led, on two occasions, to a candidate being replaced. In 1989, when the Parliament issued an opinion objecting to two nominees from a total of six, one of the two member states concerned agreed to nominate another candidate (Strasser 1992: 271). In 2004, the Cypriot government withdrew its candidate following a negative vote in Parliament. The investiture proceedings established a right of parliamentary involvement that was later followed in relation to the appointment of the Commission. According to Art. 286 TFEU (ex Art. 247 TEC), the members of the Court must be from the national external audit bodies or have 'special qualifications' for the office. The stipulation that those 'who are especially qualified' may serve means that the Court of Auditors consists mainly of a mixture of professional senior auditors, finance officials, and former politicians. This mix contrasts with the European Central Bank (ECB), the members of which are all bankers and thus constitute a more cohesive professional college.

The President of the Court is essentially *primus inter pares*: his or her authority rests on the fact that fellow members of the Court elect him or her. The President oversees the operation of the Court and is the public face of the institution, presenting the ECA's annual report to the EP and to the Economics and Financial Affairs Council (Ecofin), and representing the Court vis-à-vis national audit offices. The role of the President has been enhanced by the growing importance of financial control in the Union. Since its inception, the Court has had ten Presidents (see Table 11.1). Vítor Manuel da Silva Caldeira of Portugal was elected President of the Court in 2008 and re-elected in 2011. One of the most outspoken Presidents of the Court was André Middelhoek, who served until 1995. As a member of the Court from the outset, Middelhoek was very committed to the idea that the Court should be an EU institution, formally and legally (as it was so designated by the Maastricht Treaty). He was also determined to heighten the profile of the Court and to give greater salience to the issue of financial management. Middelhoek went on to play a major role in the 1999 Commission resignation crisis when he chaired the Committee of Independent Experts in a particularly muscular fashion.

Regardless of the personality of its President, the Court is a collegiate body characterized by a vertical hierarchy between the auditing staff and the college of members, and a horizontal division between the sectoral auditing areas. From the outset, the Court had organizational autonomy, and was solely responsible for the organization of its work and rules of procedure. In June 2010, the Court of Auditors replaced the rules of procedure under which it had operated since December 2004. It is now

TABLE 11.1 Presidents of the European Court of Auditors

President (Country)	Period
Sir Norman Price (UK)	1977
Michael Murphy (IRL)	1977–81
Pierre Lelong (F)	1981–84
Marcel Mart (Lux)	1984–89
Aldo Angioi (I)	1990–92
Andre Middelhoek (NL)	1993–95
Bernhard Friedmann (G)	1996–98
Jan O. Karlsson (S)	1999–2001
Juan Manuel Fabra Vallés (E)	2002–05
Hubert Weber (A)	2005–08
Vítor Manuel da Silva Caldeira (P)	2008–

Source: Court of Auditors, **http://eca.europa.eu**

organized into audit chambers in order to facilitate more efficient adoption of certain categories of report and opinion (see Box 11.1).[2] The areas of responsibility of each chamber are decided by the Court as a collegial body on a proposal of the President. Each chamber elects one of its members as Dean and can adopt reports and opinions, with the exception of annual reports on the general EU budget and the European development funds. For individual tasks to be carried out, such as selected audits leading to special reports, the chamber appoints a member (or members) to act as reporting member(s), thereby assuming direct responsibility for each task. Chambers have a preparatory responsibility for the adoption of documents—notably, the annual reports that are still adopted by the Court as a collegial body. This new organizational structure gives the Court more flexibility and has been designed to improve its efficiency in decision-making.

The structure of the Court has developed on the basis of one member per state, thus giving it an increasingly top-heavy structure over time. The size of the Court has grown from nine to twenty-seven as the number of member states has expanded. The Treaty of Nice made explicit provision for 'one national from each Member State' (Art. 247 TEC). Following successive enlargements, the Court gained twelve additional members and their supporting cabinets.

A second change that resulted from Nice was the provision that the Council shall adopt the 'list' of candidates put forward by the member states; prior to this, the Council took a separate decision on each nominee. It is too early to tell if this change will make it more difficult for the EP to attempt to block individuals. Given the disparate backgrounds of the members of the Court, ensuring that the College works effectively and to the highest professional standards required in an auditing institution is a genuine challenge.

BOX 11.1   Distribution of responsibilities in the Court of Auditors

Presidency: Supervision of the performance of the Court's work; relations with the institutions of the European Union; relations with the supreme audit institutions (SAIs) and international audit organizations; legal matters; internal audit

Chamber I: Preservation and management of natural resources (six members)

Chamber II: Structural policies, transport, and energy (six members)

Chamber III: External actions (five members)

Chamber IV: Revenue, research and internal policies, and institutions and bodies of the European Union (six members)

CEAD Chamber: Coordination, evaluation, assurance, and development (three members)

Secretariat-General: Human resources, finance and support, information technology, and translation

Source: **http://eca.europa.eu**

OLAF

OLAF's structure grew out of UCLAF, the office that it replaced in 1999. The key difference between UCLAF and OLAF is that the latter was given a special independent status in the regulations that led to its establishment. It remains, however, a part of the Commission under the responsibility of the Commissioner in charge of the budget. Its independence is clear in its investigative powers and OLAF's Director-General (Giovanni Kessler, at the time of writing) is independently responsible for its investigations. The Director-General is appointed by the Commission for a five-year period, renewable once following a favourable opinion from the Supervisory Committee of OLAF, the Council, and the EP. He or she may neither seek nor take instructions from any government or EU institution, including the Commission, and may uphold its prerogatives before the European Court of Justice (ECJ). The management of the Office is under the guidance of a Supervisory Committee of five persons who have no links to EU institutions and are specialists in its area of work. After its creation, OLAF underwent a process of rapid expansion and had a staff complement of 500 staff by 2010.

The relationship between the Commission and OLAF is ambiguous. On the one hand, OLAF has independent powers of investigation; on the other, it works closely with the Commission concerning its responsibility for advising on anti-fraud measures. Yet, in the conduct of its work, it has to investigate Commission officials on occasion. This hybrid nature of OLAF was raised as a serious issue in a report by the UK House of Lords (2004). It pointed to the absence of an independent investigating body in the EU and the continued contestation around the idea of a European public prosecutor.

Powers of the institutions

The European Court of Auditors

Notwithstanding its title, the ECA does not have any judicial functions. The Court performs its audits within an inter-institutional framework laid down mainly by the Treaty on the functioning of the European Union (TFEU) and a financial regulation.[3] Article 287, para. 2 TFEU states that the 'Court of Auditors shall examine whether all revenue has been received and all expenditure incurred in a lawful and regular manner and whether the financial management has been sound'. Its task is a vast one given that the EU's financial instruments are deployed in the member states and in third countries throughout the world. The Commission estimates that, in any one budgetary year, it engages in 400,000 individual budgetary transactions (Laffan 1997b).

The Court has developed a number of non-treaty-based practices. The President of the Court may issue what is known as a 'President's letter' to a concerned

institution to raise important issues arising from an audit, but which are not considered significant enough to be published as a special report. These letters, at times,
provide chilling accounts of the challenges of financial management in the EU and
reveal the politicized nature of the Commission when faced with high-level national
intervention.

Output of the Court

The Court is a prolific producer of reports (see Table 11.2). Between 2005 and 2010,
the Court produced seventy-seven reports, comprising six annual reports and sev-
enty-one special reports and opinions. The Court's work programme and auditing
cycle enters the policy process in the form of the Court's annual report, published in
the autumn of each year for the preceding year and mainly comprising the statement
of assurance, which has been drafted since 1994, specific annual reports on particular EU bodies, a myriad of special reports on policy programmes or financial processes, and opinions when requested by the Council or observations on the initiative
of the Court.

The annual report is a large document running to some 240 pages each year. It
includes detailed observations on different spending programme,s and the replies of
the Commission and other EU institutions on its observations. The length of the
report and the level of detail that it contains has been a deterrent to all but the most
eager followers of EU finances. An attempt was made to produce shorter and sharper
annual reports towards the end of the 1990s, and to focus more on special reports
dealing with the results of audits on specific sectors, such as agriculture and natural
resources, or specific aspects of financial control, such as financial regulations.
A report on the ECA by the UK House of Lords (2001) found 'the Special Reports of
generally greater value than the Annual Report, although variations in the quality of
the former were recognised'. As of 2005, there was a concerted attempt to add clarity
and consistency among chapters in order to facilitate ease of reading, and the annual
report is now supplemented by a concise introduction as a summary of the detailed
report. There has also been a recent tendency to include in the annual report issues
affecting sound financial management and not only those revolving around the traditional financial audit work.

TABLE 11.2 Reports of the European Court of Auditors 1977–2010

Years	1977–86	1987–96	1997–2004	2005–10
Annual Reports	10	10	8	6
Special reports and studies	47	55	112	71
Total	**57**	**65**	**120**	**77**

Source: European Court of Auditors, **http://eca.europa.eu**

From the outset, there has been considerable consistency in the findings of the Court. In 1981, its benchmark study of the financial systems of the European Communities (European Court of Auditors 1981) reported key findings including:

- limited staff resources devoted to financial management;
- serious delays in the clearance of European Agricultural Guidance and Guarantee Fund (EAGGF) accounts;
- financial accounts that were hardly intelligible to users;
- insufficient emphasis placed on the evaluation of results by the Commission;
- problems in the definition of the tasks of the Commission's financial controller; and
- no comprehensive strategy for computer software, hardware ,and operating staff resources.

These criticisms have been repeated regularly in the annual report, the special reports, and, since 1994, in the statement of assurance. In its report on financial year 2003, the Court asserted that it had 'no reasonable assurance that the supervisory systems and controls of significant areas of the budget are effectively implemented so as to manage the risks concerning legality and regularity of the underlying operations' (European Court of Auditors 2004: 6).[4] This statement is echoed in the Court's report on financial year 2009, in which it states that 'payments underlying the accounts for the year ended 31 December 2009 for the policy groups "Agriculture and natural resources", "Cohesion", "Research, energy and transport", "External Aid, development and enlargement" and "Education and Citizenship" are materially affected by error' (European Court of Auditors 2010a: 12).

However, progress has been made. In 2010, the Court published an opinion that stated:

In recent years, the Court has reported improvements in the internal control at the Commission and an overall reduction in the level of irregular payments. However, the Court continues to report a high level of irregular payments in substantial areas of the budget and scope for improving important aspects of diverse EU expenditure programmes and schemes.

(European Court of Auditors 2010b: 2)

(See Box 11.2.)

The Court's institutional position

In analysing the Court's position in the Union's institutional landscape, it is important to distinguish between its relationship with its auditees, on the one hand, and its place in the Union's system of financial control, on the other. Inevitably, tensions exist between the Court as an audit institution and the other EU institutions that are subject to its audits. Although the work of the Court covers all EU institutions and

BOX 11.2	Statements of assurance

Since the coming into force of the Treaty of European Union (TEU, known as the Maastricht Treaty), the Court of Auditors is required to include a statement of assurance (DAS, or SOA) in its annual report. The statement has two elements:

- an audit of the reliability of the accounts; and
- an audit of the legality and reliability of the underlying transactions.

Much has been made in the EP, national parliaments, and the media over the years of the failure of the Court to give positive assurances of the Union's accounts. Headlines such as that which appeared in 2003 in the (UK) *Daily Telegraph*—'Something still rotten in the state of Europe'—reflect the manner in which Eurosceptic media use the Court's annual report to highlight problems in the management of EU funding. A statement at a conference in 2010[5] made by Dutch MP Frans de Nerée tot Babberich reflects concerns within national parliaments:

The EU has not received positive accountancy clearance for its annual accounts for a period of 15 years, without anyone taking true responsibility. While improvements have been made, primarily in the field of agricultural funds, the present situation is impossible to explain to EU citizens.

There has been a tendency in the press and among some parliamentarians to conflate the Court's qualified assurances with fraud and corruption. In fact, there has been significant improvement in the management of EU funds, which is captured in the Court's statements of assurance since 2008. The 2009 annual report launched in November 2010 represented the third consecutive year during which the Court found the accounts to be reliable. Concerning legality and regularity, the Court found that the revenue side of the budget was free from material error, as were commitments. Payments remain the key problem area in which the Court continues to find material levels of error, particularly in relation to agriculture and natural resources, with a level of error of between 2 per cent and 5 per cent, and cohesion, with error levels of over 5 per cent. The continuing evidence of errors in these two big spending areas underlines the continuing challenges facing EU financial management, notwithstanding improvements. The complexity of the spending programmes, decentralized management systems, and a myriad of rules make improvements in EU financial management a work in progress.

bodies, the most critical relationship is the one with the Commission as the institution that is responsible for EU expenditure (even if it directly manages only a small part of it). The relationship with the Commission was very difficult for many years as the young Court strove to find its niche in the Union's institutional landscape. One of the first controversial issues with the Commission related to a 'right of reply' to the Court's observations. In the early years, the Commission never fully reconciled itself to the role of the Court in 'value for money' auditing, and clearly felt that the Court was straying from its audit function into policy or political judgments. Gradually, however, in the 1980s, the Court and the Commission developed a working relationship as the latter came to accept that the audit body was a permanent feature of the Union—a relationship that has continued to the present, albeit with the expected tensions between auditor and auditee.

Relations deteriorated again during Jacques Delors' term as President of the Commission. During the negotiations of the Delors II budgetary package (covering 1993–99), the Commission was furious at a report from the Court to the Council on management problems in the structural funds. Delors complained that the report made it more difficult for him to get the member states to agree to a larger budget.

The Santer Commission made improving relations with the Court one of its main objectives. Santer had had considerable contact with the Court during his time as Prime Minister of Luxembourg. The Santer Commission attempted to upgrade its relationship with the Court. It is paradoxical, then, that the Court contributed to the resignation of the entire Santer Commission in March 1999 when the 1996 discharge procedure became embroiled in a wider debate on management problems in the Commission (see below).

The Court is not the only cog in the wheel of financial management in the Union; such management is also the responsibility of the internal auditors in all of the EU institutions, the authorizing officers in each Commission DG, OLAF, the national authorities that manage EU finances, and the national audit offices. Given the extent and range of the Union's budgetary activities, the Court cooperates with the national audit offices, taking account of the independence of each body. Court audits in the member states are carried out in liaison with the national audit authorities, all of which have appointed a liaison official with the Court. In the period since the ratification of the Maastricht Treaty in 1993, the Court has devoted considerable energy to improving its links to the national audit offices, especially given the latter's staffing resources and responsibility for national financial interests. But a key factor has been a new (Lisbon) Treaty Article that states that:

In the Member States the audit shall be carried out in liaison with national audit bodies or, if these do not have the necessary powers, with the competent national departments. The Court of Auditors and the national audit bodies of the Member States shall cooperate in a spirit of trust while maintaining their independence.

(Article 287 TFEU)

In practice, a significant part of this cooperation happens within the annual contact committee meetings between the Court and the national audit bodies, which can be traced to a provision of a declaration in the Treaty of Nice.

The Court's formal relations with the Council and the EP take place within the so-called 'discharge procedure'. Under this procedure, the EP has the power to grant or postpone approval for the Commission's implementation of the annual budget. The Council also offers a recommendation, but the Parliament takes this decision alone. The Commission is legally bound to take the EP's discharge resolutions into account. The procedure is based on the analysis by the EP's Budgetary Control

Committee of the Court's annual report, its statement of assurance, and any special reports published during the budgetary year in question. The EP drafts a discharge report largely based on the work of the Court and hearings of Commissioners. Because of the discharge procedure, contact is continuous between the Court and the EP's Budgetary Control Committee. The Parliament refused to grant a discharge in 1984 with respect to the 1982 budget and has delayed the discharge on a number of occasions since then.

However, in spring 1998, the most politically charged discharge process in the history of the EU began. In March, the EP Budgetary Control Committee recommended that the EP delay giving the Commission a discharge for the 1996 budget following one more critical report from the Court of Auditors. The issue then became entangled with additional allegations of mismanagement involving Commissioner Cresson and, later, the European Community Humanitarian Office (ECHO). An internal Commission whistle-blower—one of an increasing number to come forward in recent years (see Box 11.3)—added to the politically charged atmosphere (see van Buitenen 2000, and Chapter 5).

The Commission survived a motion of censure, but only because a special Committee of Independent Experts was appointed to investigate the charges of mismanagement. The ultimate result was the resignation of the entire Santer Commission. In an indirect way, the Court's highly technical work of auditing therefore

---

BOX 11.3   EU whistle-blowers

A number of officials working in EU institutions have, over the last decade, made public their concerns about financial management in EU institutions. These whistle-blowers have received considerable exposure in the media, and hence have had high visibility and nuisance value to defenders of the EU's financial controls. The institutions generally responded to the whistle-blowers very defensively, although Vice President Kinnock felt obliged to establish a whistle-blowers' charter in 1999. Among the whistle-blowers were the following.

- Paul van Buitenen brought his concerns about financial management to an MEP in 1998. He was suspended from his post, but his revelations led to the downfall of the Santer Commission in 1999. Van Buitenen (2000) first wrote a book on his experiences and later (in 2004) was elected to the European Parliament.

- Marta Andreasen was appointed as chief accountant in the Commission, but was suspended in 2002 when she refused to sign off on the Commission's accounts. She was highly critical of the book-keeping standards in the Commission. The Commission did not accept her intervention as a valid case of whistle-blowing. Commissioner Kinnock considered that the Commission had already been in the process of dealing with the shortcomings in the accounting system that Andreasen had voiced (known as the 'Kinnock reforms') and that she had been suspended following a cumulative breach of staff regulations, including being absent from her post.

contributed to what was a history-making event in the politics of the Union. Most of its activity, however, is directed towards the less dramatic, but still crucial, task of improving the financial management of the EU budget by the institutions and protecting the financial interests of the Union.

OLAF

OLAF exercises the following tasks in the fight against fraud, corruption, or any other activity affecting the financial interests of the EU:

- conducting all of the investigations conferred on the Commission by Community legislation and in third countries through agreements;
- safeguarding the Community against behaviour that might lead to administrative or penal proceedings;
- exercising a coordinating role vis-à-vis the national anti-fraud authorities in the fight against fraud; and
- contributing to the development of methods for combating fraud.

To carry out these tasks, OLAF conducts external investigations in the member states and, where permissible, in third countries. It has the power to conduct internal investigations in the EU institutions when fraud or corruption is suspected.

OLAF's 2004 activity report marked the first five years of this fledgling organization's work. OLAF's case management system listed 3,992 cases during this time, including 1,423 cases that it inherited from UCLAF. The number of cases in any one year rose from 322 in 1999–2000 to 637 in 2003–04 (OLAF 2004: 17). In this period, a very high proportion, 73 per cent, related to activities jointly carried out with member state authorities (*ibid.*). This large share of cases underlines the necessity for EU-level bodies to work with national authorities in the fight against fraud (*ibid.*: 19). The pattern in more recent years has changed to one whereby two-thirds of all new cases are OLAF's own investigations and a third involve assistance to national authorities. Between 2005 and 2009, OLAF opened approximately 200 new cases per year (OLAF 2009). The Eurostat case was one of the most controversial cases involving an investigation by OLAF since its establishment (see Box 11.4).

OLAF, like all EU institutions, operates in an institutional environment that is multilevel, cross-national, and very diverse. It has to develop strategies for managing diversity and for dealing with the multiple anti-fraud agencies in Europe. It seeks to work closely with national authorities, not as a substitute for national action, but as a means of more effectively fighting fraud that is transnational in nature. As much crime and fraud in Europe today has a transnational dimension, OLAF itself is partly a response to transnational pressures. In short, legal Europe is attempting to catch up with criminal Europe.

> ### BOX 11.4 The Eurostat investigation
>
> Following the mass resignation of the Santer Commission and the stated commitment to tackling fraud by President Prodi, the emergence of serious problems in Eurostat—the Commission's statistical service—was most unwelcome. Fraud allegations emerged concerning an irregular bank account set up in Luxembourg during the 1990s, known as the 'Eurodiff account', which appeared to hold money from the sale of Eurostat publications that should have been channelled into the Commission account.
>
> Faced with mounting political pressure from the EP, the Commission and OLAF set up a special OLAF task force to deal solely with the investigation into Eurostat. A total of fourteen investigations were pursued: four external cases and ten internal cases (some of which were not yet complete at the time of writing). The task force found that most of the irregularities had their origins before 1999 (House of Lords 2004; OLAF 2004).
>
> The Eurostat investigation was the source of considerable conflict between the Commission and OLAF. The former felt that it should have been informed sooner of the investigation, because it was accountable for the agency and was itself under considerable pressure from the EP.
>
> The Commission suspended three senior Eurostat officials and terminated a number of contracts with private companies.

The institutions in context

Financial control and the larger EU system

The evolution of the Court of Auditors and OLAF in the EU system illustrates how institutions and their external environments interact. These institutions were established at different times, more than twenty years apart, in response to changes in the salience of financial management, control, and accountability in the EU system. The establishment of the Court reflected recognition of the supranational nature of the EU budget; that of OLAF, the failure of self-regulation within the Commission. Both institutions represented a strengthening of the relatively weak organizations that preceded them. The Court of Auditors had to devote considerable organizational energy to becoming a 'living institution'—that is, to becoming embedded in the EU system. The Court had to evolve a culture of auditing that was suitable to the extended scale and reach of the Union's financial activities. Like all EU institutions, it had to work with diversity: auditing cultures, attitudes to financial management, diversity of professional background, legal arrangements in the member states, and multiple languages.

No less important than internal structures are relationships with other parts of the EU system. The Court is part of the system of financial audit and control that exists in the EU, involving internal financial control, external audit, and measures to combat fraud. It is part of the Union's accountability structures in that the Parliament's

Budgetary Control Committee relies on reports of the Court for its annual discharge process. The Court has played its part, albeit a secondary one, in the unfolding drama of EP–Commission relations. The Court has gradually established working relationships with all EU institutions and its institutional status gives it the same legal status as the institutions that it audits. Its stronger, formal status in treaty terms matters in the day-to-day politics of auditing in the Union. As the salience of good financial governance has gained prominence in the Union, and received the backing of the Council and the European Council, the Court has turned its attention to enhancing its relationship with national auditing authorities.

OLAF, like the Court of Auditors, is part of the Union's accountability structure with a specific remit to combat fraud and crime. Its remit is based on the clear recognition that there is an important transnational dimension to budgetary fraud in the EU. The establishment of OLAF as an independent unit attached to the Commission, but with a separate chain of command, was a response to the problems the Commission had in conducting internal investigations when there were allegations of fraud by individuals in the Commission's services. Its future is bound up with the creation of a European public prosecutor. The idea, which was floated in 1997 in a Commission-funded study entitled *Corpus Juris* carried out by eight academic lawyers, was later backed by the Commission in a 2001 Green Paper on the protection of the financial interests of the Union.[6] The proposal re-emerged in the Convention on the Future of Europe and formed part of the Constitutional Treaty agreed by the member states in 2004. The Treaty made provision for the creation of the role of European Public Prosecutor (EPP), subject to unanimous agreement in the Council. According to the Constitutional Treaty's provisions, the EPP would be responsible for 'investigating, prosecuting, and bringing to judgement, where appropriate in liaison with Europol, the perpetrators of … offences against the Union's financial interest' (Article III-175).

The EPP provisions were controversial and were opposed by a number of countries in the negotiations—notably, the UK and Ireland, which did not want the Union to encroach on their systems of criminal law. Hence there is considerable uncertainty concerning the place of OLAF in the emerging financial architecture of the Union. The creation of the EPP, if it is established, will alter OLAF's operating environment in a fundamental manner. One could envisage that OLAF becomes an investigating arm of the EPP or that it is absorbed into a reorganized European Police Office (Europol).

Theories of integration and institutional development

From the outset, scholars of integration paid considerable attention to what they saw as the novel characteristics of the Union's institutional architecture. In fact, institutions were central to neo-functionalist analysis, as well as early studies of the EU's policy process. Not unexpectedly, the growing volume of literature on the factors driving integration—liberal intergovernmentalism, supranational governance/new institutionalism, and social constructivism—all address different dimensions of in-stitutionalization and institutional evolution in the EU.

How well do these theories of European integration explain the establishment and evolution of the ECA and OLAF? Both bodies are non-majoritarian, with a role as guardian of the EU purse in the case of the ECA and of investigating fraud in the case of OLAF. All political systems have bodies the *raison d'être* of which is supervision and control. Social constructivism draws our attention to the importance of ideas and discourse in shaping political action and structures. In the case of the two insti-tutions analysed in this chapter, established concepts of democratic government and accountability shaped the institutions from the outset. The fact that external audit was a well-established norm and practice in domestic government made it very dif-ficult for any member state to argue against the establishment of the Court of Audi-tors. By conducting audits and reporting on the findings of such audits, the ECA contributes to the diffusion of democratic practices of governance in the EU. In par-ticular, social constructivism provides a useful lens through which to analyse the normative dimension of institution-building, and the related processes of learning and socialization (Checkel 1999: 548). The Court of Auditors, together with other actors in the system, had a responsibility to strengthen the norms of sound financial management, legality, and regularity in relation to the EU budget, and did so through its recommendations and opinions on changes to financial regulation and sectoral regulations. In an effort to enhance its effectiveness, the Court of Auditors and, more recently, OLAF have promoted learning and socialization on issues of financial man-agement and fraud in the EU system.

The literature on institutionalization and supranational governance provides a lens through which to analyse the development of these institutions over time (Pier-son 1996; Stone Sweet and Sandholtz 1998: 16–20; Pollack 1998, 2009). The proc-esses highlighted in this literature, such as rule-making and institutionalization, are clearly evident in the evolution of the ECA and OLAF. The member states may have established the Court of Auditors to oversee their agent, the Commission, in its management of EU monies, but over time the Court, because of its audit remit, has had to follow the audit trail into the member states. One of the unintended conse-quences of the establishment of the Court was the manner in which national finan-cial management came under increasing scrutiny. Treaty revision and changes in financial regulation all contributed to an enhancement of the norm of sound finan-cial management in the EU and to creating a web of rules around the control of EU expenditure. The Court and OLAF are but part of the wider development of an insti-tutionalized control/accountability culture in the Union. Nor has the process been limited to these two institutions: provisions for the establishment of the office of EPP underline the tendency for institutional spill-over in the system, notwithstanding the controversial nature of this proposal.

Liberal intergovernmentalism is more concerned with why institutional delega-tion takes place rather than the consequences of such delegation. A liberal-intergovernmental analysis of the development of the Court of Auditors and OLAF would privilege an explanation based on the need for credible commitments. From this perspective, the role of both these institutions is to assure predictable, fair, and transparent compliance with the rules. However, the credibility of the commitment is bolstered by both of these institutions, not by limiting democratic involvement (a key argument in liberal intergovernmentalism), but by reinforcing democratic control, because both institutions are part of the democratic fabric of the EU polity (Moravcsik 1998). Liberal intergovernmentalism could not easily account for the establishment of the EPP if it were to be created, because it is opposed by a number of powerful players.

The impact of the institutions

Given the perennial problems associated with the management of EU finances and highlighted in successive reports of the Court of Auditors, the Commission's annual reports on *The Fight against Fraud*, and OLAF's annual reports, it begs the question: just how intractable are the problems associated with financial management in the Union? Establishing effective systems of financial management is a challenge even within states. In the EU, there are additional structural factors—notably, the range of auditing institutions, practices, and cultures in the member states and beyond, the geographical range of EU finances, and the multilingual environment within which the staff of the Court of Auditors and OLAF work.

The reports of the Court since the end of the 1970s did much to highlight management inadequacies in the first place, and the ECA's constant pressure on the Commission led to an acceptance—however tardy—that there were very real problems of financial management in the Union. The Commission responded by strengthening formal systems for overseeing the implementation of the budget. But as Levy (2000: 187) has concluded, 'moving beyond formal change is a general problem that bedevils most aspects of EU programme management'. The Commission continues to enhance its internal management processes and to strengthen its links to the member states. This effort has borne some fruit, as is evident in the annual reports of the Court of Auditors, but continuing evidence of problems—particularly in areas of shared management with the member states—underlines the continuing challenges facing the Commission. Addressing the fragmented accountability structures in the Union is a work in progress. The situation in relation to financial management has improved as a result of the 'critical juncture' of the resignation of the Commission, administrative reform of the Commission, and the enhanced commitment to financial control within the system. The Court of Auditors played a particularly important role in EU institutional politics by altering the balance in relations between the EP and the Commission. Its reports provided the EP Budgetary Control Committee with the raw material to exercise the discharge procedure in a manner that strengthened parliamentary control over the Commission. The resignation of the Santer Commission was the most dramatic event to result from the problems of self-regulation in the Commission. Without the slow drip-feed of ECA reports, it is unlikely that it would have happened. For its part, OLAF has undertaken a large number of investigations in the EU institutions, the member states, and in third countries. These investigations have led to criminal investigations in Romania, the extradition of a Lithuanian national from Lithuania to Belgium, a guilty plea by a multinational company in Lesotho, and an investigation into the use of EU monies by the Palestinian Authority (OLAF 2004: 38–40).

Conclusions

The establishment of the Court of Auditors in 1977 was dependent on the changing nature and funding of the EC budget. In turn, once the Court found an institutional identity and established its approach to auditing, it began to highlight the problems of financial management in the Union. Its effectiveness improved with the internal development of an agreed audit culture and growing human resources. For well over a decade, the Court had to fight to ensure that its findings were taken on board in the Commission, in the Council, and at national level. With the major expansion of the Union's budgetary resources after 1988 and a growing net contributors' club, financial management found its way from the margins of the agenda to centre stage. Gradually, the rules surrounding financial management were strengthened and the member states were forced to accept a tighter regime of financial control. The Court of Auditors, the institutional position of which was strengthened in this period, contributed to, but also benefited from, the growing salience of financial management in the Union. The establishment of OLAF in 1999 was a response to the problems of fraud against the financial interests of the Union and, more specifically, to the problems of self-regulation in the Commission.

The Court of Auditors and OLAF represent institutional innovation in the EU system. Subsequent provisions for a European public prosecutor suggest that the process of institutional innovation continues. Such developments bring the continuing autonomy of national criminal law systems and the need to combat transnational problems sharply into focus.

 NOTES

* The views expressed in this chapter by George Karakatsanis are entirely his own and should not be interpreted as the official views of the Court of Auditors.

1. The authors would like to thank Geoffrey Simpson, Director of the Presidency in the European Court of Auditors, for his thorough review of an earlier version of this chapter. The chapter has benefited greatly from his comments, while any fault in interpreting his corrections and observations is entirely our own.

2. This configuration puts the Court in accordance with Article 287(4) TFEU.

3. Articles 310–325 TFEU and Council Regulation (EC, Euratom) No. 1605/2002 of 25 June 2002 on the Financial Regulation applicable to the general budget of the European Communities.

4. The Court is attempting to get agreement for the Commission to establish an integrated control framework for the EU as a whole (ECA Opinion 2/2004 on the 'single audit' model).

5. The interparliamentary conference on 'Improving National Accountability of EU Funds', The Hague, 29 January 2010.

6. Com (2001) 175 final.

 FURTHER READING

Levy (1996) highlights the difficulty posed by diverse national auditing traditions for external auditing in the Union, while the same author's monograph (2000) is the most in-depth analysis available of financial management in the EU. Laffan (1999, 2003) analyses (respectively) the Court of Auditors' relationship with other EU institutions, and charts how it became embedded in the Union's institutional system and the general dynamics of financial accountability in the EU. Pujas (2003) provides insight into the governance of EU anti-fraud activities. Recent works on OLAF include Groenendijk (2004), Quirke (2010), and White (2010).

Groenendijk, N. S. (2004) 'Assessing member states' management of EU finances: an empirical analysis of the annual reports of the European Court of Auditors, 1996–2001', *Public Administration*, 82/3: 701–25.

Laffan, B. (1999) 'Becoming a "living institution": the evolution of the European Court of Auditors', *Journal of Common Market Studies*, 37/2: 251–68.

Laffan, B. (2003) 'Auditing and accountability in the European Union', *Journal of European Public Policy*, 10/5: 762–77.

Levy, R. (1996) 'Managing value for money audit in the European Union: the challenge of diversity', *Journal of Common Market Studies*, 43/4: 509–29.

Levy, R. (2000) *Implementing European Union Public Policy* (Cheltenham: Edward Elgar).

Pujas, V. (2003) 'The European Anti-Fraud Office (OLAF): a European policy to fight against economic and financial fraud?', *Journal of European Public Policy*, 10/5: 778–97.

Quirke, B. (2010) 'Fighting EU fraud: why do we make life difficult for ourselves?', *Journal of Financial Crime*, 17/1: 61–80.

White, S. (2010) 'EU anti-fraud enforcement: overcoming obstacles', *Journal of Financial Crime*, 17/1: 81–99.

WEB LINKS

http://ec.europa.eu/

The most important web link, which provides access to all of the EU institutions, including the European Parliament, which provides access to the work of the Budgetary Control Committee, which is central to the annual discharge of the budget.

http://eca.europa.eu

The website of the ECA provides access to the annual reports, special reports, and a bibliography on the Court of Auditors. It also offers access to the Budget Directorate and the Financial Control Directorate.

http://ec.europa.eu/anti_fraud

The OLAF website provides an overview of the activities of the organization, including case studies linked to issues such as cigarette smuggling, and also explains how individuals or groups can make informal contact to report fraud.

PART III

Integrating Interests

CHAPTER 12

Security Interests: Police and Judicial Cooperation

Andrew Geddes

▋ Summary

European Union (EU) member states now work together on issues such as asylum, migration, border controls, police cooperation, and judicial cooperation. These were once seen as the prerogative of member states; indeed, they are defining features of states' identities as sovereign. This chapter shows a complex process of incremental institutional change that has established new ways of working on internal security issues and reconfigured the strategic setting from which these issues are viewed. Member states have, over time, established particular working methods to support and sustain collaboration. From being a policy arena that was not even mentioned in the Treaty of Rome or Single European Act (SEA), internal security within an 'area of freedom, security, and justice' (AFSJ) is now a key EU priority. This chapter pinpoints key developments, specifies institutional roles, and explores the relationships over time between changing conceptualizations of security and institutional developments.

Introduction

European cooperation on internal security within the area of freedom, security, and justice (AFSJ) is firmly embedded as a key priority of the European Union. Significant policy development in areas such as policing, judicial cooperation, border controls, migration, and asylum has been accompanied in a relatively short period of time by institutional development, transformation, and consolidation. Policy and institutional development signify movement into areas of 'high politics' that impinge directly on state sovereignty. Institutional change has also been informed by reconceptualizations of internal security that have played a powerful role in framing institutional and policy developments. This chapter connects policies, institutions, and ideas over time to analyse the extensive, diverse, and politically contentious range of issues that usually fall within the domain of interior or justice ministries in the member states. They also tend to be seen as closely related to national sovereignty and reside within the domain of the executive branches of national governments, with tendencies towards seclusion and secrecy in decision-style.

There was no mention of internal security in the Paris and Rome Treaties or in the Single European Act (SEA). There was, though, 'informal' cooperation between states outside the Treaty framework. It was not until 1993, when the Maastricht Treaty created the justice and home affairs (JHA) pillar, that there was formal reference to internal security, including immigration, asylum, border controls, and judicial and police cooperation. In 1999, the Amsterdam Treaty proclaimed that the EU should be 'maintained and developed as an area of freedom, security and justice … within which the free movement of persons is assured' and with 'appropriate measures with respect to external border controls, asylum, immigration and the prevention and combating of crime'.

The key development post-Lisbon is the full application of Community decision rules and institutional processes to almost all internal security matters, including immigration, asylum, border controls, policing, and judicial cooperation. The Lisbon Treaty also makes the Charter of Fundamental Rights binding on member states. The Czech Republic, Poland, and the UK secured derogations from the scope of the Charter of Rights. This means that citizens of these three countries cannot use the Charter to challenge rights issues in their courts if the basis for their challenge is rights granted to them as EU citizens within the Charter. If they are to issue a challenge, then they must use national laws. The Charter cannot be used to introduce new rights into the national laws of these three countries.

Post-Lisbon institutional changes also sees the JHA portfolio within the Commission separated into 'home affairs' and 'justice' roles. That said, as will be seen, this area of policy does possess a complex and byzantine quality due to opt-out provisions, as well as the importance of 'venues' used by member states that are outside of the formal Treaty framework for policy and institutional development. Box 12.1 provides a timeline of key developments.

BOX 12.1	**Timeline of key developments in police and judicial cooperation**
1967	**Naples Convention** establishes customs cooperation to tackle fraud
1975	**Trevi** initially a response to terrorist organizations, but its remit was widened to tackle internal security issues seen as arising from single market integration
1985	**Schengen** an agreement initially between five member states (Belgium, France, Germany, Luxembourg, and the Netherlands) that became the laboratory for 'compensating' internal security measures in the single market
1986	**SEA** proposed a Europe with free movement for people, services, goods, and capital, and provided a further impetus to informal cooperation between member states outside of the formal treaty framework
1986	**Ad Hoc Group on Immigration** to explore the migration and asylum implications for non-EU nationals of free movement provisions
1988	**Group of Coordinators** established to coordinate the various informal bodies and groups dealing with internal security issues
1993	**Maastricht Treaty** formalized transgovernmental cooperation by creating the justice and home affairs (JHA) pillar
1999	**Amsterdam Treaty** created a new Title IV dealing with free movement, migration, asylum, and border controls, while leaving judicial and police cooperation in a recast judicial and police cooperation (JPC) pillar
1999	**Tampere Programme** devised by national interior minister and set an ambitious five-year agenda for internal security development
2004	The **Hague Programme** provided a further five-year plan for policy development within which increased emphasis was laid on the 'external dimension'—that is, cooperation with non-member states
2009	**Lisbon Treaty** provided for full application of Community decision rules to almost all internal security matters and made binding the Charter of Fundamental Rights to inform application of the internal security *acquis*
2009	**Stockholm Programme** laid down a further five-year plan (2010–14) that proposes, for example, a common asylum policy and sees a strong and renewed focus on the 'external' dimension of internal security

This chapter addresses two related sets of questions that link institutions, policies, and ideas. First, what impelled the development of EU cooperation on internal security? Why have developments occurred at some points in time and not at others? What impact have changes in the conceptualization of security and insecurity had on the development of policy?

The second set of questions focus on institutional form, and ask how the processes have developed and who the key actors have been, in order to ascertain where power lies in this policy area and to assess changes in its distribution.

The meaning of 'security'

Central to the analysis that follows is the relationship between institutions and ideas. This section centres on exploration of working methods, institutional form, and organizational action linked to reconceptualizations of internal security. To understand this arena of EU policy, it is important to probe the meaning of 'security'.

Various qualifiers are appended to the term 'security', such as 'internal', 'external', 'state', 'national', 'international', 'human', and 'societal'. But none help us to understand the term itself. Perhaps the EU itself can help in a quest for clarity by providing a definition of security? There is a strong commitment to develop the EU as an area of freedom, security, and justice (AFSJ). But even in key EU documents such as the Stockholm Programme (which maps the EU internal security agenda for the period 2010–14), the meaning of the term can be elusive. The Stockholm document recognizes that security concerns are important to citizens of the member states and that security needs to be 'enhanced'. Various threats that are seen to confront the member states are also identified, such as terrorism and organized crime, drug trafficking, corruption, human trafficking, people smuggling, and arms trafficking. The Stockholm Programme then discusses the need to develop an EU internal security strategy to 'improve' and 'guarantee' security. By the end of the document, it is clear that internal security has become a key EU priority, but it is still not entirely clear what is meant by the term itself.

The EU's draft internal security strategy produced by the Council in 2010[1] states that:

> The concept of internal security must be understood as a wide and comprehensive concept which straddles multiple sectors ... [and] ... to reach an adequate level of internal security in a complex global environment requires the involvement of law-enforcement and border-management authorities, with the support of judicial cooperation, civil protection agencies and also of the political, economic, financial, social and private sectors, including non-governmental organisations.

It then lists the main challenges to adequate levels of internal security: terrorism; serious and organized crime; cyber crime; cross-border crime; violence such as hooliganism; and natural and man-made disasters, such as forest fires. Great emphasis within the draft internal security strategy is laid on the gathering and sharing of data, such as biometrics.

Security is often represented in documents such as the Stockholm Programme and the draft internal security strategy as a pressing demand made by EU citizens. The development of action on internal security can then be a means for the EU to acquire legitimacy in the eyes of its citizens by taking on this role. This 'demand-side' argument suggests that political leaders are merely responding to the concerns of their citizens. It does, however, seem plausible to suggest that there is a supply side in this particular 'market', because institutions, organizations, and processes associated with EU action may themselves have helped to create cultures of insecurity, uncertainty, and risk that then form the basis for arguments for intensified policy action.

For example, in the aftermath of the end of the cold war, there were hugely over-blown claims about potential migration flows from the former Soviet Union and of the menace of transnational organized crime. These movements did not transpire on the scale that some predicted, but they did play a particularly powerful role in impelling institutional action after the end of the cold war.

There may be another way of thinking about these issues that considers whether definitional ambiguities might create political opportunities. Rather than embarking on a quest for the 'meaning' of security, it might be better to focus on its essential contestation and the ways in which various actors seek to impose their preferred understandings. This way of thinking connects issue 'framing' to mobilizations and then to the types of policy and institutional response that have developed. Such a constructivist perspective takes ideas seriously in relation to institutional development.

Finally, we need to think about the effects of policy development over time. Decisions about EU internal security cooperation and policy have been made at particular *points in time*. We can also assess the effects of cooperation *over time* and the pace, or *tempo*, of institutional development. By doing so, it is possible to assess the influence of initial decisions about institutional form on later decisions. This perspective allows us to assess the ways in which—over time—new EU-level institutional venues have been created and, in turn, how these venues have contributed to the reshaping of ideas about security and insecurity in the EU. For example, we see that working methods created in the 1970s have left powerful legacies. This approach allows us to see how dramatic external shocks, such as the 9/11 terrorist attacks, were dealt with by organizations and institutions that were already of long standing. A theoretical observation can also be made if we extend this thinking about the effects of cooperation over time. If it is the case that understandings of security and thinking about strategic challenges have been affected by cooperation, then it also would seem to be the case that national preferences can be shaped and reshaped by cooperation at the EU level as a consequence of interactions over time and the emergence of new, shared understandings of European internal security. In such circumstances, preferences are not exogenous to the process, as liberal intergovernmentalists argue; rather, they can be defined and redefined as a result of interaction.

Executive dominance

From its early origins, cooperation on internal security has centred on liaison and interaction between national interior and justice ministries, as well as national security agencies such as police forces. This configuration pinpoints the predominant position of the executive branch of national government and associated agencies. The Commission did seek to play a role in policy development, but found this effort difficult because it was confronted by a weak legal basis for its involvement. Even in the late 1990s, the Commission representatives would leave the room when member states turned their attention to the Schengen area because it was an issue from which the Commission was excluded. Supranational institutions such as the Commission, European Court of Justice (ECJ), and European Parliament (EP) were effectively excluded from the development of the Schengen system in the 1980s and 1990s. This exclusion is significant because these developments went on crucially to inform the shape and form of cooperation after the Schengen *acquis* was brought into the EU treaty framework by the Amsterdam Treaty.

We can also specify a little more clearly how cooperation worked and assess its implications. There were actually very specific forms of cooperation that were 'sectoral'—that is, focused on a range of issues linked to internal security, and involving ministers and officials from mainly interior ministries and security agencies. What this specificity means is that distinct patterns of cooperation and working methods have evolved over time. Wallace (2010) has identified internal security as an example of 'intensive transgovernmentalism', whereby functional interdependence exposes a governance dilemma as member states confront 'transboundary' policy problems with which they would struggle to deal acting alone (see also Menon and Weatherill 2006).

That an issue is 'transboundary' does not determine the shape or form that cooperation might take. Environmental issues are also transboundary and the EU has made much more significant steps towards common policies in this arena than it has in the area of internal security. By contrast, the EU has preferred to move more tentatively in the arena of internal security because of the distinct national sensitivities that member states hold for issues such as immigration, asylum, policing, and judicial cooperation. All clearly have a strong and direct relation to understandings of national sovereignty, as well as to the legitimate authority of national governments that are concerned to be seen to 'deliver' security to their citizens.

The analytical insight that can be garnered from the preceding discussion is that, instead of being locked into a supranational–intergovernmental dichotomy, the focus on transboundary problems and transgovernmental institutions provides a means of exploring the ways in which functional interdependencies can generate pressures for action. But it also shows that these pressures need not translate into a unique template for cooperation and/or policy development; rather, there are distinct policy styles and ways of working in areas as diverse as the environment and internal security that play a strong role in shaping the scope, form, and content of action.

Informal transgovernmentalism

The Trevi Group

Early traces of internal security cooperation can be found in the Naples Convention of 1967, agreed between the six founding EEC member states ('the Six') to deal with customs cooperation. This cooperation was closely linked to the common market as it sought to combat infringements of national customs legislation. Cooperation moved to a different level when member states sought greater coordination in their responses to domestic groups defined as terrorist organizations, such as ETA (*Euskadi ta Askatasuna*, the Basque separatist group) in Spain, the Red Army Faction in West Germany, the Red Brigades in Italy, and the Irish Republican Army (IRA) in Northern Ireland. National governments sought to cooperate within the Trevi Group, which was set up in 1976 by the then nine member states to promote cooperation between police, security, and intelligence agencies. There are various explanations given for the name 'Trevi': one is that it is an acronym derived from its focus on '*Terrorisme, Radicalisme, Extrémisme et Violence Internationale*'; another is that it is named after the Trevi fountain in Rome, near where the group first met. Whichever is the case, the key point is that Trevi created patterns and habits of cooperation in key areas of policy closely linked to state sovereignty. Structures created within Trevi are revealing of the kinds of working methods that have since become associated with EU cooperation on internal security. In particular, they highlight the importance of regular interactions between officials. Beneath the surface of ministerial meetings, forms of cooperation and ways of working have developed over time and have linked internal security officials in member states.

The political leadership and direction for Trevi was set by meetings every six months of interior ministers from the nine member states. This kind of political steering by national ministers is a key feature of EU decision-making, but cannot provide policy and operational details. Consequently, to prepare these ministerial meetings, senior officials from each member state would meet in May and November—that is, one month before the meeting of ministers. There was also another layer beneath this senior official level, because the detailed groundwork for these higher-level meetings was actually done in working groups. Three such groups were created in 1976. So-called 'Trevi 1' focused on anti-terrorism; 'Trevi 2' on police training, including measures to combat football-related violence. A third group dealing with civilian air travel ('Trevi 3') was largely inert and was redefined in 1985 to focus on serious organized crime, after which it became more active. Two other groups (nuclear safety and civil emergencies) were created, but never actually met. Associated with the work of Trevi in the sense of being kept informed about developments were the 'friends of Trevi': Austria, Canada, Finland, Morocco, Norway, Sweden, Switzerland, and the United States.

We can draw some lessons from these early forms of cooperation. They centred on anti-terrorism, police training, and serious organized crime. Methods of cooperation emerged outside of the formal Treaty framework with a strong transgovernmental focus and the exclusion of supranational institutions. Cooperation focused on interactions between the executive branches of national governments and security agencies. This focus meant secrecy and very limited scope for democratic or legal accountability. We see, too, the development of working groups that provide a base for interaction and the development of shared understandings between national officials, which, in turn, helped to reshape the context within which planning and decision-making occurred. Member states were not ready or willing to cede responsibility to common institutional processes, but had made evident their willingness to work together.

The impact of single-market integration

Did the Single European Act's (SEA) plan to create a European single market—defined as an area without internal frontiers within which people, services, goods, and capital could move freely—also have the effect of impelling cooperation on internal security? There are certainly important linkages between economic integration and internal security cooperation. But there was also a determination that internal security cooperation would occur outside of the Treaty framework, in transgovernmental forums with limited involvement by supranational institutions.

The key development during the 1980s occurred outside of the Treaty framework and prior to the SEA. In June 1985, the Schengen Agreement was signed by Belgium, France, (West) Germany, Luxembourg, and the Netherlands in a riverboat on the River Mosel near to the town of Schengen in Luxembourg. The location was symbolic because it is where the borders of Luxembourg, Germany, and France meet. The Schengen Agreement marked an ambitious move by five EC member states with a long-standing commitment to deeper political integration. The Schengen Agreement provided for the abolition of border controls between participating states, common rules on migration, asylum, and visas, and the creation of a database—the Schengen Information System (SIS)—to bring together information held in national databases on individuals and property. In 1990, the Schengen Implementing Convention, agreed by the same five states, sought to implement these agreed measures. Monar (2002) has argued that Schengen provided a 'laboratory' for the member states, demonstrating to them the internal security implications of free movement. In May 2005, Austria, Belgium, France, Germany, Luxembourg, the Netherlands, and Spain reached agreement in the Prüm Treaty to step up cooperation in tackling cross-border crime, illegal immigration, and terrorism, by providing reciprocal access to the DNA profiles, fingerprints, and vehicle registration data of participating states (Grabbe 2000; Pastore *et al.* 2006). The Prüm Treaty was signed before the Lisbon Treaty's provisions for 'enhanced cooperation' came into effect. But Prüm (as Schengen did before it) foreshadowed the enhanced cooperation under which a third or more of EU member states can pursue cooperation so long as it does not discriminate against other member states, furthers Treaty objectives, and is not an area that falls within the EU's exclusive competence.

The Amsterdam Treaty imported the Schengen *acquis* directly into the EU. This move points to the importance of secluded and secretive venues outside of the Treaty framework for the development of measures that are then 'imported' to form part of the EU *acquis*. By 1997, when the Amsterdam Treaty was agreed, all member states except Ireland and the UK had signed the Schengen Agreement.

Informal transgovernmental cooperation in the 1980s

Single market integration also affected the Trevi Group, which initially focused on terrorism and police training. Over time, however, its role was developed in light of the creation of the single market and the security issues that were seen as arising as a result of this deeper level of economic integration that would require the dismantling of internal frontiers. The 'Trevi 92' group worked with the 'Ad Hoc Group on Immigration' (created in 1986) to consider the security implications of single market integration. A Group of Coordinators was established in 1988, consisting of senior officials from each member state, which produced the Palma document that detailed the internal security measures that were seen as necessary to 'compensate' for single-market liberalization.

The Ad Hoc Group on Immigration drafted the Dublin Convention (1990), which is the framing document of the European asylum system, and which created key ideas and approaches that have informed policy development since. The right to asylum is protected by the Geneva Convention of 1951. Article 1 of the Convention seeks to protect anyone who:

owing to a well-founded fear of being persecuted for reasons of race, religion, nationality, membership of a particular social group or political opinion, is outside the country of his nationality and is unable or, owing to such fear, is unwilling to avail himself of the protection of that country; or who, not having a nationality and being outside the country of his former habitual residence as a result of such events, is unable or, owing to such fear, is unwilling to return to it.

At the core of the Dublin system is the idea that an asylum application be made in the first country that is entered by the applicant. Any decision made in this first country of entry is final and binding for other member states. This rule means that the European asylum system is supposed to be a 'one-stop shop' designed to prevent 'asylum shopping', with applicants moving from one member state to another. The Eurodac system—that is, the European fingerprint database—supports implementation of the Dublin Convention (and its successor the Dublin II Regulation of 2003, which formed part of the migration and asylum law developed after the Amsterdam Treaty came into force) (Lavenex 1999; Hailbronner 2004).

The context for the development of the Dublin system was the increase in asylum that occurred in the aftermath of the end of the cold war. In particular, flows of refugees from the former Yugoslavia were strongly focused on Germany. While Germany was concerned about the steep increase in numbers of asylum applicants, other member states were not ready to embrace the sharing of responsibility or of solidarity through, for example, the distribution of asylum seekers and refugees in a more proportional way across the EU.

One clear implication of the 1992 programme was the linking of immigration and asylum to the internal security frame. By the late 1980s, we can also see the emergence of European-level cooperation on anti-terrorism, police training, serious organized crime, and immigration. We see, too, the development of informal working methods that were outside of the Treaty framework, and which centred on interaction between officials from interior ministries and security agencies in the member states.

Formalized transgovernmentalism

The Maastricht Treaty and the challenges of a wider Europe

The end of the cold war provided further impetus to the development of EU internal security cooperation. We also begin to see, in the late 1980s and early 1990s, how security issues were redefined, with a move from the state security framework that had prevailed during the cold war, to a new focus on societal security and associated 'threats' such as immigration, asylum, and transnational organized crime that also cut across the traditional distinction between 'internal' and 'external' security. Institutional form and decision-making processes were heavily influenced by the patterns of interaction and cooperation created in the 1970s, and by the key role played in these by interior ministries and internal security agencies.

The 1990s saw some fairly apocalyptic predictions of large-scale migration or rampant organized crime from Eastern Europe. Some argued that as many as 25 million people might move from East to West, although the actual number was about 10 per cent of that figure (Codagnone 1999). The key point is that these perceptions of the potential scale of the threat or challenge had important effects on perceptions of internal security and were used as a rationale for strengthened EU-level action to deal with these perceived threats.

The institutional response was the justice and home affairs (JHA) pillar of the Maastricht Treaty. This step was a compromise measure that sought to reconcile states that were firmly opposed to supranational action on issues such as migration and asylum, such as the UK, with those member states, such as Belgium, France, Germany, and the Netherlands, that were more open to the idea of common policy-making on such issues at EU level. The intergovernmental JHA pillar allowed member states to cooperate in nine areas of 'common interest' (see Box 12.2)—that is, areas in which common policies were to be developed. There would also be limited involvement by supranational institutions, with the Commission only loosely associated with policy development and the EP and ECJ largely excluded.

The Maastricht Treaty brought together within the JHA pillar a variety of issues. Some of them were those on which member states had been working together since the late 1960s. It formalized this cooperation, but did so in a way that severely limited involvement by supranational institutions, and also placed constraints on legal and political accountability at either national or EU levels (Geddes 2008).

Authority was delegated to a complex five-tier structure comprising the JHA Council, the Committee of Permanent Representatives (Coreper) II, the K4 Committee of

BOX 12.2	Areas of 'common interest' in Maastricht's JHA pillar

- Asylum policy
- Border controls
- Immigration policy, including rules on entry, residence, and movement, as well as family reunion and access to employment by nationals of non-EU member states, or third-country nationals (TCNs); it also covered unauthorized immigration, residence, and work by TCNs.
- Combating drug addiction
- Combating fraud
- Judicial cooperation in civil matters
- Judicial cooperation in criminal matters
- Customs cooperation
- Police cooperation for preventing and combating terrorism, unlawful drug trafficking, and other serious forms of international crime; this also included customs cooperation, in connection with the organization of a Union-wide system for exchanging information within a European Police Office (Europol).

senior officials (named after the relevant Treaty Article), steering groups, and working groups. This set-up was later amended to a four-tier structure during the UK presidency in 1998, when steering groups were abolished. Even so, the structures were complex and opaque.

Decisions were to be made by unanimity in the JHA Council, which would be supported by Coreper and the K4 Committee. The K4 Committee and the working groups brought working methods established in the Trevi Group into the EU. In the JHA pillar, the Commission shared the right of initiative with the member states. A JHA portfolio was created within the Social Affairs Directorate-General (DG). The EP had the right only to be 'regularly informed' of developments and 'consulted' about decisions, while the ECJ had no mandatory jurisdiction over the JHA pillar.

The legal outputs that were possible from the JHA pillar were also very limited in their scope. There was no provision for issuing regulations or directives under the JHA pillar; instead, member states had to rely on other types of instrument. Joint positions and joint actions could define the EU's approach to a particular issue, while conventions in international law could be agreed, which would then need to be ratified in accordance with constitutional procedures in each member state. Three such conventions were agreed: Schengen; Dublin (dealing with asylum); and Rome (creating Europol—see Box 12.3). All took a long time to move from agreement to ratification. The process of ratification of the Schengen Agreement was delayed by the implications of German reunification, while Dublin took seven years to move from signature to ratification.

> **BOX 12.3** **Europol**
>
> The European Police Office (Europol) is based in The Hague and has more than 600 staff. Europol's early origins lie with nascent forms of police cooperation established within the Trevi Group, whose remit was subsequently expanded as a result of the perceived security challenges that became associated with single-market integration. The Europol Convention agreed in Rome in July 1995 provided a base for cooperation. Europol does not have powers of arrest. Its role is to facilitate information exchange and coordinate investigations. Around 130 liaison officers from national police forces work with Europol. Europol has complex institutional structures. It has a management board that is composed of one high-ranking representative of each member state and the European Commission. Each member has one vote. The management board meets twice-yearly to discuss a wide range of Europol issues and to adopt a general report on Europol activities. These reports are then submitted to the JHA Council for its approval. A director appointed for a four-year term supervises the work of three departments (focusing on operations, governance, and capabilities).

Partial communitarization

The Amsterdam Treaty

The Amsterdam Treaty was designed to tackle some of the inadequacies of the Maastricht 'pillar' framework. The Maastricht Treaty was an uneasy compromise born more of the need to strike a deal than of considered reflection on the best way in which to tackle perceived new security challenges. At the most basic level, it seemed that the Maastricht framework did not provide the member states with the tools needed to do the job. For example, the inability to use the Community decision-making method inhibited the effectiveness of cooperation, as demonstrated by the difficulty securing ratification of conventions agreed in international law. Opaqueness and difficulties in holding decision-makers to account were seen as exacerbating the democratic deficit.

During the Amsterdam negotiations, a core group of member states were prepared to see fuller incorporation of internal security issues within the Community, but others, such as the UK and Denmark, were not prepared to take such a step. The solution, as will be seen, was the use of 'flexibility' in the Treaty framework, which allowed the UK, Ireland, and Denmark to opt out of measures on free movement, immigration, and asylum. The UK and Ireland were not Schengen members, while Denmark was.

A key feature of the Amsterdam Treaty was the new Title IV added to the Treaty framework. It brought free movement, migration, asylum, checks at external borders, protection of the rights of nationals of non-member countries (known as third-country nationals, or TCNs), and judicial cooperation in civil matters into the scope of the Community method of decision-making. The Council remained the key decision-maker for five years following ratification of the Treaty (until 2004). This meant that:

- the power to make proposals was shared by the Commission and the member states;
- all decisions required unanimity in the Council; and
- the EP would be consulted before decisions were taken.

The ECJ also saw its competences extended to cover Title IV matters, but only following a reference from the highest court of appeal in a member state. This provision constrained the ECJ's role in making rulings based on preliminary references from tribunals in member states seeking to apply Community law.

The European Commission did not exercise jurisdiction over the JHA pillar. After 2004, the Commission had sole right of initiative in Title IV (just as in other Community areas of competence) and, following unanimous agreement by the Council, the codecision and qualified-majority voting (QMV) procedures could be applied. The 'Return' Directive of 2008,[2] covering expulsion of irregular migrants, was the first measure to be adopted using codecision (known under the Lisbon Treaty as the 'ordinary legislative procedure').

Objections from the UK and Ireland were accommodated within a protocol added to the Treaty, which made it clear that the two countries were not covered by measures under Title IV and could not be bound by decisions made by other member states. Both countries could, however, opt in to proposals. The protocol was added because the UK and Ireland reserved the right to impose controls on those entering their territory, while other member states within 'Schengenland' were removing such controls. Ireland was keen to participate so far as possible with Title IV measures, while maintaining its common travel area with the UK. The UK government, too, has opted into a range of Title IV measures, including all key asylum measures (Papagianni 2001; Geddes 2005; Adler-Nissen 2009). The UK has seen the benefits of EU-level action on those forms of migration that its policies have defined as unwanted (asylum seekers and irregular migrants), while not participating in those measures that are potentially rights-extending (such as the 2003 directive that extended rights equivalent to EU citizens for TCNs legally resident in the Union for a period of five years or more[3]) or measures that impinge on the ability to exercise border controls at the UK's frontier.

The government of Denmark also chose not to be covered by Title IV measures. Its position was different because it *is* a Schengen member state. But governments of a more Eurosceptic and anti-immigration hue were keen to be able to decide whether or not to implement decisions agreed under Title IV in national law that built on the Schengen framework.

The JHA pillar dealt with provisions on judicial and police cooperation (JPC) in criminal matters, which included racism and xenophobia, terrorism, trafficking in persons and offences against children, drug trafficking, arms trafficking, and corruption and fraud. The aim here was to promote closer cooperation, although the institutional mechanisms for doing so were weak. The instruments for policy action remained joint positions, decisions, framework decisions, and conventions.

In 1999, a DG was established within the Commission that, by 2010, employed more than 600 staff. In 2010, the remit of the JHA DG was split into two, with one new DG dealing with home affairs and another with justice. Viviane Reding, the first Justice Commissioner, made a big impact in her new role in 2010 when she labelled plans to round up and deport Roma from France to Romania 'a disgrace', and issued a letter of formal notice to the French government requesting full information on the transposition of the 2004 Free Movement Directive[4] into French law. Her intervention was grounded in a suspicion that the French were employing ethnic criteria to discriminate against Roma, which would be against EU law (Boswell and Geddes 2011: 195).

The five-year plans

On the basis of the agreement reached at Amsterdam, the interior ministers of the member states met in Tampere, Finland, to draft a five-year policy plan specifying their objectives in the area of internal security policy and cooperation. These five-year plans have become a staple component of EU internal security policy. The Tampere Programme was followed by the Hague Programme in 2004 and the Stockholm Programme in 2009.

Tampere

The Tampere Programme specified a number of objectives.[5] First, a 'common migration and asylum policy' was taken to mean efforts to promote partnership with countries of origin, to promote 'fair treatment' of non-EU nationals (TCNs), and to seek better management of migration flows with action to tackle illegal immigration. The second area identified by Tampere was creating 'a genuine European area of justice', including mutual recognition of judicial decisions. The third area was the 'Union-wide fight against crime' that sought to step up cooperation against crime. Finally, Tampere sought stronger external action, with closer integration of the external and internal dimensions of policy. This effort has become evident in what the EU calls its 'global approach to migration'. Lavenex (2006) has noted that migration—typically the domain of interior ministries—has now acquired a significant foreign-policy dimension.

Tampere was a powerful agenda-setting document. Political leaders tend not to have the time, ability, or inclination to flesh out the broad policy directions that they provide. They rely on officials to perform this function for them. On the basis of the Tampere conclusions, the Commission and the member states set to work. The Commission, in particular, was keen to stake out a role for itself, to develop credible policy ideas, and to set ambitious targets for realization of the various components of the AFSJ, identified by the Tampere document.

Particular progress was made in the development of common migration and asylum policies, but here, too, we see some distinct features of EU policy development: the dominance of the executive branch of national governments, and the existence of opt-out provisions for the UK, Ireland, and Denmark, but combined with a growing role for supranational institutions. It is important to make a distinction between free movement for EU citizens and the regulation of migration by TCNs. In 2006, around 3.5 million people settled in a new country in the EU. Of these, 3 million were not nationals of the state to which they moved (500,000 were nationals returning to their countries of origin). At first glance, we could suppose that migration of this magnitude means that 3 million immigrants moved to Europe in 2006. But this inference would be misleading, because 1.8 million of these 3 million were TCNs, while 1.2 million were nationals of other EU member states, and thus EU citizens. If we break down the 3.5 million into these three components, then we get a better sense of the composition of migration flows to the EU in 2006. We see that 14 per cent were returning nationals, 34 per cent were accounted for mobility by EU citizens, and 52 per cent represented migration by citizens of non-EU member states (Boswell and Geddes 2011: 23).

We can also think about the countries to which these people moved. First, we can consider movement by TCNs. What we see is large stocks of migrant populations in 'older' immigration countries, such as France, Germany, the Netherlands, and the UK, but we also see rapidly growing migrant populations in newer immigration countries in southern Europe. Between 2000 and 2006, Spain's TCN migrant population rose by 194 per cent to 3.1 million. In 2006 alone, 840,000 people moved to Spain, of whom 500,000 were TCNs. There has also been strong growth in the TCN populations of Italy and Greece. A key issue for these countries has been border controls and efforts to tackle 'irregular' forms of migration—more precisely, those not authorized by migration policies. There has been much slower movement on legal migration, or admissions, as Box 12.4 on the 'Blue Card' Directive illustrates.[6]

The Hague

The Hague Programme covered the period 2004–09. It sought to move the EU from standards-setting measures, such as those on asylum, to a more common approach to key internal security issues, including a common asylum policy.[7] It also sought to deal with admissions policy, which had been an area in which member states had resisted the extension of EU competencies. There was further reinforcement of measures to tackle irregular migration and to step up cooperation with non-EU member states on migration and asylum as part of the external dimension. This

---

BOX 12.4   **The Blue Card Directive**

EU institutions are formally precluded from involvement in decisions about the numbers of migrants to be admitted, but have become involved in measures that seek to approximate the rules governing admission. The 'Blue Card' Directive of 2009 covered the conditions for entry and residence by highly skilled workers, and sought to 'approximate' member state standards on the admission of highly skilled migrants. This directive does not give the EU power to intervene in decisions made by member states about numbers of migrants to be admitted. The Lisbon Treaty states that its provisions on migration 'do not affect the right of member states to determine volumes of admission of TCNs coming from third countries to their territory to seek work, whether employed or self-employed'.

The allusion in its title is to the US 'green card' system, but the EU provision is much more limited in terms of rights extended and the residence period. The US reference is, however, interesting, because it indicates how the EU has sought to position itself in relation to countries such as the US and Canada in a 'global competition' for highly skilled migrant workers. This stance was also seen as a way of countering the current predominance of migration inflows into lower-skilled forms of employment. The 'Blue Card' Directive was agreed in May 2009. The UK, Denmark, and Ireland opted out. It has been used as the template for further proposals from the Commission that seek to further expand the EU's remit in rules regulating admission to EU member states. The Commission has preferred a 'sectoral' focus, with, for example, proposals for approximation of rules governing movement by intra-corporate transferees and seasonal workers.

---

effort included measures to expel and return irregular migrants to their countries of origin. In December 2008, the 'Return' Directive, laying down rules on expulsion, was agreed. It was the first directive in the area of internal security to use the codecision procedure.

In the JPC area, the Hague Programme sought greater exchange of information, which was indicative of the emphasis laid in EU internal security on the gathering of data through systems such as SIS and Eurodac. The programme also called for greater use of Europol and Eurojust. Greater stress was laid in the Hague Programme on measures to tackle terrorism in terms of prevention, preparedness, and response.

Stockholm

The Stockholm Programme[8] and subsequent action plan[9] prepared by the Commission marked a further development of the plans for the AFSJ in light of earlier developments, and also the revised structure for internal security policy developed in the Constitutional Treaty (which was dropped following 'no' votes in referenda held in France and the Netherlands in 2005). The key internal security elements of the Constitutional Treaty were included within the provisions of the Lisbon Treaty, the main headings being: citizenship and fundamental rights, including strengthening cooperation in law enforcement; border management; civil protection; disaster management; and judicial cooperation. The importance of the 'external dimension' of internal security is a prominent feature of the Stockholm Programme. Its inclusion blurs the distinction between the responsibilities of interior and foreign ministries, and raises questions about how the EU can achieve objectives in non-member states. In the 1990s and 2000s, it was able to transpose fairly effectively its objectives into the national legal frameworks of accession states, because it was able to dangle the carrot of membership in front of them. It cannot offer a membership prospect to countries such as Morocco and Libya, but has been very keen to work with them to help to achieve objectives such as curbs on the flows of irregular migrants. Here, we see that the external dimension of internal security requires issue linkage if agreements are to be reached and if connections are to be made between issues such as migration control and border security, with issues of importance to sending and transit states, such as aid, trade, and development. As Paoletti (2011) shows, this stance gave repressive regimes, such as that in Libya, leverage and the ability to extract concession from the EU, such as funding for major infrastructural projects. These connections with the Gadaffi regime were to be a considerable embarrassment for EU leaders in the aftermath of the popular uprising that began in 2011 and subsequent NATO-led military action.

Policy development in the AFSJ

We can now examine three areas in which there has been policy development, but distinct ways of working. This distinctiveness illustrates the institutional complexities of internal security cooperation and policy-making at EU level.

Anti-terrorism

Anti-terrorism policy developed in the context of the revised JPC pillar, with a focus on cooperation outside of the Community decision-making processes and a limited role for supranational institutions. The 9/11 attacks on Washington DC and New York played a powerful role in impelling cooperation, but, as we have seen, the institutional base for such cooperation was already established, and the 'meaning' of security had been powerfully defined by interior ministries and security agencies beginning in the 1970s. Put another way, there was already a powerful institutional repertoire that provided the basis for responses to 9/11 and subsequent terror attacks, such as those in Madrid in 2004 and in London in 2005. Two common positions were agreed in 2001 on the funding of terrorist organizations and the freezing of terrorist assets. A Framework Decision on Combating Terrorism was adopted in mid-2002 that sought to create a common EU-wide definition of 'terrorist organization'. This definition was broad, going beyond that included in United Nations conventions, and thus was seen by some as having the potential to lead to the application of anti-terrorist laws to public protest more generally, with the risk of trampling on civil liberties. The Madrid attack led to the appointment of an EU anti-terrorism coordinator, an anti-terrorism action plan, and a 'scoreboard' to monitor implementation of measures in the action plan. Following the London attacks, an extraordinary meeting of EU interior ministers was held, at which it was agreed that all measures that had already been agreed should be implemented as a matter of urgency. This list included the European Evidence Warrant, the strengthening of the SIS and visa information system, biometric details on passports, stronger efforts to combat terrorist financing, efforts to prevent recruitment and radicalization, and stronger controls on the trade, storage, and transport of explosives. There have also been efforts to promote EU–US cooperation, but these have been controversial, as Box 12.5 shows.

Migration, asylum, and border controls

Migration, asylum, and border controls were located within the new Title IV, and subject to application of Community decision rules, with a transitional period until 2004. There were two key policy drives in the aftermath of Amsterdam and Tampere that reflected consolidation of EU efforts to 'securitize' migration: the development of a common asylum policy, and efforts to tackle irregular migration. By 2003, the EU had agreed the 'Dublin II' regulation, which brought the one-stop asylum procedure into the framework of EU law. Directives on temporary protection, reception conditions, qualifications to enter the asylum process, and asylum procedures were also agreed. These tended to be framed as minimum standards and gave a lot of wriggle room to member states. This flexibility resulted not because the Commission in its proposals preferred relatively low minimum standards (its proposals were usually more ambitious), but because it was what the member states in the Council were prepared to agree. Accompanying the development of asylum policy were efforts to develop stronger capacity at the EU's external frontiers as part of what the Union called its 'fight against illegal immigration'. This effort took the form of efforts to devote financial resources and expertise to newer immigration countries in southern Europe and accession states in Central and Eastern Europe. It also led to the creation of a European agency, Frontex, to assist member states with policy development and implementation.

The European arrest warrant

The European arrest warrant (EAW) shows how single-market principles in the form of mutual recognition have been applied to internal security. The EAW is a warrant for arrest that is valid throughout the EU. Building on the objectives specified in the Tampere document to step up the fight against crime and to extend the principle of mutual recognition, a framework decision of 2002 was made that entered into force on 1 January 2004. The EAW is designed to speed up the process of

---

BOX 12.5   EU–US cooperation post-9/11

Cooperation on anti-terror measures has also involved working closely with the US authorities. This area of cooperation has provided further examples of cooperation in the reserved domain of executive power, with limited legislative or judicial involvement or scope for oversight. Concerns have also been expressed about the abuse of personal data in breach of EU data protection laws. In the post-Lisbon EU, however, we see the EP flexing its muscles in this area, because it has the power to block international agreements.

Bilateral EU–US agreements on extraditions and mutual legal assistance were agreed in 2003 and implemented in the bilateral relations of the member states with the US to take effect in 2010. The extradition agreement specifies extraditable offences, the exchange of information, transmission of documents, and transit rules. It also provides protection against use of the death penalty, because extradition to the US is possible only if the death penalty will not be imposed. The mutual legal assistance agreement provides for exchange of financial information.

Cooperation was further extended when a controversial EU–US agreement, the Passenger Name Record (PNR) Directive, gave American authorities access to passenger data from European airlines. The EP obtained an annulment of the PNR Directive by the ECJ on the grounds that greater data protection measures were needed to conform with EU data protection laws. The EP also questioned the Commission's legal jurisdiction to conclude the PNR agreement. The ECJ ruled that the Commission did not have the legal authority to do so. The ECJ judgment did not deal with privacy and data protection issues, which left scope for bilateral agreements to take the place of the PNR Directive between the US and each EU member state. As part of its 'global approach' on internal security issues, the Commission announced plans in 2010 to revisit the PNR issue both within the EU and with key partners such as the US, Canada, and Australia.

Using powers granted to it by the Lisbon Treaty in 2010, the EP also acted to block an interim SWIFT data-sharing agreement between the EU and the US. SWIFT (the Society for Worldwide Interbank Financial Telecommunication) is a private company, based in Belgium, which handles international bank transfers. The Parliament's rejection would affect the ability of the US authorities to access 'bulk' data, but it would still be able to access individual data using the provisions of the agreement on mutual legal assistance. The Parliament's Civil Liberties Committee indicated that it was unlikely to look favourably on revised Commission proposals if they were not to address fundamental issues of data protection and respect for the rights of EU citizens. Later in 2010, a new version of the agreement was approved by the EP. How far these fundamental issues were resolved remains a matter of argument, but it was a dramatic example of the ability of the Parliament to change the content of a treaty signed by the Commission and all twenty-seven member states.

---

extradition and is based on the principle that warrants issued for arrest by national judicial authorities are recognized by other member states. The EAW was used to return Osman Hussain, suspected of involvement in the failed bombings in London in July 2004, to the UK from Italy. More controversially, a British national, Andrew Symeou, was sent to Greece on a manslaughter charge for alleged involvement in a death at a nightclub in 2007. Symeou denied the charge and questions were raised about the evidence, as well as allegations of mistreatment of witnesses by the Greek authorities. Symeou spent eleven months in prison before being released on bail. He was cleared of the charges in June 2011.

The Lisbon Treaty

The implications of the Lisbon Treaty for internal security are profound. The creation of an AFSJ is defined as competence that is shared with the member states. Almost all internal security matters are made subject to the Community method of decision-making, with use of QMV, codecision (under the ordinary legislative procedure) for the EP, and competence for the ECJ extended to cover the issuance of preliminary rulings in the areas of judicial cooperation in civil matters, migration, and asylum, and, following a five-year post-ratification break (until 2014), to all areas previously covered by the JPC pillar, including judicial cooperation in criminal matters, the Eurojust and Europol (see Box 12.3) agencies, and non-operational police cooperation and civil protection. Eurojust was established following a 2002 Council decision to pursue cooperation on serious crime between member states, and to allow for investigations and prosecutions covering the territory of more than one member state. Given national sensitivities in these areas, Lisbon introduced potential blocks on supranational encroachment. The 'emergency brake' mechanism provides individual member states with the power to veto measures that are seen to jeopardize its criminal justice system. A system of 'yellow' and 'orange' cards was also introduced, which gave national parliaments the right to return legislative proposals to the European Commission. This could serve as a check on EU action, but seems more likely to be a way in which legislatures can seek to influence the negotiating positions of national governments. Lisbon also made important organizational and institutional changes, summarized in Box 12.6.

BOX 12.6   **Post-Lisbon organizational changes**

A Standing Committee on Internal Security (COSI) was created to develop the EU's internal security strategy. COSI is composed of high-level officials from interior ministries.

The respective roles of the Standing Committee on Immigration, Frontiers and Asylum (SCIFA) and the Article 36 Committee (CATS) were to be reviewed by January 2012. Reporting to SCIFA and CATS are working groups on: visas; asylum; external frontiers; civil law matters; terrorism; customs cooperation; cooperation in criminal matters; cooperation in substantive criminal law; civil protection; fundamental rights; citizens rights and free movement of persons; information exchange and data protection; external relations; law enforcement; Schengen; and, finally, general matters, including evaluation.

Conclusions

The introduction to this chapter posed two sets of linked questions that explored the relationship between institutions, policies, and ideas. First, we asked what impelled these developments. We saw a range of factors linked both to the logics of European integration, such as the effects of single-market integration, as well as to the resonance of transboundary issues, such as terrorism, in the domestic politics of member states and the perceived need to seek new venues in which to develop responses to these challenges. We then asked why developments occurred at some points in time and not at others. We see the importance of certain critical junctures in policy development linked to the drive for economic integration that informed Schengen and the SEA, as well as the broader implications of the end of the cold war. But we saw, too, the need to account for the impact of systematic patterns of working together on internal security that developed from the 1970s onwards. These arrangements have changed the setting within which occur both thinking and decision-making about internal security. Thus we need to focus both on the timing of events, but also on the underlying tempo of institutional development linked to the institutionalization of organizational action at the EU level in the area of internal security.

We can now seek to factor in the role that ideas play in shaping institutional change and policy development. The chapter emphasized how changed conceptualizations of security have played a key role in shaping the EU internal security agenda. But also it is ideas about security advanced by certain actors largely concentrated within the executive branches of member state governments that have played a particularly key role in shaping the policy agenda.

This focus on the important underlying role of ideas about security leads to the second set of questions that have been addressed by this chapter. We saw that the executive branch of member state governments have been key players in policy development. We saw, too, that their role is now challenged by the developing responsibilities of the Commission, EP, and ECJ in these areas. We have seen how all three have been able to flex their muscles and challenge aspects of policy. At the same time, this area is characterized by complexity and opaque structures, with scope for innovation to occur outside of the Treaty, such as through Schengen and, more recently, the Prüm Treaty. As a result of these changes, we can now identify a rebalance in power relations between the executive, legislative, and judicial branches of government. The executive still holds the upper hand—but the EP and ECJ have scope to advocate and delineate the parameters of an AFSJ that realigns the relationship between freedom, security, and justice.

NOTES

1. Council of the EU (2010) 'Towards a European security model', Draft internal security strategy for the European Union, 5842/10, February.
2. Directive 2008/115/EC of the European Parliament and of the Council of 16 December 2008 on common standards and procedures in Member States for returning illegally staying third-country nationals.
3. Council Directive 2003/109/EC of 25 November 2003 concerning the status of third-country nationals who are long-term residents.
4. Directive 2004/38/EC of the European Parliament and of the Council of 29 April 2004 on the right of citizens of the Union and their family members to move and reside freely within the territory of the Member States.
5. Tampere European Council, 15–16 October 1999, presidency conclusions.
6. Council Directive 2009/50/EC of 25 May 2009 on the conditions of entry and residence of third-country nationals for the purposes of highly qualified employment.
7. The Hague European Council, 4–5 November 2004, presidency conclusions.
8. 'The Stockholm Programme: an open and secure Europe serving and protecting citizens', OJ C 115/01, 4 May 2010.
9. European Commission (2010) *Delivering an Area of Freedom, Security and Justice for Europe's Citizens Action Plan Implementing the Stockholm Programme*, COM (2010) 171.

FURTHER READING

The most comprehensive guide to the legal framework governing the AFSJ is provided by Peers (2011). Mitsilegas *et al.* (2003) provide a thorough account of the development of the AFSJ. Boswell and Geddes (2011) explore the implications for migration and mobility of emerging EU internal security competencies. Huysmans (2000) provides a sophisticated conceptual account of the securitization of migration, while Lavenex (2006) explores the implications for the governance of migration and asylum of 'external governance'.

Adler-Nissen, R. (2009) 'Behind the scenes of differentiated integration: circumventing national opt-outs in justice and home affairs', *Journal of European Public Policy*, 16/1: 62–80.

Boswell, C. and Geddes, A. (2011) *Migration and Mobility in the European Union* (Basingstoke and New York: Palgrave).

Codagnone, C. (1999) 'The new migration in Russia in the 1990s', in K. Koser and H. Lutz (eds) *The New Migration in Europe: Social Constructions and Social Realities* (Basingstoke: Macmillan).

Geddes, A. (2005) 'Getting the best of both worlds: Britain, the EU and migration policy', *International Affairs*, 81/4: 723–40.

Geddes, A. (2008) *Immigration and European Integration: Beyond Fortress Europe?* (2nd edn, Manchester: Manchester University Press).

Grabbe, H. (2000) 'The sharp edges of Europe: extending Schengen eastwards', *International Affairs*, 76/3: 519–36.

Hailbronner, K. (2004) 'Asylum law in the context of a European migration policy', in N. Walker (ed.) *Europe's Area of Freedom, Security and Justice* (Oxford: Oxford University Press).

Huysmans, J. (2000) 'The European Union and the securitization of migration', *Journal of Common Market Studies*, 38/5: 751–77.

Lavenex, S. (1999) *Safe Third Countries: Extending the EU Asylum and Immigration Policies to Central and Eastern Europe* (Budapest: Central European University Press).

Lavenex, S. (2006) (2006) 'Shifting up and out: the foreign policy of European immigration control', *West European Politics*, 29/2: 329–50.

Menon, A. and Weaterill, S. (2006) 'Transnational legitimacy in a globalising world: how the European Union rescues its states', *West European Politics*, 31/3: 397–416.

Mitsilegas, V., Monar, J., and Rees, W. (2003) *The European Union and Internal Security: Guardian of the People?* (New York: Palgrave Macmillan).

Papagianni, G. (2001) 'Flexibility in justice and home affairs: an old phenomenon taking new forms', in B. de Witte, D. Hanf, and E. Vos (eds) *The Many Faces of Differentiation in EU Law* (New York, Intersentia).

Pastore, F., Monzini, P., and Sciortino, G. (2006) 'Schengen's soft underbelly? Irregular migration and human smuggling across land and sea borders to Italy', *International Migration*, 44/4: 95–119.

Peers, S. (2011) *EU Justice and Home Affairs Law* (3rd edn, Oxford: Oxford University Press).

Wallace, H. (2010) 'An institutional anatomy and five policy modes', in H. Wallace, M. A. Pollack, and A. Young (eds) *Policy-making in the European Union* (6th edn, Oxford and New York: Oxford University Press).

 WEB LINKS

http://ec.europa.eu/dgs/home-affairs/index_en.htm
http://ec.europa.eu/justice/index_en.htm
In 2010, the Commission divided JHA between two DGs: the DG Home Affairs and the DG Justice.

http://www.europol.europa.eu/
The Europol website.

http://www.ceps.eu
Brussels-based think tank the Centre for European Policy Studies (CEPS) has a section dedicated to JHA at its website.

http://www.statewatch.org
The civil liberties organization Statewatch monitors the growth of the European state.

CHAPTER 13

International Interests: the Common Foreign and Security Policy

John Peterson, Andrew Byrne, and Niklas Helwig

▌ Summary

Amongst all that sets the European Union apart, its aspirations in foreign policy rank high. No other international organization claims to have a 'common' foreign policy. Leaving aside the (arguable) exception of the North Atlantic Treaty Organization (NATO), none claim an emerging defence policy. The common foreign and security policy (CFSP) seeks to combine the political weight of twenty-seven EU member states in the pursuit of common goals. But 'European foreign policy' must integrate a wide range of other policies to be effective. Likewise, any assessment of the EU's role in global affairs must consider CFSP as one policy area within a broader external relations toolkit. This chapter highlights the CFSP's relative youth (compared to other EU policies), mixed record, and uncertain future. Compared with the rest of what the EU does, foreign policy has resisted pressures for integration. Nonetheless, it has witnessed a significant degree of institutionalization and is an area in which the EU's ambitions remain high.

Introduction

The creation and development of what is now the European Union (EU) has not only promoted cooperative relations between its member states, but has also given them an opportunity to speak with a common, sometimes even single, voice in world politics. Potentially, at least, the Union has the power to influence global events in pursuit of European values and interests. By the early twenty-first century, no other international actor had such a diverse foreign policy 'toolkit' (Everts and Keohane 2003: 177). It could even be argued that the EU's power matched or exceeded that of the United States in every area besides the deployment of military force (Moravcsik 2005: 349; see also McCormick 2007).

Possessing such power is not the same as being able to deploy it effectively. The EU's capacity for common external action developed earliest and most rapidly in trade policy. From the origins of the European Economic Community (EEC), there was a clear and necessary connection between the creation of a customs union and a common commercial policy (CCP) towards the rest of the non-EU world (the former is impossible without the latter). Purely functional necessity resulted in the effective delegation by member states of trade policy authority to the EU's institutions, with the European Commission in the lead. Today, the EU acts for the member states in international trade negotiations, including within the World Trade Organization (WTO), usually managing to negotiate as a single bloc.

However, there is no obvious connection between (what has become) a single market and a common foreign policy. The EU shares representation with member states in key forums such as the Groups of Eight and Twenty (G8 and G20), and it has 'super-observer' status at the United Nations General Assembly. But it is entirely absent from others, such as the International Monetary Fund (IMF). EU member states have vastly different foreign policy capabilities, and vary sharply in their willingness to employ the EU's complex and often time-consuming procedures. One consequence is a stubborn persistence of different views about the EU's ultimate aim in foreign policy: the *intergovernmental coordination* of pre-existing national foreign policies (at a minimum), or the *supranational governance* of a single European foreign policy (at a maximum).

When decisions on foreign policy action are taken, EU member states (particularly larger ones) often act like 'normal' nation-states—that is, they reject the delegation of foreign and security policy to international bodies except on the basis of unanimity. This intergovernmental approach dominates most other international organizations, such as NATO. At the same time, however, it has become increasingly recognized within European political classes, and even more so amongst diplomats, that even the largest EU states have limited influence unless they act together with their European partners. All EU member states have accepted this reality for decades, but they have drawn different conclusions from it. Most smaller EU states, but

BOX 13.1	Defining 'foreign policy' and 'external relations'

In ordinary English, 'foreign policy' and 'external relations' mean much the same thing. However, they have quite different meanings in Euro-speak. *External relations* is used in Brussels to refer to the foreign affairs responsibilities of the Commission: in practice, trade and aid, but also external aspects of other EU policies (such as agriculture, and judicial and police cooperation, or JPC). Most decisions are taken by the Council on the basis of a Commission proposal, increasingly by qualified-majority voting (QMV) and often with a strong role for the European Parliament (EP).

In contrast, *foreign policy* refers to policies and actions in those areas that are normally in the remit of national foreign ministries and on which nearly all decisions are taken unanimously. The Commission is fully associated, not least through the High Representative, who now chairs most meetings of EU foreign ministers and is Vice-President of the Commission (see Box 13.4). But the Commission has always occupied a position of weakness compared with that of EU member states in foreign policy. The EP still has no power—besides budgetary influence and a new right to invite heads of EU delegations for exchanges of views—over the common foreign and security policy (CFSP).

CFSP proposals can be made by any member state or the High Representative (with or without the support of the Commission). In practice, the Council presidency has usually taken the lead. The first signs that this equation may change were suggested after the EU's new model High Representative, initially in the person of Catherine Ashton (formerly a British Labour politician), took up her post.

Since the 1992 Maastricht Treaty, the CFSP, along with the rest of what the EU does, has been the responsibility of a single set of institutions, or 'single institutional framework'. Thus, decisions on the CFSP and external relations are, in the end, taken by the same people—mainly foreign ministers and heads of government, with Commission support—but according to different decision rules. The Lisbon Treaty eliminated the pillar system that made CFSP decision-making distinct from other policies. But, in substance, little has changed: CFSP decisions still require unanimous approval by the European Council and the Foreign Affairs Council, with limited possibilities for QMV and the option for member states to 'constructively abstain'. The European Court of Justice (ECJ)—traditionally a motor of integration—has no jurisdiction on CFSP matters. One of the legal gurus of the EU argues that Lisbon 'confirms that CFSP remains clearly subject to different rules and procedures from the other activities of the EU. It therefore remains a second pillar as it was before' (Piris 2010: 260).

also Germany, have argued consistently for a more supranational CFSP—notably, with decisions by qualified-majority voting (QMV). Others—notably, France, Spain, Sweden, and the UK—have insisted that EU foreign policy must be made by consensus.

Even as it aspires to a *common* foreign policy, the EU has learned from experience that it is unlikely ever to have a *single* foreign policy, in the sense of an EU foreign policy that replaces national policies. The common foreign and security policy

---

BOX 13.2   The European Security Strategy

Agreed in the aftermath of painful divisions over the US-led invasion of Iraq, the European Security Strategy (ESS; see EU 2003) identifies the key challenges and threats facing the EU. It also identifies the Union's strategic objectives, throwing the EU's weight behind effective multilateralism (especially via the United Nations), democracy promotion, and respect for human rights and the rule of law. The ESS espouses the need for more active policies across the whole range of 'political, diplomatic, military and civilian, trade and development activities', and an EU strategic culture fostering 'early, rapid, and when necessary, robust intervention'. The leitmotif is multilateralism: promoting good governance, international cooperation, and the use of all the policy instruments at the EU's disposal, especially economic instruments, but not excluding force. There is little dispute that the ESS was partly, at least, a European response to the controversial 2002 US National Security Strategy (NSS), which appeared to embrace the doctrine of 'pre-emption' of threats to US security without prior consultation with European (or any other) allies.

Since then, the US has published multiple national security strategies, including one in 2010 under President Obama. The 2010 NSS signalled a course-correction in US foreign policy towards 'international engagement and collaboration as first options against national security threats' (DeYoung 2010). At this point, the EU had yet to revise its 2003 document, despite issuing a report on implementation of the ESS (see EU 2008). It played no military role in the UN-backed and NATO-led 2011 action in Libya, and its incoherence in response to the Libyan crisis suggested that EU foreign policy remained prone to painful divisions of the kind it had suffered over Iraq (see Koenig 2011). In the circumstances, debates about whether European and US security cultures remained in alignment or were diverging remained live ones (see Dannreuther and Peterson 2006).

---

remains only one element in what is often referred to as 'European foreign policy', or the sum total of all external action by EU member states, whether it is pursued via the Union itself, national channels and instruments, or other (non-EU) multilateral organizations (see Carlsnaes *et al.* 2004; Laïdi 2008a; Hill and Smith 2011). And when the perceived national interests of member states clash, such as over the 2003 Iraq war, there simply is no EU foreign policy, common or otherwise (Hill 2004).

What the CFSP offers is a mechanism for consensus-building and seizing on the 'politics of scale' (Ginsberg 1989, 2001), or the reality that the EU is far more powerful when it speaks with one voice, as opposed to twenty-seven or more. The EU has even developed something approaching a doctrine for its foreign policy, in the shape of the European Security Strategy (ESS) adopted in 2003 by the European Council (see Box 13.2). More generally, the Union has gone much further in institutionalizing foreign policy cooperation than has any other regional organization.

The origins of CFSP institutions

One of the first laws of politics is that nearly all institutions have unintended effects that their creators neither foresaw nor intended. The founding fathers of what is now the European Union had little or no ambition to create a new and unique foreign-policy power. Foreign policy was thus a bit player in the European project of the early 1950s, which began as a mostly economic enterprise, albeit with a strong political purpose: to make war impossible between Germany and France via the integration of their coal and steel industries. The next major step, the creation of a European Defence Community (EDC) in 1952, sought to harness a still-occupied and distrusted (West) Germany into a European army to bolster Western Europe's defence against the Soviet threat (see Table 13.1). But the EDC collapsed in 1954, following its rejection by the French National Assembly, leading the founding fathers once again to turn to economic integration to fulfil political objectives.

The supranational governance endemic to the European Coal and Steel Community (ECSC) and, later, the EEC, was always unimaginable in the security realm. Defence was left to the North Atlantic Treaty Organization (NATO), created in 1949, and the Western European Union (WEU) a mutual defence organization founded in 1948 (see Rees 1998), and their strictly intergovernmental institutions. However, the coming to power of Charles de Gaulle as French President led to a serious effort to 'intergovernmentalize' the EEC by grafting onto it the so-called Fouchet Plan in 1961–62. De Gaulle's clear intent was to turn the EEC into a voluntary union of member states with extensive national veto powers, and action only by unanimity in foreign and defence affairs. The Fouchet Plan was rejected by the other EEC five, partly because some (such as the Netherlands) were unhappy that it excluded the UK and partly because it was seen as a French move against NATO. In any event, the debate on the Fouchet Plan—with intergovernmental cooperation competing for support with the Community method—set a pattern for future debates about European foreign policy.

European political cooperation

Interest in foreign policy coordination did not disappear with the Fouchet Plan. Buoyed by the resignation of de Gaulle and the prospect of the Community's first enlargement, EC foreign ministers agreed the 1970 Luxembourg report and thereby established the European political cooperation (EPC) mechanism. EPC had no basis other than a political declaration (legally non-binding) of the Council. Member states agreed to consult and cooperate on issues of foreign policy, but not on defence and only outside the EEC Treaty framework. For several years, France prevented any discussion of foreign policy within an EC framework. Foreign ministers were even forced on one occasion in 1975 to hold an EPC meeting in the morning in Copenhagen and then fly to Brussels to reconvene in the afternoon for 'separate' EC discussions.

TABLE 13.1 The expansion of EU foreign policy: a chronology	
1952	EDC Treaty signed by six founding states of the EEC
1954	EDC Treaty rejected by French National Assembly Brussels Treaty for the WEU signed by six EEC states plus the UK
1958	Treaty of Rome founding the European Community (EC) enters into force
1961–62	Fouchet Plan for purely intergovernmental political cooperation rejected
1970	EPC mechanism created
1971	EPC used to present (for the first time) collective EC positions at the UN
1973	EPC used to develop collective positions toward key allies (such as the US)
1974	First institutionalized regional political dialogues (Euro–Arab)
1975	Helsinki Final Act of the CSCE, in which EPC played a key role
1977	EPC establishes Code of Conduct for EC firms operating in South Africa
1981	EPC/EC coordinated economic embargo against Argentina during Falklands War
1986	Single European Act agreed, bringing EPC into the EC treaty framework
1989–91	Communist governments fall in Central and Eastern Europe, culminating in German unification (1990) and the collapse of the Soviet Union (1991)
1992	Maastricht Treaty on European Union agreed, with provisions for a CFSP and links to the WEU
1993	Maastricht Treaty (and the CFSP) enters into effect
1995	Madrid European Council launches a set of strategies and partnerships with specific regions
1997	Amsterdam Treaty agreed, creating High Representative for the CFSP
1998	UK and France agree the St Malo Declaration on European Defence
1999	Cologne and Helsinki summits (respectively) create European Security and Defence Policy (ESDP) and agree to create Rapid Reaction Force
2003–04	Convention on the Future of Europe agrees Constitutional Treaty First ESDP police mission in Bosnia, followed by ESDP military missions (Macedonia, Democratic Republic of Congo, Bosnia)
2003	The US invades Iraq in coalition with some European Union member states; the EU is painfully divided on the issue
2005	Constitutional Treaty rejected by French and Dutch voters
2006	The Lisbon Treaty is negotiated by European leaders, retaining much of the Constitutional Treaty's content on external relations
2009	The Lisbon Treaty is ratified by all member states Catherine Ashton is appointed the first High Representative for Foreign Affairs and Security Council; Herman Van Rompuy becomes President of the European Council Russian troops move into South Ossetia and Abkhazia, sparking a conflict with Georgia; under France's Presidency of the European Council, French President Sarkozy negotiates a ceasefire
2011	A wave of democratic protests and reforms spreads across North Africa, heralding an 'Arab Spring'; the EU is forced to re-examine its strategy in the Southern Neighbourhood

Still, EPC slowly became more institutionalized, with a number of informal rules and substantive policies gradually emerging during the 1970s. There was no shortage of opportunities to put EPC to the test: common European positions were sought during this period on the Yom Kippur War in the Middle East, relations with the US, crises in Cyprus and Portugal, the Soviet invasion of Afghanistan, and the Iranian revolution. Actual policy output remained modest for two main reasons: first, all decisions were made by consensus, and just one member state could block or water down any proposal; second, EPC had no resources, policy tools, or staff of its own.[1] Some of its early participants viewed it as little more than a diplomats' dining club.

Over time, however, EPC began to produce substantive policies. The 1980 Venice Declaration on the Middle East affirmed the right of Palestinians to self-determination (in defiance of the US) for the first time. The member states, using both the EPC and EC frameworks, played a leading role in the Conference on Security and Cooperation in Europe (CSCE).[2] Despite US scepticism towards what was originally a Soviet initiative, the CSCE produced the Helsinki Final Act in 1975, a political declaration that (amongst other things) reaffirmed fundamental rights and freedoms, made border changes permissible only by peaceful means, and opened to international discussion the ways in which countries treated their citizens and cooperated with their neighbours. Later, the CSCE was regarded as an important factor in the political process leading to the end of the cold war.

From EPC to the CFSP

Despite EPC's successes, the 1970s and 1980s were mostly a time of missed opportunities for European foreign policy. Member states, including France, gradually accepted that a large part of the problem was the separation of EPC from the EC itself. EPC had begun to develop its own brand of 'soft law', which allowed its participants to refer to and (with the cooperation of the Commission) draw upon Community instruments such as economic aid and sanctions. Still, these arrangements remained mostly ad hoc and unsatisfactory.

Over time, an increasing number of member states became both less hesitant to use Community instruments and institutions to support EPC objectives, and frustrated by problems rooted in the compartmentalization of economic and political affairs. The Commission became gradually more accepted as a necessary partner in EPC in order to align Community policies with EPC-identified policy objectives. Eventually, member states decided that EPC should be given formal status within the treaties in the Single European Act (SEA) in 1986.

Even the new-model EPC was exposed as inadequate in the face of major foreign policy challenges such as the fall of the Berlin Wall, ethnic tensions and war in Yugoslavia, and the first war with Iraq. The opportunity was taken in the 1992 Maastricht Treaty to strengthen it, by bringing it into the new EU's institutional structure, and to give it, for the first time, aspirations in the defence field, all with an ambitious-sounding new name: the 'common foreign and security policy' (see Box 13.3).

BOX 13.3   CFSP policy instruments

In contrast with the purely political decisions taken under EPC, the CFSP provides for legally binding decisions. Prior to the Lisbon Treaty, there were three types of decision: *common positions* (requiring coordinated national actions); *joint actions* (using EC instruments, such as aid and trade); and *common strategies* (providing a longer-term view). Yet the lack of any clear distinction between, say, common positions and joint actions, and the tendency of common strategies to lack substance, led to the reformulation of these terms. The Lisbon Treaty cut to the quick by specifying only one legally binding act for all CFSP action: *decisions*, which could define policy Union guidelines, actions, positions, and implementation arrangements. However, there remained no provisions for giving the Commission the right to monitor implementation of the CFSP, besides entrusting the High Representative with ensuring 'implementation of the decisions adopted by the European Council and the Council'. How he or she would do so, besides 'naming and shaming' in cases of blatant non-implementation, remained unclear. Proper implementation of the CFSP thus appeared to be 'largely left to the goodwill of Member States' (Piris 2010: 264).

Maastricht integrated the hitherto-autonomous EPC Secretariat (working under the Council presidency) into the General Secretariat of the Council. It also established new CFSP policy instruments and marked the first steps towards an EU defence policy (see below). What it did *not* do was modify the strictly intergovernmental decision-making processes of the old EPC. Despite a political signal that the EU was getting its act together in foreign policy, little changed in practice.

The structure of the CFSP system

The Maastricht Treaty gave birth to a new European Union, putting into a single treaty framework the European Community, CFSP, and the newly emerging area of justice and home affairs (JHA), which later became judicial and police cooperation (JPC; see Chapter 12). But it kept these policy areas separate by giving the CFSP and JHA their own distinct decision-making procedures and 'pillars' (Pillar II for the CFSP). Maastricht also launched the EU on the road towards a military capability. It provided for a common defence policy and gave the Union the right to call on the WEU, a European-only alternative to NATO that had been kept alive for various purposes, to undertake military missions on the EU's behalf.

The new Treaty also ensured a strong measure of continuity between the old EPC and new CFSP. Responsibility for managing the CFSP remained with the rotating Council presidency, which also remained responsible for its implementation. Decisions could be taken on the proposal of any member state, as well as the Commission, but the Commission's inferior status was formalized by making it 'fully associated' only with the CFSP. While the EU appeared to embrace higher foreign-policy ambitions, it dedicated few new resources to this purpose. The CFSP remained stubbornly intergovernmental and a matter for (almost exclusively) unanimous agreement. As under EPC, the Union continued to look extensively to the policies and instruments of the EC, especially its economic tools, to realize its foreign-policy ambitions.

The European Council formally gave the CFSP strategic direction and took the highest-profile political decisions (see Chapter 3). Foreign ministers meeting monthly in the General Affairs Council (GAC) took most policy decisions. On CFSP matters, foreign ministers' agendas were prepared as under EPC by a committee of senior officials, the Political Committee (PoCo), which did the sort of preparatory work that the Committee of Permanent Representatives (Coreper) performed in Brussels for Pillar I questions. Composed of political directors—very senior diplomats—from national foreign ministries, PoCo normally met once a month on its own, usually in the capital of the presidency, as well as in the margins of foreign ministers' and European Council meetings. PoCo was serviced by a diverse array of working groups of national EU officials covering geographical regions (such as the Middle East) and functional issues (such as non-proliferation).

The CFSP also inherited the Coreu system, named after the acronym for the French *correspondant Européen*, from EPC.[3] This encrypted communications network allows for direct communications between the foreign ministries of all member states, the Commission, and the Council Secretariat, and is a critical, real-time means of exchanging information and views. The longer it has operated, the more it has become accepted that major foreign-policy problems should be discussed at the EU level before national positions are formed. Thus a 'coordination reflex' has emerged: consultation before action is the norm and unilateral action is shunned.

The 1997 Treaty of Amsterdam was an opportunity to address some of the defects in the CFSP (see Peterson and Sjursen 1998). The Treaty created a new High Representative for the CFSP, who would also retain the existing post of Secretary General of the Council, to 'assist' the presidency in managing the CFSP. A new policy planning and early warning unit was also established within the Council Secretariat, bringing together staff from the Council, Commission, WEU, and member states' diplomatic services. Some spoke of a 'nascent EU foreign ministry'; more-sober analysts noted that the new unit expanded the EU's Brussels-based foreign policy machinery, but kept it under the firm grip of the Council (Allen 1998: 54–5; see also Spence 2002).

In themselves, these changes were not far-reaching. To illustrate, the new policy unit did not supplant or even contribute much to the EU's network of national foreign ministries. What made the Amsterdam changes important, and what really changed CFSP, was less the new provisions than the way in which they were implemented. Amsterdam came into force (in 1999) when the EU was under pressure after its humiliating performance in the Balkans, where it appeared powerless without US political, as well as military, leadership to prevent extensive bloodshed, first in Bosnia and then in Kosovo (see Bildt 1998; Holbrooke 1999; Clark 2001). In particular, the exposure of Europe's institutional and military ineffectiveness in Kosovo focused minds on the Union's inability to manage a security crisis without extensive US participation.

Thus the Cologne European Council in June 1999 created a new European security and defence policy (ESDP), building on the bilateral UK–French St Malo initiative of the previous year.[4] It also appointed Javier Solana as the CFSP High Representative, thus opting for a heavyweight former Spanish Foreign Minister and NATO Secretary-General, instead of a low-profile official as many had expected. Six months later, the Helsinki European Council agreed the main features of the EU's defence policy, with substantial knock-on effects for the CFSP (of which ESDP, now called the 'common' security and defence policy, or CSDP, forms a part). The so-called 'headline goal' was agreed, specifying the military capabilities that member states would aim to put at the EU's disposal (see below), along with parallel 'civilian and conflict prevention dimensions'.[5]

New politico-military structures had to be grafted onto what was previously a purely civilian organization in order to manage the EU's new military capability. Thus a Military Committee, consisting of senior military officers representing their national chiefs of staff (similar to NATO's arrangements), was set up. It would be serviced by a new military staff made up of military personnel seconded from member states located in the Council Secretariat. On the political (CFSP) side, the Political Committee was superseded by a new Political and Security Committee (PSC), consisting of national ambassador-level officials stationed, significantly, not in their capitals, but in Brussels. The PSC would meet regularly (typically twice a week) and take responsibility, under the chairmanship of the Council presidency, for the day-to-day management of the CFSP. Uniquely in the EU's institutional set-up, it was given scope to make actual decisions (as opposed to recommendations) on the political control of military operations if the Council so mandated. In its earliest versions, member states frequently appointed relatively junior diplomats to the PSC; '[p]rogressively, however, the PSC has become a key posting for career diplomats' (Howorth 2010: 457).

These institutional changes, along with the appointment of Solana as High Representative for the CFSP, resulted in a distinct European foreign policy system. Over time, it became increasingly robust, action-oriented, and Brussels-centred. Still, foreign policy remained an area in which the EU clearly failed to punch its weight. Perhaps the CFSP's main weakness was the leadership conflicts inherent in a system in which the presidency changed every six months, a High Representative was increasingly seen as the external face of EU foreign policy, but lacked real power, and the Commission was responsible for many of the instruments needed to make CFSP effective. Thus CFSP reform emerged as a prominent theme of the 2002–03 Convention on the Future of Europe, and the new Constitutional Treaty that emerged in 2004.

Following its rejection in the 2005 French and Dutch referenda, the Constitutional Treaty looked doomed. Few were more disappointed than those for whom strengthening the EU's foreign policy was a priority. The Constitutional Treaty had proposed to abolish the rotating presidency and transform the High Representative into an EU Minister for Foreign Affairs (MFA), who would also serve as a Vice President of the Commission in charge of external relations. It also included provision for a new European External Action Service (EEAS) to assist the MFA.

The Constitutional Treaty embraced doctrinal, as well as institutional, changes. It included a 'solidarity clause' committing the EU to 'mobilise all the instruments at its disposal', including national military resources, in the event of a terrorist attack or natural or man-made disaster in any of its member states. Strikingly, given the strong obligation felt by many member states to NATO, it created for all member states the obligation to aid each other 'by all the means in their power' if any EU member state were the victim of armed aggression, although without prejudice to NATO commitments.

In the end, most of the Constitutional Treaty's provisions on foreign and security policy survived the transition to the Lisbon Treaty that came into force in December 2009. The term 'Minister of Foreign Affairs' was ditched for the less provocative (and more familiar) title High Representative of the Union for the CFSP, but the post retained nearly all of the same powers and authority specified in the Constitutional Treaty (see Box 13.4). The EEAS was launched in 2010, intended to be a 6,000-strong diplomatic service for the Union, working alongside national embassies (see Box 13.5). The launch was marred by extensive turf battles between the Commission, member states, and the European Parliament (EP) over the scope and design of the service.

Lisbon also contained 'mutual assistance and solidarity clauses', albeit with qualifications to reassure non-NATO members (such as Sweden and Ireland) and a clear statement that, for the twenty-one EU members of the Atlantic Alliance, NATO 'remains the foundation of their collective defence and the forum for its implementation' (Art. 42, para. 7 TEU). Piris (2010: 275) is clear that while the solidarity clause is 'of utmost symbolic and political importance... it does not amount to a mutual defence clause and does not change anything in the respective position of each member state vis-à-vis NATO'.

What also do not change are the basic ground rules of the CFSP—notably, that nearly all important decisions are taken by unanimity. Nor does the new-model High Representative reduce the importance of national foreign ministers or the Council presidency, whose agreement continues to be needed for each and every common policy. However, the High Representative now assumes a far stronger position than any previous European official to broker agreements and to implement them once agreed.

The CFSP system in action

One of the abiding features of the EU foreign policy system is its emphasis on consensus. No single official or body enjoys a monopoly over policy initiation, although the Council presidency traditionally has been expected to provide leadership and manage business. The new High Representative is meant to take over

---

BOX 13.4   **The High Representative**

The newly empowered High Representative of the Union, introduced by the Treaty of Lisbon, is meant to eliminate shortcomings in the 'continuity', 'coherence', and 'visibility' of the EU's action in the world. The High Representative is triple-hatted (that is, given more than one formal affiliation) as High Representative for CFSP in the Council (as before Lisbon), the Commissioner for External Relations, and President/Chair of the Foreign Affairs Council of EU foreign ministers. However, fulfilling such a wide range of tasks predictably posed a difficult challenge for the first occupant of the post, Catherine Ashton.

The European Council appoints the High Representative by qualified majority, with the agreement of the Commission President. The High Representative serves for a five-year term. As one of the Vice-Presidents of the Commission, he or she needs EP approval, together with the approval of other members of the Commission.

Taking over the job of the rotating presidency, the High Representative chairs formal and informal Council meetings of foreign ministers (the Foreign Affairs Council), including its development and defence formations. Appointees of the High Representative chair the PSC, as well as the majority of the CFSP working parties, and thus prepare Foreign Affairs Council meetings. A right of initiative in CFSP allows the High Representative to put forward her or his own proposals. The High Representative is also the interlocutor for the EP and reports to its plenary on the CFSP.

The incumbent is meant to take part in the weekly meetings of the college of Commissioners, but inevitably misses many of these because of heavy travel commitments. So, too, will the High Representative inevitably end up being abroad when the Foreign Affairs Council meet, in which case (maybe revealingly) it is chaired by the member state holding the Council's rotating presidency. If all of that were not enough, the High Representative is tasked with coordinating the external relations portfolios that are still in the remit of other Commissioners, such as those for trade, development cooperation, humanitarian aid, enlargement, and neighbourhood policy, to ensure coherence in EU external action.

The High Representative represents the Union externally on all matters relating to the CFSP. Besides undertaking a large number of diplomatic visits around the world, this duty comprises the issuing of statements on his or her own behalf or of declarations on behalf of the EU. Alongside the High Representative, the President of the European Council represents the Union 'at his [or her] level'—that is, the level of heads of state and government—on CFSP matters. The President of the Commission retains his or her own external representative role, such as representing the EU in the G8 and G20 (together with the President of the European Council). Thus the High Representative is the 'external face' of the CFSP, but not, in many settings, of the EU more generally.

---

these functions and provide leadership of a kind that the CFSP traditionally has lacked. The basic problems of multiple EU foreign-policy representatives, plus inconsistent and often weak leadership and implementation, were prime motivators of the decision to create this new post. Giving the High Representative a foot in both the Commission and Council camps has built-in institutional contradictions.

BOX 13.5   The European External Action Service

Formally launched in December 2010 as an 'autonomous body', the EEAS was still in the process of being established at the time of writing. Its staff was set to be a mix of officials from the Commission and the General Secretariat of the Council, as well as the member states' diplomatic services. To avoid duplication, entities from the Commission's former Directorate-General for External Relations (DG RELEX) and the General Secretariat of the Council was to be merged into six DGs with geographical, multilateral, and thematic desks. The same was planned for crisis management structures for the planning and implementation of CSDP missions, although they were to be kept separate from the rest of the organizational structure of the EEAS due to the unwillingness of member states to integrate this policy area. The chair of the PSC and a number of working-party chairs are now part of the EEAS, making the service crucial in decision-shaping on the CFSP. On the ground, 136 Union delegations around the world represent the EU. In its early stages of development, the EEAS faced many internal challenges, such as the consolidation of working procedures (between hierarchical levels and different policy fields), as well as challenges arising outside the EEAS (inter-institutional relations with the Commission, member states, and the EP). Whether the EEAS was really a European foreign ministry in the making, or just an institutional fudge that would ultimately preserve divisions between the Commission, Council, and national foreign ministries, remained an open question.

But it nonetheless creates at least the potential for greater coherence between political ends and economic means.

A more fundamental problem with the CFSP system is that member states are bound by agreed common approaches and have an obligation to consult each other, but retain freedom of action where there is no agreed common policy. Even where an EU agreement exists, member states may still act themselves, so long as they do so in accordance with the agreed position. This practice can be seen for example in the succession of EU foreign ministers who follow each other making the rounds in the Middle East, sometimes to the despair of Council presidencies (especially from small countries) and, presumably in future, the High Representative. Put simply, there is no obligation on a member state to conduct its foreign policy 'exclusively' or even primarily through the CFSP, or even to leave CFSP action exclusively to the High Representative (unless it has been agreed otherwise).

The difficulty of reaching common policies and/or the conviction that (especially) larger member states can achieve better results by other means sometimes leads to the creation of small groups outside the EU for the pursuit of European foreign-policy objectives. One prominent and traumatic (for the young and fragile CFSP[6]) example was the so-called Contact Group, in which France, Germany, the UK, and (eventually) Italy engaged in multilateral diplomacy after 1994 with the US and Russia on the conflict in the former Yugoslavia, with other EU member states effectively excluded. Another occurred when France, Germany, and the UK (the 'EU3') gave themselves the task in 2004 of trying to convince Iran on behalf of the EU to agree to international controls on its nuclear development programme. Sensitivities between large and small EU member states remain tender, but with enlargement to twenty-seven or more, there is an increasing—if still reluctant—recognition that some member states are more equal than others, and that similar groups are necessary if the CFSP is to function. In any event, foreign policy for all EU member states has over time become more 'Europeanized' (Wong 2011)—that is, more Brussels-based, frequently linked to EC external economic policies, and an increasingly central part of the EU's personality.

Powers of the institutions

As the rules governing EU foreign policy have expanded over the years, so too have its policy instruments and capabilities. As we have seen, EPC often involved little more than issuing declarations and coordinating diplomatic activity among EU member states. On some issues, however, the coordination of views and even common actions were quite sustained and intense. For example, the Euro–Arab Dialogue and CSCE in the mid-1970s were early examples of *institutionalized political dialogues*. Such dialogues became useful ways in which to coordinate all EPC (and, later, EC) activities toward an important region or country, such as the Mediterranean or the countries of Central and Eastern Europe. In particular, trade and cooperation agreements were linked to broad political goals, particularly democracy, respect for the rule of law, and human rights (Szymanski and Smith 2005). These arrangements also enabled the EU to promote regional integration in other key areas of the world, such as the Middle East, Latin America, and Asia (see Smith 2008: 76–110).

Each of the EU's 'positive' economic measures (financial aid or trade agreements) involves a negative component as well: the EU's ability to stop aid or to suspend trade negotiations (at a minimum), or to impose diplomatic or economic sanctions (at a maximum). During the first twenty years of the EEC's existence, economic sanctions were imposed in only two cases: against Rhodesia in 1965, and against Greece in 1967. Following the creation of EPC in 1970, the EU imposed sanctions against a growing list of countries, including Iran, the Soviet Union, Argentina, Poland, Libya, South Africa, Yugoslavia, and Iraq. In 2011, the democratic uprising in the southern Mediterranean was met with a wave of targeted sanctions against authoritarian regimes of Libya, Egypt, Tunisia, and Syria. Still, the EU generally favours diplomacy over coercion (Hill and Wallace 1996).

By the late 2000s, the EU had moved to create *strategic partnerships* with major or emerging international powers, not least as a way in which to give itself incentives to agree common positions and combine policy instruments in bilateral diplomacy (see Box 13.6). Otherwise, the objectives of these privileged dialogues were left unclear. As Herman Van Rompuy, the post-Lisbon President of the European Council bluntly put it: 'We have strategic partners, now we need a strategy.'[7]

BOX 13.6	Strategic partnerships

The EU has created a dense network of agreements and partnerships that seek not only to advance specific policy matters, but also to create a multilateral, rules-based global order, mirroring its own internal nature and habits. Partnership and cooperation agreements (PCAs) with third countries provide for cooperation on trade and economic matters, but also on issues such as climate change, poverty reduction, and political reform. The Cotonou Agreement (2000) with seventy-nine African, Caribbean, and Pacific (ACP) countries is one example.

Growing out of PCAs with countries such as Russia (1994) and China (1985) came what are now called strategic partnerships. The EU has upgraded several relationships with ten countries to this status, which might be considered the holy grail of institutionalized relations with the EU. By 2011, the Union had strategic partnerships with (in addition to Russia and China) Brazil, Canada, India, Japan, Mexico, South Africa, South Korea, and the US.

The most-developed strategic partnerships were with the US and the BRIC countries (Brazil, Russia, India, and China). For India, a 2004 agreement offered it €470 million in assistance over six years, and involvement in the EU's space satellite program Gallileo. For its part, Brazil received only €61 million in assistance through the partnership process—reflecting its lower status in the partnership pecking order.

The direction of strategic partnerships remained uncertain. Some argued that the EU's promise of the same level of partnership to Canada, Japan, Mexico, and South Africa risked undermining the privileged nature of partnerships and also suggested a lack of differentiation by the EU in its relations with third countries. In 2010, Catherine Ashton suggested that Egypt, Indonesia, Israel, Pakistan, and Ukraine could also, in time, enter the privileged club of strategic partners. Clearly, Ashton viewed these partnerships as powerful diplomatic tools in dealings with third countries. The lack of a formal treaty basis for these partnerships, however, meant that the term was left ill-defined, and sometimes meant little more than additional summits and meetings.

The lack of practical outcomes from these arrangements has been a point of criticism, suggesting that policy outcomes were not matching rhetorical ambitions. Climate change (or, in EU-speak, 'climate action') illustrates the point. After over a decade of strategic partnerships with BRIC countries, including a focus on environmental policy, the EU found itself shut out of the room by its strategic partners on the most important negotiations at the Copenhagen Climate Talks in December 2009.

Aggregating the preferences of twenty-seven member states into a framework agreement with a non-EU state, while still allowing for bilateral relations between them and individual EU states in parallel, is quite an achievement. However, meaningful and direct action has been elusive and strategic direction or linkage has been lacking. By contrast, engagement between, say, the US and China bilateral relationship is much more demanding and concentrated (Keukelaire and Bruyninckx 2011). Strategic partnerships demonstrate that the EU is increasingly active in foreign policy. But the quality of its diplomacy remains suspect.

CFSP powers

The Maastricht Treaty was important in giving the EU, for the first time, the capacity for military action via recourse to the WEU. Elaborate arrangements were thus established between the Union and WEU, as well as between the latter and NATO (so that the WEU could call on NATO assets). The only case in which the Union drew upon the WEU's resources in the 1990s was in assisting in the EU's administration of the Bosnian town of Mostar. On the one occasion on which the Union might have asked the WEU to undertake a military operation on its behalf, to defuse a crisis in Albania in 1997, EU foreign ministers were unable to agree and Italy ended up leading a coalition of the willing.

Over time, cumbersome, slow-moving, and bureaucratic procedures for EU–WEU joint action became a source of frustration. Influenced by events in Kosovo, the European Council decided in June 1999 that the EU should have its own military capability, after which the WEU's military capability simply fell away. The core tasks of the new ESDP, like those of the WEU before it, were the so-called 'Petersberg tasks'[8]—that is, humanitarian and rescue missions, peacekeeping, and crisis management, including (the curiously ambiguous task of) 'peace-making'. ESDP's military cornerstone was the 'headline goal' agreed by the subsequent Helsinki European Council in December 1999. The EU decided to equip itself with a rapid reaction force (RRF) of 60,000 troops by 2003, which could be deployed with two months' notice and sustained for at least a year. As was the case for NATO's own reaction force, the RRF would not be a standing force; rather, EU member states would earmark national troops and capabilities for the force during specific operations, thus 'double-' or even 'triple-hatting' them.

After the RRF's launch, member governments worked intensively to identify shortfalls in European military capabilities and took steps to remedy them, even though the target date of 2003 slipped to 2010. Meanwhile, experience showed that smaller forces—even more rapidly deployable, but for a shorter time—could be useful, as was demonstrated by Operation Artemis in the Democratic Republic of the Congo (see Mace 2003). Paralleling steps in NATO towards smaller and more deployable formations, the EU decided in 2004 to create 'battle groups' of up to 1,500 troops. Most combined European resources at the hard end of their military capabilities in specialized areas such as desert or jungle fighting, or dealing with a chemical weapons attack. The aim was to have the battle groups available at near-immediate notice for short-term deployments. However, none had been deployed by the time of writing. While some may argue that the specific crises requiring the deployment of a battle group had not yet arisen, questions inevitably arose as to the relevance or need to create such forces in the first place.

On the civilian side, considerable effort has been put into developing the capability to prevent conflicts before they occur, or to 'win the peace' and help failing or post-conflict states with their civilian infrastructures—particularly law and order. A headline goal for rapid-response police, as well as for administrative, judicial, and other law enforcement professionals, was established in parallel to the military headline goal. The very first ESDP operation was, in fact, a civilian police mission, which the EU took over from the UN in Bosnia in January 2003. It was followed by relatively small military operations in Macedonia and Congo later that year, but also a more substantial military commitment in Bosnia (taking over from NATO) in 2004.

Often, efforts to give substance to the dramatic 1999 foreign and security policy decisions taken in Cologne and Helsinki have lacked conviction. Member states have failed, predictably, to live up to their more-ambitious goals (such as the RRF headline goal). Defence budgets have generally fallen, rather than increased. One rough estimate is that about 70 per cent of the EU's men and women in military uniform are able to be deployed *only* within their national territory (Patten 2010: 11). When Europe chooses to act militarily, as in the case of Libya in 2011, it has continued both to rely on NATO, and to be exposed as chronically short of military assets and dependent on US support. Arguably, the gap between capabilities and expectations that has troubled the EU since the creation of the CFSP has widened, not narrowed (Hill 1993, 1998), although probably due to increased expectations of the Union as much as, or more than, the slow growth of EU capabilities.[9]

Still, there is no denying tangible progress towards more coherent EU foreign and security policies. The Union's military options, while still small-scale, are gradually widening (see Figure 13.1). CSDP (the new term for ESDP since the Lisbon Treaty was adopted) can now be deployed 'where NATO as a whole is not engaged'. Obviously, any EU-led military operation will depend on a handful of countries—in the first place, the UK and France—with expeditionary military capabilities to mount and lead them. For anything beyond small-scale operations, the EU has to call on NATO assets, but that arguably is a sign of good sense (avoiding duplication and additional cost) and not weakness. The so-called 'Berlin Plus'[10] arrangements between the EU and NATO are far less cumbersome than the old EU–WEU procedures.

To the ambitious, the EU's effort remains disappointingly slow and militarily weak. But the EU's ability to contribute to international security by combining the military and civilian dimensions of the CSDP is unique, and certainly beyond what NATO can offer. Eventually, the EU could offer the United Nations a rapidly deployable and effective military capability, thus strengthening multilateralism more generally. Gradually, the EU is buttressing its 'soft power', or ability to attract or persuade in international affairs (see Nye 2004, 2011), with hard power to coerce or deter.[11]

The EU's foreign policy record

The sum total of the EU's foreign policy activity—diplomatic, economic, and military—goes far beyond that of any other regional organization. Yet hard, even brutal, questions about whether it results in demonstrable EU influence in world politics cannot be avoided (for contrasting views, see Zielonka 1998 and Ginsberg 2001). The EU's record as a foreign-policy actor is decidedly mixed.

After early failures, the EU's chief success—in a still-continuing story—has been the Balkans. A large part of this success has come from lessons learnt from the

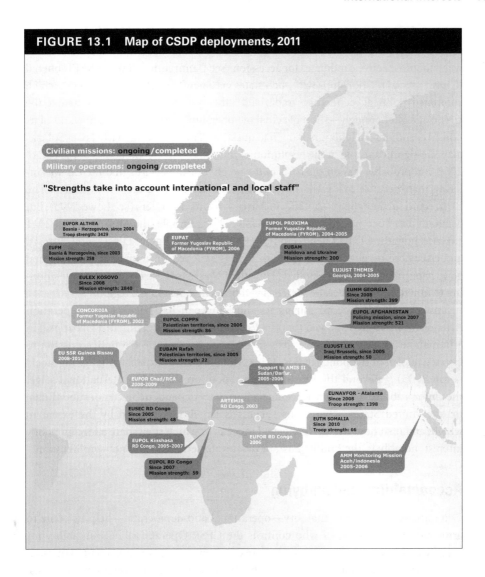

FIGURE 13.1   Map of CSDP deployments, 2011

success of using enlargement as, in a sense, a tool of foreign policy. Specifically, the promise of EU membership has been used to promote reform in Central and Eastern Europe, and had the 'demonstration effect' of establishing and consolidating democracy, liberalization, and the rule of law. Deliberately transposing this success to the Balkans, the EU has offered the prospect of accession as a way of changing behaviour. The attraction of enlargement has induced Balkan political leaders to pay heed (in many cases only intermittently) to political pressure from the EU. To illustrate, progress on curbing corruption and handing over suspected war criminals from the Bosnian War put Croatia in a position in which it was likely to become the EU's twenty-eighth member state in 2013. Thus the EU has shown itself to be more powerful because of what it *is*—a geopolitical magnet—than for anything that it actually *does*.

After the 2004–07 enlargements the Union hoped that it could achieve similar results in other neighbouring countries to the EU's east and south, even though many were not prospective candidates for accession (see Dannreuther 2004). The EU offered to form special relationships with such states via a new 'neighbourhood policy', which combined political, economic, trade, and other policy instruments. Whether the Union can offer enough—short of actual membership—to change the behaviour of its non-EU candidate neighbours is open to question. The EU (particularly Javier Solana) played a significant role in the resolution of the Ukrainian election crisis at the end of 2004, but probably less on the basis of the neighbourhood status that the EU was offering than because many Ukrainians saw themselves as future EU members. The EU's record further afield—notably in Africa—has its defenders (see Lowe 1995), but generally has been patchy and unimpressive. For example, the Arab Spring of 2011 exposed how the EU had helped to prop up dictators in Egypt, Libya, Syria, Tunisia, and elsewhere by channelling aid with strings attached on human rights and good governance that were never 'pulled'. How the EU assists these countries in transitioning to functioning democratic societies will be its next test in the region.

Similarly, CSDP's record during its short lifespan has been patchy. Operation Artemis in the Congo showed that the EU could respond quickly to a UN appeal in a humanitarian crisis and save lives in the process. But the EU police mission to oversee reform of the police in Bosnia was ridiculed as an expensive 'laughing stock' (Lyon 2005).[12] Beyond the EU's neighbourhood, on the wider international stage, the Union's ability to influence events remains very dependent on (if not subordinate to) the United States—that is, its success is largely determined by the extent to which, and if so how, the US is engaged in areas in which they share a foreign policy interest, notably in the Middle East, or on counterterrorism and non-proliferation.

Accountability and lobbying

Two dimensions of accountability—operational and democratic—help us come to grips with the question of who controls the CFSP. Operational accountability for specific CFSP policy actions varies. Where CFSP objectives are implemented through EU decisions, accountability is assured by the usual means for Community policies. However, provisions for monitoring and evaluation of CFSP decisions and implementation are much weaker than they are for other EU policies. This gap is partly a function of the foreign policy process itself and applies equally to national foreign policies, but there are problems that are particular to EU foreign policy.

One is that there are no provisions for punishing defectors from common positions. It is generically more difficult to regulate cooperation in foreign policy as compared to other domains, including trade or monetary policy. Moreover, democratic accountability in the form of parliamentary control is weak. The EP does have the right to be informed and consulted on the main lines of the CFSP, and devotes considerable energy to ensuring that these rights are respected. But the Council is under no compulsion to pay attention to the EP's views and usually—leaving aside budgetary matters—does so to the extent that it is convenient. Democratic control over the CFSP and ESDP effectively is through the accountability of foreign ministers to their own national parliaments.

There is little evidence that any of this bothers the public in most European countries. On the contrary, surveys show that European publics favour EU unity in foreign and defence policy (far more than they support other EU policies, including enlargement and monetary union), but also that ordinary citizens also show little interest in what the EU actually does in this domain. A major challenge for EU foreign policy is to increase public awareness of, and active support for, its increasingly wide range of activities.

The CFSP also mostly escapes the attention of lobbyists (the application of economic sanctions is a major exception). In fact, the most-active lobbyists of EU foreign policy are non-EU governments, such as the US, the states of the Middle East, Russia, and other players in the global system. Much of this diplomatic lobbying is directed towards the holder of the Council presidency, the High Representative, and the Commission, although—understandably—third countries often also lobby in European national capitals, especially Berlin, London, and Paris.

EU foreign policy has always been an elite-driven process. It might be argued that so are national foreign policies. Still, the CFSP's institutional system clearly insulates the national elites conducting it, let alone the Brussels elite in the Council machinery, from ordinary democratic pressures as it produces policies with increasingly powerful effects. It thus illustrates Hill's (2003: xvii) more general maxim that foreign policy has become 'a key site for responsible action, and for democratic accountability in a world where the facts and myths of globalization have obscured the locations of decision-making and confused the debate over democratic participation'.

The institutions in context

One of the CFSP's major problems is that it does not represent or dominate any specific policy problem. Unlike (say) agricultural or competition policy, in which the EU has exclusive competence, the CFSP must often compete with other actors and forums, such as functionally related EU policy domains, other international organizations, and even the independent activities of EU member states. In this sense, the CFSP must often struggle just to make itself relevant.

The CFSP in the EU system

Foreign policy is effective to the extent that its 'targets' are open to persuasion, influence, or coercion by the foreign policy actor. The EU is no different: its success depends on its ability to supply or withhold certain resources in exchange for compliant behaviour. However, the CFSP by itself has only limited resources and few instruments of its own, even if that is changing—notably, via the CSDP. It is therefore most effective when it harnesses resources available as EU instruments. In these cases, Commission involvement is essential, if only because it has the sole right of initiative. Sensitive to its prerogatives, the Commission often bridles at any suggestion that decisions might be taken in CFSP that tell it what to do or what the Union's member states want of it in other EU policy areas.

Under the Lisbon Treaty, the right of initiative in CFSP is exclusively a matter for the High Representative and the member states, although the High Representative is, after all, a Vice-President of the Commission. EU member states have gone to considerable lengths to maintain their control over CSDP, and to isolate it and their national defence industries completely from integrative pressures that might push it in the direction of the Community method. However, military and civilian crisis-management structures (such as the Military Committee, and the Crises Management and Planning Directorate) now fall under the remit of the High Representative. Furthermore, a European Defence Agency (EDA) was launched in 2004, with Solana (and then Ashton) chairing its board of directors, to begin long-overdue work on upgrading and integrating the EU's military capabilities.

As is often the case, what is most interesting is not where the EU is, but where it is in relation to where it started. Not long ago, the mere mention of an EU military capability was unthinkable; today, the CSDP is an accepted growth area for common European action. No other regional international organization possesses its own military component, although some (such as the African Union) have embryonic military capabilities or have made feeble pledges to cooperate on foreign policy issues. Despite all of its problems, the EU has gone further in security and defence policy than any other international organization.

The CFSP and national policies/ministries

Foreign, security, and defence policies are core prerogatives of nation-states. All EU member states have their own highly institutionalized foreign and defence ministries and policies (see Hocking and Spence 2002). There is little sign that they intend to abandon them. Yet the EU has become a central, although not exclusive, reference point for national foreign policies, especially for smaller EU states (Manners and Whitman 2000). Since the early 1970s, we have witnessed a gradual contraction of *domaines réservés*, in which former colonial powers regard their own interest and influence as paramount, and a simultaneous expansion of the topics considered appropriate for the CFSP (Belgium's experiences in Congo and Rwanda, where it was helpless acting on its own to prevent humanitarian disasters in its former colonial possessions, no doubt contributed). Virtually no foreign policy topic is considered off-limits for EU action, although discussions do not always lead to common action. The exception is issues before the UN Security Council, of which Iraq was a prime example: the two European permanent members of the Security Council—the UK and France—insisted that their UN obligations preclude any coordination of their positions with the EU, let alone accountability to the Union for them.

Otherwise, communication between national capitals—which is crucial to consensus-building—is now highly institutionalized. The growth of the CFSP as a policy domain and the intense networking that takes place within it often make it difficult for outsiders to determine where national foreign policy-making ends and the CFSP begins. Some would even argue that purely national foreign-policy preferences—entirely unaffected by EU deliberations—no longer exist (see Glarbo 2001).

Theorizing the CFSP

Applying theory to the practice of all of this activity, involving the EU's member states, institutions, non-member actors, and other policy domains (EU and otherwise), is a daunting task. Most theories of European integration or EU policy-making provide partial explanations at best, since the CFSP contains elements of intergovernmentalism, supranationalism, and transgovernmentalism. Equally, for theorists of European integration or international relations (IR) more generally, 'the issue of the meaning of European foreign policy cooperation for the international system, and conversely the impact of international relations on the EU, has been of marginal concern' (Hill and Smith 2011: 477).

Realists have struggled to explain the emergence of the CFSP as it challenges the assumption that nation-states remain narrowly concerned with sovereignty concerns: chiefly, their own relative power and security. From a realist perspective, Rosato (2011), however, has argued that the emergence of EPC and then CFSP represented attempts to reign in a resurgent and then reunited Germany, and that integration more generally was an attempt to balance against an external threat: the Soviet Union. Realists remain divided on the matter, however, with most arguing that CFSP remains little more than a rhetorical veil for the persistence of traditional national foreign policies.

One of the most compelling theoretical accounts of the CFSP is an institutionalist one (see Smith 2003, 2011). Institutional theory helps to explain not only what is expected, but also what is appropriate behaviour by actors in any social setting. Institutions 'filter' disparate social activities into explainable, purposeful policy outputs. Institutionalism stresses the importance of (mostly) incremental changes in terms of their accumulation: consider the High Representative's transformation into something akin to an EU minister for foreign affairs, or how the EU started with EPC and eventually equipped itself with a defence capability.

Institutionalism offers a kind of moving picture rather than a snapshot of European integration (see Pierson 1996). The differences between these two accounts of the CFSP are crucial. The CFSP began as an intergovernmental discussion forum (EPC), then developed its own complex infrastructure, and finally allowed the involvement of existing EC institutions (namely, the Commission). A process of 'learning by doing' led to the embedding of foreign policy in the EU, actively drawing upon Community resources.

Perhaps more than any other single perspective, institutionalism helps to explain why EU foreign-policy institutions have developed sufficient proficiency to make member states not only unable, but also *unwilling* to interrupt, reverse, or exit from a process of further institutionalizing foreign, security, and (now) defence policy cooperation (see Hill 2004), even if clear policy successes remain elusive (see Howorth 2010). Even theorists who reject the institutionalist account have to concede that foreign policy cooperation is now sufficiently institutionalized in Europe as to defy the assumption—which still underpins much IR scholarship—that all alliances between states are temporary and expedient. Among students of IR, consensus is beginning to emerge—slowly, gradually, and somewhat begrudgingly—that 'the EU can no longer be treated as a peculiar side-issue in international relations' (Hill and Smith 2011: 458–9). The question for the future remains, however, to what extent the institutionalization of foreign policy inputs (decision-making processes, structures) will truly shape important foreign-policy outcomes in the conduct of international relations.

Conclusion

The history of EU foreign policy is punctuated by critical junctures when the Union ran up against crises in the international arena and tried to come up with institutional responses to address them. The pattern of crisis and response is evident in the chronology of treaties since the early 1990s. The collapse of the Berlin Wall, tensions in Yugoslavia, and the first Gulf War led European leaders to try to develop greater foreign policy and military capacities through CFSP and the WEU in the Maastricht Treaty in 1992. After the crises in Bosnia and Kosovo exposed a lack of European crisis management tools, European leaders responded by creating the ESDP via the Amsterdam Treaty in 1999. The persistent inadequacies of the CFSP system— exposed by disunity on Iraq, combined with the 'Big Bang' 2004–07 enlargements and the era of new global terrorist threats after the 9/11 terrorist attacks—brought another such response in the Constitutional Treaty in 2004, and its descendant, the Lisbon Treaty. Afterwards, it was still impossible to imagine an effective CFSP without more 'coalitions of the willing' or leadership by larger EU member states (such as France during the Georgian crisis of 2008), perhaps increasingly in tandem with the High Representative. Stronger leadership was seen as necessary in itself, as well as an important means of resolving other problems—notably, tensions between small and large member states, and achieving more coherence in the EU's external policies.

There was no shortage of opportunities, and indeed demands, for the EU to speak with a single voice in the years immediately after the 2004–07 enlargements. Continued tension in the Middle East, the unfinished peace in the Balkans, problems in the Caucasus and other countries close to the EU's borders (Belarus, Moldova, North Africa, Ukraine), threats associated with terrorism and weapons of mass destruction (WMDs), the rise of China as a global actor, ongoing disputes with North Korea, tensions in transatlantic relations, and the erosion of democracy in the former Soviet Union all put pressure on the EU. There was a widespread feeling that things could not go on in foreign policy as before. The first major test of the post-Lisbon CFSP architecture came in the form of the Arab Spring in 2011. After a disappointing early response to the crisis, it remains to be seen whether the EU can employ its new institutional structures to greater effect in its longer-term strategy in the region.

As always, institutional reform was a necessary, but far from sufficient, condition for an effective CFSP. Member states, especially large ones, will always weigh the virtues of 'multiplying' their power via common EU action against the difficulties of getting others to agree, resorting instead to working with smaller groups, or even alone. Recent enlargements have made consensus-building even more delicate and time-consuming than before. The external relations provisions of the Lisbon Treaty have the potential, at least, to give the CFSP consistent leadership, with international name-recognition and authority to pull together the strengths of its member states and the Commission. The EEAS gives the EU, for the first time, 'real' embassies in important national capitals such as Washington, Beijing, and Delhi, backed up by real resources in terms of personnel and policy instruments. The EU will no doubt be faced with fresh chances to realize its potential in foreign policy. But it will no doubt fall short more often than it will act to its full potential.

Institutionally speaking, neither the Constitutional Treaty nor Lisbon were ever going to solve all of CFSP's problems, let alone problems arising from a lack of political priority being given to hammering out common policies. In a sense, the EU has tried to rely on an (adapted) institutional system that has achieved much success in economic policy, but is poorly suited for foreign policy. One of the EU's top diplomats even goes as far as to claim that '[t]he European institutions were designed for everything except foreign policy, in fact to abolish foreign policy'.[13]

Of course, having the best institutional arrangements in the world cannot guarantee the right solutions, or even solutions at all, to intractable problems. The persistence of divergent member state interests and preferences on so many key foreign-policy issues means that institutional innovations can be stymied before they are even tested. Still, Lisbon at least gives the EU a more centred and (potentially) coherent foreign policy. Its member states face stronger incentives to act collectively and to make full use of the EU's collective power in a global context in which it is widely held that 'wealth and power are moving away from the North and West to the East and South, and the old order dominated by the United States and Europe is giving way to one increasingly shared with non-Western rising states' (Ikenberry 2011: 56). But despite existing in 'an ever less European world' (Laïdi 2008b: 1), the EU has still not become 'a straightforward "pole" in a multipolar system' (Hill and Smith 2011: 456); nor have national foreign policies in Europe ceased to exist or clash.

On the one hand, EU foreign-policy coordination has been institutionalized in important respects; on the other, EU foreign has been stubbornly resistant to pressures for integration. The tension remains between reformed and complex foreign-policy inputs, and somewhat disappointing foreign-policy outcomes. As institutionalist theory tells us, institutions can shape and sustain political action, but they cannot themselves create such action.

 NOTES

1. In its first years, EPC was staffed by the foreign ministry of the holder of the Council presidency, reflecting its informal and non-institutionalized status.

2. The CSCE was renamed the Organization for Security and Cooperation in Europe (OSCE) when it was made a standing organization (rather than a 'conference') in 1995.

3. Coreu refers both to *correspondant Européen*—that is, a mid-level official in each foreign ministry, responsible for coordination of arrangements and consultations with the presidency and other colleagues—and the system used for communication on CFSP matters.

4. This bilateral summit held at a French coastal resort produced a joint declaration by Europe's two major military powers endorsing the creation of an ESDP with the means to allow the EU to act autonomously when NATO decided not to be involved in a military action (see Sloan 2005: 190–3).

5. This rather opaque phrase refers to 'civilian' (that is, non-military) policy tools, such as diplomacy or economic sanctions, and command structures (such as EU defence ministers meeting in the Council of Ministers), as well as instruments for preventing conflicts, including the addition of policing or judicial expertise to EU military missions, as was done in the Balkans.

6. Nuttall (1992: 269) notes that the Contact Group 'did after all preserve a facade of EU organizational coherence' through a variety of procedural fixes that linked the participation of EU states to the CFSP as a whole. However, the Contact Group came at a time—during the first year of the CFSP's existence—during which the EU's new mechanisms for foreign policy seemed to be failing more generally.

7. Quoted in *European Voice*, 16 September 2010, p. 11.

8. This designation arose from the Petersberg hotel outside Bonn at which WEU ministers adopted the tasks in 1992.

9. It is worth mentioning that the EU has proved capable of settling, or at least managing, open disputes that have flared with the US (about the relationship with NATO) and Turkey (primarily about Cyprus) externally, and between the UK and France internally (about the nature of what is now the CSDP and its relationship to the US).

10. 'Berlin Plus' refers to the set of rules and procedures finalized in 2002 to govern EU access to NATO planning and military assets (see Cornish 2004; Sloan 2005).

11. One of the EU's top foreign-policy officials argues that soft power is wielded only by those who also possess hard power (see Cooper 2004).

12. James Lyon is Serbia project director for the highly regarded International Crisis Group.

13. Robert Cooper, Director-General for External Affairs, Council of the EU, quoted in *European Voice*, 11–17 October 2007, p. 11.

FURTHER READING

The most comprehensive of recent works on the EU's international role is Hill and Smith (2011). K. E. Smith (2008) is a useful examination of how the EU pursues its foreign-policy objectives and McCormick (2007) makes the case that the Union has already achieved 'superpower' status. M. E. Smith (2003) offers an institutionalist treatment of the CFSP, while Bretherton and Vogler (2006) survey the EU as a global actor using a constructivist lens, and Rosato (2010) offers a provocative treatment of European integration from a realist perspective. Laïdi (2008a) and Bindi (2010) are both useful and up-to-date overviews. The ESS is analysed by Biscop (2005), and by Dannreuther and Peterson (2006). For a highly critical analysis of EU foreign policy, see Zielonka (1998).

Bindi, F. (2010) (ed.) *The Foreign Policy of the European Union: Assessing Europe's Role in the World* (Washington DC: Brookings Institution).

Biscop, S. (2005) *The European Security Strategy: A Global Agenda for Positive Power* (Aldershot: Ashgate).

Bretherton, C. and Vogler, J. (2006) *The European Union as a Global Actor* (2nd edn, London and New York: Routledge).

Dannreuther, R. and Peterson, J. (2006) (eds) *Security Strategy and Transatlantic Relations* (London and New York: Routledge).

Hill, C. and Smith, M. (2011) (eds) *International Relations and the European Union* (2nd edn, Oxford and New York: Oxford University Press).

Howorth, J. (2007) *Security and Defence Policy in the European Union* (Basingstoke: Palgrave Macmillan).

Laïdi, Z. (2008a) (ed.) *EU Foreign Policy in a Globalized World: Normative Power and Social Preferences* (London and New York: Routledge).

McCormick, J. (2007) *The European Superpower* (Basingstoke and New York: Palgrave Macmillan).

Rosato, S. (2010) *Europe United: Power Politics and the Making of the European Community* (Ithaca, NY: Cornell University Press).

Smith, K. E. (2008) *European Union Foreign Policy in a Changing World* (2nd edn, Oxford and Malden, MA: Polity).

Smith, M. E. (2003) *Europe's Foreign and Security Policy: The Institutionalization of Cooperation* (Cambridge: Cambridge University Press).

Zielonka, J. (1998) *Explaining Euro-paralysis: Why Europe is Unable to Act in International Politics* (Basingstoke and New York: Palgrave Macmillan).

WEB LINKS

http://www.consilium.europa.eu/policies/foreign-policy.aspx?lang=en

The Council's own website is the best place to start a web search on the CFSP or ESDP.

http://consilium.europa.eu/eeas/security-defence.aspx?lang=en

The Council's CSDP site has a number of resources, including details on operations, structures, and other documents.

http://ecfr.eu/

The European Council on Foreign Relations publishes topical analysis of current issues in European foreign policy.

http://www.eeas.europa.eu/

For up-to-date coverage of the activities of the High Representative and EEAS, the service's own page is very current.

http://www.iss.europa.eu

The Institute for Security Studies (ISS), the EU's own, internal, Paris-based think tank, produces high-quality analyses of foreign and security policy issues that are all available online.

CHAPTER 14

National Interests: the Committee of Permanent Representatives

Jeffrey Lewis

▌ Summary

The Committee of Permanent Representatives (Coreper) originated as a diplomatic forum to meet regularly and prepare meetings of the Council of Ministers. It quickly and quietly evolved into a locus of continuous negotiation and *de facto* decision-making, gaining a reputation as 'the place to do the deal'. This reputation is based on insulation from domestic audiences and an unrivalled ability to make deals stick across a range of issue areas and policy subjects. Most importantly, Coreper spotlights the process of integrating interests in a collective decision-making system with its own organizational culture, norms, and style of discourse. Coreper is an institutional environment in which group-community standards create what neoinstitutionalists call a 'logic of appropriateness', which informs bargaining behaviour and influences everyday decision-making outcomes.

Introduction

This chapter addresses the role of the Committee of Permanent Representatives (Coreper) in the European Union. According to one analyst, 'the caliber and effectiveness of permanent representation officials determine to a great extent how countries fare in the EU' (Dinan 2010a: 216); another claims that the members of Coreper are 'among the great unsung heroes' of European integration (Westlake 1999: xxiv). Both observations offer a useful entry point to understanding Coreper and how it functions. First, it is a pivotal actor in everyday EU decision-making. For this reason, member states consider Coreper one of the most important postings in Brussels. Second, in what may seem counter-intuitive to the first point, Coreper is less visible than most other institutions in the EU. As this chapter will clarify, Coreper's importance as an institutional actor is related to its ability over the years to avoid the spotlight, and to work behind the scenes at finding agreements and forging compromise.

Coreper is the site in EU decision-making where national interests and European solutions interact more frequently, more intensively, and across more issue areas than any other. To work effectively, the Committee relies on a culture of consensus-based decision-making—an informal, intangible quality of the institutional environment and a critical component in the EU permanent representation's ability to 'find solutions'. Coreper is also something of a chimera: to some, it resembles a bastion of intergovernmentalism; to others, it appears less like inter-state bargaining than a haven for Eurocrats to 'go native'. Neither view, in such stark terms, is accurate; nor is either view entirely wrong. In an authoritative study of the Council system, Hayes-Renshaw and Wallace (2006: 332) note 'a continuous tension between the home affiliation and the pull of the collective forum'. From a theoretical perspective, negotiation in Coreper is often a subtle blend of both the 'logic of consequences' and the 'logic of appropriateness'.[1] Viewed through a neoinstitutionalist lens, it is precisely this tension that makes Coreper so interesting to study.

According to the EU's treaties, Coreper is 'responsible for preparing the work of the Council and for carrying out the tasks assigned to it by the Council' (Art. 240 TEU). From this austere mandate, Coreper has developed into a major player in the EU system. Among its 'assigned tasks' is the remit to 'endeavour to reach agreement at its level'.[2] In essence, this means that Coreper holds responsibility for the performance of the Council as a whole. In institutionalist language, there is an obligation of result that the permanent representatives find is an unwritten part of the job description. As one ambassador explained, 'there is a high collective interest in getting results and reaching solutions. This is in addition to representing the national interest'.[3] Another said: 'If we have to take it to the Council, there is a sense that we have failed.'

Signs of this responsibility and the mandate on which it rests can be traced back to the dog days of Eurosclerosis, and the heads of state and government who innovated European Council summitry. In particular, the communiqué of the 1974 Paris Summit holds: 'Greater latitude will be given to the Permanent Representatives so that only the most important political problems need be discussed in the Council.'[4] It was during this same period that integration researchers began to observe that Coreper resembled 'a Council of Ministers in permanent session' (Busch and Puchala 1976: 240).

In many ways, Coreper is the ideal institutional site to examine national interests in the context of everyday EU decision-making. Coreper is the needle's eye through which the legislative output of the Council flows. Because a defining trait of the Council is its sectoral differentiation, pursuing the 'national interest' across its operating formations requires complex national systems of interest intermediation and inter-ministerial coordination. The permanent representatives have a cross-Council negotiating mandate that functions as an essential aggregation mechanism in everyday EU decision-making. The EU ambassadors and deputies are thus critical interlocutors in the ability of a member state to pursue what Anderson (1999: 6) calls a 'milieu goal' in Brussels, or the ability to 'ensure that government policy objectives are consistent, both within Europe and across the national and supranational levels'.

The chapter proceeds as follows. In the next section, we examine how the permanent representatives acquired such a central position in the EU system. We then sketch out the structure of Coreper, including how it works and has changed over time. Next, the Committee's main powers—namely, *de facto* decision-making and an institutional capacity for integrating interests—are examined. We move on to consider enlargement effects on the 'clubbiness' of Coreper, which to date show robust evidence of newcomers acclimating to the norm-rich, collective decision-making environment. A brief concluding section will follow, looking at the wider implications for theory of an institutional body that so explicitly straddles and *blurs* the boundary between the national and European levels.

Coreper's origins

Although no mention was made in the Treaty of Paris about the creation of a preparatory body, the need for such a body became apparent less than six months after the Treaty entered into force in July 1952. At the first meeting of the Special Council of Ministers (September 1952), the ad hoc group on the organization of the Council's work was instructed to come up with a proposal for a preparatory committee. The Coordinating Commission, or Cocor (*Commission de Coordination du Conseil des Ministres*), was the result. The formal decision to create Cocor was taken by the Special Council of Ministers in February 1953. But it was only with the Treaty of Rome that the legal basis for a preparatory committee was established (under Art. 151 TEC).

The first Cocor meeting was held in March 1953. Cocor began to meet monthly in Luxembourg, with representatives travelling back and forth from their national capitals. Cocor diplomacy was premised on mutual trust, a spirit of accommodation, and an equality of voice between big and small states. Ernst Haas (1958: 491; see also Haas 1960) drew a sharp distinction between Cocor and the brand of diplomacy found at, for example, the Council of Europe, equating the former with the 'principle of a novel community-type organ'.

From the earliest proposals to set up a permanent preparatory body, the issue of delegating formal decision-making authority was allowed to remain ambiguous. This non-debate was evident at the 1956 intergovernmental conference (IGC), where the design of a new permanent, Brussels-based committee was negotiated (see Box 14.1). Over the course of discussions, it became clear that there was agreement among the foreign ministers *not* to create a Brussels-body composed of deputy ministers; instead, they agreed that the permanent delegations should be headed by high-ranking diplomats. But there was little discussion of what substantive form the permanent representatives' role should take and the issue was left open. Articles 151 and 121 of the Treaty of Rome reflect this ambiguity, allowing simply that the Council's rules of procedure shall 'provide for the establishment of a committee composed

---

BOX 14.1   Constitutive politics and the Spaak Committee

The creation of a permanent Brussels-based body composed of high-ranking civil servants was based on a proposal from the Committee of the Heads of Delegations, popularly known as the Spaak Committee after its chair, the industrious Belgian Foreign Minister Paul-Henri Spaak. The Spaak Committee, set up by the foreign ministers at Messina (June 1955) to discuss future steps in European integration, began meeting intensively at the Château de Val Duchesse outside Brussels in July 1955. Eight months of talks produced the Spaak Report (April 1956). The recommendations of the Spaak Report were approved by the foreign ministers' meeting in Venice (May 1956) and, after further IGC negotiations (again led by the Spaak Committee), culminated in the Treaty of Rome (March 1957). In one of the lesser-known political coups in the history of the EU, it was the Spaak Committee that strongly endorsed a permanent negotiating body. For the most part, the Committee's members were the same individuals who would become the first permanent representatives.

As Noël (1967: 219) recounts, the Treaty[5] became a 'means of prolonging and perpetuating ... that rather extraordinary "club"' (that is, the Spaak Committee), which was 'both a meeting place of authorized and faithful spokesmen of the six Governments and a group of militants (even of "accomplices") dedicated to a vast and noble political undertaking' (see also Lindberg and Scheingold 1970: 242). Noël (1966: 88) hints at the novelty of this move, whereby the Spaak Committee morphed into what would become Coreper, since the Interim Committee set up in March 1957 contained many of the same personnel and 'preserved the same atmosphere and spirit'. Except for France and Italy, the Interim Committee delegates would also become the first permanent representatives in early 1958. In short, the Spaak Committee and the creation of Coreper is a striking example of 'constitutive politics' in the institutional history of European integration.[6]

of representatives of member states. The Council shall determine the task and competence of that committee'.

Early on, the open-ended nature of Coreper's authority set off alarm bells at the Commission. Following the January 1958 decision to begin the work of the Committee without precisely defining its tasks and powers, the Commission asked for clarification of Coreper's role (de Zwaan 1995: 75). In March 1958, Belgian Foreign Minister Larock, acting as Council President, defended the Council's provisional rules of procedure and assured Commission President Hallstein that they ruled out the possibility of delegating decisional authority to Coreper (Noël 1967: 228–9). There were similar questions raised in the European Parliament (EP), with some members concerned that the Committee could usurp the Commission's right of initiative (de Zwaan 1995: 75). Since these early years, the Commission—and in particular the Secretary-General's office, with Emile Noël at the helm from 1958 to 1987—would come to view the permanent representatives as potential allies in a common cause. As one Commission participant stated: 'We consider Coreper more as an ally than something we have to fight with.' Coreper is often the strategic point of inroad to the Council, since the Commission prefers to have detailed, substantive discussions with the permanent representatives, who (unlike many ministers) are also well versed in the legal intricacies of the Treaty. Jacques Delors, while Commission President, often personally appeared in Coreper to explain and 'sell' key single-market proposals to the permanent representatives before they were presented at the ministerial level.[7]

Since the late 1950s, Coreper, quietly and often unnoticed, has acquired a reputation for forging compromise and finding solutions across an ever-growing range of issues. This standing was contrary to its reputation in academic circles: integration researchers typically characterized Coreper as an embodiment of intergovernmentalism and hardball bargaining.[8] As the European Community deepened, Coreper acquired new responsibilities and general policy competences (Noël and Étienne 1971). Agricultural policy was an exception because of the highly technical nature of administering the common agricultural policy (CAP), and in 1960 the Special Committee on Agriculture (SCA) was established to take over this specialized policy field.[9] The deepening process created exponential pressures for Coreper to develop *de facto* legislative competences in order to minimize policy-making bottlenecks and impart coherence to the segmentation of the Council's work. The bifurcation of Coreper in 1962 into Coreper I and II (discussed below) was a realization of this burgeoning workload. But contrary to conventional accounts, such as Weiler's (1981: 285) claim that 'decisional supranationalism' was weakened by the addition of Coreper to the EC system, the Committee institutionalized a deliberative, consensual style of decision-making based on 'thick' bonds of trust, understanding, responsiveness, and a willingness to compromise. The ability to serve as a gatekeeper for the Council's work was not simply about paving the way for ministers to find agreements, but, increasingly, the ability to dispose of large quantities of business by forging consensus out of seemingly irreconcilable national positions.

Structure of the institution

In structural location, Coreper occupies a unique institutional vantage point in the EU system. Vertically placed between the experts and the ministers, and horizontally situated with cross-Council policy responsibilities, the permanent representatives obtain a broad overview of the Council's work. Compared with the experts meeting in the working groups, they are political heavyweights, but unlike the ministers, they are policy generalists *and* experts in the substantive questions of a file. In his classic study of Coreper, Joseph Salmon (1971: 642) referred to this unique perspective as the *vue d'ensemble*. The institutional perspective of the *vue d'ensemble* is a qualitative feature of Coreper, part of its organizational culture, and a kind of cognitive map that newcomers must learn to read and navigate to be successful.

Defined narrowly, Coreper consists of fifty-four members, who are jointly referred to as the permanent representatives. This cohort includes twenty-seven EU permanent representatives (also known as the EU ambassadors) and twenty-seven deputy permanent representatives. The Committee meets in two formats: confusingly, Coreper I (deputies) and Coreper II (ambassadors). The Commission is always represented in both Committee formats. But such a narrow definition would miss how Coreper is embedded in a much more extensive network of national delegations in Brussels, known as the EU permanent representations, or 'Permreps'. At a glance, the Permreps look like embassies, but as integration has deepened they have grown in size and coverage to become microcosms of the national governments, and 'veritable administrative melting-pots' (Hayes-Renshaw *et al.* 1989: 128). For example, most Permreps also staff an ambassador-level official for the Political and Security Committee (PSC; see Chapter 13). And most now include at least one high-ranking military officer (such as a lieutenant general, vice admiral, or colonel) for the work covered by the EU Military Committee. Permreps also become the nerve centre to manage the duties of the rotating EU presidency, and delegations often swell by 25 per cent or more to handle the workload. This expansion can be seen in Table 14.1, in which it is shown that the size of Belgium's Permrep grew by more than a third for the 2010 presidency, while the Hungarian delegation nearly doubled in preparation for its inaugural 2011 presidency.

Since 1975, a group of assistants to the ambassadors, known as the Antici counsellors (or 'Anticis'), have finalized and prepared the agendas for weekly Coreper II meetings. The Anticis also act as advisers to their ambassadors, minimizing the element of surprise by floating ideas and testing arguments before or at the margins of meetings, drafting reports to send back home, and attending European Council summits as note-takers. In 1993, the deputies formalized a similar group of assistants, known as the Mertens counsellors (or 'Mertens'). With enlargement, the Anticis and Mertens have assumed a more active role. One Antici portrayed the group as a 'full-fledged working group' for two sorts of issue: '... issues that should be dealt with close to the ambassadors, and ... issues that don't fit any other working group'. A good example of the latter is the Antici group's quiet handling of the fine print on

TABLE 14.1 Growth in the number of EU permanent representations

Year	2010	2005	2000	1995	1991	1986	1969	1965
Member state								
Austria	85	72	68	65	—	—	—	—
Belgium	89	65	46	36	31	26	18	18
Bulgaria	64	—	—	—	—	—	—	—
Cyprus	69	31	—	—	—	—	—	—
Czech Republic	80	58	—	—	—	—	—	—
Denmark	50	47	46	38	35	31	—	—
Finland	63	56	60	37	—	—	—	—
France	107	94	70	50	41	29	19	18
Germany	138	111	79	62	47	41	28	21
Greece	97	86	55	66	62	48	—	—
Hungary	97	57	—	—	—	—	—	—
Ireland	59	51	37	37	26	24	—	—
Italy	67	67	49	42	44	40	29	22
Latvia	52	36	—	—	—	—	—	—
Lithuania	54	35	—	—	—	—	—	—
Luxembourg	31	76	13	14	13	6	8	4
Malta	37	31	—	—	—	—	—	—
Netherlands	73	89	47	45	30	24	21	19
Poland	87	56	—	—	—	—	—	—
Portugal	63	50	55	48	44	36	—	—
Romania	88	—	—	—	—	—	—	—
Slovakia	62	48	—	—	—	—	—	—
Slovenia	58	34	—	—	—	—	—	—
Spain	89	76	58	54	50	31	—	—
Sweden	61	61	50	52	—	—	—	—
United Kingdom	95	77	55	50	39	45	—	—

Source: For 2010, 2005, and 2000, EU Who is Who (**http://europa. eu/who is who**); Guide to the Council of the European Communities, various years

how to implement a new EU language translation regime. The Antici and Mertens counsellors are also emblematic of a wider array of transgovernmental networking that takes place among national administrations through the Permreps. This networking extends to common foreign and security policy (CFSP) and justice and home affairs (JHA) counsellors, and, now, military attachés who work on European security and defence policy (ESDP) matters. In general, the permanent representations are a mechanism for socialization to the EU, training new generations of diplomats and policy specialists, orchestrating presidencies, and educating national administrations to open their minds to a new EU reality (Lewis 2005).

Coreper I and II

Coreper is split into two formations based on a functional division of labour (see Table 14.2). Both meet weekly and each have their own councils to prepare. Coreper II is composed of the ambassadors and is responsible for the monthly General Affairs Council (GAC), as well as issues with horizontal, institutional, and financial implications. The lion's share of weekly Coreper II agendas deal with EU external relations (such as trade, aid, and foreign policy). What is more, discussions range widely, for example shifting from canned tuna to relations with Russia. Coreper II is also closely implicated in multi-annual budget negotiations (from Delors I and II, to the present discussions on spending after 2013), and historically, with IGCs (often serving as a delegation's personal representative).[10]

TABLE 14.2 Responsibilities of Coreper I and II

Coreper II—Ambassadors

General affairs and external relations
Justice and home affairs
Multi-annual budget negotiations
Structural and cohesion funds
Institutional and horizontal questions
Association agreements and development
Accession
IGC personal representatives*

Coreper I—Deputies

Conciliation in areas of codecision ('ordinary legislative procedure')
Single European Market
Environment
Employment, social policy, and consumer affairs
Competitiveness
Transport, telecommunications, and energy
Research
Culture Council
Education, youth affairs, and culture
Fisheries
Agriculture (veterinary and plant-health questions)

* Varies by member state and IGC

Coreper I is made up of the deputies and is responsible for the misleadingly labelled 'technical' councils such as those for competitiveness, environment, and employment, social policy, health, and consumer affairs. While decisions are often 'technical', such as setting fish support prices every December for the common fisheries policy (CFP), this work is also often intensely political. Coreper I is also responsible for representing the Council during codecision (now known as the 'ordinary legislative procedure'—see Chapter 6) negotiations and conciliation committee meetings with the EP. It is estimated that as much as 50 per cent of the deputies' time is now devoted to codecision matters (Bostock 2002: 223). This places Coreper I at the heart of the Council's 'new legislative culture' with the EP (see Shackleton 2000).

As a general rule, the division of labour between Coreper I and II functions smoothly. Coreper II is generally considered the appropriate forum for any file that covers broader external relations or has inter-institutional implications. Coreper I is much more active now than it was prior to codecision. Partly, these differences stem from policy remit and the ministers' meetings for which each formation is responsible, but there are differences in status and ego between the ambassadors and deputies, with the former exuding almost limitless self-confidence to get the job done. 'We are mere mortals compared to the ambassadors,' one deputy joked.

Who are the EU permanent representatives? Ambassadors are almost invariably senior-ranking diplomats from the ministries of foreign affairs. For most member states, the deputy is also recruited from foreign affairs; exceptions include Germany, for which the deputy always comes from economic affairs, and the UK, for which the deputy frequently comes from the Department of Trade and Industry (DTI). The EU permanent representatives are selected from the highest tier of career diplomats and senior civil servants, usually with a considerable background in European affairs. The member states control appointments, and there is no approval process in Brussels. Appointments are typically made after a recommendation, or at least tacit approval, from the head of state or government. Such high-level political selection contributes enormously to the credibility (and confidence) of the permanent representatives to negotiate in Brussels. 'We don't care if he wears a nice suit,' one participant explained. 'We want to know: can he deliver?' In European diplomatic circles, Coreper is considered a top posting. EU permanent representatives rank the position on par or slightly above postings to Washington, New York, and Paris.

Coreper appointments are also noteworthy for the length of tenure and absence of partisan politics. The average appointment is five years, slightly longer than the typical three- or four-year diplomatic rotation. But some permanent representatives remain in Brussels for much longer, upwards of a decade or beyond. For example, since 1958, Belgium has had seven ambassadors; Germany, six deputies. Longer appointments provide 'continuity in the representation of interests' (de Zwaan 1995: 17). Permanent representatives usually remain insulated from electoral politics and shifts in government (although with some exceptions, such as Portugal and Greece; see Lewis 1998b: 109–13).

Contestation

Since 1958, Coreper has been the senior preparatory forum of the Council. The vertical channels of coordination have placed the permanent representatives in clear command of how files are routed to the ministers. They are undisputed gatekeepers. While, on paper, all treaty reforms have reconfirmed Coreper's senior preparatory status, two developments are gradually contesting this position in practice.

Since the early 1990s, everyday EU decision-making has seen the intensification of rivalries between preparatory bodies (Lewis 2000). There are occasional turf battles over CFSP competences with the PSC. However, the advent of the ESDP (assisted by the new Military Committee and military staff) has more sharply delineated the boundaries of where Coreper does not wish to tread. (In interviews, Coreper officials claim that the minutiae of military planning is as appealing to them as agricultural price schedules for wheat.) Some in Brussels see the coherence of EU foreign policy-making as limited by the fragmentation of preparatory authority.

In other policy areas, Coreper II has permanently conceded responsibility of the Economics and Financial Affairs Council (Ecofin) and the 'Euro Group' of eurozone finance ministers, to the Economic and Finance Committee (EFC). EFC reports are not, as a rule, even copied to the permanent representatives; they are sent directly to finance ministers. Other, less serious, boundary disputes involve the Coordinating Committee in the area of judicial and police cooperation in criminal matters (formerly the Article 36 Committee, or CATS) and JHA matters, and the Trade Policy Committee (formerly the Article 133 Committee) over administration of the common commercial policy (CCP). Over the last decade, Coreper has become more proactive in establishing policy boundaries and clarifying its senior preparatory status. The Council's Rules of Procedure are now more detailed in laying out Coreper's right to 'ensure consistency of the Union's policies and actions'.[11] We see Coreper's senior preparatory authority confirmed in the language of the General Secretariat's list of Council preparatory bodies, which describe a group such as the EFC or Employment Committee as an 'advisory body.'

A second source of contestation is the relative decline of the General Affairs Council (GAC), redesigned as a 'bicameral' General Affairs and External Relations Council (GAERC) in 2002. For the first several decades of European integration, general affairs was *primus inter pares*. But the process of deepening had the effect of raising the stature and importance of other sectoral councils. By the 1990s, the GAC had lost its claim to be providing leadership or acting as an overall coordinator of EU affairs (Gomez and Peterson 2001). Some hold that Ecofin has supplanted the GAC as the senior formation of the Council. For most member states, this shift is a reflection of the domestic inter-ministerial balance of power, which has seen a relative eclipse of foreign affairs (Hocking 1999). The weakening of the GAC (and, in turn, the foreign ministries' grip on Council leadership) is slowly having effects on Coreper as well. This impact is evident, for example, in the EFC–Ecofin (and 'Euro Group') linkages, which bypass Coreper. Some Permrep officials perceive this general pattern of contestation as weakening

Coreper's institutional role. Whether the recent bifurcation of the GAERC into 'general affairs' and 'external relations' formats really resolves these dysfunctions remains an open question (see Chapter 4).

Powers of the institution

By focusing on Coreper, we are essentially looking at what Peterson (1995) has termed the systemic level of 'policy-setting' decisions. But EU decision-making is also 'heavily nuanced, constantly changing, and even kaleidoscopic' (Peterson and Bomberg 1999: 9), with significant variation by policy sector and issue area. Within this complex and multidimensional setting, two formal and informal powers stand out at Coreper level: *de facto* decision-making, and the institutional capacities to integrate interests.

De facto decision-makers

As a continuous negotiation chamber in the EU, Coreper is a place where many decisions are effectively made. But the permanent representatives have no *formal* decision-making authority. Juridical decision-making authority is a power exclusively reserved for the ministers, and formal voting is expressly prohibited at any other level of the Council. But in practice, or *de facto*, Coreper has evolved into a veritable decision-making factory. There are ways around the formality of *de jure* voting, such as the 'indicative vote' of how a delegation would vote if the matter were put before the ministers. More common is the tactful packaging of a discussion by the presidency, in which the chair will ask 'I assume no one else requests the floor?' or state 'A sufficient majority exists'. No vote is taken. There is no raising of hands. But many agreements are reached in this manner and many decisions are thus made.

Participants claim that the overwhelming bulk of decisions are made by consensus (see Chapter 4). Even under conditions of qualified-majority voting (QMV), permanent representatives regularly spend extra time to 'bring everyone on board'. Pushing for a vote is considered inappropriate in most cases, and the 'consensus assumption' is a reflexive habit. A clear example of this consensus reflex can be seen in the legislative record of the 1992 Project. Out of the 260 single-market measures subject to QMV, approximately 220 of them were adopted unanimously, without a vote at all (de Schoutheete 2000: 9–10). Spending extra time and not pushing for a vote is considered 'the right thing to do', offering a clear illustration of the logic of appropriateness in Coreper's institutional setting.

The most surprising finding here is not that civil servants have been delegated *de facto* decisional authority, but the density of this mechanism in maintaining the output and performance across so many policy fields of the Council's work. Early evidence on the effects of enlargement confirm the principled interest in consensus-based legislative outcomes and Coreper's notoriety as the 'place to do the deal' has, if anything, become enhanced. We turn now to how Coreper is able to reach so many decisions and what is potentially the group's most valuable contribution to EU decision-making: its capacity in integrating interests.

Integrating interests

Continuous negotiation

Coreper's structural position imparts a coherence and continuity in the representation of interests that would otherwise be difficult to match. Not only is Coreper distinguishable by the intensity of negotiations, but the permanent representatives' involvement across the different domains of EU decision-making is also pervasive. In addition to weekly meetings, the permanent representatives sit beside their ministers during Council sessions, briefing them beforehand and offering tactical suggestions. They attend European Council summits and can serve as behind-the-scenes consultants. They monitor the proceedings of the working groups and offer specific points of strategy or emphasis. The ambassadors are also closely involved in monitoring cooperation and association agreements, cooperation councils (including Euro–Med conferences and Euro–Asian summits), and accession negotiations. Finally, from the beginnings of the Lomé Convention with the African, Caribbean, and Pacific (ACP) states, the ambassadors have prepared the relevant councils through the ACP–EC Committee of Ambassadors that precede yearly meetings. And while the links between the EP and Coreper II remain limited, codecision has created an intense negotiation network between MEPs and the deputies.

All of this creates a dynamic of continuity in Coreper's work, reinforced through weekly meetings. Added to this is the regular cycle of Coreper luncheons, held by Coreper II before the monthly GAC and sometimes on a more topical, ad hoc basis.[12] Lunches sometimes function as long-term strategic planning sessions, often with a European Commissioner invited as a guest. More frequently, and because attendance is so tightly restricted, lunches are used to tackle the thorniest of problems (Butler 1986: 30). Then there are the informal Coreper trips hosted by the presidency, which precede European Council summits.[13] Trips are long weekends of socializing, 'rich in food and culture', used to reinforce interpersonal relations and the bonds of trust—a kind of 'oiling of the mechanism'. This ongoingness of negotiation builds an institutional memory in Coreper from which the permanent representatives learn to draw (Lewis 1998a: 485).

Instruction and voice

Permanent representatives are under 'instruction' from their national capitals. In principle, for every agenda item, there is an instruction, setting, at a minimum, what is and is not acceptable as an outcome. Again in principle, this instruction is arrived at after domestic coordination through the relevant line ministries and often through an inter-ministerial coordination mechanism.[14] In practice, the instruction process is much more complex, especially in temporal sequence. For starters, most instructions have inbuilt flexibility. Of course, there are certain taboo areas (institutional reform; fiscal policy) and national sensitivities—but, here, permanent representatives claim not even to need instructions, because they already know what positions to take.

Much more fundamental to this story is the degree to which permanent representatives have an institutionalized voice in the instruction process itself. Some generic patterns of this include, first, departing from instructions and making recommendations back to the capital for changes. The power of recommendations obviously varies by issue area and the personal authority of a permanent representative, but they are most effective in areas in which there is a risk of becoming isolated or, under the shadow of the vote, disregarded in a possible compromise.

Second, the capitals often signal that a margin of manoeuvre exists. Sometimes, permanent representatives are told not to take an instruction seriously, or that the position in the printed instruction can be disregarded. 'Instructions are a way for [the capital] to say they have done their job,' one ambassador explained.

Third, when there is a political need to avoid confrontation or politicization at the level of the ministers, permanent representatives (sometimes even told 'avoid Council') will have a freer hand in making deals and selling success at home.

Fourth, there are times when the capital does not know or cannot decide (or does not want to decide—see below). In these instances, the permanent representatives are causally contributing to the definition of what national interests in the EU context are. As one Antici counsellor explained: 'Instructions already contain a big Brussels element in them, and sometimes they are Brussels instructions, because the first ten lines of our report imply an instruction … sometimes they just copy our reports into instructions.' A different pattern emerges when the capital does not want to decide. According to one ambassador from a large member state: 'Sometimes they don't give an instruction because sometimes the ministers don't want to be pinned down. The result of this is that we make policy often from here.'

The degree of voice that the permanent representatives can obtain is derivative of Coreper's basic mission: to find solutions. Finding collective solutions and 'getting on with it' is an unspoken job requirement that gives Coreper its reputation for being results-oriented. It can even happen that permanent representatives disregard their instructions. As one ambassador detailed:

It [disregarding instructions] happens. The first time it feels like a big deal. The second time, its easy. The problem is to know what are the interests of your country … sometimes the capital gets nervous, they have various lobbies behind it usually. We also have to keep in mind that what has been built up over the last forty years is important. That a file should go. That we should proceed forward. This is constantly a factor in what we do. Often we have much more at stake than the dossier.

While it is important to avoid an oversocialized view of the permanent representatives, one should not underestimate the relative autonomy that Coreper, as a collective decision-making forum, can obtain. The instruction process is often a two-way street, with permanent representatives able to insert a high degree of voice in their construction. And, as a group, the Committee can engage in transgovernmental bargaining tactics, such as the 'plotting' of a compromise in the collective interest of finding solutions (see below).

Insulation

One of the most distinctive features of Coreper diplomacy is the degree of insulation from the normal currents of domestic constituent pressures. The meetings themselves are treated with an air of confidentiality, and many sensitive national positions are ironed out in restricted sessions in which the permanent representatives can speak frankly and in confidence that what is said will not be reported to the capitals or the media. This can even include group discussion on how an agreement will be packaged and sold to the authorities back home. 'At our level, publicity does not exist,' an ambassador explained. 'Our body is absolutely black; we can do deals.' Another stated: 'We are better placed than the capitals to know what are the real interests of our countries. We are less exposed to the pressures, the short term problems of the time. This affects us much less'.

A structural feature of Coreper that often goes unnoticed is that insulation affords member states the capacity to reshape domestic constraints. As an ambassador put it: 'Coreper is the only forum in the EU where representatives don't have a domestic turf to defend.' 'Because of this', he went on to add:

It is often politically necessary to present a position knowing it is unrealistic. My minister of finance needs certain arguments to be presented. He has certain pressures from his constituencies. We have to make it look like we fought for this even though we both know it will lead nowhere. I will present it, and if it receives no support, I will drop it.

A dense normative environment

Coreper's institutional capacity to aggregate interests across such an array of issue areas and under such a steady workload is facilitated by a dense normative environment. While these norms are almost purely informal in character—meaning that they are unwritten, not linked directly to any clauses in the treaties, and largely self-enforcing—the group-community standards in Coreper are highly institutionalized and ingrained into the basic ethos of the Committee's work. Five mutually reinforcing norms stand out in particular.

First, there is a norm of diffuse reciprocity, or the balancing of concessions over an extended shadow of the future. 'We do keep a sense in an unspecific way of obligations to another member state,' one ambassador remarked. Diffuse reciprocity can take many forms, including concessions and derogations, or 'going out on a limb' to persuade the capital for changes or a compromise. Dropping reserves or abstaining (rather than submitting a 'no' vote) are also political gestures that can be filed away and later returned in kind.

Second, there is a norm of 'thick trust' and the ability to speak frankly. It is reconfirmed weekly through the normal cycle of meetings, trips, and lunches.[15] Thick trust is especially important during endgame negotiations and restricted sessions when the group collectively legitimates or rejects arguments based on deliberative processes, such as principled reasoning, standards of fairness, or justifications for special consideration.

Third, there is a norm of mutual responsiveness that is best described as a shared purpose to understand each other's problems. Mutual responsiveness is another form of collective legitimation, whereby arguments are accepted or rejected by the group. Mutual responsiveness works within broad normative parameters, recognizing on the one hand that everyone has certain problems that require special consideration, but on the other that no one can be a *demandeur* too often and expect anyone to listen. This rule is such a basic one in Coreper that several permanent representatives from the newest member states had already learned that it existed after attending only a few meetings.

The fourth norm is a consensus reflex. This norm is what Hayes-Renshaw and Wallace (1995: 465) refer to as 'the instinctive recourse to behave consensually'. Even under conditions of QMV, permanent representatives often spend extra time to 'bring everyone on board'.

Finally, there is a culture of compromise that is premised on a basic willingness to accommodate divergent interests and is reinforced by the other norms listed above. The normative effects of this culture include a self-restraint in the calculations and defence of interests. It is seen, for example, when delegations quietly drop reserves after failing to convince the others of their arguments (Lewis 2005).

Norm socialization and enlargement

EU norms are internalized through a multilevel process of socialization. At the microlevel, new participants in Coreper go through a process of adaptation and learning. One Mertens counsellor claimed that it takes newcomers at least six months to 'find their way', since 'they stick close to their instructions. They don't yet have all the technical knowledge of the dossiers. They cannot gauge what is whispered in their ears'. Norm socialization is especially relevant for the substantial cohort of Coreper members from Central and Eastern Europe who arrived 2004–07. Despite early estimations that increased heterogeneity and unwieldy size would pose problems for the Council's club-like settings, evidence to date underscores a conscious effort by the 'newcomers' to acclimatize to EU decision-making norms. The best overall indicator is the stability of consensus-based outcomes, with contested votes in the Council accounting for less than 15 per cent of all legislative acts, a figure that is historically very consistent (Mattila 2008, 2009; Hertz 2010). The latest findings confirm that while more and more members do tend to increase the transaction costs of negotiation, and may decrease the speed of reaching decisions, they have not altered long-standing traditions of consensus-seeking behaviour, nor have they thus far led to more contestation and reliance on formal voting (Leuffen 2010; Hertz and Leuffen 2011).

Socialization dynamics in Council forums such as Coreper track with recent international relations research that argues that institutional environments can instil 'mimicry' and 'social influence' behaviours in novices who seek, first, to get by in an uncertain environment (that is, to copy what others are doing), and second, over time, become more durably internalized as practising the accepted norms leads to influence and social capital (Johnston 2008). Indeed, the Council even has built-in mechanisms to promote norm socialization, such as the 'active observer' period, which began one year prior to formal accession and gave national delegations the opportunity to attend meetings, including Coreper, in order to learn the ropes (Lempp 2006; Juncos and Pomorska 2007). The rotating presidency is another mechanism for norm socialization. For newcomers in particular, their inaugural presidency is judged a veritable 'entrance exam' (Elgström and Tallberg 2003: 194), which involves exposing hundreds of national civil servants to EU realities, often spearheaded through the Brussels-based permanent representations and usually several years in advance. Poland began preparation for its 2011 EU presidency as early as 2008 (*The Economist* 2011: 66); in a still-commended example, Finland began preparing for its inaugural 1999 presidency in 1995 and involved around 900 civil servants in programmes such as language training and negotiation simulations (Stubb 2000: 49). Running an effective presidency is a way of proving one's European credentials, and the pattern of earnest effort by novice members tells us this is considered a clear route to building a good reputation and social capital in Brussels.

There are, however, complex social psychological factors at work, as well as background ('scope') conditions for such norm internalization to work, including a shared identification with the legitimacy of the institution and the rules in question. If a forum such as Coreper did not also have a well-endowed tradition to practise mutual responsiveness and deal with sensitive domestic concerns by spending extra time and collectively legitimating individual arguments, then we would not expect to see the levels of trust required for such consensus-based decision-making hold up for long. Of course, building such trust happens slowly. Coreper is a negotiation forum ostensibly designed to fast-track such trust-building. In 2005, a small state deputy with a long tenure in Brussels summarized his new post-accession colleagues by stating: 'They have been very silent, they have been very careful. I am not sure the silence is from fascination; they may be flabbergasted at how things work in Coreper.'

There is also evidence that Council forums such as Coreper have made new use of existing procedures to build mutual confidence and avert contested legislative outcomes. One example is the upsurge in reading formal statements into the minutes of legislative acts since 2005. Some argue that the use of 'formal statements' serves as a viable outlet for expressing political dissatisfaction without the need for contesting a vote (Hagemann and de Clerck-Sachsse 2007). In other words, an informal norm to voice dissent through formal statements helps to maintain the consensus culture, as well as to send positive signals from newcomers that they are willing to uphold existing norms.

On the other hand, interviews with the newcomers to Coreper reveal a degree of cynicism that was not apparent with the new members from northern states in the mid-1990s. One new ambassador stated: 'They are all polite, they are nice, but there is no sympathy … I would say that it is a gathering of cynics condemned to compromise.' Another reached a similar conclusion: '[The group] can say "no" quite politely, but equally strong, they can be sympathetically ungiving. And I'm not seeking sympathy! I'm assuming and view this as a tough, competitive environment and I may not enjoy it.'

As a result, some interpret enlargement as a catalyst for deeper change in the EU's normative environment. Few anticipate less reliance on informal methods. A long-standing deputy noted: 'Much has shifted to an informal circuit. I spend much more time on the telephone: "I have a point, can you support me?" [The newcomers] will have a problem doing this, the informal work.' An ambassador reached a similar conclusion: 'You do feel around the table you're not going to know them as well. In an EU of the future you will know your colleagues less well. It is inevitable that more will be done outside the meetings rather than in the room.' There are also procedural rules on working methods and a higher usage of the so-called written procedure to handle more routine administrative business. But, overall, the evidence to date points to the durability of venerable consensus-seeking norms. The incentives to build a good reputation are still strong, and compel newcomers to acclimatize and internalize collective norms.

Plotting

Plotting is a negotiation pattern found in Coreper that demonstrates how a collective rationality can reformulate individual, instrumental rationality. The basic function of plotting is using the group to redefine a national position or to reshape domestic constraints.[16] 'To get new instructions we have to show [the capital] we have a black eye,' an ambassador explained. 'We can ask Coreper for help with this; it is one of our standard practices.' According to another, 'Sometimes I will deal with impossible instructions, by saying, "Mr Chairman, can I report back the fierce opposition to this?" And sometimes fierceness is exaggerated for effect.'

An excellent illustration of plotting occurred with Coreper II negotiations to reduce the number of Council formations (following the conclusions of the December 1999 Helsinki Summit). In this case, as a participant explained:

All fifteen [ambassadors] had negative instructions. They all had their own lists of what to keep, what to cut. This is because each has its own lobbies, you know, on gender questions, and so on. We all have our own [national] coordination problems. So we met in a luncheon. I told them, 'You understand this is pointless.' And I asked them, 'Will you report back that you were totally isolated?' So each has reported home that the other fourteen are more or less in agreement.

In general, plotting and underlining opposition is a tool to deal with recalcitrant bargaining positions. Exaggerating the fierceness of opposition is also a group strategy to collectively legitimate or reject arguments.

Style of discourse

Coreper has a shared discourse with its own key phrases, such as when a delegation is signalling willingness to compromise. There is a style of presenting arguments; there is also the art of derogation, whereby permanent representatives ask for help or special consideration. Learning the discourse is an important socialization mechanism for newcomers who join the club. As Peterson and Jones (1999: 34) point out, new members to Coreper 'must learn to use the language (even rhetoric) of appeals to the "European project"'.

There is a discourse to reveal who is behind their instructions and who is not. 'I can tell,' a deputy explained, 'when someone wants to distance themselves from their instructions.' One strategy is to just read them: 'They may say, "Mr Chairman, I'd like to read you something which I myself do not understand," or "Unfortunately I have to bore you with the following . . ."' Some claim to be able to tell if a colleague agrees with their instructions by body language alone.

Discourse is also key to signalling when something is important or to request mutual understanding. According to one ambassador:

There is a Coreper language with its own code words and code phrases. When used, this language is clearly understood by everyone. For example, if I have bad instructions that I'm against, I can say, 'But of course the presidency has to take its responsibilities,' which means put it to a vote and I'll lose, I accept this.

Most importantly, arguments matter. The power of a good argument can be as compelling as a blocking minority or the shadow of the veto. The scope for persuasion and the norm of mutual responsiveness work as great equalizers in Coreper negotiations. As a result, smaller member states that articulate clear, sound arguments can often punch above their weight. A financial counsellor from a large member state drew the following contrast: 'Sweden, who is always taking part in the debate, has influence far beyond their votes. Germany is the opposite; they have less influence than votes.' An Antici echoed this sentiment: 'If you convince others, it's with good arguments. Big or small makes no difference. In fact, the big member states often have higher burdens of proof in order to convince the others.'

Accountability

There is a common perception that decision-making in Brussels is remote, opaque, and even undemocratic. Given Coreper's role in everyday decision-making, it is somewhat surprising that, in all of the discussions to address the EU's democratic deficit since the early 1990s, Coreper has remained largely unmentioned. But given Coreper's workload and the need for insulation from politicization effects discussed above, it is clear why member states are reluctant to tinker with such fine-tuned mechanisms. There are occasional suggestions that emanate from a capital that perhaps a new Coreper III of ministers or deputy prime ministers might work to democratize the system—but support for this idea has never gained much momentum.

It is also easy to push the image of an all-powerful, unaccountable group of backroom decision-makers too far. Committee members are accountable to their ministers for the positions taken in negotiations and there is always a possibility (although specific examples are extremely hard to come by) that a minister can undo a deal done at Coreper level. If permanent representatives were to stray too far or be overruled by their ministers, they would quickly lose credibility in Coreper and in the home capital. There are also signs of more direct institutional links to domestic politics, seen in the number of Permreps, who now have a formal liaison for communication with the national parliament (including Greece, Hungary, Ireland, and Latvia).

Whether such an indirect system of accountability is a sustainable form of governance can be debated. Following the 2004–07 enlargements, many believe the EU will need to rely even more on the few, but vitally important, negotiation forums that are based on a club-like and insulated atmosphere in which collective norms guide acceptable behaviour and rule out a range of instrumentality (such as pushing for a vote, making veto threats, and so on). Coreper is the exemplar of this, but it is not alone. An intriguing analogue in macroeconomic and euro area policy-making is the Economic and Finance Committee (EFC), which puts national central bank and finance officials together—in camera, with no note-takers, and under the long tradition of doing everything by consensus. Even with the veritable revolution that we have seen in the EU's legislative process—namely, the evolution of codecision into an 'ordinary' decision-making procedure—we witness a heavy reliance on informal and closed-door settings, such as the trialogue methodology, to work out areas of compromise between the Council and EP versions of a proposal. The insulated, in camera, and club-like negotiation settings in the EU offer strong confirmation for David Stasavage's (2004: 670) argument that states will often 'shun transparency' in international negotiations, since openness can act as 'an incentive for representatives to "posture" by adopting uncompromising bargaining positions'. In an EU of twenty-seven or more states, the need for a mechanism like Coreper is greater than ever.

The institution in context

The 'Janus face' of Coreper

Coreper challenges the conventional dichotomy that sharply demarcates the national and European levels. Institutionally, Coreper embodies the claim that national and European levels of governance have become amalgamated in the EU system (see Wessels 1997). As state agents, the EU permanent representatives nicely illustrate how national and supranational roles and identifications can become nested and coexist. Coreper personnel offer empirical confirmation for Wendt's (1999: 242) hypothetical question of 'whether the members of states can ever learn additional ... identities above and beyond the state, creating "concentric circles" of group identification'. Interviews with participants consistently confirm that permanent representatives obtain a distinct secondary allegiance to collective, EU decision-making, although the 'nested' identity concept does not fully capture the quality of the identity configuration found here, because permanent representatives do not self-reflectively see these as competitive or contradictory to national allegiance. They are not different hats worn at different times or held in juxtaposition to each other, so much as a broadening of the cognitive boundaries of what counts as the 'self' and the 'national interest'. One deputy claimed: 'There is a confidence that I will deliver the goods at home and a confidence to deliver the goods collectively. I must find ways to synthesize the two.' The EU permanent representatives are examples of state agents who have found a way in which to operationalize what Laffan (2004: 90–4) describes as 'double-hatting'.

While empirical findings from research on Coreper clearly show that national and supranational identities are not zero-sum commodities, some theorists still generally assume otherwise. For example, Stone Sweet and Sandholtz (1998: 6) claim to 'leave as an open question the extent to which the loyalties and identities of actors will shift from the national to the European level. There is substantial room for supranational governance without an ultimate shift in identification'. Instead of limited conceptualizations of shifts and transfers in identity, what we see in Coreper is a blurring of the boundaries between the national and the European. Describing his own job description, one deputy claimed: 'I wear a Janus face.' The metaphor of the Janus face can be detected throughout the interview data in how permanent representatives perceive their institutional roles and multiple allegiances, to represent national interests *and* participate in making collective decisions according to a deliberative process of negotiation. None of this implies that national identities and interests become marginalized or disappear; rather, what stands out is the infusion of the national with the European and vice versa. To be successful, EU permanent representatives develop a more-complex identity configuration informing definitions of self and interest. From a Janus-faced perspective, they act as both state agents and supranational entrepreneurs simultaneously. From an institutiona-design standpoint, this finding is highly significant as to how the overall system of decision-making functions. As Weiler (1994: 31) so aptly summarized, the system:

replaces a kind of 'liberal' premise of international society with a communitarian one: the Community as a transnational regime will not simply be a neutral area in which states seek to maximize their benefits but will create a tension between the national self and the collective self.

The implications of this tension for how we think of sovereignty in Europe is also significant. Waever (1995: 412) argues that the EU reconfigures conventional conceptions of national sovereignty because of the 'importance of Europe *in* national identities' in which 'the European dimension is included in national self-conceptions' (emphasis original). The cognitive blurring of boundaries between the national and European layers also fits suggestively with what Risse (2004: 251–2) describes as a 'marble cake' concept of identity, in which 'identity components influence each other' and, rather than being neatly compartmentalized, 'mesh and blend'. As high-ranking national officials, the permanent representatives offer a striking empirical example of this at the everyday level of EU decision-making.

Conclusions

This chapter has focused on integrating interests in the context of the EU and, in particular, the systemic, policy-setting level at which Coreper operates. Understanding Coreper negotiations requires being alert to the often subtle interplay of national and community perspectives. The EU permanent representatives are nation-state agents who represent national interests, but who have also internalized collective decision-making rules and norms that inform bargaining behaviour and shape legislative outcomes. The logic of action found in Coreper goes beyond cost–benefit, instrumental interest calculation, and includes a distinctive 'appropriateness' logic based on group-community standards. Given the range of early predictions about enlargement leading to gridlock or worse, it is impressive how this collective decision-making logic has persisted, which in turn supports an argument that norm socialization in forums such as Coreper is an important process-level dimension of European integration. As a key decision-making bottleneck in the Council system, Coreper embodies a culture of consensus-seeking and mutual accommodation of national preferences using group-legitimation standards.

At the same time, while the Committee's normative environment is highly institutionalized, it is also based almost exclusively on informal rules and norms. As such, it is subject to a very different process of change from, say, that of revising the treaties or changing the formal voting rules. If members were to alter the calculus of whom they appoint to Coreper (and the Permreps) and/or to begin to challenge established decision-making norms (by, say, pushing for a vote under QMV, or refusing to explain and justify positions), the Council *could* develop a more rigid 'veto culture' or divide into different voting blocks along geographic or gross domestic product (GDP) lines. In such scenarios, the organizational culture and normative environment would change. The 'double-hatting' identity configuration of the EU permanent representatives could be altered as well. If Coreper were to develop into a body in which voting weights and instrumental cost–benefit calculations ruled the day, rather than consensus-based deliberation and debate, we could see system-wide effects (and unintended consequences) on how effectively the Union can operate.

NOTES

1. March and Olsen (1989) offer the classic distinction between logics of consequences and appropriateness. In the former, 'the only obligations recognized by individuals are those created through consent and contracts grounded in calculated consequential advantage' (March and Olsen 1989: 951); in the latter, individuals are 'acting in accordance with rules and practices that are socially constructed, publicly known, anticipated, and accepted' (*ibid.*: 952).

2. Article 19, Council's Rules of Procedure, OJ L285, 16 October 2006.

3. All interview quotes come from field research conducted by the author in Brussels.

4. Bulletin of the EC, 12–1974, point 1104.7.

5. Specifically, Article 151 EEC.

6. Anderson (1997: 81) defines 'constitutive politics' as the 'processes and outcomes that establish or amend EU rules of the game', as distinct from 'regulative politics', which are the 'processes and outcomes that take place within established, routinized areas of EU activity'.

7. Interview, 15 May 2000.

8. See Webb (1977: 18–19), for example.

9. Along the same lines, other partial exemptions from Coreper's remit involve macroeconomic policy coordination (the specialty of the EFC), military planning (now managed by the Military Committee), and financial services (led by the Paris-based Committee of European Securities Regulators, or CESR, and a Securities Committee charged with 'fast-tracking' liberalization efforts). See the section on 'Contestation' for more.

10. Negotiations for the 2007–13 budget certainly needed the input of the EU ambassadors to help to keep the cauldron of issues—from the British rebate and relative size of Germany's contributions, to redistributive fairness between 'new' and 'old' members—off the boil.

11. Article 19, para. 1, with a footnote that holds 'in particular for matters where substantive preparation is undertaken in other fora' (Art. 19, fn. 2(g)).

12. Coreper I also convenes working lunches, usually two or three per presidency.

13. Trips are restricted to the ambassadors, the Anticis, and spouses.

14. Such as the Cabinet Office in the UK or the SGCI (*Secrétariat Général du Comité Interministériel pour les Questions de Coopération Economique Européenne*) in France.

15. As Putnam (1993: 171) explains, thick trust is a key interpersonal ingredient of 'social capital', which tends to develop in 'small, close-knit communities' based on 'a belief that rests on intimate familiarity with this individual'.

16. This is known as 'Chiefs of Government collusion' in two-level games research: see Evans (1993: 406–7).

FURTHER READING

For an excellent treatment of Coreper's role in EU decision-making, see Hayes-Renshaw and Wallace (2006). De Zwaan (1995) offers perhaps the most comprehensive study available in English, although it tends toward the descriptive and legalistic. Hayes-Renshaw *et al.* (1989) is a classic. See also Bostock (2002), Mentler (1996), and Westlake and Galloway (2004). For a testimonial of the EU system from the former *doyen* of Coreper, see de Schoutheete (2000). On the Spaak Committee, see Mayne (1962) and Willis (1965). For more on multiple identities and how to conceptualize different configurations of identity in the context of the EU, see Risse (2010).

Bostock, D. (2002) 'Coreper revisited,' *Journal of Common Market Studies*, 40/2: 215–34.

de Schoutheete, P. (2000) *The Case for Europe: Unity, Diversity, and Democracy in the European Union* (London and Boulder, CO: Lynne Rienner).

De Zwaan, J. (1995) *The Permanent Representatives Committee: Its Role in European Union Decision-making* (Amsterdam: Elsevier).

Hayes-Renshaw, F. and Wallace, H. (2006) *The Council of Ministers* (2nd edn, Basingstoke and New York: Palgrave).

Hayes-Renshaw, F., Lequesne, C., and Mayor Lopez, P. (1989) 'The permanent representations of the member states to the European Communities', *Journal of Common Market Studies*, 28/2: 119–37.

Mayne, R. (1962) *The Community of Europe* (New York: W. W. Norton).

Mentler, M. (1996) *Der Auschuss der Ständigen Vertreter bei den Europäischen Gemeinschaften* (Baden-Baden: Nomos).

Risse, T. (2010) *A Community of Europeans? Transnational Identities and Public Spheres* (Ithaca, NY: Cornell University Press).

Westlake, M. and Galloway, D. (2004) *The Council of the European Union* (3rd edn, London: John Harper Publishing).

Willis, F. R. (1965) *France, Germany, and the New Europe, 1945–1963* (Stanford, CA: Stanford University Press).

WEB LINKS

http://www.consilium.europa.eu

The best online resource with which to monitor Coreper's work is the Council's website, although details on meetings remain hard to come by. Links to the EU presidency offer basic information, such as dates, agendas, etc. For an online database of Coreper personnel (including valuable contact information for arranging interviews at the permanent representations), select 'IDEA—Who's who in the Council' and then choose the link 'Permanent Representatives Committee'.

CHAPTER 15

Political Interests: the European Parliament's Party Groups

Tapio Raunio

Summary

The party system of the European Parliament (EP) is dominated by the two main European party families: centre-right conservatives and Christian democrats, on the one hand, and centre-left social democrats on the other. In the early 1950s, members of the EP (MEPs) decided to form ideological groups instead of national blocs to counterbalance the dominance of national interests in the Council. Since then, the party groups have gradually, but consistently, consolidated their positions in the Parliament, primarily by introducing procedural reforms that enable them to make effective use of EP's legislative powers. At the same time, the shape of the party system has become more stable, at least as far as the main groups are concerned. Nevertheless, national parties remain influential within party groups, not least through their control of candidate selection.

Introduction

Compared with parties in EU member state legislatures, the party groups of the European Parliament (EP) operate in a very different institutional environment. While the Parliament is involved in the appointment of the Commission and can force it to resign, there is nonetheless no real EU government accountable to the Parliament. There are no coherent and hierarchically organized European-level parties. Instead, members of the EP (MEPs) are elected from lists drawn by national parties and on the basis of national electoral campaigns. The social and cultural heterogeneity of the EU is reflected in the internal diversity of the groups, with a total of approximately 170 national parties from twenty-seven member states winning seats in the Parliament in the 2009 elections. The party groups are thus firmly and even structurally embedded in the political systems of the EU member states. However, despite the existence of such factors, EP party groups have gradually, over the decades, consolidated their position in the Parliament, primarily through introducing procedural reforms that enable them to make effective use of EP's legislative powers. At the same time, the shape of the party system has become more stable, at least as far as the main groups are concerned. One can thus talk of the 'institutionalization' of the EP party system.

The chapter begins by examining the shape of the EP party system. It then analyses the structure of the party groups and the role of national parties within them, before exploring the relationship between the groups and committees, arguing that the empowerment of the Parliament has resulted in stronger links between national parties and their MEPs. We also show that the EP party system has become more competitive, with the Left–Right dimension constituting the main cleavage in the chamber. Next, we examine parties at the European level and argue that, without any executive office at stake in European elections, the vertical linkage function of the party groups—that of connecting voters to the EU policy process—remains poorly developed. However, in horizontal terms, the EP party groups and the Europarties perform an important function by integrating political interests across the Union.

The shape of the EP party system

The Common Assembly of the European Coal and Steel Community (ECSC), the predecessor of the Parliament, held its inaugural session in September 1952. Already, in the first important vote held in the Assembly, to elect its President, the members split along group lines instead of voting as national blocs. The decision to form party groups crossing national lines needs to be understood in the light of developments in the early 1950s. First, the creation of the High Authority (the predecessor of the Commission) and the Assembly marked the emergence of truly supranational institutions, in contrast to those of the intergovernmental Council of Europe (particularly its Consultative Assembly). Second, national interests in the ECSC were already represented in the Council of Ministers and the Assembly sought to counterbalance this through its ideologically based group structure.

Throughout its history up to the present day (Box 15.1 summarizes EP groups after the 2009 elections), the EP party system has been based on the Left–Right dimension, the main cleavage in all European countries. The seating order in the chamber reflects this divide, with the social democrats and former communists on the Left side of the hemicycle, the greens and liberals in the middle, and Christian democrats and conservatives on the right. Table 15.1 shows the distribution of seats between party families in the Parliament between 1979 (the date of the first direct EP elections) and 2009. Initially, the party system consisted of only three groups: socialists/social democrats (the Party of European Socialists, or PES); Christian democrats/conservatives (the European People's Party, or EPP); and liberals (the European Liberal, Democrat and Reform Party, or ELDR), the three main party families in EU member states. The Christian democrat group was the largest group until 1975, when the British Labour Party joined the Socialist group.[1]

BOX 15.1   Party groups in the 2009–14 European Parliament

European People's Party (EPP, 264 seats)

The EPP is a mix of Christian Democrats and Conservatives, joining together parties from all EU member states except the UK. The largest national party is the German Christian Democratic Union/Christian Social Union (CDU/CSU). The conservative wing of the group has strengthened over the years, with the entry of the Spanish People's Party, the Italian People of Freedom, the French (Gaullist) Union for a Popular Movement, and the British Conservatives (which left the group in 2009 to form the ECR group—see below). Despite the numerical growth of conservative forces in the group, the EPP has traditionally and consistently been strongly in favour of closer European integration.

Progressive Alliance of Socialists and Democrats (S&D, 185 seats)

This group of the Party of European Socialists (PES) brings together social democratic and socialist parties from all EU countries. The largest party delegations are the German Social Democrats, the Spanish Socialist Workers' Party (PSOE), and the Italian Democratic Party. The group supports further integration, primarily because, with monetary union, the defence of traditional goals of the Left—such as social and environmental legislation and employment policies—require European-level action to complement national measures.

Alliance of Liberals and Democrats for Europe (ALDE, 85 seats)

The liberal group consists of various liberal and centrist parties, and has come to occupy a pivotal role between the two largest groups. After the 2004 elections, the group changed its name from European Liberal, Democrat, and Reform Party (ELDR) to the Alliance of Liberals and Democrats for Europe (ALDE). The group brings together MEPs from twenty member states, with the largest national parties being the German Free Democratic Party and the British Liberal Democrats.

European Conservatives and Reformists (ECR, 56 seats)

This conservative group was formed after the 2009 elections and after the British Conservatives had broken away from the EPP group. ECR has members from nine countries, but the group is essentially a pact between the British Conservatives, the Polish Law and Justice Party, and the Czech Civic Democratic Party (ODS). The group can be categorized as Eurosceptical, but it does not share the hard-line anti-integrationist views of the EFD.

Greens/European Free Alliance (G/EFA, 55 seats)

First formed after the 1999 elections, this group is an alliance between green parties and various regionalist parties. The regionalist parties of EFA—such as the Scottish National Party and the Catalan parties—do not have enough seats to form a group of their own and thus sit with the Greens. The Greens have, in recent years, become strongly pro-EU, for similar reasons to the social democrats. The group unites MEPs from fourteen countries and the largest party is the German Alliance '90/The Greens.

Confederal Group of the European United Left/Nordic Green Left (EUL–NGL, 35 seats)

The EUL–NGL brings together a variety of Left-socialist and former Communist parties from thirteen member states. The main national party is the Left Party from Germany. EUL is divided over the desirability of further integration.

Europe of Freedom and Democracy (EFD, 27 seats)

The EFD group is the only predominantly Eurosceptic group in the Parliament, bringing together anti-EU lists and parties from nine countries, including Italy (*Lega Nord*) and the UK (Independence Party).

Note: The seat shares are from June 2011. Twenty-nine MEPs did not belong to any of the groups, sitting instead as 'independent' or 'non-attached' MEPs.

TABLE 15.1 Party groups in the European Parliament (1979–2009)

Party family	Seat distribution after each round of elections						
	1979	1984	1989	1994	1999	2004	2009
Social democrats/ socialists	113 (SOC)	130 (SOC)	180 (SOC)	198 (PES)	180 (PES)	200 (SOC)	184 (S&D)
Christian democrats/ conservatives	107 (EPP)	110 (EPP)	121 (EPP)	157 (EPP)	233 (EPP-ED)	268 (EPP-ED)	265 (EPP)
Liberals	40 (LDG)	31 (LDRG)	49 (LDRG)	43 (ELDR)	50 (ELDR)	88 (ALDE)	84 (ALDE)
Conservatives	64 (EDG) 22 (EPD)	50 (EDG) 29 (EDA)	34 (EDG) 20 (EDA)	27 (FE) 26 (EDA)	21 (UEN)	27 (UEN)	54 (ECR)
Communists/ Radical left	44 (COM)	41 (COM)	28 (EUL– LU (14)	28 (EUL– NGL)	42 (EUL– NGL)	41 (EUL– NGL)	35 (EUL– NGL)
Greens/ regionalists		20 (RB)	30 (G) 13 (RB)	23 (G)	48 (G/EFA)	42 (G/EFA)	55 (G/EFA)
Eurosceptics				19 (EN)	16 (EDD)	37 (IND/ DEM)	32 (EFD)
Extreme right		16 (ER)	17 (ER)				
Others	11 (CDI)			19 (ERA)	20 (TGI)		
Non-attached	9	7	12	27	16	29	27
Total	**410**	**434**	**518**	**567**	**626**	**732**	**736**

Note: Social democrats/socialists: SOC = Socialist Group, PES = Party of European Socialists, S&D = Progressive Alliance of Socialists and Democrats; Christian democrats/conservatives: EPP = European People's Party, EPP-ED = European People's Party and European Democrats; Liberals: LDG = Liberal and Democratic Group, LDRG = Liberal and Democratic Reformist Group, ELDR = European Liberal, Democrat and Reform Party, ALDE = Alliance of Liberals and Democrats for Europe; Conservatives: EDG = European Democratic Group, EPG = European Progressive Democrats, EDA = European Democratic Alliance, FE = Forza Europa (EDA and FE merged in July 1995 to form Union for Europe, with that group then joining the EPP in June 1998), UEN = Union for Europe of the Nations, ECR = European Conservatives and Reformists; Communists/Radical left: COM = Communist and Allies Group, EUL = European United Left, LU = Left Unity, EUL–NGL = Confederal Group of the European United Left–Nordic Green Left; Greens/regionalists: RB = Rainbow Group, G = Green Group, G/EFA = Greens/European Free Alliance; Eurosceptics: EN = Europe of Nations, EDD = Europe of Democracies and Diversities, IND/DEM = Independence and Democracy, EFD = Europe of Freedom and Democracy; Extreme right: ER = European Right (in addition, a short-lived Identity, Tradition and Sovereignty group existed between January and November 2007); Others: CDI = Technical Group of Co-ordination and Defence of Independent Members and Groups, ERA = European Radical Alliance, TGI = Technical Group of Independents; Non-attached = independent members not belonging to any party group.

For the first time since the introduction of direct elections, the EPP became, after the 1999 elections, the largest group in the chamber. The EPP has continued to be the largest group since then, a development explained partly by the difficulties that centre-Left parties have faced throughout Europe in recent years. The conservative wing of the group has been strengthened since the 1990s, but the party that had most difficulties in fitting into the group was undoubtedly the British Conservatives, the views of which, particularly on European integration, were quite different from those of the group majority (Maurer *et al.* 2008). Hence the formation of the ECR group and the departure of the British Conservatives and the Czech ODS after the 2009 elections may have eased tensions within the EPP group.[2]

The centre-Left social democratic group was the biggest in the Parliament from 1975 to the 1999 elections. The formation of the centre-Left group (S&D after the 2009 elections) presents far fewer problems, because almost each member state has an electorally significant centre-Left, social democratic party. The Liberals played a key role in the early years of the Parliament, but between 1979 and 2004 their seat share remained below 10 per cent. The group has a strongly pro-European philosophy, and this stance has occasionally created problems between the group majority and the Centre parties from the Nordic countries that are more Eurosceptical than the group majority.

The greens achieved an electoral breakthrough in 1989, and have since then formed a group of their own in the Parliament. The regionalist parties of the European Free Alliance (EFA) have never mustered enough seats to form their own group, and hence their MEPs have mainly joined forces with the greens. Communists, or the radical Left, have formed a group under various labels since 1973. The title 'Nordic Green Left' was added to the group name Confederal Group of the European United Left after the 1995 enlargement, because the Finnish and Swedish Left parties wanted to emphasize their separate identity within the then otherwise largely Mediterranean group. The group has traditionally been a quite loose alliance, and the group states in its own constituent declaration that EUL–NGL 'is a forum for cooperation between its different political components, each of which retains its own independent identity and commitment to its own positions'. Eurosceptical parties have formed a group since the 1994 elections, but such strongly anti-EU political forces have remained very much in the minority in the Parliament. The conservatives, however, a party family that displays a milder version of opposition to further integration, have formed a group under various names ever since the UK joined the then European Community. Finally, the non-attached MEPs have normally represented various extreme Right or nationalist parties (which had a group of their own between 1984 and 1994), such as the Hungarian *Jobbik* or the French *Front National* after the 2009 elections.

The EP party system has, throughout the history of the directly elected Parliament, been effectively dominated by the centre-Right EPP and the social democratic PES (Kreppel 2002). After the 2009 election, they retained control of approximately two-thirds of the seats. This duopoly is nicely illustrated by the system of electing the President of the Parliament. With the exception of the 1999–2004 Parliament, the PES and EPP have shared the presidency since 1989. For example, in the 2009–14 electoral term, the first President was the Pole Jerzy Buzek from the EPP, with an MEP from the S&D group expected to replace him at mid-term in January 2012.[3] The party system has also become more stable and predictable. In addition to the three groups that have been present in the chamber from the 1950s, the groups of the greens (including the regionalists), the conservatives, the radical Left, and the Eurosceptics have also become 'institutionalized' in the chamber since the first direct elections.

Internal organization

In the context of national legislatures, a parliamentary party group can be defined as:

an organized group of members of a representative body who were elected either under the same party label or under the label of different parties that do not compete against each other in elections, and who do not explicitly create a group for technical reasons only.

(Heidar and Koole 2000: 249)

Applying this definition to the Parliament, we note the features that distinguish the EP groups from national legislative parties. First, most—but not all—of the national parties in the two main groups were elected under the same label (EPP or PES), but these labels were hardly used in the campaigns and remain largely unknown among the voters.[4] Moreover, the larger groups in particular often contain more than one party per member state, and therefore these parties compete against each other in the elections.

The EP's Rules of Procedure, the standing orders of the Parliament, set numerical criteria for group formation. Following the 2009 elections, a political group must comprise at least twenty-five MEPs from at least a quarter of the member states.[5] Apart from ideological ties (McElroy and Benoit 2010), the availability of considerable financial, material, and procedural benefits has provided further incentives for group formation. While the money from the Parliament may appear inconsequential in absolute terms, it has nevertheless been crucial for certain smaller parties—such as regionalist and green parties—which often do not have access to comparable resources at the national level. The sum that each group receives depends on the number of MEPs and working languages in the group. Material benefits include for example office space and staff.

Group staff perform a variety of duties, ranging from routine administration to drafting background memos, following developments in committees, and drawing up whips in plenaries. In addition, each MEP has one to three personal assistants (financed from the EP budget), and both the committee and the EP staff assist groups and MEPs. Turning to procedural rights, appointments to committees and intra-parliamentary leadership positions, and the allocation of reports and plenary speaking time, are based on the rule of proportionality between the groups. Certain plenary actions, such as tabling amendments or oral questions, require the backing of a committee, a party group, or at least forty MEPs. Non-attached representatives are thus procedurally marginalized in the chamber.

Group cohesion

Three factors tend to work against cohesion within party groups in the Parliament: the balance of power between the EU institutions; the rules for candidate selection; and the internal heterogeneity of the groups. A key element in producing unitary group action in national legislatures is the fact that governments depend on the support of the parliamentary majority. Especially when the government enjoys only a small majority, both it and the opposition have strong incentives to act cohesively. The EP party groups lack this motive. While the Commission has to be approved by the Parliament and can be brought down by it (as happened indirectly in 1999), the composition of the Commission is only partly based on the outcome of the European elections.

Second, 'centralized nomination procedures should lead to greater party cohesion' (Bowler *et al.* 1999: 8). National parties, and not EP groups or Europarties, control candidate selection. Therefore national parties possess the ultimate sanction against MEPs. This applies particularly to countries using closed lists or mixed systems, in which parties present pre-ordered lists and the electors vote either for a party or an individual candidate. Interestingly, while links between national parties and their MEPs have traditionally been rather loose (Raunio 2000), more recent research indicates that the ties are gradually becoming stronger. There is greater policy coordination between MEPs and their parties, with case studies on British and German parties in particular confirming this trend, but national parties nonetheless largely refrain from 'mandating' their MEPs (Raunio 2000; Blomgren 2003; Bailer 2009). Voting behaviour in the Parliament provides further evidence of the influence of national parties. Research indicates that when MEPs receive conflicting voting instructions from national parties and their EP groups, they are more likely to side with their national party, particularly in parties in which the leadership has more or better opportunities to punish and reward its MEPs (such as through more centralized candidate selection or closed lists):

Despite the fact that the parliamentary principals in the EP control important benefits—such as committee assignments and speaking time—it is the principals that control candidate selection (the national parties) who ultimately determine how MEPs behave. When the national parties in the same parliamentary group decide to vote together, the EP parties look highly cohesive. But when these parties take opposing policy positions, the cohesion of the EP parties break down.

(Hix 2002b: 696)

Hence we can expect particularly those MEPs who are seeking re-election to be re-luctant to ignore national party guidelines, with such attentiveness to national party positions higher in the run-up to the EP elections (Lindstädt *et al.* 2011).

Finally, of all legislatures, the heterogeneity of the Parliament is probably matched only by that of the Indian Congress. Around 170 national parties from twenty-seven member states won seats in the 2009 elections. The largest group, EPP, consists of forty-one national party delegations. Such a high level of heterogeneity, not to men-tion the problems involved in communicating in over twenty official languages, presents a formidable challenge for the groups.

However, roll-call analyses show that the groups do achieve high levels of cohe-sion, with average cohesion levels of around 85–90 per cent and some groups even above 90 per cent (Hix *et al.* 2007). In comparative terms, the EP groups are on average less cohesive than party groups in the EU member state legislatures, but have tended to be more cohesive than parties in the US Congress. What accounts for this relatively unitary behaviour? Until the 1990s, one could argue that because most votes in the Parliament had little, if any, impact, it did not really matter how MEPs voted. According to this line of reasoning, the fragile foundations of group cohesion would be put to the test once the Parliament acquired real legislative pow-ers. However, in reality, group cohesion has risen, not declined, as the EP has gained new powers.

The explanation advanced here for high cohesion levels focuses on policy influ-ence, and on how group organization is tailored to face the twin challenge of internal heterogeneity and the strong position of national parties. Decision-making within groups can be described as rather consensual, with groups putting much effort into building positions that are acceptable to all, or nearly all, parties in the group. Unlike national party leaders, EP group chairs do not control or even influence candidate selection, nor can they promise lucrative ministerial portfolios or well-paid civil service jobs. Groups have whips, but they basically only remind MEPs of group posi-tions and indicate which votes are important. While the groups have fairly similar organizational structures to their counterparts in national parliaments, with leaders, executive committees, and working parties, the groups can nevertheless be charac-terized as non-hierarchical and non-centralized.

Choosing leaders

At the start of the five-year legislative term, the groups elect their leaders (chairper-sons/presidents), who usually occupy the post until the next elections or even longer. The chairs represent their group in the Conference of Presidents, the body responsi-ble for setting the Parliament's agenda and for organizational decisions. In the 2009–14 Parliament, the G/EFA and EFD groups have two co-chairs. The number of vice-chairs varies between the groups. The executive committee of the group is the Bureau, which normally includes the group chair and vice-chairs, heads, and possible additional members of national party delegations; other potential members include the treasurer or committee coordinators. The Bureau is responsible for organizational and administrative issues, and prepares policy decisions for group meetings. It plays a key role in facilitating group consensus. In their discussion on factionalism within national parties, Bowler *et al.* (1999: 15) argue that:

there are reasons for thinking that factions can help rank-and-file members discipline their leadership, either by providing faction leaders to take part in policy discussions (reporting back to their members) or by making it clear to party leaders that a block of votes will desert if some policy line is crossed. In this sense, factions help party leaders understand where their support or opposition lies within the party and the levels of this support or opposition.

The same dynamic is at work in the EP groups. When one replaces factions with national party delegations, we see that, by guaranteeing most national delegations representation in the executive committee, the group leadership learns about the positions of national parties and the intensity of their preferences. The groups convene regularly in Brussels prior to the plenary week, as well as during plenaries. The meetings in Brussels constitute a 'Group week', usually lasting two or three days. When MEPs feel that they cannot follow the group position, they are expected to make this clear in the group meetings. Party groups have also established working groups for examining specific policy areas and for coordinating group policy on those issues.

National party delegations

National party delegations are the cornerstones upon which the groups are based. Some smaller groups are indeed no more than loose coalitions of national parties, while even in the older and more organized groups, one can occasionally see divisions along national lines. Most national delegations have their own staff, elect their chairpersons, and convene prior to group meetings. However, the impact of national parties is mitigated by three factors. First, national parties are seldom unitary actors themselves. National parties throughout the EU are, to a varying extent, internally divided over integration, and these divisions are reproduced in the Parliament. Perhaps the best examples are the British Conservative and Labour delegations. Second, the EP is a committee-based legislature, with emphasis on building issue-specific majorities in the committees. Third, the majority of bills and resolutions do not produce divisions along national lines. Much of the Parliament's agenda is taken up by traditional socio-economic matters, such as internal market legislation, not by constitutional matters or redistributive decisions, such as the allocation of structural funds.

But the most important reason why MEPs and national party delegations vote with their group most of the time is policy influence. After all, the main rationale for group formation in any decision-making body is that it helps like-minded legislators to achieve their policy goals. Cohesive group action is essential for achieving the group's objectives, while cooperative behaviour within groups helps MEPs to pursue their own policy goals. Moreover, given the huge number of amendments and final resolutions voted upon in plenaries, the voting cues provided by groups, and particularly group members in the responsible EP committee, are an essential source of guidance for MEPs (Ringe 2010).

To summarize, the desire to influence EU policy and the relatively non-hierarchical group structure, based on institutionalized interaction between the leadership, the committees (see below), and the national party delegations, facilitates group cohesion. It is occasionally claimed that the accommodation of national viewpoints leads to lowest-common-denominator decisions. However, these policy compromises are a prerequisite for the Parliament to influence EU legislation.

The next section examines coalition dynamics in the chamber, focusing on the interaction between party groups and committees.

Coalition politics and parliamentary committees

Committees are established to make parliaments more efficient. They facilitate specialization, and thereby enhance a parliament's ability to influence legislation and hold the government accountable. While there is much variation among European legislatures, most parliaments have strengthened the role of committees in order to reduce the informational advantage of the executive (Mattson and Strøm 1995).

The same applies to the EP (Mamadouh and Raunio 2003). Unlike many national constitutions, the EU treaties leave it up to the Parliament to design its internal rules. The EP has structured and reformed its internal organization so as to make the most of its hard-won powers in the EU political system (Kreppel 2002). As the EP has gained new powers, the full chamber has delegated more authority to committees. The thrust of legislative work is done in committees, in which individual rapporteurs draft reports that form the basis for parliamentary resolutions. Committees are also key forums for holding institutions such as the Commission and the European Central Bank (ECB) to account, and in shaping the EU's budget and monitoring its implementation. The 2009–14 Parliament has twenty committees.

Parliament's positions are, in most cases in practice, decided in the committees before the plenary stage. Indeed, this system has enabled the EP to be successful in using its legislative and appointment powers. When explaining this success, scholars have emphasized the interaction between party groups and committees. More specifically, the rapporteurship system, with parliamentary resolutions and amendments based on reports drafted by individual members, is often identified as crucial (Bowler and Farrell 1995). As committees enjoy extensive procedural rights in processing legislation and in shaping the EP's agenda, the key question for the party groups is therefore how and to what extent they influence committee proceedings.

Representation on committees is roughly proportional to group size, with committee memberships and chairs reallocated at mid-term (after two-and-a-half years). Research on committee appointments by Bowler and Farrell (1995: 227) shows that 'the share of committee places is proportional by both nationality and ideological bloc. Within these limits, set by allocations along ideological or national lines, there is scope for the kinds of specialized membership and recruitment made in the US Congress' (see also McElroy 2006; Yordanova 2009). Within committees are four positions of authority: chairperson; vice-chairs; party group coordinators; and rapporteurs. Committees elect their own chairs, but in practice party groups decide the allocation of chairs and vice-chairs, with the d'Hondt method[6] used for distributing the chairs. Chair allocation is thus broadly proportional, again reflecting procedures used in most national parliaments (Mattson and Strøm 1995). Party group coordinators are responsible for coordinating the work of their groups in the committees. Together with the committee chair, the coordinators negotiate the distribution of rapporteurships between the groups.

Turning to the passage of legislation, when the draft act arrives in the Parliament from the Commission, a committee is designated as responsible for producing a report on the issue, with one or more committees assigned as opinion-giving committees. Committees use an auction-like points system for distributing reports to the groups, with group coordinators making bids on behalf of their groups. The allocation of reports is also roughly proportional to group strength in the Parliament. However, because the points total of each group is proportional to its seat share in the chamber, the most expensive reports (those that 'cost' the most points), such as those on the EU budget or on important pieces of codecision legislation, are largely controlled by the two largest groups, EPP and S&D (Mamadouh and Raunio 2003; Kaeding 2005; Hausemer 2006; Hoyland 2006).

The rapporteur must be prepared to make compromises. Majority-building as early as the stage at which reports are drafted helps to facilitate the smooth passage of the report in the committee and in the plenary. The draft report, together with amendments (tabled by any member), is voted upon in the committee. Before the plenary, the groups decide their positions: what amendments to propose, and whether or not to support the report. National party delegations often hold their own meetings prior to the group meetings. Finally, the report and amendments (by the responsible committee, a party group, or at least forty members) are voted upon in the plenary.

Because committees enjoy extensive procedural rights in the Parliament, it is in the interest of both the party groups and national parties to influence committee work. Party groups monitor committee proceedings, with group coordinators and working parties playing key roles. The procedures for allocating committee chairs, seats, and reports, all roughly based on proportionality, can also be seen as mechanisms for the party groups to control the committees. Importantly, national parties are key players in allocating committee seats and reports, and there are signs that they are, to an increasing extent, using committee assignments to achieve their policy goals. Nonetheless, research suggests that party-group influence within committees is ultimately based on coordinating mechanisms for overseeing committee work instead of hierarchical structures for controlling MEP behaviour in the committees. Delegating authority to backbenchers through committee work and reports can also be understood as a key way of rewarding group members and tying them into the formation of group positions (Hausemer 2006; Settembri and Neuhold 2009; Ringe 2010; Whitaker 2011).

Coalition-building at the plenary stage is more clearly driven by partisan concerns. Roll-call analyses show that the main cleavage structuring competition in the Parliament is the familiar Left–Right dimension, with the anti/pro-integration dimension constituting the second main structure of competition in the Parliament (Hix *et al.* 2007; see also McElroy and Benoit 2007).[7] While the primary decision rule in the Parliament is simple majority, for certain issues (mainly budget amendments and second-reading legislative amendments adopted under the codecision or 'ordinary' procedure), the EP needs to have absolute majorities (50 per cent plus one additional MEP). This absolute majority requirement facilitates cooperation between the two main groups, EPP and S&D, which between them control around two-thirds of the seats. Cooperation between EPP and S&D is also influenced by inter-institutional consideration, because the Parliament has needed to moderate its resolutions in order to get its amendments accepted by the Council and the Commission (Kreppel 2002). Competition on the Left–Right continuum has benefited the smaller groups. This advantage has applied particularly to the liberals: situated ideologically between EPP and S&D, the liberals have often been in a pivotal position in forming winning coalitions. Recent enlargements have not really changed either group cohesion levels or coalition patterns in the chamber. Party cohesion has remained stable, and the two main groups voted together almost exactly the same amount of times in the 2004–09 Parliament (68 per cent of the time) as in the previous electoral period (Hix and Noury 2009). But how MEPs vote hardly matters from the point of view of EP elections, as is argued in the next section.

Electoral accountability

Voting decisions in EP elections are heavily influenced by the domestic party-political environment (van der Eijk and Franklin 1996; Schmitt 2009). The primacy of domestic factors results in part from the strategies of national parties, which control candidate selection and carry out the electoral campaigns. Most national parties have so far fought EP elections on domestic issues. National parties are mainly based on the traditional social cleavages recognized in political science literature, and because the anti/pro-integration dimension tends to cross-cut these cleavages, parties often experience internal fragmentation on EU questions (see, for example, Hix and

Lord 1997; Hix 1999; Marks and Wilson 2000; Marks and Steenbergen 2004). More-over, survey data shows that parties are, on average, more representative of their voters on traditional Left–Right matters than on issues related to European integra-tion, with the parties more supportive of integration than the electorate (Mattila and Raunio 2006). Hence established parties have an incentive to contest the elections along the familiar Left–Right dimension and to downplay contestation over integra-tion. Indeed, in most member states, parties have preferred not to engage in debates over the EU—and where such debates have taken place, this contestation has often benefited smaller parties at the expense of mainstream governing parties (Szczerbiak and Taggart 2008).

Elections to the Parliament are therefore scarcely 'European'—they are held dur-ing the same week, and the candidates compete for seats in an EU institution, but there is no common electoral system,[8] constituency boundaries do not cross national borders, and campaigning is conducted by national parties on the basis of largely national agendas. So national politics is reproduced in EP elections, with the same set of actors and largely also the same set of issues. While it is true that the lack of discussion on the constitutional aspects of the EU (more or less integration) is po-tentially very damaging, the current situation is arguably not without its merits (Mair 2000; Thomassen 2009). By reproducing the ideological cleavages dividing party families at the national level, and by offering the electorates familiar faces and themes, national parties have probably facilitated electoral mobilization in EP elec-tions. One could also argue that the focus on Left–Right issues in the campaigns is a positive factor in light of the EP's powers and the representation of citizens' opin-ions: the Parliament has no formal say over constitutional questions, the group structure of the EP is based on the Left–Right dimension, and the congruence of opinions between the representatives and the voters is higher on Left–Right matters than on integration issues.

But, interestingly, recent evidence points in the direction of the EU, as an issue, becoming increasingly politicized and salient (Steenbergen and Scott 2004; Benoit and Laver 2006; Pennings 2006; Netjes and Binnema 2007). Eurosceptical parties have benefited from more negative public opinion towards the EU and also several mainstream parties—such as conservative parties—have adopted more critical views of integration (Hooghe 2007; Hooghe and Marks 2007). Analysing the 2004 and 2009 EP elections, Hobolt *et al.* (2009: 111) show how preference congruence between parties and their supporters over EU impacted on the vote shares of national parties:

governing parties may lose votes because of the disconnect between major governing parties and their voters on the issue of EU integration, and the fact that EP elections make this issue, and therefore this disconnect, more prominent. On both the contextual and individual levels, it appears that Europe can matter when voters go to the polls. Governing-party voters who are more sceptical about further integration are more likely to defect or abstain in EP elections.

However, while parties thus have a good reason to take the EU seriously, these developments need to be understood in the context of the second-order logic of EP elections, with smaller and opposition parties gaining votes at the expense of mainstream and government parties (Reif and Schmitt 1980; van der Eijk and Franklin 1996; Manow and Döring 2008; Schmitt 2009; Hix and Marsh 2011).

Parties at the European level

The main party groups in the Parliament are either officially, or in practice, the parliamentary wings of their Europarties. Article 138a of the Maastricht Treaty assigned political parties a specific role to play in the political system of the European Union: 'Political parties at the European level are important as a factor for integration within the Union. They contribute to forming a European awareness and to expressing the political will of the citizens of the Union.' This 'Party Article' has now been included in the Lisbon Treaty (Art. 10, para. 4): 'Political parties at European level contribute to forming European political awareness and to expressing the will of citizens of the Union.'

The constitutional recognition in the form of the Party Article in the Maastricht Treaty contributed to the consolidation of Europarties. With the exception of the EPP, which had already been founded back in 1976, the other federations of national parties were quickly turned into Europarties. The Confederation of Socialist Parties of the European Community (CSP), founded in 1974, was transformed into PES in November 1992. The Federation of European Liberal, Democrat and Reform Parties, founded in 1976, became ELDR in December 1993. The European Federation of Green Parties (EFGP) was established in June 1993, changing its name to the European Green Party (EGP) in 2004. In addition, a number of smaller Europarties have been established since the introduction in 2004 of public funding of Europarties from the EU's budget (Johansson and Raunio 2005).

It is still more realistic to describe Europarties as federations of national parties or as party networks (see, for example, Ladrech 2000; Bardi 2002), at least when comparing them with the often centralized and hierarchical parties found at the national level. At the same time, there can be no doubt that the constitutional and political changes that have taken place since the early 1990s have contributed to changes in the influence and organization of the Europarties. Internally, Europarties have introduced organizational reforms that reduce their dependence on individual member parties. In particular, (qualified) majority voting is now the standard decision rule in the main organs of the Europarties. The political environment in which the Europarties exist has also changed fundamentally. The empowerment of the Parliament, in terms both of legislative powers and of holding the Commission accountable, means that the Europarties' EP groups are in a key position to influence the EU policy process.

The exact policy influence of Europarties is practically impossible to measure, and depends primarily on the willingness of national member parties to pursue and implement the agreed policy objectives. However, the Europarties serve as important arenas for the diffusion of ideas and policy coordination. Particularly the meetings of party leaders, held usually at the same venue as the summits of the European Council, enable national parties to coordinate their actions prior to the summits.[9] Moreover, Europarties prepare the ground for future enlargements by integrating interests from the prospective member states. Through their membership in the Europarties, parties from the applicant countries engage in partisan cooperation that is important in nurturing wider, pan-European political allegiances (Hix and Lord 1997; Ladrech 2000; Johansson and Zervakis 2002; Lightfoot 2005; Hanley 2008).

Ideologically, the Europarties have become increasingly similar, especially after social democrats (PES) and greens (EGP) changed their attitudes to European integration. In fact, while support for deeper integration was stronger among the centre-Right parties (EPP and ELDR) until the 1990s, since the Maastricht Treaty, the centre-Left (PES and also partially the greens) have become the leading advocates of further centralization (Hix 1999; Gabel and Hix 2002). Nevertheless, when examining both the issues that the Europarties prioritize and their positions on socio-economic issues, it is obvious that the parties have different objectives. For example, in the 2009 European elections, EPP and ELDR had quite typical centre-Right programmes, with emphasis on economic competitiveness and eradicating remaining barriers to trade, with centre-Left Europarties—PES and Greens—in turn placing more emphasis on solidarity, full employment, and social and environmental issues.

In fact, advocates of supranational EU democracy argue that such differences between Europarties should be elevated to a decisive role in European governance. Indeed, there has emerged quite a lively debate about whether the EP should become a fully fledged 'federal' parliament that elects and controls a genuine EU government. The defenders of such a parliamentary model, or stronger supranational democracy in general, argue that because the EU already possesses significant authority over a broad range of policy areas, the choice of who exercises such authority should be based on competition between political forces—in this scenario, essentially Europarties contesting the EP elections (Follesdal and Hix 2006; Hix 2008). More cautious voices argue that this not the right way in which to address the democratic deficit, partly on account of the lack of common European identity and because issues that are most salient to voters are still decided nationally (Moravcsik 2002). Others have pointed out that installing party government at the EU level may not be a good solution in an era during which political parties are facing serious difficulties in the context of national democracies (Mair and Thomassen 2010).

In this parliamentary model, the government (the Commission) would be accountable to the EP and could be voted out of office by the latter—as already happens. Europarties would put forward their candidates for the Commission President (the EU's 'prime minister'). These candidates would campaign on the basis of their

Europarties' manifestos. After receiving the support of the Parliament, the winning candidate would form his or her government (Box 15.2 shows the potential governments after the 2009 EP elections), with the other party groups forming the parliamentary opposition. The party groups of the governing Europarties should be cohesive enough to enable the government to execute its programme once in office. The last point might require more hierarchical and centralized Europarties, and perhaps even giving the Europarties the right to influence or determine candidate selection in EP elections.[10]

The introduction of the parliamentary model would change fundamentally the role of the Commission by making it explicitly a party-political institution (and not anymore so much a 'neutral' defender of the common EU interest or a guardian of the treaties). However, the change might not be that big after all, because the link between EP elections and the composition of the Commission has become more direct since the early 1990s. As both the Commission and its President have to be

---

BOX 15.2   **Forming an EU government after the 2009 EP elections**

Before the elections, at least the main Europarties—EPP, PES (S&D group in the Parliament), ELDR (ALDE) group, EGP (Greens/EFA)—and potentially also other party families, such as the conservatives (ECR) and Eurosceptics (EFD), would put forward their own candidates for the Commission President. At this stage, the Europarties might also make public commitments about sharing or not sharing power with certain other parties.

   After the elections, the winning candidate would enter into negotiations with other Europarties about forming a coalition EU government. In 2009, there were essentially three alternatives for forming such a government, as follows.

Alternative 1: a grand coalition between EPP and S&D, with the Commission President coming from the EPP

This would have been the safest option in terms of building the needed majorities, but it would also have led to a weak opposition in the chamber (particularly if the liberals were also in the government).

Alternative 2: a centre-Right coalition between EPP, ALDE, and G/EFA and/ or ECR, with the Commission President representing the EPP

This coalition would have had a narrower majority, but it would probably have been also ideologically more cohesive than the grand coalition.

Alternative 3: a centre-Left minority coalition between S&D, ALDE, EUL–NGL, and G/EFA, with the Commission President representing the social democrats

Such a minority coalition, common in Nordic countries, would have been appointed by, and would rule with the support of, the opposition groups.

approved by the Parliament before they can take office, the EP has explicitly demanded and made sure that the verdict of the voters has influenced the composition of the Commission.

Since the 2004 elections, there has also been a kind of government–opposition divide in the Parliament. With the EPP, the largest group and the centre-Right groups having a majority in the Parliament (and as centre-Right cabinets have also dominated the Council), the 2004–09 and 2009–14 Commissions have leaned in partisan terms towards the centre-Right, with a clear majority of Commissioners and the Commission President representing either EPP or ELDR member parties. Not surprisingly, there has thus been a firm 'centre-Right' grip on EU politics that has certainly left its mark on legislation. Therefore the leftist party groups—S&D, G/EFA, and EUL–NGL after the 2009 elections—have been more critical of the Commission while the centre-Right groups are more supportive of it. In fact, the shift to the Right began already in the 1999 elections, when the EPP emerged as the largest group (Warntjen *et al.* 2008). Europarties may not be familiar to European voters, but party politics clearly matters in EU politics.

Conclusions

The party groups in the EP are often underestimated, or even ridiculed, by national media. Certainly, from the outside, these groups may appear to be somewhat strange creatures. After all, they bring together representatives from as many as twenty-seven countries, with a plethora of languages spoken in the Parliament's meeting rooms and corridors.

However, such characterizations are quite simply not accurate. The Parliament as an institution has structured its internal organization so as to maximize its influence in the EU. The thrust of legislative work is done in the committees, in which individual rapporteurs draft reports that form the basis for parliamentary resolutions. In a similar fashion, the party groups have designed their rules of procedure and divided labour within them so as to make the most of the Parliament's hard-won legislative powers. And research clearly shows that the EP groups have indeed mastered the art both of bargaining with other EU institutions and of achieving unitary group behaviour.

Another often-aired claim is that MEPs and their national parties live in different worlds, with lack of will and conflicting preferences over integration preventing meaningful cooperation. While there is some truth to such arguments, these divisions do not mean that MEPs are divorced from their national parties or constituencies. On the contrary, MEPs remain firmly connected to national politics through a variety of channels, with most of them holding simultaneously various offices in their parties (either at the local, district, or national level), and maintaining active links with their party organizations and voters. And, as recent evidence clearly shows, national parties are investing more resources in links with their MEPs, at least partly in order to further their own policy objectives. Moreover, it is interesting to note that, overall, the preferences of national MPs and MEPs over integration are quite similar, and that, contrary to much accepted wisdom, MEPs do not 'go native' in Brussels—that is, become considerably more pro-European than their party comrades back home (Scully 2005).

The biggest, and most demanding, challenge for the party groups is to connect with EU citizens. This point applies to both connecting vertically with the citizens in individual EU countries and to forging horizontal cross-national linkages. First, considering the lack of a common EU-wide identity and the absence of any real European government, EP elections are bound to remain 'second-order' contests in comparison with elections to national parliaments. This status means also that the party groups in the Parliament will remain unknown to most Europeans. Second, while the Europarties and their EP groups undoubtedly perform an important role by integrating political interests across the Union, this integrative function takes place almost exclusively among national political elites, thus leaving the electorate to focus on national or local politics. To put it simply, Europeans do not know how and to what extent the EP party groups influence EU policies.

 NOTES

1. For analyses of party groups in the pre-1979 Parliament, see van Oudenhove (1965), Fitzmaurice (1975), and Pridham and Pridham (1981).

2. In fact, the title 'European Democrats' was added to the EPP's group name after the 1999 elections so that the Tories could maintain their separate identity in the otherwise strongly pro-integrationist EPP group. Before the 2004 elections, the group struck a deal with the Conservatives, who had threatened to leave the group and ally with other conservative parties that are critical of further integration. This deal caused a lot of controversy in the group—and in the end resulted in a section of MEPs defecting to the ELDR after the 2004 elections. According to that deal, the Conservatives had a right to voice their own views on European constitutional and institutional matters, and had more favourable financing and staffing terms within the group, including the right to one of the group's vice-presidents.

3. This cosy pact was temporarily suspended after the 1999 elections, when a centre-Right coalition elected Nicole Fontaine (EPP) as the new President in July 1999. Imitating the deals between EPP and PES, the EPP and ELDR struck an agreement according to which the Liberals would support Fontaine and the EPP would, in turn, back the candidacy of ELDR group leader Pat Cox at mid-term in January 2002.

4. Europarty labels can be counterproductive for national parties. In their discussion on parties in the US House of Representatives, Cox and McCubbins (1993) argue that members of Congress have an incentive to be loyal to their party groups, because the

reputation of their groups is important in terms of re-election. Distancing oneself, or the national party, from the Europarty can actually be a wise electoral strategy for MEPs, especially in those member states in which the public is less supportive of European integration.

5. Groups comprising MEPs from only one country (such as Forza Europa in 1994–95) have not been permitted since the 1999 elections.

6. Named after its inventor, Belgian mathematician Victor d'Hondt, the method is used for allocating seats in electoral systems based on proportional representation. The party group winning most seats in the Parliament gets the first committee chair, and the number of seats held by that group is then divided by two and compared with the seat shares of the other groups. The group with most seats at this point receives the second committee chair. The process continues until all committee chairs have been allocated.

7. There is also a debate concerning the validity of the roll-call data. Because recorded votes represent only a sample of the totality of votes in the Parliament, the representativeness of that sample is a crucial matter—particularly when studying conflict dimensions in the EP (Carrubba *et al.* 2006).

8. The design of the electoral system impacts on MEPs' contacts with their electorates, with MEPs from more 'open' systems paying more attention to individual voters and constituency interests (Farrell and Scully 2007, 2010).

9. While scholars have paid more attention to the role of parties and party preferences in EU decision-making since the late 1990s, this strand of research is still quite undeveloped, particularly in terms of measuring and explaining party links between the EP, Council, the Commission, and even the European Council (see Lindberg *et al.* 2008).

10. For another and more detailed illustration of how such a parliamentary model would work, see Hix (2008: 166–78). An alternative approach would be that of having a direct election of the Commission President. In such a 'presidential' model, the candidates would also be put forward by Europarties (Decker and Sonnicksen 2011).

FURTHER READING

The first book to focus on the role of political parties in the EU, Hix and Lord (1997) remains relevant today, with chapters on national parties, EP party groups, and Europarties. Kreppel (2002) provides a data-rich account of the development of the EP's party system. The special issue of the *Journal of Common Market Studies* edited by Hix and Scully (2003), published on the occasion of the EP's half-centennial, contains articles by leading experts on various aspects of the Parliament, including its party system, committees, and policy influence. Comparing the electoral systems used in EP elections, Farrell and Scully (2007) analyse how the design of the electoral systems impacts on the composition of the Parliament, and the attitudes and behaviour of the MEPs. Based on a large data set of roll-call votes since the 1979 elections, Hix *et al.* (2007) explain party-group voting in the chamber, with particular focus on voting cohesion and coalition formation. Ringe (2010) examines how MEPs make decisions in the Parliament, with particular focus on the interaction between committees and party groups. Whitaker (2011) offers a systematic analysis of how the EP's committees have changed over time and analyses how national parties use the committees to further their policy objectives.

Farrell, D. M. and Scully, R. (2007) *Representing Europe's Citizens? Electoral Institutions and the Failure of Parliamentary Representatio*n (Oxford: Oxford University Press).

Hix, S., and Lord, C. (1997) *Political Parties in the European Union* (Basingstoke: Macmillan).

Hix, S. and Scully, R. (2003) (eds) 'The European Parliament at Fifty', *Journal of Common Market Studies*, 41/2 (special issue).

Hix, S., Noury, A. G., and Roland, G. (2007) *Democratic Politics in the European Parliament* (Cambridge: Cambridge University Press).

Kreppel, A. (2002) *The European Parliament and the Supranational Party System: A Study of Institutional Development* (Cambridge: Cambridge University Press).

Ringe, N. (2010) *Who Decides, and How? Preferences, Uncertainty, and Policy Choice in the European Parliament* (Oxford: Oxford University Press).

Whitaker, R. (2011) *The European Parliament's Committees: National Party Control and Legislative Empowerment* (Abingdon: Routledge).

WEB LINKS

European Liberal, Democrat and Reform Party: http://www.eldr.eu
European People's Party: http://www.epp.eu
European Green Party: http://europeangreens.eu
Party of European Socialists: http://www.pes.org

The websites of the party groups provide information on the members and national parties in the groups, and the internal organization of the groups, together with policy statements, press releases, and latest news regarding the groups. The homepages of the four main Europarties provide a brief history of the parties, their election and policy programmes, and links to national member parties, the EP party group, and affiliated organizations.

http://www.votewatch.eu
Votewatch is a constantly updated website using statistics from the EP's homepage to provide comprehensive data on the attendance, voting, and other activities of MEPs, party groups, and national parties.

http://www.lse.ac.uk/collections/EPRG/
Founded in 1998, the European Parliament Research Group (EPRG) brings together the leading scholars on the EP from Europe and North America, with the home page offering downloadable data and working papers.

CHAPTER 16

Social and Regional Interests: the Economic and Social Committee and the Committee of the Regions

Charlie Jeffery and Carolyn Rowe

▌ Summary

Since its founding moment, the European integration project has provided for the formal inclusion of social and regional interests through, first, the European Economic and Social Committee (EESC), created in 1957, and more recently, a Committee of the Regions (CoR), established in 1994. While neither has full institutional status nor any degree of codecision rights, they provide something of a focal point for organized social and regional interests. Their impact, however, remains debatable. Some minor 'successes' in shaping policy outcomes by no means suggest a role and function on a par with the European Commission, European Parliament (EP), or European Council. The validity of these EU-funded bodies has been brought into question, as interest groups have shown themselves to be able to engage in the policy process without the need for a formalized representative structure. Nonetheless, such is the symbolic force of both organizations that their future looks to be secure.

Introduction

The Economic and Social Committee (EESC) and the Committee of the Regions (CoR) are two formal bodies that were established to represent two specific sets of interests within the European Union's inter-institutional nexus— the interests of employers and employees, and regional interests, respectively. Neither enjoys full institutional status, and each instead relies largely on goodwill and informal contacts to gain access to the heart of the decision-making process. As the number of competing interests in Brussels grows, both bodies are faced with the need to maintain their relevance. Squeezed to the margins of the policy process, existential questions now cast a very large shadow over their role, function, and operation. What is their relevance in the contemporary European political system? What value do they add to EU decision-making?

This chapter considers the role and purpose of these two bodies. It begins with a historical consideration of their establishment, and examines the extent to which the context in which they were founded continues to provide a rationale and legitimacy for their operation. The chapter then looks at the manner in which the operations of both bodies have had to develop over time in response to the shifting institutional circumstances in which they find themselves. The development of both bodies tells the story of how interest mediation in the EU has expanded, pushing these formal vehicles of social and regional interest representations to the fringes of policy networks. The chapter then moves on to an analysis of the contemporary operation of both bodies, assessing how they continue to contribute to European politics and analysing their real added value.

Although launched in such different eras, the EESC and CoR have a remarkable amount in common. Much of this commonality was deliberate. The EESC served as the institutional template for the establishment of the CoR. The internal structures of the two bodies are similar, as is their advisory status. They share a newly renovated headquarters at the heart of the EU district in Brussels. More fundamentally, they had similar founding rationales: to mobilize additional input felt, at the time of their creation, to be valuable for the European decision-making process. In neither case, though, have many observers been convinced that this rationale of added value has been delivered.

The origins and history of the EESC and CoR

The EESC and CoR were each fashioned in treaty negotiations held at critical stages in the European integration process. The Treaty of Rome, which established the EESC, built out radically in 1958 from the narrow foundations of the European Coal and Steel Community (ECSC) to inaugurate a much wider project of economic integration. The Maastricht Treaty of 1992, which provided for the creation of a committee of regional interests in the EU, was an ambitious response to market deepening, new global economic pressures, and, above all, the collapse of the Iron Curtain. At such critical moments as these, negotiating agendas are fluid and windows of opportunity for new, and often unanticipated initiatives, can emerge. The EESC and CoR both fall into this category.

The idea of establishing an economic and social committee as part of the new European Economic Community (EEC) emerged only in 1956 and was finally agreed just two months before the Treaty of Rome was concluded in March 1957 (Smismans 2000: 4). It was brought onto the agenda by two of the smaller players in the negotiations, Belgium and the Netherlands. Their aim was to reproduce the corporatist models provided by their domestic social and economic councils—forums for consulting business and trade unions in economic policy-making—in the new EEC framework. The proposals fell on fertile ground: five of the founding six member states (except West Germany) had similar domestic institutions (Lodge and Herman 1980: 267). Germany originally opposed the proposal due to its negative experience of a similar economic and social body, the *Reichswirtschaftsrat*, during the Weimar Republic (Hrbek 1993: 127).

Two other factors argued for an EESC and led to its adoption against West German opposition. First, the idea of bringing in the expertise of 'social partners' of business and labour to economic decision-making was consistent with both the predominantly economic logic of the early stages of the economic integration process, and the prevailing climate of corporatist interest representation. 'Europe' could even lend its own example in the form of the Consultative Committee, comprised of representatives of employers and workers (and also of traders and consumers), which had been established to support the work of the ECSC.

Second, the proposed ECSC Assembly, the forerunner to the European Parliament (EP), was to be indirectly elected, at least initially, and limited to a consultative role. As such, it did not provide 'normal' parliamentary channels for bringing interest-group influence to bear on European decision-making. In this sense, some felt that the EESC was needed as a supplementary *representative* body for the new Community, perhaps even 'as an incipient parliamentary-legislative assembly—the third organ in a tri-cameral legislature alongside the Council of Ministers and a European Parliament linked to the Commission' (Lodge and Herman 1980: 267).

The idea to establish a committee of European regional interests developed traction throughout the 1980s. The Single European Act (SEA) of 1986 had ushered in a new suite of policy responsibilities for the European level of governance, sustained by the activist Commission presidency of Jacques Delors. This expanded agenda saw European competence creep into the spheres of authority of many of Europe's local and regional governments. Furthermore, local and regional governments found themselves responsible for on-the-ground implementation of many new European policies, decisions over which they had had little input, amidst heightening tensions over the legitimate sphere of European competence. 'Strong' regions—that is, territorial entities with their own autonomous governing capacities—were disproportionately affected by the shifts of policy responsibility upwards to the European level, following the implementation of the SEA. These regions were, understandably, in the vanguard of pressuring the European institutions for change, through some kind of formal compensation for their lost responsibilities. Those member states the regions of which had been most affected as a result—Germany, Belgium, and Spain in particular—came under domestic pressure to push at an intergovernmental level for some form of regional institution in Brussels.

Whatever the tensions over legitimacy, the SEA had created a new framework of political cooperation amongst levels of authority across the member states of the European Community. As the scope of these policies grew, regional and local governments were inevitably drawn in as desirable partners in policy-making. In certain fields–in particular, structural policy after the reforms of 1988—this role became increasingly formalized, leading to the coining of the term 'multilevel governance' (Marks 1993).

At the same time, governance within EU member states came under pressure, increasing the salience of local and regional actors within new policy paradigms. Patterns of governance within the member states were being recalibrated in ways that upgraded the significance of sub-state governments. Globalization was felt to make redundant traditional forms of economic-policy intervention by central governments, and to require more differentiated economic strategies tailored to local and regional strengths. In some member states, movements for regional autonomy (re-) emerged to prominence. In each case, the result was a growing capacity among regional and local governments to engage in policy-making processes, at both the domestic and the European levels. The new multilevel governance emerged in other words from the convergence of new trends of sub-state political mobilization launched from both above and from below. From the 'bottom up', strong regions were putting pressure on their national governments to secure a stronger and more direct foothold in the policy process of the EU. From the top down, the functional rationale supporting a regional committee—'to improve the poor implementation of regional policy by member states by involving other stakeholders in its design and execution' (Warleigh 1999: 10)—was essentially the same technocratic impulse that had earlier argued for the inclusion of the economic expertise of interest groups, via the EESC, into economic integration policy.

Many of the reasons given for the CoR's lacklustre performance on the EU institutional scene following the hype that surrounded its creation were put down by commentators to the original 'birth defects' of its creation. In the eventual compromise that secured its creation by the Maastricht Treaty, those championing a third level of European decision-making had had to give way to a watered-down format that saw local mayors and councillors sit alongside the presidents of powerful and economically mighty regions and historic nations. But this compromise also reflected a strategic political decision: that powerful sets of interests in Europe did not wish to see the CoR, or the sub-state level more broadly, develop into genuinely influential policy actors.

In the initial days of its operation, the CoR, with only a consultative role to play, depended for a large extent on its relations with the Commission, the Council, and the EP for its formal relevance (Domorenok 2009: 146). The instability of this institutional position was aggravated further by the decision to make the Committee a representative vehicle for *all* subnational territorial interests from the member states, seating presidents of the German *Länder* or Spanish *Communidades Autonomas* alongside town councillors from municipalities with around 250 residents. Common positions on policy issues were difficult to establish given the diverse sets of interests represented in the CoR.

These internal divisions threatened to tear apart the newly created consultative body. But, instead, they served merely to weaken the body's potential as a significant actor in EU affairs. Its most powerful actors, and the collective power that these could wield in cooperation with a coalition of regional interests from other member states, chose rather to pursue their interests in alternative venues. The most powerful sub-state actors simply bypassed the CoR as a real force for interest representation, and instead acted through more direct channels in Brussels, such as their own permanent representations in the city, or through coalitions of similar, powerful regional actors, such as the Conference of Presidents of Regions with Legislative Power (RegLeg), the political network of EU regions with legislative competences.

This had the overall effect of marginalizing the CoR, pushing it to the fringes of EU policy debates. Clearly, the EESC and the CoR are not the only routes available through which social and regional interests can bring their concerns to bear in Europe, and the range of alternative vehicles for interest representation has expanded greatly since the two advisory bodies were established. Both interest groups and regional and local authorities routinely use alternative routes to access EU decision-making. These alternative routes offer, for some at least, greater returns than working through the EESC or CoR alone, and are logically given preference, impacting on both the credibility and the function and operation of both organizations.

The function and operation of the EESC and COR

Both the CoR and EESC have formal roles as 'consultative committees'. The CoR was established in the model of the EESC, which pre-dated it by almost forty years. Yet both the EESC and the CoR have developed an operational remit today that takes them slightly beyond the scope of their original purpose. Because their treaty positions were circumscribed in vague terms, both the EESC and the CoR have made use of their limited degree of institutional leeway to carve out a position of some authority within shifting patterns of EU governance.

Formal powers

The EESC was not generously endowed at the outset. The Rome Treaty provided for mandatory consultation of the Committee by both the Council and the Commission, in certain specified fields, and optional consultation in other areas in which the institutions consider such consultation appropriate (see Box 16.1). The Amsterdam Treaty also opened up the possibility for the EESC to be consulted by the EP, although this happens only rarely. The list of areas in which consultation is mandatory has expanded over time, in particular since the SEA. It includes agriculture, the free movement of labour, internal market issues, economic and social cohesion, social policy, regional policy, the environment, research and technological development, employment policy, equal opportunities, and public health. The Lisbon Treaty expanded the policy areas in which the EESC must be consulted to cover sports policy, European space policy, and energy. Optional consultation allows the EESC to be consulted where the Council, Commission, or EP 'consider it appropriate', and can thus cover any other aspect of the treaties (Art. 304 TFEU). Crucially, the right to

---

BOX 16.1   **EU policy fields in which EESC consultation is mandatory**

Mandatory consultation

- Agriculture
- Free movement of labour
- Internal market
- Transport
- Harmonization of tax legislation
- Approximation of laws
- Economic and social cohesion
- Social policy
- Regional policy
- Environment
- Research and technological development
- Employment policy
- Equal opportunities
- Consumer protection
- Public health
- Sports policy
- European research area
- Energy

give opinions does not extend to a right to have those opinions heard. Neither Commission nor Council, nor indeed the EP, is obliged to give any feedback on EESC opinions, let alone take them into account.

The Nice Treaty established a new category of members to the EESC: namely, consumers. Thus the EESC's representative focus was considerably broadened. Consumers, legitimately, could be considered to constitute the most significant organized civil society representatives across the EU.

The CoR was initially given more or less the same set of powers as the EESC, although the range of policy areas on which the EU institutions were obliged to consult the CoR was smaller than that of the EESC (see Box 16.2). Mandatory referrals naturally covered a rather different group of policy fields, reflecting the CoR's local and regional remit. The initial fields for mandatory consultation related to education, training and youth, economic and social cohesion, the structural funds, trans-European networks, public health, and culture. These have been extended incrementally through treaty revision and now cover aspects of employment policy, social policy, and the environment, with the Lisbon Treaty also allowing for mandatory consultation on energy and climate change policy.

The CoR is informed when the EESC is being consulted on legislative proposals. In cases in which it considers that specific regional interests are involved, it may also issue an opinion on the matter. This provision essentially extends the fields of mandatory consultation of the CoR to match those of the EESC, particularly in issues concerning agriculture.

BOX 16.2   EU policy fields in which CoR consultation is mandatory

Mandatory consultation

- Education and training
- Youth
- Economic and social cohesion
- Structural funds
- Trans-European networks
- Transport
- Public health
- Culture
- Employment policy
- Social policy
- Environmental policy
- Civil protection
- Energy and climate change policy

The CoR also has the possibility to draft 'own initiative' opinions in areas of concern that are not covered by the list of policy fields for mandatory consultation. This right was granted to the CoR on its inception. In contrast, the EESC had to wait thirty-five years, until the signing of the Maastricht Treaty, to be afforded such an opportunity (Warleigh 1999: 20).

Composition of the EESC

The memberships of the EESC and the CoR have always mirrored each other and continue to do so. Both now have 344 members, with membership distributed according to the size of the member state. Thus France, Germany, Italy, and the UK each have the largest national delegations to each body, with twenty-four members each, whilst Malta has the smallest delegation, of only five members (see Box 16.3).[1]

The EESC was established to provide for a permanent dialogue between the principal social and economic actors in Europe, and those groupings have not changed dramatically since the body's inception in 1957. The original EESC brought together members from national socio-economic organizations, divided into three groups: (I) employers' organizations (the 'Employers' Group'); (II) trade unions (the 'Workers' Group'); and (III) 'various interests'—that is, actors who did not fall naturally into either of the other group categories, and who were drawn from a broad range of civil society groupings. This last section tends to cover fields such as the social economy, consumer and environmental organizations, agricultural organizations, groups representing small business, and so on. The groups (I, II, III) function largely along the lines of the political groups found in the EP or the CoR. Their role is principally to discuss the work programme of the EESC and to develop outline positions on proposals ahead of full consideration in plenary sessions. Since 2010, members have

BOX 16.3	National memberships of the EESC and CoR
Country	**Number of seats**
France, Germany, Italy, United Kingdom	24
Poland, Spain	21
Romania	15
Austria, Belgium, Bulgaria, Czech Republic, Greece, Hungary, Netherlands, Portugal, Sweden	12
Denmark, Finland, Ireland, Lithuania, Slovakia	9
Estonia, Latvia, Slovenia	7
Cyprus, Luxembourg	6
Malta	5

been appointed for a five-year term, aligning the EESC with the norm in the EU institutions.

The sections of the EESC are where the bread-and-butter work is carried out. In this way, they are similar to the thematic commissions of the CoR or the committees of the EP: they undertake full analysis of policy proposals from the EU institutions, and draft opinions and recommendations. Within the EESC, the sections (rather than political groups, as elsewhere) appoint an individual as *rapporteur* on a proposal, whose job it is to guide the process of drafting the opinion on that issue.

Each section is made up of a membership that cross-cuts group membership. At present, there are six thematic sections, each responsible for a set of policy areas. As the sections draw in members from all three of the groups within the EESC, it is here that the 'social dialogue' between workers and employers, which is at the core of the EESC's remit, is technically facilitated. Each of these sections is referred to informally by a three-letter acronym (see Box 16.4).

Beyond these formal subject committees within the EESC, it also sets up ad hoc groups to consider broader issues of thematic concern. For example, it recently established a Consultative Commission on Industrial Change (CCMI), three 'observatories' that monitor the single market, the labour market, and sustainable development in the EU, and a steering committee on the Europe 2020 strategy for sustainable growth. All of these act in an advisory committee and produce reports for wider consideration. Plenary meetings are held over a two-day period, around ten times per year, and take place in the EP's Brussels building. The agendas of plenary sessions tend to focus on the consideration of reports and the adoption of opinions.

Composition of the CoR

Members of the CoR are appointed by national governments, who propose lists of members to the Council for adoption. At the point of its creation, there was no obligation for members appointed to the CoR to be elected representatives in their home regional or local authority. However, most member states developed an informal system for delegation that demanded some position of elected authority, and in those

---

BOX 16.4   **Sections of the EESC**

- Economic and Monetary Union, Economic and Social Cohesion (ECO)
- Single Market, Production and Consumption (INT)
- Agriculture, Rural Development and Environment (NAT)
- External Relations (REX)
- Employment, Social Affairs and Citizenship (SOC)
- Transport, Energy, Infrastructure and Information Society (TEN)

countries with clearly defined political regions, at least half of the CoR seats were allocated to regional politicians (Nugent 2010: 231).

As in the EP, policy proposals are considered in detail in subject committees, known within the CoR as 'Commissions'. Membership of each Commission cross-cuts national and party affiliations. The CoR currently operates on the basis of six thematic subject committees, which each consider policy proposals in a certain sphere of activity (see Box 16.5). Again, these are referred to internally by an acronym.

Internally, at an organizational level, successive restructuring procedures have seen the CoR become reshaped to take on a more politicized role than that originally envisaged for it. Since 2006, the CoR has begun to approximate the political procedures of the EP, being organized internally on the basis of political groups. Between them, these political groups share out the lead roles on opinion drafting and appointing the rapporteurs for each issue on the basis of a size-related points system, as is done in the EP. The establishment of strong political groups as the basis of administration within the CoR has largely superseded the position of national delegations to the CoR; it has also facilitated stronger ties between the CoR and EP, particularly on the drafting of opinions. Overall, then, the internal organization of the CoR has become increasingly sophisticated in order to reflect the growing scope of its work (Schönlau 2008: 20).

Members of the CoR are currently organized into four political groups, alongside a small subset of non-aligned members. Three of these political groups are familiar from the EP: liberals (Alliance of Liberals and Democrats for Europe, or ALDE); socialists (Party of European Socialists, or PES); and centre-Right (European People's Party, or EPP). The CoR also has a fourth group, known as the European Alliance (EA), an ad hoc mixture of independents, greens, and minority nationalists, drawn mainly from the Baltic states, Belgium, Poland, and the UK. There are significantly fewer political groups in the CoR than in the EP, because the national systems of delegating members to the CoR introduces something of an automatic filtering process. The PPE is currently the largest political grouping within the CoR, with 125 members; the PES has 113 members; the ALDE group has forty-six; and the European Alliance has thirty-five.

BOX 16.5   **Commissions of the CoR**

- Commission for Citizenship, Governance, Institutional and External Affairs (CIVEX)
- Commission for Territorial Cohesion Policy (COTER)
- Commission for Economic and Social Policy (ECOS)
- Commission for Education, Youth and Research (EDUC)
- Commission for Environment, Climate Change and Energy (ENVE)
- Commission for Natural Resources (NAT)

Leadership of the EESC

At a planning and operational level, the EESC is guided by a managerial Bureau. The Bureau is made up of thirty-six members, along with the President and two Vice Presidents. The President has oversight for the political work of the EESC and is largely responsible for providing the guidelines for that work. The President is also the figure responsible for the external representation of the Committee, interacting with the other institutions on the Committee's behalf, as well as member states and other bodies.

The Vice Presidents support and assist the President in their roles. Vice Presidential positions are held by members of the two groups that do not hold the presidency. The distribution of functions within the Bureau, sections, and any study groups established always strives to strike a balance between the three groups (Smismans 2000). The President, two Vice Presidents, and the members of the Bureau itself are elected on a two-yearly basis, and take-up of the position rotates between the three groups. The other thirty-six members include the president of each of the functional sections and each of the representative groups.

Leadership of the CoR

The organizational structure of the CoR is very similar to that of the EESC. At a political level, the CoR is managed by a Bureau, constituted by sixty members of the Assembly. The President, elected for a two-and-a-half-year term of office since Lisbon, is supported by a First Vice President and one Vice President from each of the member states. Alongside these members, there are then four chairs of the political groups represented within the CoR. Finally, the bureau is supported by twenty-seven further ordinary members of the CoR. Overall, the composition of the Bureau reflects the national and political balances within the CoR.

The Bureau then meets around seven times per year to manage planning functions, such as the agendas for plenary sessions, to draw up the CoR's policy programme, to allocate opinions to the various subject commissions, and to decide when to draft own-initiative opinions. The CoR holds fewer plenary sessions than the EESC and there are around five per year. Like EESC plenaries, however, full sessions of the CoR are also held in the EP premises in Brussels.

The EESC in practice

Despite the limited power that it had been given, there were confident expectations in the EESC that its 'accumulated expertise would be valued and exploited by the EC's institutions' and that it would be able to develop a representative role as a 'mediator on behalf of national economic and social interests vis-à-vis the Commission and the Council of Ministers' (Lodge and Herman 1980: 269). Neither expectation was fulfilled. For the Council of Ministers, the EESC was a body to be regarded with scepticism and disdain. Its output was regarded, for the most part, as simply reinforcing the supranational agenda of the European Commission, and thus was prone to run up against the buffers of intergovernmentalism. This situation does not mean that the EESC has thrived under the Commission's protection; for Lodge and Herman (1980: 276–7) the Commission viewed the EESC as 'an unimportant and at times irritating source of work because papers must be routed to it and because it is another body whose voice insists on being heard'. Thus, the EESC remains on the fringes of the European policy debate, with a limited impact on decisions. It has effectively been relegated to the status of yet another EU lobby group, struggling to compete with other consultative bodies and organized interests in Brussels.

It has, nonetheless, had its successes and these have been widely championed. For example, an EESC report on a Community Charter of Basic Social Rights formed the basis of the Commission's proposals on the Social Charter that were accepted at the Strasbourg European Summit in 1989. This episode marked the first time in its history that the EESC had been able to set the agenda decisively and before the usual decision-making process had begun. Building on this achievement, the EESC led on the issue of fundamental rights in the EU. It continues to hold this example up as its key area of influence in the European sphere across all of its marketing literature; the EU Charter of Fundamental Rights, the EESC claims, was largely the outcome of its own internal debates and subsequent opinion on the issue of fundamental rights.

Largely in recognition of its increasing marginalization and in view also of the source of its one true success, the EESC leadership in the 1990s began to shift towards presenting itself and its own role in the EU slightly differently, as a leading representative of European civil society. Throughout the 1990s, the European Commission had begun to engage more systematically with civil society organizations in policy fields such as environmental and development policy. This mode of interaction was perceived as a legitimizing force for the Commission. It subsequently developed a new normative discourse on the role of these organizations, coining the concept of 'civil dialogue' in 1996 to plead for increased interaction with civil society organizations (Smismans 2003: 484).

It was at this point that the EESC began to stress the value that it could add to this concept of a European civil dialogue, on the strength of its own cross-national, multi-sectoral composition. Subsequent presidencies of the EESC began to give priority to the so-called 'Citizen's Europe' initiative, organizing hearings that, it was claimed, gave voice to the real aspirations of the European citizens. This approach faltered, however, given the badly focused and top-down character of the hearings (Smismans 1999: 557). Nonetheless, the EESC's new focus on civil society persevered. By the late 1990s, the EESC began to tagline itself as the 'forum of organized civil society'. Since 2003, the former Economic and Social Committee (ESC), referred to informally as Ecosoc, has called itself the European Economic and Social

Committee (EESC), largely to help to differentiate it from the numerous economic and social committees that operate in the member states.

The EESC today sees its own role as threefold and this understanding of its functions puts its status as a civil society representative body at the heart of its mission. First, the EESC believes it helps to ensure that European policies and legislation better reflect economic, social, and civic concerns, by drawing on the knowledge and expertise of its members. Second, it feels that its mere existence and operation helps to promote a 'more participatory EU', given that it acts as 'organized civil society's institutional forum'. Finally, it argues that its work advances the role of civil society organizations and participatory democracy in Europe.[2] National economic and social councils exist in twenty-two of the EU's member states, and these bodies are core partners for the EESC, providing a network for their activities and a range of contacts with whom the EESC's own committees and consultative bodies interact.

Despite its composition, the EESC does not operate as an expert body within the institutional configuration of the EU, undertaking rather a more representative role. The opinions that the EESC prepares are by no means technical; rather, they reflect a compromise on an issue between the EU's principal socio-economic actors. This representative status remains the primary self-understanding of the Committee, even if stakeholders within other institutions might prefer greater technical expertise to be reflected in their opinions.

Smismans (2000) argues that the EESC could be called a functional body rather than a representative body, because one of its principal roles is to bring together the main socio-occupational groups that are active in the European policy sphere. Rather than constituting a democratically representative body, the EESC facilitates and promotes technical and sectoral integration (Smismans 2000: 7). Its representative nature is limited, because it does not represent *all* economic and social groups with an interest in European policy development; rather, it represents only the main groups, primarily from industrial production.

The CoR in practice

The initial output of the CoR was deemed to be of little added value for the general policy-making process of the Community, underpinning further a sense of marginalization. Its opinions were widely regarded as bland, of low quality, and 'invariably call[ing] for an increased sub-national participation in the EU policy-making process, but little else' (Farrows and McCarthy 1997: 26). Some major improvements have been noted over time, however. The majority of opinions produced are delivered today on the basis of either mandatory or optional inter-institutional consultations, rather than as a result of 'own-initiative' proposals from the CoR itself (Domorenok 2009: 152). This practice has helped to achieve a degree of focus in the output of the CoR, with an increased emphasis on delivering advice where its expertise would be welcomed.

While the CoR's confused birth gave rise to a situation of ambiguity in which it was not exactly clear what it was really for, successive treaty revisions and a process of internal reordering have subtly altered the role and status of the CoR, allowing the body to define its objectives more clearly. The Amsterdam Treaty extended its remit to cover legislation in around two-thirds of the EU's policy fields. But it was the Treaty of Nice that really marked a qualitative step forward in the status of the CoR, with the inclusion of a new provision that CoR members should hold some form of electoral accountability in their home locality. The Committee was thus to consist of 'representatives of regional and local bodies who either hold a regional or local authority electoral mandate or are politically accountable to an elected assembly' (Art. 300 TFEU).

The ratification and entry into force of the Lisbon Treaty in 2009 finally delivered one of the CoR's core objectives: securing its right to defend its own prerogatives before the European Court of Justice (ECJ). Of equal note is the right, also enshrined in the Lisbon Treaty, for the CoR to bring actions before the ECJ in cases in which it views legislation as having breached the principle of subsidiarity, effectively turning the CoR into the EU's subsidiarity 'watchdog'. This move, on its own, was viewed as a hugely significant advance by the CoR's supporters. Not only did it fulfil, fifteen years after its inception, one of the CoR's longest-standing aims, but it also finally elevated the CoR above the status of the EESC. Indeed, new Rules of Procedure drafted for the CoR in the wake of the Lisbon Treaty have sought to mainstream the CoR's role as the new subsidiarity watchdog of Europe into the output of the Committee.[3] The Lisbon Treaty also provided for further changes that were perceived as having strengthened the CoR and its role in the European legislative process. First, the Treaty increased its members' term of office from four to five years, bringing the CoR in line with other EU institutions, notably the EP and the Commission. In addition, the Lisbon Treaty saw a widening of the CoR's area of consultation to include new policy areas: energy and climate change. Consultation rights were also strengthened, so that the CoR can now be consulted by the EP, as well as the Commission and Council of Ministers, in the areas of common concern set out by the EU treaties.

At a more abstract level, the Lisbon Treaty wrote into law the fundamental objective of 'territorial cohesion' in the EU. This shift marked a further step change for the CoR's inter-institutional relations, as it continues to promote territorial cohesion through its own work and operation. In a separate move that articulates this objective more precisely, the Treaty on European Union (TEU) was revised to enshrine the right to local and regional self-government in EU law (Art. 4, para. 2 TEU).

However, it is at the level of internal organization that the primary change has taken place over the course of the CoR's existence. Observers feared at the outset that internal divisions within the CoR—northern versus southern European regions; strong versus weak regions; rich versus poor; and so on—would prevent the new body from developing a clear sense of purpose. Yet while these internal disparities have encouraged the stronger, constitutionally empowered regions at the very least to prioritize alternative channels of interest mediation in the EU, dividing lines have not proven as destructive as was first feared. Indeed, despite all of these obvious lines of conflict that the CoR's original template design established, today those lines of potential conflict have been replaced by real lines of conflict between the sets of actors who strive to achieve influence within the body: the political groups and the national delegations (Hönnige and Kaiser 2003).

The CoR's original institutional composition did not include political groups. As an advisory body, *national* delegations were established to represent territorial interests on a member state by member state basis. On that model, the two most important organizational structures were the national delegations and thematic commissions. However, over the years, the operation of the CoR and its leaderships have seen the body evolve in a more 'politicized' direction, with lines of conflict opening up between the interests of party groups, much along the same lines as party groups within the EP. Today, the party groups are the most significant structures within the CoR, a development that few expected (Christiansen 1996). This development has had a substantial impact on inter-institutional relations: the operation of the main party groupings within both the CoR and the EP has inevitably led to closer links between these two bodies than with either the Commission or the Council of Ministers. Through the contacts at the level of secretariats and individual rapporteurs, the political groups try to bring the positions of the institutions closer together and thereby to increase the chance that the consultative output of the CoR is taken into account in the wider EU decision-making process.

In terms of impact, it is difficult for the CoR to improve on its engagement with the principal decision-making institutions of the EU (Commission, Council, Parliament), given that its opinions are generally only ever sent by internal post. There is no formal mechanism in place for follow-up discussions, or feedback from the decision-making institutions themselves. In recognition of this shortcoming, targeted steps have been taken to secure greater impact in the policy process. For example, on any opinion produced, a core set of the recommendations that it entails are now also printed on the outside, so that even if the opinion itself is not widely read, its overall message can have some potential impact on the desk of whichever official to whom it is sent. This change may seem minor, but it is a significant one.

Of even more significance is the degree to which links with the European Commission, the most important champion and partner of the CoR since its inception, have incrementally been strengthened. For example, a new protocol, signed with the European Commission in 2001, went some way towards improving this situation. In particular, this agreement committed the Commission to attending more of the CoR's plenary sessions, and delivering input into discussions on draft opinions. On average, two Commissioners now attend each of the CoR's plenary sessions, and the Commission President takes part at least once a year. In addition, the use of non-mandatory referrals by the European Commission to the CoR has also risen sharply (Schönlau 2008: 23).

The EESC and the CoR in context

Evidently, then, both the EESC and the CoR have developed their roles within the institutional architecture of the EU in ways that go beyond the initial activity originally foreseen for them at the moment of their founding. Their operation and functions today show that these bodies have adapted to the changing nature of European governance and how they have sought to carve out roles for themselves, whilst continuing to face calls for their closure. Dissenting views on the value added of both organizations, the CoR and EESC alike, are not uncommon and periodically make headline news. For example, in 2011, in its position paper on the new EU budget post-2013, the (liberal) ALDE group of the EP called for a both a radical shake-up of the CoR and possible abolition of the EESC (ALDE 2011).

Against this background of constant debate about their legitimacy, both the CoR and the EESC have increasingly bought into the narrative of 'participatory democracy' and 'input legitimacy' in the EU. Both have sought to maximize their civil-society and grass-roots connections as an entry ticket to wider policy negotiations. In this vein, the CoR has also sought to support initiatives that explore the concept of multilevel governance in practice, as a means to bolster its own position in the European policy process. Their representative structures, both bodies claim, facilitate better connections between Europe's decision-makers and the citizen; this claim then, is their argument for greater status as policy actors in the institutional framework of the EU. Some commentators continue to argue that the EESC and the CoR are only important at a symbolic level, in that it is useful for the EU to recognize the territorial disparity of its member states through a formal committee that discusses regional and local perspectives on policy. Others suggest that both bodies do have a legitimate role to play in European decision-making, largely on account of their representative character (Smismans 2000). These views stress that it does add something to the legitimacy of the European policy process if the decision-making system incorporates a formalized, permanent committee of economic and social interests.

This new approach has mutual benefits. For an EU polity in search of greater popular support, the potential linkages that both the EESC and CoR can offer on the ground has provided new opportunities for strengthening their own position within the institutional configuration of Brussels. First, they were active in the context of the Commission's White Paper on European governance in 2000 and subsequently in debates relating to the future of Europe undertaken by the European Convention. Both the EESC and CoR began explicitly to use the discourse on civil society and civil dialogue at the EU level as an element of legitimation for their activities and institutional position (Smismans 2003: 493).

Neither the EESC nor the CoR presses for formalized powers of codecision. Nevertheless, they have, since the Convention on the Future of Europe and subsequent enquiries into a stronger EU communications policy, including former Vice-President of the European Commission Margot Wallström's 'Plan D for Democracy,

Dialogue and Debate' agenda,[4] moved to emphasize their credentials on the basis of their civil-society status. Indeed, the EESC has launched an initiative to act as a key communicator of EU policy and goals under the umbrella of the Commission's own initiative on 'Communicating Europe'.

The EESC argues that its own value-added in the EU is to bring in a wealth of disparate views into the policy-making nexus, albeit on the fringes of institutional status. It is their history and connection—alongside their physical position today in a shared 'home' with the CoR, next to the EP, and at the heart of the Brussels policy scene—that, in the views of the institution's champions, necessitate its continued existence and operation. Their mantra is that politics in the EU 'is not just about elections', and that they offer a degree of technical expertise that the EP lacks.

Since the early 1990s, the concept of a European civil society, broadly defined, has become common currency within the EU's discourse, yet (unsurprisingly perhaps) some institutions and bodies have held on more firmly to these notions than others. For the Commission, the normative dialogue on stronger engagement with civil-society actors in social-policy decisions has gradually spread to all of its Directorates-General (DGs), and forms the basis of its policy on interaction with external representatives (Smismans 2003). For the EESC and, to a lesser degree, the CoR, the growing notion of a civil dialogue allowed them to reinforce their strategies to gain a stronger voice in European affairs, by emphasizing their connection to grass-roots concerns in the member states, both with regard to social and economic partners and to local and regional authorities. In light of this new approach, the EESC began to present itself more forcefully as an institutional expression of the organizations making up civil society (*ibid.*). In fact, the EESC currently markets itself with the strapline 'a bridge between Europe and organised civil society'.[5] It emphasizes that its operation helps to strengthen the EU's democratic legitimacy and effectiveness by enabling civil-society organizations from the member states to express their views at the European level. But the Committee's focus is not restricted to the EU member states. Like the CoR, the EESC has an active external relations agenda. It engages in civil-society dialogue such as round tables with Brazil, China, and India, and connects regularly with civil-society groups in the European neighbourhood, all carried out under an annual operational budget of around €120 million per year.

In more general terms, both organizations emphasize the validity of their engagement with the community outside the Brussels 'loop'. That community extends to European civil society and local and regional authorities. On taking office in 2010, the new EESC President Staffan Nilsson, a farmer, launched his work programme and priorities in 2010 under two headline sound bites: 'cultivating a stronger European civil society'; and 'engaging people for a sustainable Europe'.

Again, beyond the original remit set for the CoR as an advisory body, the CoR has developed a profile as a facilitator of regional engagement, leading on particular issues of note and championing certain objectives that it selects, in cooperation with various other regional stakeholders. This move has seen the CoR begin to open its doors to regional representatives and their associations to host debates, workshops, conferences, and events that consider issues of shared concern. With its new large new building and central location in Brussels, the CoR is well placed to do this, even if this new role is rather at odds with its original focus on contributing opinions to the EU legislative process. As such, this shift represents a new interpretation of the loosely defined role and scope of a CoR within the EU's institutional environment.

Chief amongst the new activities that embrace wider regional support in Brussels include regular forums on thematic issues such as communications, transport policy, and social innovation, the Europe 2020 monitoring platform, which aims to track the implementation and development of the Lisbon Strategy at the regional and local level, and a subsidiarity monitoring network. It also extends to the annual open days hosted in Brussels, and a series of workshops and seminars under a general theme with a regional and local angle, organized by both the Commission and the CoR in Brussels. The aim of these workshops and seminars is to increase awareness of regional perspectives and their popularity has grown enormously since they were first launched in the mid-2000s. These interactions with the large community of so-called local and regional 'stakeholders' in Brussels—regional representations, non-governmental organizations (NGOs), city government officials, associations of regions with shared sectoral concerns, and so on—comes in addition to the regularized interactions between the CoR and its stakeholder community in Brussels, through the more formalized system of 'structured dialogue'—that is, regularized interaction on thematic points of mutual concern.

A final issue to note is the CoR's increasing engagement not only in the sectoral policy issues and not only with a clear territorial cohesion dimension, but also in the external affairs of the Union. The CIVEX Commission in particular has a remit to consider engagement in the EU's international affairs, for example promoting the development of decentralized cooperation globally. A clear marker of the growing international ambitions of the CoR is its role in establishing the Euro–Mediterranean Assembly of Local and Regional Authorities, known more commonly by its French acronym ARLEM. This assembly provides a local and regional dimension to the EU's ongoing integration efforts in the Euro–Mediterranean area, and has been developed under the umbrella of the Union for the Mediterranean. ARLEM itself is closely modelled on the CoR as an advisory body. The CoR has thus far been steering the Assembly, establishing functional committees in its own image. Its aim is to bring local and regional actors from the three shores of the Mediterranean into some form of permanent dialogue with the EU institutions, whilst at the same time facilitating stronger cohesion between the representatives themselves. The focus of ARLEM's work is policy areas of primary concern to the EU itself, such as de-pollution of the Mediterranean, maritime and land highways, and the Euro–Mediterranean university.

All of this activity blurs somewhat the distinction between the CoR's formally prescribed role, as set out in the EU treaties, and its ambitions or, more precisely, the ambitions of recent CoR leaderships that have steered the body in this direction. With an increased emphasis on the CoR's ability to connect disparate groups and promote shared policy agendas through dialogue and discussion, the CoR begins to take on a role as something of a platform rather than an actor in EU affairs. Whilst the networking and collaborative activities do, at times, feed into the more formal work of the CoR—namely, the drafting of opinions—this is not always the case. As such, the CoR's position in the institutional configuration of the EU remains unclear, whatever the added value of these 'softer' activities in the policy sphere may be. All of this ambiguity provides further grist to the mill of those who seek to disband the organization, and fuels the drive within the CoR to outline its own impact through measurable successes and targets delivered. For the member states, the EESC and CoR present no demonstrable cause for concern, other than perhaps the financial implications of their operation, although the EESC and CoR together represent just 2.56 per cent of the EU's overall administration budget. For this reason, debates surrounding their future have limited salience in national politics, and even less so since the rise in value of 'civil society' arguments. The 'hands-off' approach to management of the EESC and CoR has provided both organizations with the scope to develop their roles in new directions since their establishment.

Overall, both the EESC and CoR continue to mobilize core sectoral alliances that periodically have fed effectively into EU policy debates. At certain times, it has proved useful for member state governments to align themselves with these representative bodies. When they have done so, it has been with the aim of portraying externally a willingness to engage with social and regional issues at the EU level.

The EESC and the CoR within the EU's institutional framework

It is, of course, a truism to note that however much they claim to add value through civil society debate, both the EESC and the CoR remain fundamentally weakened because neither has full institutional decision-making rights. Moreover, each organization is only one of a number of channels that social or regional interests can exploit to engage with the European decision-making process. Both share an uncomfortable position on the margins of EU legislative circles. Despite ambitions to shape policy outcomes, both remain restricted and challenged in that aim, largely superseded today by the vast number of 'civil society' actors that operate as independent lobbyists in the Brussels arena.

Both organizations are concerned with the widespread perception that they are only marginal actors in the European policy process. In an effort to try to counter these negative perceptions, both bodies have recently begun to carry out widespread impact assessments, whereby they attempt to monitor the process of legislation and map this process against the original policy aims and recommendations that they had proposed. These results are often publicized in the form of glossy brochures and pamphlets, which are available at their headquarters on Rue Belliard in Brussels. Taken at face value, these indicators do demonstrate a degree of impact, although the choice of highlights is curious.

According to the EESC's publicity materials on impact, in 2005 over 80 per cent of opinions submitted by the EESC to the Commission contained at least one comment that was taken up and which may be considered to have brought about specific changes to the EU's activity (EESC 2008). If anything, this indicator raises the question as to the value added of the other 20 per cent of EESC opinions. The key example cited by the EESC relates to the EU Services Directive,[6] which made its way through the institutions of the EU during 2004–05. Here, the EESC claims to have been the first EU body to point out the possible negative fallout from the unconditional application of the country-of-origin principle, and from any watering-down of existing social protection standards. Then Commissioner for the Internal Market Charlie McGreevy acknowledged that the views of the EESC prompted a Commission review of the proposed directive.

However, these claims are not reliable indicators of impact. The outcome of policy wording is a notoriously difficult process to change, with a number of different actors each able to claim that their own phrasing has been taken through to the final legislative proposals. The EESC may just have got lucky and happened to chime with the general 'mood music' of the policy environment at the time of drafting.

But one area in which both organizations have sought to improve their engagement in the policy process is through producing fewer opinions, but opinions of higher quality. The EESC still leads the way here in terms of level of output. The Committee produces a vast quantity of opinions, although this number has fallen in recent years. In 2010, for example, the EESC produced 181 opinions, a large majority of which were produced through mandatory consultation. Around a third of these opinions were produced as own-initiative opinions (EESC 2011). The CoR has also made a strategic effort to focus on a smaller number of policy briefs in order to make a more meaningful contribution to policy debate. In 2010, the CoR adopted forty-five opinions, a significant drop on the large numbers produced in the early days of the Committee's existence, and substantially lower than the number produced annually by the EESC.

The notion of impact continues to shape the activities of the EESC and the CoR. By way of example, in 2008–09, the CoR undertook wide-scale research on its own role and purpose. This task was underpinned primarily by a desire to understand better the organization's broader impact in EU circles, although ostensibly this research was to support the drafting of a 'mission statement' for that organization. Surveys were carried out with all full and alternate members, and interviews were conducted with the principal stakeholders in Brussels and in the member states—chiefly, associations of local and regional authorities—as well as with key interlocutors in the EU institutions. Overall, this survey came to the conclusion that the institutions would prefer the CoR to focus on providing technical expertise on the implementation of EU policies at regional level rather than another party-political compromise. However, the stakeholder community was largely supportive of the emerging function of the CoR as a forum for debate and the exchange of experience and ideas (Bloomfield and Moore 2009).

The mission statement itself (see Box 16.6) was launched in March 2009 on the fifteenth birthday of the CoR. It thus marked the organization's transition from childhood to adolescence. The statement chose to emphasize the civil society credentials of the CoR and to reinforce the argument that the CoR's involvement in European policy processes imbues them with a form of democratic legitimacy.

The drafting of a mission statement for the CoR, in itself, has done little to change the organization's status or to alter its inter-institutional relationship. Within the institutional architecture of the EU, interaction with the Commission is widely regarded as a useful means by which the CoR can gain influence within the policy process over and above its formal legal remit. For example, where the European Commission lacks a clear-cut view on policy development, and where it is open to innovative ideas and suggestions, the CoR is often used as a testing ground for policy proposals (Tatham 2008). Recent examples involve dossiers relating to cultural policy or regional airports legislation. Under other conditions, such as when the Commission already has a clearly focused line on policy proposals or when the dossier has already garnered an EP response before the CoR has delivered its opinion, the influence of the CoR is likely to be both 'diffuse and weak' (*ibid.*). Thus CoR policy engagement and effectiveness is variable across EU issue areas.

BOX 16.6   **Mission statement of the CoR**

We are a political assembly of holders of a regional or local electoral mandate serving the cause of European integration. Through our political legitimacy, we provide institutional representation for all the European Union's territorial areas, regions, cities and municipalities. Our mission is to involve regional and local authorities in the European decision-making process and thus to encourage greater participation from our fellow citizens. Our political action is based on the belief that cooperation between European, national, regional and local levels is essential if we are to build an ever closer and more mutually supportive union among the people of Europe and respond to the challenges of globalisation. To this end, we work closely together with the European Commission, the European Parliament and the Council of the European Union, and in the Member States with the various tiers of authority, in order also to promote multi-level governance.

Source: CoR 2009

Conclusion

The EESC and the CoR have developed roles in practice that deviate somewhat from the visions held by the initial supporters and champions of their creation. Neither has moved to take on a stronger formal position as a codecision-maker in the European legislative process. But both have cultivated niche roles that anchor them firmly in the policy circles that feed into the wider processes of thinking on European issues, and which ultimately launch new policy agendas. Both retain important symbolic functions at the EU level, and have sought to maximize the opportunities afforded to them through debates on European governance, civil-society dialogue, and multilevel governance.

Neither organization has stood still since its creation; rather, each has sought actively to secure some form of engagement in the European policy process that is appropriate to its membership and representative focus. The question remains, however: what is the added value of each of their operations in an open policy process with a burgeoning private lobbying sector and new groups of collective interests emerging all of the time? This question continues to raise the notion of 'impact' as a driver of the activities of both the EESC and CoR, even if that impact is difficult to categorize and even more slippery to pin down.

Nonetheless, both the EESC and CoR have managed to cultivate an approach to engagement in European policy issues that has some wider resonance in the stakeholder community. Each has, on occasion, managed to shape policy outcomes in its favour. This influence does suggest some degree of dynamism inherent to both organizations that should secure their future in an increasingly complex system of EU governance.

NOTES

1. The numbers per country are detailed in Protocol 36 TFEU.
2. EESC mission statement, available online at **http://www.eesc.europa.eu/?i= portal.en.about-the-committee**
3. Rule 51(2), which entered into force in January 2010, states that 'Committee Opinions shall contain an explicit reference to the application of the subsidiarity and proportionality principles'.
4. See online at **http://europa.eu/legislation_summaries/institutional_affairs/ decisionmaking_process/a30000_en.htm**
5. See online at **http://www.eesc.europa.eu/**
6. Directive 2006/123/EC of 12 December 2006 on services in the internal market.

FURTHER READING

There are few systematic investigations of either the EESC or CoR on their own; most studies put these bodies into comparative perspective or address them within the context of investigations into the nature of European governance. The analysis presented by Warleigh (1999) of the CoR is a useful start point for understanding the body itself. Smismans (2000) provides an equally insightful starting point for analysis of the EESC. Hooghe and Marks (2001) put the emergence of the CoR into a broader, comparative investigation of emergent patterns of multilevel governance in the EU. Jeffery (2000) offers some insights into the impact of increased regional representation on European governance. Rowe (2011) considers the tensions that promote regional engagement in Brussels, both through the CoR and through alternative channels of representation. Mazey and Richardson's analysis (1993) of lobbying in the EU provides some historical perspective on the role of the EESC and the CoR, and Greenwood's study (2011) of more-contemporary lobbying in the EU helps to clarify the nature of the interest mediation carried out by both the EESC and the CoR.

Greenwood, J. (2011) *Interest Representation in the European Union* (3rd edn, Basingstoke: Palgrave Macmillan).

Hooghe, L. and Marks, G. (2001) *Multi-level Governance and European Integration* (Oxford: Rowman & Littlefield).

Jeffery, C. (2000) 'Sub-national mobilization and European integration: does it make any difference?', *Journal of Common Market Studies*, 38/1: 1–23.

Mazey, S. and Richardson, J. (1993) *Lobbying in the European Community* (Oxford: Oxford University Press).

Rowe, C. (2011) *Regional Representations in the EU: Between Diplomacy and Interest Representation* (Basingstoke: Palgrave Macmillan).

Smismans, S. (2000) 'The European Economic and Social Committee: towards deliberative democracy via a functional assembly', *European Integration Online Papers No 12/2000*.

Warleigh, A. (1999) *The Committee of the Regions: Institutionalising Multi-level Governance?* (London: Kogan Page).

WEB LINKS

http://www.cor.europa.eu/

http://www.eesc.europa.eu/

Full information on the activities of the EESC and the CoR can be obtained from their respective websites.

CHAPTER 17

Conclusion

John Peterson and Michael Shackleton

▍ Summary

Uncertainty about the future of the European Union should not be allowed to obscure the enduring character of its institutions and the persistence of the difficulties that they face. They remain irrevocably interdependent, obliged to work together to deliver collective governance even as they compete to maintain or extend their prerogatives. Their capacity to govern collectively is increasingly called into question, especially given their acute problems of leadership, management, and accountability. These problems are ever more complex, with governments constantly looking for new ways of governing collectively without 'communitarization'. Analytically, no one can understand the EU, or wider debates about legitimizing international institutions, without understanding the EU's institutions.

Introduction

'We conclude at a time of unparalleled uncertainty': these were the words with which we introduced this chapter in the second edition of this book in 2006. Just as it is impossible for any moment to be more unique than another, and just as no one can be a 'little bit pregnant', uncertainty cannot be repeatedly unparalleled. Yet the continued relevance of the European Union and its institutions seemed less assured at the time of writing of this edition than it had in many years.

Five years previously, the uncertainty was generated by the 2005 referenda in France and the Netherlands, with no one knowing how the EU's institutional system could, or should, develop. The ideas of creating new institutions, such as a standing President of the European Council, or reinforcing existing ones, such as increasing the powers of the European Parliament (EP) by extending codecision, seemed to have been set aside. And yet—with the Lisbon Treaty in force—we now have a President of the European Council and the powers of the EP have been significantly extended, precisely as was proposed by the Constitutional Treaty.

The transformation of the institutional environment over the last five years should make us very cautious about making any predictions at a time when the EU is again going through a period of enormous uncertainty. Europe's slow recovery from the post-2008 global recession became manifest in a major crisis in the eurozone, with the EU scrambling—along with the International Monetary Fund (IMF)—to try to prevent outright defaults on the debts of weaker members of the euro—Ireland, Italy, Portugal, Spain, and (especially) Greece—in 2010–11. These events had a potentially profound impact on the shape of the EU and the relationships between its member states. For some observers, we were witnessing the beginnings of the collapse of the whole structure. Stephen Wall, a former UK permanent representative and certainly not a Eurosceptic, commented: 'We have seen the high point of the European Union. With a bit of luck it will last our lifetime. But it's on the way out. After all, very few institutions last forever.'[1] The annual conference of a Brussels think tank on the state of the EU in 2011 observed that 'the European integration process appears fragile and tired', and would 'soon lose relevance for its citizens' unless it were reinvigorated (Emmanouilidis *et al.* 2011: 6). An alternative perspective was offered by the first new-model European Council President, Herman Van Rompuy: '[The] state of the Union is not so bad but the mood is not so good.'[2]

This chapter seeks to lift its gaze beyond the immediate horizon (or mood). But it contains no gazing into a crystal ball; instead, it looks back over the rest of the book to identify what is enduring about the character of the EU's institutions, however fragile the wider process of European integration now seems. Chapter 1 began by stressing how unique the Union's institutions are, and how the fundamental, overriding goal of the EU—managing the enormous interdependence that links European states—gives rise to the need for collective (or 'post-sovereign') governance (Wallace 2005). Collective governance logically requires institutions that work *collectively* to offer leadership, to manage diverse tasks, and to integrate interests in the pursuit of common goals.

The EU's institutional system is widely considered more complex and arcane than its counterparts at the national level. Truly 'common' goals may seem to be a thing of the past now that the EU is a Union of twenty-seven or more. Yet it would be difficult to argue that states in Europe were ever more interdependent than they are today. It is easy to forget that Europe is an enormously diverse part of the world, characterized by a tremendous range of densely populated states (many of them small), the histories of which are closely intertwined, but marked above all by conflict (much of it bloody). More than most regions in the world, Europe must cooperate to prosper, or even survive (Dogan 1994). Collectively governing Europe is neither easy nor optional.

The historical focus of this volume's contributions reminds us that European integration as a project began with what, in retrospect, were strikingly narrow and overwhelmingly economic objectives: first, to manage jointly the production of coal and steel; then, to develop a common market. Yet the earliest moves to institutionalize European cooperation were never seen as final. They represented something new and unspecified, but which definitely went beyond the intergovernmental cooperation of, for example, the Council of Europe, with its limited agenda and resources and non-binding decision-making. From the beginning, EU institution-building had a decidedly political purpose: to make European states ever more mutually dependent on one another. Then, as now, this aim generates tensions between those who wish to reinforce the central institutions in a federalist direction and those who see them as instrumental vehicles for maximizing state interests. As Dehousse and Magnette argue in Chapter 2, this tension—reminiscent of eighteenth-century debates in the United States between 'federalists' and 'anti-federalists'—has defined European integration, but has not prevented the growth and acceptance of ever greater interdependence.

Over the last half-century, the EU has expanded to take on an enormous number of new tasks. As it has done so, it has expanded its membership to include a far more diverse collection of states than anyone could have imagined at the beginning. One crucial by-product is that it now has far more, and more disparate, members than its institutional system was ever intended to accommodate. Institutionalizing collective governance has become a steadily more politicized process, and one that dominates the calculations of European governments and increasingly touches the lives of European citizens.

Moves to extend the EU's remit to matters of monetary, foreign, defence, and internal security policies (amongst others) have led to more diverse institutional choices. Rather than simply framing the question as a straight up-or-down, black-or-white one—'Do we want to *communitarize* this policy sector or not?'—member governments have created a wider set of options for themselves. Deciding to make policy in the EU context is only a first step that leads to a set of further choices: 'Do we communitarize, *or* do we organize new cooperation using one of the existing alternative institutional mechanisms, *or* do we create an entirely new institutional solution?'

The stakes surrounding such choices are much higher now than they were in the 1950s. There are more players—more governments and affected interests, plus the EU's increasingly assertive institutions themselves—making compromises more difficult to strike. The 'permissive consensus' that allowed bold steps forward in European integration without much public protest or even attention during most of the history of the EU is now gone. Citizens' sense of loyalty to the EU institutions is generally weak, even if there is a somewhat stronger attachment to 'Europe' as a focus for collective action, especially in foreign policy (see Chapter 13). Weak loyalties cannot be separated from increased institutional complexity. Most average citizens cannot help but be befuddled by the arcane language that has characterized the treaty changes of the last decade. The idea that the response of Irish voters to the Treaty of Nice in the June 2001 referendum, when a majority rejected the Treaty and a still larger number did not bother to turn out, was an aberration was firmly knocked down in 2008, when the slogan of the (successful) 'no' campaign in the referendum on the Lisbon Treaty was: 'If you don't know, vote no.' Much needs to be done before EU citizens truly identify with the institutions of the Union as their own.

This volume has tried to cut through the complexity by approaching each individual institution in a roughly similar way. Four basic themes have emerged. First, the EU's institutions are intensely and irrevocably interdependent. Regardless of how much they compete for power and influence amongst themselves, and how divided they are about where the EU is going, they are doomed to succeed or fail together. Second, the capacity of the EU's institutions to continue to govern Europe collectively is being increasingly called into question. Recent, radical enlargement—with the prospect of adding further member states—along with the difficulties of managing the eurozone raise doubts about the ability of the system to generate policies that both work and are seen to work. Third, the process of embedding what is national into what is European has become a far more complicated process than it was when, say, the decision was taken in the 1960s to create a common agricultural policy (CAP) to replace national agricultural policies. One result is that member governments have experimented with new forms of decision-making and even new kinds of *acquis*, such as the 'Schengen *acquis*' and the 'common foreign and security policy (CFSP) *acquis*', to achieve collective governance. But in doing so they have added to the EU's dizzying complexity. Fourth, without discounting the insights that arise from the application of alternative theoretical models, this volume has shown that neo-institutionalism has a lot to tell us about the EU. In particular, it reveals that an essential first step to understanding the politics of European integration is to understand the EU's often-mystifying institutions.

We develop each of these themes below, and conclude by grappling with perhaps the most urgent question facing students of the EU's institutional system: can it be reformed to be made more accountable and more legitimate in the eyes of European citizens? Put another way: can it become a more accepted, respected pivot of political life in Europe, or must it inevitably become a target of the same populist doubts, pressures, and protests that have affected other international organizations, such as the World Trade Organization (WTO) or IMF? Our essential argument is that, regardless of the answers to these questions, the EU's institutions remain at the vanguard of efforts to legitimize international institutions that have become increasingly powerful regulators of economic and political life globally.

Institutional interdependence

A constant theme of this book has been that none of the EU institutions is independent and free to act autonomously; all are interlinked and interdependent. Every contribution to this volume has focused on the relationship between the institution(s) in question and its counterparts elsewhere in the EU system. The effect has been to highlight the *collective* responsibility that the Union's institutions assume for EU policies. It is not only the members of the Commission's College (see Chapter 5) who must formally and publicly support all decisions of the Commission; more generally, if often informally, all components in the EU's institutional system are cogs in a *system*, or network of mutually reliant actors (see Keohane and Hoffmann 1991: 13–15).

Even bodies that appear to be independent—and are assured a very large measure of independence in their statutes, such as the European Central Bank (ECB; see Chapter 9)—need links with the rest of the EU institutional system and, moreover, the outside world to prosper. To deny this need is to invite the opprobrium of other institutional actors and popular disillusion with what the EU does more generally. Witness the damaging (not least to the value of the euro) and now-notorious statement of ECB President Wim Duisenberg in reponse to pleas for lower interest rates to spur economic growth back in 2001, 'I hear but I do not listen', which met with the ire of (particularly) the EP, as well as many others beyond Brussels. Arguably, much the same could be said about the intervention of the ECB in Spanish and Italian bond markets in the midst of the eurozone crisis in 2011, which led the German President to attack the moves as 'legally and politically questionable' and the German Bundesbank to charge that they lacked 'democratic legitimacy'.[3]

In fact, the design of the EU's institutional system virtually *demands* that actors within each of its individual institutions both hear *and* listen to actors in the other institutions. Even the European Court of Justice (ECJ), the deliberations of which remain shrouded in secrecy and which fosters an image of distant independence, ultimately depends on the goodwill of the member states and of their courts to implement its judgments (see Chapter 7). Whatever talk there may be of the decline, permanent or not, of the Commission, it is hard to see how the Council could prosper without a Commission strong enough to make suggestions, broker deals, and sometimes accept criticism for the results. In particular, the need for collective governance to maintain the Union's economic clout internationally is sometimes so clear that EU member governments are essentially obliged to defend the institutional system that they have created, warts and all, when its basic authority is questioned.

A good example is the quotas agreed on the import into the EU of Chinese textiles after the decades-old international Multi-Fibre Agreement was discontinued at the end of 2004. All EU member governments publicly supported the Commission's attempt to protect against a flood of Chinese imports (or at least did not condemn it) when the quotas were initially agreed, despite the preference of several member states for a more liberal approach, allowing more imports in to satisfy consumers. Later, the Commission, and especially Trade Commissioner Peter Mandelson, were blamed by EU governments when the quotas were filled far faster than projected by mid-2005, leaving many European retailers howling. Yet it was European governments that had effectively mandated the Commission to negotiate the quotas, and which were themselves integral parts of the Brussels system that was attacked by most of the European press and public for the chaos of the 'bra wars'.

Of course, the reality of collective responsibility does not mean that turf-battling is not a primary feature of the EU's institutional system; it is surely one of its most harmful pathologies. At times, the EU's institutions can seem more concerned with expanding their own remits than with ensuring that the EU turns out effective policies. Yet as Hooghe and Kassim (see Chapter 8) show, there is compelling evidence to suggest that even the European Commission—often alleged to be the most fervent turf-battler and remit-expander—is populated by officials who mostly want the EU to work better. Of course, as much as they compete for turf, the Union's institutions also compete for credit for policies (such as the single market) that do prove to be effective, thus revealing how the fortunes of the EU's institutions have become more closely linked over time.

Moreover, the EU's institutions have become collectively *accountable*, and probably increasingly so, for the work of the Union and at virtually every level. Within Council working groups, as Hayes-Renshaw points out (see Chapter 4), as well as in the Committee of Permanent Representatives (Coreper)—as shown by Lewis (see Chapter 14)—national views are merged into an agreed position. Afterwards, national actors are staunchly reluctant to reveal to others the range of views that preceded decision. The Council often collectively and stubbornly defends its position in codecision with the EP, even if it has been accepted with difficulty by some member states.[4] But after negotiation produces agreement, it becomes often very hard to separate out who was responsible for what. As one of us has argued (see Chapter 6), codecision has not only become (literally) the EU's 'ordinary' decision procedure, but has also firmly established that most major legislative decisions are made more or less collectively by the EU's three main legislative institutions: Commission, Council, and Parliament. The first enjoys a virtual monopoly of formal legislative initiative; the other two act as twin branches of a bicameral legislature; all are obliged to defend legislative outcomes in the ECJ in the case of a legal challenge. The more general point is that the future of the European project—to create a more prosperous and unified Europe—depends as never before on the ability of the EU's institutions to work together, as elements in a *system*, to offer collective governance.

Capacity: decline or renewal?

A second underlying theme of the book has been the emergence of new questions about whether the EU's institutions are up to the job that they have been given. Even before the Union's membership expanded to twenty-seven member states, it had become tempting to ask whether the EU's institutional system had worked in the past about as effectively as it ever *could*, and in a way in which it never *would* in the future. That is, even if it has fostered and consolidated international cooperation of a kind unprecedented in modern history, do we have to accept that it can never work as well again? Are *immobilisme* and decline now inevitable in a radically enlarged EU of twenty-eight (after Croatia joins, as is foreseen for 2013) or more? It is worth reviewing the arguments presented in this volume that give rise to such stark and disturbing questions.

The leadership problem

This book has highlighted the pluralistic, non-hierarchical character of the EU, and its lack of both government and opposition. No political party or coalition of parties can really claim to govern the Union. There is no Cabinet, no true executive.[5] As de Schoutheete (Chapter 3) argues, the European Council may seem to sit at the top of a pyramid structure, acting as a sort of board of directors for the EU. Yet its capacity to give strong political impulse to the Union's affairs has, in recent years, appeared to decline. Here, however, we may find that one of the Lisbon Treaty's institutional innovations, wedded to urgent necessity, has acted to enhance leadership capacity: the European Council has begun to meet more regularly under the chairmanship of Van Rompuy, who himself was intimately involved in successive decisions taken to try to cope with the eurozone crisis, including agreeing the mandate given to him by EU heads of state and government to improve crisis management in the eurozone. It was widely agreed that Van Rompuy 'provided continuity and gave the work of the European Council the appearance of seamlessness and flow at an unexpectedly challenging time' (Dinan 2011: 110).

Still, the EU will probably never stop falling short of strong or clear political leadership (see Hayward 2008). Leadership remains a contested commodity, as we can see if we look at the various institutional candidates to provide it: the Commission, the Council presidency, or the European Council. The Commission looks more and more like an international bureaucracy, and less and less like a proto-government. The Council presidency can act only within a limited mandate and cannot go further than the other states will let it. Its position has been conspicuously weakened since the Lisbon Treaty in that it is no longer responsible for organizing European Councils and has lost 'ownership' of CFSP to the High Representative. Again, the most likely candidate to supply leadership in the years to come is probably the European Council. Nevertheless, it is only able to achieve what the member states want it to achieve with agreements often hammered out bilaterally beyond its walls. For example, the deals struck by the European Council that pulled the eurozone back from the brink of crisis (at least temporarily) in July and December 2011 were, in fact, agreed (mostly) bilaterally between France's Nicolas Sarkozy and Germany's Angela Merkel 24 hours before the EU summits convened. Moreover, the incident illustrated that having Van Rompuy as chair cannot—and will not—prevent EU leaders from sending mixed messages, as evidenced by Sarkozy's claim that '[w]e are creating the beginnings of a European monetary fund' and the counter-claim of Dutch Prime Minister Mark Rutte that '[t]here is no question of creating a European monetary fund'.[6]

It might be argued that institutions do not lead; leaders must lead—that it is up to the EU's member governments, individually or in alliances with one another, to provide political direction to the European project. If we take this view, we inevitably end up asking whether past sources of leadership—such as the Franco–German alliance—can be resurrected. Two of the fundamental lessons of this volume help us to frame, if not answer, this question. First, we have seen that powers are now more widely shared amongst the EU's institutions than ever before, making it more difficult for one member state or any group of them to give political impulses that resonate across the Union's institutional system. Second, while crises may still give scope for Franco–German leadership (see above), it is clear that strong, decisive action at the EU level often requires political agency from multiple sources. Thus, again, a strong Council requires a strong Commission. The EU's multiple presidents—of the European Council, Commission, and Council—must inevitably put aside their egos and own institution's agendas to negotiate and deliver common political messages. Confusion about who really speaks for the EU shapes calculations made by non-Europeans about how important the Union really is, as starkly illustrated at the 2009 Copenhagen international summit on climate change, when the EU was not even invited to attend the final negotiations that determined its result. More generally, the evolution of the EU towards a more diverse political and institutional system casts new doubts about whether the Union of the future can rely on past sources of political leadership.

The management problem

The EU's lack of hierarchy has benefits. It sustains participation by many parties because the policy agenda seems (in appearance, at least) remarkably open. No one wins all of the time, and even losers in policy debates can often become winners by shifting the agenda towards new policies that mitigate or cancel out past ones. Ultimately, collective governance is unsustainable in the absence of compromise: we can expect all to be willing to compromise today only if all can hope for better results tomorrow.

Yet the EU's lack of hierarchy creates problems of management, as well as political drift. At earlier stages in its evolution, the EU's business might have been managed effectively by the Hallstein and Delors Commissions, or by its largest and most committed member governments (again, especially the French and German) when they held the Council presidency (although a now-familiar claim is that small states tend to run more successful presidencies—see Hayes-Renshaw and Wallace 2006). In any case, the reality is now different: no genuine hierarchy of policy goals exists and there is no body or institution able to impose one. It often seems that too many voices must be accommodated at every turn, and that everyone has a say, without anyone being able to get the final word. The US delegation headed by George W. Bush that visited Brussels in early 2005 was reportedly bemused by the approximately seventy different speeches to which they were subjected by various EU representatives in the course of only a few days of meetings.

The severity of the management costs arising from the EU's hyperpluralism has been highlighted perceptively by Metcalfe (2000). Put simply, the EU's institutional system—whatever its virtues—is also a recipe for *undermanagement*. Regardless of how high and mighty the European Council looks to the untrained eye, much EU governance occurs in practice within horizontally structured and often highly autonomous policy networks that preside over individual policy sectors (see Peterson and Bomberg 1999; Peterson 2009). The EU's main institutions are well represented in most of them (especially since codecision marked a substantial upgrade in the EP's powers), and inter-institutional politics can be lively: agents of the Commission, EP, and Council can be relied upon to defend their institutions' prerogatives and priorities staunchly.

Yet responsibility is shared widely both for policy outputs and outcomes. As such, none of the EU's individual institutions have strong incentives to invest in the capacity of policy networks to manage the policy agenda—that is, to set priorities, to follow up past initiatives, to ensure effective implementation, and so on. Moreover, even leaving aside the effects of enlargement, the Union's management problem almost naturally gets worse over time since:

a combination of factors operating within the EU's institutional framework creates political incentives to take on more tasks while imposing constraints on the acquisition and development of capacities for managing them effectively. In the Council, political decision-makers too readily assume the existence of management capacities and governance structures to implement policies or dodge the difficult issues about who should provide them. The Commission has been more interested in staking out new territorial claims than insisting on the resources for discharging responsibilities effectively.

(Metcalfe 2000: 824)

The wide 'spread' of the roots of the EU's management deficit means that all of the Commission's recent efforts to make itself more organizationally efficient (see Chapters 5 and 8) cannot, by themselves, produce more effective EU governance.

Weak management means poor coordination and a lack of clear priorities. Witness Hayes-Renshaw's (Chapter 4) discussion of the General Affairs Council (GAC) and its increasing inability to impose direction on or set priorities for EU policy-making.

Perhaps some kind of permanent council of European affairs ministers could help to close the management deficit? (Indeed, some member states already send such a minister to represent them in the GAC.) Yet it remains difficult to foresee EU governments collectively biting the bullet and single-tasking senior, heavyweight cabinet ministers with the job of making the EU work better. To do so, they would have to defy the system of incentives that encourages all actors in EU decision-making to focus on winning today's policy argument, as opposed to ensuring that the policy agenda does not become too crowded or that yesterday's decisions are implemented properly. And when European leaders had the opportunity to focus on closing the management deficit in debates on the European Constitution and those on the Lisbon Treaty that followed, they chose to focus on other priorities.

The problem of integrating interests

Until the 1980s, the task of integrating interests was a relatively simple one of integrating the *national* interests of its member states. The then European Community (EC) dealt only with narrowly circumscribed areas of policy marked out for collective governance, such as the CAP and external trade. Policy-making was an elite-driven exercise, more or less monopolized by national executives working with the Commission. The EP was an assembly of seconded national parliamentarians. The European Economic and Social Committee (EESC) was a pseudo-corporatist talking shop. Both were easily ignorable by the Council. The Commission was always less ignorable, and took pains to ingratiate itself with broad social and political interests while trying to integrate them into Europe-wide associations. But not until the Delors era did the Commission ever successfully integrate pan-European interests into its work to the point at which it was able to 'use' them to challenge the Council or to encourage member governments to accept its own policy agenda.

Now, of course, the problem of integrating interests is far more acute. The EU's policy agenda has expanded enormously, and continues to do so. More societal interests both have a stake in EU policy-making and demand a voice in the process. One of us noted in the 1990s that the EU had (at the time) only recently been transformed from 'a system concerned with the *administration of things* to one concerned with the *governance of people*' (Shackleton 1997: 70; emphasis original). The speed of developments is such that this moment now seems a very long time ago. Since then, the EU has become a far more important purveyor of public goods. Yet the Union has made far fewer and shorter strides towards integrating societal interests compared to the steps it has taken to subject policies to collective governance.

Two caveats must be offered here. One is that, as we have seen, the EU system does a remarkably proficient job of integrating the *institutional* interests of its main institutional players. No important EU policy can be agreed—outside of very few sectors, such as competition or agriculture—without a very large measure of consensus spanning the Council, the Commission, and EP. Even the EU's more recent institutions, which tend to privilege national interests and are overwhelmingly staffed by national officials, provide the Commission and EP with channels for input. A good example is the Hague Programme on justice and home affairs (JHA), which brings together both national foreign affairs and JHA officials to assess terrorist threats from particular countries, but with annual assessments of whether liaison on counter-terrorism with foreign governments is effective being carried out by the Commission.[7] Collective institutional responsibility for EU policy, which must be a central goal of any effective system of collective governance, is something that the EU does rather well.

Second, the EU's institutional system has, over time, become increasingly innovative in the task of integrating different *sectoral* interests. One of the central features of the shift to so-called 'post-sovereign' political structures in response to globalization is the 'sectoral unbundling of territoriality in various functional regimes' (Ruggie 1998: 27; see also Slaughter 2004)—that is, the emergence of various kinds of policy-specialized transgovernmental networks, populated by actors who have more in common with each other than with officials who specialize in other policy areas in their own nation-states. The implication for the EU is that it now must integrate a far wider diversity of more differentially concerned 'national interests' than was the case for most of its history. On this test, the EU again scores quite well. Lewis (Chapter 14) portrays Coreper as a remarkably effective integrator of the interests of increasingly more divided and less single-minded national civil services. Coreper is widely viewed as an effective broker of 'political' and 'technical' interests, although (as is the case with all EU institutions) its ability to continue to work so well following enlargement is less clear. Meanwhile, Kelemen and Majone (Chapter 10) are convincing in arguing that the growing popularity of strong, independent agencies offers a potential mechanism for the effective integration of functional interests in an era of 'sectoral unbundling'.

At the same time, Part III of this volume also contains plenty of proof of the EU's failure to integrate many wider societal interests very effectively. Raunio (Chapter 15) bluntly suggests that pan-European party groups in the EP are very far from commanding the loyalty and support of European citizens, who in large part do not understand the influence that the groups can have on EU policies. Jeffery and Rowe (Chapter 16) strain to conclude that the EESC is even worth having. At best, the Committee of the Regions (CoR) is one of a number of channels open for regional interests to make their mark, and by no means obviously the most important one.

The problem of the EU's limited capacity to integrate societal interests can easily be overstated. Those who view it as a major pathology of the Union sometimes neglect the essential distinction between input and output legitimacy (see Lord and Magnette 2004; Risse 2007). Input legitimacy comes from ensuring that a large number of voices are heard in the policy process. Output legitimacy, more simply, comes from ensuring that policies work, in the sense of bringing the greatest good to the greatest number of citizens. If the EU manages to produce policies that work, then it may not matter that much how they are made (see Scharpf 1999). Advocates of this view contend that however much the EU's policy remit has expanded, its competences remain tiny compared with those of its member states. What is less often stated, although it is clearly implied by such arguments, is that integrating more interests into EU policy-making could well be counterproductive to the goal of producing effective policies, since the Union is already so fundamentally reliant on compromise.

The prospects for renewal

Despite all of the EU's problems—institutional and political—that we have highlighted, there are good reasons to believe that European integration is not permanently stalled, the EU is not moribund, and that its institutions are not doomed to atrophy. One is the EU's proven capacity for improvization (see Peterson and Bomberg 2001: 58–9). Traditionally, only when faced with a crisis has the Union been able to innovate. The EU's response to the eurozone sovereign debt crisis is a case in point. Debate raged across Europe about whether measures taken to contain the crisis—such as creating (what became) the European stability mechanism (ESM) to support eurozone countries that experience financial difficulties—were in the best tradition of EU improvization or instead revealed a failure of European leaders to get 'out ahead' of powerful market forces. But the debate also placed on the EU's agenda previously unimaginable proposals to move towards shared fiscal liability, via the creation of common 'eurobonds', as well other steps towards more common economic governance, even including a common eurozone treasury. Most such moves towards greater fiscal integration inevitably would require transfers of considerable economic sovereignty from national capitals to Brussels, and for that reason met with the ire of many commentators (see, for example, Issing 2011). Yet they also reflected what UK Chancellor George Osbourne (hardly a staunch European integrationist) termed the 'remorseless logic' of the need to grasp the nettle in the face of the inexorable pressure of markets.[8] How much improvization was either needed or likely to save the euro was unknowable as this book went to press. But the EU's historical track record suggests that placing any bet on European integration stalling or reversing is a risky move.

Another good reason to think that European integration is considerably more than an historical artefact is the wide variety of new methods for embedding the 'national in the European' that have been embraced, some quite successfully, in recent decades. Most have eschewed the traditional Community method of decision-making and thus circumscribed the powers of the Commission, EP, and others in new areas of policy-making, much to the chagrin of admirers of that method. But these methods at least have signalled that EU member governments remained willing to extend collective governance to the point of institutionalizing new policy cooperation, even if new institutions are often strange and awkward creatures. The section that follows confronts these new, mostly 'open' methods of policy coordination and assesses their implications for the EU's institutional system.

Embedding the national in the European

One of the central themes of this book is how much more varied and complex the institutionalization of collective governance has become in Europe over time. The eclecticism of recent responses to demands for the extension of collective governance is striking. Take, for example, the arrangements for enforcing the stability and growth pact (SGP; Chapter 9), the 'dirty communitarization'—at least pre-Lisbon Treaty—of JHA policy (Chapter 12), the Lisbon process for economic reform and Europe 2020 programme to promote 'smart and sustainable' economic growth (Chapter 5), or the common security and defence policy (CSDP; Chapter 13). Of course, it is wrong to lump together these and other non-traditional modes of collective governance, because significant differences exist between them (see Wallace 2010). Yet what most (if not all) have in common is that they preserve a role for individual member states that is stronger, more inscrutable, and less challengeable by the EU's institutions than is the case under the Community method (applied when policy is truly communitarized, and according to which the Commission—exclusively—proposes, while the EP and Council amend and dispose).

In retrospect, we can see that the Community method, in its pure and unadulterated form, has been under threat since the early 1990s (see Devuyst 2005). Moreover, there is nothing new about the EU being used for narrow and ostensibly 'national' purposes 'to extend the policy resources available to the member states' (Wallace 2010: 89). But the increasingly frequent institutionalization of collective governance in ways that preserve national prerogatives and priorities more explicitly has been a spur to a burgeoning new literature on 'Europeanization' (see Börzel 2005; Bulmer and Lequesne 2005; Graziano and Vink 2007; Sedelmeier 2011; Wong 2011). Contributors to this literature have struggled to come up with a definition of Europeanization (much as institutionalists strain to define 'institution'[9]) that is broad enough to convey the eclecticism of the process, yet specific enough to be meaningful. Ladrech (1994: 69) does as good a job as any, defining Europeanization as a 'process reorienting the direction and shape of politics to the degree that E[U] political and economic dynamics become part of the organizational logic of national politics and policy-making'.

The point for any student of the EU's institutions is simple. To privilege or preserve national practices and goals when reorienting national policy processes to the European level—especially in sensitive areas such as policing, defence, and fiscal policy—could be viewed less as a *barrier* to the success of the EU than as an essential *precondition* of its success. Here, we come to grips with the relationship between the new, post-Maastricht politics of European integration and the recent institutionalization of new forms of policy cooperation. In an abstract sense (as well as, we suspect, an empirical one), it would be difficult to imagine cases in which any set of democratically elected governments would choose to transfer powers, in a straight and linear way, from themselves to an international organization in a period during which the secular trend is towards declining public support for the latter. As such, it should not surprise us that we have not witnessed a straightforward communitarization of newly Europeanized policy areas, such as the CSDP, JHA, or employment policy. What is perhaps more surprising is that the trend towards *more* collective governance in Europe—albeit via methods that were unfamiliar until recently—has been effectively unbroken despite the disappearance of the 'permissive consensus'. Understanding why EU member governments have chosen to embed the national in the European in such a dizzyingly diverse number of ways starts with acknowledging that unless European governments can see their own practices and goals in some way reflected in Brussels policy-making, and can convince their citizens that this reflection is genuine, they are unlikely to accept new shifts of competence to Brussels.

The power of the general imperative to retain national levers of control even as new policies are Europeanized is abundant in this volume. Perhaps the prime illustration is the increasingly ubiquitous role of the European Council in the full range of what the EU does, even if de Schoutheete's (Chapter 3) analysis casts doubt as to how much it really controls (or even effectively monitors). Another is the enhanced role of national parliaments in EU decision-making, manifest (for example) in how the Polish Council presidency invited national parliamentarians—for the first time—to join representatives of all EU member states, the EP, and the Commission at an extraordinary summit to discuss the 2014–20 multi-annual financial framework in late 2011. To these examples could be added the way in which Coreper has assumed such an essential role at the interface between what is Europeanized and what is communitarized, and incidentally has gone from being a collection of 'bad guys' to one of 'good guys' in the eyes of those who are most enthusiastic about European integration. Even the most ardent of European federalists realize that sustaining the project requires embedding the national in the European, because simply replacing the former with the latter simply does not happen anymore.

Even where Europeanization has, over time, produced genuine communitarization, levers for national influence have been retained and guarded very jealously. Monetary policy, as Hodson (Chapter 9) shows, is one such area. There is now a single currency, as well as very live debates about more integrated economic governance in Europe. But the structures of the ECB reflect the imperative to preserve channels for national influence, and even some measure of control for national central banks. Even the development of Community law reveals a similar pattern. It can be argued that the EU has achieved such strength as a legal system only because national courts are so intimately involved in interpreting and enforcing EU law, and because no democratic state can resist the injunctions of its own courts (see Weiler 1999).

Analytically, some suggest that 'Europeanization' has become an alternative to 'communitarization' as a response to pressures for collective governance (see Laffan *et al.* 2000: 84–90). According to this view, European integration no longer has any clear teleology (if it ever had one at all). The EU is likely to become an increasingly more complex, differentiated, and polycentric institutional system over time.

Others portray Europeanization as a step on the path towards communitarization, as in the cases of JHA, environmental, and research policies. Advocates of this view argue that the emergence of new and different methods of embedding the national in the European does not imply that European integration has lost its purpose in institutional terms. They predict that 'the basic EU ... set-up will remain and evolve as the major channel for dealing with an increasing number of public policies ... [because] no real alternative is available' (Wessels 2001: 215).

We cannot predict with any certainty where the EU is headed in institutional terms. But it is clear that the Union and its member states will face many more new and hard choices about how cooperation is institutionalized in the years ahead. We hope that this volume helps its readers to make up their own minds about whether Europeanization is replacing communitarization, or merely signals the inevitability of the latter over time.

EU institutions and the new institutionalism

If this book has grappled with one theoretical question above all others, it is this: do institutions matter? In line with the teachings of the new institutionalist literature, we have seen that institutions—how they are constructed, how they work, and how they interact—are a powerful determinant of EU politics. A close reading of this volume yields one heuristic point above all others: the process of collective governance in Europe cannot be understood without intimate knowledge of the EU's institutions, and how they work both individually and together as a system. Moreover, the main themes that emerge from a careful scan across the full landscape of the EU's institutions are all, we would submit, central to the study of the EU more generally. They include the following.

- *The considerable scope for institutional agency in EU politics inevitably makes inter-institutional competition a primary feature of EU policy-making.* We have seen that new mechanisms, such as trialogues, inter-institutional agreements, and the European External Action Service (EEAS) have had to be constructed to channel and control conflict between the EU's institutions over time. In one sense, fiercer inter-institutional competition is the product of the empowerment of the Commission and the EP after the 1980s (and the Court before and after that) to the point at which the Council can agree relatively little of importance without their consent. As such, the main cleavages in EU policy debates have become as much inter-institutional as intergovernmental.

- *The EU's institutional system generates multiple identities, the importance of which cannot be discounted in EU policy debates.* Virtually all actors in EU policy-making must balance or at least reconcile different identities. Consider a few random, imagined examples: what motivates a socialist minister from the Spanish foreign office who hails from Catalonia when the Council debates a move to centralize decision-making on the structural funds? What advice does a German cabinet official give to her Commissioner (for monetary policy) on a proposal to reprimand the German government for breaching the GSP targets for budget deficit, and which incidentally sets a precedent for rapping future *coupables* on the knuckles? Recent attempts to develop accounts of EU policy-making that draw on constructivist theory and ascribe causal importance to questions of identity have met with some (modest) success (see Jupille *et al.* 2003; Sedelmeier 2005; Risse 2009). Such accounts leave open the question of which out of various multiple identities motivates key actors in the policy process at any given time. Constructivists insist that identities, and thus interests, are 'constructed' as part of the process of repeated interactions between actors in Brussels. Regardless of how accurately (or not) they portray the EU policy process, there is no doubting that the EU's institutions are a crucial, additional source of identity—along with nationality, party affiliation, and so on—for actors in EU policy-making, who often go to considerable lengths to defend the agenda, prerogatives, and dignity of their institution in policy debates. Two upshots are that the Council (in all of its forms) is far from being purely intergovernmental and that there exists plenty of scope for the defence of national interests within the Union's ostensibly supranational institutions.

- *Path dependence is so powerful in the EU's institutional system as to make it hard not to be pessimistic about the system's ability to cope with the Union's enlargement.*   One theoretical implication is that institutionalism is an impressive predictor of the extent to which the EU's institutions—and, equally if not more so, their national counterparts—often resemble generals meticulously prepared to fight the last war (see Peters 1999: 40). Witness the tendency of the EESC (see Chapter 16) to defend a corporatist model of state–society relations that was never accepted across Europe even in its heyday.

  Path dependency is especially acute in a system that, after all, remains quite young and thus relies heavily on past precedents—political and, above all, legal—to define the scope for future action. More generally, the EU provides plenty of grist for the institutionalist mill in the way in which it has embraced the values of openness, transparency, and democratic accountability only slowly and often reluctantly. This volume has uncovered much to validate the basic institutionalist assumption that 'an inconsistency in cultures is likely to develop across time as an institution recreates an internal value system that is incompatible with a changed environment' (Peters 1999: 40).

- *A crucial implication of the strength of path dependence in the EU is that principal–agent relationships are often troubled and contested, with inevitable policy costs.*   Kelemen and Majone (Chapter 10) show how member states

have been unwilling to give new European agencies the degree of autonomy
necessary to enable the system to prosper, not least because they remain
stuck with a doctrine that severely circumscribes the autonomy of European
regulatory bodies from the Commission. As they suggest, the burgeoning of
new European agencies might be taken as evidence that both the
Commission and EU member governments are slowly coming to grips with
the mismatch between regulatory needs and old, anachronistic doctrines
about delegating powers. But it remains possible to cite a lengthy list of
policy areas—food safety, JHA policy, financial control, and the CFSP among
them—in which half-hearted or disorderly delegation from member states to
the EU's institutions (principals to agents) has produced confused and/or
ineffective policy.

This survey of the EU's institutions, like the new institutionalist literature itself,
might seem to paint a generally sombre, downbeat, pessimistic picture of modern
politics. Prominent themes include inertia, pathology, inconsistency, turf battles,
and so on. Yet, as is suggested by work that applies institutionalist theory to international organizations (see Keohane 1998; Peters 1999: 126–40; Ikenberry 2001), it is
possible to view international institutions—including those of the EU—as *the* leading purveyors of innovative solutions to the problems of modern governance. While
they may be trapped by path dependency in important respects, the EU's institutions
are usually better able than European national governments to develop, embrace,
and promote long-term solutions to problems such as global warming, the ageing of
the European workforce, or fostering civil society in central Asia. It is in the nature
of politics that governments, the calculations of which are governed by four- or five-
year electoral cycles, have great difficulty in thinking beyond short-term time hori-
zons and investing in policies that will pay off only long after the next election. To
illustrate the point, however much the Union's star as an international environmental actor had dimmed post-Copenhagen, it was difficult to imagine that there would
have been a Kyoto Agreement in the first place if the EU had not acted together to
make the necessary deals required with states such as Canada, Japan, and Russia,
which were reluctant to act without the United States.

Moreover, an important insight of the institutionalist literature is that different
institutional traditions in different polities reflect the values held most dear by the
societies in question. In the continental European tradition, which remains the basic
leitmotif for the EU, an abiding principle is that 'the State is linked organically with society and society is significantly influenced by the nature of the State' (Peters 1999: 6).
Whatever the inadequacies of the EU's institutions, which are often laid bare by the
application of institutionalist theory, this principle offers at least a set of aspirations
to guide institutional reform. One hopes that it also motivates governments to think
about how the relationship between the EU and its citizens can be made more
organic.

Conclusion: the accountability conundrum

If there is one single, burning question that arises from studying the EU's institutions, it is the vexed accountability question: how can the Union's institutions, in the absence of a truly European polity, become more accountable to European citizens and thus a more legitimate level of governance? In our view, it is difficult to imagine that the problem can be solved simply with a dose of direct democracy, such as by instituting the direct election of the President of the Commission, empowering national parliaments in EU decision-making, or spending more to foster truly pan-European political parties. It might be rather easier to envisage the future election of governments able and willing to do a better job of selling the EU's institutions to average citizens as both necessary and competent agents in the tasks of governing Europe, and defending its interests in a new, modern, and increasingly globalized world. According to one view, the post-Delors, Kohl, and Mitterrand generation has shown little inclination to take political risks to build Europe (see Paterson 2008). But an alternative view is that twenty-first-century Europe's political class is populated by articulate and committed pro-Europeans, such as Angela Merkl, who was crucial to political agreement on the Lisbon Treaty and staunch in insisting that the defence of the euro was in the German interest, however much it appeared to be costing German taxpayers during the eurozone crisis. Moreover, some amongst the most fluent political communicators during this period—Barroso, Van Rompuy, Trichet—held posts in the EU's institutions that did not exist or which had been transformed since the 'heroic' epoch of European integration in the 1980s. Again, the EU's institutions are enmeshed in, and springboards for, Europe's politics.

Still, the EU's accountability problem persists and might be seen as a conundrum. Member governments accept the need to pool sovereignty at the EU level to achieve collective governance. But they refuse to create clear, straight, simple lines of accountability of the sort that allow citizens in democratic systems to throw out a government that they themselves have elected and substitute an opposition (see Peterson 1997). It is a conundrum that could lead to the conclusion that the EU's institutional system is on the verge of breakdown, especially given enlargement to include generally poorer states, the citizens of which are hungry for rapid economic development, combined with declining enthusiasm for the EU in Europe's more mature democracies and growing unrest over the consequences of the decisions being taken to defend the euro. The result is a classic collective action problem, in which 'free-riders' (consider the case of Greece) fail to act in the interests of the collective (see Olson 2002).

Of course, the collective action problems of all successful international organizations grow as their membership increases. But no international organization is as powerful as the EU and thus none faces such demands for accountability according to democratic standards. The problem of 'scaling up' democracy to suit a more integrated and globalized world is by no means unique to Europe; rather, the problem of

subjecting global governance to democratic controls is one of the most vexing problems facing governments everywhere. Robert Dahl (1994), a shrewd student of democracy, has posed the problem as an essentially generic one (see also Rodrik 2011).
To simplify only slightly, the closer that governments work to the citizen, the more
they must respond to the needs and preferences of average people. However, small-
scale governments cannot hope to cope with problems such as international terrorism, nuclear proliferation, financial crises, or humanitarian tragedies that are
solvable—if they are solvable at all—only through the collective efforts of states
working through international organizations. Above all, the problem of governing the
global economy in a political world in which the overwhelming majority of governments believe in the virtues of open commerce requires global rules and adjudication
of conflicting interests. In this context, the EU may be seen as an essential, driving
force behind the freeing of international trade, however much it frustrates its trading
partners with its frequent backsliding towards protectionism, but also a staunch defender of values that are easily trammelled by free trade, such as environmental protection or core labour standards. The European economy could be seen as a prototype
for the global economy of the future, in which the main factors of production become
basically borderless, but remain subject to supranational regulation.

Taking the analogy further, the EU's institutions could be viewed as prototypes for
global institutions that might one day govern something like a 'single' global market. It is easy to stretch this analogy too far and to be seduced by the same naive,
Wilsonian vision of world government that was widely embraced in the interwar
period, only to be exposed by realist international relations theorists in the 1950s as
intellectually bankrupt. Yet it was precisely then that the EU embarked on its extraordinary mission of institution-building in the pursuit of collective governance.
One long-term effect, certainly foreseen by none of the EU's founding fathers, has
been to mark out the EU's institutions as models suitable for emulation by other international organizations that need to be made more accountable and subject to
democratic controls. The view of Keohane (1998), perhaps the most influential of all
international relations scholars, is that the task of democratizing international organizations is not that much more challenging than was the task of creating and institutionalizing democracy at the domestic level during the passing of the era of the
'divine right of kings' in the seventeenth and eighteenth centuries. This view might
be dismissed as overly naive (and peculiarly American), but its existence shows us
both that there is much about the EU's institutional system that is admired (as well
as much that is heartily disliked) internationally *and* that the Union's democratic
conundrum reflects wider problems of democratizing global governance.

Meanwhile, there exists no consensus about the severity of the EU's democratic
deficit (see Moravcsik 2003; Corbett 2012). When compared with other international organizations, the Union even appears to be a relatively 'democratic' one. It
overrepresents its smaller member states in a way that, say, the United Nations or
WTO never could. It does not discriminate against poorer states, as the IMF is frequently accused of doing. All of its constituent political units, at least for now, are

entitled to representation in the College of Commissioners in a way that, say, the individual US states are not in the US cabinet. Maybe its most distinguishing feature is that it is subject to increasingly close and powerful scrutiny by the world's only democratically elected, multinational parliament.

In this context, it is worth recalling the view of the so-called 'new governance' school of policy analysts, for whom Majone (1996) is a primary spokesperson. According to this view, the EU's democratic deficit is overblown by its critics, who fail both to recognize that the Union's competence is relatively narrow compared to that of its member states *and* that the EU's core tasks of regulating economic activity are rarely subject to majoritarian democratic controls in national polities. Some of the collective goods provided by the EU—free trade, fair competition, healthy food, a single currency—could not be provided without insulating policy-makers from short-term political pressures (see also Moravcsik 2003).

Even if we conclude that the new governance school is too complacent about the democratic deficit, there is at least some evidence to suggest that the problem of fragmented accountability alongside collective responsibility is beginning to be tackled by new and creative solutions. One is to subject all EU institutions to stand-ard sets of rules or procedures, or scrutiny by agents who are both dedicated to a single task and also responsible for applying it across the entire EU institutional system. A good example is the European Ombudsman, who has figured little in this book, but who has begun to appear as an important figure in forcing the institutions to march to the sound of a single drum on a range of issues of (mal)administration.[10] Or, as Karakatsanis and Laffan (Chapter 11) suggest, the empowerment of the Euro-pean Court of Auditors (ECA) and the creation of the European Anti-Fraud Office (OLAF) could be taken as evidence that, from a rather modest beginning, the EU has adopted a much tighter and uniform regime of financial control in recent years.

None of this is to deny that the EU's institutions do not suffer from severe prob-lems, many of which could be legitimately called pathologies, of the same kind that plague international organizations generally. Especially given the EU's enlargement to twenty-seven members or more, the Union's institutions often appear ill-suited to the modern tasks of European governance and more likely to stifle innovation than to encourage it. There is a clear need for analysts of the EU's institutions to embrace normative thinking about how the Union's institutional system could work better.

However, there is another side to the ledger. As we have seen, the EU's institu-tions—regardless of their problems, both collective and individual—often facilitate collective governance on divisive issues such as migration, market liberalization, and the EU's relations with its near abroad in ways that are often just short of miracu-lous. When the EU's institutions work well together, the Union's policy process takes on a sort of epileptic charm, much like good jazz music, blending European tradi-tions, languages, and experiences. We cannot tell yet, but it may happen far less often in an enlarged EU than it did in the past. But, historically, it has happened often enough to ensure that the European Union remains the champion of those who wish and hope for more and more effective collective governance internationally.

NOTES

1. Quoted in *The Guardian*, 24 June 2011, p. 35.

2. Quoted in *European Voice*, 23 June 2011, p. 13.

3. Quoted in Evans-Pritchard (2011).

4. The importance of this rule in the Council was underlined in the spring of 2001 when Germany withdrew its support from the common position that had been agreed unanimously one year earlier on the Takeovers Directive (Directive 2004/25/EC of the European Parliament and of the Council of 21 April 2004 on takeover bids). This was the first time in the history of the EU that a member state had acted in this way and it caused enormous consternation amongst other states, particularly when the EP rejected the Directive in July 2001. One member state had been able to overcome the opposition of the (then) other fourteen.

5. As Weiler (1999) has argued tirelessly, the tiny share of EU policy for which the Commission is responsible for implementing, and the almost as small percentage of the EU budget that it spends, means that is far from being a true 'executive'. According to this view, the Council has more right to be termed the executive of the Union than does the Commission (see also Metcalfe 2000: 825).

6. Quoted in Wishart (2011).

7. See 'The Hague Programme: Ten Priorities for the Next Five Years', available online at **http://europa.eu/legislation_summaries/human_rights/fundamental_rights_within_european_union/l16002_en.htm.** See also Carrera and Guild (2006).

8. Quoted in *Financial Times*, 12 August, p. 1.

9. Note, for example, that almost every chapter in Peters' (1999) survey of different variants of institutionalism includes a section entitled 'What is an institution?' and manages to limit rational choice theorists alone to no fewer than four different, alternative definitions (*ibid.*: 53).

10. The Ombudsman has assumed extensive powers under Art. 228 TFEU to examine cases of maladministration and, more generally, has felt free to criticize the way in which the institutions operate. They have, in turn, felt obliged to respond and to improve their working methods, such as recruitment procedures or the response to requests for information from the general public.

REFERENCES

Adler-Nissen, R. (2009) 'Behind the scenes of differentiated integration: circumventing national opt-outs in Justice and Home Affairs', *Journal of European Public Policy*, 16/1: 62–80.

Allen, D. (1998) 'Who speaks for Europe?', in J. Peterson and H. Sjursen (eds) *A Common Foreign Policy for Europe* (London: Routledge).

Alliance of Liberals and Democrats for Europe (ALDE) (2011) 'ALDE position paper on EU budget post 2013', available online at **http://www.alde.eu/fileadmin/2010_site-docs/documents/publications/Budget/EU-Budget-January2011-EN-web.pdf**

Allison, G. T. and Zelikow, P. (1999) *Essence of Decision: Explaining the Cuban Missile Crisis* (2nd edn, London: Longman).

Alter, K. (2001) *Establishing the Supremacy of European Law* (Oxford and New York: Oxford University Press).

Amtenbrink, F. and Van Duin, K. (2009) 'The European Central Bank before the European Parliament: theory and practice after ten years of monetary dialogue', *European Law Review*, 34/4: 561–83.

Anderson, J. (1997) 'Hard interests, soft power, and Germany's changing role in Europe', in P. J. Katzenstein (ed.) *Tame Power: Germany in Europe* (Ithaca, NY: Cornell University Press).

—— (1999) *German Unification and the Union of Europe: The Domestic Politics of Integration Policy* (Oxford: Oxford University Press).

Andrews, D. (2003) 'The Committee of Central Bank Governors as a source of rules', *Journal of European Public Policy*, 10/6: 956–73.

Armstrong, K. and Bulmer, S. (1998) *The Governance of the Single European Market* (Manchester: Manchester University Press).

Arnull, A. (2006) *The European Union and its Court of Justice* (2nd edn, Oxford: Oxford University Press).

Atkins, R., Scheherazade, D., and Parker, G. (2005) 'Eurozone ministers say rates must stay on hold', *Financial Times*, 30 November.

Bailer, S. (2009) 'The puzzle of continuing party cohesion in the European Parliament after Eastern Enlargement', in D. Giannetti and K. Benoit (eds) *Intra-Party Politics and Coalition Governments* (Abingdon: Routledge).

Balint, T., Bauer, M., and Knill, C. (2008) 'Bureaucratic change in the European administrative space: the case of the European Commission', *West European Politics*, 31/4: 677–700.

Balthasar, S. (2010) '*Locus standi* rules for challenges to regulatory acts by private applicants: the new art. 263(4) TFEU', *European Law Review*, 35/4: 542–50.

Bardi, L. (2002) 'Parties and party systems in the European Union', in K. R. Luther and F. Müller-Rommel (eds) *Political Parties in the New Europe: Political and Analytical Challenges* (Oxford: Oxford University Press).

Barnett, M. A. and Finnemore, M. (1999) 'The politics, power and pathologies of international organizations', *International Organization*, 53/4: 699–732.

Barroso, J. M. (2007) 'Better institutions for better results', Speech 07/203 before the European Parliament on 28 March, available online at **http://europa.eu/rapid/press ReleasesAction.do?reference=SPEECH/07/203&format=HTML&aged=1&language= EN&guiLanguage=en**

Bauer, M. W. (2002) 'Reforming the European Commission: a (missed?) academic opportunity', *European Integration Online Papers 6/18*, available online at **http://eiop. or.at/eiop/texte/2002-008.htm**

Benoit, K. and Laver, M. (2006) *Party Policy in Modern Democracies* (Abingdon: Routledge).

Best, E., Christiansen, T., and Settembri, P. (2008) (eds) *The Institutions of the Enlarged European Union: Continuity and Change* (Cheltenham and Northampton, MA: Edward Elgar).

Better Regulation Task Force (2004) *Make it Simple, Make it Better: Simplifying EU Law* (London: HMSO).

Bildt, C. (1998) *Peace Journey: The Struggle for Peace in Bosnia* (London: Weidenfeld and Nicolson).

Bindi, F. (2010) (ed.) *The Foreign Policy of the European Union: Assessing Europe's Role in the World* (Washington DC: Brookings Institution Press).

Biscop, S. (2005) *The European Security Strategy: A Global Agenda for Positive Power* (Aldershot: Ashgate).

Blinder, A. (2007) 'Monetary policy by committee: why and how?', *European Journal of Political Economy*, 23/1: 106–23.

Blomgren, M. (2003) *Cross-Pressure and Political Representation in Europe: A Comparative Study of MEPs and the Intra-Party Arena* (Umeå: Department of Political Science, Umeå University).

Bloomfield, J. and Moore, C. (2008) *Communicating European at the Local and Regional Level* (Brussels: CoR).

———— (2009) *Connecting Europe: The Future of the CoR* (Brussels: CoR internal report).

Borràs, S. and Jacobsson, K. (2004) 'The open method of coordination and new governance patterns in the EU', *Journal of European Public Policy*, 11/2: 185–208.

Börzel, T. A. (2005) 'Europeanization: how the European Union interacts with its member states', in S. Bulmer and C. Lequesne (eds) *The Member States of the European Union* (Oxford and New York: Oxford University Press).

Bostock, D. (2002) 'Coreper revisited', *Journal of Common Market Studies*, 40/2: 215–34.

Boswell, C. and Geddes, A. (2011) *Migration and Mobility in the European Union* (Basingstoke and New York: Palgrave).

Bouchard, C. and Peterson, J. (2011) 'Conceptualising multilateralism: can we all just get along?', *MERCURY e-paper 1* (January), available online at **http://www.mercury-fp7.net/ fileadmin/user_upload/E_paper_no_1__Revised_Version.pdf**

Bowler, S. and Farrell, D. M. (1995) 'The organizing of the European Parliament: committees, specialisation and co-ordination', *British Journal of Political Science*, 25/2: 219–43.

————, ————, and Katz, R. S. (1999) 'Party cohesion, party discipline, and parliaments', in S. Bowler, D. M. Farrell, and R. S. Katz (eds) *Party Discipline and Parliamentary Government* (Columbus: Ohio State University Press).

Bretherton, C. and Vogler, J. (2006) *The European Union as a Global Actor* (2nd edn, London and New York: Routledge).

Bribosia, H. *et al.* (2009) 'Revising the European Treaties: a plea in favour of abolishing the veto', *Notre Europe, Policy paper N° 39*, available online at **http://www.notre-europe.eu/uploads/tx_publication/Policy-Paper37-en-Hbribosia-Revising_European_treaties.pdf**

Brittan, L. (2000) *A Diet of Brussels: The Changing Face of Europe* (London: Little Brown and Company).

Buiter, W. (1999) 'Alice in Euroland', *Journal of Common Market Studies*, 37/2: 181–209.

—— (2009) 'The proposed European Systemic Risk Board is overweight central bankers', *Financial Times*, 28 October.

Bulmer, S. (1994) 'The governance of the European Union: a new institutionalist approach', *Journal of Public Policy*, 13/1: 351–80.

—— and Lequesne, C. (2005) (eds) *The Member States of the European Union* (Oxford and New York: Oxford University Press).

—— and Wessels, W. (1987) *The European Council* (London: Macmillan).

Burrows, N. and Greaves, R. (2007) *The Advocate General and EC Law* (Oxford and New York: Oxford University Press).

Busch, P. and Puchala, D. (1976) 'Interests, influence, and integration: political structure in the European Communities', *International Organization*, 47/1/Winter: 41–76.

Butler, M. (1986) *Europe: More than a Continent* (London: William Heinemann).

Cain, B. E. (2000) 'Is the democratic deficit a deficiency? The case of immigration policy in the US and EU', available online at **http://www.igs.berkeley.edu/reports/democraticDeficit.html**

Campbell, J. (1983) *Roy Jenkins: A Biography* (London: Weidenfeld and Nicolson).

Carlsnaes, W., Sjursen, H., and White, B. (2004) (eds) *Contemporary European Foreign Policy* (London and Thousand Oaks, CA: Sage).

Carrera, S. and Guild, E. (2006) *The Hague Programme and the EU's Agenda on Freedom, Security and Justice: Delivering Results for European Citizens?* (Brussels: Centre for European Policy Studies), available online at **http://www.ceps.eu/book/hague-programme-eu%E2%80%99s-agenda-freedom-security-and-justice-delivering-results-europe%E2%80%99s-citizens**

Carrubba, C. J., Gabel, M., Murrah, L., Clough, R., Montgomery, E., and Schambach, R. (2006) 'Off the record: unrecorded legislative votes, selection bias and roll-call vote analysis', *British Journal of Political Science*, 36/4: 691–704.

CEPS/Egmont/EPC (2007) *The Treaty of Lisbon: Implementing the Institutional Innovations*, available online at **http://www.ceps.eu/files/book/1554.pdf**

—— (2010) *The Treaty of Lisbon: A Second Look at the Institutional Innovations*, available online at **http://www.ceps.eu/ceps/download/3736**

Checkel, J. (1999) 'Social construction and integration', *Journal of European Public Policy*, 6/4: 545–60.

Christiansen, T. (1996) 'Second thoughts on Europe's third level', *Publius: The Journal of Federalism*, 26: 93–116.

—— (1997) 'The Committee of the Regions at the 1996 IGC Conference: Institutional Reform', *Regional and Federal Studies*, 7/1: 50–69.

——, Jorgensen, K. E., and Wiener, A. (2001) (eds) *The Social Construction of Europe* (London and Thousand Oaks, CA: Sage).

Christoffersen, P. S. (2011) 'The creation of the European External Action Service: challenges and opportunities', in *The European Union after the Lisbon Treaty* (Maastricht: Monnet Lecture Series Three).

Clark, W. K. (2001) *Waging Modern War* (New York: Public Affairs).

Clegg, N. and van Hulten, M. (2003) *Reforming the European Parliament* (London: Foreign Policy Centre).

Cockfield, A. (1994) *The European Union: Creating the Single Market* (Chichester: Chancery Law Publishing).

Codagnone, C. (1999) 'The new migration in Russia in the 1990s', in K. Koser and H. Lutz (eds) *The New Migration in Europe: Social Constructions and Social Realities* (Basingstoke: Macmillan).

Coen, M. and Thatcher, D. (2008) 'Reshaping European regulatory space: an evolutionary analysis', *West European Politics*, 31/4: 806–83.

Commission (European) (2000) *Reforming the Commission: A White Paper*, 1 March, available online at **http://ec.europa.eu/reform/refdoc/index_en.htm**

——— (2001) *European Governance: A White Paper*, COM (2001) 428 final (Luxembourg: Office for Official Publications of the European Communities).

——— (2002) *Reforming the Commission: Recruitment of Senior Managers to the Commission Staff*, available online at **http://ec.europa.eu/reform/2002/selection/chapter10_en.htm**

Committee for the Study of Economic and Monetary Union (1989) *Report on Economic and Monetary Union in the European Community* (Brussels: European Community).

Committee of Independent Experts (1999a) *First Report on Allegations Regarding Fraud, Mismanagement and Nepotism in the European Commission*, 15 March (Brussels: European Parliament).

——— (1999b) *Second Report on Reform of the Commission: Analysis of Current Practice and Proposals for Tackling Mismanagement, Irregularities and Fraud*, 10 September (2 vols, Brussels: European Parliament).

Committee of the Regions (2009) 'Mission statement', available online at **http://www.toad.cor.europa.eu/ViewDoc.aspx?doc=cdr%5Cnouveau+mandat% 5C2010-2015%5C2010%5CEN%5CCDR56-2009_FIN___DECL_EN. doc&docid=2696988**

Coombes, D. (1970) *Politics and Bureaucracy in the European Community: A Portrait of the Commission of the EEC* (London: George Allen and Unwin).

Cooper, R. (2004) 'Hard power, soft power and the goals of diplomacy', in D. Held and M. Koenig-Archibugi (eds) *American Power in the 21st Century* (Oxford: Polity).

Corbett, R. (1993) *The Treaty of Maastricht* (Harlow: Longman).

——— (2012) 'Democracy in the European Union', in E. Bomberg, J. Peterson, and R. Corbett (eds) *The European Union: How Does it Work?* (3rd edn, Oxford and New York: Oxford University Press).

———, Jacobs, F., and Shackleton, M. (2005) *The European Parliament* (6th edn, London: John Harper).

———, ———, and ——— (2011) *The European Parliament* (8th edn, London: John Harper).

Cornish, P. (2004) 'NATO: the practice and politics of transformation', *International Affairs*, 80/1: 63–74.

Costa, O. (2001) *Le Parlement Européen, Assemblée Délibérante* (Brussels: Editions de l'Université de Bruxelles).

——— and Magnette, P. (2003) 'Idéologies et changement institutionnel dans l'Union Européenne: pourquoi les gouvernements ont-ils constamment renforcé le Parlement Européen', *Politique Européenne*, 9/Winter: 49–75.

Cowles, M. G. and Curtis, S. (2004) 'Developments in European integration theory: the EU as "other"', in M. G. Cowles, and D. Dinan (eds) *Developments in the European Union II* (Basingstoke and New York: Palgrave).

Cox, G. and McCubbins, M. (1993) *Legislative Leviathan: Party Government in the House* (Berkeley: University of California Press).

Craig, P. and De Búrca, G. (2011) (eds) *EU Law: Text, Cases and Material* (5th edn, Oxford: Oxford University Press).

Cram, L. (1999) 'The Commission', in L. Cram, D. Dinan, and N. Nugent (eds) *Developments in the European Union* (Oxford: Oxford University Press).

Dahl, R. A. (1994) 'A democratic dilemma: system effectiveness versus citizen participation', *Political Science Quarterly*, 109/1: 23–34.

Dannreuther, R. (2004) (ed.) *European Union Foreign and Security Policy: Towards a Neighborhood Strategy* (London and New York: Routledge).

—— and Peterson, J. (2006) *Security Strategy and Transatlantic Relations* (London and New York: Routledge).

De Gaulle, C. (1970) *Discours et Messages: Tome IV: Pour l'Effort* (Paris: Plon).

De Grauwe, P. (2007) *The Economics of Monetary Union* (7th edn, Oxford: Oxford University Press).

De Haan, J., Eijffinger, S., and Waller, S. (2005) *The European Central Bank: Credibility, Transparency, and Centralization* (Cambridge, MA: MIT Press).

De Ruyt, J. (1987) *L'Acte Unique Européen* (Brussels: Editions de l'Université Libre de Bruxelles).

de Schoutheete, P. (2000) *The Case for Europe: Unity, Diversity, and Democracy in the European Union* (London and Boulder, CO: Lynne Rienner).

—— (2009) 'La crise et la gouvernance Europeénne', *Politique Étrangère*, 74/1: 33–46.

—— (2011) *El Consejo Europeo in Tratado de Derecho y de Politicas de la Union Europea* (vol. III, Madrid: Aranzadi).

—— and Wallace, H. (2002) *The European Council* (Paris: Notre Europe, Research and European Issues #19).

de Zwaan, J. (1995) *The Permanent Representatives Committee: Its Role in European Union Decision-making* (Amsterdam: Elsevier).

Decker, F. and Sonnicksen, J. (2011) 'An alternative approach to European Union democratization: re-examining the direct election of the Commission President', *Government and Opposition*, 46/2: 168–91.

Dehaene, J.-L., von Wiezsäcker, R., and Simon, D. (1999) *The Institutional Implications of Enlargement: Report to the European Commission*, 18 October (Brussels: European Commission).

Dehousse, R. (1988) 'Completing the single market: institutional constraints and challenges', in R. Bieber, R. Dehousse, J. Pinder, and J. H. H. Weiler (eds) *1992: One European Market? A Critical Analysis of the Commission's Internal Market Strategy* (Baden-Baden: Nomos).

—— (1995) 'Constitutional reform in the European Community: are there alternatives to the majoritarian avenue?', *West European Politics*, 18/1: 118–36.

—— (1998) *The European Court of Justice: The Politics of Judicial Integration* (Basingstoke: Palgrave).

Dehousse, R. (2004) *La Stratégie de Lisbonne et la Méthode Ouverte de Coordination: 12 Recommandations pour une Stratégie à Plusieurs Niveaux plus Efficace*, 28 February (Paris: Notre Europe), available online at http://www.notre-europe.eu/fr/axes/competition-cooperation-solidarite/travaux/publication/la-strategie-de-lisbonne-et-la-methode-ouverte-de-coordination-12-recommandations-pour-une-strateg/

———— (2005) *La Fin de l'Europe* (Paris: Flammarion).

———— and Majone, G. (1994) 'The dynamics of European integration: from the Single European Act to the Maastricht Treaty', in S. Martin (ed.) *The Construction of Europe, Essays in Honour of Emile Noël* (Dordrecht: Kluwer).

Delors, J. (2004) *Mémoires* (Paris: Plon).

Deroose, S., Hodson, D., and Kuhlmann, J. (2007) 'The legitimation of EMU: lessons from the early years of the euro', *Review of International Political Economy*, 14/5: 800–19.

Devuyst, Y. (1999) 'The community method after Amsterdam', *Journal of Common Market Studies*, 37/1: 109–20.

———— (2005) *The European Union Transformed: Community Method and Institutional Evolution from the Schuman Plan to the Constitution for Europe* (Brussels: P.I.E./Peter Lang).

Deyoung, K. (2010) 'Obama redefines National Security Strategy, looks beyond military might', *Washington Post*, 27 May, available online at http://www.washingtonpost.com/wp-dyn/content/article/2010/05/27/AR2010052701044.html?nav=emailpage

Dimitrakopoulos, D. G. (2004) (ed.) *The Changing European Commission* (Manchester: Manchester University Press).

Dinan, D. (2000) (ed.) *Encyclopaedia of the European Union* (London: Macmillan).

———— (2010a) *Ever Closer Europe: An Introduction to European Integration* (4th edn, Boulder, CO: Lynne Rienner).

———— (2010b) 'Institutions and governance: a new treaty, a newly elected Parliament and a New Commission', in N. Copsey and T. Haughton (eds) *JCMS Annual Review of the European Union in 2009* (Oxford: Wiley Blackwell).

———— (2011) 'Governance and institutions: implementing the Lisbon Treaty in the shadow of the euro crisis', in N. Copsey and T. Haughton (eds) *JCMS Annual Review of the European Union in 2010* (Oxford: Wiley Blackwell).

Dogan, M. (1994) 'The decline of nationalisms within Western Europe', *Comparative Politics*, 26/3: 281–305.

Domorenok, E. (2009) 'The Committee of the Regions: in search of identity', *Regional and Federal Studies*, 19: 143–63.

Doutriaux, Y. and Lequesne, C. (2002) *Les Institutions de l'Union Européenne* (4th edn, Paris: La Documentation Française, Collection Réflexe Europe).

————, ————, and Ziller, J. (2010) *Les Institutions de l'Union Européenne après le traité de Lisbon* (Paris: Lavoisier).

Duchène, F. (1994) *Jean Monnet: The First Statesman of Interdependence* (London and New York: Norton).

Dumoulin, M. (2007) (ed.) *The European Commission, 1958–72: History and Memories* (Brussels: European Commission).

Dyson, K. and Featherstone, K. (1999) *The Road to Maastricht: Negotiating Economic and Monetary Union* (Oxford: Oxford University Press).

Easton, D. (1971) *The Political System: An Enquiry into the State of Political Science* (2nd edn, New York: Alfred A. Knopf).

Eberlein, B. and Grande, E. (2005) 'Beyond delegation: transnational regulatory regimes and the EU regulatory state', *Journal of European Public Policy*, 12/1: 89–112.

———— and Kerwer, D. (2004) 'New governance in the European Union: a theoretical perspective', *Journal of Common Market Studies*, 42/1: 121–42.

The Economist (2005) 'Those Ozymandian moments', 11 June.

———— (2011) 'Poland and the European Union: presidential ambitions', 25 June.

Egeberg, M. (2003) *Organising Institutional Autonomy in a Political Context: Enduring Tensions in the European Commission's Development* (Oslo: ARENA Working Paper Series 04/02).

Elgström, O. and Tallberg, J. (2003) 'Conclusion: rationalist and sociological perspectives on the Council Presidency', in O. Elgström (ed.) *European Union Council Presidencies: A Comparative Approach* (London and New York: Routledge).

Elster, J. (1998) 'Deliberation and constitution-making', in J. Elster (ed.) *Deliberative Democracy* (Oxford: Oxford University Press).

Emmanouildis, J. A. and Janning, J., with Balfour, R., Martens, H., Pascouau, Y., and Zuleeg, F. (2011) *Stronger after the Crisis: Strategic Choices for Europe's Way Ahead* (Brussels: European Policy Centre), available online at **http://www.epc.eu/documents/uploads/pub_1300_strategy_paper.pdf**

Eurogroup (2000) *Communiqué de l'Eurogroupe*, 8 September, Versailles.

European Court of Auditors (1981) 'Study of the financial system of the European Communities', OJ C342-24, 31 December.

———— (2004) 'Annual report concerning the financial year 2003', OJ C293-47, 30 November.

———— (2010a) 'Annual activity report 2009', available online at **http://eca.europa.eu/portal/pls/portal/docs/1/7842816.PDF**

———— (2010b) *Improving the Financial Management of the European Union Budget: Risks and Challlenges*, Opinion No. 1/2010.

European Economic and Social Committee (EESC) (2008) *The Impact of the European Economic and Social Committee*, CESE-2008-02-EN (Brussels: EESC).

———— (2011) 'Discover the European Economic and Social Committee', available online at **http://www.eesc.europa.eu/resources/docs/esc-11-012-en.pdf**

European Investment Bank (EIB) (2011) *Annual Report 2010, Vol. 1: Activity Report* (Luxembourg: EIB Group).

European Parliament (2004) 'Activity report of the delegations to the Conciliation Committee for the period 1 May 1999 to 30 April 2004', Presented by Vice-Presidents G. Dimitrakopoulos, C. Cerderschiöld, and R. Imbeni, available online at **http://www.europarl.europa.eu/code/information/activity_reports/activity_report_1999_2004_en.pdf**

———— (2009a) 'Activity report 1 May 2004–13 July 2009 of the delegations to the Conciliation Committee', PE 423.893, available online at **http://www.statewatch.org/news/2009/sep/ep-activity-report-2004-2009.pdf**

———— (2009b) *Dehaene Report on the Impact of the Treaty of Lisbon on the Development of the Institutional Balance of the European Union*, EP Session Document A6–0142/2009, 17 March.

European Union (2003) *A Secure Europe in a Better World: European Security Strategy*, December (Brussels: European Union), available online at **http://www.consilium.europa.eu/uedocs/cmsUpload/78367.pdf**

———— (2004) *Facing the Challenge: The Lisbon Strategy for Growth and Employment*, November (Brussels: High Level Group chaired by Wim Kok), available online at **http://ec.europa.eu/research/evaluations/pdf/archive/fp6-evidence-base/evaluation_studies_and_reports/evaluation_studies_and_reports_2004/the_lisbon_strategy_for_growth_and_employment__report_from_the_high_level_group.pdf**

European Union (2008) *Report on the Implementation of the European Security Strategy: Providing Security in a Changing World*, S407/08, 11 December (Brussels: Council of Ministers), available online at **http://www.eu-un.europa.eu/documents/en/081211_EU%20 Security%20Strategy.pdf**

Evans, P. (1993) 'Building an integrative approach to international and domestic politics: reflections and projections', in P. Evans, H. Jacobson, and R. Putnam (eds) *Double-edged Diplomacy: International Bargaining and Domestic Politics* (Berkeley, CA: University of California Press).

Evans-Pritchard, A. (2011) 'Germany fires cannon across Europe's bows', *Daily Telegraph*, 29 August, available online at **http://www.telegraph.co.uk/finance/ financialcrisis/8720792/Germany-fires-cannon-shot-across-Europes-bows.html**

Everts, S. and Keohane, D. (2003) 'The European Convention and EU foreign policy: learning from failure', *Survival*, 45/3: 167–86.

Farrell, D. M. and Scully, R. (2007) *Representing Europe's Citizens? Electoral Institutions and the Failure of Parliamentary Representation* (Oxford: Oxford University Press).

—— and —— (2010) 'The European Parliament: one parliament, several modes of political representation on the ground?', *Journal of European Public Policy*, 17/1: 36–54.

Farrell, H. and Héritier, A. (2005) 'A rationalist-institutionalist explanation of endogenous regional integration', *Journal of European Public Policy*, 12/2: 273–90.

—— and —— (2007) 'Codecision and institutional change', *West European Politics*, 30/2: 285–300.

Farrows, M. and McCarthy, R. (1997) 'Opinion formulation and impact in the Committee of the Regions', *Regional and Federal Studies*, 7/1: 23–49.

Fitzmaurice, J. (1975) *The Party Groups in the European Parliament* (Farnborough: Saxon House).

Fligstein, N. (2008) *Euro-Clash: The EU, European Identity and the Future of Europe* (Oxford and New York: Oxford University Press).

—— and McNichol, J. (1998) 'The institutional terrain of the European Union', in W. Sandholtz and A. Stone Sweet (eds) *Supranational Governance: the Institutionalisation of the European Union* (Oxford and New York: Oxford University Press).

Follesdal, A. and Hix, S. (2006) 'Why there is a democratic deficit in the EU: a response to Majone and Moravcsik', *Journal of Common Market Studies*, 44/3: 533–62.

Freedman, O. (1978) *Crisis and Legitimacy* (Cambridge: Cambridge University Press).

Gabel, M. J. and Hix, S. (2002) 'Defining the EU political space: an empirical study of the European elections manifestos, 1979–1999', *Comparative Political Studies*, 35/8: 934–64.

Garrett, G. (1995) 'The politics of legal interpretation in the European Union', *International Organization*, 49/1/Winter: 171–81.

Gatsios, K. and Seabright, P. (1989) 'Regulation in the European Community', *Oxford Review of Economic Policy*, 5: 37–60.

Geddes, A. (2005) 'Getting the best of both worlds: Britain, the EU and migration policy', *International Affairs* 81/4: 723–40.

—— (2008) *Immigration and European Integration: Beyond Fortress Europe?* (2nd edn, Manchester: Manchester University Press).

Gerardin, D., Munoz, R., and Petit, N. (2005) (eds) *Regulation through Agencies: A New Paradigm of European Governance* (Cheltenham: Edward Elgar).

Ginsberg, R. H. (1989) *Foreign Policy Actions of the European Community: The Politics of Scale* (London and Boulder, CO: Lynne Rienner).

—— (2001) *The European Union in International Politics: Baptism by Fire* (Oxford: Rowman & Littlefield).

Giscard d'Estaing, V. (1988) *Le Pouvoir et la Vie* (vol. 2, Paris: Compagnie 12).

———— (2002) 'Introductory Speech by President V. Giscard d'Estaing to the Convention on the Future of Europe', 26 February, available online at **http://european-convention. eu.int/docs/speeches/1.pdf**

Glarbo, K. (2001) 'Reconstructing a common European foreign policy', in T. Christiansen, K. E. Jørgensen, and A. Wiener (eds) *The Social Construction of Europe* (London and Thousand Oaks, CA: Sage).

Goebel, R. (2006) 'Court of Justice oversight over the European Central Bank: delimiting the ECB's constitutional autonomy and independence in the *Olaf* judgment', *Fordham International Law Journal*, 29: 600–54.

Golub, J. (1999) 'In the shadow of the vote? Decision-Making in the European Community', *International Organization*, 53/4: 733–64.

Gomez, R. and Peterson, J. (2001) 'The EU's impossibly busy foreign ministers: "no one is in control"', *European Foreign Affairs Review*, 6/1: 53–74.

Gouldner, A. W. (1957–58) 'Cosmopolitans and locals: towards an analysis of latent social roles, I and II', *Administrative Science Quarterly*, 2: 281–306 and 444–80.

Grabbe, H. (2000) 'The sharp edges of Europe: extending Schengen eastwards', *International Affairs*, 76/3: 519–36.

Grant, C. (2002) 'Restoring leadership to the European Council', *Bulletin of the Centre for European Reform*, 15 April, available online at **http://www.cer.org.uk/publications/ archive/bulletin-article/2002/restoring-leadership-european-council**

Gray, M. and Stubb, A. (2001) 'Keynote article: the Treaty of Nice—negotiating a poisoned chalice?', *The European Union: Annual Review of the EU 2000/2001 (Journal of Common Market Studies)*, 39: 5–23.

Graziano, P. and Vink, M. P. (2007) (eds) *Europeanization: New Research Agendas* (Basingstoke and New York: Palgrave Macmillan).

Greenwood, J. (2011) *Interest Representation in the European Union* (3rd edn, Basingstoke: Palgrave Macmillan).

Griffith, R. T. (2001) *Europe's First Constitution* (London: I. B. Tauris).

Groenendijk, N. S. (2004) 'Assessing member states' management of EU finances: an empirical analysis of the annual reports of the European Court of Auditors, 1996–2001', *Public Administration*, 82/3: 701–25.

Groenleer, M. (2009) *The Autonomy of European Union Agencies: A Comparative Study of Institutional Development* (Delft, The Netherlands: Eburon).

Gronbech-Jensen, C. (1998) 'The Scandinavian tradition of open government and the European Union: problems of compatibility?', *Journal of European Public Policy*, 5/1: 185–99.

Gros, D. (2003) 'Reforming the composition of the ECB Governing council in view of enlargement: an opportunity missed', *CEPS Policy Brief No. 32*.

Haas, E. B. (1958) *The Uniting of Europe: Political, Social, and Economic Forces, 1950–1957* (Stanford, CA: Stanford University Press).

———— (1960) *Concensus Formation in the Council of Europe* (Berkeley, CA: University of California Press).

Habermas, J. (2009) *Europe: The Faltering Project* (Cambridge and Malden, MA: Polity Press).

Häge, F. M. (2007) 'Committee decision-making in the Council of the European Union', *European Union Politics*, 8/3; 299–328.

Hagemann, S. (2008) 'Voting, statements and coalition-building in the Council from 1999 to 2006', in D. Naurin and H. Wallace (eds) *Unveiling the Council of the European Union: Games Governments Play in Brussels* (Basingstoke: Palgrave Macmillan).

Hagemann, S. and de Clerck-Sachsse, J. (2007) *Old Rules, New Game: Decision-Making in the Council of Ministers after the 2004 Enlargement*, CEPS Special Report.

Hailbronner, K. (2004) 'Asylum law in the context of a European migration policy', in N. Walker (ed.) *Europe's Area of Freedom, Security and Justice* (Oxford, Oxford University Press).

Hall, P. A. (1997) 'The role of interests, institutions and ideas in the comparative political economy of the industrial nations', in M. Lichbach and A. Zuckerman (eds) *Comparative Politics: Rationality, Culture and Structure* (Cambridge: Cambridge University Press).

—————— and Taylor, R. C. R. (1996) 'Political science and the three new institutionalisms', *Political Studies*, 44/5: 936–57.

Halliday, F. (1983) *The Making of the Second Cold War* (London: Verso).

Hanley, D. (2008) *Beyond the Nation State: Parties in the Era of European Integration* (Houndmills: Palgrave Macmillan).

Hausemer, P. (2006) 'Participation and political competition in committee report allocation: under what conditions do MEPs represent their constituents?', *European Union Politics*, 7/4: 505–30.

Hayes-Renshaw, F. (1999) 'The European Council and the Council of Ministers', in L. Cram, D. Dinan, and N. Nugent (eds) *Developments in the European Union* (Basingstoke and New York: Palgrave).

—————— and Wallace, H. (1995) 'Executive power in the European Union: the functions and limits of the Council of Ministers', *Journal of European Public Policy*, 2/4 December: 559–82.

—————— and —————— (1997) *The Council of Ministers* (Basingstoke and New York: Palgrave).

—————— and —————— (2006) *The Council of Ministers* (2nd edn, Basingstoke and New York: Palgrave).

——————, Lequesne, C., and Mayor Lopez, P. (1989) 'The permanent representations of the member states to the European Communities', *Journal of Common Market Studies*, 28/2: 119–37.

Hayward, J. (2008) (ed.) *Leaderless Europe* (Oxford and New York: Oxford University Press).

Heidar, K. and Koole, R. (2000) 'Parliamentary party groups compared', in K. Heidar and R. Koole (eds) *Parliamentary Party Groups in European Democracies: Political Parties behind Closed Doors* (London: Routledge).

Héritier, A. (1999) *Policy-making and Diversity in Europe: Escape from Deadlock* (Cambridge: Cambridge University Press).

—————— (2007) *Explaining Institutional Change in Europe* (Oxford: Oxford University Press).

Hertz, R. (2010) 'Still pedalling? The impact of Eastern Enlargement on European Union decision-making', Unpublished dissertation, ETH Zurich.

—————— and Leuffen, D. (2011) 'Too big to run? Analysing the impact of enlargement on the speed of EU decision-making.' *European Union Politics*, 12/2: 193–215.

Hill, C. (1993) 'The capability–expectations gap, or conceptualizing Europe's international role', *Journal of Common Market Studies*, 31/3: 305–28.

—————— (1998) 'Closing the capabilities-expectations gap?', in J. Peterson and H. Sjursen (eds) *A Common Foreign Policy for Europe?* (London and New York: Routledge).

—————— (2003) *The Changing Politics of Foreign Policy* (Basingstoke and New York: Palgrave).

—————— (2004) 'Renationalizing or regrouping? EU foreign policy since 11 September 2001', *Journal of Common Market Studies*, 42/1: 143–63.

———— and Smith, M. (2011) (eds) *International Relations and the European Union* (2nd edn, Oxford and New York: Oxford University Press).

———— and Wallace, W. (1996) 'Introduction: actors and actions', in C. Hill (ed.) *The Actors in Europe's Foreign Policy* (London: Routledge).

———— and ———— (2011) (eds) *The International Relations of the European Union* (2nd edn, Oxford and New York: Oxford University Press).

Hix, S. (1998) 'Elections, parties and institutional design: a comparative perspective on European Union democracy', *West European Politics*, 21/3: 19–52.

———— (1999) 'Dimensions and alignments in European Union politics: cognitive constraints and partisan responses', *European Journal of Political Research*, 35/1: 69–106.

———— (2002a) 'Consitutional agenda-setting through discretion in rule interpretation: why the European Parliament won at Amsterdam', *British Journal of Political Science*, 32/2: 259–80.

———— (2002b) 'Parliamentary behavior with two principals: preferences, parties, and voting in the European Parliament', *American Journal of Political Science*, 46/3: 688–98.

———— (2008) *What's Wrong with the European Union and How to Fix It* (Cambridge: Polity Press).

———— and Lord, C. (1997) *Political Parties in the European Union* (Basingstoke: Macmillan).

———— and Marsh, M. (2011) 'Second-order effects plus pan-European political swings: an analysis of European Parliament elections across time', *Electoral Studies*, 30/1: 4–15.

———— and Noury, A. G. (2009) 'After enlargement: voting patterns in the sixth European Parliament', *Legislative Studies Quarterly*, 34/2: 159–74.

———— and Scully, R. (2003) (eds) 'The European Parliament at Fifty', *Journal of Common Market Studies*, 41/2 (special issue).

————, Noury, A. G., and Roland, G. (2002) *How MEPs Vote* (Brighton: ESRC and Weber Shandwick Adamson).

————, ————, and ———— (2007) *Democratic Politics in the European Parliament* (Cambridge: Cambridge University Press).

Hobolt, S., Spoon, J-J., and Tilley, J. (2009) 'A vote against Europe? Explaining defection at the 1999 and 2004 European Parliament elections', *British Journal of Political Science*, 39/1: 93–115.

Hocking, B. (1999) (ed.) *Foreign Ministries: Change and Adaptation* (New York: St Martin's Press).

———— and Spence, D. (2002) (eds) *Foreign Ministries in the European Union* (Basingstoke and New York: Palgrave).

Hodson, D. (2010) 'Economic and monetary union', in H. Wallace, M. Pollack, and A. Young (eds) *Policy-making in the European Union* (6th edn, Oxford: Oxford University Press).

———— (2011) *Governing the Eurozone in Good Times and Bad* (Oxford: Oxford University Press).

Holbrooke, R. (1999) *To End a War* (New York: The Modern Library).

Hönnige, C. and Kaiser, A. (2003) 'Opening the black box: decision-making in the Committee of the Regions', *Regional and Federal Studies*, 13: 1–29.

Hood, C. (1991) 'A Public Management for All Seasons?' *Public Administration*, 69: 3–19.

Hooghe, L. (2001) *The European Commission and The Integration of Europe: Images of Governance* (Cambridge: Cambridge University Press).

Hooghe, L. (2005) 'Several roads lead to international norms, but few via international socialization: a case study of the European Commission', *International Organization*, 59/4: 861–98.

———— (2007) (ed.) 'What drives euroscepticism?', *European Union Politics*, 8/1 (special issue).

———— (2012) 'Images of Europe: how Commission officials conceive their institution's role'. *Journal of Common Market Studies*, 50/1: 87–111.

Hooghe, L. and Marks, G. (2001) *Multi-level Governance and European Integration* (Oxford: Rowman & Littlefield).

———— and ———— (2007) (eds) 'Europe's blues: understanding euroscepticism', *Acta Politica*, 42/2–3 (special issue).

———— and ———— (2009) 'A postfunctionalist theory of European integration: from permissive consensus to constraining dissensus,' *British Journal of Political Science*, 39/1: 1–23.

House of Lords (2001) *The European Court of Auditors: The Case for Reform*, 12th Report, 3 April (London: HMSO).

———— (2004) *Strengthening OLAF, the European Anti-Fraud Office*, 24th Report, 13 July (London: HMSO).

Howarth, D. and Loedel, P. (2005) *The European Central Bank: The New European Leviathan?* (Basingstoke: Palgrave Macmillan).

Howorth, J. (2007) *Security and Defence Policy in the European Union* (Basingstoke and New York: Palgrave Macmillan).

———— (2010) 'The EU as a global actor: grand strategy for a global grand bargain?', *Journal of Common Market Studies*, 48/3: 455–74.

Hoyland, B. (2006) 'Allocation of codecision reports in the fifth European Parliament', *European Union Politics*, 7/1: 30–50.

Hrbek, R. (1993) 'La function consultative dans la République Fédérale d'Allemagne', in J. Vandamme (ed.) *Fonction Consultative Professionnelle et Dialogue Social dans la Communauté Européenne* (Brussels: Presses Universitaires Européennes).

Huysmans, J. (2000) 'The European Union and the securitization of migration', *Journal of Common Market Studies*, 38/5: 751–77.

Ikenberry, G. J. (2001) *After Victory: Institutions, Strategic Restraint, and the Rebuilding of Order after Major War* (Princeton, NJ: Princeton University Press).

———— (2011) *Liberal Leviathan: The Origins, Crisis, and Transformation of the American World Order* (Princeton, NJ, and Oxford: Princeton University Press).

Issing, O. (1999) 'The Eurosystem: transparent and accountable or "Willem in Euroland"', *Journal of Common Market Studies*, 37/3: 503–19.

———— (2008) *The Birth of the Euro* (Cambridge: Cambridge University Press).

———— (2011) 'Slithering to the wrong kind of union', *Financial Times*, 9 August, p. 9.

Jacqué, J. P. (2004) 'Les principes constitutionnels fondamentaux dans le projet de traité établissant la constitution européenne', in L. S. Rossi (ed.) *Vers une Nouvelle Architecture de l'Union Européenne* (Brussels: Bruylant).

Jeffery, C. (2000) 'Sub-national mobilization and European integration: does it make any difference?', *Journal of Common Market Studies*, 38/1: 1–23.

———— (2005) 'Regions and the European Union: letting them in, and leaving them alone', in S. Weatherill and U. Bernitz (eds) *The Role of Regions and Sub-national Actors in Europe* (Oxford: Hart).

Jenkins, R. (1989) *European Diary: 1977–1981* (London: Collins).

Joana, J. and Smith, A. (2002) *Les Commissaires Européens: Technocrates, Diplomates ou Politiques?* (Paris: Presses des Sciences Po).

Joerges, C. and Vos, E. (1998) *EU Committees: Social Regulation, Law and Politics* (Oxford: Hart Publishing).

Johansson, K. M. and Raunio, T. (2005) 'Regulating Europarties: cross-party coalitions capitalizing on incomplete contracts', *Party Politics*, 11/5: 515–34.

—————— and Zervakis, P. (2002) (eds) *European Political Parties between Cooperation and Integration* (Baden-Baden: Nomos).

Johnston, I. (2008) *Social States: China in International Relations, 1980–2000* (Princeton, NJ: Princeton University Press).

Jørgensen, K. E. (2000) 'Continental IR theory: the best-kept secret', *European Journal of International Relations*, 6/1: 9–42.

Josselin, D. and Wallace, W. (2001) (eds) *Non-state Actors in World Politics* (Basingstoke and New York: Palgrave).

Judge, D. and Earnshaw, D. (2003) *The European Parliament* (London: Palgrave Macmillan).

—————— and —————— (2008) *The European Parliament* (2nd edn, London: Palgrave Macmillan).

Juncos, A. and Pomorska, K. (2007) 'The deadlock that never happened: the impact of enlargement on the Common Foreign and Security Policy Council working groups,' *European Political Economy Review*, 6/March: 4–30.

Jupille, J., Caporaso, J., and Checkel, J. T. (2003) 'Integrating institutions: rationalism, constructivism, and the study of the European Union', *Comparative Political Studies*, 36/1–2: 7–40.

Kaeding, M. (2005) 'The world of committee reports: rapporteurship assignment in the European Parliament', *Journal of Legislative Studies*, 11/1: 82–104.

Kassim, H. (2004a) 'EU member states and the Prodi Commission', in D. G. Dimitrakopoulos (ed.) *The Changing European Commission* (Manchester and New York: Manchester University Press).

—————— (2004b) 'The Kinnock reforms in perspective: why reforming the Commission is an heroic, but thankless task', *Public Policy and Administration*, 19/3: 25–41.

—————— and Menon, A. (2004) 'EU member states and the Prodi Commission', in D. G. Dimitrakopoulos (ed.) *The Changing European Commission* (Manchester and New York: Manchester University Press).

——————, Peterson, J., Bauer, M., Connolly, S., Dehousse, R., Hooghe, L., and Thompson, A. (2012) *The European Commission of the 21st Century* (Oxford and New York: Oxford University Press).

Kelemen, R. D. (2002) 'The politics of "Eurocratic" structure and the new European agencies', *West European Politics* 25/4: 93–118.

—————— (2005) 'The politics of Eurocracy: building a new European state?', in N. Jabko and C. Parsons (eds) *The State of the European Union Vol. 7: With US or Against US? European Trends in American Perspective* (Oxford and New York: Oxford University Press).

—————— and Tarrant, A. (2011) 'The political foundations of the Eurocracy'. *West European Politics*, forthcoming.

Kenen, P. (2006) 'Comment on central banks, governments and the European monetary unification process', *Bank for International Settlements Working Papers No. 201*.

Keohane, R. O. (1998) 'International institutions: can interdependence work?', *Foreign Policy*, 110/Spring: 82–96.

Keohane, R. O. and Hoffmann, S. (1991) (eds) *The New European Community: Decision-making and Institutional Change* (Boulder, CO: Westview Press).

Keukeleire S. and Bruyninckx, H. (2011) 'The European Union, the BRICs, and the emerging new world order', in C. Hill, and M. Smith (eds) *International Relations and the European Union* (Oxford and New York: Oxford University Press) 2nd edition.

Kingdon, J. W. (1984) *Agendas, Alternatives, and Public Policies* (New York: Harper Collins).

Koenig, N. (2011) *The EU and Libyan Crisis: In Quest of Coherence?*, 19 July (Rome: IAI Working Paper 11), available online at **http://www.iai.it/pdf/DocIAI/iaiwp1119.pdf**

Kohler-Koch, B. (2000) '"Framing": the bottleneck of constructing legitimate institutions', *Journal of European Public Policy*, 7/4: 513–31.

———— and Eising, R. (1999) (eds) *The Transformation of Government in the European Union* (London and New York: Routledge).

Kreppel, A. (2002) *The European Parliament and the Supranational Party System: A Study of Institutional Development* (Cambridge: Cambridge University Press).

Lacroix, J. (2010) '"Borderline Europe": French visions of the European Union', in J. Lacroix and K. Nicolaïdis (eds) *European Stories: Intellectual Debates on Europe in National Contexts* (Oxford and New York: Oxford University Press).

Ladrech, R. (1994) 'Europeanization of domestic politics and institutions: the case of France', *Journal of Common Market Studies*, 32/1: 69–88.

———— (2000) *Social Democracy and the Challenge of European Union* (Boulder, CO: Lynne Rienner).

Laffan, B. (1997a) *The Finances of the Union* (London: Macmillan).

———— (1997b) 'From policy entrepreneur to policy manager: the challenge facing the European Commission', *Journal of European Public Policy*, 4/3: 422–38.

———— (1999) 'Becoming a "living institution": the evolution of the European Court of Auditors', *Journal of Common Market Studies*, 37/2: 251–68.

———— (2003) 'Auditing and accountability in the European Union', *Journal of European Public Policy*, 10/5: 762–77.

———— (2004) 'The European Union and Its Institutions as "Identity Builders"', in R. Hermann, T. Risse, and M. Brewer (eds) *Transnational Identities: Becoming European in the EU* (Lanham, MD: Rowman and Littlefield).

————, O'Donnell, R., and Smith, M. (2000) *Europe's Experimental Union: Rethinking Integration* (London and New York: Routledge).

Laïdi, Z. (2008a) (ed.) *EU Foreign Policy in a Globalized World: Normative Power and Social Preferences* (London and New York: Routledge).

———— (2008b) 'European preferences and their reception', in Z. Laïdi (ed.) *EU Foreign Policy in a Globalized World: Normative Power and Social Preferences* (London and New York: Routledge).

Lamfalussy, A. (2006) 'Central banks, governments and the European monetary unification process', *Bank for International Settlements Working Papers No 201* (Basel).

Lavenex, S. (1999) *Safe Third Countries: Extending the EU Asylum and Immigration Policies to Central and Eastern Europe* (Budapest: Central European University Press).

———— (2006) 'Shifting up and out: the foreign policy of European immigration control', *West European Politics*, 29/2: 329–50.

Lempp, J. (2006) 'COREPER enlarged: how enlargement affected the functioning of COREPER', Paper presented at the ECPR Third Pan-European Conference, Istanbul, 21–23 September.

Leonard, M. (2005) *Why Europe Will Run the 21st Century* (London and New York: Harper Collins).

Lequesne, C. (1996) 'La Commission Européenne entre autonomie et dépendance', *Revue Française de Science Politique*, 46/3: 389–408.

Leuffen, D. (2000) *Implementing European Union Public Policy* (Cheltenham: Edward Elgar).

——— (2010) 'The impact of Eastern Enlargement on the internal functioning of the EU: why so much continuity?', Paper presented at the Conference, 'Europe Twenty Years after the Cold War: The New Europe—New Europes?', Graduate Institute, Geneva, 14–15 October.

Levy, R. (1996) 'Managing value for money audit in the European Union: the challenge of diversity', *Journal of Common Market Studies*, 43/4: 509–29.

——— (2000) *Implementing European Union Public Policy* (Cheltenham: Edward Elgar).

Lewis, J. (1998a) 'Is the "hard bargaining" image of the Council misleading? The Committee of Permanent Representatives and the Local Elections Directive', *Journal of Common Market Studies*, 36/4: 479–504.

——— (1998b) 'Constructing interests: the Committee of Permanent Representatives and decision-making in the European Union', Unpublished dissertation, University of Wisconsin-Madison.

——— (2000) 'The methods of Community in EU decision-making and administrative rivalry in the Council's infrastructure', *Journal of European Public Policy*, 7/2: 261–89.

——— (2005) 'The Janus face of Brussels: socialization and everyday decision making in the European Union', *International Organization*, 59/4: 937–91.

Lightfoot, S. (2005) *Europeanizing Social Democracy? The Rise of the Party of European Socialists* (Abingdon: Routledge).

Lindberg, L. N. (1963) *The Political Dynamics of European Integration* (Stanford, CA: Stanford University Press).

——— and Scheingold, S. A. (1970) *Europe's Would-be Polity: Patterns of Change in the European Community* (Englewood Cliffs, NY: Prentice-Hall).

———, Rasmussen, A., and Warntjen, A. (2008) (eds) 'The role of political parties in the European Union', *Journal of European Public Policy*, 15/8 (special issue).

Lindner, J. and Rittberger, B. (2003) 'The creation, interpretation and contestation of institutions: revisiting historical institutionalism', *Journal of Common Market Studies*, 41/3: 445–73.

Lindstädt, R., Slapin, J. B., and Vander Wielen, R. J. (2011) 'Balancing competing demands: position taking and election proximity in the European Parliament', *Legislative Studies Quarterly*, 36/1: 37–70.

Linz, J. J. (1998) 'Democracy's time constraints', *International Political Science Review*, 19: 19–37.

Lodge, J. and Herman, V. (1980) 'The Economic and Social Committee in EEC decision-making', *International Organization*, 34/2: 265–84.

Lord, C. and Magnette, P. (2004) 'E pluribus unum? Creative disagreement about legitimacy in the EU', *Journal of Common Market Studies*, 42/1: 183–202.

Lowe, D. (1995) 'The development policy of the EU and the mid-term review of the Lomé Partnership', *The European Union 1995: Annual Review of Activities* (*Journal of Common Market Studies*), 33: 15–28.

Ludlow, P. (1992) 'Europe's institutions: Europe's politics', in G. F. Treverton (ed.) *The Shape of the New Europe* (New York: Council on Foreign Relations Press).

Ludlow, P. (2000) *A View from Brussels: Briefing Notes on the European Councils* (Brussels: EuroComment).

———— (2001) *The European Council at Nice: Neither Triumph nor Disaster*, Background Paper, CEPS International Advisory Council, 1–2 February, Brussels.

———— (2002) *The Laeken Council* (Brussels: EuroComment).

———— (2010) *A View from Brussels: Briefing Notes on the European Councils* (Brussels: EuroComment).

———— (2011) *A View from Brussels: Briefing Notes on the European Councils* (Brussels: EuroComment).

Lyon, J. (2005) 'EU's Bosnia police mission is "laughing stock"', *European Voice*, 15 September, pp. 15–21.

Mace, C. (2003) 'Operation Artemis: mission improbable?', *European Security Review*, 18 July, available online at **http://www.isis-europe.org**

MacMullen, A. (1999) 'Fraud, mismanagement and nepotism: the Committee of Independent Experts and the fall of the European Commission', *Crime, Law and Social Change*, 31/4: 193–208.

———— (2000) 'European Commissioners 1952–1999: national routes to a European elite', in N. Nugent (ed.) *At the Heart of the Union* (2nd edn, Basingstoke and New York: Palgrave).

Maduro, M. and Azoulai, L. (2010) (eds) *The Past and Future of EU Law* (Oxford: Hart).

Maes, I. (2006) 'The ascent of the European Commission as an actor in the monetary integration process in the 1960s', *Scottish Journal of Political Economy*, 53/2: 222–41.

Magnette, P. (2001) 'Appointing and censuring the Commission: the adaptation of parliamentary institutions to the Community context', *European Law Journal*, 1/3: 289–307.

———— (2005a) *What is the European Union?* (Basingstoke: Palgrave).

———— (2005b) 'In the name of simplification: coping with constitutional conflicts in the Convention on the Future of Europe', *European Law Journal*, 11/4: 434–53.

———— and Nicolaïdis, K. (2004) 'The European Convention: bargaining under the shadow of rhetoric', *West European Politics*, 27/3: 381–404.

Mair, P. (2000) 'The limited impact of Europe on national party systems', *West European Politics*, 23/4: 27–51.

———— and Thomassen, J. (2010) 'Political representation and government in the European Union', *Journal of European Public Policy*, 17/1: 20–35.

Majone, G. (1996) *Regulating Europe* (London: Routledge).

———— (2000) 'The credibility crisis of Community regulation', *Journal of Common Market Studies*, 38/1: 273–302.

———— (2003) (ed.) *Risk Regulation in the European Union: Between Enlargement and Internationalization* (Florence: European University Institute).

———— (2005) *Dilemmas of European Integration: The Ambiguities and Pitfalls of Integration by Stealth* (Oxford: Oxford University Press).

Mamadouh, V. and Raunio, T. (2003) 'The Committee system: powers, appointments and report allocation', *Journal of Common Market Studies*, 41/2: 333–51.

Mandelson, P. (2005) 'The idea of Europe: can we make it live again?', UACES Lecture on the Future of Europe, Brussels, 20 July, available online at **http://www.uaces.org**

Manners I. and Whitman, R. (2001) (eds) *The Foreign Policy of the EU Member States* (Manchester: Manchester University Press).

Manow, P. and Döring, H. (2008) 'Electoral and mechanical causes of divided government in the European Union', *Comparative Political Studies*, 41/10: 1349–70.

March, J. G. and Olsen, J. P. (1989) *Rediscovering Institutions: The Organizational Basis of Politics* (New York: The Free Press).

Marks, G. (1993) 'Structural policy and multi-level governance in the EC', in A. Cafruny and G. Rosenthal (eds) *The State of the European Community, Vol. 2: The Maastricht Debates and Beyond* (Boulder, CO: Lynne Rienner).

—— (1996) 'An actor-centred approach to multilevel governance', *Regional & Federal Studies*, 6/2: 21–36.

—— and Hooghe, L. (2001) *Multi-level Governance and European Integration* (Boulder, CO: Rowman & Littlefield).

—— and Steenbergen, M. R. (2004) (eds) *European Integration and Political Conflict* (Cambridge: Cambridge University Press).

—— and Wilson, C. (2000) 'The past in the present: a cleavage theory of party response to European integration', *British Journal of Political Science*, 30/3: 433–59.

——, Hooghe, L., and Blank, K. (1996) 'European integration from the 1980s: state-centric v. multi-level governance', *Journal of Common Market Studies*, 34/3: 341–78.

Mattila, M. (2008) 'Voting and coalitions in the Council after enlargement', in D. Naurin and H. Wallace (eds) *Unveiling the Council of the European Union: Games Governments Play in Brussels* (New York: Palgrave Macmillan).

—— (2009) 'Roll call analysis of voting in the European Union Council of Ministers after the 2004 Enlargement'. *European Journal of Political Research*, 48/6: 840–57.

—— and Raunio, T. (2006) 'Cautious voters—supportive parties: opinion congruence between voters and parties on the EU dimension', *European Union Politics*, 7/4: 427–49.

Mattson, I. and Strøm, K. (1995) 'Parliamentary committees', in H. Döring (ed.) *Parliaments and Majority Rule in Western Europe* (Frankfurt and New York: Campus and St. Martin's Press).

Maurer, A., Parkes, R., and Wagner, M. (2008) 'Explaining group membership in the European Parliament: the British Conservatives and the movement for European reform', *Journal of European Public Policy*, 15/2: 246–62.

Mayne, R. (1962) *The Community of Europe* (New York: W. W. Norton).

Mazey, S. and Richardson, J. (1993) *Lobbying in the European Community* (Oxford: Oxford University Press).

McCarthy, R. (1997) 'The Committee of the Regions: an advisory body's tortuous path to influence', *Journal of European Public Policy*, 4: 439–54.

McCormick, J. (2007) *The European Superpower* (Basingstoke and New York: Palgrave Macmillan).

McCubbins, M. D., Noll, R. G., and Weingast, B. R. (1987) 'Administrative procedures as instruments of political control', *Journal of Law, Economics and Organization*, 3/2: 243–77.

McElroy, G. (2006) 'Committee representation in the European Parliament', *European Union Politics*, 7/1: 5–29.

—— and Benoit, K. (2007) 'Party groups and policy positions in the European Parliament', *Party Politics*, 13/1: 5–28.

—— and —— (2010) 'Party policy and group affiliation in the European Parliament', *British Journal of Political Science*, 40/2: 377–98.

McNamara, K. (1998) *The Currency of Ideas: Monetary Politics in Europe* (Ithaca, NY: Cornell University Press).

—— (2002) 'Rational fictions: central bank independence and the social logic of delegation', *West European Politics*, 25/1: 47–76.

Menon, A. and Weatherill, S. (2006) 'Transnational legitimacy in a globalising world: how the European Union rescues its states', *West European Politics*, 31/3: 397–416.

Mentler, M. (1996) *Der Auschuss der Ständigen Vertreter bei den Europäischen Gemeinschaften* (Baden-Baden: Nomos).

Metcalfe, L. (2000) 'Reforming the Commission: will organisational efficiency produce effective governance?', *Journal of Common Market Studies*, 38/5: 817–41.

Milton, G. and Keller-Noëllet, J. (2005) *The European Constitution: Its Origins, Negotiation and Meaning* (London: John Harper).

Milward, A. (1992) *The European Rescue of the Nation-state* (London: Routledge).

Mitsilegas, V., Monar, J., and Rees, W. (2003) *The European Union and Internal Security: Guardian of the People?* (New York: Palgrave Macmillan).

Monar, J. (2002) 'Institutionalising freedom, security and justice', in J. Peterson and M. Shackleton (eds) *The Institutions of the European Union* (Oxford and New York: Oxford University Press).

Monnet, J. (1978) *Memoirs* (New York and London: Doubleday and Collins).

Moravcsik, A. (1991) 'Negotiating the Single European Act: national interests and conventional statecraft in the European Community', *International Organization*, 45/1: 19–56.

———— (1998) *The Choice for Europe: Social Purpose and State Power from Messina to Maastricht* (London and Ithaca, NY: UCL Press and Cornell University Press).

———— (2002) 'In defence of the "democratic deficit": reassessing legitimacy in the European Union', *Journal of Common Market Studies*, 40/4: 603–24.

———— (2003) 'Reassessing legitimacy in the European Union', in J. H. H. Weiler, I. Begg, and J. Peterson (eds) *Integration in an Expanding European Union* (Oxford and Malden, MA: Blackwell).

———— (2005) 'The European constitutional compromise and the neofunctionalist legacy', *Journal of European Public Policy*, 12/2: 349–86.

———— and Nicolaïdis, K. (1999) 'Explaining the Treaty of Amsterdam: interests, influence, institutions', *Journal of Common Market Studies*, 37/1: 59–85.

———— and Schimmelfennig, F. (2009) 'Liberal intergovernmentalism', in A. Wiener and T. Diez (eds) *European Integration Theory* (2nd edn, Oxford and New York: Oxford University Press).

Morgenthau, H. J. (1948) *Politics among Nations* (Chicago, IL: Chicago University Press).

Narjes, K.-H. (1998) 'Walter Hallstein and the early phase of the EEC', in W. Loth, W. Wallace and W. Wessels (eds) *Walter Hallstein: The Forgotten European?* (Basingstoke and New York: Macmillan and St Martin's Press).

Naurin, D. and Wallace, H. (2008) (eds) *Unveiling the Council of the European Union: Games Governments Play in Brussels* (Basingstoke: Palgrave Macmillan).

Nelsen, B. F. and Stubb, A. (1998) (eds) *European Union: Readings on the Theory and Practice of European Integration* (2nd edn, Basingstoke and Boulder, CO: Palgrave and Lynne Rienner).

Netjes, C. E. and Binnema, H. A. (2007) 'The salience of the European integration issue: three data sources compared', *Electoral Studies*, 26/1: 39–49.

Noël, E. (1966) 'The Permanent Representatives Committee', Lecture delivered to the Institute of European Studies, Université Libre de Bruxelles, 19 and 21 April, reprinted in *A Tribute to Emile Noël: Secretary-General of the European Commission from 1958 to 1987* (Luxembourg: Office for Official Publications of the European Communities).

———— (1967) 'The Committee of Permanent Representatives', *Journal of Common Market Studies*, 5/3: 219–51.

———— and Étienne, H. (1971) 'The Permanent Representatives Committee and the "deepening" of the Communities', *Government and Opposition*, 6/4/Autumn: 422–47.

Norman, P. (2003) *The Accidental Constitution: The Story of the European Convention* (Brussels: Eurocomment).

——— (2005) *The Accidental Constitution: The Story of the European Convention* (2nd edn, Brussels: Eurocomment).

Nugent, N. (1999) *The Government and Politics of the European Union* (4th edn, Basingstoke and New York: Palgrave).

——— (2000) (ed.) *At the Heart of the Union* (2nd edn, Basingstoke and New York: Palgrave).

——— (2001) *The European Commission* (Basingstoke and New York: Palgrave).

——— (2010) *The Government and Politics of the European Union* (7th edn, Basingstoke and New York: Palgrave).

Nuttall, S. (1992) *European Political Cooperation* (Oxford: Clarendon Press).

——— (2000) *European Foreign Policy* (Oxford: Oxford University Press).

Nye Jr, J. (2004) *Soft Power: The Means to Success in World Politics* (New York: Basic Books).

——— (2011) *The Future of Power* (New York: PublicAffairs).

OLAF (2000) *Report by the European Anti-Fraud Office (OLAF): First Report on Operational Activities, 1 June 1999–31 May 2000*, available online at **http://ec.europa.eu/anti_fraud/reports/olaf/2000/rep_olaf_2000_en.pdf**

——— (2004) *Report by the European Anti-Fraud Office (OLAF): Fifth Activity Report for the Year Ending June 2004*, available online at **http://ec.europa.eu/anti_fraud/reports/olaf/2003-2004/en2.pdf**

——— (2009) *Tenth Activity Report of the European Anti-Fraud Office (OLAF)*, available online at **http://ec.europa.eu/anti_fraud/reports/olaf/2009/en1.pdf**

Olsen, J. P. (2002) 'Reforming European institutions of governance', *Journal of Common Market Studies*, 40/4: 581–602.

——— (2003) 'Reforming European institutions of governance', in J. H. H. Weiler, I. Begg, and J. Peterson (eds) *Integration in an Expanding European Union: Reassessing the Fundamentals* (Oxford and Malden, MA: Blackwell).

Olson, M. (2002) *The Logic of Collective Action: Public Goods and the Theory of Groups* (Cambridge, MA and London: Harvard University Press).

Padoa-Schioppa, T. (1999) 'EMU and banking supervision', Lecture delivered at the London School of Economics, Financial Markets Group, 24 February.

———, Emerson, M., King, M., Milleron, J. C., Paelinck, J. H. P., Papademos, L. D., Pastor, A., and Scharpf, F. W. (1987) *Efficiency, Stability, and Equity: A Strategy for the Evolution of the Economic System of the European Community* (Oxford: Oxford University Press).

Page, E. (1997) *People Who Run Europe* (Oxford: Clarendon Press).

Palmer, J. (2005) 'After the Dutch referendum', *Political Europe* (Brussels: European Policy Centre), available online at **http://www.epc.eu**

Paoletti, E. (2011) 'Migration and foreign policy: the case of Libya', *Journal of North African Studies*, 16/2: 215–31.

Papagianni, G. (2001). 'Flexibility in justice and home affairs: an old phenomenon taking new forms', in B. de Witte, D. Hanf, and E. Vos. (eds) *The Many Faces of Differentiation in EU Law* (New York: Intersentia).

Parsons, C. (2003) *A Certain Idea of Europe* (Ithaca, NY, and London: Cornell University Press).

Pastore, F., Monzini, P., and Sciortino, G. (2006). 'Schengen's soft underbelly? Irregular migration and human smuggling across land and sea borders to Italy', *International Migration*, 44/4: 95–119.

Paterson, W. (2008) 'Did France and Germany lead Europe? A retrospect', in J. Hayward (ed.) *Leaderless Europe* (Oxford and New York: Oxford University Press).

Patten, C. (2010) 'What is Europe to do?', *New York Review of Books*, LVII/4 (11–24 March): 11–12.

Pedler, R. and Schaeffer, T. (1996) (eds) *Shaping European Law and Policy: The Role of Committees and Comitology in the Political Process* (Maastricht: European Institute of Public Administration).

Peers, S. (2011) *EU Justice and Home Affairs Law* (3rd edn, Oxford: Oxford University Press).

Pennings, P. (2006) 'An empirical analysis of the Europeanization of national party manifestos, 1960–2003', *European Union Politics*, 7/2: 257–70.

Pescatore, P. (1987) 'Some critical remarks on the Single European Act', *Common Market Law Review*, XXIV/1: 9–18.

Peters, B. G. (1999) *Institutional Theory in Political Science* (London and New York: Continuum).

Peterson, J. (1995) 'Decision-making in the European Union: towards a framework for analysis', *Journal of European Public Policy*, 2/1: 69–93.

—— (1997) 'The European Union: pooled sovereignty, divided accountability', *Political Studies*, 45/3: 559–78.

—— (1999) 'The Santer era: the European Commission in normative, historical and theoretical perspective', *Journal of European Public Policy*, 6/1: 46–65.

—— (2002) 'The College of Commissioners', in J. Peterson and M. Shackleton (eds) *The Institutions of the European Union* (Oxford and New York: Oxford University Press).

—— (2004) 'The Prodi Commission: fresh start or free fall?', in D. G. Dimitrakopoulos (ed.) *The Changing European Commission* (Manchester and New York: Manchester University Press).

—— (2006) 'Conclusion: where does the Commission stand today?', in D. Spence and G. Edwards (eds) *The European Commission* (London: John Harper).

—— (2008a) 'Enlargement, reform and the European Commission: weathering a perfect storm?', *Journal of European Public Policy*, 15/5: 761–80.

—— (2008b) 'José Manuel Barroso: political scientist, ECPR member', *European Political Science*, 7/1: 64–77.

—— (2009) 'Policy networks', in A. Wiener and T. Diez (eds) *European Intergration Theory* (2nd edn, Oxford: Oxford University Press).

—— and Bomberg, E. (1999) *Decision-making in the European Union* (Basingstoke and New York: Palgrave).

—— and —— (2001) 'The EU after the 1990s: explaining continuity and change', in M. G. Cowles and M. Smith (eds) *The State of the European Union, Vol. V: Risks, Reform, Resistance or Revival?* (Oxford and New York: Oxford University Press).

—— and Jones, E. (1999) 'Decision making in an enlarging European Union', in J. Sperling (ed.) *Two Tiers or Two Speeds? The European Security Order and the Enlargement of the European Union and NATO* (Manchester: Manchester University Press).

—— and Sjursen, H. (1998) (eds) *A Common Foreign Policy for Europe?* (London: Routledge).

Pierson, P. (1996) 'The path to European integration: a historical institutionalist analysis', *Comparative Political Studies*, 29/2: 123–63.

—— (2004) *Politics in Time: History, Institutions, and Social Analysis* (Princeton, NJ, and Oxford: Princeton University Press).

Piris, J.-C. (2010) *The Lisbon Treaty: A Legal and Political Analysis* (Cambridge and New York: Cambridge University Press).

Pollack, M. (1997) 'Delegation, agency and agenda-setting in the European Union', *International Organization*, 51/1: 99–134.

—— (1998) 'The engines of integration? Supranational autonomy and influence in the European Union', in A. Stone Sweet and W. Sandholtz (eds) *European Integration and Supranational Governance* (Oxford: Oxford University Press).

—— (2003) *The Engines of European Integration: Delegation, Agency, and Agenda Setting in the EU* (Oxford and New York: Oxford University Press).

—— (2006) 'Rational choice and EU politics', in K. E. Jørgensen, M. A. Pollack, and B. Rosamond (eds) *Handbook of European Union Politics* (London and Thousand Oaks, CA: Sage).

—— (2009) 'The new institutionalisms and European integration', in A. Wiener and T. Diez (eds) *European Integration Theory* (2nd edn, Oxford and New York: Oxford University Press).

Pollitt, C. and Bouckaert, G. (2004) *Public Management Reform: A Comparative Analysis* (2nd edn, Oxford and New York: Oxford University Press).

Pridham, G. and Pridham, P. (1981) *Transnational Party Cooperation and European Integration: The Process towards Direct Elections* (London: Allen & Unwin).

Priestley, J. (2011) 'Right question: wrong answer'. *European Voice*, 28 July.

Prodi, R. (1999) 'Speech to the European Parliament', 4 May, available online at http://europa.eu/rapid/pressReleasesAction.do?reference=BIO/99/191&format=HTML&aged=1&language=EN&guiLanguage=en

Puetter, U. (2006) *The Eurogroup: How a Secretive Circle of Finance Ministers Shapes European Economic Governance* (Manchester: Manchester University Press).

Pujas, V. (2003) 'The European Anti-Fraud Offfice (OLAF): a European policy to fight against economic and financial fraud?', *Journal of European Public Policy*, 10/5: 778–97.

Putnam, R. (1993) *Making Democracy Work: Civic Traditions in Modern Italy* (Princeton,NJ: Princeton University Press).

Quaglia, L. (2008) *Central Banking Governance in the European Union: A Comparative Analysis* (London: Routledge).

—— (2009) 'Political science and the Cinderellas of economic and monetary union: payments services and clearing and settlement of securities', *Journal of European Public Policy*, 16/4: 623–39.

Quermonne, J.-L. *et al.* (1999) *The European Union in Pursuit of Legitimate and Effective Institutions* (Paris: Commissariat général du plan).

Quirke, B. (2010) 'Fighting EU fraud: why do we make life difficult for ourselves?', *Journal of Financial Crime*, 17/1: 61–80.

Randzio-Plath, C. (2000) 'A new political culture in the EU: democratic accountability of the ECB', *Center for European Integration Studies Working Paper B-04/2000*.

Rasmussen, A. (2000) 'Losing independence or finally gaining recognition? Contacts between MEPs and national parties', *Party Politics*, 6/2: 211–23.

—— (2007) 'Early conclusion to the co-decision legislative procedure', *European University Institute Working Papers, MWP 2007/31*.

Raunio, T. (2000) 'Losing independence or finally gaining recognition? Contacts between MEPs and national parties', *Party Politics*, 6/2: 211–23.

Raz, J. (2002) 'On the authority and interpretation of constitutions: some preliminaries', in L. Alexander (ed.) *Constitutionalism: Philosophical Foundations* (Cambridge: Cambridge University Press).

Rees, W. R. (1998) *The Western European Union at the Crossroads* (Oxford and Boulder, CO: Westview Press).

Reif, K. and Schmitt, H. (1980) 'Nine second-order national elections: a conceptual framework for the analysis of European election results', *European Journal of Political Research*, 8/1: 3–44.

Rhodes, R. A. W. (1995) 'The institutional approach', in D. Marsh and G. Stoker (eds) *Theory and Methods in Political Science* (Basingstoke and New York: Palgrave).

Ringe, N. (2010) *Who Decides, and How? Preferences, Uncertainty, and Policy Choice in the European Parliament* (Oxford: Oxford University Press).

Risse, T. (2004) 'European institutions and identity change: what have we learned?', in R. Hermann, T. Risse, and M. Brewer (eds) *Transnational Identities: Becoming European in the EU* (Lanham, MD: Rowman and Littlefield).

—— (2007) 'Assessing the legitimacy of the EU's treaty revision methods', *Journal of Common Market Studies*, 45/1: 69–80.

—— (2009) 'Social constructivism and European integration', in A. Wiener and T. Diez (eds) *European Integration Theory* (2nd edn, Oxford and New York: Oxford University Press).

—— (2010) *A Community of Europeans? Transnational Identities and Public Spheres* (Ithaca, NY: Cornell University Press).

Rittberger, B. (2001) 'Which institutions for post-war Europe? Explaining the institutional design of Europe's first community', *Journal of European Public Policy*, 8/5: 673–708.

—— (2005) *Building Europe's Parliament: Democratic Representation beyond the Nation-state* (Oxford: Oxford University Press).

—— and Wonka, A. (2010) 'Credibility, complexity and uncertainty: explaining the institutional independence of 29 EU agencies', *West European Politics*, 33/3: 730–52.

Rodrik, D. (2011) *The Globalization Paradox: Why Global Markets, States and Democracy Can't Co-exist* (Oxford and New York: Oxford University Press).

Rosato, S. (2010) *Europe United: Power Politics and the Making of the European Community* (Ithaca, NY: Cornell University Press).

—— (2011) 'Europe's troubles: power politics and the state of the European project', *International Security*, 35/4: 45–86.

Ross, G. (1995) *Jacques Delors and European Integration* (New York and London: Polity Press).

Rowe, C. (2011) *Regional Representations in the EU: Between Diplomacy and Interest Representation* (Basingstoke: Palgrave Macmillan).

Ruggie, J. G. (1998) *Constructing the World Polity: Essays on International Institutionalization* (London and New York: Routledge).

Salmon, J. (1971) 'Les representations et mission permanentes auprés de la CEE et de l'Euratom', in M. Virally, *et al.* (eds) *Les Mission Permanentes Auprés des Organisations Internationales* (vol. 1, Brussels: Dotation Carnegie pour la Paix Internationale).

Sanders, D. (2010) 'Behavioural analysis', in D. Marsh and G. Stoker (eds) *Theory and Methods in Political Science* (3rd edn, Basingstoke and New York: Palgrave).

Sanders, E. (2006) 'Historical institutionalism', in R. A. W. Rhodes, S. A. Binder, and B. A. Rockman (eds) *The Oxford Handbook of Political Institutions* (Oxford and New York: Oxford University Press).

Sauger, N., Brouard, S., and Grossman, E. (2007) *Les Français contre l'Europe? Les Sens du Referendum du 29 Mai 2005* (Paris: Presses de Sciences Po).

Sbragia, A. (1991) (ed.) *Europolitics* (Washington DC: Brookings Institution).

Scharpf, F. (1999) *Governing in Europe: Effective and Democratic?* (Oxford and New York: Oxford University Press).

Schmitt, H. (2009) (ed.) 'European Parliament elections after Eastern Enlargement', *Journal of European Integration*, 31/5 (special issue).

Schönlau, J. (2008) 'The CoR at 15: what role in a multi-level democracy?', Unpublished paper, RECON.

Scully, R. M. (2005) *Becoming Europeans? Attitudes, Behaviour and Socialization in the European Parliament* (Oxford: Oxford University Press).

Sedelmeier, U. (2005) *Constructing the Path to Eastern Enlargement* (Manchester and New York: Manchester University Press).

—————— (2011) 'The differential impact of the European Union on European politics', in E. Jones, P. M. Heywood, M. Rhodes, and U. Sedelmeier (eds) *Developments in European Politics* (2nd edn, Basingstoke and New York: Palgrave Macmillan).

Settembri, S. and Neuhold, C. (2009) 'Achieving consensus through committees: does the European Parliament manage?', *Journal of Common Market Studies*, 47/1: 127–51.

Shackleton, M. (1997) 'The internal legitimacy crisis of the European Union', in A. W. Cafruny and C. Lankowski (eds) *Europe's Ambiguous Unity* (Boulder, CO, and London: Lynne Rienner).

—————— (2000) 'The politics of co-decision', *Journal of Common Market Studies*, 38/2: 325–42.

—————— (2005) 'Parliamentary government or division of powers: is the destination still unknown?', in C. Parsons and N. Jabko (eds) *The State of the European Union: With US or Against US* (Oxford and New York: Oxford University Press).

—————— and Raunio, T. (2003) 'Codecision since Amsterdam: a laboratory for institutional innovation and change', *Journal of European Public Policy*, 10/2: 171–87.

Shapiro, M. (1997) 'The problems of independent agencies in the US and the EU', *Journal of European Public Policy*, 4/2: 279–91.

Siedentop, L. (2000) *Democracy in Europe* (Harmondsworth: Penguin).

Skach, C. (2005) 'We, the peoples? Constitutionalizing the European Union', *Journal of Common Market Studies*, 43/1: 149–70.

Skocpol, T. (1985) 'Bringing the state back in: strategies of analysis in current research', in P. B. Evans, D. Rieschemeyer, and T. Skocpol (eds) *Bringing the State Back In* (Cambridge: Cambridge University Press).

Slaughter, A.-M. (2004) *The Real New World Order* (Princeton, NJ: Princeton University Press).

Sloan, S. (2005) *NATO, the European Union and the Atlantic Community* (2nd edn, Oxford and Boulder, CO: Rowman and Littlefield).

Smismans, S. (1999) 'An Economic and Social Committee for the citizen, or a citizen for the Economic and Social Committee?', *European Public Law*, 5: 557–82.

——— (2000) 'The European Economic and Social Committee: towards deliberative democracy via a functional assembly', *European Integration Online Papers 4/12*, available online at **http://eiop.or.at/eiop/texte/2000-012a.htm**

——— (2003) 'European civil society: shaped by discourses and institutional interests', *European Law Journal*, 9: 482–504.

Smith, J. (1999) *Europe's Elected Parliament* (Sheffield: Sheffield University Press).

Smith, K. E. (2008) *European Union Foreign Policy in a Changing World* (2nd edn, Oxford and Malden, MA: Polity).

Smith, M. E. (2003) *Europe's Foreign and Security Policy: The Institutionalization of Cooperation* (Cambridge: Cambridge University Press).

——— (2011) 'A liberal grand strategy in a realist world? Power, purpose and the EU's changing global role', *Journal of European Public Policy*, 18/2: 144–63.

Spaak, P. H. (1969) *Combats Inachevés* (2 vols, Paris: Fayard).

Spence, D. (1991) 'Enlargement without accession: the EC's response to German unification', *RIIA Discussion Paper 36* (London: Royal Institute of International Affairs).

——— (2000) 'Plus ça change, plus c'est la meme chose? Attempting to reform the European Commission', *Journal of European Public Policy*, 7/1: 1–25.

——— (2002) 'The evolving role of foreign ministries in the conduct of European Union affairs', in B. Hocking and D. Spence (eds) *Foreign Ministries in the European Union* (Basingstoke and New York: Palgrave).

——— (2006) (ed.) *The European Commission* (3rd edn, London: John Harper).

Stacey, J. (2003) 'Displacement of the Council via informal dynamics? Comparing the Commission and Parliament', *Journal of European Public Policy*, 10/6: 936–55.

Stark, J. (2008) 'Does the Eurozone need an economic government?', Statement delivered at the HEC European Executive Campus, Brussels, 22 January, available online at **http://www.ecb.int/press/key/date/2008/html/sp080122_1.en.html**

Stasavage, D. (2004) 'Open-door or closed door? Transparency in domestic and international bargaining', *International Organization*, 58/2: 667–703.

Steenbergen, M. R. and Scott, D. J. (2004) 'Contesting Europe? The salience of European integration as a party issue', in G. Marks and M. R. Steenbergen (eds) *European Integration and Political Conflict* (Cambridge: Cambridge University Press).

Stein, J. (1981) 'Lawyers, judges and the making of a transnational constitution', *American Journal of International Law*, 75/1: 1–27.

Steinmo, S. (2004) 'Néo-institutionnalismes', in L. Boussaguet, S. Jacquot, and P. Ravinet (eds) *Dictionnaire des Politiques Publiques* (Paris: Presses de Sciences Po).

Stevens, A. with Stevens, H. (2001) *Brussels Bureaucrats: The Administration of the European Union* (Basingstoke: Palgrave).

Stewart, R. (1975) 'The reformation of American administrative law', *Harvard Law Review*, 88: 1667–813.

Stone Sweet, A. and Sandholtz, W. (1998) 'Integration, supranational governance, and the institutionalization of the European polity', in W. Sandholtz and A. Stone Sweet (eds) *European Integration and Supranational Governance* (Oxford: Oxford University Press).

Strasser, D. (1992) *The Finances of Europe* (7th edn, Luxembourg: EC Official Publications).

Stubb, A. (2000) 'The Finnish Presidency', *Journal of Common Market Studies*, 38/Annual Review/Sept: 49–53.

Szczerbiak, A. and Taggart, P. (2008) (eds) *Opposing Europe? The Comparative Party Politics of Euroscepticism: Vols 1 and II* (Oxford: Oxford University Press).

Szymanski, M. and Smith, M. E. (2005) 'Coherence and conditionality in European foreign policy', *Journal of Common Market Studies*, 43/1: 171–92.

Tallberg. J. (2004) 'The power of the Presidency: brokerage, efficiency and distribution in EU negotiations', *Journal of Common Market Studies*, 42/5: 999–1024.

———— (2008) 'The power of the chair: formal leadership by the Council Presidency', in D. Naurin and H. Wallace (eds) *Unveiling the Council of the European Union: Games Governments Play in Brussels* (Basingstoke: Palgrave Macmillan).

Tatham, M. (2008) 'Going solo: direct regional representation in the European Union', *Regional and Federal Studies*, 18: 493–515.

Taulègne, B. (1993) *Le Conseil Européen* (Paris: P.U.F).

Thelen, K. and Steinmo, S. (1992) *Structuring Politics: Historical Institutionalism in Comparative Analysis* (Cambridge: Cambridge University Press).

Thomassen, J. (2009) 'In conclusion: the legitimacy of the European Union after enlargement', in J. Thomassen (ed.) *The Legitimacy of the European Union after Enlargement* (Oxford: Oxford University Press).

Tsakatika, M. (2005) 'The European Commission between continuity and change', *Journal of Common Market Studies*, 43/1: 193–220.

van Buitenan, P. (2000) *Blowing the Whistle: One Man's Fight Against Fraud in the European Commission* (London: Politico's Publishing).

van der Eijk, C. and Franklin, M. N. (1996) (eds) *Choosing Europe? The European Electorate and National Politics in the Face of Union* (Ann Arbor, MI: The University of Michigan Press).

van Oudenhove, G. (1965) *The Political Parties in the European Parliament: The First Ten Years (September 1952–September 1962)* (Leyden: A. W. Sijthoff).

Vedel, G. (1972) *Report of the Working Party Examining the Problem of the Enlargement of the Powers of the European Parliament* (Brussels: Bulletin of the European Communities, Supplement 4/72) (the 'Vedel Report').

Verdun, A. (1999) 'The role of the Delors Committee in the creation of EMU: an epistemic community?' *Journal of European Public Policy*, 6/2: 308–28.

———— and Christiansen, T. (2000) 'Policies, institutions and the euro: dilemmas of legitimacy', in C. Crouch (ed.) *After the Euro: Shaping Institutions for Governance in the Wake of European Monetary Union* (Oxford: Oxford University Press).

Waever, O. (1995) 'Identity, integration and security: solving the sovereignty puzzle in EU studies', *Journal of International Affairs*, 48/2: 389–431.

Wallace, H. (1980) *Budgetary Politics: The Finances of the European Union* (London: Allen and Unwin).

———— (2002) 'The Council: an institutional chameleon', *Governance*, 15/3: 325–44.

———— (2010) 'An institutional anatomy and five policy modes', in H. Wallace, M. A. Pollack, and A. Young (eds) *Policy Making in the European Union* (6th edn, Oxford and New York: Oxford University Press).

———— and Wallace, W. (2000) (eds) *Policy-making in the European Union* (4th edn, Oxford and New York: Oxford University Press).

————, Pollack, M. A., and Young, A. (2010) (eds) *Policy-making in the European Union* (6th edn, Oxford and New York: Oxford University Press).

Wallace, W. (2005) 'Post-sovereign governance: the EU as partial polity', in H. Wallace, W. Wallace, and M. A. Pollack (eds) *Policy-making in the European Union* (5th edn, Oxford and New York: Oxford University Press).

Waltz, K. (1979) *Theory of International Politics* (Reading, MA: Addison-Wesley).

Warleigh, A. (1999) *The Committee of the Regions: Institutionalising Multi-level Governance* (London: Kogan Page).

Warntjen, A. (2008) 'Steering but not dominating: the impact of the Council Presidency on EU legislation', in D. Naurin and H. Wallace (eds) *Unveiling the Council of the European Union: Games Governments Play in Brussels* (Basingstoke: Palgrave Macmillan).

—— (2010) 'Between bargaining and deliberation: decision-making in the Council of the European Union', *Journal of European Public Policy*, 17/5, 665–79.

——, Hix, S., and Crombez, C. (2008) 'The party political make-up of EU legislative bodies', *Journal of European Public Policy*, 15/8: 1243–53.

Wasserfallen, F. (2010) 'The judiciary as legislator? How the European Court of Justice shapes policy-making in the European Union', *Journal of European Public Policy*, 17/8: 1128–46.

Webb, C. (1977) 'Introduction: variations on a theoretical theme', in H. Wallace, W. Wallace, and C. Webb (eds) *Policy-making in the European Community* (Chichester: John Wiley & Sons).

Weigel, G. (2004) 'The new Europe: no Catholics need apply', available online at **http://www.catholiceducation.org/articles/persecution/pch0071.html**

Weiler, J. H. H. (1981) 'The Community system: the dual character of supranationalism', *Yearbook of European Law*, 1: 268–306.

—— (1994) 'Fin-de-siecle Europe: on ideals and ideology in post-Maastricht Europe', in D. Curtin and T. Heukels (eds) *Institutional Dynamics of European Integration: Essays in Honour of Henry G. Schermers* (Dordrecht: Martinus Nijhoff Publishers).

—— (1999) *The Constitution of Europe* (Cambridge: Cambridge University Press).

Wendt, A. (1999) *Social Theory of International Politics* (Cambridge: Cambridge University Press).

Werts, J. (1992) *The European Council* (The Hague: TMC Asser Instituut).

Wessels, W. (1997) 'An ever closer fusion? A dynamic macropolitical view on integration processes', *Journal of Common Market Studies*, 35/2: 267–99.

—— (2001) 'Nice results: the millennium IGC in the EU's evolution', *Journal of Common Market Studies*, 39/2: 197–219.

Westlake, M. (1999) *The Council of the European Union* (London: Cartermill International).

—— (2011) *The European Parliament's Committees: National Party Control and Legislative Empowerment* (Abingdon: Routledge).

—— and Galloway, D. (2004) *The Council of the European Union* (3rd edn, London: John Harper Publishing).

Whitaker, R. (2011) *The European Parliament's Committees: National Party Control and Legislative Empowerment* (Abingdon: Routledge).

White, S. (2010) 'EU anti-fraud enforcement: overcoming obstacles', *Journal of Financial Crime*, 17/1: 81–99.

Willis, F. R. (1965) *France, Germany, and the New Europe, 1945–1963* (Stanford, CA: Stanford University Press).

Wishart, I. (2011) 'Talks pull eurozone back from the brink', *European Voice*, 28 July, pp. 4–5, available online at **http://www.europeanvoice.com/article/imported/talks-pull-eurozone-back-from-the-brink-/71740.aspx**

Wong, R. (2011) 'The Europeanization of foreign policy', in C. Hill and M. Smith (eds) *International Relations and the European Union* (2nd edn, Oxford and New York: Oxford University Press).

Wright, V. (1997) 'The paradoxes of administrative reform', in W. J. M. Kickert (ed.) *Public Management and Administrative Reform in Western Europe* (Cheltenham: Edward Elgar).

Yordanova, N. (2009) 'The rationale behind committee assignment in the European Parliament: distributive, informational and partisan perspectives', *European Union Politics*, 10/2: 253–80.

Zielonka, J. (1998) *Explaining Euro-paralysis: Why Europe is Unable to Act in International Politics* (Basingstoke and New York: Palgrave Macmillan).

Zilioli, C. and Selmayr, M. (2000) 'The European Central Bank: an independent specialized organization of Community law', *Common Market Law Review*, 37/3: 591–643.

Zwart, T., and Verhey, L. (2003) (eds) *Agencies in European and Comparative Law* (Antwerp: Intersentia).

■ INDEX

A

Accountability, 399–402
  comitology 139
  and the Commission 185–9
  and Coreper 332–3
  and the Council 90–1
  and the ECB 213, 216
  electoral accountability, EP
      party groups 350–2
  and European agencies 236–7
  financial 242, 255–8
  Lisbon Treaty 151
ACER see Agency for the
      Cooperation of Energy
      Regulators
Adenauer, K. 98
African, Caribbean, and Pacific
      (ACP) states 325
African Union 308
AFSJ see Area of Freedom,
      Security, and Justice
agencies see regulatory agencies
Agency for the Cooperation of
      Energy Regulators
      (ACER) 223, 229
Agency for Fundamental rights
      (FRA) 222
Agriculture and Fisheries
      Council (AgFish) 71,
      77
Aigner, H. 244
Alliance of Liberals and Democrats
      for Europe (ALDE)
      341–2, 368, 374,
  See also European Liberal,
      Democrat and Reform
      party
Alternative Investment Fund
      Managers Directive 138
Amsterdam Treaty 28, 29, 127
  Commission President 101,
      111, 112, 130, 135
  judicial co-operation 266
  negotiations on 29, 61
  Schengen agreement 272
  Title IV 276
  TNC's 276–7
Amtenbrink F. 214

Anderson, J. 317
Andreasen, M. 242, 253
Andreotti, G. 63
Ansiaux, H. 209
Arab spring (2011) 306, 311
Area of Freedom, Security, and
      Justice (AFSJ) 265,
      281–4
  Amsterdam Treaty 266
  European Council 56
  Lisbon Treaty 266, 284–5
  See also internal security
      policy; JHA
Ashton, C. 12, 75, 89, 106, 113,
      290, 293, 299, 302,
      308

B

Bank of Japan Act (1997) 203
Barcelona European Council
      (2002) 64
Barnier, M. 111
Barroso Commission 116–17
  Barroso I Commission 16,
      111–12
  Barroso II Commission
      112–14, 118
  (Rocco) Buttiglione affair, 108
  cabinets, appointment of 115
  enlargement 107, 118–19
  'Europe 2020' programme
      118
  leadership 112
  Secretariat General 105
  voting 112
Barroso, J. M. 12, 61, 104, 106,
      107, 399
  Constitutional Treaty 33
  and European Parliament, 131,
      135
  and Lisbon Treaty 105
  Presidency compared 108–10
battle groups 304
behaviouralism 5–6
Berlin Plus arrangements (EU
      and NATO) 304
Blair, T. 12, 64, 140

Blinder, A. 211
Blue Card directive 279–80
BNP Paribas 211
Bosnia
  CSDP deployment 296, 304,
      306, 310
Bowler, S. 347, 349
Brazil 12, 375
Bretton Woods institutions 5
Brussels Summit
  (October 2003) 32
  (December 1993) 58
BSE (Bovine Spongiform
      Encephalopathy) 139,
      235–6
Budgetary Treaties (1970 and
      1975) 127–8, 243
Buiter, W. 204
Bush, G.W. 390
Buttiglione, R. 105, 108
Buzek, J. 49, 344

C

Caldeira, V. M. d. S. 246
Cameron, D. 49
CAP see Common Agricultural
      Policy
Cassis de Dijon case (1979) 26, 36
CCP see Common Commercial
      Policy
CEEC see Central and Eastern
      European countries
Central and Eastern European
      countries (CEECs), 28–9
CEPOL see European Police
      College
CFCA see Community Fisheries
      Control Agency
CFI see Court of First Instance
  See also General Court
CFP see Common Fisheries
      Policy
CFSP see Common Foreign and
      Security Policy
Charter of Fundamental Rights
      30, 32, 165, 370
  See also Lisbon Treaty